PLATO'S PENAL CODE

PLATO'S PENAL CODE

Tradition, Controversy, and Reform
in Greek Penology

Trevor J. Saunders

CLARENDON PRESS · OXFORD
1991

Oxford University Press, Walton Street, Oxford OX2 6DP
Oxford New York Toronto
Delhi Bombay Calcutta Madras Karachi
Petaling Jaya Singapore Hong Kong Tokyo
Nairobi Dar es Salaam Cape Town
Melbourne Auckland
and associated companies in
Berlin Ibadan

Oxford is a trade mark of Oxford University Press

Published in the United States
by Oxford University Press, New York

British Library Cataloguing in Publication Data
Saunders, Trevor J. (Trevor John), 1934–
Plato's penal code: tradition, controversy, and reform in
Greek penology.
1. Greece. Law. Ancient Period
I. Title
343.8
ISBN 0-19-814893-3

Library of Congress Cataloging-in-Publication Data
Saunders, Trevor J., 1934–
Plato's penal code: tradition, controversy, and reform in
Greek penology.
Includes bibliographical references and index.
1. Punishment—Greece—History. 2. Criminal law (Greek law)
3. Plato—Views on punishment. 4. Plato—Views on criminal law.
I. Title.
HV8523.S28 1991 364.6'0938—dc20 90-49681
ISBN 0-19-814893-3

Typeset by Joshua Associates Ltd., Oxford
Printed in Great Britain by
Bookcraft (Bath) Ltd., Midsomer Norton, Avon

TO
TERESA
con amore

ACKNOWLEDGEMENTS

'Big book, big evil', remarked Callimachus; and if that is true then this bulky book is very bad indeed. But it is not only great in extent: it has also been unavoidably long in the making. Indeed, if it were not for the timely generosity of several benefactors, it would not even now be complete. In 1971–2, thanks to a visiting membership of the Institute for Advanced Study at Princeton, I carried out an extensive programme of preliminary reading. During the next dozen years or so I was able to publish several articles on Greek penology; but these were the trailers, not the film. It was not until the mid-1980s that the opportunity occurred for further sustained effort. In 1985–6 the Research Committee of the University of Newcastle upon Tyne, by financing replacement teaching, set me free for an invaluable six months' work; and in 1986 a research fellowship at the Humanities Research Centre of the Australian National University provided a most pleasant and profitable four months of study and writing in Canberra. Finally, in the autumn term of the same year, I again enjoyed the matchless hospitality and facilities of the Institute for Advanced Study, and virtually completed a first draft of the entire book. The University of Newcastle upon Tyne kindly granted me leave of absence for the appropriate periods. To all these bodies I express my cordial gratitude.

It is an agreeable duty to thank most warmly Professor D. M. MacDowell, Professor P. J. Rhodes, and Dr S. C. Todd, who read an early version and made many wise suggestions. The no doubt numerous imperfections that survive are not to be laid at their door.

I also thank Penguin Books Ltd. for permission to reproduce and in some cases to modify slightly passages from *Plato: The Laws, Translated with an Introduction by Trevor J. Saunders* (Penguin Classics, Harmondsworth 1970, copyright © Trevor J. Saunders).

T.J.S.

December 1989

CONTENTS

REFERENCES AND ABBREVIATIONS

References to modern works are given by author and date alone; full details will be found in the bibliography.

Certain references to ancient authors are given in abbreviated style. Those of the form XVII. 146 refer to Homer's *Iliad*; those of the form xvii. 146 refer to his *Odyssey*. References to the works of Plato also are given bare of author (e.g. simply '*Hipp. Maj.* 303a'), and references to his *Laws* are given bare of title also (e.g. simply '642c'). The authors of a few other bare references will be obvious from the context. The Aristotelian *Athēnaiōn Politeia*, 'Constitution of the Athenians', familiarly known as 'the *Ath. Pol.*', is referred to by the plain *AP*.

Almost all the texts which I cite are readily available in English translation, usually in the Loeb Classical Library or the Penguin Classics. Some fragments, however, cause difficulty: a very few have not been translated at all, others only rarely; in selecting texts from which to cite the latter I have had regard to the presence of a translation. Both the fragments and the works surviving complete of the orators Andocides, Antiphon, Demades, Dinarchus, Hyperides, and Lycurgus are cited from the Loeb *Minor Attic Orators*, i (And., Ant.) ed. K. J. Maidment, 1941, and ii (the rest) ed. J. O. Burtt, 1954 (London and Cambridge, Mass.).

The abbreviations 'p.' and 'pp.' refer to pages of *this* book.

The abbreviations I use for ancient authors and their works are given below.

Ael.	*NH*	Aelian	*Nature of Animals*
	VH		*Varia Historia*
Aes.	*Agam.*	Aeschylus	*Agamemnon*
	Choe.		*Choephori*
	Eum.		*Eumenides*
	Pers.		*Persians*
	PV		*Prometheus Vinctus*
	Se.		*Seven against Thebes*
	Supp.		*Suppliants*

Fragments cited are in H. W. Smyth, *Aeschylus*, ii (Loeb edition, London and Cambridge, Mass., 1957), either in the main section, or in the Appendix by H. Lloyd-Jones.

Aesch.		Aeschines	
Aesop		A. Hausrath, *Corpus Fabularum Aesopicarum* (Teubner edn., Leipzig 1956–9; 2nd edn. by H. Hunger, 1970).	
Alc.		Alcaeus Cited from D. A. Campbell, *Greek Lyric*, i (Loeb edn., London and Cambridge, Mass., 1982).	
And.		Andocides	
Ant.	*Tetr.*	Antiphon (orator)	*Tetralogies*
Apol.	*Bibl.*	Apollodorus	*Bibliotheca*
Ap.Rh.		Apollonius Rhodius	
Ar.	*Cl.*	Aristophanes	*Clouds*
	Eccl.		*Ecclesiazusae*
	Kn.		*Knights*
	Plut.		*Plutus*
	Thes.		*Thesmophoriazusae*
		The fragment cited is in C. Austin, *Comicorum Graecorum Fragmenta in Papyris Reperta* (Berlin and New York 1973).	
Arist.	*HA*	Aristotle	*Historia Animalium*
	NE		*Nicomachean Ethics*
	Pol.		*Politics*
	Rhet.		*Art of Rhetoric*
		The fragment cited is in V. Rose, *Aristotelis qui ferebantur librorum fragmenta* (Teubner edn., Leipzig 1886; repr. 1967).	
[Arist.]	*MH*		*On Marvellous Things Heard*
	Prob.		*Problems*
Arch.		Archilochus, ed. M. L. West, *Iambi et Elegi Graeci*, i (Oxford 1971).	
Call.	*Dem.*	Callimachus	*Hymn to Demeter*
Dem.	*Fun. Sp.*	Demosthenes	*Funeral Speech*
Democ.		Democritus	
Din.	*Arist.*	Dinarchus	*Against Aristogeiton*
	Dem.		*Against Demosthenes*
	Phil.		*Against Philocles*
Diod. Sic.		Diodorus Siculus	
Diog. Laert.		Diogenes Laertius	
DK		H. Diels (rev. D. Kranz), *Die Fragmente der Vorsokratiker* (3 vols., 6th edn., Berlin 1951–2).	
Emped.		Empedocles	
Eur.		Euripides	
	Bac.		*Bacchants*

	El.		*Electra*
	Herac.		*Children of Heracles*
	Hipp.		*Hippolytus*
	HF		*Hercules Furens*
	IT		*Iphigenia among the Taurians*
	Med.		*Medea*
	Or.		*Orestes*
	Supp.		*Suppliants*
	Tr.		*Women of Troy*

FGrH   *Die Fragmente der griechischen Historiker*, ed. F. Jacoby (Berlin and Leiden 1923–).

Gorg.	*EH*	Gorgias	*Encomium of Helen*
Harp.		Harpocration	
Her.		Herodotus	
Hes.	*Astr.*	Hesiod	*Astronomy*
	Cat.W.		*Catalogue of Women*
	GW		*Great Works*
	Th.		*Theogony*
	WD		*Works and Days*

The first three of these are fragmentary, and are cited from H. G. Evelyn-White, *Hesiod* (Loeb edn., London and Cambridge, Mass., 1936).

Hipp.	*Epid.*	Hippocrates	*Epidemics*
	Morb. Sacr.		*The Sacred Disease*
Hom. H.			*Homeric Hymns*
Hyg.	*Fab.*	Hyginus	*Fabulae*
Hyp.	*Dem.*	Hyperides	*Against Demosthenes*
	Eux.		*In Defence of Euxenippus*
	Phil.		*Against Philippides*
IG			*Inscriptiones Graecae*
Is.		Isaeus	

Fragments cited from E. S. Forster, *Isaeus* (Loeb edn., London and New York 1927).

Isoc.	*Let. Phil.*		*Letter to Philip*

Lex. Seg.   *Lexicon Iconographicum Mythologiae Classicae* (Zurich and Munich 1981–).

Lex. Seg.   *Lexica Segueriana*, ed. I. Bekker, *Anecdota Graeca*, i (Berlin 1814).

L+S   Liddell, H. G. and Scott, R., *A Greek–English Lexicon*, 9th edn., Revd Jones, H. S. (Oxford 1940).

Lyc.	*Leoc.*	Lycurgus	*Against Leocrates*
Lys.		Lysias	

		Fragments cited from T. Thalheim, *Lysiae Orationes* (2nd edn., Leipzig, 1913).	
Nic. Dam.		Nicolaus of Damascus	
Ovid	*Met.*		*Metamorphoses*
Paus.		Pausanias	
Pind.	*Ol.*	Pindar	*Olympians*
		Fragments cited from J. Sandys, *The Odes of Pindar* (Loeb edn., London and New York, 1919)	
Plato	*Ap.*		*Apology of Socrates*
	Ch.		*Charmides*
	Crat.		*Cratylus*
	Crit.		*Critias*
	Eu.		*Euthyphro*
	Euth.		*Euthydemus*
	Gorg.		*Gorgias*
	Hipp. Maj.		*Hippias Major*
	Phaed.		*Phaedrus*
	Phil.		*Philebus*
	Polit.		*Politicus*
	Prot.		*Protagoras*
	Rep.		*Republic*
	Soph.		*Sophist*
	Symp.		*Symposium*
	Th.		*Theaetetus*
Plut.		Plutarch	*Lives of:*
	Ages.		*Agesilaus*
	Alex.		*Alexander*
	Dem.		*Demosthenes*
	Di.		*Dion*
	Lyc.		*Lycurgus*
	Per.		*Pericles*
	Sol.		*Solon*
	Tim.		*Timoleon*
	LVD		*On the Late Vengeance of the Deity*
Pol.		Pollux	
Sol.		Solon, ed. M. L. West, *Iambi et Elegi Graeci*, ii (Oxford 1971).	
Soph.	*Aj.*	Sophocles	*Ajax*
	Ant.		*Antigone*
	El.		*Electra*
	OC		*Oedipus Coloneus*
	OT		*Oedipus Tyrannus*

	Phil.		*Philoctetes*
	Tr.		*Trachiniae*

Fragments cited from A. C. Pearson, *The Fragments of Sophocles* (3 vols., Cambridge 1917).

Stes.   Stesichorus

Cited from J. M. Edmonds, *Lyra Graeca*, ii (Loeb edn., London and Cambridge, Mass., 1924).

Theog.   Theognis, ed. M. L. West, *Iambi et Elegi Graeci*, i (Oxford 1971).

Thuc.   Thucydides

Xen.	*Ages.*	Xenophon	*Agesilaus*
	Anab.		*Anabasis*
	Con. Lac.		*Constitution of the Lacedaemonians*
	Cyr.		*Cyropaedia*
	Hell.		*Hellenica*
	Hunt.		*On Hunting*
	Mem.		*Memorabilia*
	Oec.		*Oeconomicus*
[Xen.]	*AP*		*Constitution of the Athenians*
(the 'Old Oligarch')			

INTRODUCTION

The principles of moderation, of the rule of law, and of the rule of philosophy—these are κτήματα ἐc αἰεί ['possessions for ever'], and it is Plato in the *Laws* who first set them forth in their full range and potency.

G. R. Morrow, *Plato's Cretan City*, 593

The *Laws*, Plato's last and longest work, depicts in vivid detail a blueprint for an ideal state called Magnesia, which is to be founded in the South of Crete under guidance from the Academy. 'Ideal' does not imply the perfection of the state described in the *Republic*: Magnesia is simply the best state that Plato considered capable of realization in the circumstances of the Greek world in the middle of the fourth century BC.[1] Though in that sense a utopia, it is a realistic and practical one; it must expect to have crimes and criminals. It therefore stands in need of a penology and a penal code. Indeed, to judge from the sheer amount of space Plato devotes to these two topics, he regards them as of central importance to the entire enterprise.

His penology combines the 'rule of law' with the 'rule of philosophy' to powerful effect. His fundamental inspiration is the Socratic paradox, 'no one does wrong willingly'. If a man does do wrong, it must be because of some psychic mistake; and mistakes are not the kind of thing one can reasonably *punish*. Our treatment of a criminal, therefore, should never look backward to his crimes, but always forward, to the 'cure' of his mental and moral 'disease'. We must of course ensure that he pays compensation to the injured party; but that is not a penal matter. As his punishment, we may make him suffer, or employ any other measure we think likely to be effective; but our purpose must always be strictly reformative:

When anyone commits an act of injustice, serious or trivial, the law will combine instruction and constraint, so that in the future either he will never again dare to commit such a crime voluntarily, or he will do it a very great deal less often; and in addition, he will pay compensation for the damage he has

---

[1] 739a ff. Briefly, the difference between the two states is that the former is governed by the unfettered discretion of philosopher-kings, the latter by an extensive body of civil, constitutional, and criminal law.

done. This is something we can achieve only by laws of the highest quality. We may take action, or use speech; we may grant pleasures, or cause pain; we may confer honour, we may inflict disgrace; we can impose fines, or even give gifts. We may use absolutely *any* means to make him hate injustice and embrace true justice—or at any rate not hate it.[2]

Such a resolutely utilitarian policy is askew to the orthodoxies of Plato's day. It is a striking anticipation of certain modern views,[3] and has important moral and legal implications. We shall have to ask whether Plato himself appreciated them fully.

If it is to be put into practice, a new model penology needs a new model penal code embodying its principles. Accordingly, Plato equips Magnesia with a substantial and detailed code of criminal law.[4] It is not easy reading; at times it is quite pixilatingly complex; and few scholars have been prepared to venture far into the thickets. Indeed, what point could there be in bothering? For its provisions seem at first sight to be far removed from the theory which officially underpins them. Blood-curdlingly vengeful terminology mingles with a welter of penalties that are the same in range and kind, and apparently in retributive purpose, as those prescribed by contemporary Attic law. This is not at all what we are led to expect by the forward-looking, medically-inspired language of 'cure' that permeates the penal theory. It is tempting to be cynical, and to conclude that Plato is a mere armchair penologist.[5] But that would be methodologically facile. With a flourish of trumpets, Plato announces a new penology and in certain parts of his code applies it clearly enough. We have a duty to consider how from his point of view, on his assumptions, he could have supposed himself to be utterly consistent throughout.

It is the thesis of this book that if we examine Plato's penology and penal code closely, in the light of (i) the historical development of Greek penal assumptions and practices, (ii) his own psychological, medical and physiological theory, a striking consistency does emerge. He has adopted and adapted, abandoned or expanded, and in general re-calculated and reshaped a vast range of criminological ideas and practices in such a way as to combine intense conservatism with radical innovation. He has compounded an amalgam, not simply thrown together a loose mixture of inconsistent elements. As a political craftsman, he has skilfully, systematically, and on the whole successfully utilized the material that lies to hand, to answer his own purposes.

---

[2] 862de.

[3] See Saunders (1975).

[4] The terms 'code', 'crime,' and 'criminal' are theory-laden, but my use of them is entirely pragmatic: a 'code' is simply a *de facto* assemblage of laws, however unsystematically formed, and a 'crime' is simply an offence against one or more of them.

[5] Cf. Flew (1973) 119 n. 22.

Part I of this book is therefore an attempt to trace the development of Greek[6] penal ideas and practices from Homer to the mid-fourth century. It is emphatically not a complete description or history or analysis of the many and varied individual punishments which the Greeks inflicted on each other, or of their distribution in time and place, or of the patterns of their attachment to the various offences. There is plenty of raw material here for somebody's book, but not mine. My enquiry into the pre-Platonic evidence is strictly for the purpose of understanding Plato, by setting out the 'inherited conglomerate'[7] of assumptions and principles which he had to take into account when constructing Magnesia's penal code according to his own tenets. In brief, the focus of Part I is not individual punishments as such, but the circumstances of their infliction, the manner in which they are calculated, their justifications and their purposes. The same holds for my detailed examination, in Part II, of the relationship between the prescriptions of major parts[8] of Plato's penal code and the prescriptions of contemporary Athenian law: for the changes Plato makes to his historical models are for precise penological reasons. It is these reasons, and the changes to which they give rise, that are my primary interest.

Chapters 1–4 necessarily range far, into a very diverse collection of evidence and themes. If any reader of these parts feels that Plato is taking an unconscionably long time to come into view, I can only ask him to hold his soul in patience until Chapters 5–16, which from time to time refer to Chapters 1–4 in order to elucidate Plato's intentions, problems and solutions.

Though it is, I hope, not insensitive to vocabulary, this is not a lexically-based study. Punishment is a special aspect of retaliation, the meeting of aggression with counter-aggression, and such situations are not only extremely various in themselves but lend themselves to widely different descriptions according to the perceptions of the observer. The Greeks seem to have felt that these descriptions sufficed; at any rate, they had no single word for 'punishment'. The more notable terms are:

1. *kolasis*   'check', 'chastening', 'chastisement'
   kolazein   'to chastise'

---

[6] The evidence is however, chiefly Athenian. Lack of hard information makes it difficult to judge whether the laws of all Greek states form some sort of collective unity in any fundamental way: see Cartledge *et al.* (1990) 7–11 for a discussion.

[7] Dodds (1951) 207 ff.

[8] That is to say, those parts on which Plato himself lavishes most attention. There are many offences of lesser moment for which he legislates quite briefly, and to which I refer when they become relevant; but I have not attempted to cover the code exhaustively. This is not quite the dereliction it may appear, if we assume, as we must, that Plato intends to apply, *mutatis mutandis*, the same penological principles according to the same criteria throughout his code. Cf. pp. 334–5.

2. *timōria*	'help' given to the *timē* ('wealth', 'status' etc., see pp. 11, 20) of an injured party in retaliation against an aggressor, and in that sense the 'punishing' of the latter
timōrein	'to take vengeance' on someone, or 'to help the injured party's *timē*', hence 'to avenge' him
timōreisthai	'to help your own or another's *timē* against, to seek *timē* from', an offender, hence to exact penalty/vengeance from him; *timōreisthai* may also be passive: 'to have *timē* sought from you', 'be punished'
3. *paschein*	'to suffer', by way of retaliation, hence 'be punished'
4. *poinē*	'requital', 'recompense', in concrete or other form
5. *tisis*	'conferring, returning, of *timē*' in concrete or other form; verb *tinein* and compound forms
tinesthai	'to exact *timē* from, in return' (all these words, and *poinē*, are etymologically related)
6. *zēmia*	'hurt', 'damage', especially loss of money, suffered by offender by way of retaliation, hence 'penalty'
zēmioun	'to damage', 'to fine'

The term most Protean in meaning, however, is *dikē*, commonly translated 'justice', or 'penalty'. I discuss its semantic field in Chapter 2.

All these words describe retaliatory procedures in terms of ideas which we can indeed use today; but in each case we would find it natural to say also that someone is being 'punished'; and we may still wish to do that even when, as often happens in the ancient texts, *none* of these ideas occurs in the description of the retaliation. That is why I concentrate on the dynamics of aggression and counter-aggression, rather than on the words used to describe them. How far the Greeks, in performing the actions they described by those words, that is to say in retaliating, regarded themselves as doing what we would now call 'punishing', is a question best left until (in Chapter 1) we frame a definition, necessarily somewhat arbitrary, of 'punishment'.

Penal theory is commonly discussed by reference to several cloudy concepts on which I have sought to impose consistency of usage. 'Talionic', 'mirroring', and 'crime-specific' I discuss in Chapter 3. In my usage, 'recompense' is that which is transferred, usually but not invariably from the offender, and usually but not invariably to the injured person, in order to make good the damage or loss inflicted by the former; 'satisfaction' is used to refer only to the *feeling* of contentment thereby occasioned in the latter. 'Retribution' is punishment whose justification is sought retrospectively, in the loss or damage caused. 'Revenge', 'vengeance', and the adjective 'vindictive' refer to punishments designed wholly or chiefly to afford the injured party 'satisfaction', particularly in the form of pleasure taken in the offender's suffering. A 'deterrent' punishment is intended to discourage the offender from further offences by inculcating in him fear of further suffering, and those who witness the proceedings from committing offences themselves; a 'reformative' punishment is calculated to prevent further offences by improving morally the offender's opinions and character.

These simple usages suffice for my purposes; for the conceptual framework sufficient for an understanding of ancient Greek penology in general and Plato's in particular is, to my mind, not complex. And for that reason among others, this enterprise is innocent of much theory. Greek penology, like modern penology, does of course generate many problems of moral philosophy; but they are not my central concern. They have been explored by M. M. Mackenzie, in her stimulating book *Plato on Punishment*. My work is quite different in method, scope, and emphasis from hers, and indeed from the work of other writers too on Plato's penology.[9] Its purpose is to understand how the penal ideas and practices of the Greeks took shape, and how one man sought to reform them root and branch.

---

[9] Publications from 1920 until early 1979 are listed in my [1979] § B8. Since then, Stalley (1983, 137–50) has provided a brief but useful survey, and Schöpsdau has re-examined in detail the penological excursus in book IX.

I

FROM HOMER TO THE MID-FOURTH CENTURY

I

PUNISHMENT IN HOMER

IS HOMER USABLE?

In his *Laws* and elsewhere Plato advanced a radical new penology, sharply different from any penology practised or advocated down to his day. The ideas and practices which he sought to modify or displace were those of the Athenian legal system of the fifth and fourth centuries. They have their first attestation in Homer; and so too have certain elements in Plato's attempted reform of them.

To Homer, then, we must betake ourselves; and difficulties arise immediately. The *Iliad* and the *Odyssey* are generally thought to have been composed shortly before 700 BC. The stories they tell are set in a society whose historical existence is uncertain. For the poems witness only to themselves; little independent check on their testimony is available. If they do describe some historical society, it is not one contemporaneous with their date of composition. Homer inherited a vast mass of poetic material that had accumulated over a long period, and by selection and adaptation constructed the two full-scale epic poems. Hence the picture he gives us may well not be of a single historical period or even of a single society, but of some composite.

Any attempt to reconstruct 'Homeric' society is open to further distortion from the nature of the poet's themes. His stories focus on the exploits of aristocratic 'heroes', and have little to say about the common man. The *Iliad* is set in a foreign country during a long and exhausting war, when conduct among the heroes may well be unusually harsh and aggressive; while the *Odyssey*, although its scenes are more domestic and set in times of peace, contains many episodes of folk-tale and imaginative invention.

Hence the Homeric poems are probably something of a distorting-mirror, and if we wish to use them as sociological sources we have to bear in mind that we may unwittingly be working with grotesqueries. Indeed, there is some temptation to throw up one's hands and abandon the poems as plausible fiction. Such methodological gloom seems, however, hardly justified.[1]

[*See p. 10 for n. 1*]

1. Even a fictional society, provided it is constructed with internal consistency—that is to say, provided the ideas and practices ascribed to it remain consistent from episode to episode and do not vary wildly and randomly as a result of unbridled fancy on the part of the composer— may be reconstructed more or less systematically.

2. The Homeric poems do in fact exhibit a high degree of such internal consistency; and this is the more impressive in that the poet's concerns are quite other than sociological or analytic. He is concerned to tell a story, and perhaps point a moral; the information which emerges about ideas and practices he gives us unselfconsciously; it is not subject to selection or distortion arising from the grinding of any sociological axe.

3. Even though the Homeric poems may have portrayed a world which was wholly or partly unhistorical, the Greeks nevertheless plainly regarded them as commending and legitimizing certain norms of conduct in their own society. The influence of Homer on moral sensibility was accordingly pervasive. Certainly in matters penological it is demonstrable that there is a direct line of continuity from the pattern of beliefs and conduct found in Homer down to that discernible in the classical period. Now if in fact the Greeks allowed themselves to be influenced in their beliefs and conduct by a description of a fictional society or of a historical society depicted with gross distortion, that may be remarkable and perhaps deplorable. But for my purposes it will not matter crucially; and here I merely record *en passant*, for what it is worth, my impression that the assumptions and practices described in Homer are all too life-like.

HOMERIC SOCIETY

The account of Homeric society which I adopt is in general that of Moses Finley (1979), in *The World of Odysseus*. Briefly, the basic unit is the 'home' or 'estate' (*oikos*); it consists of a 'hero' at its head, his wife, children, first workmen and slaves, and their families. The terms 'lord' or 'squire' catch something of his position. The struggle for livelihood and the competition for resources are intense. The members of the *oikos* look to their lord for leadership, and expect under him to achieve security and

---

[1] See in general M. I. Finley (1979), especially App. I and 48: 'Essentially the picture offered by the poems of the society and its system of values is a coherent one'; cf. Adkins (1971) 1–2. However, we ought not to look for total uniformity and consistency in any sphere of conduct; presumably there were inconsistencies and variations in procedure, not only across time and space, but within the 'system' of values itself. On the dating of Homeric society, see now the important article by Morris (1986): he argues that the poems reflect eighth-century conditions and a conscious aristocratic ideology.

prosperity. His role, therefore, is not one of ease and privilege; he needs a high degree of self-reliance and self-assertion; and he is judged by results. His overriding need is to gain *timē*, in the concrete sense of 'possessions' or 'wealth', for use by himself and his *oikos*; and it is his *timē* in this sense that is the foundation for his *timē* in a second sense, the 'honour', 'status' or 'clout' which he possesses both within the *oikos* and in his relations with other heroes and the world in general. For there is a scale of *timē*, with the hero at the top, and strangers and beggars at the bottom; for the latter do not contribute to the prosperity of the *oikos*, and receive only such allowance of *timē* as it chooses to give them. More extended associations, of several or many *oikoi*, are glancingly noticed, but how powerful they were socially and politically is not at all clear. The title 'king' (*basileus*) denotes a leader of such a wider grouping. *Ad hoc* military alliances, obviously, were possible (witness the colossal Greek expedition against Troy).

A regular and established system of law-enforcement backed up by a systematic infliction of punishment after due process of law is nowhere to be seen. To be sure, law did exist in some sense: it was certainly not written, but consisted of customary conduct reinforced partly by the *dikai* ('judgements') and *themistes* ('layings-down'), delivered by the kings or others,[2] and partly by direct communal action.[3] But for the most part we find only certain types of hostile encounters between the heroes, and between them and others, which flare up from time to time in the course of the informal private enterprise of their social, military, religious, and family activities. That is why I shall start by considering the widest possible range of hostile relationships, and in particular the widest possible range of *measures of retaliation* visited by anyone (including gods)[4] on anyone, whether those measures are described as actual, foreseen, threatened or merely wished or imagined. Somewhere in all this we may hope to isolate, so far as one can, the principles and practice of punishment in Homeric society. In order not to beg questions, therefore, I shall in the next section not use the word 'punishment' at all, even as a first approximation, except in the final paragraph.

[2] See pp. 35 ff. below.
[3] xxiv. 415 ff.; further examples in Calhoun (1927) 20 ff.; cf. Bonner and Smith (1930) i. 22 ff., MacDowell (1978) 21–3.
[4] Homer assumes that the same desires and motivations, and patterns of aggression and retaliation, exist among gods as among human beings, and therefore also in the relationships between the two: see Adkins (1972b).

AGGRESSION AND RETALIATION

(a) Staying the hand

A hero who suffers or thinks he suffers any kind of harm, either to his person or to his property or reputation, may get some help from his relatives or community.[5] But often the remedy lies in his own hands: he must himself take steps to assert his position or claim, and to recover the ground he has lost. If he believes himself to be in a weak position,[6] or if he has something to gain from restraint,[7] he may simply hold his hand, at least for the moment.[8] Retaliation, if it comes, may spring from sheer anger; but anger may be overridden by calculation.

(b) Persuasion

Calculation appears also in a certain tendency to resort to persuasion, which is explicity distinguished from force.[9] An injured party may decide that, initially at least, the situation may be remedied by honeyed words, or threats, or a combination of both. The structure of some of the speeches made on such occasions contains three elements: (1) an attempt to talk the offender round by gaining his good-will; (2) a statement of the injured party's request; (3) a threat of certain unpleasant consequences if the request is not met. Chryses, coming to ransom his daughter, first prays that the Atreidae may conquer Troy, then asks for his daughter, then hints at the displeasure of Apollo if the Atreidae fail to comply; and his request is backed by the Achaeans at large.[10] Menelaus uses more formal tactics: when defeated by Antilochus' guile in the race held at Patroclus' funeral games, he first asks the leaders of the Argives to judge between them, but then changes his mind and tells Antilochus to take an oath that he had not cheated.[11] There is some recognition that peaceful reconciliation of the parties, or at least deterrence of one by the other, is superior to retaliation. Homeric society does know ways of taking the heat out of conflict. To that extent, retaliation is a deliberate, calculated response; it is not the only option.

(c) Blaming the right person

Further careful and sometimes subtle calculation in retaliation is evident in the attention paid to blaming the right person. If one blames, and then

---

[5] iv. 164-7.

[6] xvi. 71-2, IX. 453-61; cf. XIV. 256-61 (of a god, Zeus).

[7] I. 187-221.

[8] xx. init.

[9] XV. 106; cf. IX. 428-9.

[10] I. 15-23; cf. xviii init., xix. 482 ff.

[11] XXIII. 570 ff., cf. M. I. Finley (1979) 108 ff.

retaliates against, someone other than the person responsible (*aitios*), not only does the latter escape, possibly to repeat his offence, but one has made an enemy out of the other person. Such a mistake is thus not only dangerous: it can invite the ridicule of others, to the detriment of one's standing. Patroclus notes that Achilles is precisely the sort of man to blame the blameless; but Achilles is perfectly clear-eyed about where responsibility for offending him lies: with Agamemnon, not with Agamemnon's servants, nor indeed with the Trojans.[12] Considerations of equity can apparently arise: Poseidon argues to the gods on Aeneas' behalf that he was innocent (*anaitios*) and pious, and did not deserve to die for the griefs of others.[13] Some ascriptions of responsibility are on the tendentious side.[14] But at any rate getting the target for retaliation right is of recognized importance.[15]

(d) Retaliation against third parties

Nevertheless, in a competitive world, to locate the proper target for blame is not always to locate a proper target for retaliation. The offender himself may for some reason not be available; even if he is, his relatives or *oikos* or wider community may well feel threatened, and so represent a danger; in any case they can be plausibly supposed to have contributed to the offence by encouraging or succouring the offender. So if a hero who has lost *timē* can regain it from some source close to the offender, even if not from the offender himself, that may be the best he can do. Agamemnon tells Peisander and Hippolochus that he will kill them in return for the offence of their father Antimachus. He can hardly *blame* them; but to kill them is the only way he can hit back at their father, and to that extent feel that by their sufferings he has restored his own *timē*.[16] It is most commonly the offender's wife and children who thus suffer retaliation vicariously, more or less defenceless as they are; but reprisals can sometimes extend to huge numbers, as when Apollo sends a plague on the whole Greek army at the beginning of the *Iliad*, for the offence of its commander. There is no notion of equity here: that third parties are innocent is irrelevant. Yet the conflict between suffering and desert did not go entirely unnoticed: Agamemnon twice says that even 'workers of good' among women as yet unborn will have their reputation besmirched by the offences of Clytemnestra.[17]

---

[12] I. 152 ff., 335–6.
[13] XX. 297–9.
[14] ii. 87 ff.
[15] On *aitios*, see also Cantarella (1979) 273 ff., and cf. III. 164, XV. 137, XXI. 275, xx. 135, *Hom. H.* 2. 78.   [16] XI. 142; cf. III. 288–301, IV. 162 ff. XXIV. 605 ff., 735.
[17] xi. 434, xxiv. 202, in effect suffering which arises from a species of 'guilt by association'.

(e) Relative strengths

Having decided on the desirable target for retaliation, the offended party has another calculation to make. Is the offender stronger? If so, ought he to be left alone, or should an attempt at retaliation be made nevertheless? Homeric society is intensely combative; who is stronger or better than who is a question of vital and perennial interest. Poseidon advises Aeneas not to fight Achilles, who is stronger and dearer to the immortals. Achilles, supposing that he has made Aeneas withdraw, boasts that Aeneas will not 'try him out' again.[18] Achilles is indeed stronger than all mortal men, hence Agenor's anguished debate whether it would not be prudent to retreat; eventually he decides to 'try him out'.[19] These situations are military; but in non-military contexts too calculations of relative strength enter into retaliatory or prospectively retaliatory relationships. Zeus boasts that he will retaliate by plunging into Tartarus any god who thwarts his wishes, which will show the other gods that he is the most powerful of them all; if they doubt it, let them try him out. The gods took the point.[20] Ares, however, got his calculation wrong: seeking to retaliate upon Athene for a past offence, he was knocked senseless by her; presumably he did not hear her then say, 'Fool, not even now have you realized how much mightier I claim to be'.[21] A person who has suffered more from retaliation than he has gained from offending is a person who has tried it *on* another by trying him *out*, and has lost.

(f) Excuses

Can anything induce an injured party to mitigate the vigour of his response? His need to assert himself in a decisive and unmistakable manner may well make him disinclined to enter into nice calculations about the offender's motives and intentions. The injury has been done, *timē* has been lost, and that's that; action is called for. Indeed, it has long been accepted that in Homeric society good intention, or lack of bad intention, does not absolve from consequences. In spite of that, excuses do crop up fairly frequently in Homer, though admittedly they vary in effectiveness.[22] But the fact that they are there at all is significant: no man makes excuses if excuses are never effective; and even when an excuse fails in its purpose, it may nevertheless be a perfectly *justified* excuse, in the eyes of its maker and others, even if not in the eyes of the offended party.

[18] XX. 332-52.
[20] VIII. 1-37; cf. I. 80, XXI. 225-6, 486.
[19] XXI. 553-82.
[21] XXI. 391-411.
[22] For discussions see Maschke (1926) *init.*, Adkins (1960*a*) 10 ff., 5, Long 124 n. 9, Cantarella (1979) 264 ff.

The range of possible excuses in Homer is as follows:

1. *Tender years.* In general, the poems are censorious of the foolishness and instability of the young.[23] Patroclus, however, in addition to mentioning that when he committed murder he was foolish (*nēpios*) and angry over a game of dice, and lacked intent (*ouk ethelōn*, 'not wanting'), says he was 'only a kid'—presumably in some hope of exculpation, or at least as a bid for pity.[24] Antilochus, having offended Menelaus, asks him to be forbearing, since he (Antilochus) is younger and therefore foolish and impulsive. Menelaus accepts the plea, but alters it slightly: youth, he says in effect, is an excuse not in general, but only when it prompts acts untypical of the offender (Antilochus had previously been reliable).[25] That an offence may be untypical of the offender is a nice observation,[26] and characteristic of the rather gentlemanly tone of the dispute at the funeral games.

2. *Inadvertence and forgetfulness.* One cannot be sure that such excuses were in fact ever urged; but we do find, once, 'either he forgot or did not notice'.[27] Such a precise distinction between two somewhat similar states of mind is quite likely to have arisen from a desire to exculpate, though that is not actually stated in this case.

3. *Accident/lack of intent or premeditation.* We noted lack of intent in the Patroclus passage:[28] his anger got the better of his youthful character; presumably he either intended to injure but not kill, or to kill indeed, but without premeditation. The suitors suppose Odysseus killed Antinous without intending to: presumably if they had thought he had done so deliberately, they would have killed him immediately, and his apparent lack of intent gave them pause.[29] Menelaus challenges Antilochus to swear that in impeding the chariot 'he did not intend to cheat', i.e. it happened by accident.[30] When Priam comes to collect the body of his son Hector, Achilles, well aware of the tenseness of the situation and of the danger of 'flashpoint' between Priam and himself, contrives the arrangements with considerable care; he knows that strong influences like anger can lead one to actions which are contrary to one's considered intention.[31]

4. *Over-persuasion, or* force majeure. The minstrel Phemius successfully urged that he entertained the suitors not from any wish or craving, but under constraint (*anankē*); Telemachus on the strength of this calls him

[23] e.g. III. 108, vii. 294, xx. 309-10.
[24] XXIII. 85 ff. On this passage see Maschke (1926) 5-6. Patroclus is appearing after death to Achilles, in a dream. His plea falls, of course, on sympathetic ears; one can only speculate what his pursuers would have made of it. [25] XXIII. 586-90, 603-4.
[26] Cf. Dodds (1951) ch. 1, on 'unaccountable' errors. [27] IX. 537.
[28] XXIII. 85 ff. [29] xxii. 31.
[30] XXIII. 585; cf. xiii. 276-7. [31] XXIV. 568-70, 582-6, 599-601.

blameless (*anaitios*), and he was spared.[32] Noemon admits he gave Telemachus a ship willingly, not under pressure and against his will.[33]

5. *Lack of physical power* may be an excuse for not fighting.[34]

6. *Past services*. This plea evidently helped to save the herald Medon.[35]

These excuses are all of 'ordinary life'; they are not claims that a god may have intervened to override the offender's intention. They are therefore to be distinguished from the kind of plea made by Agamemnon,[36] that 'it is not I that am at fault, but Zeus and Moira and Erinus that walks in darkness, who cast upon my soul grievous *atē* (blindness, delusion)'. Such rueful, face-saving and exculpatory laments are not urged as reasons for exempting the human offender from unpleasant consequences;[37] hence they constitute a further category of cases in which the agent to be blamed is identified, but for various reasons does not suffer retaliation.[38]

The harvest of excuses one can garner from some 28,000 lines of poetry is not large; and it is difficult to judge their effect in practice. Even so, it is clear that the rigours of 'absolute liability' could be modified; for the very existence of the excuses argues that they were effective at least sometimes. In the nature of the case, excuses count for less in war than in peace, and much of Homer is after all set in military context; to that extent our impression of the number and effect of excuses in Homeric society is probably distorted. At any rate, the elaborate excuse-theory of later times is present in Homer in embryo; Plato develops it even further, but in his own special way.

(g) Aggravations

Contrariwise, certain features of an offence may be held to aggravate it. An injured party who can show that the offender took the initiative unprovoked, and an offender who can show that he offended only by way of retaliation, can put himself in a strong debating position. Hence the frequent claims that the other 'started it',[39] that the victim had not provoked the offence,[40] and that the offender acted 'on his own responsibility' (*autos*),[41] so that he will experience suffering which he will have 'brought upon himself'.[42] Secrecy and deception are also apparently thought of as aggravations.[43]

[32] xxii. 350 ff.   [33] iv. 645-9.   [34] XIII. 786-7.

[35] xxii. 357-8; cf. xxiii. 21-4 for an allowance made to old age.   [36] XIX. 86-8.

[37] Adkins (1960) 13 ff., 23 ff.; Dodds (1951) 2 ff.   [38] Cf. (c) and (d) above.

[39] III. 100, 299, 351, IV. 236, 271, xx. 394, xxi. 133; cf. II. 378.   [40] xvii. 566-7.

[41] I. 356, 507, II. 240, of Agamemnon, who admits the point at XIX. 89, cf. 183.

[42] xviii. 73, xxiv. 455, 462.

[43] IV. 168, VII. 243, XXIII. 576, 585, iii. 250, iv. 92, xi. 422. Deceit and cunning are of course in the eye of the beholder: see Athena's indulgent attitude to Odysseus, xiii. 291 ff., cf. 270. What is cleverness in me is deceit in you.

(h) Restraint

Even if no excuse is available in mitigation, it is not true that the injured party may resort to any measure he wishes. Sometimes we find protests against excessively savage or extreme retaliation; and as in the case of excuses, it seems likely that such protests presuppose a certain receptiveness in their audience. At all events, Homeric characters do seem occasionally to assert or admit that there are certain limits to be observed, which of course vary according to circumstances, but which retaliation should not exceed. There is an instinctively recognized rough equivalence. The point is evident in the expression 'make appropriate recompense' (*tinein aisima*), i.e. appropriate in amount or scale,[44] which may indeed be great, but should not be unlimited. The implicit claim is that there should be some reasonable correlation between offence and retaliation.[45]

The probable origin of such a belief is a prudent recognition that the animosity of some injured parties would, if unchecked, be destructive to the community. Some men, fiercely proud and sensitive to slight, will kill in reprisal for a trivial theft or minor insult, because they see it as a substantial impairment of their *timē*;[46] the dangers of massive retaliation are great, and must be coped with. Hence the existence in Homeric society of a strong revulsion against extreme behaviour.[47] The unsqueamish Odysseus is horrified at the scenes of murder on Heracles' belt;[48] and instinctive pity finds some place in calculating a limit to reprisal, as in Priam's appeal to Achilles, in Apollo's protection of Hector's body,[49] and in his reproach of Achilles for loss of pity and for excessive retaliation.[50] The notion that enough is enough is prominent in the episode of the appeals to Achilles: he is told that Hades is the most hated of the gods because he never yields, he is urged in his own interests to show kindliness, and is reminded that even gods can bend: he should overcome his great anger/spirit (*thumos*), and not have a relentless heart, since Supplications, the daughters of Zeus, need to be received graciously.[51] In

---

[44] viii. 348; for *aisima* in more general applications cf. vii. 310, xiv. 84, xv. 71. Hyperion fears that he will not receive 'fit repayment' (*epieikea amoibēn*), xii. 382: obvious shortfall is as objectionable as excess (cf. *antaxion*, 'of equivalent worth', at I. 136, and the same idea, in a military context, at XIV. 471). At the end of the *Odyssey* (xxiv. 477 ff.) Zeus recommends cessation of reprisals as 'seemly'. Cf. Cantarella (1984) 44–5.

[45] Some sort of grading is evident in the wide variety of forms of retaliation in Homer. They range from, for example, a beating, through enforced recompense of varying amounts, to physical mutilation, exile, and death. [46] Cf. Adkins (1960*b*) 29–30.

[47] Cf. Long (1970) 129 ff. [48] xi. 613–4.

[49] XXIV. 19, 504. On pity, justice, propriety, etc. in Homer see Schofield esp. 16–22, 28.

[50] XXIV. 44–54; cf. in general xii. 258–9, xiv. 82. At xxii. 411 ff. Odysseus rebukes Eurycleia for exulting noisily over the dead suitors: she should 'restrain' herself (cf. XVII. 19), on grounds of piety.

[51] IX. 158, 256, 496 ff.; cf. XV. 202–3 (Poseidon), XXIII. 611 (Menelaus), XXIV. 157 (Achilles).

short, Achilles is told that in refusing to accept vast compensation out of pity for the army he is breaking the 'rules of the game': in effect there seems to be at some point an obligation of some kind on him not to persist in damaging the Greeks.[52] The exceptional length and elaboration of the appeals to him are dictated by his exceptional obduracy. They do not necessarily suggest that Homeric man found strange the idea that one's desire for recompense and satisfaction should be subject to considerations other than self-interest. In short, some realistic restrain ts, in part brought to bear by public opinion,[53] are discernible.

(i) Appropriateness

That retaliation should be apt is a frequent theme in Homer, and indeed in primitive law in general; it is a special application of the wider notion of appropriateness as a standard of conduct in Homeric society.[54] It is very dear to the heart of Homeric man that retaliation should lend itself to being expressed in some ironic or grimly humorous way (e.g. 'to don a coat of stone' as a description of a stoning, and the suitors' 'dinner', i.e. death, than which nothing could be more unwelcome).[55] The *manner* in which retaliation is carried out or described is part of the satisfaction the injured party gets; for instance, the twin facts that reprisal comes after appearing never to come at all, and that it comes late, often contrary to the expectation of the offender, are just as important to the injured person as the reprisal itself.[56]

In many cases, such retaliation is 'appropriate' in the sense that in somehow specifying the offence it serves to establish, however crudely, some limiting ratio: an eye for an eye, but not *more* than an eye. Its general influence is therefore similar to that of the inclination to restraint discussed in (h) above.[57]

(j) Anger and glee

Other and related feelings of satisfaction can enter into a retaliator's calculations. To strike back in anger is natural and normal.[58] To pacify or gratify one's indignation or resentment is entirely legitimate: these are

---

[52] Cf. Lloyd-Jones (1983) 16 ff.; cf. XXIII. 176.

[53] Cf. IX. 460, ii. 65–6, 101–2, 199, xxii. 39–40; Long (1970) 126–7, 137; Schofield (1986) 28–9. Even Zeus is open to public pressure, XVI. 439 ff. (though this is not a retaliatory context).

[54] See Jolowicz (1926), and Long (1970) 135–9, esp. 138.

[55] III. 57, xx. 392.   [56] e.g. IV. 161.

[57] However, crime-specific retaliation stands somewhat apart from the main stream; see ch. 3 for a discussion, and Appendix.

[58] I. 81–3, where the anger is nursed; xxii. 59. The paradoxical pleasure of anger is described at XVIII. 107–10.

not emotions to be ashamed of.[59] The pleasure of a good gloat over successful retaliation, and over the offender's sufferings and impotent rage, is actively sought.[60] One may invite others to share one's mocking triumph, as Hephaestus invites the gods to join him in gloating over his binding of Ares and Aphrodite.[61]

(k) Publicity and deterrence

To draw the attention of third parties to successful retaliation has an important purpose: to deter the offender and potential offenders for the future, by demonstrating superiority and by marshalling public opinion against them. The Achaeans predict that Thersites, having been beaten for stepping out of line, will not offend them again; Menelaus prays to Zeus that what he does to Paris will deter even posterity from injuring hosts; and Achilles is furious that Apollo, being a god, does not fear vengeance/repayment (tisis).[62] The heroes also know that the most effective way to deter is to produce a conviction that offences against themselves will not pay.[63] 'Seeing' and 'knowing' are the key concepts. Agamemnon, for instance, threatens to take Briseis from Achilles by force 'so that you may know that I am stronger than you, and so that anyone else too may hesitate to argue with me and liken himself to me to my face'.[64] Hera is reminded by Zeus that he is the stronger, so that she may 'see' that amorous wiles are weaker than brute force.[65] When the heroes taunt each other with witlessness, they commonly mean precisely a lack of empirical knowledge of relative strengths: 'the fool learns when the deed is done', as Menelaus reminds an adversary.[66] The formula '. . . so that others too (or, these people too) may know', when used in retaliatory contexts, shows clearly that the same realization is intended to take place in others besides the offender.[67]

It has long been argued, by Dodds and others,[68] that character and behaviour in Homer are explained in terms of knowledge. In so far as

[59] IX. 632 ff., XIV. 132. The word in these passages is thumos, something more than plain anger: 'spirit', 'pride', 'resentment', 'self-assertion'. To gratify one's feelings by seeing an offender suffer is nowadays regarded as bad form; but as Honderich (1969, 17–19, 30) points out, the desire for such satisfaction is a powerful stimulus to retributivism. Cf. Soph. El. 1503–4.

[60] I. 139, ii. 192–3, ix. 413, 459–60, 492 ff., xxii. 177, 408; cf. the limited relief of anguish at XVII. 538–9.   [61] viii. 306 ff.; cf. III. 43 ff.

[62] II. 276–7, III. 351–4, XXII. 19–20; cf. xiv. 400.

[63] The need to demonstrate superiority decisively accounts in part for the fact that retaliation frequently exceeds the original injury: see (h) above. Indeed, it can lead to the elimination of the offender, by death or exile.

[64] I. 186–7; cf. 302. By contrast Medon, in order that he may 'know' the superiority of good deeds over bad, is let off, xxii. 373.   [65] XV. 32; cf. VIII. 17, 406, XXI. 479 ff.

[66] XVII. 32, XX. 198; cf. I. 411–12, VIII. 111, 532 ff., XVI. 273.

[67] I. 302–3, xviii. 30; cf. VIII. 515, XXIII. 610, viii. 306 ff. Unbearable publicity after an offence: xi. 274.   [68] Dodds (1951) 16–17; cf. O'Brien (1967) 22 ff.

this is true, we have at least part of the reason: character and behaviour are determined by knowledge of relative strengths. Such knowledge produced by being worsted by retaliation is one possible means in Homer of altering the outlook and character, or at least the behaviour, of the offender. Antilochus is to behave better after being put in his place by Menelaus.[69] A god, too, may inflict damage on human beings whose conduct threatens his *timē*, in order to induce them to reform that conduct in the interests of that *timē*.[70]

(*l*) *Restoration of* timē

When a hero retaliates, his central purpose is the restoration, and often the enhancement, of his *timē*, his property, power, and prestige.[71] A cluster of related words in such contexts makes it clear that what he seeks is *recompense* or *repayment (tisis)*. The offender has subjected the victim to the process of *atiman*, to deprive of *timē*; and *timē* is 'something concrete, something which may be transferred, *apotinein*, from one person to another'.[72] The person exacting such payment in retaliation exacts *tisis* or *timē* for himself (*tinesthai* and related words).[73] This process increases, that is to say restores, the *timē* of the injured party to its original level, and often beyond it; conversely, the *timē* of the offender is thereby diminished to the level at which it was before the offence, and often below it. The injured party who retaliates successfully emerges with his property, self-esteem and public status restored or enhanced.

(*m*) *The character of Homeric retaliation*

This survey of the dynamics of aggression and counter-aggression in the epic poems demonstrates that retaliation in Homeric society was a matter of many calculated variables. The injured party, in adopting counter-measures, had a lot to think about: the right target for blame; relative strengths; the possibility of restraint, or of resort to persuasion; the likely reaction of third parties, families and the community; excuses, aggravations; intentions and dispositions of the offender; appropriateness; the likely degree of publicity and deterrent effect; and many others. Therefore, if Homeric retaliation (as I shall claim) necessarily incorporates certain characteristics which we are entitled to call 'punishment', then punishment, even at this early stage, will itself, to that extent, be

---

[69] XXIII. 605.
[70] VII. 446 ff. and xiii. 128 ff., discussed by Adkins (1972*b*) 3–5, 7.
[71] In this paragraph I draw heavily on the fundamental work by Adkins (1960*b*).
[72] Adkins (1960*b*) 27.
[73] For a fuller survey of usage, see Adkins (1960*b*) 28.

effectively a matter of uncertainty, debate, and calculation. We shall have here the ground from which sprang the controversies about punishment that arose in forensic and other contexts in the classical period; and these were in turn the controversies addressed by Plato.

IS THERE PUNISHMENT IN HOMER?

(a) The criteria of punishment

Provided it is agreed that the patterns of aggression and retaliation in Homer are as I have described them, there is in a sense little point in disputing what particular label we should attach to the element of retaliation. It would be possible to describe it, vaguely enough, by reference to terms such as 'punishment', 'penalty', 'revenge', 'vengeance', 'recompense', 'retribution', or 'compensation', without diminishing the broad intelligibility of the patterns. But in recent years there have been two separate but related claims that 'punishment' does not exist in Homer. I believe both to be mistaken.

The concept of punishment is slippery; but for many years now attempts to define it have centred on Flew's five criteria.[74] For an act to qualify as a punishment 'in the primary sense',

1. 'it must be an evil, an unpleasantness, to the victim';
2. 'it must (at least be supposed to) be for an offence';
3. 'it must (at least be supposed to) be of the offender';
4. 'it must be the work of personal agencies';
5. 'it has to (be at least supposed to) be imposed by virtue of some special authority, conferred through or by the institutions against the laws or rules of which the offence has been committed.'

A further criterion, suggested by Benn and Peters,[75] may conveniently be added:

6. 'The unpleasantness should be an essential part of what is intended and not merely incidental to some other aim.'

With certain variations of wording this list of 5 (or 6) criteria forms the basis of discussion by Samek, McPherson, McCloskey, Hart, and Kasachkoff. (2) and (4) present no difficulty; (3) is however violated in Homer in cases of punishment of third parties. That apart, to consider whether the punishment exists in Homer, we need to focus first on (1) and (6) together, then on (5).

---

[74] Flew (1954) 85-7.
[75] Benn and Peters (1959) 174.

(b) Punishment as suffering (criteria 1 and 6)

Enforced restoration of *timē* entails the deliberate infliction of pain or suffering on the offender.[76] It therefore satisfies the first two criteria for a punishment, and moreover does so without in the least ceasing to be restoration of *timē*. For to inflict pain for an offence is, in part, the means of the restoration: one restores a commodity, *timē*, by inflicting pain, which is in a sense a commodity. I say 'in part', and 'in a sense', because if the restoration takes the form of an accession of goods from the offender to the retaliator, the goods are just goods and not in themselves pain. But their enforced relinquishment by the offender is also an inevitable, foreseen and deliberate infliction of pain by the retaliator. And to the offender, it is not only the loss of goods as such that is a pain: it is also a pain to be forced to increase the *timē* of another relatively to one's own, and to know that the other party is laughing or gloating. On some occasions there may be no goods transferred, and the pain he inflicts may be effectively the only satisfaction or repayment the punisher gets.[77] In practice, then, pain and *timē*-restoration are a unity, as unsplittable as Epicurus' atoms.

(c) The argument from assimilation

Adkins has argued powerfully and persuasively that the prime purpose of retaliation by a Homeric hero is the restoration or increase of his *timē*. What cannot be accepted, however, is his further claim that punishment does not exist in Homer, because it is assimilated to that purpose. Adkins juxtaposes two passages.[78] In the first, Alcinous and the Phaeacian counsellors propose to restore their *timē*, their bank-balance as it were, depleted by gifts to Odysseus, by collecting valuable objects from the Phaeacian people. Adkins rightly says that no one would now describe this example of *tinesthai* as 'punishment', but that Orestes' killing of Aegisthus in the second passage, and his recovery of his kingdom and all its *timē*, could be so described. Restoration of *timē* is common to these two situations, and Adkins comments: 'Since *timē* is so important, a basic essential of Homeric existence, these transactions, which appear different to us, appear in the same light to Homeric society. Punishment, in fact, as we know it, did not exist in Homeric society: it is assimilated to other modes of behaviour . . .'

The assimilation of the two transactions is curious. Alcinous did not

---

[76] Cf. the *Concise Oxford Dictionary*: To punish is to 'cause (offender) to suffer for offence'.

[77] e.g. ix. 413. This is obviously so when he inflicts death, e.g. XIV. 482–4; cf. Adkins (1972b) 7 n. 16 on xii. 377 ff.

[78] xiii. 14 ff. and iii. 194 ff., in (1972a) 14–15; cf. (1960b) 27–8, 30.

regard the Phaeacian people as aggressors, and his recouping of his *timē* from them is entirely non-penal. Nevertheless Orestes' obviously penal recovery of *timē* from the aggressor Aegisthus is to be 'assimilated' to that transaction; for both are the restoration of *timē*. The implication of 'assimilated', apparently, is not that the Homeric hero could not distinguish between hostile and non-hostile recovery of *timē*—clearly he could; but that nevertheless the recovery is all in all to him, and that there is nothing else in the transaction that matters. In Homer, therefore, we find restoration of *timē*; we do not have punishment 'as we know it'.[79]

But the word 'assimilate' is misleading. If two transactions share a common feature, however unimportant to one or both, they may indeed be 'assimilated', in the literal sense of 'likened' or 'compared'. Similarity, however, is not identity: neither situation has absorbed or subsumed the other. They remain distinct, but with a common feature; and in other respects they may be quite dissimilar. Adkins's use of 'assimilated' ignores the possibility that retaliation in Homer may have other—however subsidiary—purposes, in addition to restoration of *timē*. If I take to my bicycle primarily in order to go to work, but also, virtuously, in order to give myself some exercise, I should be rather crestfallen to be told that I am not really getting any exercise, since it is assimilated to another mode of activity, namely transport.

The sixth criterion was: 'The unpleasantness should be an essential part of what is intended and not merely incidental to some other aim.' Presumably 'incidental' means here 'arising unsought', like pain in medical treatment. But unpleasantness or pain caused by Homeric retaliation is not like that at all; for clearly it *is* sought. If however 'incidental' is to be construed as 'means to an end', then it could be argued that in Homer the restoration of *timē* is the end, and the suffering imposed is merely a means; for in some cases it is *by* inflicting pain on the offender that *timē* is restored: by diminishing the other man one increases oneself. But there is no reason to suppose that, even if the pain is to be interpreted in this way, as a means, it cannot be punishment. Punishment is punishment, whether or not it has a purpose beyond itself.[80]

The plain fact is that retaliatory and enforced restoration of *timē* inescapably entails the infliction of suffering. The offender will be reluctant, chagrined, and resentful; he will suffer by losing face, and perhaps by being openly mocked; and in particular he will suffer by deprivation

---

[79] In (1960 *a*) 54, however, Adkins talks without strain of 'punishment' in Homeric society.

[80] McPherson (1967–8, 21) notes the predominantly retributive flavour of the first five criteria and asks, 'Why should a definition of punishment look only to past and present (as does the received definition) and not to the future?'

of whatever it is he is forced to yield to his opponent, even if it is no greater than the loss which he himself inflicted. In such cases suffering is the inevitable *concomitant* of loss. In others, the suffering may *be* the loss: *timē* is restored by the sheer fact that the offender visibly suffers, for that suffices to demonstrate the retaliator's superiority, in his own eyes and those of society. In other words, the retaliator may obtain either recompense in the form of goods, or satisfaction in the form of the knowledge or actual spectacle of suffering; and both[81] assuage his anger or indignation, and restore his *timē*.

Moreover, the infliction of suffering is quite deliberate. No Homeric hero is high-minded enough to say to an offender: 'I shall go to all possible lengths to recoup my *timē* from you; but that is enough for me, and if you find the process grievous, I do apologise.' The fact that often the suffering is inescapably entailed by the restoration of *timē* does not mean that it is not sought; indeed it is an inextricable part of the restoration. The heroes know it, and acknowledge it.[82] They also know that the infliction of suffering serves to deter,[83] in a way which the mere restoration of *timē* would not. It is because *timē*-restoration is disagreeable that it deters; what deters is not the restoration *simpliciter*, i.e. considered, if that were possible, in isolation from the suffering it causes. A doctor tries to cure without causing pain; the Homeric hero restoring his *timē wants* to cause it.

The central drawback of the argument from assimilation is that it treats *timē*-restoration as so dominant a concern that the suffering entailed is relegated to an unrealistically subordinate position.[84] Further, in ignoring the calculations and restraints I have described, it obscures the extent to which the infliction of suffering, i.e. punishment, is already in Homer a matter of reflected and considered policy. *Timē*-restoration is indeed crucial; but the argument from assimilation is simplistic.[85]

It may seem, on my account, that punishment and retaliation are the same thing. But I would plead for a distinction. As the Latin root of the word indicates (*talis*, 'such', 'like'), to retaliate is to hit back, to do as you are done by. Suppose A takes B's cow, and so (in Homeric terms) increases his own *timē* relatively to B's, and then B enforces its return, or

---

[81] See Adkins (1960*b*) 27 on the two forms, in XVI. 398 (death of the offenders) and IX. 632 ff. (evidently goods); the latter is literal payment, the former metaphorical (cf. XIX. 260, XXII. 271–2, XXIV. 212–14, i. 43).

[82] See pp. 18–19 above.

[83] See pp. 19–20 above.

[84] Indeed, the reader of Adkins's (1960*b*) could be forgiven for not realizing that *timē*-restoration is painful: see 30, where punishment in Homer is described as 'merely an adjustment of goods, status and prestige between two competitive and autonomous units'; the clause beginning 'save that' a little later buries the issue.

[85] Cf. Mackenzie's view (1981, 106–12) that 'payments' (in Homer) become 'penalties' (later): the truth in this is oversimplified.

the surrender of something of a similar value, so as to increase *his timē* relatively to A's. B has retaliated: he has treated A 'like' A treated him. Considered in this bare and formal way, the transaction involves no pain. But of course in so acting B is *punishing* A: he makes him suffer for suffering inflicted; and almost invariably he intends so to do. The return of the cow, and the suffering the return brings, are linked but distinct elements in the proceedings. Punishment is the suffering which retaliation entails.[86]

(d) Recompense and extra

Let us linger for a moment in the company of the cow. Suppose B not only enforces restitution of the cow but takes a bull as well. The distinction between 'basic' and 'extra' is fundamental, and recognized by the heroes themselves;[87] but the relationship or ratio between the original injury and the subsequent adjustment is not always readily expressible. Eurymachus offers Odysseus 20 oxen per suitor and bronze and gold 'till your heart be warmed'.[88] Agamemnon is offered threefold and fourfold recompense[89] for the loss of the girl; for that loss is a sort of injury, at which Agamemnon is recognized to be justified in feeling aggrieved. Calchas demands the restoration of the girl to her father without ransom; this is presumably simple recompense, the extra being a hecatomb at Chryse.[90] Euryalus is to add a gift to his apology for his insult to Odysseus.[91] Again, Antilochus offers to Menelaus something over and above the prize Menelaus had been in danger of losing.[92] Sometimes the restitution seems formally less than the injury: to Achilles, Hector's death alone is recompense for the many companions of his whom Hector had killed.[93] Adequacy of recompense is a matter for the judgement and feelings of the punisher, and Achilles hates Hector so much that Hector's death seems to him 'equivalent' to those of many Greeks.[94] By contrast, the recompense offered Achilles in *Iliad* IX is, for special reasons, enormous. In fact, both the recompense and the extra can have various relationships to the offence, and take various forms. The suitors have plundered Odysseus' property: in return, they

---

[86] It would of course be possible to identify the element which is 'reciprocally such' as simply the suffering, in which case punishment and retaliation would indeed be the same thing. But that would be unhelpful, since it robs the word 'retaliation' of reference to the act or mode of operation—cow exacted for cow, etc.

[87] Adkins (1960*b*) 30 and (1972*b*) 6 in effect, but fleetingly, notes the distinction.

[88] xxii. 55–9.   [89] I. 127–9, 213.

[90] I. 99–100. When Achilles wants Briseis back, he stipulates gifts in addition: XVI. 85–6; cf. IX. 638–9.

[91] viii. 396–415: honeyed words cancel out insulting words, but a concrete object is needed on top.   [92] XXIII. 592–5; cf. III. 284–7.

[93] XXII. 271–2.   [94] Cf. XVII. 538–9.

themselves are killed, their deaths are (gratifyingly) impossible to avenge, and their own estates will be plundered by Odysseus to replenish his possessions.[95] In short, injured *timē* requires recompense massively beyond the scale of the actual technical offence (plunder).

What is the status of the extra? If one regards the basic as restoration of *timē*, and not as punishment, then presumably one will regard the extra in the same light: the injured party's feeling of insult and loss of status is so great that *timē* can be restored to its original level only if recompense is made on an enhanced scale; there will be nothing essentially punitive in it.[96] However, if simple restitution leading to restoration of *timē* inescapably entails the infliction of suffering, the same must be even more true of restitution enhanced beyond the scale of the original injury. For without ceasing to be enhanced restitution, it also necessarily entails enhanced suffering; indeed, precisely because it entails enhanced suffering, it in part *constitutes* enhanced restitution. That is inherent in the very animosity of the relationship between offender and injured party.

On the basic, it is possible to put some measure or limit, however approximate or notional, that would reflect the seriousness of the damage and hence loss of *timē*, in the concrete sense of the term. But personal distress is different, for loss of reputation or status is impossible to measure precisely; hence the demand for extra recompense or satisfaction in terms of goods or feelings is potentially infinite. In the simple sense that huge recompense entails huge suffering, the extra has a far stronger penal import than the basic.[97] At some point, however, the discrepancy between the extent of the original damage and the amount of recompense demanded or exacted will become obvious, not only to the offender but to society at large, which, as we have seen, is perfectly capable of distinguishing basic and extra, and of curbing the latter. To draw such a distinction, to ask, that is, 'what did he *really* lose?', is a natural response to extreme retaliation. Society comes to feel involved, because the greater the restitution demanded the greater will be the likely effect on the offender's *oikos* and wider community. If the community then decides that, if only in its own interests, the extra should be curtailed, we have in effect, in a wholly rudimentary manner, public involvement in the criteria for the infliction of suffering on

---

[95] i. 376–80, xxii. 55–9, xxiii. 356–8.

[96] Mackenzie (1981) 76 n. 19 seems to suggest that I regard the basic as mere recompense and the extra as punitive. But I do not wish to argue anything as bald as that. Moreover, to say as she does that colossal recompense is mere restoration of *timē* is to betray a startling readiness to accept a hero's own estimate of his own loss of *timē*. It is clear that Homeric society was not thus ready, or not always (see below and pp. 17–18 above).

[97] The point is recognized by M. I. Finley (1979) 66, who describes Agamemnon's gift to Achilles as 'amends with a penal overtone'; cf. 117, 'penal gift'.

offenders. That involvement centres on the extra, not the basic. In that sense, the extra is central to all subsequent Greek penology.

(e) The argument from authority

Criterion (5) is glossed by Flew as (i) 'direct action by an aggrieved person with no pretensions to special authority is not properly called punishment, but revenge'; (ii) 'we should not insist . . . that [punishment] is confined to either legal or moral offences, but [we should] allow the use of the word in connection with any system of rules or laws—state, school, trades union, trade association, etc.'

Hart, however, restricts criterion (2) to offences 'against *legal* rules', and (5) to an 'authority constituted by a "*legal system*"' against which the offence is committed' (my italics in both cases); offences falling under Flew's gloss (ii) he relegates to 'sub-standard' or 'secondary' status.[98]

Adkins claimed that punishment 'as we know it' does not exist in Homer. Mackenzie goes further, asserting roundly, 'In the *Iliad* there are no punishments.'[99] Like Adkins, she sees Homeric retaliation as simply the restoration of the *status quo* for the *timē* of the injured party. She also relies, and relies heavily, on what she sees as the failure of retaliation in Homer to satisfy Flew's fifth criterion, but essentially in the strong form preferred by Hart: 'It [punishment] must be imposed and administered by an authority constituted by a legal system against which the offence is committed.' She herself defines punishment as 'suffering deliberately inflicted, by a penal authority, upon a criminal for his crime, in so far as he is responsible for that crime'.[100] Of that penal authority she demands:[101]

1. that it be impartial, in particular that it be other than the aggrieved party; for aggrieved parties exact not punishment but revenge;
2. that it be institutionalized, and operate in accordance with statutory and publicly known rules or laws;
3. that it must be appointed on the basis of its 'superiority or excellence in some respect';
4. that it be recognized as an authority *before* the exercise of its powers.

It is not clear whether *all* these conditions have to be satisfied before an infliction of suffering can qualify as a punishment. But on any showing

---

[98] Hart (1968) 4–5.

[99] Mackenzie (1981) 88, cf. 106. The *Odyssey* plays a fairly small role in her account, for reasons she gives on pp. 95–6. My own inclination is not to drive a wedge between the *Iliad* and the *Odyssey* in the matter of punishment.

[100] Ibid. 69.   [101] Ibid. 6, 11–12, 91–2.

they are very strong, and obviously derive from modern penal theory and practice. For another version of them, we may turn to Rawls:

... a person is said to suffer punishment whenever he is legally deprived of the normal rights of a citizen on the ground that he has violated a rule of law, the violation having been established by trial according to due process of law, provided that the deprivation is carried out by the recognised legal authorities of the state, that the rule of law clearly specifies both the offence and the attached penalty, that the courts construe statutes strictly, and that the statute was on the books prior to the time of the offence.[102]

Mackenzie's requirements are somewhat less elaborate than these; even so, clearly she is using, on a colossal scale, a device which she observes in others: the 'definitional stop', that is to say the claiming of the 'privilege of a "definition"',[103] in order to restrict the range of application of a term within predetermined limits. No one employing her criteria will find it difficult to stamp punishment out of Homer altogether.

What is it that the definitional stop stops? It is the use of the term 'punishment' to describe retaliatory actions in any society that does not have a formal legal system. In particular, less formally structured associations such as family, school, club, or trade union will be excluded, or at any rate allowed to be inflicting punishment on their members only in some secondary or non-standard sense—a sense which is secondary or non-standard only because it fails to fit the criteria.[104] Hence disquiet has rightly been expressed at the arbitrary restriction of the term 'punishment' to the penalties imposed by authorities operating under formal legal systems.[105]

Particularly objectionable is the notion that I may not punish an offender for an offence against myself on the grounds that if I do, I inflict not punishment but revenge; whereas if an authority takes it upon itself to punish on my behalf, that *is* punishment. Yet the penalty I impose may be precisely what the authority would have imposed. Whether or not that is so, the fact that it may be unjustified or unfair does not rob it of its status of punishment, any more than an unjustified or unfair punishment meted out by an authority would be robbed of that status for that reason. Impartiality is no doubt desirable, and its absence deplorable; but partial and impartial punishments are alike punishments, that

---

[102] Rawls (1969) 111-2.
[103] Mackenzie (1981) 13 n. 36, 32 etc.
[104] Kasachkoff (1973) 364 n. 4, 374-5.
[105] e.g. McCloskey (1962) 321-3, Samek (1966) *init.* and 219 ff. Honderich (1969) 1 cautiously admits that 'If there are practices governed by generally accepted rules, where the injured man or his family exacts the penalty, these approach to being practices of punishment.' Many other writers too display unease in admitting the existence of punishment in societies based on custom-law.

is to say the infliction of suffering on an offender for his offence. Nothing is gained by stigmatizing punishments imposed by the injured party himself as 'revenge', which is a disapproving and 'emotionally loaded'[106] word inappropriate when those punishments are perfectly justified and reasonable in scale. Does a court which itself punishes for contempt of court (i.e. itself) inflict only 'revenge'? That would be contrary to usage. 'Revenge' would be better reserved for a 'personal' punishment of which one disapproves, because the injured party acts with undue viciousness and places undue stress on the gaining of satisfaction for himself. In the Homeric context, the disapproval would occur at the point when social restraint begins to operate.[107]

Nor is it necessary that the offence should be against publicly known rules. Any informal or personal system of rules will suffice; indeed, at an extreme, an injured party may reasonably be said to 'punish' for an offence against himself even if it is not forbidden by any rule at all.

What we must not do is to confuse the marks of a *system* of punishment with the marks of the *concept* of punishment;[108] for there may be many systems, with and without authorities, each embodying the concept. Kasachkoff puts the matter as follows:[109]

the error which underlies [the] introduction of 'a real or supposed authority' into the criteria requirements for punishment is twofold: (1) an extension of the criteria for punishment operative in legal contexts to contexts beyond that realm; and (2) confusion of the defining criteria of the *concept* of punishment with the grounds for the *moral* justification of its infliction. Together these confusions lead to the mistaken view that the concept of punishment cannot *apply* to offences which merit a punishment for which there is no legitimate authority.... outside of the legal or quasi-legal sphere, the authority with which one inflicts punishment bears only on the justifiability of one's act; it does not, on account of its *moral* relevance, acquire any *conceptual* force.

Mackenzie laid down four requirements to be satisfied before punishment could be said to exist in Homer, or at any rate in the *Iliad*; she found them not satisfied, and denied, with no qualification that I can see, that Homeric society knew the practice of punishment. I hope to have shown that, posed in that way, the problem virtually dictates its own answer. Nevertheless, it will be instructive to see how far her requirements, though strict, may nevertheless be met. The two central ones are *recognized and impartial authority* and *publicly known rules*.

What authorities are there in Homer? We learn of 'kings' and others delivering *dikai* and *themistes*.[110] Whatever else *dikai* and *themistes* were, they were presumably decisions of some kind in cases of dispute

---

[106] Adkins's term, (1960b) 24.   [107] See pp. 17–18 above.
[108] I take the terminology from Samek (1966) 219.
[109] Kasachkoff (1973) 375, cf. 377.   [110] See pp. 35 ff. below.

between two sides. Sometimes, presumably, the decision took the form of a direction that a given amount of *timē*, in the sense of goods, should be transferred, or allowed to be transferred by seizure, from the person against whom the decision was given to the person in whose favour it was given; and such a transfer would inevitably have brought with it the transfer of *timē* in the sense of 'standing'. The losing party suffers, that is, damage and grief; and to the extent that this is the result the winning party wants to achieve, and does so by appealing to a king, both he and the king may be said to be inflicting punishment; and the king is, ostensibly at least, impartial between the two sides. All parties know, and the complainant intends, that if the king finds against the alleged offender, suffering will be inflicted on him for his offence. Conversely, a complainant who fails to persuade the king will himself suffer, by losing face. The very winning and losing of the day, whichever way the decision goes, confers and takes away *timē*; for the event is public, or at any rate before some sort of audience. If that is right, we have an institutionalized form of the one-to-one conflict between individuals. The kings have recognized authority, though they are probably much influenced by the shouted interventions of the people. But much of this is conjecture: we simply do not know how systematic, regular, and effective such occasions were. In particular, we cannot know whether such 'courts' felt it to be their business to distinguish between 'basic' and 'extra', or to consider excuses and aggravations and a whole host of other factors.[111]

As for rules and laws, 'statutory' implies writing, which was not yet in general use; but obviously this does not entail that Homeric society had no norms at all. Clearly it did have a code of behaviour, which rested on a prudent combination of habit and convenience, reinforced by teaching, direction, and pressure[112] from 'heroes' and 'kings' acting in their various spheres of conduct (*oikos*, army, 'court', etc.), and in relation to various categories of person (other heroes, wife, children, slaves, foreigners, etc.). Firmly entrenched notions of 'the fitting' constituted more general guides to conduct.[113] One of the more obviously prudential 'rules' would have been 'do not offend someone stronger than yourself—for he may strike back, and it may well happen that no one will be able or willing to stop him doing as he wants with you'.

That, surely, is the point. Society gives to private self-help and retaliation its acquiescence, licence and approval.[114] The individual—any

---

[111] These early courts are discussed in more detail in ch. 4; for the trial scene on the shield of Achilles (XVIII. 497 ff.), see p. 90 n. 7 below.

[112] See in more detail pp. 90–1 below. [113] See pp. 17–18 above.

[114] Cf. Wolff (1946), Latte (1931), in Berneker (1968) 263–5. Mackenzie (1981) 86 concedes the 'traditional acceptance' of the patterns of aggression and retaliation as between individuals in Homer. 'But authority in the meaningful sense of the external and statutory agent of punishment is entirely lacking . . .'

individual, not just a hero—is his own authority; and this authority is conferred on him by society, which sanctions, in part because it has only imperfect means of preventing it, the exercise of his power, his 'superiority or excellence' in Mackenzie's words (her criterion (3)). The authority of an individual is certainly not impartial; yet he cannot afford entirely to ignore certain restraints.

The preceding paragraph may sound like an attempt to meet Mackenzie's criteria; but it is not, as I have no concern to meet them, since I believe them to be arbitrary and misapplied. But I do suggest that in Homer we find rudimentary approximations to them.

(f) The character of Homeric punishment

How ought we to describe punishment in Homer? He himself has no single comprehensive word for it. What he did recognize was suffering inflicted on an offender for an offence, either as a concomitant of timē-restoration, or as itself constituting the restoration; and he described the many specific means by which this suffering was caused, and the various forms it could take. Similarly he has no single term for 'reward', in the general comprehensive sense of 'good done to doer of good in return for good done'; he has only a series of particular concrete ways in which people are rewarded.[115] Nor has he general adjectives to describe the character or purpose of 'suffering inflicted on an offender for an offence'. But he knows that in its various manifestations it can be retributive or deterrent or both. In so far as it is calculated to be compensatory, i.e. to restore the status quo, it is retributive in the literal sense of the word, and thus strongly utilitarian;[116] it is utilitarian also in being deterrent; and if to be deterrent is to be calculated to improve not only an offender's conduct but his character, it is also reformative. How far it is retributive in a moral sense, i.e. dictated by the feeling that an offender ought to suffer in principle, for reasons independent of the satisfaction it affords the punisher, is a question best faced in the next chapter when we consider the influence of the idea of 'justice', particularly in Hesiod and Solon.

(g) Conclusion

In discussing punishment in Homer both Adkins and Mackenzie employed tools that were too blunt for the job. In response, I have adopted a kind of reductionist view of punishment, treating it in its basic

[115] Cf. Lloyd-Jones (1983) 26: 'in Homeric Greek ... if the word [for 'duty' or 'loyalty'] is lacking the thing is not'.
[116] Quinton (1969) 56.

dictionary-definition sense of 'suffering inflicted on an offender for an offence'. Adkins claims punishment does not exist in Homer 'as we know it'. True enough, for its institutional forms have changed radically; but it exists. In particular, the constraints and decisions that face the punisher in Homeric society are clear anticipations of the controversies about punishment that developed later. Greek penology starts in Homer.

2

ANXIETIES AND SURROGATES

In the varied literature of the roughly three centuries that separate Hesiod and Plato, three processes went on simultaneously. (i) The mode of operation of surrogate punishers of several kinds is described and elaborated in vividly imaginative forms; (ii) a formal system of courts came into being, with their own characteristic purposes, procedures, and provisions for punishment; (iii) reflection about equity and moral responsibility, and their implications for punishment, developed considerably in a variety of legal, political, and philosophical contexts. These three developments affected each other. In order, therefore, to preserve clarity of outline in a long and complex period of history I shall in this and the next two chapters attempt to say something about each of the three in turn, and to examine some of their relationships. We shall then be in a position to approach Plato.

At the root of the development of Greek penology lies anxiety lest the offender escape scot-free. This no doubt is a universal human worry; but in Greek thought it is conspicuous. Naturally; for remedies lay, at least in archaic times, largely in self-help, and victims could easily find that through weakness or other circumstances they could not retaliate effectively; and such courts as existed at any period were not without expense, open to various kinds of corruption, and of variable and unpredictable effectiveness. The result of the anxiety was a series of vivid constructs of the imagination, designed partly for purposes of deterrence, but also to assure a victim that whatever his own weakness, the offender would be caught and punished in the end by some over-whelmingly powerful surrogate.

GODS AS PUNISHERS

Greek literature exhibits everywhere the general belief, often passionate, unreflecting, and with no tinge of doubt,[1] that the gods, especially Zeus,

---

[1] For instance, Orestes in Eur. *El.* 583–4 is made to say that if injustice triumphs over justice, then the gods must be supposed not to exist. This is in effect to say that if gods exist, as they do, then

punish offenders, even if only after an interval, and even if only their descendants or other third parties. The offences are often stated explicitly to be against 'justice', which is conceived in various ways. Sometimes it is a kind of world-order, which the gods, being at its apex, wish to protect in their own interests; at other times it is a peaceful and equitable relationship between men, whose disruption is thought of as a disruption of the world-order itself. No firm boundary between offences against the order and offences against men can be drawn; nevertheless my focus is on the latter kind, and on the role of the gods in inflicting punishments for them, in addition to or instead of those inflicted by men themselves. I make no attempt to rehearse the evidence exhaustively,[2] but simply concentrate on authors and passages which discuss the matter openly or seem in some way revealing.

(a) The Homeric assumptions

In the analysis of Homeric aggression and retaliation in the previous part I treated gods as being very much on all fours with human beings in their motivations. For gods too feel anger, and have *timē* to defend. However, in virtue of their immortality and superior strength certain other functions are ascribed to them; and the way in which they are thought to discharge these functions provokes problems.

In Homeric society, to retaliate against, and thus to punish, an offender is largely a matter for the individual injured party. But some offenders are stronger than the parties they injure, and conversely some injured parties are able to retaliate with extreme violence. The battery of restraints brought to bear on what could all too easily be a relationship in which might was right is very evident in the poems. These restraints took two forms: (i) a general social insistence on 'seemly' and 'moderate' conduct; (ii) the institutionalized enforcement of that conduct. (i) I have described already,[3] but some further description is now needed of (ii); for both seem to enjoy some divine protection.

There is plenty of evidence for (i), both in the *Odyssey* and in the *Iliad*; but for (ii), and for the role of the gods in punishing offenders against both (i) and (ii), the evidence is appreciably more abundant in the *Odyssey*. Presumably that is because of the nature of its theme, but

---

of course they punish injustice (cf. *HF* 841–2). No doubt such reasoning would have struck many Greeks as entirely cogent.

[2] Here is the merest sample, varying widely in context, expression, and purpose: Pind. *Ol.* 1. 64, Soph. *Phil.* 1040 ff., Aes. *Supp.* 733, Ar. *Cl.* 395–7, *Thes.* 668 ff., Xen. *Hunt.* 1. 11, Isoc. 1. 50 (but 5. 117 treats the Olympians as benefactors, and confines punishing to other gods, presumably those of the underworld), Lys. 6. 20, 34. 10; cf. Dem. 19. 71, 239, 25. 11.

[3] See pp. 17–18 above.

possibly also because of a slightly later date, when questions of justice were becoming urgent preoccupations. Hence certain passages of the *Iliad* have been taken to be interpolations. The most conspicuous passage has fallen under grave suspicion:[4] Zeus sends torrential rain when he is angry and rages against men who by violence in the marketplace, *agora*, judge crooked ordinances, *themistes*, and drive out *dikē*, paying no regard to the vengeance, *opis*, of gods. Admittedly, this sounds Hesiodic, as we shall see; but so too do several other (but shorter) passages, particularly in the *Odyssey*. But that proves nothing.[5] Evidence external to the poems themselves for the hypothesis of interpolation is entirely lacking, and the danger of begging the question is obvious. I see no reason not to believe that the beliefs and practices I discuss were a going concern as early as (say) the ninth century.

It is clear that 'kings', and probably other persons making up the great and the good in Homeric society, were expected to deliver judgement in cases of dispute which were referred to them. The manner of the referral, the procedure during the hearing, and the form taken by the judgements, are obscure, and in any case not relevant here.[6] What is crucial is the pair of terms *themis* (pl. *themistes*) and *dikē*. They have been studied intensively, and I state as succinctly as possible what I understand to be their nature. A *themis* is some general 'laying down',[7] or formulation of a standard of conduct, some more or less lapidary statement of normal, expected and desirable behaviour in some department of life.[8] Its application is presumably not limited to 'courts': it constituted a basis in which a king would ground or justify his advice and policy in particular circumstances. In a 'court', its use would be to provide some intelligible reasons for a *dikē*, a specific decision between competing claims; it would be that general consideration in the light of which the

---

[4] XVI. 384–8.

[5] Cf. Lloyd-Jones (1983) 18, 35–6.

[6] MacDowell (1978) ch. 1 is a good brief account of these primitive 'courts'. For the celebrated trial scene on the shield of Achilles (XVIII. 497–508), see esp. Bonner and Smith (1930) i. 31–41, Wolff (1946), Gagarin (1986) 26–33 and p. 90 n. 7 below.

[7] *Tithēmi*, 'I ordain or lay down'. Obviously some *themistes* fell on deaf ears or failed in their purpose for some other reason: see IX. 156 and 298, 'rich' or 'fruitful' *themistes*, implying that some were not so.

[8] II. 206: 'one king, to whom the son of Cronus has given .... *themistes*, so that he may give them [his people] counsel' (the word 'counsel' is not quite certain, but cf. IX. 99, ix. 112 ff.). It is sometimes said that no *themis* is recorded. But surely the frequent interjection of the words 'which is *themis*', or 'it is not *themis*', to give a general explanation or justification of a particular course of action, shows pretty exactly the nature of the *themistes* delivered by the kings. For example, Eumaeus justifies greeting Odysseus by claiming that it is not *themis* to slight any stranger at all; and that Odysseus is noticeably 'lowly', he argues, does not exclude him from the benefits of the injunction that all strangers and beggars are from Zeus (xiv. 55 ff., cf. XI. 779). In effect, he argues for a specific application, which *prima facie* offered some difficulty, of a general rule. Cf. II. 73, IX. 33, x. 73, xxiv. 286, for some presumably more straightforward applications of a *themis*.

dikē is given; and the *dikē* expresses how the norm is to be observed in practical terms in a particular case.

Dikē, however, has many meanings:

1. 'Way', 'manner', 'characteristic behaviour', 'clear pattern of regular and normal conduct', of some category of person, e.g. slaves, gods, kings.[9]

2. The 'proper way' in which people and things *should* behave; this meaning arose from the natural and common feeling that what is normal ought to continue to be so.[10]

3. A 'showing' or 'demonstration' or 'marking out' of (2), by king or judge, or indeed other person, in a particular case; *dikē* is apparently to be derived from *deiknumi*, 'I show or mark out'.[11]

4. 'Recompense' or 'settlement'; hence 'penalty', since (3) will usually constitute a decision against one of the contending parties.[12]

5. All or part of the formal process of (3) and (4): 'trial', 'case', 'suit', 'prosecution', 'litigation'.

6. The principles and standards of propriety or fairness dictating and embodied in (3), (4), and (5); in effect the concept 'justice'.

7. A goddess, 'justice' personified.

In Homer, meanings (1) and (3) are strongly marked; and (2) is implied, as obviously the kings' decisions in (3) must depend for their acceptability and effectiveness on generally held notions of propriety and obligation. Meaning (6) *may* be present in one or two passages.[13]

Themis and *dikē* thus cohere intimately. They are both formal expressions of those moral norms and restraints which are enjoined and enforced informally in society at large; but *themis* expresses them generally, *dikē* in particular situations. But since both express and reinforce the same norms, either may be used to describe procedure in a 'court': the elders 'gave *dikē* (*dikazon*) and 'spoke' it; Minos 'gives *themistes*' to the dead, who ask for *dikai* from him; *dikaspoloi* protect *themistes*; and the judges 'judge crooked *themistes* by force and drive out *dikē*'.[14] Essentially the same procedure is being described in all these cases: the giving of a *dikē* by reference to one or more *themistes*. A just

---

[9] iv. 691, xiv. 59, xix. 43.

[10] As when Penelope reproaches the suitors for having departed from precedent in the *dikē mnēstērōn*, 'the way of suitors', xviii. 275. 'Der Gegensatz zwischen blosser Konvention und ethisch wertvoller Sitte besteht für die homerische Zeit nicht' (Hoffmann (1914) 41) is, however, an exaggeration.

[11] XVI. 542, XVIII. 508, XXIII. 542, ix. 215, xi. 570. The verb *dikazō*, 'I give a *dikē*, XVIII. 506. *Dikazomai*, 'I seek a *dikē*, xii. 440. *Dikaspolos*, 'giver of *dikai* (pl.)', I. 238, xi. 186. On the derivation from *deiknumi*, see Palmer (1950).   [12] XIX. 180.

[13] Probably XVI. 388 and xiv. 84, though in both places 'the institution or process of the giving of *dikē*' may be the sense (5) intended.

[14] I. 238-9, XVI. 387-8, XVIII. 506, xi. 569-71.

man, *dikaios*, is therefore one who has a sense of just conduct, and who therefore does not need *dikē* to be imposed on him.

What are these 'moral norms'? Evidently decent, restrained behaviour directed by practical sagacity. Ares is described as 'foolish' or 'mad' (*aphrōn*), and as not 'knowing' or 'observing' any *themis*; a lover of civil strife is *athemistos*, 'without *themis*'; the Cyclops, who 'knows' or 'recognizes' neither *dikai* nor *themistes*, is 'savage' (*agrios*); the use of force and strength are opposed to observance of *themis*; some suitors may be *athemistoi*, others *enaisimoi*, 'of fitting or righteous conduct'.[15] Odysseus couples 'arrogant' (*hubristēs*), 'savage', and 'not *dikaios*', i.e. 'not observing *dikē*'; the suitors are neither 'knowing' (*noēmones*) nor *dikaioi*;[16] and when Agamemnon has been brought to recognize his mistake and has recompensed Achilles, he will in future be 'more *dikaios*', i.e. 'more regular or conventional'.[17]

The reflection that Zeus is angry with a judge who judges crooked *themistes*[18] brings us to the role of the gods. For just as both the informal standards in ordinary life and the formal constraints of the 'courts' existed in order to mitigate the harshness and potential excesses of self-help, so too the gods were reckoned to act, in some manner which we shall examine in a moment, as overseers and enforcers of both categories of norms and constraints. The evidence for this concern on the part of the gods is fairly abundant, particularly in the *Odyssey*, and is of three kinds:

1. Statements that *themis/themistes* and *dikē* originate from the gods and are protected or revered by them.[19]
2. General censure of the failure of various offenders to have regard to the *mēnis* (anger) of the gods and their *opis* (vengeance); the need to be god-fearing (*theoudēs*).[20]
3. Implications that the gods retaliate against breaches of *themis* and *dikē*, and other transgressions of various kinds.[21]

---

[15] V. 761, IX. 63–4, ix. 215 (cf. 106), xvii. 363, xviii. 139–41.

[16] ii. 282, vi. 120; cf. iii. 52, 133, 244, viii. 575, ix. 175, xiii. 201, 209.

[17] XIX. 181; cf. XIII. 6, the Abians, 'people without force', *bia*, are 'most *dikaioi*', and XI. 832, Chiron as the 'most *dikaios* of the Centaurs' (who were a wild bunch; presumably Chiron is relatively civilized, as he is Achilles' teacher). Note also the opposition of *dikaios* to *huperbion* ('insolently'), xiv. 90–2. [18] XVI. 387.

[19] I. 238: *themistes* are from Zeus (or, conceivably, 'the *dikaspoloi* guard them at Zeus' behest'); II. 206: [let us have one chief, one king], 'to whom the son of Cronus has given *themistes*', cf. IX. 99; xiv. 84: 'the gods do not love cruel (*schetlia*) action, but revere (*tiousi*) *dikē* and the seemly deeds of men (*aisima erga*)'; xvi. 403: *themistes* that are of Zeus.

[20] XIII. 624–5; XVI. 388: [corrupt judges] 'do not pay regard to the *opis* of the gods'; ii. 66–7; xiv. 82, 88, 283–4; xx. 215; xxi. 28. 'God fearing': vi. 121, ix. 176, xiii. 202, xix. 109. On *mēnis*, see Considine (1986).

[21] IX. 502 ff.: Zeus injures inflexible transgressors; XVI. 384–8: corrupt judges attract Zeus' anger; xvii. 485–7: gods roam the earth observing the *hubris* and good order (*eunomiē*) of men. The Erinues (if they may count as gods) pursue offenders against family law (XV. 204, IX. 454, 565–72, ii. 135, xi.

The gods, then, are believed to punish offenders against various social norms, and against *themis* and *dikē*. But obviously the belief is based on wishful thinking rather than hard evidence. The poet, of course, can 'know' that an offender has been punished by a god, but the offender himself cannot: he can only surmise. And even if he has not, to his own knowledge, committed an offence, he may not unreasonably infer that he has in fact done so unwittingly, from the mere fact that he is suffering. For Zeus does not suddenly pop up in front of (say) a perjurer, rap him smartly over the knuckles with some celestial cane, and then disappear. The perjurer who subsequently experiences some suffering, whether at the hands of his fellow men or in some other fashion, is at liberty to interpret it as a divine punishment; but if nothing untoward happens he may naturally suppose that Zeus has not noticed the perjury, or has forgotten, or does not care. The general belief that gods punish is not necessarily a belief that they do so invariably, in every case;[22] nor does the mere fear of their anger entail a belief that it is inescapable. To plug such holes in the theory that the gods punish misdeeds is the purpose of certain assurances which are obviously calculated to comfort victims and deter potential offenders: (i) that the gods have eyes and see all over the place,[23] (ii) that although punishment may come late, it does come in the end,[24] and that (iii) perjurers are made to pay *after death*.[25]

But the fundamental flaw in the belief in divine punishment is that it has insufficient rationale. Clearly both gods and men have *timē*, and a powerful interest in defending it; in particular, the gods resist insults, or encroachment on their spheres of activity, and have their special favourites and enemies among mankind. Accordingly, for various injuries, gods punish gods and men, and men punish men (they can hardly punish gods). That is all intellectually coherent. The trouble starts when one moves on from the comforting belief that gods punish offences against the family, the social order, or whatever, and begins to ask *why* they do so.

No doubt Zeus has a 'sphere of interest', in beggars, oaths etc., and dislikes having his name taken in vain. But why does he take an interest in the first place? Are we to suppose that he takes a 'disinterested interest', out of a sheer passion for moral virtue? The only model for punishment available in the human world is one in which the punisher is angry, because of an injured interest; but how the gods' interests can be

---

280) and breakers of oaths (XIX. 259), and perhaps protect beggars (xvii. 475). Zeus too has certain special functions, notably to punish oath-breakers (eg. IV. 158) and offenders against strangers and suppliants (XIII. 625, vii. 165, 181, ix. 270, xvi. 422).

[22] Athena believes that in general Zeus rewards good kings, but that in a particular case (Odysseus) he has failed to do so, v. 7 ff. [23] IX. 502 ff., xvii. 485-7.
[24] IV. 161. [25] III. 278-9.

injured is not always clear. For they are immortal and blessed, and may presumably, if they wish, remain unaffected by men who offend against each other; so why should they be so furiously angry as to punish them? A general and remote answer could be that if human society were even more violent and chaotic than it is, the gods would receive less worship and fewer sacrifices; and that would give them their interest in punishing crime.[26] But even this approach is of limited use. The gods themselves lead lives that are not particularly edifying,[27] and to envisage them as punishing men for what they themselves do is perhaps implausible or even outrageous. And of course they may simply not notice particular offences, or, for reasons they deem sufficient in their own interests, turn a blind eye; and if that is so, the general supposition that they punish invariably would crumble. Some crumbling can in fact be detected in Homer.[28]

In short, invariability needs either to be guaranteed by some exceptionally powerful private interest and motivation on the part of the gods, or to be based on some plausible reason for supposing them capable of rising above the self-interest which actuates them normally. The latter possibility was not envisaged immediately; but the task of demonstrating invariability based on self-interest was undertaken by Hesiod (*fl. c.* 700).

(b) Hesiod's use of the Homeric assumptions

At a first reading of Hesiod's two major poems, the *Theogony* and the *Works and Days*, we seem to be in a very familiar world. In the *Theogony* especially, the gods retaliate on each other for offences very much as in Homer, and in the same sort of spirit (e.g. Zeus punishes Prometheus in anger).[29] The punishment of mortals also seems to be broadly on the Homeric model. Zeus fashions a penalty (*dikē*) for *hubris* and cruel deeds,[30] and *Dikē* herself invisibly visits society and brings evil to those who spurn her.[31] Zeus evidently runs a spy service: 30,000 immortal watchers roam the earth and take note of unjust deeds.[32] As in Homer, these personal agencies are not, evidently, *disinterestedly* interested in the enforcement of justice. Hesiod does not or cannot rise to this. These

---

[26] I. 74–100, V. 177–8: gods may retaliate against failure to worship them properly.

[27] As Xenophanes later complained (B11 DK).

[28] Telemachus is far from sure that the gods will help him against the *hubris* of the suitors: i. 378–80, iii. 205–9, 223–8, xvii. 50–1. There may be irony in xvi. 263–5. xvi. 129 implies the gods may or may not bestir themselves.

[29] *Th.* 521 ff., 561, *WD* 47, 53. 138. Aptness: *Th.* 561 ff., and references in West (1966) on 562. Initiative: *Th.* 172.   [30] *WD* 239.

[31] *WD* 220 ff.; compare Paus. 5. 18. 2, and contrast the administrations of Peace 'abroad in the land' (228).

[32] *WD* 252–5, backed up by 256 ff., where Justice, *Dikē*, sits beside Zeus and tells him of the unjust minds of men. Zeus may also have a familial reason for supporting her: she is his daughter.

'persons' enforce justice not out of zeal for moral virtue but because they are themselves personally involved: the gods punish transgressors because they are angry.[33] Good men are loved by the gods, who have to be propitiated by sacrifices etc.[34] Hesiod's celebrated insistence on justice and her divine guarantors sounds an elevated thing; but he operates very strictly within a tight framework of personal motivation, of injury, and of anger and counter-injury. Divine punishment is retaliation by the stronger party.

Nevertheless, Hesiod has something new and important to say, and he says it by systematically exploiting Homeric themes. In a preliminary way, we can see this process in Hesiod's handling of the concept of knowledge. In Homer, the *dikaios* man was also *noēmon*, 'knowing'.[35] What did he 'know' or 'realize' or 'understand'? Presumably, as a matter of practical prudence, the prevailing pattern of restrained and civilized behaviour, justified by *themistes* and enforced from time to time by individual *dikai*. The Homeric heroes learned, sometimes painfully, who was 'stronger'; and the gods, by virtue of their superior strength, had the general role of punishing transgressors. A strong sanction, one might think; yet their efficiency, willingness, and motivation were not beyond doubt. But Hesiod writes an explicitly didactic poem, the *Works and Days*, and has a more general and comprehensive point to make. His purpose is not simply to convince Perses (the addressee)[36] that some person, or even some god, is stronger than he is. He urges him to 'realize'[37] a crucial fact about the very nature of social life: it is constructed in such a way that injustice cannot pay. Not merely does it not pay on particular occasions, it *never* pays. The unjust Perses must see that Hesiod, or rather his message, or rather the nature of the social world which the message describes, is 'stronger'.

Hesiod's intention that Perses should grasp that justice is stronger than injustice, as a matter of truth and sheer fact, emerges from a series of passages in which he reproaches Perses for his foolishness and urges him to 'get wise' to the truth. At the beginning of the poem he says, 'I'll tell you true things,' and proceeds immediately to explain the light that

---

[33] *WD* 333; cf. 251, 303.   [34] *WD* 336 ff.
[35] e.g. ii. 282, iii. 133; cf. Tsouyopoulos (1966) 30–1 and p. 37 above.
[36] It is sufficient for my purposes that Hesiod represents Perses as flouting *dikē*. The exact historical situation is not easy to fathom; indeed we may have only fiction or literary convention: see Gagarin (1974*a*) and West (1978) 33 ff.
[37] *WD* 9, 12, 397, *et saepe*; cf. 107: Hesiod himself 'knows'. On *noeō*, 'to come to realize', see the articles by von Fritz (1943, 1945, 1946). The kings too need to 'take note', 248; cf. 202, where they are said to 'know' or 'be aware' already—unlike Perses, who at 218 is in danger of 'finding out' too late that injustice does not pay: 'the fool knows by experience or suffering'. This is a maxim found in a slightly different form in Homer, XVII. 32, XX. 198. But in Homer it is put into the mouth of one hero telling another to yield to a stronger, i.e. to himself. In Hesiod, the 'stronger' is 'the system', 'the way of the world,' the way it is made.

has dawned on him about the two strifes, 'So then, after all/in the event/ in fact/contrary to earlier supposition (which is the force of *ara* in line 11),[38] there are not one but two strifes upon the earth'. One is brute polemical strife, getting one's own way by force; the other is the whole-some spirit of emulation and competition, which makes a man work hard. Devotees of the former are fools, for they do not know that its results are, in practical and prudential terms, worse than those of the latter: they do not *know* how much more the half is than the whole, nor what great advantage there is in mallow and asphodel,[39] i.e. in a modest competence rather than in riches. Hesiod does not present these arguments or assertions as opinions, but as plain facts; and these facts function as substitutes for persons or things which might force Perses' hand. In other words, just as a Homeric hero tries by words or deeds to produce in his adversary knowledge or conviction of his (the hero's) superior strength, or of someone prepared to fight on his behalf, Hesiod tries by words alone to convince Perses that certain forces of irresistible strength operate or will operate on Hesiod's side;[40] so let Perses desist— not, be it noted, directly or simply because it is just to do so, but simply in his own best interests. Hesiod's message is not 'crime is wicked'. It is, 'crime does not pay'. As he himself says,[41] 'may I *not* be just ... if the injust man is going to get more *dikē*,' i.e. do better out of *dikē* than the just man. But justice is strong and does pay, while injustice is weak and does not; and the *Works and Days* is essentially a large-scale version, and a lineal descendant, of one of those Homeric speeches that says in effect, 'If you try it on, you'll learn that you are weaker'. Hesiod's advice to Perses is therefore essentially prudential: 'You great chump, Perses, I'm going to tell you sound sense, for your own good'. Perses is a chump who needs to be told that to do hurt to others is to do it to oneself, and that evil plots harm the plotter most.[42]

Hesiod, then, recommends *dikē* to Perses in the most emphatic terms. What does he mean by the word? Often he means a 'showing', or judicial decision,[43] expressing a *themis* and capable of being arrived at 'straightly' or 'crookedly';[44] and since a decision entails a settlement, or a penalty imposed on the one side or the other, we naturally find it in that sense.[45] On a few occasions it seems to indicate the principles or standards of fairness or propriety that ought to inform the 'showings'.[46] It is opposed,

---

[38] *WD* 10-11; the reference is presumably to *Th.* 225.

[39] *WD* 40-1.

[40] Consider the repeated keynote word, *WD* 5 ff.: 'easily' ('with his little finger') does Zeus humble the proud etc.; cf. 105, 'it is impossible to escape his will'; 267 'he sees everything'; 217, '*Dikē* is stronger than *Hubris* in the end'.

[41] *WD* 270-2.   [42] *WD* 266.

[43] *WD* 39, 221, 264; cf. p. 36 above.   [44] *WD* 219, 262, 264.

[45] *WD* 238, 249.   [46] *WD* 213, 275.

as in Homer, to *hubris* and violent conduct in general;[47] and it is palely personified as a goddess.[48]

With colossal confidence, Hesiod asserts that Zeus himself punishes injustice; and he seems to mean by 'injustice' every particular case of it.[49] If he does mean that, truly Zeus must have a busy time of it. But he does not actually want to make the larger claim that Zeus intervenes personally on every occasion. For he believes that Zeus punishes every case of injustice at one remove, through the instrument of a particular pattern of life he has imposed on men, which works automatically.

That pattern of life is one characterized by much trouble and hard work, *which is itself a punishment*.[50] Prometheus deceived Zeus; Zeus hit back with grievous cares for men[51] by depriving them of fire; Prometheus stole fire and restored it to men; thereupon Zeus contrived that Pandora be given to men, who of course released upon them further 'grievous cares', which include 'hard work'.[52] The myth of the five ages, which now follows, describes the successively more degenerate races of men; the sequence culminates in the present day, in which men's life is described in the same terms as before: it is full of labour and sorrow, and the gods will give them grievous cares, mingled with some good.[53] Eventually Zeus will destroy this race for its violence and injustice.[54] The lugubrious description of the present day[55] is pointedly followed by the fable of the hawk and the nightingale: the hawk (Perses and the corrupt *basileis*) may be stronger than the nightingale (Hesiod), but implicitly Zeus is more powerful than either, and men cannot escape punishment for their misdeeds.[56]

---

[47] *WD* 213, 217, 275.

[48] *WD* 220–4, 256 ff. On the meaning of *dikē* in *WD* see also Rodgers ('keeping out of trouble'), Gagarin (1973) (various constituents of 'legal process', without 'general moral sense'), and Dickie (1978), who rightly stresses that the notions of fairness and propriety must be present. It is sometimes difficult to see what sense Hesiod intends; the above is not intended as a complete review, for which see Gagarin.

[49] *WD* 248 ff. (Zeus has 30,000 watchers of men), 267 (he realizes everything); cf. 105. In 268 we find '. . . and he looks upon these things too' (i.e. relations between Hesiod and Perses) 'if ever he wishes'. This kind of formula is used, as West on *Th.* 28 says, to explain why a god 'does not always do what he is supposed to be able to'. If Hesiod has not simply used a formula carelessly, and does mean seriously to imply that Zeus does not always wish to intervene personally, that would be consistent with his wider view, as I indicate. More probably, the point did not occur to him: the 'if ever he wishes' formula and the like are frequently used to suggest that a god has only to wish to achieve something, and he can do it with ease (e.g. X. 556, iii. 231, x. 22, and some of West's other references). The notion of Zeus' power and care is prominent in *WD* 3 ff., and I take it this is the point of 268.

[50] But not one without prospect of reconciliation. Just as an offender regains the friendship, *philotēs*, of his victim by paying recompense, *dikē*, so a man who works is dearer, *philteros*, to the gods: *WD* 309, 711–13.   [51] *WD* 42–9.

[52] *WD* 91, 95, 100.   [53] *WD* 176–8; the first race had no need to work, 109–20.

[54] *WD* 180–201.   [55] Or rather, prediction by extrapolation from present trends.

[56] *WD* 202–12 with 265 ff. and Zanker (1986) 31–2. Or is the hawk Zeus, and Perses the nightingale? See Welles (1967) 17 ff. and Jensen (1966) 20–2.

Hard work is thus a Zeus-sent punishment, which it is impossible to escape; for Zeus has built it permanently into the very nature of human life.[57] The just man is not exempt from the need to work; indeed the very fact that he works constitutes the punishment imposed on the race by Zeus; it is by work that he wins virtue.[58] But the unjust man attempts to escape that punishment: by fraud and violence he tries to live a life without work, i.e. without undergoing the punishment the race must suffer.[59] Perses does this; but he is a fool, because he does not see that the world is so constructed that for attempting to escape the punishment of Zeus he will in effect be punished further; for the attempt ineluctably brings suffering. Work supplies food; gods and men feel indignation (*nemesis*) with the idler, and idling brings the disagreeable social consequence of disgrace.[60] To covet other men's wealth to escape work simply brings poverty, the need to beg and to grovel to others, and crippling retaliation from the gods.[61]

Hard work to win wealth of one's own, and keeping one's hands off that of others; restrained and non-violent conduct; a willingness to settle disputes by straight *dikai* and not crooked ones; all this adds up to the strenuous pattern of life imposed on men by Zeus as a punishment for Prometheus' offence. The notion that failure to toe this line brings an inevitable 'backlash' is pervasive.[62] For instance, crooked judgements bring social disorder, and evil planned recoils upon the plotter.[63] Just as Pandora brought ills upon mankind, so a wife brings, or can bring, ills to her husband; but avoiding them by remaining a bachelor has its own grave disadvantages.[64] Neglecting hard work on the land leads to hunger; you must plough at the right time or there is no crop. Correct husbandry is correct ethics.[65] That misdeeds often come to grief is of course a common enough observation;[66] but Hesiod builds it into a comprehensive theory of conduct.[67]

---

[57] He has set the good strife (*eris*) 'in the roots of the earth,' *WD* 19; he has hidden livelihood from men, 42; and he has ordained *dikē* as a way of life for them, 276–80.

[58] *WD* 230–1, 289–92. On work as justice, see further Bongert (1982).

[59] *WD* 189, 192, 'might is right'. Note the echoes of language: 398, the gods have ordained (*dietek-mēranto*) work for men; 239, Zeus ordains (*tekmairetai*) punishment (*dikē*) for violent men (violence being a way of avoiding work); 229, Zeus does not *tekmairetai* war for just men.

[60] *WD* 298–313; cf. 352 ff.

[61] *WD* 314–26, 391–404. "Grovelling" = *aidōs ouk agathē*, 'respect for others which is not good' (i.e. not good for the person who has to do the respecting).

[62] 'Toeing the line' may take two forms, *WD* 293 ff.: having one's own discernment, and merely obeying good advice (a somewhat Platonic distinction).

[63] *WD* 220 (*rhothos* is the angry murmur of the people in protest), 265–6.

[64] *WD* 373–80, 695–705, *Th.* 590–612.

[65] *WD* 225–47, 298 ff., 383 ff. *passim*, e.g. 394–404, 413, 493–501. The relationship between justice and agriculture *may* be part of the point in xix. 111. At XVI. 384 ff. the connection is explicit, though only in a context of individual punishments by Zeus, and without overt theory; but the passage may be a 'Hesiodic' interpolation, Walcot (1963) 17 ff.   [66] e.g. viii. 329.

[67] The social prohibitions embodied in the series of specific pieces of advice from *WD* 706

The strenuous life is a punishment from Zeus; the strenuous life is also the just life; and the unjust life, being therefore the avoidance of that punishment, is ineluctably attended by painful consequences. The comprehensive boldness of this scheme is remarkable. In the service of justice Hesiod utilizes a crude and savage punishment inflicted on mankind's benefactor through, or in the person of, those whom he benefited. For human beings were not originally offenders against Zeus; although benefiting from Prometheus' offence, they were third parties. Further, the punishment is of the kind in which the only recompense or satisfaction available to the injured party is the spectacle of suffering—the suffering, be it noted, of the descendants of third parties, rather than that of the offender.[68] That spectacle assuages Zeus' anger; and he laughs at the thought of what mankind will suffer.[69]

Paradoxically, therefore, the prudence of observing justice is rooted in, and is indeed the same thing as, the prudence of not attempting to escape a colossal punishment inflicted on third parties by Zeus.[70] In effect, justice is protected by a measure which seems to us monumentally unjust. It is, of course, myth; and how far Hesiod believed in its literal truth is impossible to say. But even if he did believe it to be literally true, it would not have offended his sense of justice; for it was not until after his time that substantial protests against the punishment of third parties arose. The idea of justice did not originate in moral outrage created by third-party punishments: it was eventually extended to embrace it. Hesiod would not have been sensitive to the paradox.[71]

Hesiod's passionate advocacy of *dikē* was, I suggest, stimulated not merely by corrupt practice in his own day, but by the suspect credentials of anthropomorphic gods as guarantors of justice and punishment of the unjust. Without actually excluding the possibility that individual gods punish individual offenders for offences, he puts forward a once-for-all system, contrived by Zeus, under which no offender can ever escape. Neither Zeus nor any other god needs to take any action at all. The belief that they do act individually on at least some occasions has of course to be reckoned with, and indeed the poem opens with resounding

onwards have fundamentally the same purport: do *x*, and such-and-such a disaster follows; for it is the way the world is made.

[68] The suffering of Prometheus himself is only hinted at in the *Works and Days* (56); cf. *Th.* 507–616. The infliction of Pandora on the human race is 'instead of' fire, to counterbalance it (57); Zeus gets no recompense except glee at the thought of what she will do to mankind.

[69] *WD* 59.

[70] Adkins (1960*a*, 72), on *WD* 214–18, comments: 'Even the successful man, *esthlos*, should avoid injustice, since he will almost certainly suffer for it in the end. These lines are merely prudential. Here, then, the link between *dikaios* and *agathos* remains tenuous.' On the contrary, it is of the tightest: *dikē* is *essential* to continued success, and 'merely prudential' diminishes the central point.

[71] Cf. *WD* 240–1, 260–1.

statements that Zeus blasts the proud and straightens the crooked, which a believer in individual punishments would understand in that sense. Similarly, Dikē's personal complaints to her father Zeus belong to the older frame of thought; so too do assurances that nothing escapes the eyes of Zeus' 30,000 'watchers of mortal men'.[72] Hesiod's language is often ambiguous;[73] and in any case the two concepts are not mutually exclusive.

Hesiod thus employs a deeply conservative set of concepts in the service of innovation: he offers a much-needed demonstration, not just a hope or an assertion, that there is some method by which all wrongdoers are punished, on every occasion. But he achieves his result at a high price. When a god punishes on his own behalf, he can recover *timē*: the process, without ceasing to be punishment, is rectificatory. When the gods punish as surrogates, however, the emphasis falls inevitably on the *fact* of punishment; for the belief that gods punish as surrogates arises from anxiety that offenders will escape punishment by mortals. But what interest can they have in so acting? The mortal injured party does have an interest; but it is not he who does the punishing. When a Homeric hero restores his *timē*, and thereby or in addition inflicts suffering and so punishment, retributive punishment and rectificatory punishment effectively coincide; when a god inflicts suffering on behalf of a mortal, they tend to diverge. The result is this: of the two senses of retributive punishment, recompense and suffering, the first comes to be lost sight of, and the second has to suffice instead of it, or simply to function *as* it; literal satisfaction is replaced by metaphorical 'satisfaction'.

In Hesiod, where the effective punisher is the 'way of the world', the divergence is pronounced. The message is overwhelmingly 'offenders assuredly suffer', not 'victims are assuredly compensated'. Compensation is no doubt taken as read, being included among the blessings of straight *dikai*; but the overwhelming emphasis, so far as Zeus' activities are concerned, lies on 'grievous cares, evils, inflictions' and the like for the offender. For one does not give recompense to a punisher when the punisher is a 'system'.[74] In short, the focus changes, as between Homer and Hesiod, from the rectificatory purposes which punishment is supposed to achieve, to the achieving of punishment in itself. This

---

[72] *WD* 248 ff.

[73] e.g. *WD* 238-47, 274 ff., 388: is the 'mode of life' (*nomos*, see Ostwald (1969) 21), which Zeus has given to men, enforced by his action on each occasion of violation, or is it the 'way of the world', that works automatically?

[74] Words indicating 'repayment' are frequent in Homer, but rare in the *Works and Days*. *Apotino* occurs at 260, in a context of individual punishment, but it is not clear what the *apotisis* would consist of, nor to whom it would be paid. The same is true of 'requital' (*amoibē*) at 334. At 711 we hear of twofold recompense (*tinusthai*) exacted by one man from another.

preoccupation will become very apparent in the treatment of punishment in the literature that follows Hesiod.

Two other developments are implicit in Hesiod's approach. In Homer, Zeus' will is inscrutable: he is believed, both in a general way and in particular areas such as oath-taking, to punish injustice; but his mode of operation is unclear, and indeed to a sceptic could appear uncertain and unreliable. Hesiod makes Zeus' mode of operation scrutable; for it is firmly anchored in the workings of the world as observed by anyone. He takes the first step towards making Zeus and the other gods redundant as surrogate punishers, because punishment becomes explicable by reference to the 'system', irrespective of who created it; punishment begins in effect to be secularized. A similar shift is observable in the role of the kings. Hesiod asserts not that Zeus has given kings *themistes*, but that he has given *dikē* to men at large.[75] Kings can no doubt assist *dikē*; but if they judge crookedly, then *dikē*, which operates independently of them, is stronger than they are. Hesiod's thrust is to make *dikē* and punishment for infractions of it less divine and royal, and more secular, examinable and challengeable. The process has a long way to go; but it is unmistakable.

(c) Post-Hesiodic literature

Solon (c.640–after 561)

Solon represents Zeus and Justice as exacting heavy and wholly inescapable payment (*tisis*) for injustice and *hubris*. By 'justice' he means, in brief, an equitable political policy in the interests of all sections of the community, and conduct inspired not by greed and excess but by a peaceable spirit of reasonable moderation. Unreasonable and excessive conduct has disastrous consequences both for the *polis* and for the individual.[76] But in spite of his insistence on divine activity, Solon seems to treat justice as a sort of natural system with its own self-governing mechanisms. As Vlastos puts it, 'he describes its operation in Fragment 4 strictly through the observable consequences of human acts within the social order'.[77]

---

[75] Contrast Il. 204–6 with *WD* 276 ff.   [76] See esp. frr. 4, 5, 6, 13, 36.

[77] Vlastos (1946) 65, referring especially to 4. 17–20; in this piece Justice is confined to three lines (14–16). Fragment 13 is fuller in expression, but its implications are hard to assess: the inevitable displacement of bad weather by good is the model for the inevitable displacement/rectification of injustice by Zeus' justice, but does that tell us anything about the workings of the *social* order? Certainly there is no passage which might describe the workings of the 'social order' which could not also imply or assume direct divine intervention. Nevertheless, Zeus' activity does seem decidedly generalized and remote: he looks to the *end result*, in the *long run* (ll. 15, 17, 28). As Vlastos puts it (65 n. 5), 'justice merges with the wisdom and power of Zeus'. Cf. the section on Hesiod, pp. 45–5 above: the ambiguities are the same, as indeed they are in Theog. 197–208, which is reminiscent of Sol. 13. 9 ff.

The similarities to Hesiod's account of the workings of justice are obvious. Justice is personified; she and Zeus somehow see everything.[78] But apparently they sit in their heaven and operate at long distance, and do not intervene predictably and promptly to punish individual offenders; indeed Solon claims that Zeus does not get cross with every little thing in the short term.[79] The process by which offenders against justice are punished normally must then be a human and social one: human misdeeds attract human retaliation.

The differences between Hesiod and Solon are however considerable. In Hesiod, Zeus has (i) a motivation and interest: Prometheus' offence; there is no counterpart in Solon, except possibly a glancing reference to Zeus' long-term 'anger'.[80] Hesiod also gives him (ii) a mechanism: work, and the reaction of the 'social order' against the lazy and unjust; but what the relation of that order to Zeus is in Solon it would be hard to say. Most interestingly, Hesiod provides Zeus with (iii) some form of interest, and *tisis*: the pleasure of watching men work. To be sure, in Solon *Dikē* comes to take vengeance for herself, *apoteisomenē*, and Zeus exacts *tisis*.[81] This is language appropriate to gods and humans whose interests are involved, or who at least enjoy the sight of offenders suffering; yet no interest or enjoyment is mentioned, and the language is to that extent empty, though perhaps 'purer', in that it may indicate 'disinterested' divine punishers. Similarly if Folly or Ruin (*Atē*) is to be taken as personified,[82] what *tisis*, arising from what interest, has such a person? The notion of 'payment back' has become a metaphor: the human offender may well feel he is losing or suffering something, and hence 'paying for' his offence; but the 'payment' seems not to be 'handed over' in any meaningful sense: somehow it never leaves him, and seems to have only the vaguest of destinations.

So fast and so casually does Solon move between the divine level and the human that the lack of real connection all too easily escapes us.[83] The activity of Zeus is a matter of faith, hope and aspiration; it comes close to being the subject of mere protreptic.[84] Solon moves on a markedly lower or at any rate vaguer intellectual level than Hesiod, perhaps as befits the practical statesman that he was.

Solon threatens the retribution of Zeus and Justice, and to that extent his message will be deterrent to certain readers or listeners. But if that retribution is ever inflicted, the main point of it, apparently, is to inflict

---

[78] 4. 15; 13. 17, 27. [79] 13. 25-6.
[80] 13. 26. [81] 4. 16, 13. 25. [82] 13. 75-6.
[83] 4. 16-17, for instance, are connected only by a vague 'this', and 13. 16-17 only by 'but'. Zeus and Justice's mode of operation is wholly unspecified, though we do learn that, if slow, it is certainly sure: 13. 17 ff.

[84] Note for instance the amplitude of the meteorological model, 13. 14 ff., and the elaborate invocation of the Muses.

suffering, not to achieve recompense or an improvement in conduct.[85] At any rate these purposes are not mentioned; the emphasis is wholly on the suffering. That is typical of punishing by surrogates: it is the achievement of punishment in itself that matters overwhelmingly.

At this point, someone may object: 'Why do you lay such emphasis on the gap between human activity and divine? Why should we *expect* Solon to bridge it? After all, Greek thought commonly displays "double determination": the same act can be described both as the result of a human decision and as the result of divine intervention;[86] and the latter explains anything mysterious or strange in human conduct.'[87] That is true enough; but it is not the point. Once human beings feel, on the human level, that they are too weak to retaliate against offences, and out of anxiety project the function of punishment on to gods, in virtue of their superior knowledge and powers, then necessarily something is done on the divine level that is not done, because it cannot be done, on the human. The two levels then become separated, and questions must arise about their relationship. These questions occurred to Hesiod, but not, it seems, to Solon. He is typical of believers in divine punishment in presenting it simply as suffering. But he also seems to think of punishment as part of the workings of the 'social order'. It may be, then, that punishments on the human level acquire an even stronger vindictive flavour from the punishments thought to be inflicted by divinities; for the two are of course the same thing, in that any given punishment can be thought of now as a human infliction, now as a divine.

Aeschylus (525–456) *fr. 282*

This celebrated fragment bears a general similarity to Hesiod *WD* 217 ff., 256 ff., and Solon 4. 15–16. Dikē aided Zeus and is much honoured by him; he sends her among men to reward the just; the offences of the 'reckless' she writes on a tablet of Zeus, who presumably then takes action against them.[88] There are three points of interest.

1. Zeus received help from Dikē against Cronus because his cause was just, Cronus having 'started it'. The honouring of Dikē is only a personal *quid pro quo*, not, apparently, a disinterested passion for what she represents.[89] The parallel with Hesiod is instructive. Both he and Aeschylus wish to establish that justice is an incalculable power among

---

[85] 4. 5, 8, 17 ff.; 13. 13 and 75, *atē* ('ruin'). There is some talk of a 'foolish' state of mind (e.g. 13. 33 ff.), but none of learning better; contrast Hesiod.   [86] Cf. Lloyd-Jones (1983) 44.

[87] As indeed it is used by Solon, to explain *delay* in retribution, and its extension to innocent third parties (13. 25 ff.); cf. Vlastos (1946) 76 n. 80, and fr. 17.

[88] Probably after an interval, the purpose of the tablet being to aid memory: see fr. 251, *Eum.* 275, and Solmsen (1944); cf. Dem. 25. 11.   [89] Cf. Lloyd-Jones (1956) 60.

men; naturally Zeus is to enforce and guarantee it; but the only reason they can think of why Zeus does so is bound, by comparison with the grandeur of the enterprise itself, to look selfish or inadequate or even spiteful.

2. Zeus sends Justice to those to whom he has goodwill. If these are men who are just antecedently, they hardly need the accession of Justice. If they are some men but not others, what are the grounds of selection? If they are all mankind, *why* does Zeus bear them goodwill?

3. Justice asserts that she implants a sober or sensible mind in the reckless, and to her interlocutor's query whether by persuasion or force, talks simply of the eventual opening-up of the tablet. Presumably persuasion is not excluded; but the implication of the answer *seems* to be chastisement by Zeus. But if so, it evidently produces a 'sensible mind': it is not mere suffering, but suffering for a purpose, and learning of better ways. As we know from the *Oresteia*, that is a theme which interested Aeschylus. However, since the passage may come from a satyr-play, one ought perhaps not to try to extract too much from the medley of ideas it contains; in any case, one has to rely on a fairly high proportion of conjectural restoration in the crucial lines.[90]

Theognis (mid-6th cent.?) *373–92 and 731–52*

Theognis is very far from having the confidence of Hesiod and Solon that Zeus has a concern for justice. Indeed he vigorously reproaches Zeus for the fact that offenders flourish and the righteous suffer. In doing so, he puts his finger on one important attribute of Zeus that might furnish confidence that he enforces justice: his power. He *has* great power, grumbles Theognis,[91] but he does not use it. He pays no attention to desert: just men do not get just treatment.[92] This dereliction of duty by Zeus then sets up a vicious circle: the unrighteous prosper and the righteous grow poor, which prompts them in turn to commit offences.[93] Zeus' failure to punish not only forces them, however unwillingly, to engage in deceit etc., presumably to keep body and soul together, but also stimulates the belief that crime does pay, because the gods are indifferent to it.[94] Zeus' sin of omission is made worse by the fact that punishment is not only not visited on offenders, but *is* inflicted on their descendants, however just they may be.[95]

These forty passionate lines are dynamite to faith in the justice of Zeus.[96] Theognis' time-scale is short: he wants punishment for offenders

---

[90] As to the 'sensible mind' (19), Lloyd-Jones's σώφρονας φύω] φ[ρένας is supported by Soph. *El.* 1463, (ώς) ἐμοῦ κολαστοῦ προστυχὼν φύσῃ φρένας; cf. *OC* 804–5.

[91] 374.   [92] 385, 746; contrast Hes. *WD* 270–3.

[93] 385 ff.   [94] 747 ff.   [95] 731 ff.; cf. Arch. 127.

[96] Lloyd-Jones's (1983) discussion of them (46) is very brief. Their force and importance remain even if they were written at a time when, as he suggests, belief in *post-mortem* punishments was

quickly and visibly; not for him the comforting reflection that Zeus will punish ineluctably in the long term.[97] His objections are theological, moral and social; it is difficult to see how they could be put more trenchantly; and it is as if Solon, perhaps fifty years earlier, had never written.[98] Whether Theognis was speaking only for himself cannot now be known; but his points, however forceful, are after all not very difficult to think of. But they are not made as often as one would expect, at any rate before Euripides.

Euripides (485–406)

That the gods themselves are capricious, or unjust themselves in spite of punishing offences, or unduly harsh as punishers, are well known *topoi* in Euripides.[99] Three passages are of special interest.

1. *Hecuba* (1029–30). As Hecuba enters the tent in which she will blind Polymestor, who had killed her son, the chorus predict that he will now probably pay the penalty. 'For where liability (*hupenguon*) to *dikē* and to the gods coincide, it is a deadly, deadly evil' (for the offender).[100] Evidently the chorus believe that in this case they do coincide, and that the penalty will be greater than it would if they did not. What seems to be envisaged is a liability to justice (Justice?) which is not a liability to gods, in the sense that they take no, or diminished, trouble to see that it is discharged, presumably because they have no personal interest in it, or rather, in this case, because it does not fall within the bailiwick of a particular god, Zeus Protector of Suppliants. (The possibility then exists that the liability to gods could 'not coincide' in the sense of itself leading to an unjust exaction; but that line of thought is not explored.) The implication of these two lines seems to be that gods do punish offences against justice, but not invariably.

---

beginning to spread. Theognis does *not* say, 'Oh, but all this doesn't really matter: offenders will be punished in the next world, and that will vindicate the justice of Zeus after all.' He says nothing about *post-mortem* punishments, not even at 207–8, where we might expect it. The plain fact is that Zeus gets 'a straight talk' (Dodds (1951) 33).

[97] What then ought we to make of 197–208? When an unjust man escapes *tisis* 'on the occasion', either he is made to pay his 'debt' (later? see 202) by the gods without leaving it to his children, or he dies before *dikē* catches up with him. The implication seems to be that the 'mind' (*nous* 203) of the gods is dilatory or unreliable: some offenders suffer late, others do not suffer at all.

[98] I adopt a 6th-century date for the passages I have quoted, but the chronology of the poems in the Theognidean corpus is a minefield of controversy (see West (1974) 40–71); a date *earlier* than Solon is conceivable.

[99] e.g. *Ion* 437 ff., *IT* 560, *Hipp.* 1400, *HF* 339 ff.; cf. pp. 38–9 above.

[100] Reading οὐ συμπίπνει, not οὖ, which would yield an expression of *outrage* at particular or invisible non-coincidence: 'they do not coincide—a deadly, deadly evil'. But in the context such a remark makes no sense. The notion of the double offence is anticipated at 850–3, where Polymestor is said by Agamemnon to have been impious, 'in respect of gods and justice', presumably Zeus Protector of Suppliants, and human justice.

2. *Supplices* (594–7). Theseus, about to march against Thebes, draws a slightly different conclusion. 'The only thing I need is to have (the support of) such gods as reverence justice; for when these (gods and justice) are on one's side, one gains victory. Valour is no use to mortals if it/one does not have (the support of) the wish of the god'. Some gods revere justice, it seems, while others do not.[101]

3. *Electra* (737–46). The chorus express extreme scepticism about the story that Zeus changed the course of the sun, in anger at Thyestes' crime, 'for the sake of' (i.e. in order to uphold) 'human justice' (*or* 'to punish mortals').[102] They comment: 'But stories frightening to men are profitable: they are an encouragement to worship the gods.' I take it that this is yet another possible response to the gods' apparent inefficiency as punishers of injustice: to maintain a rational scepticism about myths exemplifying their concern for justice and their chastisement of men for offences against it, but to urge the usefulness of fearful belief as an aid to piety and deterrence.

Critias (*c.*460–403) B25 DK

A character, probably Sisyphus, in Critias'[103] satyr-play of that name, goes further. The very reason for the 'invention' of the gods, he argues, was anxiety that secret crimes, which could not be detected and punished by human agents, would reduce life to chaos; but the gods see and hear and understand everything. Their existence was dreamt up by some surpassingly clever person at some point in history, as a deliberate but beneficent fiction designed to produce in men fear of awful punishers.

Conclusion

As a solvent of anxiety lest offenders should escape punishment, belief in divine punishment is imperfect; for divine punishment can all too often appear arbitrary, inefficient or even unjust. Hence the very wide spectrum of ways in which the belief can be handled:

1. Justification by elaborate mythology showing that divine punishment is inescapable, being built into the very structure of society (Hesiod) by contrivance of a god with a strong motive to act.

---

[101] Read φέρει 596. To take ὅσοι in 594 as restrictive seems to me unavoidable. As Conacher (1956) 21–2 points out, Theseus' hesitation is matched by that of the chorus, 612–18, who then announce at 731–3 that their doubts are now dispelled.

[102] 741–2. 'Human justice', *thnētē dikē*, could I suppose mean 'justice as practised among mortals'; but perhaps the sense of 'penalty' is more likely.

[103] Or Euripides': see Davies (1989, with text and translation) and Sutton for discussions of this vexed matter. Sutton 38 compares Isoc. 11. 24–5.

2. Justification by passionate assertion, and on the basis of the workings of society (Solon).
3. Justification by reference to myth alone (Aesch. fr. 282).
4. Protest at apparent arbitrariness and inequity (Theognis, and elsewhere in Greek literature, especially Euripides).
5. Rudimentary attempts to *account for* the arbitrariness by reference to variable distribution of concern among the gods (*Hecuba*, *Supplices*).
6. Scepticism of the truth of the belief, in spite of its usefulness (*Electra*).
7. Explicit denial of its truth, in an account of its utilitarian origins (Critias).

In sum:

(*a*) In 1–5 the overwhelming emphasis is on punishment as suffering: that the offender should not escape it matters almost exclusively.
(*b*) When the belief is impugned as *untrue*, and rationalized in terms of its origins and/or usefulness, the purpose of deterrence attains exclusive prominence (7, perhaps 6).
(*c*) The pattern of belief and conjecture is obviously extremely various. In due time Plato will select and adapt certain parts of it in a systematic attempt to impose coherence and uniformity.

POST-MORTEM PUNISHMENTS

The belief that one survives after death in some sentient and intelligent form is widespread; it is implied in many funeral and grave practices, and openly assumed in literature. About the precise nature of *post-mortem* existence, and about the total environment of the next world, the agreement is of course much less.[104] In particular, the belief that one is punished in the next world for misdeeds committed during life is attested only patchily. This could be merely a misleading result of the random distribution of the surviving sources; but on the whole it seems a fair reflection of the varied and unsystematic character of Greek religion. The most we can say is that some people in some places at some times held the belief, others being hostile or indifferent to it. Nor are we entitled to look for consistency between one account and another: to variation in imaginative speculation there are no limits.

---

[104] Note the dispelling of Achilles' doubts (XXIII. 103–4): after his dream of the ghost of Patroclus he exclaims, 'so there is, then, some *psuchē* and *eidōlon* (spirit and phantom) even in Hades, but without *phrenes*' (a bodily organ, 'guts', as Guthrie (1950) 279 puts it).

According to Homer, the dead exist in Hades, a dark and gloomy subterranean place. They have some resemblance to their former persons, but are now mere tenuous and feeble spirits. They still enjoy some capacity to remember, and take an interest in the world they have left; they desire, quarrel, and speak, or at least twitter; they have some feelings, notably a morose awareness of being dead. Once arrived in Hades, they never return.[105]

The generally unbridgeable chasm between the worlds of the living and the dead entails that no *post-mortem* punishment can be imparted by living men direct: they need surrogate punishers to act for them, and so too do Zeus and the other gods of Olympus. For the Olympian and the Chthonian gods are distinct: neither trespass on the others' domain. If an Olympian god wishes to punish a dead person, then like any human being he has to rely on some denizen of the underworld to act as his agent. Hence in all cases:

1. A surrogate needs to be identified, and given some motive for acting.
2. The punishments the surrogate inflicts must be purely vindictive; for the offender cannot now give recompense to the injured party except in the form of the latter's confidence that the infliction takes place.
3. Since there seems no particular reason, death being eternal, for supposing that *post-mortem* punishments need ever stop, the only plausible way of imposing a *limit* on them, or of giving them some forward-looking *purpose* of deterrence or reform, is to resort to some doctrine of reincarnation.

(a) Homer

1. *Odyssey* (xi. 568–627).[106] Odysseus observes the frightful torments undergone by three celebrated offenders against the gods: Tityus, Tantalus and Sisyphus. The punishments are simply 'there': the emphasis is on the grisly detail and the extremities of suffering; only in one case (Tityus) is the offence specified; the offended parties (Olympian gods) are *not* stated to have actually contrived the punishments.

This lack of information is in one way natural, as two of the punishments described, once set up, do not need an agency to keep

---

[105] This picture is of course composite, which is all that is necessary for my purposes. See XVI. 857, XXIII. 62–107, x. 490–5, xi. 216–22, 476, 487 ff., 568–71, xxiv. 1 ff.; cf. Ar. *Frogs.*

[106] At the start of this sequence Minos gives judgements to the dead, in litigation between themselves; he is not judging them for offences committed while alive. The whole passage is almost certainly an interpolation (see Kirk (1962) 236–7 and Stanford (1947, 1948) ad loc.); I take it to reflect belief of the 6th century. Cf. also Keuls (1974).

them going. In the third case (Tantalus) the punishment does have to be kept going—but that is done simply by a *daimon*. The author of these lines knows he cannot import the Olympians into Hades; but he is either incurious about the punishing agents or at a loss to identify them; and he is in any case overwhelmingly interested in the punishments themselves, which are essentially vindictive.

2. *Iliad* (III. 278–80). Agamemnon invokes (i) Zeus, Helios, rivers, and earth, (ii) 'you twain who punish (*tinusthon*) dead men below, whoever has sworn a false oath'. The 'twain' are probably the Underground Zeus and Persephone;[107] but elsewhere[108] it is the Erinues, after an invocation to Zeus, Earth and Helios, whom Agamemnon identifies as the punishers of perjurers. Persephone, Underground Zeus[109] and the Erinues act because Olympian Zeus himself cannot; their motives are not stated, they are simply given the function; and again the punishment, though it is not described, seems surely vindictive.

Adkins[110] attempts to minimize these *post-mortem* punishments in (1) as being simply for colossal and 'unparalleled' offences against the gods' personal interests; they are not 'human offences' or 'instances of immorality'. For if they were to be so interpreted, then to that extent Adkins's general thesis, that there was only modest force in the claims of the quiet virtues and in the sanctions applied to protect them, would be weakened. But this is to ignore the psychology underlying punishment ('revenge', as Adkins calls it) inflicted by gods. The gods are after all constructs of the human imagination; but they have a social purpose. Imagined in an anthropomorphic fashion, they do indeed have 'personal' interests, like any human; and for offence against these interests they punish not only men but each other. That is the model on which men, out of anxiety that 'human' offences may go unpunished, ensure (by make-believe, or wish-fulfilment, or powerful fiction, as you will) that some stronger party does in fact punish them. With varying plausibility, the gods have attributed to them an interest in so doing. Offended mortals pretend (so to speak) to Zeus that in punishing offenders against themselves he is punishing offenders against himself; they deliberately blur the distinction between the two kinds of operation. To commit an offence against Zeus personally is dangerous not only to oneself but to one's community; to break an oath is socially undesirable; in the fiction, Zeus punishes *both* kinds of offences as offences against himself; and the real point of the exercise is to rope him in as a punisher of 'human' crimes. Zeus is brought to do the morally 'advanced' thing, punishing evildoers, for selfish or obscure reasons; as we have noticed before, the basis on

---

[107] IX. 457.   [108] XIX. 259–60.

[109] Cf. Aes. *Supp.* 228–31: 'another' Zeus judges last judgements for the dead. The Doppelgänger Zeus is of course Hades himself.   [110] Adkins (1960a) 67 and n. 14.

which a moral advance is made cannot really bear the weight put upon it.[111] But that such beliefs, however unconvincing to us, can have had no social purpose or effect is a quite unwarranted assumption. The offences described in (1) above may indeed be 'unparalleled'; so too are the penalties; and potential offenders may find them exemplary.

It must be admitted, however, that these few passages from forty-eight books of epic poetry are no great harvest. The poems are fairly full of indications[112] that the gods punish misdeeds this side of the grave; but that they, or rather their surrogates, do so beyond it seems an embryonic notion, perhaps dating (by interpolation) from some subsequent period. The possibility must remain, however, that the idea was indeed common enough in Homeric society, but that Homer had little need or desire to refer to it in the poems.

(b) The simple pattern of post-mortem punishments

Belief in the pattern found in Homer, of a single set of offences committed in this life punished by a single but apparently eternal set of punishments in the next, is fairly well attested in the sixth, fifth, and fourth centuries, though the precise extent of its diffusion is not now knowable.[113] It is especially prominent in Aeschylus;[114] and Plato and Democritus refer to it as though it were quite common.[115]

(c) The complex pattern: the mystery-religions

Alongside the simple pattern, however, a more complicated conception of post-mortem punishment was developed, at least as early as the sixth century, by certain religious movements. The identity of these movements is a matter of contention, but irrelevant to my purposes.[116] Nor do I presume to attempt a reconstruction of their social and religious origins and their tenets in general. My concern is with the strictly penological element in their ideas about the after-life.

[111] Cf. pp. 48–9 above.   [112] pp. 34 ff. above.

[113] e.g. Theog. 1036, Alc. 38A. 8–10; see in general Brandon (1967) 79 ff. and Dover (1974) 261–8. Cf. Adkins (1960a) 145 ff. on Pausanias' description (10. 28 ff.) of Polygnotus' painting of Hades (mid-5th century), and the confusion of belief which it exhibits. Exceptionally, one punishment is said to have stopped: that of Tityus, apparently because he had been worn away to insubstantiality (29. 3).

[114] e.g. Supp. 228 ff., Eum. 267 ff.

[115] Rep. 330d-331b; Democ. B199, B297 DK; contrast Lys. 6. 20, who implicitly confines divine penalties to this life. Cf. Dem. 25. 52.

[116] The history of the mystery-religions is a soup: it is almost impossible to identify which movement believed exactly what, since syncretism was so common: see e.g. Her. 2. 81, West (1983) 259 ff. Much remains obscure (Burkert (1972), 133 ff.), and the opportunities for confusion are immense: see e.g. Ion of Chios B2 DK and Dodds (1951) 147 ff. I am much indebted to Dr N. J. Richardson for useful comment and bibliography on this section.

The simple pattern, though obviously modelled on ordinary patterns of offence and retaliation and therefore readily intelligible, suffers from three major defects. First, it is extremely frightening. Imaginative speculation about the hideous horrors of the punishments inflicted in the next world could well have outraged the instinct of restraint we have seen operating in the infliction of punishment in Homer; their savagery makes them unlike anything practised in this life. Second, the punishment is again unlike human punishments in having no time-limit. The punisher is not a human injured party whom one may expect to satisfy in the end, but some divine eternal being who can apparently never be satisfied and inflicts punishment on the offender for ever. Third, *post-mortem* punishment differs yet again from the punishments of this world in having no future reference. The punished soul cannot, by learning who is 'stronger', adopt better conduct: he just goes on being punished. Perhaps it is not too much of a speculation to suggest that such reflections must have induced feelings of resentful hopelessness. One commits an offence; one tries to make restitution, and one may suffer an earthly punishment; one does not know if the gods are appeased or not; one dies—and may be punished eternally. *Quem ad finem? Cui bono?* Christianity too threatens eternal punishment; but the threat is tempered by abundant opportunities for avoiding sin and for repentance, thanks to the love and grace of God. But the Greek gods offered nothing like that; they did not have a warm concern for the welfare of all mankind. They had their favourites; but that is very different.

Certain features of the complex pattern of belief are, I suggest, intelligible as responses to the dismal thoughts which I have attempted to reconstruct. The sources, which have to be pieced together on the hopeful assumption that they represent different aspects of broadly the same framework of thought,[117] are chiefly certain passages of Pindar which probably reflect the beliefs of his aristocratic patrons, and the texts of gold leaves of various provenances and dates, which appear to stem from beliefs whose diffusion started about the sixth century.[118] These leaves were placed inside graves, and contain instructions to the dead person about what he should do and say on arrival in Hades, and at

---

[117] Cf. Lloyd-Jones's conclusion (1985, 277), though our reconstructions differ in important ways.

[118] The ideas expressed in the text of the plates are generally regarded as 'Orphic', though Zuntz (1971) 87, 321–2, 337 ff. has argued that they are Pythagorean. The Hipponium gold plate, however, published in 1974, which is in the same tradition as those analysed by Zuntz in 1971, suggests Orphism: see Kirk–Raven–Schofield (1983) 29–30; *contra*, Zuntz (1976) 146–9. Cf. Cole (1980) 225 ff., and other references in 223 n. 3. A firm Dionysiac connection now emerges: see e.g. Lloyd-Jones (1985) 263 ff., Tsantsanoglou and Parassoglou (1987) 7, cf. West (1982) 21. Janko (1984) attempts a stemma of the B fragments. The literature on the leaves is vast, and I make no attempt to rehearse it all.

his judgement by Persephone. They have been extensively discussed, notably by Zuntz. Different sheets describe different stages of the procedure to be followed; I select the points which seem crucial for our purposes.[119]

1. (B1 and B2) Avoiding a certain spring, presumably that of forgetfulness, the dead person is to approach the spring of memory and tell its guardians that he is the 'son of Earth and Starry Heaven'.

2. Pleading thirst, he must then ask them for permission to drink from the spring (B1 and B2), which they will grant (B1).

3. Appearing before Persephone, he is to claim that he has come 'pure from the pure', and that he is 'of your blessed race' (A1, A2, A3).

4. At this point, one of two things happens: (a) The dead person confidently asserts that he has escaped the 'grievous and tearful cycle', has attained the 'longed-for crown', and has refuge with Persephone (A1), who then says 'happy and blessed one, you will become a god instead of a mortal' (A1, cf. A4). (b) The dead person claims he has paid the requital for unjust deeds, and that he now supplicates Persephone to send him to the 'abodes of the holy' (A2 and A3). (These texts end here. *Conjecturally*, he will be reincarnated eventually as a successful and eminent human being.[120])

5. As an alternative to 4(b), one supposes,[121] Persephone may deny the claim and dispatch the person to some grim and grimy place, there presumably to be punished. What then happens to him is not clear. It would be natural to suppose that he too is reincarnated, though probably as some lowly person.[122] Certainly reincarnation in Orphism and Pythagoreanism seems to apply to *all* souls: I can find no hint that those

---

[119] I use Zuntz's numeration (1971).

[120] The distinction between 4(a) and 4(b), the rewards of a higher and a lower level of moral attainment respectively, seems broadly paralleled by Pind. *Ol.* 2. 56 ff., 4(a) in 68 ff. and 4(b) in 61–7: see Zuntz (1971) 336, Solmsen (1968a). If B1 l. 11 refers to 4(a), the greater reward, and promised heroization rather than godship, that is closer to Pind. *Ol.* 2. 68 ff., which promised only heroization, than outright godship is (A1 and A4); but the difference may not be significant: see Rose (1936) 92. On godhead in connection with two gold leaves found in 1985, see Tsantsanoglou and Parassoglou (1987) 7. Pindar fr. 133 I take to refer to 4(b), to the state after reincarnation to 'the upper sun' (i.e. this world) 'in the ninth year'. As to 4(a), 'the experience you have not experienced before' in A4 refers probably to the completion of the third earthly life free of injustice, mentioned in Pind. *Ol.* 2. 68 ff. (on 'three times' here, see Bluck (1958b) and Lloyd-Jones (1985) 266 n. 37), and thus to an escape from the 'grievous cycle' of A1 (see Zuntz (1971) 320 ff., 331, 336), so that the person now experiences, for the first and only time, promotion to godship—or, as Pindar puts it, 'the isles of the blest' (for which cf. Ar. *Wasps* 636–41, Dem. 60. 34; Hes. *WD* 170–3 apparently sees them as a more desirable residence than the subterranean abodes of the silver race, 140–1). Fr. 137 refers quite generally to the pleasant existence after death awaiting an initiate into the *Eleusinian* mysteries.

[121] One can hardly suppose that Persephone 'nods through' everyone to godship or the abodes of the holy. Clearly she is being supplicated, and could say 'no'; indeed, fr. 133 implies that from some persons she *refuses* to accept requital. The 'purity' of step 3 could be merely ritual purity; but the 'unjust' deeds of 4(b) suggest she makes some kind of moral assessment: note Pind. *Ol.* 2. 67.

[122] Or indeed as an animal, e.g. Emped. B127 DK.

punished are detained in Hades for ever.[123] Both virtuous and wicked seem to be reborn, and may equally use ceremonies of purification to win eventual release from the cycle of suffering—presumably by living virtuously and achieving divine status, as described on the plates.[124]

But in any case the gold plates are obviously not the sort of document in which one would expect to find mention of, let alone stress on, *post-mortem* punishment. For details of that we have to rely on the allusions chiefly of Pindar (who also had an interest in reticence, not wishing to hold out such a prospect to his patrons), and on the hints and picturesque detail given by, for example, Aristophanes.[125]

In brief, on this necessarily hazardous reconstruction, Persephone 'interviews' three categories of persons: (i) those who are then promoted to godhead; (ii) those who after nine years are returned to earth for either their second or their third virtuous life; (iii) those who are to be punished, and only then returned to earth.

It is clear that the eschatological belief described on the sheets was fundamentally a belief of aspiration. The dead person says he is 'son of Earth and Heaven', that is to say a half-god; and he claims to be, potentially, a full god: 'I am of your blessed race'. *Post-mortem* punishment exists in the system; but it is balanced by the possibility of aspiring to escape it by a life of 'purity', and indeed of ascending to some higher status. Evidently those who have three times led blameless lives become gods; those with lesser achievements are sent to the 'abodes of the holy' before being again reincarnated; and perhaps at their next death they will succeed in becoming full gods. Hence the need of memory,[126] to preserve continuity of experience and perception between

---

[123] The 'ever-flowing' mud of Ar. *Frogs* 145-6 does not imply that the sinner's sojourn in it is permanent: it is just creepily vivid detail. Eternal *post-mortem* punishment is however known in the *Eleusinian* religion (*Hom. H.* 2. 367), for failure to give proper worship to Persephone. For a discussion of what the 'injustice' of these sinners consists in, see Richardson's commentary *ad loc.*

[124] Cf. *Crat.* 400c, incarnation as punishment. For Pythagoreanism, *Gorg.* 493a and Dodds's (1959) edition *ad loc.*, Philolaus B14 DK.

[125] Pind. *Ol.* 2. 56 ff., 67 and fr. 130; Ar. *Frogs* 145 ff., 273-5, Soph. fr. 837; cf., in reference to the Eleusinian mysteries, Isoc. 4. 28, *Hom. H.* 2. 480-2. In 3. *verso* 2-3 of a late 'Orphic' *katabasis* ('descent'), which lists sinners in Hades, we have *misthos* (pay) and *amoibē* (requital)—but these may well be rewards, not punishments (text in Merkelbach (1951) 10; discussion of *amoibē* in Solmsen (1968*b*)).

[126] Cf. Dodds (1951) 173 n. 107, Zuntz (1971) 380-1. I do not see, however, why, *pace* Zuntz, the opportunity to drink of the fountain of memory should be granted only to 'the perfected' (cf. Lloyd-Jones (1985) 271). Our sources have a good deal more to say about those in this category than those in category (iii), the punished, so inferences as to belief about the latter's ability to drink the waters of memory are hazardous. But if they are reincarnated without memory, then all we can say is that such efforts as they then make to be initiated and/or improve morally will be to that extent handicapped. Or perhaps they are reincarnated as plants or lower forms of animal life, which may be supposed not to have a faculty of memory anyway. Cole (1980) 238 supposes that 'the point of the appeal to Mnemosune is to guarantee that the initiate remember to seek the benefits that initiation promised'.

this world and the next. The waters of forgetfulness would interrupt that continuity. One wishes to be able to relate the quality of one's destination in the next world to one's present life in this, and conversely to relate one's present life in this world to one's previous destination in the other. This is to say, those who are reincarnated (4(*b*) above) must realize that by the living of a 'pure' life, there is 'promotion' to be gained after death.

What are the 'unjust deeds'? They may refer to the primeval fault at the foundation of the human race, the 'Titanic' element in us, or to common-or-garden offences in this world. In the former case, having lived in this world of suffering could itself constitute the requital accepted by Persephone for her 'ancient grief'.[127] But if that is all, simply having lived and died would guarantee Persephone's acceptance of requital, and one's ultimate status as a god. The Pindaric fragment (133), however, implies that there are some from whom she does not accept requital. These can only be those who have not endured their punishment to her satisfaction, that is by appropriate ritual and by at least paying penalties in this world, for crimes committed in it; for the primeval flaw *accounts for* such crimes, being the psychological propensity to commit them.[128] In the plates, a man who has superhumanly avoided injustice completely claims accordingly to become superhuman, a god, after death. But 'those from whom Persephone accepts requital for her ancient grief', i.e. those who have committed injustice in this life but who have paid requital for it,[129] she sends back in that ninth year to the 'upper sunlight', which I take to be this world) for a period; for though 'pure', they have shown themselves to be less than superhuman.[130] In this reincarnation they will by virtue of memory draw upon their experience in the other world, and strive the harder to live a blameless life. *Mutatis mutandis*, so too will those punished in the next world; for with the memory—if they have it—of that punishment they gain the

---

[127] Rose (1936) 85 ff. on Pind. fr. 133, Lloyd-Jones (1985) 260, Seaford (1986) 4–9. For life on earth as itself a punishment, see also West (1983) 22–3, *Crat.* 400c, and Empedocles' series of re-incarnations, frr. B115, B117, B146–7 DK. 'Empedocles views life on earth as an exile from an earlier and more ideal state . . .' (Wright (1981) 69); cf. Guthrie ii (1965) 249 ff.

[128] 701bc, cf. 854b; Dodds (1951) 155–6.

[129] Conceivably, however, the requital in fr. 133 may be requital in the next world, after which (i.e. 'in the ninth year') the person is sent to the 'upper sun'; but the plates themselves have nothing about it (cf. Bluck (1958*a*) 161 n. 4, Rose (1936) 90). In any case, a period in a 'purgatory' cannot automatically qualify one for Persephone's favour, for fr. 133 implies that she discriminates; and this can only be on the basis of life in this world. (If the plates are Pythagorean in inspiration, then the requital will presumably be in terms of mere 'suffering in return', said by Aristotle, *NE* 1132^{b}21 ff., to be Pythagorean.)

[130] The 'upper sun' I take to be the sun said in fr. 129 to shine, during our night, in the underworld, where to judge from *Ol.* 2. 61–2 days and nights are of equal length (but the language is mysterious: cf. Ar. *Frogs* 455–9, and see Solmsen (1968*a*) 504 n. 1, Lloyd-Jones (1985) 254–5).

incentive to aspire at least to the paying of requital for offences before their next death.

The whole arrangement is a sort of grand learning-system, constructed in the belief that both rewards and punishments exist in the next world, and projected on to an alternation of life and death. It offers what ordinary punishments can achieve, and what *post-mortem* punishments of the 'simple' kind cannot:[131] the prospect of learning. Punishment thereby recovers one of its ancient purposes, and in a context which is not only deterrent but encouraging of better conduct.

This system of belief is of great importance in the history of Greek penology. Though we should not suspect it until our very fragmentary and scattered sources are put together in a certain way, it seems that from the sixth century onwards there were uncertain numbers of persons who believed that a certain type of punishment, viz. the infliction of suffering after death, *for a limited period*, was not blind retaliation, nor merely the giving of satisfaction to an injured party, nor even simply a device of deterrence, but an additional incentive to good conduct. For by simultaneously suffering after death and seeing then what one might have enjoyed given a different previous life-style, one is in a sense educated for a better life after reincarnation.[132]

What is the relevance of the rites and initiation ceremonies? Perhaps there were grades of initiation, depending upon the relative moral 'purity' of one's life; in that case the person might appear before Persephone able to assert, thanks to the spring of memory, that he had attained a given grade,[133] conferred, in virtue of his moral standing, by his fellow company of the pure; and the wording of the sheet placed in the grave would differ accordingly, and so too would the words he would have to say. Naturally we wish to ask whether a virtuous man who has not gone through the rituals would be at a disadvantage in his 'interview' with Persephone. Contrariwise, a rogue who *had* gone through them ought not to be at an advantage. Or was Persephone simply expected to know? Hardly, or what would have been the point of the rituals and of using the right formulae when meeting her? But this is speculation.

The belief that our suffering in this world constitutes a punishment

---

[131] Solmsen (1968a) 503–6 argues that in Pind. *Ol.* 2. 56 ff. a new idea of multiple lives seems to have been grafted on to an original idea of reward and penalty after only one life.

[132] Cf. Keuls's (1974) interpretation of the myths of the water-carriers in the next world as undergoing purification *through* punishment.

[133] Cf. Adkins (1975) 240. A system with a strong formal content of rites, initiations, etc. can become empty and legalistic, whatever its moral intention. In practice, there would be a good deal of confusion between moral conduct and ritual practice, mere fulfilment of the latter being thought to constitute the former. But note the emphasis in A2 and A3 on justice, and the connection between ritual and abstention from murder in Ar. *Frogs* 1032; cf. (in spite of the burlesque) 355 ff. No doubt the beliefs could be mediated on a popular level by charlatans, as Plato complained (*Rep.* 364e–365a).

inflicted by some divinity for some offence is not peculiar to the mystery-religions. In Hesiod, Zeus imposed the necessity to work; seeing our toils and tribulations was his recompense for the offence of Prometheus. But there are some instructive differences: (i) Hesiod represents the suffering as inflicted on innocent and hapless third parties, whereas in the mystery-religions it is inflicted on the actual offender, the man himself, who feels in some way responsible: he has something of the Titanic in his make-up, or has spilt blood in some other existence, or whatever. (ii) Hesiod's vision is bleak and limited: man suffers and dies. The mystery-religions offer aspiration to a second chance, the opportunity to learn better in another existence. The individual matters. But what these religions and Hesiod have in common is the prospect of an alleviation of suffering *by moral conduct*; and the religions go further by promising not merely alleviation, but some sort of eventual divine felicity.

CURSES, OATHS, ERINUES

A *curse* is a prayer of malign purpose, addressed to a god or other non-human agency, by an injured party against an offender. The former prays that the latter may be made to suffer in a general or specific way, by that agency, in return for an offence, which may lie in the past or be anticipated in the future.[134] A curse may be personified, and have a sort of independent life and power of its own; it may attract picturesque adjectives which express its inescapability and terrible effects.[135] Curses may be pronounced by private individuals; but they are very often delivered, with more or less ceremony and publicity, by persons in authority in state or family, in the family or communal interest. Such curses are felt to have corporate weight behind them, and to be particularly effective for that reason; and they embrace a wide range of actual and potential offences.[136] No doubt the god or gods addressed in the curse were supposed to be active in punishing the offender, but obviously a curse served in part the function of expressing communal fear or anger, which could result, where the offender was known, in direct communal action in the form of stoning or driving into exile.[137] Such action is variably efficient, however; and the appeal to a god can only consign to him, in a hopeful spirit, the function of supplementing or even replacing human effort.

---

[134] e.g. I. 33 ff., IX. 453 ff.; for a fuller account of curses, see Vallois (1914).

[135] Soph. *OT* 417–18, 'double-striking, terrible of foot', Aes. *Agam.* 237, *Se.* 840–3, Parker (1983) 198: a curse has an 'intrinsic power'. The curser's imagination runs free, and the evils he conceives can easily outstrip those of ordinary life, as Dem. 14. 36 implies.

[136] Parker (1983) 7–8, 192 ff., citing *inter alia* the comic comprehensiveness of Ar. *Thes.* 332 ff. Cf. Aes. *Agam.* 457.   [137] Parker (1983) 194–7.

Curses inscribed on sheets of lead (*Defixionum tabellae*) are however confined largely to private life. Two main categories existed in the
fifth and fourth centuries:[138] (1) those containing simply the name
(pierced by a nail) of the cursed person(s), and of the underworld
deities to whom they are consigned for the infliction of suffering; (2)
those whose text attempts to 'bind', i.e. immobilize, the enemy's
mental and verbal faculties; often the text was accompanied by a small
doll of the 'target', with large genitals vulnerable because of hands tied
behind the back; again underworld powers are invoked, sometimes at
length.

Presumably both categories may be inspired by simple animosity, or a
desire to win some dispute or competition by hook or by crook; that
cursers felt themselves antecedently *wronged* is not clear; at any rate,
only in relatively few cases is the claim made explicitly. But given the
ease with which men rationalize and justify to themselves hostility to
others by adducing some imagined injury, *defixionum tabellae* probably
have punishment as their purpose more often than may appear.[139]

There is some but not conclusive evidence to suggest that the texts
were commonly placed in graves of persons dead prematurely.[140] If so,
the practice presumably rested on a belief that they had not expended
their life-energy in a life of normal length, and therefore had available,
perhaps only until their natural time of death, a fund of energy greater
than that usually enjoyed by the dead.[141] This energy could be used in a
hostile manner against the living: it was an expression of the dead's
anger at being dead, and could be used in particular by victims of murder
to trouble their killers. By placing the objects in the grave the curser
hoped to harness the dead person's resentful energy and divert it against
the cursed person; the dead person desired revenge, the sight of *somebody* suffering, even if not an offender against himself. His energy was
like a bolt of undischarged electricity, potentially just as effective against
an innocent target as against a guilty one. The names in the tomb as it
were prompted the dead to think of the curser's target as deserving
malevolent attention.

An *oath* is a conditional curse directed against oneself; its purpose is to
offer strong assurance. It expresses a wish that *if* what the speaker
asserts to be true is not true, or *if* he does certain things which he is

---

[138] See Faraone (1985) for a summary and references to collections. Some 5th-century examples
are discussed by Jeffrey (1955) 72 ff.

[139] Cf. Parker (1983) 198, citing Wünsch's (1897) appendix, nos. 98, 102, 158, in which the curser
explicitly claims to have been wronged.

[140] Jordan (1985) 152.

[141] Cf. 865e1: the 'freshly dead' man, an expression which perhaps implies his fury at being killed
will subside in time.

undertaking not to do, some specific or general suffering should fall on him, usually sent by a god or other non-human agency.[142]

An *Erinus* is an implacably hostile female; her function is to inflict extreme suffering on offenders. She lives in the underworld, but is not confined to it; she may attack both living and dead.[143] She may operate independently and on her own initiative, sometimes for inscrutable reasons,[144] or on receipt of a prayer from an injured party. Any misfortune overtaking an offender may be supposed, either by himself or by his victim, to be the work of an Erinus. She often works by deranging the mental state and judgement of the offender, so that he makes imprudent decisions and comes to grief (*atē*).[145] She is particularly malevolent towards perjurers,[146] towards crimes as between members of the same family,[147] and more generally towards all offences which affect *moira*,[148] the proper role and standing of the injured party; an even wider concern with limit and order is occasionally attested.[149] Sometimes mentioned or invoked as a solitary, she nevertheless commonly pursues in packs or relays with her fellow Erinues.[150] They do not replace other gods as agents of punishment: either or both may be mentioned indifferently as the addressee of a prayer or oath and as its 'fulfillers'.[151] They are sometime called *alastores*, 'avengers', or *prostropaioi*, 'those to whom one turns [as agents of vengeance]'.[152] Like curses, with which they are at least twice identified,[153] they may be described with picturesque vividness.[154]

Clearly this whole network of belief is an expression of weakness felt by an injured party, arising for whatever reason (he himself may now be dead, or the offender may be, or unknown, and therefore not reachable by normal means).[155] Curses and Erinues are explicitly stated to be 'helpers';[156] Erinues see everything, have long memories, and cannot be

[142] XIX. 258 ff. III. 276 ff. with 299 describes an oath on behalf of both the Greeks and the Trojans. Eur. *IT* 747 ff., Xen. *Anab.* 2. 5. 7, 3. 2. 10, Her. 6. 86 (verse).

[143] XIX. 259–60, XXI. 412, Aes. *Eum.* 388, 417.   [144] XIX. 86 ff.

[145] Cf. Dodds (1951) 38 ff.; XIX. 86 ff., Aes. *Eum.* 376, *Choe.* 402–4. *Atē* is both 'addled judgement' and the disaster that springs from it; cf. Lyc. *Leoc.* 91–3.

[146] XIX. 259–60, Hes. *WD* 803–4. Even gods are punished in the underworld for perjury: *Th.* 793 ff., cf. Emped. B115 DK.

[147] IX. 571, XV. 204, ii. 135, xi. 280, Eur. *Med.* 1389. They also have the particular role of pursuing those who *fail* to punish offenders within the family: Aes. *Choe.* 269 ff.

[148] Aes. *PV* 516, *Se.* 977–9, *Eum.* 392, and in general Fraenkel (1950) on 1535 ff.

[149] XIX. 418, Heraclitus B94 DK.

[150] Aes. *Eum.*, in which they are the chorus; Eur. *IT* 79.

[151] IX. 453 ff. and 565 ff., v. 184–5, xvii. 475, Aes. *Se.* 69–70, 790–1.

[152] Ant. *Tetr.* 3b. 8.   [153] Aes. *Se.* 70, *Eum.* 417.

[154] See esp. *Eum.* 46 ff. For the iconography, see *LIMC* iii. 1 and 2, and Prag (1985).

[155] Soph. *El.* 1392: Orestes is the helper of the dead (Agamemnon), the injured party; he is 'of stealthy foot' (cf. similar descriptions of the Erinues, e.g. Aes. *Se.* 791). On weakness and strength cf. Theog. 349–50, Aes. *Se.* 76; xvii. 475 admits the possibility that even beggars may have Erinues.

[156] Soph. *OC* 1376–81, *Aj.* 835, cf. Aes. *Se.* 76, 979.

evaded;[157] they constitute the guarantee which the victim needs, that the offender will suffer; the victim projects on to an imaginary personalized agency his own wish to punish the offender, and the ability, which he himself does not possess, to do so.

PUNISHMENT OF THE LIVING BY THE DEAD

Anxiety lest an offender go scot-free in this world is alleviated by belief that the gods will punish him sooner or later; anxiety lest he escape for ever is alleviated by belief that he will indubitably be punished after death, by the nether gods or by Erinues; and the latter have the power to leave the nether world and pursue him in this life too. But the principle that still-living offenders may be punished by inhabitants of the under-world is not confined to Erinues, who are surrogates: deceased injured parties themselves also have the power to punish living offenders directly. The deceased who have this power in a conspicuous degree[158] are persons who by virtue of the prowess they displayed on earth may be presumed to be strong and effective even after death, when they attain the status of semi-divine 'heroes'.[159]

Heroes wish to protect justice against aggression,[160] feel anger against offenders, and may curse them[161] (perhaps enforcing the curse by their own actions, not through agencies). They can inflict all manner of suffering, which is occasionally described to comic effect;[162] equally, of course, they can confer benefits.[163] They are open to appeals from injured parties, to lend aid in attempts to punish offenders;[164] and like living men, they can perhaps be gratified by any suffering which offenders experience at the hands of injured parties.[165] Like Erinues, they can wander abroad and be encountered in this world;[166] indeed, the similarity of their function to that of the Erinues themselves at least once causes a hero or (rather his shade) to be called an Erinus.[167]

There is one striking case in which both the offender and the victim are dead: in Polygnotus' painting of Hades (mid-fifth century) a man is

---

[157] Soph. *Aj.* 836, 843, 1391, *Ant.* 1074, Aes. *PV* 516, *Choe.* 383. *Eum.* 383.

[158] The dead in general apparently have this ability: *Hipp. Maj.* 282a; cf. Xen. *Cyr.* 8. 7. 18 ff.: they may also *send* avenging deities. Mutilation of corpses is sometimes intended to prevent the dead person from undertaking retaliation: Her. 4. 62 *fin.* Lyc. *Leoc.* 136 is not quite sure whether the dead retain sensation and take an interest in earthly affairs; Dem. 19. 66 entertains the possibility.

[159] On heroes, see Burkert (1985) 203–8.

[160] Thuc. 2. 74, Soph. *OC* 1518 ff.; cf. Ar. fr. 58, in which they appear as punishers of offenders in general, not only of offenders against themselves.

[161] Aes. *Choe.* 326, 406, Soph. *Tr.* 1202.   [162] Ar. fr. 58, cf. Hipp. *Morb. Sacr.* 4.

[163] Soph. *OC* 1518; cf. Merkelbach (1967).

[164] Aes. *Choe.* 315 ff., 476 ff.; Soph. *El.* 1060 ff. with Kells's (1973) note on 1066.

[165] Soph. *El.* 355–6.   [166] Ar. *Birds* 1482 ff.   [167] Aes. *Se.* 979.

portrayed strangling his son, who had wronged him.[168] This is a wholly exceptional transfer to the next world of a punishment that might have been inflicted in this, i.e. by the dead person on the still-living offender.

POLLUTION

In Greek society a wide variety of acts, some of them offences (notably homicide), were supposed to produce pollution (*miasma*) in the agent; and a variety of purification rituals were available and enjoined. Yet pollution is not in itself a penalty. To an offender, pollution is no doubt a disagreeable consequence of an offence; but not all disagreeable consequences are punishments. For punishments are *imposed*, either by an injured party or by someone acting on his behalf. Pollution, by contrast, is generally imagined to occur automatically, simply in virtue of the offence. Nor is its purpose to impose suffering. Pollution simply marks out the commission of an abnormal and damaging act which threatens the order and stability of the family and/or community; purification is a conspicuously enacted rite of passage which re-establishes the offender in the good graces and normal functioning of society; for he now ceases to infect it and expose it to the risk of divine anger provoked by the presence of the pollution.[169]

Nevertheless, there are certain senses in which pollution can take on something of the nature and purpose of punishment. (1) Both the offender and the injured party may regard it, like the actual penalty, as an imposition, and to that extent as a punishment in a special guise. He who pays a fine is out of pocket; so too is he who pays the expenses of purification rituals. Like punishment, pollution may be threatened as the undesirable consequence of an act, by way of deterrence.[170] (2) A murderer who believes that his victim has some *post-mortem* powers which he may use in order to inflict suffering in return will feel apprehensive, and regard himself as polluted in the sense of being a possible target of malevolence, in effect liable to punishment. Yet this feeling of being in danger, 'polluted', is not in itself the punishment the dead person ideally wishes to inflict (which is presumably something more drastic); the apprehension by the killer of that punishment is distinct from, or is at most only part of, the punishment itself. (3) Just as a penalty may be diminished or waived in consideration of the

---

[168] Paus. 10. 28. 1; but cf. Plut. *LVD* 567de.

[169] The summary in this paragraph of this diverse and complicated phenomenon relies heavily on Parker (1983), and Burkert (1985) 75 ff.; cf. Adkins (1960a) 86 ff.

[170] Dem. 20. 158 so interprets Draco's regulations on pollution. Cf. Aesch. 3. 110–11, 121, Soph. *OT* 269 ff.

circumstances of an offence or the offender's state of mind, so too pollution, despite the objective commission of the offence, may in the light of similar considerations be deemed not to have taken place, or to have occurred only on a minor scale; and purifications may then be diminished or dispensed with. Conversely, like punishment, pollution may be enhanced, in the case of exceptionally heinous offences, by multiples of itself.[171] (4) While a penalty is intended to 'wipe the slate clean' legally, so far as the rights, property etc. of the injured party are concerned, purification has the purpose of restoring the *status quo* socially and religiously. However, it rehabilitates the offender the more easily in that unlike punishment it is not calculated to impose suffering (such suffering as it may impose is indirect—see (1) and (2) above); and it therefore fails, or should fail, to arouse the resentment and hostility which impede a return to amicable normality.

Pollution is of crucial importance in Plato's homicide law, and we shall have to look at certain aspects of it more closely in that section.

THE *ORESTEIA*

Interpretation of the moral issues raised by the series of killings described in the *Oresteia* is apt to focus either on the purely human motivation and responsibility of the characters, or on the elaborate and persuasive apparatus of divine influence on human action. To scrutinize the human dilemmas and choices of the characters is indeed illuminating; but it can attenuate the divine activity to mere abstractions. Hammond, for instance, presents Agamemnon as a character who in the end decides to sacrifice his daughter because he hypocritically believes it proper (*themis*) to put military and political considerations first; such a decision offends against *moira*, the sheer facts of the apportionment of privilege and status in the world at large, and provokes inevitable backlash.[172] The backlash is the will of Zeus, as indeed is all the suffering that is said to lead to 'good sense'. On this view, Zeus operates at a rather remote distance: he seems to be effectively only the personification of certain essentially impersonal forces or facts. On the other hand, the view that Zeus intends to enforce his justice by himself provoking and using, in pursuit of his 'grand design', the disastrous decisions made by the characters, seems, if pitched in too strong a form, to reduce them to puppets.[173] The fundamental reason for such dilemmas of inter-

---

[171] Ant. *Tetr.* 3d. 10–11, cf. V. 88, 91, VI. 6.   [172] Hammond (1965) 47, 50–2.

[173] e.g. Lloyd-Jones (1962) 187–99: 'Agamemnon cannot refuse [to sacrifice Iphigeneia], for it is Zeus' will that the fleet sail; and Zeus sends Ate to take away his judgement and *force* him to consent' (199, my italics). But cf. id. (1983) 201 n. 78.

pretation is of course the 'double determination' that is so characteristic of Greek thought. The responsibility for any act may be ascribed either to the agent himself or to some god, depending on the beliefs and purposes of the speaker in his situation.[174] The divergence among interpreters is roughly parallel: some concentrate on the human agent and his character and dilemmas in a human and social framework, while others see the hand of Zeus everywhere.

Neither view seems to me to do full justice to the *Oresteia*, at least in matters penological. The first thing to be clear about is that when the text represents the characters as describing the existence, nature, and activities of surrogate punishers—Zeus, Apollo and the Erinues—it means exactly what it says.[175] Easterling, on the other hand, argues:[176] '. . . a divine explanation of human conduct . . . is a *diagnosis of something actually observed in human behaviour*, and not a piece of mumbo-jumbo independent of observed phenomena. . . . we should not use language that implied supernatural causation, though we should be seeing the same phenomenon. I conclude that when a character behaves oddly in an Aeschylean play it is not enough to say "he is in the grip of *Atē*". We must also ask ourselves what kind of *human intelligibility* the oddity has . . . To say "he behaves in this extraordinary way because a *daimon* is at work in him" and assume that one has explained the oddity, [is like] pretending that two ways of saying the same thing stand in a causal relation to one another.'

But that the supernatural activity of a surrogate punisher must (be supposed to) stand in some causal relation to the phenomenon it is intended to 'diagnose' is evident from the very nature of surrogate punishing. For a surrogate punisher is a creation of the imagination of an injured party who, because of his own real or supposed weakness, projects on to the punisher the will and the power to act in his stead. What he cannot do to the offender on his own behalf, the surrogate must do, i.e. punish; otherwise the surrogate has no use. If the injured party had the power, there would be no question but that he would himself do something to the offender; and this doing—punishing—would indeed be causally related to the suffering the offender then experienced. The surrogate punisher is simply (supposed to be) the substitute agent. Such an agent, being supernatural, may work directly on the offender, as the Erinues invoked by Clytemnestra do on Orestes; or, over a longer timescale, by *utilizing* the character of the offender when trapped in a

---

[174] Note how the Ethiopian in Her. 2. 139 feels that the gods are *tricking* him into committing an offence. Essentially the same thought recurs, unexpectedly, in Dem. 24. 121 (see Dover, (1968a) 272, on 1458 ff.): to commit a crime (and so be punished) is itself a visitation or punishment from a god. Cf. Lyc. *Leoc.* 91-3, And. 1. 113.

[175] Cf. Dodds (1951) 39 ff.   [176] Easterling (1973) 5-6.

dilemma: Zeus punishes Agamemnon (the inheritor of the curse Thyestes laid on Atreus) by sending on him *Atē* which ensured that he yielded to his ambition to sack Troy, and so sacrificed his daughter, and so was killed by Clytemnestra. If Agamemnon is to be thought of as killing Iphigeneia solely because of pride or ambition, what relevance has all the talk of the curse and the *Atē* which Zeus sends?[177] The plain fact is that surrogate punishers are conceived as *causing* something to happen to offenders that could not be brought about by the injured parties themselves. These parties do not reckon merely that a disaster suffered by an offender just because of his own character or foolish decision is what is 'meant' by punishment from Zeus or the Erinues; for that, surrogates are unnecessary; and in any case few injured parties have the faith that their offenders will come to some disaster unprompted. Rather, they believe that some active intervention is required from agents more powerful than themselves. The relation between the offender's character and decisions on the one hand, and the intervention of the surrogate on the other, is inevitably left vague.[178] But a strong belief, particularly on the part of the characters in the *Oresteia*, in some causal intervention seems to me clear.[179]

In other ways too surrogates mirror the wishes, intentions and character of the injured party. First, since often the only recompense available to him takes the form of the suffering of the offender, surrogates are essentially vindictive.[180] This is evident on almost every page of the *Oresteia*; the Erinues, moreover, like most human punishers, enjoy inflicting what they inflict.[181] Second, since injured parties rarely admit that they have suffered justly, their surrogates, as projections of their views, concentrate on the sheer fact of the injuries inflicted on them. Excuses or justifications are not entertained; hence the Erinues suppose that once Orestes has admitted to having killed Clytemnestra, no more needs to be said.[182] Third, surrogates are thought to be zealous to visit suffering on human beings who fail, or may fail, to punish offenders.[183] Such persons can feel, therefore, a strong compulsion to punish, even if on other grounds they would prefer to desist. Fourthly, a person who punishes on behalf of

[177] From this it will be evident that I adopt substantially Lloyd-Jones's view (1983, 90 ff.) of Zeus' fulfilment of Thyestes' curse. I am unmoved by Hammond's (1965) objection (42 ff.) that we hear of nothing to do with the curse until 'the *Agamemnon* is two-thirds done' (1193). To delve far back into the past for the original cause of Agamemnon's death at this latish stage seems to me perfectly effective, both dramatically and intellectually.

[178] See *Agam.* 1505–8: the *alastōr* may be a *sullēptōr*, 'accomplice'.

[179] Dodds (1960a repr. 1973) 55 speaks of the Erinues' 'reality and causative activity' as 'a presupposition of the story as Aeschylus unfolds it'.

[180] Cf. pp. 52 ff. above, and e.g. in the chorus's comments at *Agam.* 1430, *Choe.* 309 ff.; cf. 'additional note' below.   [181] *Eum.* 253, 560; cf. *Agam.* 1447, 1581.

[182] *Eum.* 585–9.   [183] e.g. *Choe.* 269–96.

another, and is therefore his *human* surrogate, can attribute to himself, in his own belief, the frightful qualities, powers, and functions of super-human surrogates, as Clytemnestra does.[184]

The network of belief in surrogate punishers, which was originally intended to afford injured parties some comfort and faith that offenders would in the end be punished by some agency stronger than themselves, became, by a sort of rebound into real life, a force justifying and demanding punishments of a wholly vindictive kind, without reference to motive, circumstances, or excuses. Produced by a penological purpose (a desire for recompense) that was vindictive in part, it cannot but have reinforced that element in that purpose. Its tendency to stimulate a long and in principle endless sequence of offences and counter-offences, killings and counter-killings, was, *if* the evidence of the *Oresteia* is anything to go by, very strong;[185] and it probably played a large part in the development of the predominantly vindictive tone which, as we shall see, is characteristic of the penology of the courts.

Now in the absence of belief in supernatural surrogate punishers, a sequence of killings and counter-killings may cease at any time, if the next person in line to kill simply does not act. He may be negligent or powerless, or see his interests differently; the killing he is supposed to punish may be as unjust as you like; but if for some reason he does not act, the sequence does at any rate stop. To ask what the characters in the plot of the *Oresteia would* have done or failed to do had they not believed in supernatural surrogate punishers is to commit the 'documentary fallacy';[186] but it is to be noticed how often the killings which form the subject-matter of the trilogy are somehow related to such a belief. (i) The Erinues are angry with Thyestes for seducing Atreus' wife;[187] Atreus retaliates, then (ii) Thyestes curses Atreus and his house;[188] (iii) Apollo instructs Orestes to punish Clytemnestra;[189] (iv) the Erinues, cheered on by Clytemnestra, seek to punish Orestes.[190] (v) Zeus wishes to have Troy punished for the crime of Paris, and (vi) Artemis wishes to see Agamemnon punished for sacking Troy.[191] The causal effect these agencies are supposed to have had is clearer in some cases than in others; but at any rate the *Oresteia* could not be what it is if the surrogate punishers were subtracted from it: they play a large and integral role and constitute, I suggest, a major part of its overall significance.

The chorus bewail the sequence of killings, and Clytemnestra wishes

[184] *Agam.* 1497 ff. (see Fraenkel (1950) on 1501).   [185] See pp. 70–1 below.
[186] But see next paragraph.   [187] *Agam.* 1188 ff.   [188] *Agam.* 1600–2.
[189] *Eum.* 84, *Choe.* 269 ff., cf. 925. But it is not quite clear that Apollo qualifies as a surrogate punisher. He may only give peremptory advice: 'Kill Clytemnestra rather than be cursed by Erinues for *failing* to do so.'   [190] *Eum.* 94 ff.
[191] *Agam.* 60 ff., 134 ff., 338 ff., 537, 810 ff., Lloyd-Jones (1962) 190, Hammond (1965) 46.

it to stop with the death of Agamemnon;[192] and the *Oresteia* does indeed portray a cessation, not at that point, but at the death of Clytemnestra herself. Now Clytemnestra, even without a belief in the supernatural surrogates she thinks support her, had powerful 'human' motives for killing Agamemnon: the death of Iphigeneia and her own liaison with Aegisthus.[193] But Orestes' case is somewhat different: clearly he is an *unwilling* killer of his mother. Aeschylus goes to some trouble to analyse his motivation for us:

1. *Choe.* 269–305, summed up by 299, 'many impulses coincide to lead to one result'. They are:

(*a*) the orders, or at least peremptory advice, of Apollo;[194]
(*b*) the threat of assault by the Erinues, that is to say pollution and the disagreeable social consequences of it, if he fails to act;[195]
(*c*) grief for his father;[196]
(*d*) poverty;[197]
(*e*) the thought that such despicable persons as Clytemnestra and Aegisthus should rule the glorious conquerers of Troy.[198]

The weight of the passage lies on (*a*) and (*b*). In spite of a passing mistrust of oracles of the type he has received,[199] Orestes must surely play it safe; *ergo*, 'the deed must be done'—and we are then, rather cursorily, informed of (*c*), (*d*), and (*e*), which are evidently subsidiary.

2. *Eum.* 84, 579–80, 622 ff. Apollo explicitly says that it was he who 'persuaded' Orestes to kill his mother, and he therefore accepts responsibility for that killing; similarly he admits to giving Orestes such an instruction, on the ultimate authority of Zeus himself.

3. *Choe.* 900–2. When Orestes momentarily yields to pity for Clytemnestra and hesitates to kill her, Pylades resolves his doubt by reference to Apollo's oracles, 'better to have all men your enemies than the gods'. Orestes takes the point, and kills her.

I conclude that if the sequence of killings was going to stop anywhere, it would have stopped as a result of a refusal by Orestes to kill his mother. But it did not stop there; he did kill her, and the crucial and decisive factor in his decision to do so was the pressure he felt under from supernatural surrogate punishers.

How far is this a reflection of a *historical* problem? In Homer, killers commonly go into exile, sometimes pursued by their victims' relatives;

[192] *Agam.* 1568 ff., cf. 1654. It could have stopped there, perhaps, if she had gone into exile: 1410 ff. At *Choe.* 481–2 Electra hopes to 'escape' after the killing of Aegisthus; at 1075–6 the chorus wonder when the end of the sequence will come.
[193] Who will take over the kingdom: *Agam.* 1638–9.
[194] *Choe.* 270 ff., 300.
[195] Ibid. 270–96, cf. 925, 1017, 1029–33: Parker (1983) 106 ff.
[196] *Choe.* 300.
[197] Ibid. 301, cf.275.
[198] Ibid. 302–4.
[199] Ibid. 297–8.

but 'no homicide in the epics gives rise to a vendetta'.[200] It is possible that long chains of killings for killings never or rarely took place, and barely existed outside the imagination of Aeschylus. Nevertheless, if belief in supernatural surrogates was ever sufficiently strong to stimulate action, then there must have been at least a potential difficulty. For if murder, like other offences, was to be brought under the control of the state courts—and we know it was so brought—one of the hindrances must have been the belief that surrogate punishers demanded blood for blood, exacted either by themselves or by human agents acting under their instigation; for such a belief could do nothing to curb murders but everything to multiply them. It was clearly desirable that the case of any single murder should be closed by the punishment (or non-punishment, for that matter) of the murderer. When belief in surrogates prevails, the killer of a killer *may* attract a further killer; but if a court kills a killer the matter is likely to end, for no one can in turn kill a court. To put the point sharply, it is possible that surrogates and courts *competed for* the punishment of offenders.

It is this process which is dramatized in the *Oresteia*. Orestes is polluted by the murder of his mother and by the onslaughts of his mother's Erinues; and the essential step is to negate these onslaughts by purifying him. This Apollo and others do.[201] The Erinues are furious at Apollo's protection of Orestes, but they cannot stop him; the most they can do is acquiesce in Orestes' trial before Athena's new court, with strong hopes that it will judge him by the same criteria as those by which they themselves judged him: the objective fact that he killed Clytemnestra, without regard to motives, circumstances and pressures.[202] As for Orestes himself, the way is now clear for him, purified and in a fit state to enter society without danger of polluting it in turn, to be tried by a human court and become liable to human penalties, if found guilty, without reference to the blind automatic operation of surrogate punishers, and without danger of provoking further killings. The court, one has to assume, took account of Apollo's confession of responsibility and Orestes' purification, though the verdict was 'a damn close-run thing'.

The position achieved at the end of the *Oresteia* is then in essence what we find in the Athenian homicide law in the classical period: purification rituals and legal processes operate side by side. Under the new dispensation introduced in the *Eumenides,* the Erinues, at Athena's urging, are to exercise for Athens' benefit their powers for good—powers

[200] Gagarin (1981) 10, 18.
[201] *Choe.* 1059–60; *Eum.* 235 ff., 280 ff., 445 ff., 474, 578. It is not clear when and where the purifying takes place: see Dyer (1969), Taplin (1977) 381–4, Brown (1982) 30–2.
[202] *Eum.* 585–9 (in spite of 202).

which sound as if they are over and above their power to refrain from inflicting evil.[203] However that may be, their strictly penological functions change—but precisely how? In one respect nothing seems to change: for Athena and the Erinues concur in holding that fear is essential to the formation of a moderate life-style, midway between anarchy and despotism;[204] and it is clear, though naturally the Erinues' benevolent functions take pride of place in the latter part of the *Eumenides*, that they will continue to represent and assist *to deinon*, i.e. that which is formidable or fearful. So offenders may still expect to receive punitive visitations from them.[205]

The crucial change is to be found in what Athena tells the Erinues they must *not* do: implant incentives to bloodshed, which are harmful to the young, nor Ares (War) among her citizens.[206] How then shall the Erinues avoid producing such socially damaging results? By accepting one crucial limitation to their role.[207] In the past, *all* injured parties, even aggressors when punished, had their own Erinues, who could be expected in turn to injure the punisher, sometimes, at least, acting through some human being who is regarded *as* an Erinus; but the punished punisher too has his Erinues, and so on. But if the sole function of the Erinues is now simply to punish, but not in the role of *agent* of any injured party of any kind, then the offender will be punished and that may well be that, for he will not have the supernatural stimulus or means to punish his own punisher. To the extent that punished offenders cease to believe they have their own Erinues, sequences of offence and counter-offence will become less likely.[208]

In short, the Erinues will continue to be fear-inspiring supernatural punishers, but they will cease to be private surrogate punishers, the personal agents of injured persons. Nowhere in the admittedly limited hints of their future punitive functions given by themselves and by Athena are they said to be 'attached to' or 'of' anyone or associated with

[203] *Eum.* 902 ff. *saepe.* By a natural but illogical polarity, beings supposed to have large capacity to do evil are thought to have an equal capacity for good. Cf. Podlecki (1989) 6–7.

[204] *Eum.* 517 ff., 691 ff., cf. Lloyd-Jones (1983) 92–4. At 517 *to deinon* has a political relevance, because political moderation and stability depends on moderation in individuals, which (the Erinues think) is induced by fear; cf. Dover (1957) 231–2.

[205] *Eum.* 934–7 as elucidated by Sommerstein (1990b), cf. 954–5.

[206] *Eum.* 858–63, on which see Sommerstein (1990b). The Erinues duly deprecate 'vengeance-disasters of reciprocal murder', 981–2.

[207] Some limitations of role is implied at Eum. 698, where Athena says 'do not banish *to deinon* from the state *completely* (*pan*)'. The Erinues themselves admit that *to deinon* is not invariably appropriate (*Eum.* 517).

[208] Mackenzie (1981), in her useful discussions of the *Oresteia* (104–6, 121–5), rightly stresses that such sequences can be stopped only if the principle is accepted that some injuries—i.e. punishments—are not to be regarded as offences. But she misses the crucial point that the 'element' of retribution that has to be 'lifted' (122) is the role of the Erinues not merely as proponents of a 'blunt *lex talionis*' (123) but as agents of *persons*. Cf. now Lloyd-Jones (1990).

any particular crime,[209] and nothing is said of their being applied to by injured parties. Their role has been emptied of the injured parties' personal spleen which they formerly embodied and expressed, and generalized into the limited one of simply deterring and punishing offenders; and as such, of course, it is merely an ancillary duplicate of that of the Areopagus itself.[210] The Erinues cease to be agents of the injured parties, and become agents of the state. The limitation on their function is simply the *psychological* expression of the loss by punished parties of the right to regard the punishment as a crime, itself meriting punishment in turn.[211] Such a loss was essential to the development of courts.

Finally, we may note that the restriction on the role of the Erinues, which is achieved by the acquittal of Orestes, depends on more of the 'arbitrary reasons' we have noticed before. The Erinues' claim that Clytemnestra was not a blood relation of Agamemnon is 'capped' by Apollo's claim that Clytemnestra is not really a 'parent' of Orestes; and Athena's preference for male over female decides her casting vote.[212] By such arbitrary arguments and preferences are moral advances justified in myth.

Additional note: Learning by suffering in the Oresteia

This celebrated doctrine, of which much has been made,[213] occurs several times in the *Oresteia*, chiefly in apparently related passages of moralizing sung by the choruses. In its complete form, which is however found in no one passage, it has four propositions:

(*a*) That the doer *suffers*.[214]
(*b*) That (*a*) constitutes *justice*.[215]
(*c*) That in so suffering the doer *learns* 'sense' or 'wisdom'.[216]
(*d*) That (*a*)–(*c*) have been laid down by Zeus as a universal law for mankind.[217]

(*a*) and (*b*) are merely the ordinary notion[218] that an offender should suffer, as a matter of justice.[219] (*c*) is obviously in the tradition of such

---

[209] *Eum.* 927–37, 950–5, and cf. n. 204. Contrast XV. 204, XXI. 412, xi. 280, xvii. 475, *Agam.* 1190 with Fraenkel's note, *Choe.* 283–6, *Eum.* 508–16.

[210] Note 'quick to anger' (to punish?) of the Areopagus (*Eum.* 705, cf. 698), and 'hard to please' of the Erinues (928): both bodies value the instillation of fear, *to deinon*; cf. 990.

[211] For instance, Clytemnestra's appeal at *Eum.* 94 ff. will no longer be entertained.

[212] *Eum.* 605, 657 ff., 734 ff.   [213] e.g. by Dodds (1960*a*, repr. 1973) 59 ff.

[214] *Agam.* 250, 1562–4, *Choe.* 312–13.

[215] *Agam.* 250, *Choe.* 311.   [216] *Agam.* 175–81, cf. Soph. fr. 229.

[217] *Agam.* 177–8, 1563.   [218] e.g. *Agam.* 1527.

[219] All parties in the *Oresteia* claim to have justice on their side, and they all think that it is satisfied by retributive suffering: *Agam.* 1432–3 (Clytemnestra); 1607–11 (Aegisthus); *Choe.* 142–8, 244, 394–9 (Electra); 554–9, 988–9, 1026–8, cf. *Eum.* 439, 610 (Orestes); *Eum.* 154, 272, 312, 516 (Erinues); 615 ff. (Apollo).

remarks as 'the fool learns late, to his cost' in Homer and Hesiod.[220] In these earlier contexts the maxim is always to specify relationships: the offender discovers from bitter experience who is 'stronger', and is supposed to learn to desist from offending him in the future. Similarly, Aegisthus threatens the chorus that they will learn 'wisdom', i.e. to obey him, by various sufferings he will impose on them.[221] Presumably by repeatedly learning (however unwillingly)[222] in the many various aspects of life what conduct does or does not attract punishment from a stronger, the punished person may be said to have gradually acquired 'wisdom' and to be 'morally improved'.[223] The moralizing of the choruses in the *Oresteia* similarly applies the maxim to the specific persons and actions of the play.[224]

(*d*) Certainly 'learning by suffering' has the sanction of Zeus. The chorus does not doubt that it is laid down and enforced by the strongest of all beings. Furthermore, they see it as a *benefit* conferred on men by Zeus: it is a 'favour of divine powers conferred by violence'.[225] Zeus is, as for example in Solon, a punisher of wrongdoers.

I therefore find it difficult to see what justifies Fraenkel's airy view,[226] 'with φρονεῖν ['wisdom', 'sense'] as the goal of man's journey we are on a much higher plane of ideas than is reached by the traditional verdict παθὼν δέ τε νήπιος ἔγνω ['the fool learns by suffering'] or in proverbial expressions such as παθήματα μαθήματα ['sufferings = learnings'] and the like.' In comprehensiveness of vision and grandeur of expressions the 'plane' on which Aeschylus moves is, no doubt, 'high'; but the component 'ideas' seem commonplace and traditional. In any case, several of the characters in the *Oresteia*, as Lloyd-Jones and others have pointed out, suffer by dying; and even if we suppose that they live just long enough to realize their mistake, it is difficult to term such learning a 'favour'. The truth is that 'learning by suffering' can be an exceedingly savage doctrine in which the notion of 'learning' is meaningless. If I punish someone by killing him, I may say, on thrusting home my sword, 'That'll teach you'; but that is a grim jest, not moral theory.[227]

At all events, it is clear that the policy of *pathei mathos* (learning by suffering) is precisely the policy which will be followed by the Erinues. They represent justice of a mainly vindictive kind; their role will be to

[220] XVII. 32, XX. 198, *WD* 218.
[221] *Agam.* 1617-24. 1632, 1642, 1649-50 (cf. Clytemnestra, 1425).   [222] *Agam.* 180-1.
[223] Perhaps that is the implication of *Agam.* 176-7: Zeus puts or leads mortals 'on the *path*' of wisdom.
[224] On the specific applications of the doctrine in the *Oresteia*, see Gagarin (1976), app. A.
[225] *Agam.* 182-3.   [226] On *Agam.* 176.
[227] Cf. Eur. *Tr.* 1040-1, *Bac.* 859. At Her. 2. 177 Egyptians are 'straightened' or 'put right' by death.

ensure that offenders suffer; and that, they hope, will have a deterrent effect on others, as well as teach punished persons 'wisdom'.[228]

THE OVERALL EFFECTS

As we look back over this survey of surrogate punishers we ought not to forget that we are considering not reports of real life, but constructions of the imagination. By this, I do not mean that the literature—chiefly drama, epic, and lyric—has no relation to life: clearly it does portray historical or fictional personalities of a kind we could actually encounter, the emotions they experienced, their friendships and conflicts, and their beliefs. But belief in surrogate punishers is *false*: the gods and the Erinues do not exist, curses and *defixiones* do not have intrinsic and automatic effects, and the dead cannot affect the living; and in particular there are no *post-mortem* punishments, since there is no life after death—or at any rate we do not know that there is. Such beliefs can, of course, and doubtless did, affect actual conduct; but they are not built on fact. The point is crucial for the character of the punishments which surrogates are supposed to inflict. For a belief that they ensure recompense would invariably be falsified; it is therefore not held. But a belief that they sooner or later inflict retribution, in this life or the next, is not falsifiable; it is therefore held widely and indeed passionately. In many cases the only recompense available to an injured party was satisfaction at the sight or thought of the suffering of the offender; and surrogate punishers, who spring from the injured party's resentful feeling of weakness, and whose power to punish is limited by imagination alone,[229] are admirably fitted to supply that sort of satisfaction. Consequently, since surrogate punishers are intended to fulfil justice, the notion that justice itself is reciprocal, retributive, and destructive receives powerful reinforcement.[230]

Belief in supernatural surrogates can be effective at three stages:

(*a*) it can deter a potential offender;
(*b*) it can give powerful satisfaction to an injured party;
(*c*) it can deter for the future an actual offender who supposes that he has in fact been punished by some surrogate.

In Greek literature, and conjecturally in life, its role is commonly restricted to (*b*). But in Hesiod, the mystery religions, and the *Oresteia*

---

[228] *Eum.* 521, cf. 1000 (which may however not be penological but refer to Athens' acquisition of wisdom during history: see Dodds 1960*a*, repr. 1973) 53.
[229] The limits were of course almost limitless: see e.g. *Choe.* 269 ff.
[230] Retributive and destructive *reciprocity*, Soph. *Ant.* 1074–6, fr. 962, Aes. *Choe.* 274.

we have three very different attempts to reinterpret it creatively, and to endow it with some positive, forward-looking moral and social purpose. In Hesiod, Zeus punishes mankind for Prometheus' offence against himself; thus far he is not a surrogate punisher, though mankind is a surrogate punishee. But he punishes men by imposing a life of hard work, in which the industrious (i.e. just) man always prospers, and the lazy (i.e. unjust) man always comes to grief. Thus Zeus is in effect the former's *utterly reliable* surrogate punisher when offended against by the latter. In the mystery-religions Persephone apparently exacts punishment which is (i) not eternal, and thus not infinitely vindictive, (ii) encouraging of moral reform. In the *Oresteia*, the Erinues lose their role as agents in the service of individuals, and acquire a general retributive and deterrent role in the service of the state.

3

CRIME-SPECIFIC PUNISHMENTS

In Greek penal thought and practice there is a class of punishments known variously as 'talionic', 'mirroring', 'crime-specific' and 'analogous'. They exhibit bewildering variety; and the four terms themselves are often employed confusingly, more or less as synonyms. Our first task is to sharpen usage by imposing certain distinctions.

1. *Talio*. The essential feature of a talionic punishment is 'like for like'. The standard examples are 'an eye for an eye' and 'a tooth for a tooth': the offender suffers exactly and literally what he has inflicted. Thus if a man's eye is gouged out because he has robbed someone else of his eye, the penalty is purely and strictly talionic.

2. *Talio with Mirror*. But if the offender's eye is gouged out with the same implements, or in the same way, or in the same circumstances, or in the same place, or by the offended person himself, or some such significant detail, then the penalty, without ceasing to be talionic, becomes mirroring also.

3. *Mirrors*. If some other part of the offender's body, instead of the eye, is destroyed, or if some other loss or damage is inflicted on him, *but with the same implements*, etc., then the penalty again mirrors the offence; it ceases to be talionic, however, because the offender loses not that which he has made his victim lose, an eye, but something else; he has not suffered exactly what he inflicted.

A talionic punishment is therefore one in which the notion of 'aptness' or 'appropriateness' is expressed by pointed *identity* of offence and penalty; a mirroring punishment is one in which that notion is expressed by pointed *associative detail* reminiscent or indirectly descriptive of the offence. Whereas a talionic penalty can take only one form, a mirroring penalty, by suggestively distorted reflection, may take any number; consequently mirroring penalties lend themselves to ingenious elaboration. My conception of a mirroring punishment is in fact fairly broad: it embraces any punishment which is apt or pointed or ironic, so that the observer smiles inwardly and relishes its appropriateness to the offence.

This notion of appropriateness is not confined to penology, but has very wide application in Greek culture.[1]

In different ways, all three punishments are 'crime-specific'. (1) specifies the offence itself; (2) specifies both the offence and certain circumstances of its commission; (3) specifies circumstances only. 'Crime-specific', therefore, is a general term, of which 'talionic' and 'mirroring' are subdivisions. For the vague term 'analogous' I find no use.

In order to convey the flavour of crime-specific penalties, I first describe two instances in some detail.

1. Herodotus, 1 189 (case A24 in the Appendix): Herodotus describes how Cyrus, ruler of Persia, on his march to Babylon in about 540 BC, prepared to cross the river Gyndes. One of his white horses, which were sacred to the Sun, was a high-spirited creature, which dashed into the water and in trying to swim across was swept away and drowned. Cyrus, in a fury, vowed he would make the river so weak that even a woman could get across in future without wetting her knees. Accordingly he spent a whole summer on the job: he made his army divide Gyndes into 360 channels, each of course very shallow. Then, having punished the river, he resumed his march.

The point of this elaborate procedure was that since the horse was sacred to the Sun, and the Sun divides the year into (approximately) 360 days, it was possible to punish Gyndes by enfeebling him in a peculiarly apt way, by making the number of channels 360, thus specifying against whom the offence was committed—the Sun, whose protection and goodwill Cyrus presumably hoped to win or retain by acting on his behalf.

2. *Odyssey*, viii. 266–369 (case B1): Demodocus the singer of tales relates how Ares, the swift and strong and handsome god of war, seduced Aphrodite, the goddess of love and wife of Hephaestus, the lame god of handicrafts. Sneaking off to bed during the chance absence of Hephaestus, Ares and Aphrodite were taking their pleasure, when to their alarm they found themselves bound fast to the bed—and, presumably, in rather close proximity to each other. Homer says they could not in any way move or raise their limbs. For Hephaestus, who had got wind of what they were up to, had previously draped the bed with invisible and unbreakable bonds. Drawing them tight—perhaps at the crucial moment, though Homer is delicate enough not to say so—he called the other gods to come and look; and in Homer's magnificent expression, they laughed an unquenchable laughter. And only on

---

[1] e.g. in the significant naming of people and places (e.g. *Hom. H.* 5. 198, and Stanford 1947, 1948) p. xxi with the indices, s.v. 'significant name', and Dodds (1960*b*) on l. 367); for ethics, note particularly Long (1970) 135 ff., and cf. p. 18 above.

promise of payment by Poseidon of the fine due to an aggrieved husband did Hephaestus consent to release Ares and Aphrodite from their bonds.

The punishment of Ares and Aphrodite is a particularly brilliant example of a mirroring punishment, because it mirrors the crime *exactly*: the punishment *is* the offence, and the (forcibly continued) offence constitutes the punishment. There is a precise formal continuity and identity of the two. Obviously such formal identity is rarely possible, primarily because the continuation or repetition of an offence, at least against the original injured party,[2] can in the nature of the case only rarely function as its punishment. In any event, the setting up of such a punishment can be very demanding in terms of time and resources; not many of us, after all, finding our wife misbehaving, have the technical resources to bind her up with her paramour in invisible bonds.

The hallmarks of a mirroring punishment are that it is vivid, picturesque, and amusing. For although technically the penalty for adultery in Demodocus' story was payment to the injured husband, in this case it is not clear that the offender actually pays it, and it plays only a subsidiary part in the narration. The whole weight of the tale is on the exquisite torture of being caught in the act and being forcibly exhibited in an acutely embarrassing posture. And it is apt, too, in other ways which Homer represents the guffawing gods as appreciating keenly: they say, 'Bad deeds do not prosper. See how the slow overtakes the swift, just as now Hephaestus, slow as he is, has caught Ares, although he is the swiftest of the gods who hold Olympus. Lame though he is, he has caught him by his skills: hence Ares owes the fine of an adulterer.' It is pretty clear that the real punishment is less the fine itself than the personal ironies and humiliating embarrassment of the situation.

Neither the river Gyndes nor Ares suffers a strictly talionic punishment: for the river does not possess a horse of which he could be robbed, and Ares, if his punishment is to qualify as talionic, would have to provide his own wife (not that he has one) to be violated by Hephaestus.[3]

The collection of examples on which the argument of this chapter is based, if rehearsed here, would be intrusively bulky. It is therefore relegated to the Appendix, where readers who catch an interest in the topic may browse in the curious detail. A synoptic view of the material suggests the following reflections.

---

[2] In Her. 8. 105–6 (case A7b) part of the penalty for castrating is to castrate—not however oneself, but one's own sons.

[3] For examples of this practice see Walcot (1978).

DISTRIBUTION

(a) Categories

The list of cases is considerable but not overwhelming. Even if a good many more examples were found, one would still be dealing with a feature of Greek culture that would be localized rather than pervasive. Most ancient Greek punishments, formal or informal, were inflicted without reference, or at least overt reference, to considerations of crime-specificity. Nevertheless, instances are too numerous to encourage the hypothesis that they have all been reported to us simply because they are wildly unusual; rather do they suggest a practice which is moderately common but not frequent. And if crime-specific punishments were not entertaining, we should hear a good deal less of them.

Strictly talionic punishments are rare (only cases A1, A7a, c,[4] A19 (vaguely), B1). Killing for killing is of course strictly talionic, but it is so common as to be undistinctive: its pointedness is dulled by its frequency.

Mixed cases, or at any rate clear ones, are hard to come by. A7b is complex, with perhaps double talio and double mirror: the castrated person himself enforces (mirror) the castration (talio) of the castrator, and the castration is actually carried out (talio) by the castrator's own sons (mirror) whom the castrator has just castrated. The castration of the original offender is talio from the point of view of *two* injured parties. In the two cases in A28 the talionic principle is used in forensic contexts—fleetingly, but apparently with serious intent, not just by way of rhetoric. In B1 the bed is the same in both offence and penalty. Crime-specific punishments seem then to be overwhelmingly mirroring, not talionic. That is natural enough: to contrive an associative detail is easy, to reproduce exactly a whole offence is commonly difficult.

(b) Literature and life

Consider first the orators. They use all their agitated rhetoric, their sophisticated reasoning, and righteous indignation, to argue before the Athenian courts for or against the infliction of penalties of almost exclusively the non-mirroring kind. The penalties they have in view are mainly financial, capital, corporal, residential (exile), or civic (various forms of political disfranchisement). Such penalties are essentially non-specific; that is to say, although they have *some* relationship to offences, notably one of proportion or gravity (minor penalties for minor crimes,

---

[4] A7a is talionic in the sense that what one does to the woman of someone else is then done to one's own.

for instance), the relationship is not vivid, picturesque, apt, ironical, or amusing; you cannot so to speak read what the crime was in the very form of the punishment, or in the manner of its infliction, or in some significant detail of it. In general, the orators who pleaded before the courts which enforced the penal code of the law of classical Athens betray scant interest in crime-specific punishments of any kind at all. When they do show some interest, it is nearly always by way of anecdotal example or rhetorical adornment, not because such punishments formed a significant part of the penal system within which they were operating. The mirror of punishment was not, it seems a part of Athenian life, at any rate of life as affected by the courts and the legal code.

What is the significance of the distribution of crime-specific punishments? The most frequent locations are Homer, Herodotus, and the tragic dramatists. Elsewhere they are rare or absent. In particular, there is a marked paucity of crime-specific punishments in the sources which could reasonably be thought to provide evidence for 'real life': comic drama, Xenophon, and Thucydides. It is true that Herodotus is fairly rich in examples; but are his tales true or tall? Much of his narration is in any case not about Greeks of the fifth century but about foreigners of the sixth. Epic may tell us something about 'Homeric' society; but tragic drama and the eschatological myths of Plato would be treacherous evidence for the historical practice of the fifth and fourth centuries.

These swift generalizations point to the conclusion that crime-specific punishments are a feature of imaginative and didactic literature, not of Greek life. And is that surprising? 'Everyone knows', we may say dismissively, 'that the ancient Greeks had nastily inventive imaginations; so what could be more natural than that their imaginative writers should from time to time dwell on mirroring punishments, because they are apt and amusing and picturesque, and offer peculiarly keen satisfaction of that strong instinct we all have, to see evil done in return for evil, tit for tat—poetic justice, so to say?' On that hypothesis, their presence in Greek literature would tell us no more about Greek culture than their occasional presence in (for example) films today, in an age when they are entirely absent from the penal code, tells us about our own culture.

But a moment's reflection reveals the implausibility of this view. It is true that some mirroring punishments, particularly those in myths about the gods, are utterly fantastic and cannot in themselves reflect life; but the principle of mirror-punishments is sufficiently prominent in Greek literature to make it perverse to suppose that there is nothing here to be learned of Greek life and culture. What matters is that the idea is there.

POINTERS TO EARLY LAW

I believe there are a number of indications that the examples of crime-specific punishments we find in Greek literature are distant witnesses to an early period in the development of Greek society when crime-specificity in punishments was in some modest vogue. I do not mean to imply that crime-specific punishments were the *only* punishments in use in that period—for obviously they can perfectly well coexist with other kinds in the same society, and indeed new ones can be contrived at any date, according to the ingenuity of the punisher. Nor of course, do I suggest that they were confined to formal penal codes.

1. In Athens, an adulterer caught in the act, if he was not actually killed by the husband, could be forced to endure a 'radish'[5] being stuffed up his backside. Such a punishment reproduces symbolically, in a rough and ready and indeed painful way, the action of the offence, and it symbolically and ironically effeminizes the offender.[6] It was not compulsory: the aggrieved husband could accept financial compensation instead, as indeed Hephaestus eventually did in Homer. Such a situation suggests that the crime-specific punishment, if indeed it was ever in vogue, is on its way out, in favour of a financial one, which is easier to administer and obviously less risky for the husband than the further alternative, that of killing the adulterer, which, though permitted, might nevertheless lead to an accusation of murder.[7] I conjecture that radishing has survived from some earlier period when self-help was more common. This is just where one would expect survival of mirroring punishments, in private sexual matters,[8] where passions run high and injured parties need powerfully charged satisfaction of their affronted feelings.

'Radishing' neatly demonstrates the readiness with which mirroring punishments can be expressed in a kind of shorthand or symbolism. For unlike strictly talionic punishments, mirroring punishments are flexible; and this presumably gave them a certain survival value.

---

[5] Case A6. Presumably the root was larger than what we call a radish, and elongated; cf. Dover (1968a) 217. It is uncertain whether the practice was a matter of formal law or of custom only: see Xen. *Mem.* 2. 1. 5 and Is. 8. 44, who may or may not be referring to it. Cohen (1985) well points out that the evidence for radishing is confined to comedy, and casts doubt on its frequency; he does not consider the possibility that we may have only a jocular reference to a grisly practice once indeed in use but surviving chiefly in folk-memory. (Cf. 'off with his head' nowadays.)

[6] Cf. case A13.

[7] Compensation: Lys. 1. 25; killing: Dem. 23. 53; accusation of murder: Lys. 1, and cf. ibid. 37 with the code of Gortyn, Col. 2. 44–5 for the possible allegation of enticement.

[8] Cf. Paoli (1948) 155–6, and cases A2, A3, A6–9.

2. One of the rare passages in Demosthenes[9] that mention talionic punishments is an intriguing and instructive anecdote about Locri, a Greek city founded about 700 BC in the toe of Italy. Apparently Locri had an exceptionally conservative legal code. Anyone who wished to propose a new law had to do so with a noose around his neck, and if his proposal was accepted, well and good; if not, then not well and good. Demosthenes tells us that in 200 years only one new law had been passed. An existing law provided that anyone who destroyed another man's eye had to have one of his own knocked out; and Demosthenes adds, interestingly, that there was no alternative of a fine; his implication, I suppose, is that fines are a later development. One day a one-eyed man was threatened with the loss of his eye at the hands of an enemy; in much alarm he therefore proposed that anyone who knocked out the eye of a one-eyed man should have not just one but both of his own eyes knocked out, so as to suffer the same: total blindness. The proposer put his head in the noose, proposed his new law, and survived. Now here we seem to have, in the unreformed law, an historically attested talionic punishment, dating presumably from the time of the lawgiver Zaleucus in the seventh century. However, it is possible to dismiss Demosthenes' report as more edifying than believable.

3. Devereux has argued, following Freud, that the self-blinding of Oedipus is symbolical self-castration; for Oedipus had killed his father and married his own mother. The eyes are of course potent sexual weapons, and there are many examples in Greek mythology, and some in 'real life', of persons being blinded for various kinds of sexual offences (e.g. that of Teiresias).[10] If Devereux is right, then we have, as he says, a far stronger reason for the peculiar form of Oedipus' self-inflicted penalty that the series of reasons given in the text of Sophocles' play, which Devereux describes as 'neither sufficient nor very convincing', e.g. that in Hades after death he would not have to look upon his parents.[11]

But even if this interpretation is right (as I think it probably is), how much does it really tell us about actual Greek culture? Devereux claims[12] that the sequence 'sexual trespass–blinding' is 'culturally patterned'. I am not sure whether this amounts to a claim that at some historical period this punishment was regularly exacted for this range of crimes. At any rate, there is a possibility that somewhere in Greece, at some period, symbolical castration was inflicted on males for some sexual offences; for in its own peculiarly revolting way it is very crime-specific indeed.

4. Mirror-punishments often depend, as in the case of Oedipus, on crude associations of number, shape, and size which we no longer find interesting or natural. So lest my suggestion about early Greek practice

---

[9] Case A1.   [10] Devereux (1973) 41, 44–5; but cf. Buxton (1980).
[11] Devereux (1973) 39 on Soph. *OT* 1371 ff.   [12] Ibid. 41.

should seem wholly improbable, I offer some reassurance from comparative legal anthropology. S. Roberts[13] mentions a report that among the East African Gisu, when a man was killed, his kinsmen sometimes waited, presumably for years if necessary, until the son of the killer was of the exact age of the person killed before 'like retaliatory action'. This is a striking example of the incredibly obsessive lengths to which a society can go in order to attain a precise and significant match between the offence and the retaliation. Jolowicz[14] goes so far as to claim that 'ancient systems deal with tort and the damages for it not so much quantitatively as qualitatively. . . . The penalty is made to fit, not the amount of damage . . . but the nature of the tort itself. . . . The principle of appropriateness comes out most clearly in . . . 'mirroring' punishments, . . . [such as] the punishment of arson by burning, of coining by boiling, of removal of a boundary-stone by ploughing off the offender's head, all of which occur in medieval German law. Such again is the common practice of punishing the member [limb] which has sinned, as where the perjurer loses the hand or the two fingers he raised in swearing . . . or where castration is inflicted for sexual offences.'[15]

ORIGINS

What frame of mind, or process of reasoning, or social or religious practices, give rise to crime-specific punishments? Should we look for one origin, or more than one? I suspect there is a fairly complex story to reconstruct, and that we should no more look for a single origin for such punishments than we should look for a single origin for myth. A further complication is the likelihood that, while actual practice was reflected and embroidered in stories, stories in turn sanctioned and influenced practice; and which came first, the practice or the stories, is a chicken-and-egg question. As possible origins, the following seem worth considering:

1. The anthropomorphism and compartmentalism of Greek gods (cases in B7). Each has or shares a special area (or areas) of activity, and naturally retaliates in that area against offences in that area. Aphrodite punishes sexual offences by making the offender or some third party impotent, or adulterous, or repugnant to the other sex (case B7, Stesichorus), *not* by (say) causing a storm or producing a flood, which would be the province of some other god. Such a pattern of activity leads

---

[13] S. Roberts (1979) 57.
[14] Jolowicz (1926) 204–5; cf. Evans (1906) 167–8, 182, Ives (1914) 54–7.
[15] Cf. Foucault (1973) 104–6.

to a certain aptness or appropriateness in punishments: they become neatly and significantly related to their respective offences.

2. Punishments as preventive of a repetition of the offence.[16] Has a man slandered someone? Then cut out his tongue. Has he committed a sexual offence? Then castrate him.[17] Here too a significant relationship is set up between offence and punishment.

3. The didactic impulse. In the days before literacy, money and prisons, early law-enforcers (kings, generals, etc.) would find the picturesque relationship between offence and punishment, inherent in talionic and mirroring penalties, useful for purposes not only of recompense and deterrence, but of publicity and instruction.[18]

4. The desire to limit retaliation, on the grounds that the unbridled private enterprise of self-help is socially destructive: it leads to feuds and vendettas. It is well known that talionic punishments can be statements of maxima: 'an eye for an eye' may enjoin 'not *more* than an eye for an eye'. To fix on the damage done as a measure of the punishment is to establish a handy form of tariff; it is to impose a reasonable ratio between an offence and its punishment.[19]

HISTORICAL DEVELOPMENT

At some period in the early history of Greece, then, way back beyond Homer, mirroring and talionic punishments may have then played a limited but distinct role in Greek life.[20] If so, it is not difficult to see why both virtually disappear from the Greek law of the classical period; and why literature preserves the idea or principle of the mirror in imaginative and indeed fantastic forms.

Let us look first at their disappearance from life. A highly pemmicanized history of Greek, or at any rate Athenian, law would run as follows. Self-help, in which the individual or his family or tribe retaliated against aggressors, using their own resources, and inflicted whatever penalties they liked, provided only that they won the battle and had the power, gave way gradually to the referral of disputes to kings and chiefs for decision, and finally to fully constituted courts of law, with juries and a regular system of formal accusation and defence, the state enforcing the juries' decisions and exacting a wide variety of penalties. Into this

[16] Cf. cases A9, 11–12.
[17] Cf. Devereux (1973) 43 ff.   [18] Cf. cases in A13, esp. Diodorus.
[19] Cf. Latte (1931) 304 (Berneker). Note in case A1 that a very strong case had to be made before the Locrians would agree to destroy two eyes for the loss of only one.
[20] Aeschylus, after some talionic jingles, *Choe.* 309–14, claims that 'the doer should suffer' is a 'thrice-aged story', *trigerōn muthos*; cf. *Agam.* 1560–4.

sequence the virtual disappearance of talionic and mirroring punishments slots neatly enough.

(a) Talio

In Homer, no strictly talionic punishment can be found *imposed on human beings* (with the single conspicuous exception of death for killing). If talionic punishments were ever in vogue historically, in the society Homer describes they have already been superseded. In so far as the function of talio is to impose some *limit*, the Homeric heroes seem not to need it: at least, they seem almost instinctively to recognize in theory (without always observing in practice) the general desirability of not going too far.[21]

Moreover, this notion of limit can be applied flexibly. That is to say, it is easy[22] to gloss 'like for like' with 'same or equivalent worth or value', and thus to argue that (say) my theft of a cow calls not only for repayment to the owner of its value in money, but for the same amount again, to compensate him for his grief, the same yet again to compensate the community for the trouble I have caused, and the same yet again or even more because I 'deserve' to suffer, and a severe punishment in some sense 'fits' my base motives and moral turpitude; or repayment even greater than that, to deter me and others in the future, or to encourage me to reform. One can now develop the distinction between recompense/reciprocation pure and simple on the one hand, and strictly penal exaction on the other.[23] At any rate, the principle of exacting a multiple of the damage is clear in Homer.[24] Once the notion of 'equivalence' is substituted for that of 'sameness', a wide variety of punishments on a long spectrum from mild to severe can be applied as somehow 'fitting' the crime. Complex penal codes can then develop, such as we find in the fifth and fourth centuries—aided of course by the invention of money as a medium of exchange. Before that could happen, the principle of strict talio, as far as it was in use, had to be dropped as inflexible; and *if* it ever was in general use, it was largely dropped, I suggest, even before the development of the society reflected in Homer. For Homer is not primitive; he is relatively advanced.

---

[21] See pp. 17–18 above.
[22] Indeed necessary, for practical reasons: see Aristotle's discussion (*NE* 1132^{b}21 ff.) of the inadequacies of the Pythagorean formulation of justice as 'simple reciprocal suffering'. As he says, the same point applies to 'the justice of Rhadamanthus': 'if a man were to suffer what he inflicted, that would be straight justice' (Hes. (fr.) *GW* 1). In both cases the underlying notion of the 'same' is ambiguous as between 'same suffering, both in amount *and form*' and 'same in amount (only)'.
[23] Cf. Arist. *NE* 1132^{b}28–30.
[24] See pp. 25–7 above.

(*b*) *Mirror*

So much for talio. What of mirror punishments? In literature they have a long history, appearing prominently in the distant worlds described by Homer and the tragedians; they appeal because they are colourful and offer scope for entertaining fantasy. But more importantly, they serve as legitimizations and reinforcements of the crucial principle of retribution. Whereas the notion of strict likeness in talio suggests primarily equivalence and limit, the vividness of the mirror suggests rather a neat and satisfying retrospective connection between offence and penalty. Mirroring punishments exhibit a certain aesthetic and intellectual elegance, which suggests that retribution is somehow right and natural.

CONCLUSIONS

Positing an early period of Greek law when crime-specific punishments (among other kinds) were in use, I diffidently suggest for modification or refutation, the following bifurcation of development down to the fourth century BC:

Strictly *talionic* punishments, both in life and in imaginative literature, become rare as such; but at some stage they were influential in encouraging restraint and limit in punishing, and hence reasonable ratios between punishments and offences.

Mirroring punishments similarly become rare in life, but are used in imaginative literature as a means of promoting belief in the inevitability and/or desirability of retribution.

4

HISTORICAL PRACTICE AND CONTROVERSY

The evolution of the Athenian courts of the sixth, fifth, and fourth centuries is complex and controversial. We need to review, in a very summary manner, first the importance in Greek legal practice of the frequent opportunities to parade competing arguments in public forum, secondly the nature and evolution of the courts, and finally the very various procedures which they followed.

PUBLIC FORUM

Injured parties who are too weak to retaliate effectively have two recourses. The first is to suppose that certain powerful beings, divine or at any rate supernatural, have a concern to redress injury by the infliction of suffering on offenders, even if only a long time after the offence. Such hope or faith is evident in Homer, and is prominent in imaginative literature down to the fourth century. Its chief characteristic, apart from picturesque descriptions of surrogate agencies and the savage punishments they inflict, is a strong sense of reciprocal justice, the infliction of suffering in return for suffering inflicted. Such vindictive retribution, the diminution of the offender's *timē* in relation to the injured party's, constitutes the latter's only 'satisfaction'; for surrogate punishers cannot supply recompense in any other form. The comforts of believing in them are real and strong; but no amount of belief will restore to an injured party what he had been deprived of, or its equivalent, or give him recompense in some concrete form for damage done.[1]

The other recourse is not imaginative but practical. It is to invent some system by which offenders are to provide some sort of restitution— this being itself, to the offender, a form of suffering, a form which is gladly witnessed by his victim. Such requitals gained by injured parties

---

[1] He may of course interpret a piece of good fortune as compensation sent by a surrogate punisher in lieu of satisfaction; but then the punisher would not be *punishing* the offender, except in the most oblique manner (chagrin at seeing his victim flourish).

are of this world, not of the realms of faith, and are accordingly much greater; yet they are obviously also much more difficult to achieve than the others, which call only for an effort of thought. How then to achieve them? If you are too weak to act effectively on your own, you will naturally call on friends and/or relatives for assistance. This procedure is obvious in Homer,[2] and is in principle no more than an elaborate form of self-help, in which generalized argument, as distinct from an indignant conviction that *this* damage, *this* violation of *this* social norm ought to be redressed, may play little or no role. The crucial development comes when the conflicting parties[3] can be persuaded or constrained to appear before some audience and/or authority to fight it out in words; for some of the words may relate to the principles on which that authority ought to base his decision.

Yet in a sense the matter is not so clear-cut. As we saw in chapter 1, the Homeric hero who retaliates against an offender has a fairly precise and consistent set of assumptions and aims: briefly, to restore by some means his *timē*, and in so doing to vent his spleen on the offender by making him suffer for his offence, i.e. to punish him. But in so doing he was subject to a network of constraints, brought to bear by common-sense and public opinion. In other words, justifications for inflicting punishment were already both articulated and in competition; they did not need any formal system of courts to bring them into being or into conflict.

The impact on penology of the rudimentary 'courts' found in Homer is initially likely to have been slight. The authority of the 'judges' clearly depended in part on their sensitive adherence to customary assumptions and usage, and probably did not extend to systematic power of execution. That is to say, the judges pronounced in favour of the one side or the other, and left the victorious party to exercise self-help from a position of publicly sanctioned and therefore enhanced strength.[4] Moreover, it is likely that early judges relied heavily on the oaths of the parties and the statements of witnesses, and wished to reach a conclusion quickly, rather than embark on a nice calculation of competing penological principles and purposes.[5] All this represents restraints on self-help over and above those already operating informally, not necessarily an advance in penological sophistication.

Nevertheless, a step has been taken which is of the last importance for the development of Greek penology. Where there is no 'court', such

---

[2] e.g. iv. 164–5.

[3] Sometimes, presumably, only one appears, in which event he is less a litigant than a complainant.

[4] Even in the classical period execution could be uncertain and hazardous: Harrison ii (1971) 185–90.   [5] Cf. Arist. *Pol.* 1268ᵇ36 ff.; but see now Gagarin (1990) 26–9.

arguments as are deployed in the course of a dispute may well take the form of impassioned and abusive exchanges between the parties and their supporters. Disinterested third parties may become involved, and may have some effect on the outcome, being influenced by what they hear; but if they do, they are governed by no formal procedure. The rights and wrongs of particular disputes may at the time or subsequently become the topic of general discussion. But once a 'court' is established the parties necessarily address someone other than each other: they have a forum. They are obliged not merely to engage in abusing one another to the 'judge', but to make rational representations to him. Some of the representations will be likely to concern the justification and purposes of the suffering which the losing party ought to undergo. In other words, the arguments will be partly, in effect, penological.

THE COURTS

These considerations are little more than *a priori*, and it is time to turn to the actual form of what I have called 'courts'. Down to the time of Solon's legislation in 594, the common method of deciding disputes which were not decided by fighting or negotiation between the parties seems to have been to consign them to the judgement of a single person, chosen for his eminence in society and/or his reputation for sagacity and fair dealing. In Homer and Hesiod (to deal summarily with time down to c.700) these persons are often the *basileis*, 'kings', local chieftains or squires, and sometimes other persons of uncertain status, styled variously, e.g. *dikaspolos*, 'giver of judgements', or *istōr*, 'knower'.[6] The hearings would commonly be held in the market-place, in the presence of bystanders, who naturally made known their views. Sometimes, it appears, there was a 'bench' of such persons, who made a point of responding to the views of the crowd.[7] Although the institution of settling disputes before kings and others seem to have been sufficiently common for it to be alluded to quite as if it were an everyday event, we

---

[6] e.g. I. 237–9, XXIII. 486; cf. iii. 244–5, xii. 439–40. Floyd (1990) now argues that *istōr* means simply 'convener'.

[7] XVIII. 497 ff., the scene on the shield of Achilles. After prolonged controversy, it is still uncertain whether the issue at this 'trial' is a *penal* one. But as Andersen (1976) points out (12–13), a debate about merely whether *poinē* had or had not been paid would hardly have aroused such lively interest among the populace. Cf. Gagarin (1981) 14. The most thorough examination of the passage is by Wolff; cf. Macdowell (1978) 18–21, whom I think to be broadly right in arguing that the dispute is about 'the lengths to which revenge may be taken'. The one party, the killer, claims to have paid 'in full', i.e. the full blood-price of the killed man; the other, a relation of the deceased, refuses to accept anything, and wishes instead to kill the killer. If that is right, then clearly the occasion would naturally give rise to penological arguments—probably, if the evidence in chapter 1 is anything to go by, arguments of aggravation (advanced by the relative) and in mitigation (advanced by the killer).

know nothing of the type of argument deployed. Since the bystanders' view would presumably influence the verdict, litigants had to argue their case simultaneously to a single judge, or a group of them, and to the bystanders. There is no need to suppose detailed uniformity of practice and procedure.

Throughout the seventh century the function of judging disputes seems to have been, in Athens at any rate, in the hands of aristocratic but publicly elected officials who had taken over the political role of the displaced hereditary kings. These officials were the 'nine archons', i.e. the three archons proper and the six *thesmothetai*, who divided up the cases between them according to their respective areas of responsibility. We still seem to be dealing with a situation in which litigants had to argue their case to a single[8] judge, with bystanders perhaps contributing pressure. Again, we can discover nothing about the speeches made; conjecturally, fairly few cases were tried, forensic oratory was in its infancy, and the degrees of penological sophistication was not great.

Gagarin[9] has well insisted that in such situations the judge is likely to aim less at a clear-cut decision for one party and against the other, in the light of an established breach of a single precise rule, than at an *ad hoc settlement* between the parties, arrived at by cajolery, flattery or threats, and with regard to several competing social norms and personal relationships. For example, if *a* had indisputably stolen *b*'s cow, then if *b*, against his better judgement, is somehow pressurized into accepting a settlement entailing restoration of less than his loss, he is likely to feel that he has been made to suffer, i.e. been punished, for some considera-tion, e.g. his unpopularity or wealth, other than what he regards as the real matter at issue (the cow). He will be even more resentful if he observes variability in settlements, such as if *c*, who had suffered similar loss, receives full recompense. Such discontents, arising from a sense of outraged justice, must have fuelled demands for the precision of written law.[10]

The crucial change comes with Solon. In his time, feeling among the people was much exacerbated by what was thought to be corrupt and partisan political and economic domination by aristocrats; for obviously their judicial power could subserve that domination, and we may reason-ably believe that 'crooked' verdicts were not unknown, and led to inadequate or excessive penalties.[11] Probably also unease was felt at

---

[8] This seems to be among the implications of *AP* 3. 5: 'they [the archons] had sovereign power to impose final judgement'. 3. 6, however, speaks of the Areopagus too as chastising and fining offenders; see MacDowell (1978) 27–9.   [9] Gagarin (1986) 4 ff., 105 ff.; Hes. *Th.* 80 ff.
[10] Cf. p. 93 below, Solon 36. 18–20, Eur. *Supp.* 429 ff., Arist. *Pol.* 1270\u1d4730, 1272\u1d4338; Humphreys 239–40, Latte (1946, in Berneker) 90; but cf. Thomas.
[11] On the possible role of the Areopagus in such cases, see Bonner and Smith ii (1938) 232 ff. (But *AP* 4 may be inauthentic: see Rhodes (1981) 84 ff.)

substantial variations in penalty for the same offence from one official to another. At any rate, Solon, while apparently not abolishing the power of individual officials to give judgement alone, provided for appeal from their decisions to the *heliaia*, a meeting of the assembly (*ekklēsia*) held for judicial purposes—a measure which may itself have made the officials more sensitive to argument, including penological argument, than they had been before (though obviously fear of reaching an unexpected or unpopular verdict could have inhibited such a development). Such appeals were naturally introduced to the larger body by the official concerned; and in time, as a result of the growth of judicial business, it came to be common practice that the official held only a preliminary hearing and consigned the effective trial of the case to a *dikastērion*, a large body of jurors empanelled from and representing the whole body of citizens.[12] In cases of political importance, this whole body, the assembly, could sit together as court. This was the system which prevailed in the fifth and fourth centuries.

Here then are the very large audiences before which most of the forensic speeches that have come down to us were delivered. Such occasions obviously encouraged special pleading, playing on emotions, and exploitation of popular assumptions and personal prejudices. The Athenian orators took full advantage of these opportunities, as we shall see, to urge juries to accept or reject a large number of propositions about the justification, nature, and purpose of punishment. In brief, they argued for the enhancement or diminution of particular penalties in particular cases by reference to general principles. However, we rarely know the verdicts and penalties in the cases for which the surviving speeches were delivered, and even when we do we cannot know what went on in the jurors' minds. We can only infer that the orators expected their arguments to have at least some effect on at least some jurors.[13]

Homicide, however, a sensitive part of the legal system, was always handled rather differently. Together with certain other offences, it was the province of the Areopagus, a council of venerable antiquity, originally having very wide political and legal functions but in the classical period confined chiefly to the latter. It was composed in that

---

[12] *AP* 9. 1, Rhodes (1981) 160-2, 318-19, 730. MacDowell (1978, 29 ff.) has an excellent sympathetic account of the process I have here savagely condensed. As he says (32), it is likely that the nine archons, plus a host of other and minor officials, many dating from a time later than the 7th century, continued to give final judgement in trivial cases (cf. 25-6, 27, 30). However, there is controversy about the *origins* of the process: Hansen ((1975) 51-2, (1978a) 141-3, (1981-2)) denies the identification of the *hēliaia* with the assembly, and sees the former as a 'people's court' dating, with its divisions, the *dikastēria*, from as early as Solon.

[13] Some of the orators' works were however composed for other kinds of audience: see Dover (1974) 8-14 for a discussion of the corpus and its interpretation. On the legal system as a battleground in the social and political life of Athens, see Osborne (1985).

period of ex-archons, who in their year of office would have presided over courts and so gained a higher degree of legal expertise than that possessed by the average member of the large popular juries. Perhaps that is at least part of the reason why the Areopagus was greatly respected. Further, the members held office for life, which probably conferred a measure of independence and consistency on their decisions.[14] The Areopagus as a whole (probably about 200 persons) tried cases of intentional homicide of citizens; various types of homicide of lesser seriousness were tried in certain other courts before panels of 51 *ephetai*, whom I take to have been (the matter is unfortunately uncertain) simply members of the Areopagus delegated to those duties as occasion demanded.[15] Here again, then, by our standards, the juries were large: either c.200 Areopagites or 51 *ephetai*; and again the procedure must have allowed discursive argument by litigants from general principles to particular cases.

LEGISLATION

Customary law can be a powerful influence on decisions made by a judge; it is a flexible instrument, and at its best can be used to fine-tune resolutions of disputes. But it suffers from the corresponding disadvantage of requiring that a great deal of individual personal judgement be allowed in interpreting and applying it. The discretion, if the evidence of Hesiod in particular is anything to go by, was not always exercised by 'kings' wisely and fairly;[16] and evidently in Athens at the end of the seventh century pressure was building up for a *written* code dealing with at least the major offences. Such a code was laid down by Draco, probably in 621/0.[17] Those of his laws relating to homicide seem to have been adopted and perpetuated in a further comprehensive round of written lawgiving carried out by Solon in 594; others were at that time modified or replaced.[18] In the seventh and sixth centuries several other lawgivers in other cities are known; the extent to which they adopted and adapted existing customary law is uncertain;[19] at any rate a high degree of detailed precision could be attained.[20]

After Solon, laws seemed to have been laid down by simple majority vote of the popular assembly, after a vetting by the *boulē* along with the

---

[14] *AP* 3. 6, cf. 8. 4; Dem. 23. 65 ff.; see MacDowell (1963), 39–47, Rhodes (1981) 106, 108.
[15] MacDowell (1963) 51–3; Harrison ii (1971) 41–2; Rhodes (1981) 647–8; for a different view of the development, see Sealey.
[16] Cf. Her. 3. 31, 5. 25, 7. 194.   [17] *AP* 41. 2, Stroud (1968) 66–70.
[18] Solon 12, 21–3, *AP* 7. 1, Stroud (1968) 75 ff., Rhodes (1981) 109 ff.; but cf. Ruschenbusch (1960) 147–52 and (1968) 11–15.   [19] Bonner and Smith i (1930) 67 ff., esp. 74–5.
[20] Arist. *Pol.* 1274^{b}7, on Charondas (6th century); cf. Gagarin (1986) 64–5, 110.

other business which it considered and proposed to that body. Some systematization of the mass of laws that had accumulated took place at the end of the fifth century. Fourth-century procedure varied in complex and elaborate ways. Proposals to introduce, modify, and repeal *nomoi* (laws) were still laid before the assembly, but had to be finally ratified by a specialized board of legal commissioners called *nomothetai*; yet many punishable offences were still created by *psēphismata* (decrees), i.e. *ad hoc* or short-term resolutions of council or assembly, of more limited application than *nomoi*.[21]

At all stages of this historical development it is obvious that there was ample scope for reflection and decision on matters we would now call penological. For to lay down a law is to specify a crime and its penalty (or the range within which the penalty must fall). Somebody—the individual Athenian commending or attacking customary law in the seventh century, or the individual lawgiver, or the members of the assembly subsequently, or those of the *boulē*, or the *nomothetai* of the fourth century—must have had to ask, in the light of all circumstances and motives, is *this* penalty right for *this* crime?[22] With the advent of written law in particular, the relationship of penalty to crime presumably became a matter of reflection and policy. Not that the ancient legislator could have been so preoccupied by penology as his modern counterpart, who has a wealth of theory and systematic empirical data to take into account.

Reflection about punishments could take a wide variety of forms and was certainly not confined to the courts.[23] Indeed, the continuity of assumptions, experience, and argument as between forensic and non-forensic situations is total. Any man could observe and indeed undergo many varieties of punishments inflicted informally in everyday life; orators in the courts devoted a great deal of effort to describing, and arguing for or against, particular penalties inflicted under the law; and philosophers and historians could record and comment reflectively on both kinds of situations. Forensic punishments developed from non-forensic punishments, and are but a specialized application of them.[24] The juror who left his ordinary life to sit in court for a day took with him

---

[21] See MacDowell (1975), (1978) 48–9, Rhodes (1981) 329, 512–3; further references in Hansen (1985).

[22] Cf. Gernet (1984) 25. Notably, the general tendency to modify the harshness of the penalties of Draco (see e.g. Lysias fr. 10) betokens penological reflection; presumably the necessity for severity was felt to have passed (cf. Stroud (1968) 78–9).

[23] It was sometimes historically based: Arist. *Pol.* 1268^b38 ff. regards the early use of oaths as naïve, and Plut. *Sol.* 17 records a comment by Demades (late 4th century) on the severity of Draco's legislation; cf. Arist. *Pol.* 1274^b17.

[24] For instance, the notion of 'chastisement' (*kolasis*) appears in political, military and forensic contexts: Thuc. 1. 40. 5, 41. 2, 6. 38. 4, Xen. *Hell.* 5. 2. 1, 3. 7, Lys. 28. 3, and often in the orators; so too 'vengeance'/'punishment' (*timōria*), Xen. *Hell.* 4. 8. 25, Lys. 13. 84. Cf. Lys. 25. 22, Dem. 2. 30, 8. 61. Formal and informal punishment: Dem. 21. 118.

a set of penological assumptions and expectations, some of them unconscious, which the orators sought to articulate and exploit, and occasionally to change.

Furthermore, the members of the popular assembly who approved the laws were the same people as the jurors who enforced them by verdicts in the popular courts, or imposed penalties when acting as minor officials. They had experience, to an extent almost unimaginable today, both of legislation, of deciding what the penalty or range of penalties ought in principle to be for a particular crime, and of deciding what it should be in a particular proven case of that crime. The more thoughtful of them presumably realized at least some of the problems.[25]

For problems there certainly were. Inspection of the penological principles employed both in 'real life' and in the courts reveals that none are beyond dispute and several are in conflict with each other. Sometimes the conflict is recognized; more often one principle is advanced at one time by one speaker or writer, and its opposite by another speaker or writer on a different occasion. Such variation is of course frequently tendentious: the orators in particular use whatever principle suits their book in the case on hand, and are indeed not above contradicting themselves in the same speech. No doubt that is still true nowadays; yet our juries do little more than reach verdicts, and we have more or less settled penological policies, which are applied by a professional corps of legal specialists; there is an *Apparat* which ensures, within rough limits, consistency of practice throughout the country. But in ancient Athens the juries' discretion was quite unfettered: they themselves interpreted the law, assessed the alleged facts of the cases, and settled not only the verdicts but the penalties,[26] and there was no body of legal experts to impose a uniform policy.[27] Litigants were therefore in a hazardous position: no one could be sure that today's jury would adopt the same principle as yesterday's, for much would depend on the unpredictable collective mood, emotions, and prejudices of large audiences, and their

[25] MacDowell (1975) 63–5 argues from Dem. 20. 89 ff. that the *nomethetai* concerned with new laws were for a period early in the 4th century required to be already jurors for the current year— perhaps a recognition that law-making needs some recent experience of law-enforcement.

[26] The speeches on either side commonly included both matter designed to influence the verdict itself and arguments to enhance or diminish any penalty awarded. In 'estimated' cases, however (see p. 101 below), when the verdict was 'guilty', supplementary speeches were made (on their length, see MacDowell (1985)), devoted entirely to the question of the penalty. That is to say, arguments which we should now regard as purely of mitigation or aggravation were advanced as part of the total ensemble of arguments on the substantive issue. Nowadays such considerations are more firmly separated off into the sentencing procedure, *after* a verdict of 'guilty'. If we may believe Lysias 27. 16, an adverse verdict did not necessarily lead to the imposition of a penalty.

[27] I wonder, nevertheless, whether the *mnamōn*, 'rememberer', attached to Gortynian judges could have been required to supply information not merely about rules of procedure but about *precedents* in sentencing (Gortyn code, Col. 9. 32).

willingness to listen to and reflect on the penological principles advanced, persuasively and skilfully or otherwise, by the orators. The upshot is that the penology of the courts, let alone that of ordinary life, was exceedingly fluid. An orator could advance precedents for this or that penalty imposed for this or that crime, and deploy principled arguments which had apparently swayed juries in the past; but the impact he made would have been far more uncertain than in a modern court. Indeed, much was said and much was argued that in a modern court would be ruled irrelevant and out of order.

CONTROVERSY

(a) The decline of self-help

It may be doubted whether in any society self-help has existed in an entirely unrestricted form—that is to say, subject to no check whatever on the ability of the injured party, provided only that he be stronger, to punish an offender. For restraints there must always be: protection of the offender by his friends or relatives, perhaps, or fear of his animosity in the future, or dissuasion from some motive of prudence or friendship, by the punisher's own family or group. Nor, for that matter, can we easily imagine a society where there is *nothing* which an offended party is entitled to do on his own account: presumably he is always at least able to resist at the time of the offence, and to put the matter in the hands of some authority, however little he may be involved thereafter. It would accordingly be naïve to think of Greek law as proceeding from pure[28] self-help to all-embracing communally-enforced law. As we have seen, even the Homeric hero was subject to many prudential constraints, and conversely the legal system of the classical period preserved substantial remnants of self-help.[29] Nevertheless, the general tendency in Greek law, for a variety of social and political reasons, was to replace self-help by prosecution and punishment of crime by publicly appointed state courts and officials.[30]

---

[28] Even those cases of allowing, apparently unrestrictedly, an injured party to inflict or exact according to his own assessment, which Latte (1931, in Berneker) 265 cites in connection with early self-help, must have been subject to sharp practical limitations: obviously something had to be exacted that could realistically be given (Her. 6. 139, 9. 93; Ar. *Wasps* 1417–20 is comic fantasy). The point is not that unlimited demands may be made, but that the injured party himself, not some other person, is entitled to assess the penalty.

[29] e.g. the right of an offended party, in certain circumstances, to arrest an offender (*apagōgē*). For a less evolutionary view of the development of Greek law, see Hansen (1976) 113 ff.

[30] See Latte (1931, in Berneker) *init.*

Assertion of state control

First and most fundamentally, even when at an early stage[31] the penalty imposed on the losing party was in effect a licence for the winner to pursue the self-help checked by the referral of the dispute to a 'judge', the very referral presumably entailed that no decision could then be given in the absence of some sort of hearing. At any rate, by the classical period there was a clear and widespread acceptance of the principle that punishments for publicly forbidden offences should be imposed only after due legally-sanctioned process (which did however vary considerably and could in some circumstances be quite summary).[32]

Nevertheless, the power of the state was sometimes challenged or flouted, and had to be asserted. In 366 one Euphron, a Sicyonian, arrived in Thebes and was assassinated by his Sicyonian political enemies.[33] The officials prosecuted them before the Council, arguing *inter alia* (*a*) that it was the Council members who had supreme authority to decide who should die, whereas the killers had 'made their own decision'; (*b*) that 'anyone who wishes' is not entitled to kill a man before the purpose of his coming to the city has become clear. The point of (*b*), I take it, is to recognize that, exceptionally, an individual may kill a person who is patently attempting a tyranny or committing treason.[34] It is (*a*) that is crucial: those extreme emergencies apart, the *state* has power of life and death, not private individuals. The only one of the killers to admit the deed, while recognizing the Council's authority to deal with him as it wished, accordingly urged in his defence not merely the alleged offences of Euphron (treason and attempted tyranny), but pointed to a precedent of the year 379,[35] when certain plotters were killed as enemies by the Thebans, 'without waiting for a vote'. The relative merits of the dispute need not concern us; the essential point is that the Theban state reserved to itself powers of life and death,[36] and in the absence of a clear emergency the independent action of Euphron's killers infringed that principle, and also the principle that there should be no such penalty inflicted without a trial—as indeed they themselves were tried (but acquitted).

[31] See Wolff (1946), esp. 49 ff.

[32] And. 4. 3, Dem. 25. 87. Sparta: Plut. *Ages.* 32. 6. For discussions, see Rhodes (1981) 537–9 on *AP* 45. 1, and Carawan (1984). Hansen (1976) 119 stresses the numerous summary procedures; but the point is that they were defined and permitted *by public law*. Breaches of the principle attracted notice, mostly censorious: Thuc. 2. 67, 8. 48. 6; Xen. *Anab.* 5. 7. 28–9, 6. 6. 25; Isoc. 7. 67, 12. 66; Dem. 23. 76, 85, 215; Lys. 22. 2. Double jeopardy forbidden: And. 4. 8–9, 36, Dem. 20. 147, 38. 16, but cf. Hyp. frr. 28–9.   [33] Xen. *Hell.* 7. 3. 4 ff.

[34] Cf. ibid. 7. Cf. the position at Athens, at least after 410, where it was legally permitted to kill with impunity anyone attempting a tyranny or betraying the state or overthrowing the democracy (And. 1. 96, Lyc. *Leoc.* 125; see further Rhodes (1981) 220 ff.).

[35] Xen. *Hell.* 5. 4. 2 ff.   [36] Cf. Hyp. *Dem.* fr. 3 *init.*

Impartiality

It became a cardinal point of policy that a trial should be impartial as between the litigants: wealth, power, and social status should not influence either the verdict or the calculation of the level of penalty or recompense.[37] As many passages make clear,[38] this principle was a democratic one: it was a weapon in the political attack on the 'stronger' i.e. aristocrats and their power and privileges, whether acting as individuals or (in the early period) as judges. It was to some degree an attack on self-help, for self-help can all too easily lead to an unjust victory of him who is stronger in political or social terms. That the attack did not go unresisted (it did after all threaten one element in a certain power-structure) is also obvious;[39] nevertheless it was successful. In theory at least, verdicts were arrived at in the Athenian courts after impartial hearing of both litigants.

Penologically, that is an important victory; and it may seem to imply that the penalties also would be the same for same and equal offences, whatever the status of the losing litigant.[40] In practice, however, all sorts of social and political considerations entered into the calculation of penalties, as we shall see in subsequent sections.[41] For the moment, however, it suffices to note that such variations in penalties did not arise from any recrudescence of sentiment in favour of self-help; their causes were many and various, and self-help was not an issue.

Mode of pleading

In courts, since the decision about the penalty, and in particular about its severity, is not in the hands of the prosecutor, any prosecutor keen to inflict a high penalty must achieve his desire by persuading the jury that it is justified; he had to get *them* to inflict a high penalty. Now what prompts a savage penalty is anger; and in Homer it is thought perfectly normal and proper to nurse anger and to vent it in imposing swingeing punishment; indeed to satisfy one's anger is part of one's recompense.[42]

---

[37] Latte (1946, in Berneker) 91, Sol. 36. 16–20, Dem. 21. 183, 24. 111–12, 151, 45. 67, 51. 11–12, cf. Ar. *Wasps* 724–5, Eur. *Herac.* 179–80, And. 4. 35, Dem. 21. 123–5.

[38] Dem. 19. 296, Isoc. 20. 19 ff., Eur. *Supp.* 399 ff., esp. 437, and for the thought cf. Soph. *OC* 880.

[39] See Theognis 53 ff., and Euripides in previous note. But no source actually represents anyone as arguing for self-help in principle. Since it involves potential inequity, it is a hard thing to defend when justice is an increasingly powerful concept. It is easier to defend—as the herald in Euripides' *Supplices* does—political inequality on grounds of the inferior wisdom of the common man, 409 ff.

[40] As implied by Eur. *Supp.* 429 ff., Isoc. 2. 18, though with specific reference to a monarch as judge; cf. 18. 38, 43.

[41] Lys. 1. 1 ff. implies that the social standing of a litigant could indeed affect verdicts and penalties, according to the political regime which prevailed.

[42] XIV. 132, ii. 192–3; cf. pp. 18–19 above.

What then could be more natural than that prosecutors in courts should lavish attention on whipping up anger and hatred in juries? This is in fact precisely what happens: the prosecutor seeks to transfer, so to speak, his own anger to those who have power to inflict the penalty. The orators are brutally frank about the matter. In his speech against Leocrates, Lycurgus says quite openly that he would like to parade those who had been wronged by Leocrates, so that the jury would reach a harsher verdict.[43] At the beginning of his speech against Demosthenes, Dinarchus explicitly tells the jury that he will say some things twice in order to provoke in them an increased anger. Demosthenes[44] firmly links hatred and *timōria*; and he claims that the jury should feel *on the plaintiff's behalf* anger against the defendant, by putting themselves in the plaintiff's position.[45] Such remarks, and implications that anger and hatred in a jury are legitimate and desirable, are very frequent in the orators. A conspicuous feature of a personal mode of punishment survives and flourishes in the court system of the classical period.

But there are occasional expressions of dissent and criticism. The speech attributed (falsely) to Demades deprecates anger provoked by prosecutors as an obstacle to clear thinking.[46] Demosthenes recognizes that anger can go too far.[47] Lysias notes that defendants judged when the jury's anger has cooled stand a better chance of being let off, because the jury is now prepared to listen to reason; that is to say, anger can lead to hasty and unjust verdicts.[48] No wonder the orators made so many appeals for a calm hearing, without anger, as indeed Lysias himself does.[49] Yet these protests are generally themselves tendentious: they are attempts to soothe anger in the interests of a particular case. Nevertheless behind all the rhetoric is a distinction, deliberately blurred by those who seek to whip up anger and sharpened by those who protest against it, between the facts of a case, and the prejudices of those who judge those facts. Implicit controversy about the legitimacy of allowing anger, of prosecutor or jury, to determine the verdict or severity of a punishment arose not simply because men are unscrupulous, and in the jousting atmosphere of a popular court will use any and every means to get their own way, but crucially because the Athenian legal system is an uneasy amalgam of two sets of assumptions: (1) the assumption of the older, unreflecting acceptance of anger as normal and legitimate; (2) the new assumption, at least implicit in the formal legal machinery, that the

---

[43] Lyc. *Leoc.* 141. On anger in general cf. Isoc. 18. 4, 36, 42; Aesch. 3. 197-8; Ar. *Wasps* 406, 424, 560, 727, 878 ff.   [44] Dem. 19. 289.

[45] Dem. 54. 42, cf. Isoc. 20. 21, Lys. 1. 1.   [46] *On the Twelve Years*, 3-4.

[47] Dem. 26. 17, cf. Lyc. *Leoc.* 116, Isoc. 15. 19, 31.

[48] Lys. 19. 6; cf. 22. 2, 25. 5, Xen. *Hell.* 5. 3. 7, *Anab.* 2. 6. 9, Dem. 6. 34.

[49] Lys. 19 *init.*

facts are paramount.[50] The severity of any punishment one inflicts will be vitally affected according to which of these two assumptions one makes.

Restrictions on execution

At least for the most serious offences,[51] exaction of the penalty became a public function, not the private privilege of the litigant who won the day; and such a restriction entailed an increasingly sharp limitation on the range and severity of punishment. Gradually, as the option to resort to a judge or court becomes a custom, and custom becomes compulsion,[52] the injured party, however strong, finds that the penalties he can exact at his own discretion are limited by an increasing number of offences embraced by law and punished by persons other than himself, and that the punishments are themselves prescribed and limited, sometimes by elaborate 'tariffs', and by reference to criteria he may not himself wish to adopt. Draco, for instance, probably provided that a man who killed without premeditation, and who duly kept clear of the agora etc. while awaiting trial, could not be killed with impunity; at any rate, if on a verdict of guilty he then went into exile, he enjoyed that protection on certain analogous terms. Hence if the relatives of the victim nevertheless wished to kill the killer, regardless of his lack of intent to kill, they would to that extent find their freedom of action inhibited. Both the severity of the penalty they could inflict for this offence, and the range of offences for which they could inflict what they wished, were restricted.[53]

The inability of a successful litigant to control the punishment and to inflict what he wishes is explicitly attested in two Demosthenic speeches. In the speech against Meidias,[54] Demosthenes replies to the *suggestio falsi* of Meidias 'Do not hand me over to Demosthenes', by twice pointing out that the laws do not permit it: 'You never hand over a criminal to any accuser; for when someone has been wronged, you (the jury) do not inflict the penalty in the manner which the injured party presses for'; and he argues in effect that it is the right of the laws, not of the prosecutor's own angry judgement, to prescribe penalties. Again, in the speech against Aristocrates,[55] Demosthenes argues that a prosecutor has no power over even a convicted murderer (much less *before* conviction at a

---

[50] Cf. Humphreys (1983) 248.

[51] I exclude from these certain special cases in which an injured party was entitled to kill the offender on the spot: see pp. 101–2.

[52] We cannot trace the growth of compulsion with much precision, and there is sharp controversy; for a summary, see Harrison ii (1971) 69–72. At XVIII. 501 'both' litigants wish to resort to judgement before an *istōr*; if only one had so wished and if the other had refused, rather than merely acquiesced, then presumably the session would not have taken place. Later, resort to the legal system by only one party would suffice to activate it. Her. 1. 96–100 shows how judicial power, once established by popular demand, could develop into a system of enforcement; cf. Gagarin (1986) 19 ff.   [53] IG I³. 104. 11–29; Gagarin (1986) 112–14, esp. n. 34.

[54] Dem. 21. 29–31, 76, cf. 54. 19.   [55] Dem. 23. 27–8, 69, 71, 79–80, 216.

trial): he may watch the penalty being imposed, but no more. He may watch, and (presumably) feel his satisfaction—an interesting survival of a more personal mode of punishment; but the actual infliction of the penalty is not in his hands; it is formal and impersonal. In the middle of the fourth century, apparently, it was still necessary on occasion to assert the subordinate status of self-help, and to defend the penology enshrined in law against the animus of successful litigants.

Survivals of self-help[56]

In one way, however, Attic law did allow self-help some influence in the fixing of penalties. For some crimes, the penalties were fixed: the trials were termed *agōnes atimētoi*, 'contests in which no estimation is required'. But others were *timētoi*, 'in need of estimation'. In such cases, to describe the procedure briefly, if there was a conviction, the prosecutor suggested and argued for one level of damages or penalty, and the defendant suggested another (naturally lower). The jurors had simply to decide which of the two amounts to award; only these two alternatives were allowed. The successful prosecutor had this very limited degree of self-help permitted him, that if he thought the court would support him and if he felt sufficiently aggressive, he could press for a penalty far in excess of the real damage or offence. There was, obviously, risk; but there does seem to be here some recognition of the older system.[57] In the fifth century, the necessity to decide between the two alternatives attracted criticism from Hippodamus, as being crude: the jurors should be free to fix a compromise verdict, and hence (presumably) a compromise penalty.[58]

In a limited number of special cases, notably adultery and certain types of theft, Attic law continued to allow an extreme degree of self-help: the offended party could kill the offender on the spot. A man catching the

---

[56] I focus here on the ability of the litigant to influence the penalty directly, rather than indirectly by procedural means. As Osborne (1985) stresses (43, cf. 49 ff.), the variety of actions and remedies available could result in different penalties being imposed for the same offence, according to the procedure under which the case was tried. The *dikē exoulēs*, suit for ejectment, *inter alia* enabled a plaintiff to overcome resistance to his taking, by 'licensed self-help', property adjudged to him by a court, and so in a way remedies the relative weakness of state agencies for enforcement; but it does not change the court's award as such, nor its automatic doubling if the alleged resister is found guilty; see Harrison i (1968) 217 ff., MacDowell (1978) 153–4.

[57] On the two categories of case, see Harrison ii (1971) 80–2. It is not clear to me whether there was some principle or principles which determined into which category a particular action would fall. If one could be found, it might rule out my interpretation of *agōnes timētoi* as an older form embodying the principle of self-help in restricted or even token form. Were *agōnes atimētoi* deliberate and later departures from that principle? The variability of punishments inflicted in *timētoi* contests makes it impossible to say whether their severity was in general greater or less than that of punishments in *atimētoi* contests; Aesch. 3. 210 seems to imply that it was less.

[58] Arist. *Pol.* 1268[a]1 ff., [b]4 ff.

seducer of his wife in the act was permitted alternatively to exact recompense in money, or to 'radish' him.[59]

(b) The state as an injured party

In early Greek society disputes arising from offences could of course be purely private in the sense of being confined to two individuals, the offender and the offended party; yet the family or wider community of one or both would naturally often have and claim an interest in the outcome. Then with the development of the *polis* as the predominant form of political organization, and with pride and loyalty focused increasingly upon it, there was a natural tendency to broaden the range of interested parties, and to think of the community of people who constituted the *polis* as an entity with interests of its own in the actions and disputes of its members, interests which could be defended and punished in a court, just like those of a private individual; and such a view could only be strengthened by the fact that the growing legal apparatus was organized centrally by the *polis* itself.[60]

In the classical period the division of cases into public and private is standard;[61] but it is employed variously. In effect, there are three categories:

1. Cases in which, though the state lends its assistance to the injured party, it does not claim a specifically public interest, or at any rate no interest requiring a penalty to be paid to it; the criteria governing compensation to the injured party are nevertheless publicly controlled, by law.[62]

2. Intermediate cases, in which an offence against a private person is treated, in varying degrees, are *also* an offence against the common interest, so that the state demands some penalty additional to that imposed for the private wrong.[63]

3. Exclusively political or public cases, in which the penalty is thought of as not only inflicted by but paid to the state as an injured party.[64]

The effect of establishing 'public interest' is an enhancement of the penalty; for an offence against those interests is an aggravation of it.[65] In

---

[59] Lys. 1. 25, 29, 49; Harrison i (1968) 32–3 ff.; on 'radishing' see Ar. *Cl.* 981, 1083, Dem. 23. 53; Cohen (1985) voices doubts about the historical reality of the practice. See further pp. 246–8.

[60] e.g. Lys. 12. 26: 'give *dikē*, satisfaction, to me and these people [the jury]'—but this was a case with a strong political flavour; And. 4. 18.

[61] e.g. Dem. 46. 26; *AP* 67. 1; Harrison ii (1971) 75 ff., MacDowell (1978) 57 ff., Hansen (1990) 231 ff.   [62] e.g. the suit for damage (*blabē*), Dem. 21. 42–3; cf. MacDowell (1978) 151.

[63] Dem. 21. 43 ff., cf. Plut. *Sol.* 21. 1.

[64] e.g. *AP* 54. 2; Dem. 24. 192–3 argues for enhanced penalties for political offences.

[65] This is clear from Dem. 21. 42 ff. (cf. 19. 284), on which Harrison's account and mine of public and private cases rely heavily; cf. Rhodes (1981) 718. *Pace* Harrison, the purpose of the passage is

effect, the old distinction between recompense and extra, which we found in Homer, has found a new application: in some disputes the extra no longer goes to the injured party, but to the state. Indeed this tendency went so far as to deny to the injured party, at least in cases of *hubris* (arrogantly violent ill-treatment), any satisfaction at all except that of seeing the offender pay the whole of the fine to the public treasury.[66] As in modern English criminal law, the interests of the injured party come to some extent to be disregarded in favour of the penalty exacted by and for the state.

Athenian law also distinguished between *dikai* and *graphai*.[67] A *dikē* was a suit which could be brought only by the injured party or his representatives specified by law; a *graphē* could be brought by 'anyone who wishes' (*ho boulomenos*). The latter originated in the legislation of Solon; its purpose was to afford help and protection to injured parties who for some reason were in no position to enter suits on their own behalf.[68] Democratic sentiment held that it was a matter of public concern that such persons should be thus protected by law.[69] Accordingly, acting under the *graphē* procedure, prosecutors (who in the classical period might be injured parties themselves) frequently claimed, whether frankly or not, to be bringing suit from public-spirited motives. To the extent that they were believed, the public interest came into consideration in the calculation of penalties for a large group of offences.[70]

Hence it would be an error to think of *dikai* as defending only 'private' interests, and of *graphai* as defending only 'public' ones. Homicide, for instance, which is a matter of major public concern as well as of private, was normally[71] prosecuted by a *dikē*; and the *graphē hubreōs* was commonly brought for attacks on individuals.[72] Both private interests and public could, according to the perspective one adopted, be held to enter into practically any *dikē* and practically any *graphē*. The frequency with which the public interest was urged in the courts suggests that it

not primarily to divide offences into private and public; it is to distinguish aggravated offences from simple ones. Aggravated offences are marked by premeditation or violence; the first (as in deliberate homicide, and in refusal to accept the verdict of a court, 43–4) may be an affront to the state, which then exacts its own and additional penalty; or it may not (the double fine in cases of deliberate damage presumably goes to the private injured party, 43). But the latter aggravation, violence, is *always* an offence against the common weal, and so always demands an enhanced penalty. (It is sometimes hard to discover the destination of a fine/penalty: plaintiff, state, or partly the one and partly the other. The orators seem simply to assume that one knows.)

[66] Dem. 21. 45, Pol. 8. 42.
[67] Harrison ii (1971) 76 ff., Osborne (1985) 40–4, cf. 55–8.
[68] *AP* 9. 1; Ruschenbusch (1968) 47 ff.
[69] Cf. Humphreys (1983) 238–9.
[70] Even displacing, as we saw, the penalty for the injured party, in the *graphē hubreōs*.
[71] See pp. 218–19 and 240 n. 116.   [72] Dem. 21. 45.

had considerable force—the juries addressed, after all, *were* in effect the state, and direct appeals to their self-interest are common, particularly in cases with political implications.[73]

If we attempt to analyse the types of penalties imposed by Athenian courts according to the presence or absence of the public interest, we find it impossible to see a clear pattern.[74] Naturally, recompense to private parties commonly took the form of money to the value either of the assessed damage or of some multiple; and offences of an exclusively public or political kind could appropriately be punished not only by huge fines but by *atimia*, some form of deprivation of the rights of a citizen.[75] But the intermediate type of case was common, and in them the claims of the public interest and the private were recognized and apportioned in a bewildering variety of ways. It is more useful to think of damage to public interest as something capable of being urged as an aggravation of an offence, and as likely to lead to a verdict of guilty and/or a more severe penalty, than as a determinant of any specific *type* of penalty.

Only occasionally is it possible to find some realization that appeals to the self-interest of juries, in the guise of appeals to the public interest, could be out of place. The speaker of a pseudo-Demosthenic oration[76] complains that certain cases of theft of public money and property have been interpreted by certain orators as threats to the democratic regime; he admits the crimes are serious and deserve the death penalty; but he asserts that the real danger to democracy lies elsewhere, in lack of military preparedness against external enemies. Such passages are rare. Once the public interest had been urged by one side, or the interests of the political regime supported by the jury, the other side would be at a decided disadvantage, whatever the facts of the case.[77]

(c) Gradation, mitigation, and aggravation[78]

If an adverse effect on the public interest is one potential aggravation, there are many others; and conversely there are many possible pleas of mitigation. We face, in fact, the tangled question of the relationship

---

[73] Lys. 22. 19–22, 29. 8–10, Aesch. 1. 192, Lyc. *Leoc.* 15, 26, Dem. 22. 37, 35. 54. Aristotle's distinction (*Rhet.* 1. 13. 3) between unjust acts against (i) a specific individual, (ii) the common interest, represents the realities of the courts only crudely. Xen. *Lac. Con.* 10. 4–6 distinguishes private and public offences idiosyncratically. Sometimes the distinction could be represented as residing in the motive of the prosecutor: Lys. 7. 20.   [74] Cf. Harrison ii (1971) 78.

[75] See Hansen (1977) for a limited number of cases of *atimia* for *private* debt, and cf. Diod. Sic. 12. 12. 1.

[76] [Dem.] 13. 14 ff.   [77] e.g. Isoc. 16. 2–3, 11, 44.

[78] The fullest accounts are by Maschke (1926) and Dorjahn (1930) (the latter's classification has influenced my own). The following survey is less than exhaustive: it is not simply descriptive, but concentrates on explicit and implicit tensions and controversies in historical practice; and it draws on non-forensic as well as forensic evidence (see pp. 94–5 above).

between an offence and its punishment. In Homer, as we have seen, punishments were inflicted largely at the discretion of injured parties strong enough to inflict them; several informal restraints were recognized, but no doubt were only randomly effective; and the judges who preceded the first lawgivers must have exhibited considerable variability, either of excess or deficiency, in the penalties they awarded. There are some indications that the lawgivers thought it important to introduce a large measure of simplification and consistency. According to Strabo,[79] before Zaleucus (seventh century) it had been left to the judges to settle/ define (*horizein*) the penalties for each injustice (*adikēma*); but Zaleucus now 'settled'/'defined' the penalties in his code, believing that the judges ought to have the same opinions about the same things/offences. This procedure seems to indicate a certain naïvety about the notion of 'same': for two offences may be the same in formal or concrete terms, yet differ greatly in the manner and circumstances of their commission. Simplicity and consistency were perhaps initially purchased at the cost of flexibility, commonsense, and equity.[80]

Many passages in the orators contain arguments which imply that severe penalties should be visited on great offences, and mild penalties on lesser ones; the notion of gradation is implicit and fundamental; and outrage is expresssed when it seems not to apply in practice.[81] Lycurgus, in arguing for disregard of circumstance and therefore gradation, is not typical.[82]

By the late fifth century the orators are using and elaborating on a host of more or less stock arguments, often in a partisan and tendentious manner, calculated to introduce differentiation in verdicts and punishments, often according to criteria not specified in the wording of the law.[83] They make frequent pleas that a defendant must be punished justly, to an extent which is 'worthy' (*axiōs, kat' axian*) of the crime,[84] and presumably had reason to suppose that their reasoning would be found plausible in principle, even if the jury should decide that it did not apply to the facts of a particular case. Often the argument from 'desert' or 'worthiness', *axia*, is used to urge that the defendant must be punished

[79] Strabo 6. 1. 8, on the authority of Ephorus.

[80] Similarly Deioces (*c.*700) judged 'according to *axia*, value, of each *adikēma*', apparently as though the amount of the injury or damage were the only thing that mattered (Her. 1. 100); but perhaps *axia* means something more flexible: 'desert' rather than 'value'. A similar effort of systematization is evident in Diocles' law-giving in Syracuse at the end of the 5th cent.: on an elaborate scale, he thought each offence worthy of a 'fixed' (*hōrismenē*) penalty (Diod. Sic. 13. 35). Isoc. 2. 18 (cf. 18. 26) and Lyc. *Leoc.* 120 stress consistency in sentencing policy. Influence of precedents: Lys. 14. 4, Aesch. 3. 193.

[81] e.g. And. 4. 18, Dem. 21. 37, 92, 105, 128 ff., 182–5, 51. 9–12.   [82] *Leoc.* 64 ff.

[83] Apart from the orators themselves, there is evidence in Aristotle's *Ars Rhetorica*, and in the tips to pleaders contained in Anaximenes' *Rhetorica ad Alexandrum*.

[84] e.g. Din. *Dem.* 3, 10, Dem. 19. 8, 302.

adequately or *fully*, and that anything less than what is demanded would not represent 'desert'.[85]

(*d*) *Gradation of punishment*

The frequent references to what a criminal should 'suffer or pay', *pathein ē apotinein*, indicate a distinction between penalties affecting his person (e.g. death, exile, imprisonment) and those affecting his property. Severity over the entire range could be calculated in several ways. The first was to distinguish between punishments which, though not commensurable in kind, obviously differ in point of severity—death, for instance, being more severe than a fine. Another was to use the injury or damage done, or an assessment of it, as the unit of calculation, and impose various multiples of it to achieve the desired level of severity; doublings are common, but much larger multiples are known. The basic unit was commonly thought of as recompense, as distinct from the 'extra' of the multiples.[86] Another was to impose *atimia*, disfranchisement, which could take many different forms and be of greater or less severity.[87] But in general punishments could vary in severity somewhat capriciously, in that some crimes could be prosecuted under more than one procedure, and different procedures entailed different penalties.[88] There is no evidence of any systematic attempt to rationalize.

(*e*) *Gradation of offences*

The general assumption is then that the severity of punishment should be in direct ratio to the magnitude of the offence. But gradation of offences is notoriously complex. The following criteria may be used singly or in combination; they centre on (i) the offence, (ii) and (iii) the offender, (iv) and (v) wider considerations of equity and social policy.

(i) *Objective seriousness*

This criterion is employed widely in all sorts of contexts in the rough and ready way already noticed in the gradation of penalties: a murder is more

---

[85] So too the modern plea that 'the punishment must fit the crime'. See e.g. Thuc. 3. 39. 6 and 40. 7; cf. Lyc. *Leoc.* 8 *et passim*.

[86] Isoc. 16 and Dem. 24. 114–15 treat the basic as recompense and the extra as deterrence. For single or double fines in the suit for damages, see p. 319 below. Twofold or threefold: Dem. 24. 105 (see Harrison i (1968) 207 n. 2). Tenfold: Dem. 24. 82–3, 111 and Hyp. *Dem.* fr. 6; cf. *AP* 54. 2. For multiples in Homer, see pp. 25–7 above, and for Charondas' code (6th cent.), see Bonner and Smith i (1930) 78. Cf. also Soph. *Ant.* 927–8, Her. 1. 22 (*two* temples).

[87] See MacDowell (1962) 106–7, (1978) 73–5, Hansen (1976) 72 ff.

[88] Hansen (1976) 120–1.

serious than theft, for instance.[89] But an offence can be aggravated by various factors in the manner of its commission and in its likely effects. We have already noted one major aggravation: damage to public interests; under this heading come offences committed by holders of public office, in the course of the duties of that office.[90]

(ii) Status of offender

Political or social status. An offence committed by a slave against a free man, especially his master, was regarded as aggravated by insult to a superior by an inferior, and therefore more serious than such an offence committed by a free man.[91] Conversely, an offence committed by a free man against a slave was regarded less seriously than one committed against a free man.[92] Offences against foreigners too were probably regarded less seriously than offences against citizens; for foreigners, though free, are similar to slaves in having lesser status, and lesser opportunity to protect themselves.[93] Sometimes an orator attempts to discourage social prejudice, at other times to arouse it.[94] A passage in Demosthenes hints at popular feeling against a non-native-born citizen who by successful prosecution sends an Athenian to his death.[95]

How far were such considerations enshrined in law? Most punishments of slaves were presumably inflicted informally, within the family; and the wide discretion of Athenian courts no doubt permitted extra severity to be shown to them[96] and to foreigners, if the jury felt so inclined. But there seems to have been no formal provision requiring it.[97] As for the protection of these categories, however, two formal discriminations are known: (i) persons fined for *hubris* were imprisoned until they paid only if their victim had been a free man;[98] (ii) the murder of a metic or other foreigner, even if intentional, was punished not by death but only by exile.[99]

---

[89] Cf. Her. 2. 120 *fin.*, 2. 137. The orators naturally make free with claims that the offences they are prosecuting are of prodigious seriousness: Isoc. 20. 1-3, Lys. 6. 15, Dem. 19. 292 ff.

[90] Cf. Xen. *Ages.* 11. 6, *Con. Lac.* 8. 4, Hyp. *Dem.* fr. 6, Dem. 26. 4; Isoc. 12. 146 and 7. 27, presumably referring to corruption. Similarly offences committed against persons acting on public business are particularly serious: Dem. 21. 31 ff., 47. 40-1.

[91] Implied by Her. 1. 114-15, Dem. 45. 86-7; cf. Xen. *Cyr.* 4. 2. 47; see further Dover (1974) 283-8.

[92] At any rate [*Xen*]. *AP* 1. 10 alleges fear of striking a free man in mistake for a slave: obviously striking a slave would not matter much; cf. *Gorg.* 483b.

[93] Aesch. 1. 195 (cf. Lys. 3. 5), on the assumption that homosexual advances are a species of aggression; further references and discussion in Dover (1974) 279-83.

[94] Lys. 16. 18, Dem. 35. 40 ff.   [95] Dem. 53. 18.

[96] Slaves could be prosecuted in court, at least in some circumstances: Morrow (1939) 72, Harrison i (1968) 174.

[97] *AP* 59. 5 may conceivably *imply* it, for slander of a free man by a slave.

[98] Dem. 21. 46-9, esp. end of 47; but cf. Aesch. 1. 15, Hyp. fr. 37. On a slave's inability to protect himself by going to law on his own behalf, see Morrow (1939) 75-6, Harrison i (1968) 167 ff.

[99] MacDowell (1963) 58 ff., Harrison i (1968) 196-9.

Certain types of bodily penalty, e.g. fetters and whipping, were thought inappropriate for free men, and suitable only or chiefly for slaves.[100] A free man, remarks Demosthenes,[101] is actuated by shame, a slave by bodily constraint. A free man subjected to bodily constraint feels shame at being treated effectively as a slave.[102]

Wealth and Poverty. Orthodox democratic sentiment was strongly against abatement or remission of penalty on grounds of the offender's wealth.[103] Demosthenes, decrying indulgence to the rich,[104] generalizes the point by urging the jury to 'show your anger on the same basis against all'. But Isocrates protests at the severity with which the 'same' penalty falls upon a poor man as compared with its lack of impact on a rich man, and Lysias argues that offences by the poor or disabled are treated with indulgence as 'involuntary'.[105] A rich man might well receive less 'pity'.[106] There was a general hostility towards the rich, but its practical effect is hard to gauge.[107]

In some oligarchies fines were imposed on the wealthy for failure to perform certain civic functions, but on the poor either no fines were imposed or only smaller ones, with a view to ensuring that the state should remain under oligarchic control.[108] These measures, however, were obviously political rather than penological.

Youth and Age. The normal relationship is of course the chastisement of the young by their elders; and Aristophanes exploits the comic potential of a reasoned argument by a son to the effect that he should beat his father.[109] When youth offends against age, two reactions are possible: (1) to treat the offence as an example of the headstrong insolence of the young, and as more serious than an offence between contemporaries;[110] (2) to palliate it by reference to the witless impetuosity of young people ('boys will be boys').[111]

---

[100] And. 4. 17–18, Aesch. 1. 139, Dem. 21. 180, 22. 55, 24. 167; Thuc. 8. 74. 3, and in general Glotz (1908), Morrow (1939) 66 ff.

[101] Dem. 8. 51. Cf. Isoc. 5. 16: persuasion for Hellenes, compulsion for barbarians.

[102] Dem. 24. 87, 115, cf. 21. 71–2. Shame is greater than any loss: Dem. 1. 27. Slaves to be trained like animals: Xen. *Oec.* 13. 9.

[103] Dem. 51. 11; cf. the complementary principle 'equal compensation for all victims', Isoc. 20. 19 ff. Further references, p. 98 above. (Contrast Gelon's high-handed partiality towards rich offenders, Her. 7. 156, for *raisons d'état*).   [104] Dem. 21. 183.

[105] Isoc. 16. 47, Lys. 31. 11.   [106] Dem. 27. 53.

[107] At Dem. 21. 182 a plea of poverty, if made, was *not* effective.

[108] Arist. *Pol.* 1294ª35 ff., 1297ª14 ff., 1298ᵇ17 ff.; cf. *AP* 4. 3, 30. 6.

[109] *Cl.* 1410 ff.; cf. Isoc. 11. 50.   [110] Ant. *Tetr.* 3a. 6.

[111] Dem. 54. 21; cf. 38. 20, where young litigants are said to be at an advantage.

(iii) *Excuses and intentions*

This general heading covers an extremely wide range of palliatives; we have already noted them, so far as they exist, in Homer.

Involuntariness. This plea, as we saw, occurs in Homer just occasionally. Athens' first lawgiver, Draco, enshrined in his code the distinction between voluntary and involuntary homicide;[112] no doubt this provision reflected existing tendencies; and throughout Greek law it is a common ground of extenuation recognized both by statute and in pleading in the courts, into which it has obviously been imported from ordinary life.[113] In general terms, the plea of involuntariness is a powerful one, which orators are at pains to press or dismiss as suits their book.[114] Its power is also suggested by the not always convincing redefinitions of certain other palliatives or excuses *in terms of* involuntariness.[115]

Ignorance. Ignorance may of course be culpable; and Andocides implies that ignorance of the law would not absolve from punishment for an offence.[116] However, ignorance is in principle recognized as an excuse. Xenophon allows that acts done in ignorance count as involuntary; and Demosthenes is prepared to be indulgent to ignorance arising from lack of guile or experience.[117] However, he subjects the principles to some restriction: he says he acquits Aeschines if he acted through ignorance or stupidity or naïvety, but then takes back the concession and argues that in *public* life such excuses are not 'just'; and in fact Aeschines (he claims) knew exactly what he was doing.[118]

Blunder and mishap. Even Croesus recognized mishap when his son was slain by Adrastus, and found the 'cause' in a god;[119] and Adrastus' remorse and willingness to die were both a sign of innocent intent and in themselves a 'penalty'. The point that bad luck and bad conduct are two distinct things is generally recognized,[120] although in a particular case the apportionment of responsibility between them could be controversial.[121] Yet Dinarchus is prepared to argue that a consistent history of

---

[112] See Gagarin (1981) 30.

[113] *Hipp. Maj.* 372a, 373b. Her. 1. 35, 2. 151; Lys. 3. 41 ff., 4. 6-7, 18, 31. 10-11, Ant. 1. 27, *Tetr.* 2a. 1-2, 3a. 6, Dem. 18. 274-5, 21. 43, 24. 49. Occasionally intent matters above all, as when the attempt to offend has failed or is only prospective: Her. 1. 124, 6. 86, Thuc. 6. 38. Contrariwise *good* intent can palliate even formally heinous offences: Xen. *Hell.* 1. 3. 19.

[114] Some dismissals: Lys. 13. 29, 31, 52, Isoc. 16. 44.

[115] Poverty and physical disablement: Lys. 31. 11; inexperience: Dem. 58. 24; ignorance: Xen. *Cyr.* 3. 1. 38.   [116] And. 1. 113.

[117] Xen. *Cyr.* 3. 1. 38; Dem. 58. 24, 59. 80 ff.; cf. *Hipp. Maj.* 372a.

[118] Dem. 19. 102-5, 109-10, 119.   [119] Her. 1. 43 and 45, Lys. 31. 10.

[120] Thuc. 5. 75. 3, Dem. 56. 42-3.   [121] Xen. *Hell.* 1. 7.

bad luck is itself punishable;[122] presumably it can be held to show divine ill-will.[123]

Indirect or remote action. The fundamental principle, claimed by Andocides to be enshrined in law, is that principal and agent are equally liable to punishment; neither can shelter behind the other.[124] Hence he who carries out an illegal act cannot shelter behind an order given for that act by an official.[125] The principle is readily extendible to encouragement, connivance, concealment, or simple failure to prevent an offence.[126] Lysias claims that information given to the Thirty, which led to the murder by them of the persons informed against, makes the informer guilty of murder.[127] A peculiarly wide extension of the principle, applied in a decree reported with approval by Lycurgus, provided that even to speak in defence of Phrynichus, who was to be tried *post mortem* for treason, should be liable to the same penalty as the treason itself.[128]

Under this heading there seems also to have been some thought given to the culpability of juries for mistaken decisions to punish or not to punish defendants.[129]

Hitting back. To claim that one injured in self-defence is a frequent and powerful plea,[130] though Demosthenes notes that 'pleas of necessity' (which in the context seems to mean provocation) should not be given too much weight.[131]

The passions. Strong passions can cause a person to act uncharacter-istically, and to that extent his offences can be said to be unintended, i.e. not what he 'normally' or 'really' wished to do.[132] Anger in particular can be seen indulgently, as Lysias is well aware.[133] An offence committed in anger can be more or less brushed aside, presumably because anger fades; but offences repeatedly committed over a period argue a set intent.[134]

---

[122] Din. *Dem.* 31, 41, 74, 77, 91-3; as he admits, he ignores the distinction between luck and responsibility (93). Cf. Thuc 6. 17 (and Gomme's note, IV. 249), and 6. 103 (375-6). Contrast [Demades] *On the Twelve Years* 15, and see Demosthenes' own view of the matter in *Letter* 4 (if genuine), and 18. 189, 194, 252 ff.

[123] *Dem.* 91; cf. Adkins (1971) 5 n. 25.   [124] And. 1. 94, cf. Ant. 1.

[125] Lys. 22. 10; his wording suggests that this was not actually a law.

[126] Lys. 29. 11; Aesch. 2. 115, 3. 121-2; Dem. 54. 22, 25, Isoc. 3. 53. Not all these passages refer to formal provisions.

[127] Lys. 13. 33, 42, 87, 92, 95—and at 88 ff., in spite of the amnesty (*AP* 39. 6).

[128] Lyc. *Leoc.* 112-16, cf. 135 and 138.   [129] Ibid. 146; Ant. *Tetr.* 3a. 4, 5. 91, 6. 6.

[130] Ant. *Tetr.* 3b. 1 ff., 3d. 7, Dem. 23. 60; law of assault: 47. 7-8, 15, 35, 38-40, 47, 54. 33; 21. 74-6 makes play with his restraint in not retaliating against Meidias' attack on him. Cf. Isoc. 8. 79, 9. 28, 16. 44.

[131] Dem. 54. 17.   [132] Ar. *Wasps* 1002: 'I did it unintentionally and out of character.'

[133] Lys. 10. 30, cf. Arist. *Rhet.* 2. 3.   [134] Dem. 21. 41 ff., cf. 66.

Drunkenness. It is notoriously hard to know whether to treat a crime committed in a state of intoxication as more or less blameworthy than one committed in sobriety. No doubt the offender was not in full control of himself, and in a sense not fully aware of what he was doing; yet his having got into such a state is itself culpable.[135] Not surprisingly, the opposing arguments are deployed in our sources. Some indicate that intoxicated criminals could be treated with a certain indulgence.[136] But the argument could cut the other way: intoxication could constitute or lead to an aggravation.[137] The most intriguing passage concerns Pittacus, ruler of Mytilene for ten years in the early sixth century. Aristotle's report[138] is not quite clear either in its expression or its implications; but it seems to say that while Pittacus accepted drunkenness as some kind of excuse, he nevertheless decided, since there were more drunk offenders than sober, to override equity on social grounds and punish the former offenders more heavily than the latter.

Force majeure. Whether a man should be punished for an offence which he committed against his wishes and better judgement, under severe pressures, but which he *could* have refused to do, is a long-standing moral problem. Sometimes we find insistence on the freedom of action, at other times on the pressures.[139]

Recidivism. Recidivism argues inveterate wickedness, and calls for relatively high penalties. In a suit for perjury a third conviction led to loss of citizen rights (*atimia*); earlier convictions were punished only by a fine.[140] The orators often dwell indignantly on persistence in wrongdoing by the defendant and others.[141] Demosthenes reports as general advice that persistent offenders do not deserve indulgence.[142]

[135] Cf. *NE* 1113^{b}30 ff., cf. 1110^{b}25 ff.

[136] Dorjahn (1930) 165, citing Arist. *Rhet.* 2. 25. 7 as showing that the drunkard's plea could be in effect one of ignorance, and Hyp. *Phil.* 3, Dem. 21. 38, 73, 180; contrast xxi. 287 ff. Cf. William Penn, *A Description of Pennsylvania* (1683), xxiv: 'It is rare that they fall out, if sober; and if drunk, they forgive it, saying, it was the drink and not the man that abused them.'

[137] Ant. *Tetr.* 3d. 6, cf. Dem. 54. 25, 33.

[138] *Pol.* 1274^{b}18 ff.—if this chapter is indeed Aristotle's. Murray (1983) suggests that Pittacus' law was directed against packs of drunken aristocrats who beat up their social inferiors (see *Pol.* 1311^{b}23 ff.). Cf. Murray (1990) 144.

[139] Isoc. 24. 12, 30, Ant. 5. 76, Lys. 12. 29, 50, 90–1, 13. 31, 52, 22. 5–6. *Un*constrained acts do not deserve pardon (implying that constrained ones do): Xen. *Cyr.* 5. 1. 13. Over-persuasion: Is. 2. 19–20 *et saepe.* 'Inability' to obey a decree: Dem. 18. 38. There is a distinction at Dem. 45. 62 between committing an offence on one's own initiative and at the request of another—not that the latter is intended as exculpation. On *force majeure* in the law of homicide, see MacDowell (1968).

[140] And. 1. 74. Hyp. *Phil.* 11 argues that having been twice convicted on a charge of making illegal proposals, for which the penalty for a third conviction was *atimia*, is *not* a reason for acquittal on the third occasion (presumably from a wish not to inflict *atimia*), but a ground for conviction: the defendant has shown his character twice before.

[141] e.g. Dem. 21. 128 ff., cf. Xen. *Oec.* 14. 8.   [142] Dem. 58. 24; cf. 26. 21, and Din. *Arist.* 3.

Deceit. Deceit and secrecy are frequently mentioned as an intolerable aggravation when practised, and as an excuse when suffered.[143] That an offence was committed publicly can also be urged as an exacerbation.[144]

Repentance and confession. Andocides argues ingeniously that what causes crime is opinion, or state of mind, *gnōmē*, not the person (body); since his opinion has now changed, his former (guilty) state of mind is no longer available to be blamed.[145] Apart from that, there is a striking rarity of any claim that repentance is a ground for diminution of penalty. However, on one occasion confession attracted a lower penalty than brazening it out.[146]

Absolute liability. Liability 'incurred independently of intention or negligence'[147] seems not to be part of Athenian law. However, a few passages attempt to apply the principle.

1. Antiphon[148] sharply reminds us that it is all very well to punish accidental murder less harshly than voluntary, but that it is an injustice to the dead man, who is robbed of *timōria*—presumably the knowledge of the killer's death in turn, which the victim needs as recompense, whether his killer acted voluntarily or involuntarily.

2. The late fifth-century Syracusan lawgiver Diocles specifically disallowed ignorance or any other mitigation if a man appeared in the agora wearing a sword.[149] Such severity may have seemed prudent in the political circumstances of the time, but clearly goes against the general trend.

3. In Egypt, the intentional killing of sacred animals was punished by death, the unintentional by something less, at the priests' discretion; but the ibis and hawk were protected absolutely, and even their unintentional killing was punished by death, so highly were they valued.[150]

(iv) *Instinctive limitation*

We saw how in Homer instinctive pity seems to have had some part to play in restraining the savagery of retaliation.[151] Pleas based on simple

---

[143] Dem. 59. 81–3; cf. 47. 46, 50, 75, 82.   [144] Dem. 21. 71 ff.

[145] And. 2. 24.   [146] Aesch. 1. 113; cf. 91 for severe discouragements to confession.

[147] Hansen's words (1976) 69–70, 119, alleging it was 'a well-known phenomenon'; but his attempt to argue that it applied to defaulting state-debtors seems overstated, since the cause of non-payment is not always *inability* to pay.

[148] Ant. *Tetr.* 2c. 7. Apparently the claims of a dead person could be urged without implausibility: Ant. 1. 21, 25–7, 5. 10, 88 (but contrast 95); Is. 2. 47.

[149] Diod. Sic. 13. 33; cf. 35. 4 and 12. 19, perhaps confusing this Diocles with an otherwise unknown archaic Syracusan lawgiver of the same name.   [150] Her. 2. 65.

[151] pp. 17–18 above. The topic is frequent. There is some speculation about the psychologicial causes of extreme severity: Her. 3. 27–9, 32, 33, 35–6, 38. Restraint at slight offence (words not deeds): Her. 9. 79 *fin.*; the offence was to suggest a 'tit-for-tat', which was unseemly and more

human fellow-felling could certainly be made in the courts, by an emotional plea of the defendant's family, and in some cases had a decisive effect.[152] On the other hand, there are examples of 'hawks' arguing that if a charge is once proved, the penalty ought to follow without any mitigation whatever,[153] or that extreme severity is appropriate for all crime, whether for social reasons or for reasons of vindictive justice, or both.[154]

(v) *The defendant's record*

A litigant's record may be used to suggest that he must be telling the truth, or that he is not.[155] But it may also be employed to argue for reciprocation. To commit any offence, even if only against an individual, as distinct from the state, is, even if remotely, to harm the common interest represented by juries. Jurors were therefore, not unnaturally, prepared to entertain representations to the effect that, whatever the truth or justice of his case, a litigant or someone closely connected with him who would be affected by the verdict, had deserved well[156] or ill[157] by meritorious or reprehensible character and conduct, by public service or disservice.[158] Such pleas were not confined to the stage after the verdict, as they are in a modern court, when the level of penalty is assessed: they were heard before the verdict, and were professedly calculated to influence it.[159]

The notion of 'compensation' sounds straightforward, but in practice it can generate difficult calculations. Three principles come into play:

1. that the verdict and the penalty should be based strictly on justice, i.e. on the facts of the case on hand;[160]

worthy of a barbarian; cf. 1. 137. In *Letter* 3. 25 Demosthenes deprecates indefinite punishment as inexpedient. Herodotus believes excessively severe penalties are odious to the gods, 4. 205. Plutarch *Solon* 17 reports Demades' (late 4th century) apparently disapproving or at least wondering remark that Draco's laws were written not in ink but blood, since they punished nearly all offences by a single penalty, death; cf. Ar. *Rhet.* 1400^{b}19, *Pol.* 1274^{b}15–18. These reports tell us something about sentiment on the point in the 5th and 4th centuries. Dem. 22. 57 claims pity and indulgence as proper to free men. Cf. 'Lemnian savagery' at Her. 6. 138; also Dem. 21. 182, 58. 70, 59. 6–8, Din. *Dem.* 57, Eur. *Supp.* 511–12, Plut. *Lyc.* 18. 3.

[152] *Ap.* 34b–35d, Lys. 20. 34–6, Lyc. *Leoc.* 141, Hyp. *Phil.* 9.
[153] Dem. 19. 283, 58. 24 (quasi-hardline), 59. 117; cf. Democ. B262 DK.
[154] Isoc. 7. 34 alleges with approval that contractual defaulters in olden days were treated with greater severity by their judges than by their victims.   [155] Dover (1974) 293–4.
[156] Isoc. 18. 66, Dem. 21. 128, 151 ff., 25. 76 ff., Hyp. *Phil.* 10 ff.; Lys. 6. 35.
[157] Isoc. 18. 47, Lys. 14. 23 ff.,
[158] Din. *Phil.* 17 (cf. 21) $\doteqdot$ *Dem.* 14 uses a quasi-technical term, *antikatallattesthai*, 'to balance' or 'to compensate'; for the idea without the term see Dem 20. 81. The calculation is 'commercial' and recriprocal, and it is found in non-forensic contexts also, e.g. Her. 1. 137, 7. 194 (Persia), Xen. *Anab.* 6. 6. 31. At Thuc. 1. 86. 1 and 3. 67. 2 a hitherto virtuous record is treated as a reason for *enhancing* a penalty; Gomme (i. 251) calls it a 'sophism', but it is natural for offended parties to feel not only injured but betrayed.   [159] Cf. in general Dover (1974) 292–5, and p. 95 n. 26 above.
[160] See the juror's oath, Dem. 24. 149–51 (cf. n. 174 below).

2. justice should be reciprocal, i.e. 'one good or bad turn deserves another' (the penalty should be modified by reference to the defendant's *record*);
3. that the penalty imposed, if any, should be modified in such a way as to serve the jury's (i.e. the public's) interests in the future; that is to say, the offender is in a position to confer benefits or harm, and his record is urged in prognostication, rather than as a matter of reciprocal justice based on an existing record.

On this analysis, pleas based on records are essentially a means of allowing, at the discretion of the jury, considerations of justice according to the law to be overriden by considerations of social policy.

The justice which may or may not be overridden is rather complex. It is clear that a plea based on a record is a plea based on some notion of desert. A man may deserve for his offence, strictly on the facts and on the law, a certain penalty; but his good record (which may not consist of explicitly public services, but merely of a blameless private life[161]) may indicate a just entitlement[162] to its remission. It is only at this point, at least in most cases, that the jury has to consider whether, in the public's future interest, on grounds of expediency, the remission should be granted. The record has a dual aspect: it indicates that a man deserves something, reciprocally, in return for past actions; and it also indicates what his actions may be in the future. In some cases desert may suffice to override strict justice, without reference to the future; in others, the future may itself influence the decision.

A passage of Lysias reveals the dual aspect of the record.[163] He lists three considerations that might be reasons for acquitting Nicomachus:[164] the courage he has shown in military service, the contributions he has made to public funds, and his ancestors—for even for this reason some men have gained the sympathy (or indulgence, *sungnōmē*) of juries. 'Or,' he goes on, 'is this your reason, that he will repay favours in the future?' Here the distinction between granting indulgence (acquittal) *for* past actions, and granting it in *expectation* of future return, is obvious. The principle of compensation on grounds of desert comes first; the calculation of public advantage supervenes upon it and keeps the question open. Another speaker (defending under the restored democracy his fitness for office: there is no question of punishment here[165]) urges (i) his record of public service, intended to enhance his reputation and ensure

---

[161] e.g. Dem. 21. 128, 'moderate and humane life', a 'decent and moderate person'; cf. 25. 76.

[162] e.g. Dem. *Letter* 2. 12: 'justly think it right' to be acquitted on the ground of good service; cf. *anaxion ad fin.*, and Lys. 3. 47–8.

[163] Lys. 30. 26–7, cf. And. 1. 146–50.

[164] Lysias says that the reasons do not in fact apply, for Nicomachus has been a rogue; but that does not affect the logic of what would be the case if they did apply.   [165] Lys. 25. 13–17.

better success in court, (ii) his democratic sympathies, (iii) his likely civic virtue and generosity in the future. Here again the calculation of public interest supervenes on the calculation of credit, desert or entitlement.[166]

In short, strict justice may be overridden by desert alone or by expediency alone,[167] or by desert and expediency in combination; and even where desert does apply it too may be overriden by expediency.

But the propriety of overriding (1) in favour of (2) and/or (3) did not go unchallenged.[168] Dinarchus urges the condemnation of Demosthenes and others, however notable they may be, on the basis of strict justice and deterrent effect.[169] In the speech against Neaera the jury is urged to remember approvingly how Archias, in spite of high birth, eminent position and the pleas of friends and relatives, was nevertheless punished on the sole grounds of his guilt.[170] Demosthenes in his speech against Meidias argues that Meidias' record is irrelevant to the need to punish him for his *hubris*.[171] Certainly pleas based on records did not always succeed.[172]

On the other hand, the priority of (3) is sometimes explicit.[173] More often, the appeal is only implicit: a good record betokens a person whose services the public interest cannot afford to do without.

The justification of punishment, or exemption from it, on the basis of the competing claims of strict justice, compensatory justice, and public interest led to a state of continuous tension in Athenian legal proceedings. The arguments and their context are invariably *parti pris* and tendentious; nevertheless Athenian juries were constantly faced with weighing the claims of justice and expediency—though it is of course doubtful if the average juror would have been able to articulate precisely why, and how strongly, he preferred one claim to the other; certainly litigants could never know in advance to which consideration the jury would collectively give priority.[174]

---

[166] Cf. Hyp. *Phil.* 10: the jury is represented as first dismissing the argument from entitlement, and *then* contemplating acquittal on grounds of expediency. Din. *Phil.* 21 urges that admitted *charis* to defendants should be outweighed by expediency of conviction on grounds of strict justice.

[167] Dem. *Letter* 3. 24-6, Laches (expediency), Mnesibulus (desert, *axios*).

[168] See in general Demosthenes' invective against capricious reasons for acquittals and light penalties, 23. 206. Cf. Dover (1974) 294-5.

[169] Din. *Dem.* 14-17, 26-7; cf Xen. *Hell.* 5. 4. 24 ff., Hyp. *Phil.* 7.

[170] Dem. 59. 117; cf. 25. 76 and the insistence on facts at 19. 296, described as 'the democratic thing to do'.   [171] Dem. 21. 160.

[172] Din. *Dem.* 14, Dem. 24. 134 ff. Dem. 24. 127 turns a plea based on an encomium of the defendant's father by saying that the criminal son of such a father deserves punishment all the more; cf. 133, where a good record is treated as a confidence-trick.

[173] Lys. 14. 43, cf. 6. 43, Thuc. 5. 63. Appeals to the jury's immediate self-interest could sometimes even take the extreme form, 'find guilty, or the source of your fees, the fines, will dry up': Ar. *Kn.* 1359, Lys. 27. 1.

[174] Presumably it is for this reason as well as others that orators like to assure juries that the verdict to which they are being urged is *both* just *and* expedient, e.g. Hyp. *Phil.* 13. Cf. in general

To consider a defendant's record of action naturally leads to a summary estimate of his moral character. Orators often speak as though they believe defendants ought to be punished for their character alone; but presumably in such cases the 'character/moral state', is only a handily compendious term for the record itself;[175] for as in English, abstract nouns such as 'vice' and 'depravity' and their cognate adjectives may refer either to a moral disposition or the actions prompted by it.

Inspection in court of a man's general record of conduct is in principle similar to *dokimasia*, assessment of fitness for office before entering upon it,[176] and to *euthuna*, 'scrutiny' or 'audit' of conduct during it. All three inspections permit *inter alia* a judgement of the sort of person he is.[177] In trials and *euthunai*, where penalties can be imposed, such a judgement contributes to assessment of desert; in trials, and more explicitly in *dokimasiai*, it permits intelligent conjecture about likely future conduct;[178] and the result of *euthuna*, a procedure which technically concerns only the past, becomes itself a part of the record in the future. In brief, forensic reviews of conduct are all of a piece with the wider assumptions and procedures of Athenian democracy.

Occasionally Demosthenes makes an implicit distinction between offenders who are evil by nature and those whose depravity has been acquired;[179] the latter he regards as more serious.[180] In a more elaborate classification he distinguishes (1) men who are best and most moderate, thanks to nature herself, and who willingly do what they should; (2) men who are not to be termed wholly bad, and are cautious about doing wrong, from fear and from apprehension of disgrace and reproach; (3)

Thuc. 6. 60 *fin.*, [Xen.] *AP* 1. 13. It is hard to assess the purport and influence of the juror's oath (Dem. 24. 149–51), which enjoined *inter alia* verdicts based strictly on the charge: clearly many or most jurors saw no inconsistency between that and taking into account a litigant's 'record'. But the oath probably also provided that a juror should decide by 'the most just judgement', at any rate in cases governed by no law (Dem. 39. 40, cf. 23. 96); as Harrison remarks (ii (1971) 48), 'the general tenor of the oath suggests that the juror is to vote according to his conscience'. See further Bonner and Smith ii (1938) 152–5.

[175] See Isoc. 20. 4 (*ponēria*, vice = putative offences), 7 (punish for *tropos*, character, as source of modest offences and potentially of disastrous escalation), 13–14 (desirability of punishing the depraved pre-emptively, on evidence of small offences, before they commit serious ones); it is sometimes hard to gauge whether arguments of this kind actually envisage punishing character independently of offences actual or prospective (cf. Din. *Phil.* 11, Hyp. *Phil.* 11, Dem. 21. 219 ff., 24. 138). The interesting argument in And. 2. 24–6 stresses character/opinion, but admits they have to be judged by actions; cf. Dem. 21. 160 ff.

[176] See e.g. Din. *Arist.* 10, and in general Adelaye (1983).

[177] A distinction needs to be made. The assessment of *motives* (above, pp. 108 ff.) is similar in nature to an assessment of character, but refers to states of mind in the commission of single acts, and functions as an *excuse* or an *aggravation*. The assessment of character, on the other hand, is a generalization intended as 'compensation' or prediction. The character assessment can nevertheless also be deployed also as *ad hoc* mitigation or aggravation, e.g. Dem. 59. 81–3.

[178] e.g. Dem. 21. 186.   [179] Dem. 58. 17, 40, cf. *Exordia* 28.
[180] Dem. 21. 186.

men called utterly depraved and moral outcasts, whom people say learn wisdom/sense by misfortune/suffering. The defendant (Aristogeiton) falls outside all categories, so surpassing all men in depravity that not even suffering deters him from crime.[181]

There is one speech whose argument seems at first sight to have been worked out on the basis of some systematic thought about the relationship between a crime and its punishment. This is Lycurgus' speech against Leocrates,[182] who left Athens hurriedly in 338 after Chaeronea and was accused of treason. Lycurgus does indeed argue from expediency in a sense: for example he says that the punishment of the guilty is an incentive to virtuous conduct; and as Adkins[183] notes, he does not actually deny that good services are relevant considerations. But he also harps on the necessity of putting justice first, of excluding irrelevance, and of requiring witnesses to give evidence uninfluenced by bribes and favour. The facts, he say, come first, and speak for themselves: 'justice is straightforward, the truth is easy, the proof is brief'—so if the charge is true, why does he not meet with the *timōria* laid down by law? He argues for a direct and simple sequence from crime to punishment, without the intervention of other considerations such as motive or innocent intent. He even cites with approval the practice of old but unnamed lawgivers who made no allowances for the relative gravity of crimes, but punished all by death. The act alone matters (though the reading is disputed at this point), not whether Leocrates sinned alone or with others—i.e. there must be no clemency on the grounds that being alone in his action he did not really constitute a threat. The only ground Lycurgus will accept for acquittal is a demonstration that Leocrates did *not*, in point of sheer fact, leave Athens. He believes it an advantage that Leocrates is available for punishment in Athens, for then a close and immediate connection between his crime and his punishment will be obvious; if he were punished abroad, the connection would be lost. He sees divine intervention in the fact that Leocrates is available for punishment by the very people he had wronged—a nice appeal to the old feeling that punishments should be inflicted by the injured party in person. Normally, he says punishments follow a crime; but in the case of aspiring to tyranny or trying to overthrow the democracy, they should precede it.[184]

This remarkable series of arguments constitutes a systematic attempt to maintain a hardline penology, without reference to the motives and circumstances of the accused, and allowing considerations of public good to influence the verdict only against him. The principle for which Lycurgus argues has a certain austere appeal; but it is very likely to have

---

[181] Dem. 25. 93-5.
[183] Adkins (1960) 214.

[182] Esp. Lyc. *Leoc.* 10-13, 20, 34, 64-7, 90, 139.
[184] Lyc. *Leoc.* 125-6.

been as opportunistic as any other. Probably Leocrates left Athens *before* it became illegal to do so; hence Lycurgus' only hope is to hammer the sheer fact that he did leave, from cowardice, and so divert attention from the chronology.[185] Perhaps some members of the jury were aware of the tactic. At any rate, *fiat justitia ruat caelum* is a sentiment in general alien to Attic legal practice, and the number and elaboration of Lycurgus' attempts to argue in that spirit perhaps suggest just how much he was going against common assumptions.[186] Yet he made some impact: Leocrates was acquitted by a single vote.[187]

(vi) *Conclusion*

In their opportunistic way, the Greek orators used and abused every conceivable argument in excuse and in aggravation; and many of these arguments are parallel to those employed in difficult situations of ordinary life. Some of them are double-edged. For example, drunkenness, or youth, can be advanced either as an aggravation or as an excuse. A great number of issues were raised of jurisprudence and of what we would now call 'sentencing policy'; and their very number and variety indicate the extreme fluidity of practice: no orator could be sure that an argument found effective yesterday would prevail today. Accordingly, in the absence of a consistent policy which they could be confident would be pursued by the courts, they resorted to grapeshot, in the hope that some jurors would find some arguments persuasive.

(f) *Third parties*

As early as Homer the inequity of punishing third parties in lieu of the offender provoked some small but discernible unease, when their connection with the offence was remote or non-existent. Nevertheless the practice of inflicting suffering on third parties either instead of or in addition to the offender continued to be taken for granted.[188] Hesiod does not think it worthy of special remark: indeed his 'theology of work' depends on it.[189] Solon notes, but does not protest against, the punishment by Zeus of the innocent descendants of an unjust man.[190] Yet the unfairness of the practice did attract notice, and some censure,

---

[185] Petrie (1922) pp. xxvii–xxix.

[186] Demosthenes' tough line may be compared, 22. 17 ff. Ant. *Tetr.* 1c. 8 rightly points out that public services are evidence of wealth, but do nothing to show innocence of the charge (murder)— but then attempts to push the argument against the defendant by suggesting that he may well have murdered in fear of *losing* his wealth.   [187] Aesch. 3. 252.

[188] Her. 1. 144, 3. 11, 45, 50, 4. 84, 9. 120; In military situations, for obvious reasons, any group among enemies or even neutrals could easily attract the retaliation more strictly directed against the more direct offender: Thuc. 3. 32. A *recherché* Spartan application of the principle: Plut. *Lyc.* 18. 4.

[189] *WD* 56, 240, 284; cf. (fr.) *Cat. W.* 67.   [190] Sol. 13. 31–2; cf. Theog. 205–6, Arch. 127.

often by way of a remark that the punished third parties are 'blameless' (*anaitioi vel sim.*)[191] The most celebrated protest is that of Theognis.[192] Xenophon records, possibly with a raised eyebrow, that in 379 the Thebans seized and killed 'even' or 'also' (*kai*) the children of certain punished persons.[193]

The orators argue both for and against, as occasion demands, which suggests that public opinion was ambivalent. A speaker in Isocrates argues against allowing his father's offences to prompt a verdict against himself too.[194] Demosthenes decries prosecuting third parties in place of the real offender, and argues against punishing children for their father's misdeeds;[195] Lysias roundly asserts that the gods do no such thing, but visit punishment exclusively on the offender, *when the offence is against themselves*.[196] But none of this amounts to a challenge to third-party punishment in the general run of cases.

Indeed the older principle was strongly asserted, especially in contexts with a religious flavour. Lysias insists that descendants can be punished for the offences of ancestors; evidently the speaker sees himself as the instrument of a god.[197] Elsewhere he asks us to believe that to kill both offenders and their (innocent) children is justified in return for the deaths of the jury's relatives (including children) caused by the offenders.[198] Demosthenes argues that though children should be accountable for their father's offences, the principle should be restricted to those cases where the (now dead) father had actually been charged.[199] He notes clemency extended to the children of the 30 tyrants, and ascribes it to Athenian philanthropy.[200]

These arguments seem somehow to go against the grain: they either invoke religion, or resort to *lex talionis*, or betray unease and seek to restrict or palliate. They have the air of special pleading.

What legal provisions were there? Successful litigants in the Palladium included their household in the oath they took that the correct verdict had been reached after true testimony from themselves; the household was therefore at risk if the testimony was false.[201] Unpaid debts to the state (e.g. fines) were inherited by the defaulter's heir, along with the *atimia* (disfranchisement) incurred by the non-payment; and *atimia*

---

[191] Her. 1. 155, 4. 200 (third parties as *metaitioi*, 'accessories'), 9. 88. Cf. Plut. *Tim.* 30 *fin.*

[192] Theog. 731-52, discussed above, pp. 49-50.

[193] Xen. *Hell.* 5. 4. 12.   [194] Isoc. 16. 2-3, 11, 44.

[195] Dem. 18. 15-16, *Letter* 3. 13-20. Aesch. 2. 178 protests at the arbitrariness of punishing only one offender out of many.

[196] Fr. 53. Presumably the gods find satisfaction in seeing the offender himself suffer.

[197] Lys. 6. 20; cf. Lyc. *Leoc.* 79. Aesch. 3. 134-6 suggests that Athens suffers at the hands of the gods for the offences of one man, Demosthenes.

[198] Lys. 12. 36, 82-4; Dem. 19. 310 has a similar argument of talionic reciprocity. For a 'pointed' punishment of a third party which is a *surrogate* (a statue) see Lyc. *Leoc.* 117-19.

[199] Dem. 57. 27.   [200] Dem. 40. 32.   [201] Aesch. 2. 87.

imposed for other reasons too could extend to descendants.[202] In general, however, the assumption of Attic law seems to have been that only offenders should be punished.[203]

Punishment of third parties is to be distinguished from any suffering which relatives and friends may undergo as a consequence of the punishment of the offender himself.[204] Demosthenes claims that juries on finding guilty make provision for the family of the criminal;[205] *if* true, this implies some recognition of their plight.

(g) Purposes

If one had asked the average plaintiff in an Athenian court what purposes he supposed would be served by the penalty he was demanding, he would have mentioned at least one of these three:

1. to gain compensation for himself or other victims, preferably in excess of the injury or damage, however assessed;[206]
2. to afford himself or other victims the satisfaction and pleasure not only of the recompense but of having their anger assuaged by *timōria*, in the shape of knowledge or sight of the offender's suffering, either by his being forced to give that recompense in concrete form or in some other way—in short, by suffering evil for evil;[207]
3. to deter through fear the offender and others for the future, by making them learn that the law is stronger and that therefore crime does not pay—in short to 'improve' them; in general terms, to serve the public interest by upholding the law, by the repression of crime, by getting rid of the criminal, and avoiding pollution; these considerations tend to be presented in various combinations and impassioned medleys.[208]

The standard penology of the courts was thus strongly retributive and deterrent. These purposes originate in Homer, and are influential in

---

[202] MacDowell (1978) 74, Harrison ii (1971) 175, Hansen (1976) 71-2, 118, Dem. 21. 113, 23. 62, 58. 2.   [203] Cf. pp. 12-13 above.

[204] Ant. 5. 82. See the belief common to Xen. *Cyr.* 8. 1. 25, Aes. *Se.* 602-4, Eur. *El.* 1355.

[205] Dem. 27. 65, contrast 21. 182. When a defendant paraded his family in court in order to excite pity, that pity was for the prospective misery of the family if he were found guilty.

[206] e.g. Dem. 55. 28. 'In excess' is for obvious reasons not admitted outright by plaintiffs themselves; but consider the implications of the plea for swingeing damages at Isoc. 20. 1, 5-6, 16, 19, and indeed of the whole procedure in 'estimated' suits (see p. 101 above).

[207] Dem. 53. 2, 59. 1, 8, 14, 126; cf. Isoc. 15. 13, a rather special case.

[208] Ant. *Tetr.* 1c. 11, Lys. 1. 47, 6. 53, 14. 12, 45, 15. 9-10, 22. 19-20, 24. 27; Aesch. 1. 34, 36, 191-2, Lyc. *Leoc.* 10, 27, Dem. 19. 343. Public interest: Aesch. 3. 8; Dem. 22. 37 virtually claims that a verdict of guilty would be called for in the public interest, even if the defendant were not guilty as charged. Getting rid of offender: Dem. 25. 92, 96 (by imprisonment for debt). Deterrence: Dem. 58. 64 attacks the common view as a fallacy in certain circumstances.

non-forensic contexts, from which they have been taken.[209] In imaginative literature, in real life, and in the courts there was gain and glory in triumphing over an opponent.[210]

Litigants look for tangible and visible recompense and satisfaction, not the unseen or future comforts of the religious faith that gods or other supernatural beings will bring offenders to book. Hence sustained religious argument is fairly rare. Lysias 6, which attacks Andocides for impiety, treats the committing of an offence as prompted by a god and as being in itself a punishment (in that it will be punished); hence that punishing is a religious duty of certain persons, which may itself attract punishment if not carried out.[211] The similarity of these notions to those found in the *Oresteia* is obvious. Antiphon has the notion that however accidental a killing, pollution is ineluctably present.[212] Aeschines, however, rationalizes aggressively: the *Poinai* (goddesses of *poinē*) do not pursue and punish (*kolazein*) wrongdoers with blazing torches, as in tragedy; they are simply each man's own impulse to do wrong in the hope of pleasure and gain.[213] The tone and arguments of the orators are in fact predominantly secular; as Demosthenes remarks, the business of the courts is to punish offenders they have in their power; it is undetected offenders who may be left to the gods to deal with.[214]

The orators only rarely raise their sights, and envisage using leniency to achieve reform of character or at any rate of conduct; but when they do mention such a possibility, it is only to scout it, often arguing that the policy has failed in the past.[215] This may itself be significant: prosecutors may know from experience that the jury may be influenced by that sort of plea in the mouth of the opposing litigant. At all events, juries are often exhorted not to be 'soft'.[216]

Andocides has some reflections on the usefulness of exile,[217] which the speaker clearly regards as a species of punishment, imposed under the

[209] e.g. Thuc. 7. 68, *Rep.* 332b, Theog. 341–50; Xen. *Anab.* 2. 6. 10 (note 'he punished *gnōmēi*', 'on principle').

[210] Eur. *Bac.* 877 ff., *Med.* 810, Her. 1. 129 *init.*, 7. 5, 9. 79. 2 *timōria* = *timē*, cf. *Symp.* 179e–180a). The jury itself can be encouraged to enhance its reputation for meritorious service by showing zeal in punishing criminals: Lys. 30. 33.

[211] Lys. 6. 11, 13, 19–20, 31–2; cf. 53; this piece also uses (32) the political argument that faith in religion is impaired when religious offenders are observed to go unpunished. See also And. 1. 113, Ant. *Tetr.* 2c. 8, 2d. 10; Dem. 59. 109, 126; more generally, Lys. 13. 3. On Lys. 6, see Dover (1968*b*) 78 ff.   [212] Ant. *Tetr.* 2a. 2, 2c. 11–12; cf. Lys. 6. 53.

[213] Aesch. 1. 190–1.   [214] Dem. 19. 71.

[215] Din. *Arist.* 3–4; Aesch. 1. 113–14, 3. 88–9, 129; Dem. 21. 186, 26. 21; 51. 12, Lys. 15. 10, 28. 16. The distinction between better conduct (because of fines or blows) and better conviction is drawn at Xen. *Mem.* 1. 2. 18; cf. the passing optimism in Dem. 23. 188.

[216] Dem. 23. 204 ff, 24. 192–3, 218; cf. Thuc. 7. 68. 3, Isoc. 6. 39, Aesch. 1. 192. Isaeus (8. 43) notes lack of punishment as an encouragement of further offences; and in 44 he concludes from an offender's failure to be deterred by punishment not that punishment does not deter, but only that the offender is very villainous.

[217] And. 4. 4 ff.; W. D. Furley (1989) argues that this piece is a political pamphlet of the year 415.

ostracism procedure: it does not go far enough, in that it permits a rogue to plot against the city, and too far also, since it banishes good citizens, to the joy of the city's enemies.

The orators give, then, an impression of almost unrelieved vindictiveness, which was no doubt the natural result of the highly combative nature of their situation. In non-forensic contexts, however, there are occasional adroit uses of punishment, or its remission, dictated in part by an irenic spirit and calculated to prevent trouble for the future, or to serve some other socially useful purpose. Herodotus records that offenders in Egypt, during the rule of Sabacos (eighth-seventh century), were made to raise embankments, in proportion to the gravity of their offence.[218] Such policies are however characteristic of single rulers with power and discretion; they are alien to the courts.[219] Xenophon, particularly in the *Cyropaedia*, has an eye for enlightened penology. Cyrus, he says, realized that training and force of example can prevent offences,[220] that men will not be affected by punishment if they think that the rules are not in their interests,[221] and that the fear inculcated by punishment is best combined with the gratitude aroused by remission, conciliation, and incentives.[222]

CRITICISM BY INTELLECTUALS

The preceding section was labelled 'Controversies'; and it may be felt that the word is used in a somewhat extended sense. For although the passages cited concern punishment, because pleaders have to persuade juries to inflict or not to inflict it, and although they exhibit conflicting assumptions about it and related matters, the controversy is indirect, informal, latent, and spasmodic. It never confronts one: it has to be elicited. Penology as such in fact never became a recognized topic of public debate, and was never taken up, so far as we know, by any group concerned to press for changes in practice: ancient Greece had no Howard League for Penal Reform. Not until the end of the fourth century or even later was a treatise written on the topic: according to Diogenes Laertius,[223] Theophrastus wrote a work in 2 books, *On*

---

[218] Her. 2. 137.

[219] Arbitrators, on the other hand, could prescind from apportioning blame, and seek to reconcile the parties: Is. 2. 30–2.

[220] Xen. *Cyr.* 1. 2. 2 ff., and especially the 'practice courts' at 6, which cover the moral 'offence' of ingratitude; force of example: 1. 2. 8; punishment of children trains their habits (though this is mere conventional wisdom, cf. *Prot.* 325c ff., pp. 133 ff. below): 1. 6. 33.

[221] Xen. *Cyr.* 1. 6. 21.

[222] Ibid. 3. 1. 8 ff., 29, 6. 1. 35 ff., 7. 2. 4 ff., *Anab.* 2. 3. 11. Incentives: *Cyr.* 1. 6. 20, *Oec.* 14. 3 ff., cf. *Mem.* 3. 4. 8. Magnanimity: *Anab.* 1. 4. 8–9. Remission: Her. 9. 79 ff.

[223] Diog. Laert. 5. 45.

Punishment (timōria). Later still we have Plutarch's *On the Late Vengeance of the Deity*, and some remarks in Dio Cassius.[224] But in general there was a certain lack of awareness of punishment as specific problem: the 'injury for injury' pattern was simply taken for granted; the very universality of the pattern in peace and war, internal relations and foreign, discouraged recognition of penology as an issue. A legal system with the origins described could not but discourage reflection on the topic: the excited atmosphere of the courts, and the need of pleaders to win with whatever arguments, militated against principled debate. Further, the absence of a professional judiciary which might have begun to reflect on sentencing policy must also have inhibited the development of penology. Nor was there in Athens, so far as we know, a clerk of the court to remember precedents and guide decisions on the relative severity of punishments.[225] The very direct and personal nature of the system also retarded the emergence of the idea of punishment as reform, in the sense not of mere deterrence but of character-improvement: that can emerge only when angry or triumphant plaintiffs demanding vengeance can be kept at arm's length by some disinterested authority. No man's character will be reformed if he knows his opponent is gloating over his discomfiture. And since the Athenians had no probation service, and precious little by way of prisons, the range of problems of punishment they had to face only partly overlaps with ours today, when we worry about an offender's environment and motives, and about probation, parole, the relative merits of prison and fines, and so on.

Yet clearly many things that worry us worried them too. What, for instance, is a valid excuse? What are valid mitigations? What may be urged as an aggravating circumstance? When should pity be shown? What ratio should there be between the seriousness of a crime and the severity of its punishment? What attention should one pay to the social origins of crime? Should the social status of the offender affect his penalty? How should one cope with recidivism? Should one temper a punishment in the hope of reform? These and other issues (some now largely dead, such as the justice of inflicting suffering on innocent third parties, usually the offender's family), were fought over in the sort of judicial context I have sketched: and the key to understanding a good many of the controversies is the realization that an informal and personal mode of punishment is in tension with a formal and ostensibly impersonal one.

Yet these controversies, though they were important in practical terms to particular prosecutors and particular defendants, and for the development of the Athenian legal system, are all essentially peripheral.

---

[224] Dio Cassius 55. 14 ff.   [225] On 'rememberers' at Gortyn, see p. 95 n. 27 below.

For however much room there was for dispute about the purposes or efficacy of punishment, or its justification, or the validity of excuses or whatever, the institution itself of punishment was never questioned, so desirable and natural did it seem. I know of no passage in which an orator mentions the possibility of resorting to some measure other than punishment, i.e. suffering; and, as we saw, the possibility that leniency or forgiveness could affect a criminal for the better is commonly treated as something so utterly risible as to be hardly worth consideration.[226] The idea that punishment might be quite misguided in principle, or socially vicious, or ineffective, or that it might be better to try to break out of the cycle of injury and counter-injury, and deal with criminals in some non-penal manner, is wholly foreign, I think, to Greek *forensic* thought. Yet these ideas did exist; there was radical criticism both of punishment as an institution and of the fundamental assumptions that controlled its infliction—not all of it direct criticism, and not all of it systematic and coherent, but it was there; and it cut far deeper than anything one can find in the orators. It existed in the thought of certain intellectuals.

(a) Gorgias[227]

The orators regarded responsibility, *aitia*, as something that could be measured on a sliding scale: an offender could be fully responsible for this action, and therefore fully punishable, or, in virtue of various excuses such as ignorance and constraints, responsible only in part, or indeed not at all. Gorgias, in his *Encomium of Helen*,[228] goes much further: he argues that Helen, and by implication anyone else, is not responsible at all for at least some of their actions, on the grounds that they commit them in a state of having been overcome by various forces stronger than themselves, such as persuasion or love. His argument depends on marrying two modes of psychological analysis:

1. The *combative* analysis of decision-making originating in Homer (which is obviously modelled on the combative nature of Homeric society), whereby a decision depends on a confrontation between the person and his emotion or mental organ, typically his *thumos* (spirit); usually the person 'wins', in the sense that calculation overcomes impulse; but the essential principle is that the stronger of the two forces prevails, and dictates resultant action.[229]

2. The later view of the *psychē*, 'soul', as the all-purpose locus of emotions, reflections, desires, and decisions.[230] By treating the soul as essentially weak, and helplessly and automatically subject to the

---

[226] See pp. 121–2 above.   [227] I draw here on the early pages of my 1986 article.
[228] B11 DK.   [229] e.g. IX. 255, 496, XVIII. 113, XIX. 66, xi. 105.
[230] Guthrie (1962–81) III. 467 ff., Ant. *Tetr.* 3a. 7.

influence of various forces,[231] Gorgias is able to argue that Helen, whatever her will may be, is not responsible for her actions and that it would be unjust to blame her.[232]

This extreme version of certain types of excuses offered in the courts poses in an acute form the problem of the relationship between responsibility and punishment; for if a person's actions are merely the automatic 'function' of the state of his soul and the pressures bearing on it, in what sense can it ever be just to *punish* him for them?[233] On the face of it, Gorgias' argument, unless refuted, would bring the work of the courts to a stop. A prosecutor could however argue for punishment, not indeed on grounds of desert, but simply as in itself a force or pressure, which if powerful enough will determine the future decisions of the criminal for the better, and which would therefore be justified in utilitarian terms. Gorgias does not explore the issue; but his *Encomium* has some similarity with Socrates' position 'no one does wrong willingly',[234] and in principle has the same implications for anyone seeking to justify punishment.[235]

(b) Antiphon

The papyrus fragments of *On Truth* have a good many radical things to say about punishment, but interpretation is difficult and controversial. I have given a complete translation and a detailed exposition elsewhere;[236] here it must suffice to state my conclusions and invite the reader to consult Antiphon's difficult text (it is only about three pages).

Antiphon draws a sharp distinction between *phusis* (nature) and *nomos* (law), and is strongly concerned to decry the latter. His criticism centres on a lack of parallelism between on the one hand the painful consequences, 'punishment', inflicted on us by nature when we violate

---

[231] *EH* 6, 8, 11–13, 15–17, 19.   [232] e.g. *EH* 2, 20.

[233] As Adkins (1970) 122 says, his analysis would 'serve to acquit anyone of anything.' In the last words of the *Encomium* Gorgias describes it as a *paignion*, a *jeu d'esprit*. i.e. (presumably) a piece of sophistical showing-off. But that hardly indicates it is not to be taken seriously: it derives its force, after all, not only from the apparent unanswerability, on a 'knock-you-down' level, of its arguments, but also from the conflict between the conclusions and the practical necessity to praise and blame both in ordinary life and in the courts. Gorgias could hardly have been unaware of the implications.

[234] See Calogero (1957). Guthrie (1962–81) III. 271 n. 1 is too dismissive of the likenesses. The essential similarity is that in both cases a person is *prevented* from carrying out his presumed will by forces overmastering the soul—persuasion etc. in the view of Gorgias, ignorance of moral values in the view of Socrates.

[235] See pp. 142 ff. below. At *EH* 7 he says it is Helen's abductor that deserves punishment, *zēmia*. But if the abductor has been overcome by Helen's beauty, what justifies punishing *him*? However, perhaps *zēmia* points merely to recompense. Gorgias seems content to throw up paradoxical implications without thinking his position through.

[236] B44 DK; Saunders (1977–8). Some criticism of my reconstruction may be found in D. J. Furley (1981); cf. Moulton (1972).

her—say by some attack on or abuse of the body—and on the other the literal punishments that are inflicted or should be inflicted on us by *nomos* when we violate it. The pain inflicted by nature is (1) automatic and inevitable; (2) useful: it teaches us to avoid the harmful, by (as we know) giving us warning of it; (3) confined to the 'offender'. But legal 'pains', i.e. punishment, are obviously (1) *not* automatic and ineluctable (rogues escape often enough); (2) *not* particularly efficient in teaching the offender not to offend again; (3) *not* confined to the offender, being inflicted at the ironic and unacceptable cost of setting up in society patterns of aggression between punisher and culprit, and between the culprit and those who witnessed against him; for their witnessing against him is an *unjust* act, as they themselves have not been wronged by him. In brief, Antiphon attacks punishments not as painful and therefore unnatural, for violated nature is also painful, but as not natural enough: even when they are 'just', which often they are not, they cannot be guaranteed, they are inefficient, and they entail socially harmful repercussions. Antiphon's criticism of punishment as an institution thus arose within the context of his exploration of the relationship or contrast between *phusis* and *nomos*, not, it seems, from any humanitarian feeling: and it arose from the observation of a radical discontinuity between the mechanisms of adjustment in nature, and those adopted, and adopted vainly, by human society.

Gorgias and Antiphon, radical critics of punishment though they both are, nevertheless differ sharply. Gorgias by implication attacks punishment as unjust; whereas Antiphon apparently regards it as perfectly just, and concentrates his fire on the inefficiency of the manner and distribution of its infliction, in contrast with the efficiency of the 'punishments' of nature. But perhaps the greatest importance of these two thinkers is their subjection of the institution of punishment to critical examination, in a society in which it was very much taken for granted. In particular, Antiphon's opposing of natural and social mechanisms of adjustment is part of the celebrated contrast between nature and convention, and obviously owes much to observation of the inequity and inefficiency of the legal system and of the punishments imposed by the courts. Part of that inequity and inefficiency was the fact that punishments, however well deserved, were not inevitable. Contrast the view of Hesiod and others that the world simply is constructed in such a way that they were precisely that: ineluctably sent by Zeus or some other god, even if after a long interval, and possibly visited on the offender's descendants. On this view, the disjunction between nature and civilization is far from sharp—indeed, the latter can be seen as an analogue of the former.[237] Antiphon, writing at a time when the Greeks had

[237] Sol. 13, Hes. *WD* 213-47, esp. 230, cf. pp. 39-48 above.

gained experience of the fallibilities of a formal legal system, and the contrast between *nomos* and *phusis* was a commonplace that could be applied to many different topics, applied it to punishment. Precisely because he does not have the eye of faith of a Solon, who saw punishment as the inevitable correlate of sin, and never questioned its status, Antiphon comes to examine its justifications, purposes and effects. His conclusion, if my reconstruction of his position is on the right lines, is that punishment, though just, is an institution of doubtful worth; while to Gorgias, inevitable or not, it was indefensible on grounds of justice.

(c) Diodotus

In 427, after crushing the revolt of Mytilene, the Athenians decided in a fit of anger to kill not only those responsible but also all adult males, and to enslave the women and children. The next day, however, the extreme cruelty of this measure provoked a feeling of revulsion, and the matter was reopened in the Assembly.[238] Cleon spoke in favour of adhering to the original decision, Diodotus in favour of punishing only the guilty parties. I cannot go into the historical accuracy of the two speeches which Thucydides gives us: I merely assume that he did not think up the opposing arguments *de novo*, but that either they were in fact used on that occasion, or that at least Thucydides from time to time heard them deployed in some form, and used them for the purposes of composing or reconstructing the speeches.[239] In either case his account is evidence for the currency in the late fifth century of differing views on the wisdom of inflicting severe punishment.[240]

Cleon is a hard-liner, who maintains that severity is dictated by the very nature of Athenian rule: it is a tyranny imposed on unwilling subjects. He argues as follows:[241]

1. Pity is dangerous, and wins no gratitude; it (and equity) do no good to a ruling power.
2. Delay dulls anger and reduces the chances of ensuring that the penalty matches the offence.
3. The Mytileneans had 'started it': they had been well treated by Athens, and had revolted gratuitously and with premeditation; they were under no compulsion from others.

[238] Thuc. 3. 36.
[239] See Gomme (1956–81) ii. 324.
[240] Cf. Diod. Sic. 13. 19 ff., the debate in Sicily in 413 on the fate of the captured Athenians; but there are powerful reasons to doubt this source as a reliable indication of penological sentiment at the end of the 5th cent.: see Drews (1962), 385–7.
[241] Thuc. 3. 37–40.

4. They were not deterred by the example the Athenians had made of others who had revolted, but preferred to rely on force rather than justice.
5. Strict justice (which is how he regards the punishment he recommends for the Mytileneans) and expediency coincide; there is no room for 'namby-pamby' things such as equity, which must be overridden if (as he assumes) the Athenians are determined to maintain their power.
6. Swingeing punishment for wilful revolt will deter potential defectors among Athens' allies.

This is a powerful address. It appeals to strict justice and to communal self-interest, and represents pity and equity as paradoxes of weak-kneed intellectuals or as the specious pleas of sophistical and corrupt orators. *Mutatis mutandis*, it is obviously similar in tone and substance to many of the arguments advanced in the courts.

Accordingly, Diodotus devoted a good deal of effort to dispelling the implied suggestion that he is activated by corrupt motives, and to justifying an unprejudiced hearing for rational argument. He replies as follows:[242]

In agreement with Cleon: That any punishment visited on the Mytileneans must be forward-looking, and subserve the advantages of Athens, defined as the maintenance of her power.

Against Cleon: In the penalty proposed by Cleon justice militates against expediency.[243] But the most expedient policy is in fact one of *epieikeia*: 'reasonableness', 'moderation', 'understanding', 'equity'.[244] In particular:

1. Speed of decision and anger, which lead to heavy penalties, are bad counsellors.
2. Swingeing penalties are not effective as deterrents; for *errare est humanum*, because of various social and psychological pressures; indeed, the prospect of suffering extreme punishment simply serves to stiffen resistance, if it is seen that repentance will make no difference; and that would cause trouble and expense to Athens. A better policy is to *prevent* revolt, by vigilance.
3. A moderate penalty, so far from showing weakness, will ensure that the state which has revolted will survive in a condition in which it is able to pay tribute in the future. Accordingly, blame should be

---

[242] Thuc. 3. 42–8.   [243] Ibid. 47. 5.

[244] This is *in effect* what his recommendations amount to. Cleon decried pity and *epieikeia* at Thuc. 3. 40. 2, and Diodotus in referring to the point at 3. 48. 1. is careful to say that 'not too much' influence should be allowed to them. On his reasons for being wary, see below.

placed on as few persons as possible, not on entire free populations; that will secure the good-will of the *dēmos*.[245]

Clearly Diodotus is no humanitarian or idealistic dreamer, who has ethical objections to retaliation or thinks that in principle one should turn the other cheek.[246] On the contrary, as he is at pains to stress, his penology is a practical one, intended to be advantageous to Athens' interests. The crucial difference between him and Cleon is that whereas Cleon thinks that in order to secure those interests equity must be over-ridden,[247] Diodotus, though he would be prepared to override it if he were convinced that those interests demanded it,[248] believes that they are in fact best served by moderation.[249] The issue is entirely out of calculation of advantage: is it best served by strict justice or by equity?

Although Diodotus believes that individuals and states are activated by the same motives when doing wrong, he tries to persuade the assembly *not* to apply the same kind of punishing policy it might use if it were dealing with an individual offender in court: that is to say, it should forgo strict justice in the interest of political advantage over other states.[250] The implication is that *not* to forgo justice in court is perfectly reasonable. Yet it is difficult to see why, given the plain implications of the speech that individuals and states are psychologically comparable, one should not forgo justice in a court too, in order to obtain social advantage *within* a state.[251] I suspect that Diodotus, and anybody of the opinion he represents, does believe this, but that he carefully avoids making a universal claim for his policy, so as not to strain the credulity and the goodwill of the assembly. If so, it is a measure of how difficult it could be, on occasions when opinion was inflamed, for the Athenian audience to accept any penological assumptions or policies other than those they heard in the courts. Diodotus won the vote because his arguments for the forgoing of strict justice were presented in a hard-headed utilitarian way, and had the advantage of falling on the receptive ears of an assembly which felt an emotional revulsion from the extreme harshness of the penalty it had decreed the day before.[252] On that occasion Diodotus, using we know not what arguments, had lost the vote. Now, however, he wins because he provides his audience with good practical reasons for acting on their feelings.

[245] Cf. Aesch. 2. 117 for a policy of punishing only those responsible, not whole cities, and Plut. *Sol.* 21. 1 *fin.*

[246] At Thuc. 3. 47. 5. he does say that Athens should be prepared to be wronged—but in the interests of her rule. *Pace* Macleod (1978) 77, I see nothing 'hollow' in this, merely a wry recognition that sometimes one has to 'roll with the punch', in the interests of long-term advantage.

[247] Thuc 3. 40. 2.

[248] Ibid. 44. 2, speaking however not of *epieikeia eo nomine*, but *sungnōmē*, 'pardon', 'indulgence'.

[249] Cf. Thuc. 4. 19.

[250] Thuc. 3. 44. 4, 45. 6–7, 47. 5.

[251] Cf. Dem. 6. 37.

[252] Thuc. 3. 36. 4, 49. 4.

What exactly is Diodotus' position, and how frank is he? It is tempting to suppose that he represents a body of opinion that was outraged by the penalty Cleon favoured, on grounds of equity, but that he felt the only way of selling this policy to the assembly was to present it as identical with advantage: by a sort of clever *praeteritio*, he says in effect, 'I do not urge equity on you for its own sake;[253] but equity (which he nevertheless describes at length) is in fact in your own best interest'— and the description then in effect makes its appeal for equity on two levels, both for its own sake and as constituting advantage.[254] If this hypothesis is correct, then Diodotus is perhaps a kind of liberal penologist, anxious on moral grounds to uphold that variety of justice that is represented by equity, whether advantageous or not, but who skilfully disguises himself as a hard-headed pragmatist.[255] On the other hand he may, as I suspect, mean exactly and only what he says: that equity pays. In that case, he is simply a shrewd pragmatist who sees that extreme punishments are counterproductive, and who is prepared to exploit arguments from equity to prevent them. I suppose that would make him rather less 'liberal' than if he were actuated by moral considerations alone. But I see no way of divining what he really thought: since he limits himself to the claim that equity is the most advantageous policy, he has no need to argue the larger and more risky thesis, that equity should prevail irrespective of advantage.

At any rate, J. H. Finley's description of Diodotus' ideas as 'conspicuously enlightened',[256] that is if 'enlightened' implies 'untypical', seems exaggerated: the whole episode shows that there was a considerable body of opinion in Athens prepared to support him, on this occasion at least, on grounds either of equity or simple human fellow-feeling, and/or of plain expediency.[257] *Pace* Moulton,[258] he does not call punishment as an institution into question on the ground that it cannot (by deterrence) prevent offences; on the contrary, he takes punishment for granted,[259] and argues merely that when a man is set on something, strong penalties are no deterrent.[260] That is a valuable observation, but does not amount to a claim that no punishments deter anyone. Nor does he question punishment as retributive. His 'enlightenment' seems to me to reside in two points only: (1) his desire to restrict blame to as few per-

---

[253] See his careful assurance, 3. 48. 1; the point of πλέον is that pity and equity are being allowed to operate no 'more' than is consistent with expediency.

[254] Cf. Gomme (1956–81) ii. 324 and Andrewes (1962) 72: there must have been expressions of simple moral revulsion (see 3. 36. 4. and 49. 4), but no one voices them in Thucydides.

[255] At 3. 43. 1–3. Diodotus recognizes the need for deviousness; cf. Macleod (1978) 73–4. (It is hard to fathom the *political* sympathies that underlie his argument: was he concerned to save the skins of the Mytilenean oligarchs in particular?)

[256] J. H. Finley (1942) 175.

[257] Cf. Gomme's notes on 3. 41 and 3. 49. 4.

[258] Moulton (1972) 365.

[259] See 3. 43. 5.

[260] Thuc. 3. 45. 7.

sons as possible—i.e. to prevent punishments which are extreme in distribution,[261] as well as punishments which are extreme in kind; (2) his awareness of the utility of measures of prevention.

Diodotus' speech offers, then, some evidence for late fifth century reflection on penal history and policy, and the psychology of offenders, in a spirit of hard-headed moderation. He does not mount an attack on punishment as such. His position is rather the traditional instinctive revulsion from extreme measures, a revulsion based on prudent calculation and given some intellectual underpinning in the shape of general reflection on human nature and considerations of equity. Hence I doubt whether Moulton's attempt to compare Diodotus' line on punishment with the much more radical and intellectual view of Antiphon can take us very far,[262] for it depends on the view that both are hostile to punishment in principle. As I have argued, Antiphon believes in punishments, but objects to their maldistribution and ineffectiveness (as well as to certain unfortunate by-products of the legal system); Diodotus merely decries extreme penalties, not all penalties. No doubt they would agree that punishments are badly distributed; but we should all agree to that, and as a basis of comparison it is quite general. Antiphon's criticism is that of a philosopher, Diodotus' that of a practical man. However, taken together, they amount to evidence for principled unease about punishment as administered in the fifth century.

(d) Isocrates

Diodotus' views are echoed in the following century by Isocrates. In his letter to Alexander in 342 BC he remarks with approval that Alexander is engaging in studies that will enable him to be a good ruler;[263] in particular, Alexander will be able, thanks to his training in rhetoric, to honour and punish/chastise (*kolazein*) properly. Taken by itself, this is not strong evidence for the study of penology in Isocrates' school; but at least it betrays some awareness of it as a topic or as an area of policy. I believe Isocrates did think systematically about punishment, at least a little, especially when writing the *Areopagiticus*, which for a few pages[264] is almost a treatise on penology and sociology. Here are the salient points he makes in his corpus as a whole:

1. In penal policy, mildness is all. Penalties should be less than the offence, and kept as low as possible;[265] but indulgence should not be easy to win.[266]

---

[261] There are of course implications here, not spelled out, for the punishment of third parties.
[262] Moulton (1972) 360 ff.   [263] *Letter* 5. 4 (if genuine).   [264] Isoc. 7. 39 ff.
[265] Isoc. 2. 23–4, 3. 32; 4. 101–2; cf. 5. 116–17, 9. 49. 7. 67 approves of punishing only those *chiefly* responsible for the oligarchic revolution in 403. Cf. Is. fr. 37.   [266] Isoc. 7. 47.

2. Crime has various origins, not only genetic, but economic and social. Prevention is emphatically better than cure, and prevention must be achieved by sound economic and social policy, notably by the elimination of poverty, by moral education, and by ensuring that young men have plenty to keep them busy, so that they do not turn to crime through sheer boredom.[267]

3. Certainty and speed of detection and punishment are superb preventives.[268]

It is of course difficult to assess the status of these recommendations. Isocrates frequently seems to float in a sort of private stratosphere several miles above real life, and the *Areopagiticus* is after all an idealization of what the Areopagus was or could become. And in other places he is perfectly capable of making remarks about punishment that sound quite conventional. Like Antiphon and Protagoras, he does not disapprove of punishment as such; but his view of it is askew to popular views, and is all of a piece with his general advocacy of decent, moderate, and civilized standards of conduct.

(e) Drama and other literature

It is quite possible that Isocrates' ideals in the matter of punishment sprang entirely from his own musings about life; yet certain trains of thought in the literature of the preceding century seem to me to suggest that these ideals were shared by at least some of the Athenian public, or were at any rate familiar to it. Greek drama, for instance, is essentiallly concerned with conflict, with aggression and counter-aggression, and at many points in the plays we find reflections and arguments which may broadly be termed penological. In Euripides' *Supplices*, for instance, Theseus seems to embody all that is restrained and civilized in penology: to punish, but not in excess; to take reasonable recompense, but then to stay the hand;[269] and to refrain from anger when wronged.[270] Excessive retaliation is a form of *hubris*, says the chorus.[271] Athena, by contrast, at the end of the play, is a penological primitive, who insists on further and unnecessary suffering being inflicted on Thebes by Argos.[272] As we have seen, the notion of proper limit in punishing can be traced right back into Homer: it is a lesson that Achilles learned the hard way. It is also implicit in the expression *axia dikē* in the orators: the *dikē* should be

---

[267] Isoc. 7. 42 ff., 55, 83, 12. 27, 15. 236. Cf. Arist. *Pol.* 1267[a]2 ff. on poverty as a cause of crime, and *Rhet.* 1372[b]25. On prevention, cf. Hyp. fr. 8.

[268] Isoc. 7. 47, 11. 25; cf. 18. 3. On belief in certainty of detection, cf. Archytas B3 DK *fin.*

[269] Eur. *Supp.* 528 ff., 724-5.   [270] Ibid. 555-7.

[271] Ibid. 511-12.   [272] Ibid. 1213 ff.; cf. Lys. 2. 10.

axia, but not more than *axia*.[273] It is this kind of traditional thought that lies behind the high-minded ideals of Isocrates.

(*f*) *Protagoras*

Clear evidence of penological reflection is to be found in some views put into Protagoras' mouth by Plato, which there seems no reason to suppose were not those of the great 'sophist' himself. They occur in the long speech he makes in his attempt to demonstrate that virtue/excellence (*aretē*) is teachable.[274] He argues that punishment is relevant to those qualities over which a man has control (unlike, say, congenital physical deformity):[275] it is an incentive to better conduct in the future, and hence a tool in the teaching of virtue, as well as a form of social hygiene.[276] The crucial passage runs:[277]

For consider, if you will, Socrates, the influence of chastisement upon those who commit injustice (*adikein*), and the institution itself will show you that men regard excellence as something which can be acquired. For no one chastises anyone because of the fact that he has committed an injustice and with *that* in mind, unless he is inflicting unreasoned punishment as one might upon a brute beast. No, the man who tries to inflict reasoned chastisement does so not because of the past injustice—a deed once committed cannot be undone—but for the sake of the future: to deter him, or another who sees him chastised, from committing a further injustice. And since he has this belief, it follows that he believes that excellence can be inculcated; at any rate, in inflicting chastisement his purpose is deterrence. This, then, is the opinion of all those who impose punishment, whether on their own or on the city's account; punishment and chastisement are in fact imposed by all men, and foremost among them by the Athenians, your fellow-citizens, upon those they believe guilty of injustice. It follows, therefore, on this argument, that the Athenians are also among those who believe that excellence is something which can be inculcated and taught.[278]

Up to a point, this is merely conventional wisdom. As we have seen,[279] the orators are full of statements that punishment, suffering, will make a man 'better'. By this, however they mean no more than brute deterrence; they do not mean that a criminal's moral convictions will be affected, only that he will refrain from crime through fear of the consequences. Does Protagoras mean any more? Admittedly he makes free with words like *nouthetēsis* ('admonition'), which need not imply the infliction of

---

[273] Cf. pp. 105–6 above, and Aristotle on *epieikeia*, equity, *Rhet.* 1374^{b}2 ff.

[274] *Prot.* 320c–328d.   [275] Ibid. 323c–e.   [276] Ibid. 325d5, 325ab.

[277] Ibid. 324a–c. The following account of Protagoras' views on punishment draws on my 1981*b* article.

[278] Trans. B. A. F. Hubbard and E. S. Karnofsky, *Plato's* Protagoras: *A Socratic Commentary* (London 1982), with some alterations, chiefly to render *kolazein* as 'to chastise' and *timoreisthai* as 'to punish' consistently throughout.   [279] See p. 120 above.

suffering; but words such as *kolazein* ('chastise') and *timōreisthai* ('punish'), which he uses indifferently, certainly do; and he says outright that punishment is for the sake of prevention or deterrence. Thus far, his views are utterly ordinary: they could have been endorsed by any man in the Athenian street.

But embedded in these unexciting observations is a remarkable claim that punishment ought not to be inflicted with an eye to the past. Whereas Protagoras states his main thesis, that punishment is inflicted for the sake of the future, in a mere three lines, he elaborates on the dismissal of the past at some little length;[280] and the wording of the passage strongly implies that the ordinary man is in fact committed to the 'rational' policy of ignoring the past.[281] The implication seems calculated to flatter Protagoras' bearers into regarding themselves as rational punishers; but it is quite false. For the ordinary man clearly *did* believe that punishment should be inflicted with a view to the past: at any rate, he certainly approved of recompense and satisfaction. Moreover, the dismissal of the past is simply unnecessary to Protagoras' thesis: he could have admitted its relevance, and still claimed the relevance of the future; and his position would have perhaps been stronger for the omission of the implausible insinuation that the 'opinion' of the ordinary man is the same as the 'belief' of the rational punisher.

Why does Plato represent Protagoras as going to such lengths? Perhaps the reason is merely tactical: Protagoras may have felt, and Plato knew he felt, that to admit the relevance of the past weakened the relevance of the future; therefore deny the former, and the latter is left holding the field. That is to say, in his extreme anxiety to stress the future perhaps Protagoras merely stumbled into an unnecessary dismissal of the past. But however arrived at, by accident or by ratiocination, his thesis is amazing; for to cut the connection between a punishment and the past is in effect to deny that an offence can *justify* a punishment. He seems to claim that if punishment were not effective in improving the offender, and had no other purpose either, there would be no justification for inflicting it at all. At one blow he severs the link between offence and punishment, injury and counter-injury, tit-for-tat, with the inevitable personal animosities, that was so deeply ingrained in Greek thought, and indeed still is in ours.

What were the antecedents of Protagoras' belief? Probably the

---

[280] It occupies nearly five lines, and expresses the disregard for the past twice (in expressions that seem to mean more or less the same thing, 'because of' and 'with that in mind'); it parades a double insistence that policy should be rational, a vivid detail about a wild beast, and the adage 'what's done can't be undone'. References for the adage are given in my (1981*b*) article, 140 n.27.

[281] See my 1981*b* article, 131, for an examination of the Greek.

frequent piecemeal and *ad hoc* decisions, in Greek law and in other contexts, to relax or to tighten the general principle that an offender should suffer in return for the suffering he inflicted; for as we have seen, all sorts of reasons can be found for departing from the principle of strict reciprocation, in the interests sometimes of equity, but sometimes for forward-looking considerations of expediency. Such tendencies needed only to be crystallized by induction into a general doctrine that the purpose of punishment is to look to the future.

Yet is the notion of a non-backward-looking punishment coherent? A punishment must be *for* something; one cannot punish unless there has been an offence; it is an offence that licences the punishment. In some sense a punishment must always look to the past. Presumably Protagoras would reply: 'Quite so; but the connection between crime and punishment need not be the infliction of suffering in return for suffering inflicted. When I see an offence committed, I have evidence of a lack of some social virtue; the way I cure that is to inflict suffering, in the expectation of reforming the offender's conduct; that is what I call 'rational' punishment: it is non-retributive, non-vengeful, and utilitarian. However,'—he would hasten to add—'I do not deny that the victim deserves his recompense, and in that sense I do look to the past; but that is not punishment, only the making-good of damage. Nor do I deny that the seriousness of the offence *may* be a guide to the scale of the offender's social vice, and so *may* indicate the severity of suffering he needs by way of cure. What I do deny is that a man's infliction of damage or suffering is in itself a reason for inflicting suffering on him; if we are to do that, we must have some utilitarian, forward-looking justification. And that justification lies in the effectiveness of pain as a means of influencing conduct, and of social control.'

Protagoras believes, conventionally enough, that punishment does indeed deter, and is an efficient tool of education. He does not face the fact that to judge by results it is a very imperfect tool;[282] nor does he pay attention to the possibility that it may be more efficient to affect a criminal's moral beliefs, not merely his conduct; and therefore he does not envisage that the methods by which moral beliefs may be affected—argument, persuasion, cajoling, or indeed any other measure that *does not consist of the infliction of suffering*—might be used. The nearest he gets to this is in his account of the use of words like *didaskō* (teach) and *nouthetēsis* (admonition),[283] which may mean anything and may certainly imply

---

[282] 'Men do not become penitent and learn to abhor themselves by having their backs cut open with the lash; rather they learn to abhor the lash.' (George Eliot, *Felix Holt*, ch. 42)

[283] It is on this that J. H. Finley (1972, 176) relies when he says, 'We know from Plato's *Protagoras* (324a–c) that the retributive theory of punishment was being given up in these years in favor of the view that offenses can be checked only by diminishing their causes.' But there is nothing about

something not wholly pleasant.[284] But in fact he makes it clear that the
disobedient become better by chastisement, and that to be chastised, to
be taught, and to become better are the same process.[285] In spite of the
radicalism of his view about the relevance of the past, he seems to take
punishment as suffering for granted, and merely seeks to justify it on
utilitarian grounds. This latter point is an important adumbration of the
position adopted by Plato himself.

diminishment of causes in this passage; that is a thought which belongs to Diodotus and Isocrates.
Protagoras speaks of admonition after an offence committed *after* education has failed. As for the
'giving up' of the retributive theory, Finley has been conned by Protagoras' quite false implication
that the ordinary man believed the past should be ignored.

[284] Cf. Isoc. 11. 3, 12. 271.
[285] *Prot.* 325a.

II

PLATO'S PENOLOGY AND PENAL CODE

5

PLATO'S MEDICAL PENOLOGY

It is a good working principle that when the information Plato gives us about a political or social or legal institution in the *Laws* is sparse, it is a sign that he is prepared to accept the main features of its contemporary counterpart; but that when the argument and detail are abundant, he wishes to make alterations on a large scale. On this criterion, it is clear that penology is of the highest importance to Plato, and that the changes he wishes to make in contemporary assumptions and practice are radical and extensive. For he devotes to his discussion of his theory of punishment over seven Stephanus pages of most careful argumentation; and he embeds it firmly in the context of his laws governing some of the most serious crimes in the calendar.[1]

Passage 1

This passage, the longest of all, runs from 857a2 to 864c9. It is rather ploddingly written; presumably the Athenian Stranger wishes to make quite sure that the none-too-bright Cleinias and Megillus fully understand and accept the new penology at which they arrive in the final paragraphs. I have already argued in print my interpretation of the sequence as a whole, and of many of its more important details.[2]

Step 1: 857a2–b8. Should all thefts attract the same penalty? We have just learned, in the few lines immediately preceding, that in certain procedural and other respects a 'single' law is to apply to treason, sacrilege (i.e. robbery from temples), and subversion. The Stranger now

---

[1] The sequence of topics in book 9 is: sacrilege, procedure in capital cases, subversion, treason, *penology* (introduced by some remarks about theft), homicide, wounding, assault.

[2] Saunders (1968), (1970) 361, 367–9. On the main issues, at any rate, Schöpsdau's (1984) long and commendably thorough analysis of the whole passage is fairly close to my own. Ripostes on detail would not be appropriate here. The two major points on which I would disagree are: (i) the irrelevance which he alleges of the seriousness of the offence to the psychic state of the offender (109; see also pp. 179, 191–5 below); (ii) his denial of the status of *adikia* to *agnoia*, the third 'cause' of crime at 863cd (123 ff.; so too Roberts (1987), though on different grounds; see appendix to my discussion of passage 1, steps 7 and 8, below).

states that a 'single' law will apply to all robbers without exception: repayment of twice the value stolen, or imprisonment until either repayment or success in persuading the victim (or the state, when the theft is from public sources) to waive the penalty. Cleinias protests that such a law fails to discriminate between the various categories of theft, which call for *differing* punishments.[3]

Comment. The Athenian Stranger is clearly trailing his coat, for the law of theft, both in Athens and in Magnesia, does contain various distinctions, and his proposal is a bold simplification.[4] It amounts to an invitation to disregard motives and circumstances, to focus on the fact that what all thieves have in common is theft, and to conclude that they thus deserve the same punishment.[5]

Step 2: 857b9–859c5. Penology is essential to a penal code. The Stranger acknowledges that Cleinias' point is a good one: it is yet another indication that the business of establishing a legal code has never been properly thought out. He then commends their earlier[6] parallel between those for whom legal codes are currently produced, and the patients of doctors who have picked up the skill empirically: for both categories of 'client' are bullied and threatened rather than enlightened and persuaded. But the good doctor is something of a philosopher: he discusses with his patient the source of the disease, and physiology in general. Anyone who legislates 'as we are doing now' is *educating* the citizens. Happily, we are in no hurry to legislate: we may do so at leisure, after mature reflection on the best laws that seem practical. Hence we have time to compile legal advice, before choosing actual laws; and such advice, compiled by a legislator, should be of high quality, and written in non-threatening terms; it deserves more attention than the advice on the conduct of life given by poets.

Comment. The passage is over-long for its essential point, which is simply that just as efficient medicine depends on some understanding of physiology, so efficient law-giving depends on some understanding of penology. Further, such a grasp of theory is necessary not only to the doctor and legislator, but to patient and citizen: both need education. The implications are important. Whatever Plato's penology will in the next few pages turn out to be, it is not to be commended to the intellect of Magnesia's legislators only, or even to that of senior and sapient powers in the land; it is to be a single publicly understood and publicly

---

[3] Contrast Lyc. *Leoc.* 65–6.
[4] See more fully under 'theft' below: step 1 is not serious penology.
[5] Repayment of twice the amount stolen: hence the penalty *would* vary, automatically (so at 857b4–5 Cleinias is perhaps muddled).
[6] 719e ff.

adopted policy, built into the penal code and applied by every citizen in his capacity as a juror.[7]

The contrast with the wealth of conflicting penological arguments provided by the orators in the Athenian courts is striking. True, in the courts there was a broad area of rough agreement, both explicit and implicit, on the nature and purpose of punishment; but by no stretch of imagination could it be called a unitary and uniform policy, either in conception or in application.[8] The extraordinary length and elaboration of step 2, therefore, prepares Cleinias not simply for a penology which will be different from the rough orthodoxy of the courts, but for the principle of having a single consistent penological policy at all. To persuade someone that your solution to a problem may be better than his may be difficult, but at least there is common recognition that a problem exists; to persuade someone who has not realized there is a problem to be solved is more ticklish. Nevertheless that is the position to which, gingerly, Cleinias has been brought by the end of step 2: in effect he agrees that such questions as 'should all thieves attract the same penalty?' need to be raised and answered as a preliminary to substantive law-giving. Until that is done, legislation is incomplete.[9]

Step 3: 859c–860c3. Justice and fineness. The Stranger now begins to prepare the ground for penology by complaining about inconsistencies in ordinary language. To deny the description 'fine' *(kalon)* to someone with 'a most just disposition', simply on the grounds that his *body* is 'shaming' *(aischron,* presumably because it is ugly or misshapen) would be wrong.[10] Now men *do* many things *(poiēmata,* 'actions'), and many things are done *to* them *(pathēmata,* 'experiences', 'sufferings'). To deny the description 'fine' *(kalon),* to a just *pathēma,* simply on the grounds that it is 'shaming' *(aischron)* would be equally wrong. So if a *pathēma* which is a punishment is just, it must be fine; its shamefulness (presumably whipping *vel sim.)* affects its goodness as little as the shamefulness of a misshapen body affects the fineness of man with a just disposition. The terms 'just' and 'fine' must not be 'torn apart'.[11]

Comment. The purpose of this step seems to be to prevent Kleinias and Megillus from thinking that the shamefulness of a just punishment is a bar to its infliction; for as readers of the *Gorgias* are already aware, a just punishment is 'fine' in the sense of being a benefit to the punished person. Now this paradox will indeed prove fundamental to the

---

[7] 861c3–6.
[8] Cf. Plato's attacks on orators for aiming to win regardless of the justice of their case, 937d ff.
[9] 859bc, cf. 861c2, d1.
[10] *Kalon* is ambiguous: 'handsome' (physically), 'splendid' or 'good' in any context, including assessment of moral character. So too *aischron,* 'ugly', 'shameful', 'dishonourable'.
[11] 860c1–2.

penology of the *Laws* also; but at this stage the Stranger refrains from stating it explicitly. Instead, he insists only that it is 'discordant' to do as 'the many' do, namely to divorce 'just' and 'fine'. That is to say, *if* a thing is just, *then* it is 'fine'. If it is non-fine (e.g. 'shameful'), it must be in some sense that does not lead to 'discord'; the fineness and the non-fineness must be related to different aspects of it, which must not be brought into collision.

Step 4: 860c4–861d9. The Socratic paradox as an obstacle to legislation. The Stranger now poses a puzzle. He maintains, as a point of principle,[12] that all 'bad' or 'wicked' men (*kakoi*) are in that state 'unwillingly' or 'involuntarily' (*akontes*). Yet he has to recognize that many wicked acts[13] are performed voluntarily, which seems to conflict with the principle. If we are to legislate, we need to achieve some consistency of language. We must be prepared to say whether we adopt a distinction between voluntary and involuntary offences, imposing heavier penalties on the former than on the latter, or whether we impose the same penalty on all, on the assumption that voluntary offences simply do not exist, so that there is only one category of offences to deal with. But all legislators adopt such a distinction, and it behoves us to maintain it, but in a different form, so that everyone will be able to judge the propriety of any given punishment imposed on either category of offence. If then the proposition that all crimes are involuntary is not to be abandoned, what new factor permits a legitimate distinction between the two categories?

Comment. This section plays off the 'Socratic' paradox that 'no one does wrong willingly'[14] against the necessary assumption of a penal code, that voluntary crimes exist; for if no crimes are voluntary, no crimes can be punished, except on a very strict doctrine of absolute liability, which the Stranger does not even contemplate. Although all offences are in the Socratic sense involuntary, evidently at least some of them may be punished on the ground that they are nevertheless voluntary in some relevant sense.

Step 5: 861e1–862b6. The new distinction. By a flick of the wrist, the Stranger now solves the problem by importing a new distinction, between injuries (*blabai*) and injustices (*adikiai* or *adikēmata*). Injuries can be inflicted voluntarily or involuntarily; but those that are committed involuntarily, i.e. without an *unjust intent* to injure, are not to be

---

[12] Cf. 731c, 734b.

[13] He now in effect discusses *poiēmata*, dropped in step 3 in favour of a discussion of *pathēmata*.

[14] The paradox appears in the form 'no one is willingly bad' (*kakos*), which then becomes immediately (860d5) 'no one is willingly unjust' (*adikos*, presumably because of the legal context: *adikein*, 'do injustice', is standard terminology in the courts for 'be guilty').

described as 'involuntary injustices', since they are not injustices at all. For an injustice springs from an unjust character, which is never acquired voluntarily. Conversely a benefit, if improper in the sense of being conferred by an unjust man, *is* an 'injustice'. The justice or injustice of an act, whether it be a benefit or an injury, depends entirely on the state of mind of the agent. Damage and injustice are the two fundamental factors to which the legislator must pay attention.

Comment. The 'Socratic' paradox that no one does wrong willingly (*oudeis hekōn hamartanei*), if indeed Socrates maintained it, depends on the two assumptions, here unstated,[15] (*a*) that doing wrong is less advantageous to the agent than doing right, (*b*) that the state of mind which leads to wrong action cannot, therefore, have been chosen by him. Any wrong act he does commit is therefore involuntary, in that it springs from a state of mind that he has acquired against his will, i.e. his 'real' will as it would have been if he had *known* that that mental state was not in his interests. On the other hand, the actual injury he commits may be voluntary, in the sense that, blinkered as he was by lack of moral knowledge, he wished to do it; or it may be involuntary, because of accident or some similar cause. In brief, an act which is voluntary as damage is involuntary as an expression of involuntary psychic *adikia*: one and the same act attracts contradictory descriptions.

It is now possible to discern what steps 3, 4, and 5 have in common. All are concerned to show how to avoid drawing false inferences from the simple fact that the same thing may attract contradictory predications. The avoidance is what the Stranger means when he refers to the 'harmony' or 'concord' of language.[16]

Step 3. (*a*) A man with a 'most just' disposition is (therefore) 'fine'; but (*b*) is also *not* fine, in respect of his 'shameful' body. (*a*) and (*b*) are not inconsistent: the contradictory adjectives refer to different aspects of him. Both statements are legitimate.

Step 4. (*a*) An unjust man performs bad actions voluntarily (in the ordinary sense); but (*b*) he performs them *not* voluntarily (in the Socratic sense). Here too (*a*) and (*b*) are both legitimate: they refer to different aspects of his actions.

Step 5. (*a*) An injury caused by an unjust man is an injustice; but (*b*) when it is caused by a just man it is *not* an injustice. (*a*) and (*b*) are again both legitimate, since they refer to different aspects or causes of the injury's commission: the unjust psychic state in (*a*), the just state in (*b*).

---

[15] Cf. 660d–663d.

[16] 860c2, 'discordant' tearing apart of 'justice' and 'goodness', picked up immediately in the opening question of step 4 at 860c4–5, about the possible 'concordance' or 'consistency' of their views 'about these very same matters'. Cf. 861a10.

In all these cases, the mistake would be to suppose that (*a*) and (*b*) cannot be true simultaneously. Essentially the same fallacy of predication is set up and resolved three times, to make three penological points.[17] The augmentation is both elementary and repetitive, appropriate to Cleinias and Megillus, plain men both.

Step 6: 862b6–863a2. The purpose of punishment. The legislator has to repair the damage caused by an offence, by seeing that recompense is made in some appropriate form; and he must attempt to reconcile offender and victim.

The Stranger now describes[18] his policy for dealing with *adikia*, the criminal's state of mind. This passage is so important that full quotation is called for.

ATHENIAN: Now to deal with unjust injuries (and gains too, as when one man's unjust act results in a gain for someone). The cases that are curable (*iata*) we must cure (*iasthai*), on the assumption that the soul has been infected by diseases (*nosoi*). We must, however, state what general policy we pursue in our cure (*iasis*) for injustice.

CLEINIAS: What is this policy?

ATHENIAN: This: when anyone commits an act of injustice, serious or trivial, the law will combine instruction (*didaskein*) and constraint (*anankazein*) so that in the future either he will never again dare to commit such a crime voluntarily, or he will do it a very great deal less often; and in addition, he will pay compensation for the damage he has done. This is something we can achieve only by laws of the highest quality. We may take action, or use speech; we may grant pleasures, or cause pain; we may confer honour, we may inflict disgrace; we can impose fines, or even give gifts. We may use absolutely *any* means to make him hate injustice and embrace true justice—or at any rate not hate it. But suppose the law-giver finds a man who's beyond cure (*aniatos*)—what legal penalty will he provide for this case? He will recognize that the best thing for all such people is to cease to live—best even for themselves. By passing on they will help others, too: first, they will constitute a warning (*paradeigma*) against injustice, and secondly they will leave the state free of scoundrels. That is why the lawgiver should prescribe death in such cases, by way of punishment (*kolastēs*, 'punisher') for their crimes—but in no other case whatever.

Comment This passage has a fair claim to be the most radical penological manifesto ever written. Apart from the implicit assumption that punishments look to the past in the sense that they can hardly be inflicted except *for* crimes already committed, the relevance of the past is reduced to a single point: the restoring of the damage.[19] The main

---

[17] Cf. *Euth.* 293a ff.   [18] 862c6 ff.
[19] Described in some detail in 862b6–c3; see also 843cd for the distinction between restoration of damage and psychic cure.

emphasis is forward-looking and utilitarian. The criminal must be made a better man, not simply in his conduct but in his character: he must be brought to hate injustice and embrace justice (or, as the Stranger says, modifying his optimism, not to hate it). No restriction is placed on the measures which may be used: they include honour, gifts, 'speech', suffering, and disgrace. They are summed up under two headings, 'instruction' and 'constraint'. The whole process is described as the 'cure' of psychic 'disease', i.e. injustice; and the nature of this condition is described in step 7.

The penultimate sentence acknowledges a deterrent purpose in punishment (cf. passage 7), and also a purpose of 'social hygiene'; on the latter, compare passage 4.

Step 7: 863a3–864a8. Analysis of psychic injustice. Cleinias, not unreasonably, now asks for a clearer explanation of the difference between injury and injustice, and of the elaborate account that has been given of voluntary and involuntary acts—presumably of the difference between them, though the text does not quite say that. The Stranger's reply has 3 stages:

1. *Three causes of crime, 863b1–d4.* These are: *anger*, an irrationally violent factor innate in the soul; it causes much havoc; *pleasure* (personified, it seems), who wields an opposite kind of force and achieves her will by 'persuasion with violent deceit'; *ignorance*, divided into (*a*) the 'simple' kind (the cause of trivial faults), and (*b*) the 'double', which is ignorance reinforced by a conceit of wisdom; when this 'double' kind has force and power at its command, the resultant offences are to be treated as very serious (*b*i); when it does not (*b*ii), the attitude of the laws will be very gentle and indulgent.

Comment. Initially Cleinias hardly gets what he asks for: the Stranger says nothing special about injury, but enumerates at length three psychic states. Both anger and pleasure work by force, the latter in the sense that it supplies specious reasoning to justify one's (bad) desires, reasoning which is irresistibly compelling; hence the oxymoron 'violent deceit'.[20] The analysis of ignorance poses a problem that will recur: if the purpose of punishment is to cure psychic states, and (as it seems) the same ('double') ignorance causes both serious and trivial crimes (depending merely on the contingent power of the agent), why should their punishments differ?

2. *Intellectual and emotional causes, 863d6–e4.* To speak of being 'master of' or 'stronger than' anger and pleasure is ordinary language; but to speak of being 'stronger than ignorance' is not. But at any rate we do say

---

[20] For a defence of this interpretation see Saunders (1968) 425–6.

that they all often prompt a man in a direction contrary to the one he wishes.

Comment. This last remark needs to be understood in the light of the Socratic paradox. The agent does wish to do this (bad) act, prompted by anger etc.; but this act is not what he really wishes, because according to the paradox a bad act is not advantageous to him; he is therefore acting contrary to what he *would* wish if he were not ignorant, and/or in thrall to anger and pleasure. The Stranger thus meets, rather glancingly, Cleinias' request for a further account of the terms voluntary and involuntary: the bad act is indeed voluntary in the ordinary sense, but involuntary in the deeper sense of the Socratic paradox.

The following summary[21] combining (1) and (2) above demonstrates the elaborate neatness of the Stranger's analysis of injustice.

(*a*) *Three causes*: Anger—Pleasure—Ignorance (subdivided).
(*b*) *Pleasure different* from anger: she persuades and deceives with a show of reason (whereas anger is irrational).
   Pleasure similar to anger: her persuasion is nevertheless *forceful*.
(*c*) *Ignorance* is different from anger and pleasure: one cannot conquer or be conquered by it.
(*d*) *All three* are similar: they all drag a man contrary to his real desires.

3. *Injury and injustice, 863e–864a8.* Cleinias now receives a reply to his request for a clearer statement of the difference between injury and injustice. The latter is simply the tyranny in the soul of 'anger, fear, pleasure, pain, envy, and desire', *whether or not it does any damage.* Similarly and conversely,[22] provided correct moral opinion rules in the soul, any act done in accordance with it is 'just', even if that opinion is not *wholly* correct; it would be wrong, therefore, to call any damage thereby caused 'involuntary injustice'.[23]

Comment. The upshot is that acts attract their moral labelling from the state of mind of the agent. Earlier, we learned of the paradox of the injustice of conferring a benefit;[24] so too here we learn of an injury that is to be termed 'just'.

Poor Cleinias has now had, in these swift and obscurely written remarks, an answer to his request for a clearer account of the distinction between injury and injustice. Injury is an act or a state of affairs; injustice

---

[21] Cf. p. 426 of my 1968 article.
[22] Confusingly, the Stranger now switches from *agnoia*, the item missing from the preceding list, to its opposite: knowledge, or rather its everyday version, 'correct opinion'. The lines that now follow, 864a1–8, are mysteriously written and contain many difficulties of interpretation. I give my own view, which is defended in detail in my 1968 article, pp. 428 ff.); cf. Mackenzie (1981) app. II.
[23] i.e. it would not be injustice at all. Cf. 862a2–6, with the echoed *tēn toiautēn blabēn*, 'such injury'.
[24] 862ab.

is a state of mind. Injury may be voluntary or involuntary in the ordinary sense; injustice, which prompts a man to do damage, is always involuntary, in the sense intended by the Socratic paradox; therefore no one does injury/wrong voluntarily. The paradox no longer stands as an obstacle to legislation, whose purpose (after the making good of any damage) is the cure of 'involuntary injustice' in the sense indicated.

Step 8: 864a8–c9. Recapitulation. The Stranger closes the discussion by summarizing the three causes of crime in the following terms: a painful one,[25] called anger and fear; pleasures and desires; expectations and opinion—'a shot at the truth about the best' (an *unsuccessful* shot, i.e. amounting to ignorance).[26] If ignorance is subdivided (as in step 7 (1)), we have five categories, requiring different laws; and these laws in turn require division into two further categories, those dealing with open and violent crimes, and those dealing with crimes committed in secrecy and with deceit; crimes combining both circumstances call for very harsh laws indeed.

Fuller comment on those indications about the nature of the laws required is best reserved until all Plato's statements on penology in the *Laws* have been reviewed in order, and we can assess their implications.[27]

Appendix to steps 7 and 8

The third cause of crime is said at 863c1 ff. to be ignorance. But what kind of ignorance? Schöpsdau (1984, e.g. 113), like some earlier commentators, supposes it to be non-moral *technical* ignorance, of the means by which a morally correct opinion about moral ends may be put into practical effect; such action, though well-intended, is mistaken and so causes involuntary damage, which the agent did not seek, and for which he is therefore not punishable—for unlike emotions, ignorance is not something one can *resist* (863d10–11). This, according to Schöpsdau, is the point of (i) τὴν δὲ τοῦ ἀρίστου δόξαν ... κἂν σφάλληταί τι (864a1–4), and of (ii) ἐλπίδων δὲ καὶ δόξης τῆς ἀληθοῦς (= subjective genitives) περὶ τὸ ἄριστον ἔφεσις (864b6–7): morally right opinion, aiming to achieve the best in action, fails through lack of non-moral technical competence. The resulting damage, *blabē*, is commonly called 'involuntary injustice'—but wrongly, for it is not injustice at all, which is the term for the domination of emotion, appetite, etc., in the soul

---

[25] Why painful? Obviously fear is painful (see further p. 176 n. 110); how can anger be? See Arist. *Rhet.* 2. 2: anger is a striving, accompanied by pain, for revenge for a slight: the slight causes the pain; cf. 866d ff.

[26] See appendix to steps 7 and 8, below, and cf. *Phaed.* 237de.

[27] See pp. 178–95.

(863c5–864a1). The ignorance in question is therefore *not* a species of psychic *adikia*.

To reduce the *agnoia* so elaborately analysed by reference to the offender's opinions and power (863c1–d4) to the level of mere practical mistake or miscalculation is patently implausible. The passage 863a8–d4 is fairly clear evidence that in suitable contexts Plato could still use a *Republic*-style threefold analysis of the soul and its parts or states (b3): accordingly, we have (i) θυμός and (ii) ἡδονή *et al.* (b1–10); then (c1 ff.) we read, at considerable length, a description of (iii) a further state, ignorance, which—presumably—affects the topmost 'part' of the soul, the intellectual part. Now Plato's chief interest in the intellect is its potential ability to attain either knowledge or right opinion of moral concepts, propositions, and ends. Can our long paragraph really be devoted to an analysis of a relatively trivial matter, namely the various 'ignorances' that lead to the many kinds of everyday practical blunders that by definition are not morally culpable offences at all, and so hardly call for penal measures, much less a gradation of them (d3–4)?

On the contrary, it seems to me clear that the *hamartēmata* in the passage *passim* are just as much *hamartēmata*, moral offences springing from psychic injustice, as the *hamartēmata* for which death was the penalty just before (863a1–2), and just as much as the offences caused by *thumos* and pleasure etc. Plato is catering for offenders who act from mistaken moral beliefs. If he is *not* doing that, he is excluding from consideration one important 'cause' (863c2) of *hamartēmata*. Is this likely? Elsewhere in the *Laws* he shows considerable interest in persons who act from moral ignorance, e.g.:

1. Notably, the atheists in book 10, who are 'ignorant' (e.g. 886b, 903d1, 905b7, c2) of the theological truths of the universe and the duties they impose; their beliefs lead them to crime (885b–e).
2. Persons who believe theft is acceptable, since the gods commit it themselves (941b).
3. Persons who believe that virtue and happiness do not go together (66od ff.).
4. Persons who suppose wealth is the supreme good (870ab).
5. Persons who ignorantly believe it wise to be selfish (732a).
6. The imaginary gods who don't *know* that they have an obligation to be solicitous of the universe (902a).

In short, I see *all* ἀδικία, whether 'spirit', emotions, or moral opinions, as (in the Socratic sense) 'involuntary'; but that does not prevent the crimes to which they lead from being *punishable*, by way of 'cure' of the unjust state of soul which occasioned them; compare the judges' job at 957e, to remove from bad men *amathia* (ignorance), incontinence, cowardice, and injustice in general. Ignorance is indeed not 'beherrschbar' (Schöpsdau 126); but moral ignorance is still punishable by way of cure, whereas technical ignorance is not.

Schöpsdau's view of *agnoia* as purely non-moral leads him (113 n. 24) to associate the children and old men of 863d1-2 with those of 864d4-5. Those in the latter passage are indeed non-responsible morally. But those in the former are not: they are foolish people, without power, whose conceit of wisdom causes little harm, which the lawgiver will '*treat as*' the offences of infantile and senile persons.

J. Roberts (1987) too interprets the passage in broadly the same way as I do; but like Schöpsdau she doubts whether all the pyschic causes of crime can be termed 'unjust'. Again it is the third of them, ignorance, that provokes controversy. She claims that Plato makes 'a distinction between injustice and ignorance' (23), and she points to the difference between (i) the ignorance which arises from the domination of reason by appetites and emotions, and (ii) the kind which is 'purely intellectual' (23), e.g. as seen in the well-intentioned heretics in book 10 (see pp. 306-7). She argues that only (i) qualifies as 'injustice', since it is accompanied by a desire to harm; (ii), though 'serious', is 'compatible with justice' (27), and is 'a different kind of psychic fault' (26), responsible for only *involuntary* offences, since the agent is not committing 'knowing harm' (29): he is like someone who causes damage simply by accident.

The comparison is interesting, but I doubt if it forms part of Plato's thinking. Accidental damage signals exactly nothing about the agent's psychic state; but the propagation of heresy, however well-intentioned the heretic, does signal something about his soul, which can hardly be that knowledge or at any rate right opinion is in charge of it. It would therefore be hard to describe his soul as having a just balance of its component elements. True, his *ēthos* (affective disposition) is just (908b5); but that does not by itself entail that his *intellectual* state is just. Indeed, the implication is if anything the other way round: the restriction of the description 'just' to his *ēthos* suggests that his intellectual state is *not* just. Moreover, his *ēthos* is just only *by nature* (908b5), presumably confirmed by habit *(ethos,* 792e1-2). His justice is therefore a relatively fragile thing, constantly in danger of being corrupted by his heretical opinions. In that event, his soul would become dominated by the bad desires and emotions suggested by his heresy, and unjust action would follow. Even at present, there is a lack of concord between his reason and his emotions; therefore he cannot possess virtue (653bc). So I see nothing to be gained from insisting that he is *intellectually* not unjust; if he were, why does Plato say that he deserves punishment *(dikē,* 908b3-4, d1)? For the function of *dikē* is precisely to make the unjust just. Even if he is entirely benevolent in his heresy (but note his mockery, 908c8), the damage he does is involuntary in only one sense, the Socratic—exactly the same sense in which the damage done by unjust persons under the domination of pleasure and emotion is involuntary; that sense apart, the damage will be voluntary, i.e. springing from an unjust psychic state in the ordinary way. Roberts's thesis seems therefore not to help the interpretation of the passage.

So much for passage 1, the central penological manisfesto. The remaining passages are shorter, but offer valuable supplementation. I present them in the sequence in which they appear in the *Laws*.

Passage 2 (728b2–c5)

You see, practically no one takes into account the greatest 'judgement' (*dikē*, as it is called), on wrongdoing. This is to grow to resemble men who are evil, and as the resemblance increases to shun good men and their wholesome conversation and to cut oneself off from them, while seeking to attach oneself to the other kind and keep their company.[28] The inevitable result of consorting with such people is that what you do and have done to you is exactly what *they* naturally do and say to each other. Consequently, this condition is not really a 'judgement' (*dikē*) at all, because justice (*to dikaion*) and judgement are fine things: it is mere punishment (*timōria*), suffering that follows a wrongdoing (*adikia*). Now whether a man is made to suffer or not, he is wretched. In the former case he is not cured (*ouk iatreuomenos*), in the latter he will ultimately be killed[29] to ensure the safety of many others.

Comment. Unfortunately this passage, which is obviously crucial, is ambiguous and has proved controversial.[30] Is the man made to suffer (by punishment) the one who is not cured, so that the one who does not suffer is killed? Or is the one who suffers killed, so that the one who does not suffer is not cured? The above translation incorporates my own view, which is that the former alternative is correct. My footnote in the Penguin ad loc. still seems to me to express what I take to be Plato's full meaning:

Absence of punishment (suffering) will mean you are not deterred from crime and will go from bad to worse until you have to be executed as incorrigible, and as an example to deter others from inviting the same fate. But if you are made to suffer, you will become resentful and turn to crime again. 'Judgement' is a scientifically designed measure to cure vice; retributive 'punishment' is only the infliction of suffering.

What does seem to emerge at minimum is that penal measures, *timōria*, that consist simply of suffering are not a fine thing: whether a criminal undergoes it or escapes it, he is wretched; and there is some

---

[28] Cf. *Th.* 176d ff.
[29] i.e. executed: cf. the use of *apollumai* at Dem. 19. 110, 302, 24. 207.
[30] Saunders (1963), Mackenzie (1981) 196 n. 62, Saunders (1984) 23–4.

sharp distinction to be made between *timōria* and *dikē*.[31] Presumably
'judgement' is some measure designed to restore the offender to a state
of psychic 'justice'.

Although the Stranger speaks of the possibility that a criminal may
escape suffering punishment (in fallible legal systems that is only too
likely), his deeper doctrine is that *timōria*, in the sense of suffering the
backlash of the evil the criminal has done, is unavoidable. The long
sequence[32] in which our passage occurs is devoted to recommending the
'honouring' of the soul. A man who 'dishonours' his soul by giving in to
his base desires fills it with 'misery and repentance',[33] and all the wealth
in the world is worth less than virtue.[34] The 'judgement', *dikē*, on evil
conduct is to grow like bad men, and to do as they do and be done by as
they are.[35] Here is the familiar Socratic paradox, that willy-nilly injustice
is less profitable than justice.[36] But this kind of suffering comes under the
same censure as retributive penalties under formal laws:[37] it is mere
timōria, not *dikē*; for *dikē* aims at the relief of misery by the cure of
injustice.[38]

Passage 3 (731 b3–d5)

This occurs in the general preamble to the legal code, as distinct from
the special preambles to the various sections of it.

Every man should combine in his character high spirit with the utmost gentle-
ness, because there is only one way to get out of the reach of crimes committed
by other people and which are dangerous or even impossible to cure (*dusiata*):
you have to overcome them by fighting in self-defence and rigidly punishing
(*kolazein*) them, and no soul can do this without righteous indignation. On the
other hand there are some criminals whose crimes are curable (*iata*), and the
first thing to realize here is that every unjust man is unjust against his will. No
man on earth would ever deliberately embrace any of the supreme evils, least of
all in the most precious parts of himself—and as we said, the truth is that the
most precious part of every man is his soul. So no one will ever voluntarily
accept the supreme evil into the most valuable part of himself and live with it
throughout his life. No: in general, the unjust man deserves just as much pity as
any other sufferer. And you may pity the criminal whose disease is curable
(*iasima*), and restrain and abate your anger, instead of persisting in it with the
spitefulness of a shrew; but when you have to deal with complete and

---

[31] At *Gorg.* 472de, however, which seems akin to this passage, *dikē* and *timōria* seem to be used
indifferently; and here the criminal who is not punished is *more* wretched than the one who is
punished (cf. *Rep.* 591a). On the 'fineness' of a punishment, see passage 1, step 3 above.

[32] 726–728d.   [33] 727c, cf. 731c.   [34] 728a.

[35] 728bc, at the start of our passage; cf. 656b. What the offender needs is to be exposed to the
social and moral pressure of *good* men, 854bc.

[36] 660e ff., cf. *Gorg.* 472d ff., 507c ff.

[37] For the decrying of retribution, see esp. passage 12.

[38] If you wish to make someone suffer, encourage him in his wrongdoing and avoidance of
punishment: *Gorg.* 480e–481b. *Kolasis* and *dikē* linked in popular thought: *Soph.* 229a.

unmanageably vicious corruption, you must let your anger off its leash. That is why we say that it must be the good man's duty to be high-spirited or gentle as circumstances require.

Comment. The word for 'punish' is the standard word of the Athenian courts: *kolazein*, 'check', 'chastise'. The medical terminology is applied both to criminal acts and to criminal states.

Again we have the Socratic insistence that crime is involuntary, since it entails misery: in effect a criminal brings on himself his own punishment (see on passage 2 above).

Passage 4 (735d8–736a3)

Like drastic medicines, the best purge is a painful business: it involves chastisement (*kolazein*) by justice (*dikē*) allied to punishment (*timōria*), and takes the latter, ultimately, to the point of death or exile. That usually gets rid of the major criminals who are incurable (*aniatoi*) and do the state enormous harm. The milder purge we could adopt is this. When there is a shortage of food, and those who have no property show themselves ready to follow their leaders in an attack on those who do, they are to be regarded as a disease (*nosēma*) that has developed in the body politic, and in the friendliest possible way they should be (as it will tactfully be put) 'sent out to a colony'.

Comment. The Stranger is discussing the selection of citizens for the new foundation, Magnesia, and remarks that a legislator faced with that task would be glad to be able to carry out even a mild purge. The above remarks refer, however, to a state which has already been founded, in which criminals need to be controlled or even got rid of. The distinction between judgement and punishment, *dikē* and *timōria*, seems reminiscent of passage 2: the best purge 'leads on to chastisement by justice allied to punishment'. Here the two methods seem to be employed together, whereas in passage 2 they were opposed, *dikē* being a good thing, *timōria* a bad one.

Passages 5a (777e4–6) and 5b (793d7–794a2)

5a [We should refrain from ill-treating our slaves.] Even so, we should certainly punish (*kolazein*) slaves if they deserve it (*en dikēi*, 'justly'), and not spoil them by simply giving them a warning, as we would free men.

5b ATHENIAN: Up to the age of 3 the early training of a boy or girl will be helped enormously by this regimen (literally 'these things'), provided it is observed punctiliously and systematically. In the fourth, fifth, sixth, and even seventh year of life, a child's character will need to be formed while he plays; we should now stop spoiling him, and resort to discipline (*kolazein*), but not so as to humiliate him. We said, in the case of slaves, that discipline (*kolazein*) should not be enforced so high-handedly that they become resentful, though on the other hand we mustn't spoil them by letting them go uncorrected (*akolastos*); the same rule should apply to free persons too.

Comment. Presumably chastisement/punishment becomes appropriate at the age when the child becomes rational enough to make a systematic connection between its conduct and the treatment it attracts from his elders. To punish someone who could not make that connection would be pointless (cf. passage 8 and pp. 190–1).

On the differentiation of treatment on the basis of social class, see chapter 15.

Passage 6 (853b4–854a3)

ATHENIAN: The very composition of all these laws we are on the point of framing is, in a way, a disgrace: after all, we're assuming we have a state which will be run along excellent lines and achieve every condition favourable to the practice of virtue. The mere idea that a state of this kind could give birth to a man affected by the worst forms of wickedness found in other countries, so that the legislator has to anticipate his appearance by threats—this, as I said, is in a way a disgrace. It means we have to lay down laws against these people, to deter (*apotropē*) them and punish (*kolasis*) them when they appear, on the assumption that they will certainly do so. However, unlike the ancient legislators, we are not framing laws for heroes and sons of gods. The lawgivers of that age, according to the story told nowadays, were descended from gods and legislated for men of similar stock. But we are human beings, legislating in the world today for the children of humankind, and we shall give no offence by our fear that one of our citizens will turn out to be, so to speak, a 'tough egg', whose character will be so 'hard-boiled' as to resist softening; powerful as our laws are, they may not be able to tame such people, just as heat has no effect on tough beans. For their dismal sake, the first law I shall produce will deal with robbery from temples, in case anyone dares to commit this crime. Now in view of the correct education our citizens will have received, we should hardly want any of them to catch this disease (*nosos*), nor is there much reason to expect that they will. Their slaves, however, as well as foreigners and the slaves of foreigners, may well make frequent attempts at such crimes. For their sake principally—but still with an eye on the general weakness of human nature—I'll spell out the law about robbery from temples, and about all the other similar crimes which are difficult or even impossible to cure (*dusiata, aniata*).

Comment. A certain truculence of language is discernible: some Magnesian punishments will be designed to 'soften' the 'tough', and will therefore have to be harsh. Though some are indeed more severe than the corresponding penalties in Attic law, others are less severe; and we shall enquire into the reasons for the variation.

Again there is a social distinction between offenders; here, and sometimes elsewhere, the foreigner is grouped with the slave; but in some other passages he is bracketed with the citizen. The reasons will be discussed in chapter 15.

Passage 7 (854c2–855a2, extracts)

Conclusion of the preamble addressed to those tempted to rob from temples:

But run away from the company of the wicked, with never a backward glance. If by doing this you find that your disease abates (*lōphai nosēma*) somewhat, well and good; if not, then you should look upon death as the preferable alternative, and rid yourself of life. [*The penalty for a slave or foreign offender is now specified.*] Perhaps paying this penalty will teach him restraint (*sōphronizein*) and make him a better man: after all, no penalty imposed by law has an evil purpose, but generally achieves one of two effects: it makes the person who pays the penalty either more virtuous or less wicked. But if a citizen is ever shown to be responsible for such a crime . . . the penalty is death. The judge should consider him as already beyond cure (*aniatos*); he should bear in mind the kind of education and upbringing the man has enjoyed from his earliest years, and how after all this he has still not abstained from acts of the greatest evil. But the least of evils will be what the offender suffers; indeed, he will be of service to others, by being a lesson (*paradeigma*) to them when he is ignominiously banished from sight beyond the borders of the state.

Comment. The medical terminology is here extended beyond the adjectives 'curable' and 'incurable' to the semi-technical verb 'abate' (*lōphan*). The 'tiny evil' one suffers when executed as incurable is presumably the loss of life, in which one might go on getting even worse, with a correspondingly worse fate in the next world. Later (passage 16) death is called a 'cure' for the incurable, by way of grim paradox; presumably it *is* a cure, however, in as much as it prevents further deterioration into vice and misery. The death penalty is used by Plato rather freely, and is discussed later (pp. 181–3).

The final sentence recognizes a deterrent purpose in punishment: cf. passage 1, step 6.

Passage 8 (864c10–e3)

This passage provides that insanity at the time of the offence, or effective insanity arising from illness, senility, or childhood, dispenses from penalties for certain serious crimes, but not from the duty to supply simple recompense, nor to undergo a period of exile in cases of murder.

Comment. These provisions come immediately after passage 1, and their careful concern with motives and intention gains from the stress of that passage on states of mind. Again, there is a sharp distinction between recompense and penalty, the latter being described as 'the other *dikaiōmata*', 'just measures' (or perhaps 'rectifications').[39]

As in passage 5b, penalties may not be inflicted on persons incapable of understanding their justification.

[39] Cf. Arist. *NE* 1135ª13, and see below, p. 217.

Passage 9 (866d5–868a1)

In this passage, 'anger' translates *thumos* or *orgē*.

If someone kills a free man by his own hand, but the deed is done in anger, we must first make an internal distinction within this type of crime. Anger is common to (1) those who kill a man by blows or similar means, owing to a sudden impulse here the action is immediate, there is no previous intention to kill, and regret for the deed follows at once; (2) those who have been stung by insults or opprobrious actions and who pursue their vengeance until, some time later, they kill somebody: they *intend* to kill, and the deed causes no repentance. So it looks as if we have to establish two categories of murder; broadly speaking, both are done in anger, but a proper description would be 'falling somewhere midway between "voluntary" and "involuntary"'; however, each type comes closer to one or other of these extremes. The man who nurses his anger and takes his vengeance later—not suddenly, on the spur of the moment, but with premeditation—approximates to the voluntary murderer. The man whose anger bursts forth uncontrollably, whose action is instant, immediate, and without premeditation, resembles the involuntary killer. Yet even so, he is not an entirely involuntary killer: he only resembles one. It is therefore sometimes difficult to categorize murders done under the influence of anger, and to know whether to treat them in law as voluntary or involuntary. The best course, which corresponds most closely to reality, is to classify them both under what they most resemble, and to distinguish them by the presence or absence of premeditation. We should lay down comparatively severe penalties (*timōriai*) for those who have killed in anger and with premeditation, and lighter ones for those who have killed on the spur of the moment without previous intent. Something which resembles a greater evil should attract a greater punishment (*timōria*), whereas a lesser penalty should be visited on that which resembles a lesser evil. . . . If someone kills a free man with his own hand, and the deed is done in a fit of anger, without previous intent, his penalty (*paschein*, 'suffering') should in general be that appropriate to a man who has killed without anger; but in addition he should be obliged to go into exile for two years, by way of a curb for his anger. If a man kills in anger, but with premeditation, his penalty should in general be that inflicted in the previous instance; but his exile should be for three years as against the other's two, the period of punishment being longer because of the intensity (literally, 'scale', 'size') of his anger.

In such cases, regulations for the return from exile should run as follows. (It is not easy to make hard and fast rules: sometimes the fiercer criminal as defined by the law may turn out easier to manage, whereas the man who is supposedly more manageable may turn out to be a more difficult case, having committed a murder with some savagery; the other, conversely, may have dispatched his victim without brutality. However, my account does describe the cases you'll find are typical.) The Guardians of the Laws should act as assessors of all these points, and when the period of exile prescribed for either category has come to an end, they should send twelve of their number, as judges, to the borders of the country. During the time that has elapsed these twelve should have made an even more exact investigation into the exiles' actions, so as to decide whether to grant pardon and permission to return; and that exiles are bound to acquiesce in the judgement of these authorities.

Comment. Homicide in anger is a category unknown to Attic law: it is a Platonic innovation. It entails a fairly elaborate inspection of the criminal's psychology and conduct at the time of the crime. The penalties are explicitly graded in severity to reflect the seriousness of the mental state, which is gauged by reference to the circumstances and manner of commission of the offence. As the passage itself indicates, there are difficulties; for the mode of commission may or may not be an accurate indicator of psychic state. This problem points to the wider issue of the relationships (*a*) between the gravity of the offence and the assessment of psychic state, and (*b*) between the seriousness of that state and the penalty to be awarded. Both issues are the concern of passage 14, and are discussed on pp. 179 and 191-5 below.

Passage 10 (880d7–881b2)

Some laws, it seems, are made for the benefit of honest men, to teach them the rules of association that have to be observed if they are to live in friendship; others are made for those who refuse to be instructed and whose naturally tough natures have not been softened enough to stop them turning to absolute vice. It will be they who have prompted the points I am just going to make, and it is for their benefit that the lawgiver will be compelled to produce his laws, although he would wish never to find any occasion to use them. Consider a man who will dare to lay hands on his father or mother or their forbears by way of violent assault. He will fear neither the wrath of the gods above nor the punishments said to await him in the grave; he will hold the ancient and universal tradition in contempt on the strength of his 'knowledge' in a field where he is in fact a total ignoramus. He will therefore turn criminal, and will stand in need of some extreme deterrent (*apotropē*). Death, however, is not an extreme and final penalty; the sufferings said to be in store for these people in the world to come are much more extreme than that. But although the threat of these sufferings is no idle one, it has no deterrent (*apotropē*) effect at all on souls like these. If it did, we should never have to deal with assaults on mothers, and wicked and presumptuous attacks on other forbears. I conclude, therefore, that the punishments (*kolaseis*) men suffer for these crimes here on earth while they are alive should as far as possible equal the penalties (*kolaseis*) beyond the grave.

Comment. The punishment eventually laid down[40] for assault on one's parents is permanent rustication from the central city and banning from sacred places. But since this is far less severe than the penalties traditionally associated with the next world, the Stranger's point may

---

[40] 881d.

well be more *recherché*: just as death is removal from life, so too the penalty in this world will be 'removal from life', in another sense.

This indignant passage is a curious exercise in the logic of deterrence: since the man disbelieves in punishment in the next world, and so cannot be deterred by that prospect of it, he must be given a crime-specific punishment in this world, in which he cannot disbelieve, so that then he may be deterred—but from assaulting his relatives, whom he will now, because of rustication, never meet again anyway. At all events, the passage does seem to show faith in the efficacy of deterrence implied by contemplating future punishment (here rustication). Does it also show faith in deterrence inspired by the experience of *being* punished? If so, is that all Plato means by 'cure'?

Passage 11 (907e6–909c4)

The law of impiety runs:

When verdicts of 'guilty' are returned, the court is to assess a separate penalty (*timēma*) for each impious act of each offender. Imprisonment is to apply in all cases. The state will have three prisons: (1) a public one near the market-place for the general run of offenders, where large numbers may be kept in safe custody. (2) one called the 'reform centre' (*sōphronistērion*) near the place where the Nocturnal Council assembles, and (3) another in the heart of the country-side, in a solitary spot where the terrain is at its wildest; and the title of this prison is somehow to convey the notion of 'punishment' (*timōria*).

Now since impiety has three causes,[41] which we have already described, and each is divided into two kinds, there will be six categories of religious offenders worth distinguishing; and the punishment (*dikē*) imposed on each should vary in kind and degree. Consider first a complete atheist: he may have a naturally just character and be the sort of person who hates scoundrels, and because of his loathing of injustice is not tempted to commit it; he may flee the unjust and feel fondness for the just. Alternatively, besides believing that all things are 'empty of' gods, he may be a prey to an uncontrollable urge to experience pleasure and avoid pain, and he may have a retentive memory and be capable of shrewd insights. Both these people suffer from a common failing, atheism, but in terms of the harm they do to others the former is much less dangerous than the latter. The former will talk with a complete lack of inhibition about gods and sacrifices and oaths, and by poking fun at other people will probably, if he continues unpunished, make converts to his own views. The latter holds the same opinions but has what are called 'natural gifts': full of cunning and guile, he is the sort of fellow who will make a diviner and go in for all sorts of legerdemain; sometimes he will turn into a dictator or a demagogue or a general, or a plotter in secret rites; and he is the man who invents the tricks of the so-called 'sophists'. So there can be many different types of atheist, but for

---

[41] The three heresies formally presented at 885b and briefly described in the course of this paragraph; they are refuted at length in book 10.

the purpose of legislation they need to be divided into two groups. The dissembling atheist deserves (*axios*) to die for his sins not just once or twice but many times, whereas the other kind needs a simple admonition (*nouthetēsis*) combined with incarceration. The idea that gods take no notice of the world similarly produces two more categories, and the belief that they can be squared another two. So much for our distinctions.

Those who have simply fallen victim to foolishness and who do not have a bad character and disposition should be sent to the reform centre (*sōphronistērion*) by the judge in accordance with the law for a term of not less than five years, and during this period no citizen must come into contact with them except the members of the Nocturnal Council, who should pay visits to admonish (*nouthetēsis*) them and ensure their spiritual salvation.[42] When his imprisonment is over, a prisoner who appears to be enjoying mental health (*sōphronein*) should go and live with sensible *sōphrones*) people; but if appearances turn out to have been deceptive, and he is reconvicted on a similar charge he should be punished (*zēmioun*) by death. There are others, however, who in addition to not recognizing the existence of gods, or believing they are unconcerned about the world or can be bought off, become sub-human (*thēriōdeis*). They take everybody for a fool, and many a man they charm among the living; and by claiming to use charms on the dead and by promising to influence the gods through the pretended magic powers of sacrifices and prayers and charms, they try to wreck completely whole homes and states for filthy lucre. If one of these people is found guilty, the court must sentence him to imprisonment as prescribed by law in the prison in the centre of the country; no free man is to visit him at any time, and slaves must hand him his ration of food fixed by the Guardians of the Laws. When he dies, the body must be cast out over the borders of the state unburied.

Comment. The extensive quotation necessary shows how a penology that stresses mental disposition and its reform comes into its own when applied to offences which have a strong intellectual dimension, as well as an emotional or appetitive one. For the way in which one may be 'cured' of an emotion or appetite (as distinct from merely being deterred from acting on it) is not immediately clear; but obviously one can be 'cured' of an opinion by being argued out of it. Yet even here the elaborate description of mental states has a pronounced emotional and appetitive flavour: the honest atheist loves just men and hates injustice, and the dissembling kind is dominated by a desire to experience pleasure and avoid pain.

It is an index of the supreme importance Plato attaches to correct theological opinion that he goes to the length of proposing two extra prisons, one with a name suggesting *timōria*, something which in the light of passage 2 we should not expect Plato to countenance; we shall discuss the implications of this curious point later. Confinement in this

---

[42] Literally, 'safety of soul'.

prison seems intended to achieve, in addition to social hygiene, a measure of publicity and deterrence; for it is difficult to see what other reason Plato can have for letting the more harmful offenders go on living, when he has explicitly said that they 'deserve' to die many deaths. The imprisonment of the less harmful heretics is not so much a punishment as a measure to ensure that they cannot avoid re-education.

Passage 12 (933e6–934c2)

When one man harms another by theft or violence and the damage is extensive, the indemnity he pays to the injured party should be large, but smaller if the damage is comparatively trivial. The cardinal rule should be that in every case the sum is to vary in proportion to the damage done, so that the loss is made good (*iasêtai*, literally 'is cured'). And each offender is to pay an additional penalty (*dikē*) appropriate to his crime, to encourage him to reform (*sōphronistus*). Thus if a man has been led to do wrong by the folly of someone else, being over-persuaded because of his youth or some similar reason, his penalty should tend to be light; but it is to be heavier when his offence is due to his own folly and inability to control his feelings of pleasure and pain—as when he has fallen victim to cowardice and fear, or some deep-rooted jealousy or lust or fury. This additional penalty (*dikē*) is to be inflicted not because of the crime (what is done cannot be undone), but for the sake of the future: we hope that the offender himself and those that observe his punishment (literally, 'see him made just, put right,' *dikaioumenon*) will either be brought to loathe injustice unreservedly or at any rate recover (*lōphan*) appreciably from this misfortune. All these reasons and considerations make it necessary for the law to aim, like a good archer, at the size of the punishment (*kolasis*), for the sake of each [offence?] and especially at the deserved (*axias*) one.[43]

Comment. This passage is a plain statement of the sharp distinction Plato draws between recompense, which is non-penal, and the 'extra', which is the penalty proper and is intended to encourage moral reform. Further, there is to be some direct correlation between the seriousness of the psychic state and the severity of the penalty. There are just two touches of medical vocabulary, the first (curing of damage) obviously metaphorical.[44] The remark that the past cannot be undone is reminiscent of Protagoras.[45] The purpose of deterrence of observers is clearly recognized.

Passage 13 (938b5–6)

[A person charged with perverse pleading or criminal advocacy]... should be tried ... and if he is found guilty the court should decide whether it thinks his motive is avarice or contentiousness.

---

[43] 'at the deserved one' renders some ambiguous Greek: see p. 193 n. 191.
[44] Cf. Dover (1981 in 1987 repr.) 40.
[45] See pp. 133–4.

Comment. This is a brief example of Plato's concentration on motive and state of mind, in the service of the special values of his state (the penalties which follow show that he regards avarice as more heinous than pugnacity).

Passage 14 (941c4–942a4)

Every thief of a piece of public property, a large piece or even a small one, needs the same penalty/justice (*dikē*). *For* the thief of something small has stolen with the same lust (*erōs*), but with less power/effect/drive (*dunamis*), and he who makes off with the greater thing when he has not deposited it is unjust (*adikei*) to the full. *Therefore*, in the eyes of the law, one man deserves a lighter penalty (*dikē*) than another, not because of the amount of the theft, but in virtue of the probability that the one would still be curable, while the other would not be. [So then, a slave or foreigner should have a penalty or fine assessed on the assumption that he is probably curable; but the citizen will have betrayed his education and must be executed as well-nigh incurable.]

Comment. There is apparent precision in 'for' and 'therefore', but the ambiguities of *dikē* and *dunamis* in the first two sentences, and the uncertain reference of 'one . . . another' in the third, make this passage hard to interpret with certainty. Two trains of thought seem possible.

1. The two thieves need the same curative penalty, *dikē* (as opposed to *timōria*, see passage 2); for while they share a common lust (to steal public property), that of the one has less drive/intensity than that of the other, and the greater thief's (psychic) injustice is complete (that of the other being *less* than complete). The pilferer ('one man', 'the one') would thus probably be curable, while the serious thief ('another', 'the other') would probably not be; we differentiate the severity of their penalties by reference to these probabilities, not directly by reference to the value of what they steal. On this criterion of curability, slaves and foreigners are probably curable, whereas citizens are not.

If that is right, we are given *two* pairs of indicators of psychic states, which indicate in turn comparative curability, which is in its turn the determinant of severity of punishment: (*a*) pilfering/serious theft, (*b*) citizen/non-citizen status. In (*a*), however, though the amount of the theft is a *prima facie* (hence 'probably') guide to psychic state and hence curability, it would not in itself be the reason for variations in punishment, only the reason for variation of recompense: for only comparative curability of psychic state can be the reason for variations in penalty.

The main advantage of this reading is that it gives full weight to Plato's general wish to assess criminal psychic states by reference to their intensity or drive (*dunamis*),[46] not by reference to damage done. As

---

[46] Cf. 870a: 'yearning' (*himeros*) is a *dunamis* which implants desires (*erōtas*) for gain.

against it, (i) 'scientific punishment' is a lot to read into the first occurrence of (*dikē*) in the passage, especially when on its second it indisputably means simply 'punishment', quite ordinarily; (ii) it is disconcerting
that the actual penalties prescribed are not, in the event, distinguished
by reference to pilfering and theft of large amounts, but only socio-
logically; (iii) there is no differentiation of penalties within the category
of citizens: all are executed.

2. The second view is simpler and harsher:[47] the *citizen* pilferer of
public property and the *citizen* large-scale thief of it deserve the same
penalty, as having the same lust, but different physical power or
opportunity to indulge it. The latter is a criminal to the full, and so too,
by virtue of having the same lust, is the pilferer: he was simply a less
efficient thief. Hence 'one man' (the citizen) is incurable; but 'another'
(slave or foreigner) is curable. In other words, a citizen, whether pilferer
or greater thief, is incurable if he steals any amount whatever, however
small, of public property. This is not true of the slave and foreigner ('one
man', 'the one'); for here betrayal of education cannot apply.

This interpretation, if correct, is almost fantastic. But I fear it may well
be right: in Plato's eyes, to steal anything, however small, from public
sources simply is a heinous crime. He would not deny, presumably, that
the citizen pilferer may well lust with less intensity than the citizen
serious thief, and in that sense be psychically less unjust. But even a
minimum desire to steal from public sources indicates injustice so
intense as to be incurable. Thus when he says the pilferer acts from the
'same' lust as the other thief, he is not equivocating, by implicitly denying
the possibility of varying intensity in that lust. He means only and exactly
what he says: both thieves wish to steal public property, and in that
simple respect both deserve to die. That same principle, it seems, applies
to sacrilege.[48]

We have here an extreme application of the principle that the scale of
the actual injury is irrelevant to the assessment of psychic state. A citizen
who steals a piece of public property, however small, is striking at the
polis itself; such a man is beyond cure.

Passage 15 (944d2–3)

Plato has a long discussion of the culpability of those who lose their
weapons in battle and other circumstances; he stresses that there is a
world of difference between deliberately throwing them away because of
cowardice and being robbed of them against one's will when struggling
against overwhelming force, or through mishap. Here again is emphasis
on state of mind and intent: 'It is the bad man you need to punish

---

[47] I am grateful to Professor P. J. Rhodes and Dr J. G. F. Powell for suggesting this interpretation
to me.   [48] See 854de: the differentiation of penalties is again sociological.

(*kolazein*), to reform him (literally, 'so that he may be better'), not someone who has been unlucky.'

Passage 16 (957d7–958a3)

[The good judge will keep the writings of the legislator as a kind of antidote (*alexipharmaka*) against other writings, and he] will confirm and strengthen (literally, 'provide permanence and increase to') the virtuous in the paths of righteousness, and do his best to banish (*metabolē*) ignorance and incontinence and cowardice and indeed every sort of injustice from the hearts of those criminals whose outlook can be cured (*iasimos*). However—and this is a point that deserves constant repetition—when a man's soul is unalterably fixed in that condition by decree of fate, our erudite judges and their advisers will deserve the commendation of the whole state if they cure (*iama*) him by imposing the penalty of death.

Comment. On death as 'cure' see comment on passage 7, and pp. 181–3. The passage has a strong medical flavour, perhaps extending to *monē* ('permanence'), *epauxēsis* ('increase'), and *metabolē* ('change'), which can function in technical medical senses—though since much technical medical vocabulary is simply ordinary language used in special applications, it is impossible to be sure.

PLATO AND PROTAGORAS[49]

Protagoras and Plato share a single central insight: that punishment should not look to the past but to the future. Both indicate the pointlessness of backward-looking punishment by citing the maxim 'what's done cannot be undone'.[50] That is to say, punishment should not be vengeful or retributive: its purpose is not to inflict suffering on an offender in return for the suffering he has inflicted, but the reformative effect it should have on him henceforth.

Now it is possible to maintain this position without being committed to any practical innovations whatever. One can continue to 'punish' as before, and explain to anyone who will listen that one is not doing so 'for' an offence, but simply regarding it as evidence of a lack of virtue, which can be remedied by making the offender suffer so that he becomes a better man because he will be deterred from offending again. As we have seen, Protagoras seems to go no further than that. Plato's thoughts are immeasurably richer.[51]

[49] See also pp. 133–6, and again my 1981*b* article.
[50] *Protagoras* 324b, *Laws* 934a (passage 12). In the latter passage Plato signals the common ground between himself and Protagoras, an attempt, presumably, to rally Protagoreans to his own cause.
[51] Though to be fair to the historical Protagoras we must recognize that he may have had more to say about penology than Plato represents him as saying.

1. He clears off the question of recompense by treating it as a simple non-penal transaction which should do something to reconcile the parties.[52] In this he shows he realizes that, because recompense and extra (the penalty proper) are so often in the same package, the offender's resentment aroused by the penalty carries over into the recompense and poisons his future relationship with his victim. Conversely, the victim, by receiving precisely the value of the damage he suffered, and by seeing the extra as a purely forward-looking measure, ought to be discouraged from regarding the suffering inflicted on the offender as part of the recompense; in brief, there will be that much less temptation for him to triumph and gloat and take pleasure in the suffering.

2. Protagoras of course argues that punishment is inflicted not for evils beyond a man's control (like congenital deformity), but in respect of evil actions which he can choose to do or not to do;[53] and Plato, on the everyday level, makes the same assumption. But his deeper position is that punishment affects something which no man would ever choose to have: a state of injustice in his soul, which (if only he knew it) is disadvantageous to him.

Plato therefore wishes to make better by punishment not simply bad conduct, but the state of mind which leads to it. Hence his elaborate sketches, if one may put it thus, of the many varieties of injustice which may be present in the soul, and his insistence that each individual offender's punishment must be calculated to reform that particular variety of injustice from which he is suffering. There is a psychological emphasis here, a concern to reform convictions and character, which is missing from Protagoras, who seems to have thought in conventional terms only, of brute deterrence through punishments of the traditional kind, consisting essentially of the infliction of suffering. This concern with psychology apparently prompts Plato to contemplate in principle measures other than the infliction of suffering, as being a suitable way of treating certain persons in certain mental states.[54]

3. By treating psychic injustice as acquired involuntarily Plato makes his description of it as 'disease' thoroughly plausible; for disease too is something which we never acquire voluntarily, and always want to be rid of. Accordingly, punishment will be 'cure'. Here too Plato appears to go a long way beyond the usage of Protagoras, the orators and Greek literature in general. The description of an offence as something requiring a 'remedy', or as ' incurable', is common;[55] to describe an offender himself, or his feelings or character or state of mind, as a disease

---

[52] 862bc, cf. 933e (passages 1 and 12).
[53] *Prot.* 323d ff.   [54] 862d (passage 1).
[55] e.g. Aesch. 3. 69, 114, 156, Dem. 31. 70, 54. 5, Isoc. 4. 110, 114.

or as diseased or as incurable, is rather less common;[56] and only very rarely, if ever, are the implications of the terminology explicitly followed up by a suggestion that the disease could be cured by punishment.[57] In Plato, by contrast, medical language is pervasive. How seriously does he mean it and what effect does it have on his penal code?

MEDICAL PENOLOGY: THEORY

Medical language is often metaphorical. In penology, it may indicate no more than a claim that *just as* medicine cures a patient of disease, *so too* does punishment 'cure' the criminal of a 'disease' (his evil conduct, habits, disposition or character). Such an analogy is natural enough, and it has a certain humane and persuasive force. Nevertheless, in point of content it is trivial, misleading, and defective. (*a*) Trivial, because penology and medicine are only two cases among very many (e.g. repairing cars) of applying remedies to faults, and any such case, in so far as it is just a case of putting right something that is wrong, could be a paradigm for any other. Medicine has no special status. (*b*) Misleading, because it assumes what is entirely uncertain, namely that mind and body are similar or parallel or even identical in nature or structure or function, so that the same or significantly similar treatment may be applied to each. (*c*) Defective, because medical cure inflicts pain as little as possible, and pain is neither its instrument nor its purpose. Punishment is essentially painful, cure only incidentally so, i.e. when it cannot be avoided.[58] The more a punishment approximates to a cure, the less of a punishment will it be.

(*c*) points to the first of three criteria which I suggest must be met by any penology claiming to be medical in a sense that is more than metaphorical:

1. It must provide that its procedures ('punishment') cause pain, if at all, only as an unavoidable concomitant or consequence of the cure.
2. It must be based on a human psychology and physiology of a kind such that the criminal state can be identified and remedied by the application of medical or medically-related procedures.
3. These procedures must be expressible in some form of law capable of being administered by non-medics, i.e. laymen judges.

---

[56] According to Protagoras, a criminal may *be* a disease or *have* a disease (*Prot.* 322d5, 325a8). Cf. Dem. *Letter* 3. 28; 18. 324, 25. 95; Aes. *PV* 378, Eur. *Hipp.* 394, 405, 766, 1306, Aesch. 2. 177, 3. 81.

[57] Dem. 26. 26, Isoc. 8. 39–40 come close.

[58] Modern doctors go to considerable trouble to avoid causing pain. In the days before anaesthetics, doctors no doubt accepted pain as inevitable; and seeing no way of not inflicting it probably took a rather casual attitude to it. But even then it was not their *purpose* to inflict pain.

These requirements are strong; but I believe that Plato's penology can largely meet them.

Gorgias

The use of the medical analogy is extensive and elaborate,[59] but remains for the most part metaphorical, in that the various expressions for punishment (e.g., *dikēn didonai* of the punishee, *kolazein* of the punisher) mean only what they normally mean: the infliction of pain in some form or other (whipping, fines, etc.). Offenders, one assumes, learn that the wages of sin are taxed at more than 100 pence in the pound, and so desist, having become 'better'. But in Plato's eyes this is of course simply to substitute one mental illness for another. In the *Phaedo*[60] this sort of 'commercial' calculation of advantage is roundly condemned. No man can be mentally healthy if he refrains from bad conduct simply through a calculation of pleasure and pain, without the guidance of moral reasoning.[61]

It is perhaps for this reason that there are in the *Gorgias* a few hints that genuinely 'curative' punishment must consist of something other than pain, even if pain is ineluctably caused in the process. The point emerges in the course of a parallel drawn between the cure of disease by doctors and the cure of injustice and licentiousness by courts.[62] The argument relevant to our purposes moves as follows:

1. Medicine relieves us from disease, and justice (applied in the shape of punishment, *kolazein*) relieves us from injustice.
2. Medical treatment is beneficial, but painful; patients nevertheless endure the pain in order to be rid of a great evil.
3. To pay a penalty (*dikēn didonai*) is to be relieved of vice, for which the medicine is justice (*dikē*): it makes us more just; so too does being 'reproved' (*noutheteisthai*) and 'reprimanded' (*epiplēttesthai*).
4. Unjust persons who *escape* reproof, punishment (*kolazein*), and paying penalty are like those who escape their doctors' 'penalties for transgressions of the body' by fearfully refusing to submit to cautery or incision, on the grounds that they are painful. Such unjust persons observe 'the painful element' (*to algeinon*) of being punished, but are blind to the benefit (*to ōphelimon*). The proper thing for the unjust to do is to approach their judges, precisely as they would their doctors, to find the cure of 'the disease of their injustice' in their souls. They should 'pay the penalty and become healthy', bravely submitting, just as they would to cutting and burning, to whipping, imprisonment, fines, banishment, or death, in

---

[59] e.g. 478d, 480a–c.
[61] Cf. *Rep.* 554c–e, 619c–e.
[60] 68d–69c.
[62] 478a–480d.

pursuit of what is 'good and fine'; and in so doing they must 'not take into account' (*hupologizesthai*) 'the painful element' (*to algeinon*).

It is not quite clear whether this last proviso[63] describes the state of mind of the person being medically cured or that of the person being punished; but since the latter state is to be modelled on the former, it seems that in either case the person who is punished is to ignore or make light of that which is painful in that process. Clearly this is nonsense, for what point can there be in a whipping etc., if not to cause pain? Cutting and burning would be just as effective even if pleasant; but it is hard to see how the same could be said of a whipping. True, Socrates probably means only 'not take into account the painful element (*to algeinon*) *in comparison with* the beneficial result (*to ōphelimon*)', i.e. justice in the soul, implying that the benefit is an immeasurably greater good than the admitted pain is an evil.[64] But even that does not dispel the difficulty: to the extent that the pain it causes is made light of, punishment must diminish in effectiveness, because it consists of nothing *except* pain.

In medicine we have (1*a*) the end, health, achieved in the unhealthy by (1*b*) cutting and burning, which is (1*c*) inevitably painful. For the parallel to operate on all fours, we need in penology, (2*a*) the end, justice, achieved in the unjust by (2*b*) punishment, which is (2*c*) inevitably painful. By the use of the expression 'the painful element' in being punished, Socrates just leaves the door ajar for punishment to be something other than the infliction of pain—something which, as it happens, is pain*ful*. The expression is something into which he has stumbled in an attempt to follow through the parallel with medicine in every respect; but having stumbled on it he cannot or does not say what apart from pain (2*b*) could be. He has in fact hit on the inadequacy of treating punishment as cure on the purely metaphorical level.

A further lack of rapport between the two sides of the analogy may however suggest something other than pain which could be punishment. Later in the *Gorgias*[65] the door Socrates left ajar is pushed open a little further. Here *kolazein*, to punish, earlier described in terms of whipping etc., that is to say essentially the infliction of suffering, is now called 'the *restraining* of the soul from its [licentious] desires and not allowing it to do anything except what will contribute to its improvement';[66] and the verbal connection between *kolazesthai* (to be punished) and *akolasia* (i.e.

---

[63] 480c7–8, in a passage which (*pace* Rosen 53) does something to describe 'the perspective of the person punished', as distinct from that of 'the practitioner of the *technē* of justice'.

[64] See 'pursuing the good and the fine,' 480c7, and cf. *Ap.* 28b and *Laws* 702c for 'not *hupologizesthai* in comparison with' something.   [65] 505ab.

[66] Twice, the second time without 'and not . . . improvement'.

lack of *kolasis*, permitting licentiousness) is exploited to make the point. Now of course this may imply no more than deterrence; but 'actions which contribute to improvement' suggests some sort of training or regimen. If the soul then finds it disagreeable, as it doubtless would, to be denied its evil gratifications, then here we have a form of punishment— habituating of the soul to do good actions and so *become* good—which does not *consist* of pain but just happens to be painful.

This same passage also contains a parallel between (*a*) the bodily desires to eat and drink, and (*b*) the desires of the soul. Now presumably the prevention of the 'doing' which the soul desires is the prevention of actions carried out by the body; but this is nevertheless supposed to make the soul 'better'—presumably because it is thus constrained by frustration to give up wishing for bad actions. The remarks are too brief to build much on, but if that is right they suggest that physiological training can affect psychology, and curative 'punishments' can consist of bodily regimen.

Republic

The idea that *kolasis* is moral regimen is, as we have seen, present in the *Gorgias* only hazily and by implication; indeed the word *diaita*, regimen, does not even occur.[67] In the *Republic*, by contrast, regimen is a prominent theme of the celebrated passage on bodily and mental health,[68] a passage which is the basis of certain later remarks on the way in which acts of a certain kind lead to psychic states of the same kind.[69] Socrates argues that just as virtue is the health of the soul, vice, the state of civil war between the parts of the soul, is its disease. Just as health is generated in the body by doing healthy actions, so virtue is generated in the soul by following good practices. That is to say, psychic states are *induced*, by the performance of actions of the appropriate kind.[70] A man whose soul is unjust, therefore, needs positively to do, presumably repeatedly, just actions; and to facilitate that may be the function of *kolasis*, which now seems not simply to restrain bad actions, but perhaps actually to play some role in promoting good ones; at any rate, some brief implicit link is made between moral regimen (*diaita*) and penology.[71] In none of these passages is there any mention of pain, and certainly not of pain as the essential instrument of making one better—and for good reason: it is simply not suggested, immediately at any rate, by the medical model of regimen.

---

[67] Only *diaitōmenoi*, 'living by a regimen', the means by which sick persons may recover health (449e).   [68] 403c–412b.

[69] 443e–445b, esp. 404e, 410d, 411d.

[70] Cf. 591bc, 618de, *Crito* 47e7, and Arist. *NE* 1103ª14 ff.   [71] 444e–445b.

Sophist

The description of *elenchus*, philosophical 'examination' or 'refutation', takes us a little further.[72] It is conceived on the analogy of medical purging: it purges persons suffering from ignorance by convincing them that their opinions are unsatisfactory, so that they become angry with themselves and gentler to others; their souls can benefit from teaching. The context of the passage is not explicitly penological; but in the anger felt with oneself *elenchus* is a painful process. Yet it is not essentially so: it would presumably be equally or more effective if pleasurable.

Transition to the Timaeus

So far, we have seen two possible senses of 'punishing' a criminal in such a way as to preserve the medical analogy of curing without the deliberate infliction of pain: (*a*) the moral regimen of repeated good actions (*Republic* and possibly *Gorgias*), which *may* cause pain, but which does not depend on it, or use it as the tool of reform; (*b*) *elenchus* in the Sophist. But (*a*) is still metaphor: just as medical regimen restores health to the sick, so too moral regimen (repeated virtuous actions) leads to moral health, i.e. virtue; the theory can be medical only if virtue has some physiological basis. And (*b*) could relate only to intellectually-based crimes; we hear nothing of offences springing from bad emotional or appetitive states. However, both (*a*) and (*b*) do amount to significant foreshadowings of Plato's genuinely medical penology, which can be reconstructed by splicing the penal code of the *Laws* to the physiology of the *Timaeus*.

Timaeus

In this dialogue Plato divides the human soul into the three parts familiar from the *Republic*. The rational and immortal part is located in the brain, the spirited part in the heart, and the appetitive in the stomach. The three parts are linked in various ways, notably by what Plato regards as in some sense an extension of the brain, namely the spinal fluid and the marrow of the bones. Impulses both from outside and from inside the body—blows, sensations, emotions associated with the two lower and mortal parts of the soul—are transmitted by physical means through the various organs from one part of the body to another, and depending on their nature and strength may ultimately penetrate to the seat of reason, the brain.[73]

Soul and body are thus intimately connected, and the state of each affects that of the other. A soul whose circles of the Same and the Other

---

[72] 230b–d; cf. Anton.
[73] 44d, 61c ff., 64a ff., 69c ff. Cf. 934d: madness caused by physical disease; also Her. 3. 33.

are revolving as they should and whose moral convictions are therefore correct, will firmly and rationally control its two mortal parts, and the body will then be well-ordered and virtuous. If the body is well-nourished and properly exercised, and is not unduly influenced by the irrational impulses of the two lower parts of the soul, it will not resist rational guidance from the brain, and will not infect, by sheerly physical disorder, the physical seat of reason, and hence reason itself. The point is that this interdependence is given some precise physiological description.[74] Indeed, Solmsen remarks in connection with the lowest part of the soul that Plato takes 'a pretty large step in the direction of making his soul parts biological'.[75]

The description of bodily diseases goes into some detail.[76] They arise from three causes: (a) a defect in the number or arrangement of the basic triangles going to make up the constituents of the body (blood, flesh, etc.), leading to (b) a reversal of the normal processes of nutrition: instead of blood contributing to the formation of flesh, flesh to that of bone, and bone to that of marrow, the later creations collapse back into the earlier so that for instance the blood in the veins becomes clogged with detritus of flesh. (c) Most seriously, such corruption, typically bile or phlegm, can be diffused over the divine circuits in the head and throw them into confusion (Plato calls this, by a neat twist, the 'sacred disease');[77] and when bile penetrates the marrow it can even, in Plato's words, 'loose the soul from its moorings',[78] which presumably means death. Conversely, the soul itself, by excessive enthusiasms, can induce the body to over-indulge some action and so suffer some disorder.[79]

Plato's description is dynamic: soul and body each has its own proper motions, which make the proper constitution of each a moving one. Hence the insistence on constant movement as a means to health,[80] preferably self-motion, e.g. gymnastics, which help to shake the body into its proper motions; for sloth simply slows up those motions, so that the processes of waste and repair become clogged up; and this unnatural retardation can in turn affect the ideally circular motions that characterize the rational soul.

Now in such a system it is obvious that by 'disease of the soul'[81] it is not simply disorder due to intellectual error that is meant. In some physiological sense, Plato believes that just as a body can suffer disease, so too can a soul, fundamentally because of its incarnation in the world of becoming, with all the constraints on rational activity implied thereby,

---

[74] 81e–89d, esp. 86b ff.　　　　　　　[75] Solmsen (1955) 157.
[76] 81e ff. A good account is by Miller (1962).　　　[77] 85b.
[78] 85e.　　　　　　　　　　　　　　[79] 87e ff.
[80] 88d ff.　　　　　　　　　　　　　[81] 86d.

but also precisely because of those diseases of the body.[82] But a diseased soul, or at any rate a soul diseased in its rational part, which is made of special divine and presumably incorruptible stuff,[83] is not a soul that is vitiated in its own constitution. A diseased rational part is a part vitiated in its *operation:* the body it is supposed to control is less amenable because the bodily functions are impaired by physical disease. And under the heading of physical disease we are to include immoderate feelings of pleasure and pain in desires and in their satisfaction; for all these impede the power of reason.[84] Sexual incontinence, which arises from the super-production of seed by the marrow itself, has a peculiarly savage effect on the soul, making it sick and senseless.[85] Enfeebled in function, it is powerless to control the moral actions of the person, by directing what is so to speak the tool of those actions, the body.

What then constitutes the cure, i.e. punishment, of a diseased soul? Obviously it will consist in restoring the body to its proper constitution and functions; and this will automatically enable the soul the better to control it, at least in so far as the soul's ability so to do is not itself impaired by false opinion about moral standards and actions. How then is the body restored? Clearly by ordinary medical methods. Hence the convicted criminal before his judge and punisher is in principle in a condition no different from that of a sick person before his doctor. For that person, Plato recommends regimen rather than drugs, and the exercise of the body, by self-induced motion rather than imparted motion,[86] in order to approximate to divine motion, and achieve a balance and harmony of the body's motions with those of the soul. Special attention should be given to the circuits of the divine part of the soul, so that they may approximate to the divine circular movement of the 'all'.[87]

Flew has a sustained attack on those, including Plato, who, he says, treat criminal conduct as itself proof of sickness, and argue that if a man commits a crime, he must, by that very fact, be mentally sick.[88] He points out that many criminals are on the face of it perfectly sane, and their

---

[82] 86b–87b. But at 86b1–2 Plato does *not* claim that '*all* mental disorders are *solely* due to bodily states' (as Cornford (1987) 346 rightly observes). Cf. Arist. *NE* 1148[b]25.

[83] 69c ff. It may be that the constitution of the two 'mortal' parts of the soul *can* be vitiated, but not to the point of destruction. Robinson (1990) argues that the tripartite soul in the *Timaeus* is everlasting but not immortal.   [84] 86c.

[85] 86d. Cf. 728e for the effect of excessive bodily conditions on psychic states.

[86] 89a ff. In the ancient controversy about the relative merits of regimen and drugs, Plato consistently favours regimen: see Taylor (1928) ad loc., Cornford (1937) 352, and Hipp. *Epid.* 6. 5. 1, where the notion that bodily constitutions are in certain respects their own healers is similar to Plato's at *Tim.* 89bc.

[87] 46e ff., 89a, 90cd. This is presumably the principle of the constant movement, especially in Corybantic cures, described in *Laws* 789a ff. Cf. Skemp (1947), esp. 56–7.

[88] Flew (1973).

criminal conduct may be no more than the result of perfectly rational choices, however eccentric or mistaken. He argues that for a criminal to be accounted mentally sick it must be shown not simply that his state of mind is peculiar or anti-social or vicious, but that it is 'relevantly incapacitating', in the sense that it incapacitates him to do non-criminal actions, just as the illness of a sick man incapacitates him for work. In so far as this criticism is aimed at Plato, it goes wide of the mark. Plato's fundamental postulate is the Socratic paradox that no one does wrong willingly.[89] If a man commits a crime, it must be because he is indeed 'relevantly incapacitated', by being mentally sick; and mental sickness arises when the rational soul, in this rugged and awkward physical world in which its activities are inevitably hampered, finds itself locked in a body whose physical derangements impede rational and virtuous action. In these circumstances, criminal conduct may well occur. For Plato, if the incapacity did not exist, neither would the criminal action; and the criminal action does in fact show mental incapacity. So much, I believe, follows from the account of body and soul in the *Timaeus*.[90]

The central points in Plato's physiology, as Tracy says,[91] are then 'the interdependence of body and soul', and the '*close parallel of basic structure in the bodily and psychic organism*' (his italics). There is a continuity between the mental and the physical, the moral and the physiological. Mental and moral states are describable conditions[92] of the soul. The regimen of the body clearly affects not only the state of the body but that of the soul; and what seems to be a regimen of the soul, good nurture and following virtuous pursuits and studies, is indicated briefly.[93] The Socratic paradox is emphatically appealed to in support of the claim that bad mental and moral states are involuntary:[94] they arise from a poor condition of the body, or bad nurture by parents and educators (who are of course themselves, by definition, in a poor physical shape which affects their own moral condition and hence ability to educate properly).

[89] 86de.
[90] Cf. Kenny (1969) 249, 'Plato was deliberately assimilating a moral concept to a medical one', and Gosling (1973) 82 ff.
[91] Tracy (1969) 133. Cf. *Ch.* 157ab. It is amusing to speculate what Plato would have said faced with an out-and-out criminal who was also in superb physical health. He could make one or both of two replies: (*a*) that the man's opinions are wrong in some strictly intellectual sense, and that his twisted soul is able to utilize a healthy body for bad ends; or (*b*) that his body really is diseased, but latently, in some deep-seated way that vitiates the operation of his soul; and that in principle there must be some regimen, perhaps as yet unknown, which would eliminate that disorder—and in a way which would initially cause him some pain.
[92] See the pairs of states at 86e–87a, which are 'examples typical of each level [i.e., 'part'] of the soul' (Tracy (1969) 123 ff., esp. 132, cf. Segal (1962), esp. 104 ff. on Gorgias' *Helen*). Note too the parallels at 906c: excess or encroachment of some element is the same thing in bodies (disease), in weather and seasons (plague), and in cities and constitutions (injustice); the last item connects with the first, since it presupposes citizens with some kind of imbalance or excess in their souls.
[93] 87b, cf. 88b, where it is firmly linked with that of the body.   [94] 86de, 87b.

In Plato's works as a whole, then, and particularly in the combined physiology and psychology of the *Timaeus*, we find (*a*) *physical* disease, prevented or cured by medical regimen (movement, health-inducing actions), (*b*) *psychic* disease, prevented or cured by moral regimen (education, morality-inducing actions). The cure of the body assists also the health of the soul, and vice-versa. Within the penology and penal code of the *Laws* we find, (*c*) *psychic* disease, which results in criminal action, and which is to be cured by punishment.

Is (*c*) in the same realm of discourse as (*a*) and (*b*)? The criminal states of mind of (*c*) are diseases. Are they diseases in the same literal sense as those of (*a*) and (*b*)? It is hard to see why not. Admittedly, the *Timaeus* does not even mention penology,[95] and the *Laws* has little to say about physiology; perhaps Plato, himself suffering from a mental disease we may call philosophical schizophrenia, never related the two. But it would be very strange if the mental illness that leads to *criminal* action were not exactly the same kind of thing as that general mental illness that leads to immoral action in the widest sense.

If that is so, we have to ask how punishment can function as a cure which is regimen. For punishment aims to cause pain, regimen does not. So in what sense can one be said to apply regimen, when the instrument of the application is a penal code? Now in passage 1 (step 6) we are told that 'the law will teach and compel' the criminal.[96] As so often in the *Laws*, Plato applies a mixture of two principles. Hence the eight possible measures (actions, words, pleasures, pains, honour, dishonour, fines, gifts) are not exclusive: the judge is not confined to only one, and in fact is virtually obliged to use at least two, a 'compelling' measure and a 'teaching' measure. The latter, presumably, needs time to take effect, in that the criminal cannot be expected to change his character overnight, from a hater of justice to a lover of it. To achieve this, he will have to change his mode of life from a doer of evil deeds to a doer of good, or, in less black-and-white terms, at least refrain from the former. What we hope to see, therefore, is a change in his regimen: we hope that, by doing good actions only, he will become just. These measures of 'teaching', in effect persuasion and inducement by *logoi*, 'words', 'addresses', 'talking to', or by gifts, honours, etc., seem to be long-term follow-ups to the other side of the treatment, the 'compelling' one.[97] Such long-term influences are amply provided for in Magnesia: the citizens are surrounded by them, in the shape not only of their education, but of the legal

---

[95] Moral training in general is reserved for 'a different style of discussion', 87b.

[96] 862d, cf. 964bc.

[97] At 864c certain crimes will call for laws which will be 'most harsh', 'if they are to have their proper part/role'—perhaps with the implication that *something else* has some other part/role in punishing.

'preambles', the art forms and religious observances and orthodoxies, in short the whole social and educational ethos Plato tries to create in his second-best utopia.[98] To this extent, Plato's 'punishments' are indeed non-penal, in that they do not consist essentially of the infliction of pain (in addition, of course, to being non-retributive).

Now as part of, or as preparation for, such a change of regimen, the 'compelling' part of the treatment makes every sort of sense in terms of Plato's physiology. For when a person changes his regimen in some respect, the process is in its early stages painful; and the same is true, it seems, when one has to change one's outlook and personality:[99]

Change, we shall find, except in something evil, is extremely dangerous. This is true of seasons and winds, the regimen (*diaita*) of the body and the character (*tropoi*, 'ways', 'habits') of the soul—in short, of everything without exception (unless, as I said just now, the change affects something evil). Take as an example the way the body gets used to (*sunēthē*) all sorts of food and drink and exercise. At first they upset it, but then in the course of time it is this very regimen that is responsible for its putting on flesh. Then the regimen (*diaita*) and the flesh form a kind of partnership, so that the body grows used to (*sunēthē*) this congenial (*phila*) and familiar system, and lives a life of perfect happiness (*hēdonē*, pleasure) and health. But imagine someone forced (*anankazein*) to change again, to one of the other recommended systems (*diaita*): initially, he's troubled by illnesses (*nosōn*), and only slowly, by getting used to (*sunētheia*) his new way of life, does he get back to normal. Well, we must suppose that precisely the same thing happens to a man's outlook (*dianoiai*, 'thoughts') and personality (*tas tōn psuchōn phuseis*, 'the natures of souls'). When the laws under which people are brought up have by some heaven-sent good fortune remained unchanged over a very long period, so that no one remembers or has heard of things ever being any different, the soul is filled with such respect for tradition that it shrinks from meddling with it in any way.

This pain of a change of bodily or mental condition has of course, as we know from the *Timaeus*, a physical base: the constituent matter of the soul is moving in a set of established patterns to which it has grown accustomed and finds congenial. To adopt a fresh set, in order to change the regimen or outlook, demands that the existing set be broken up and to a greater or less extent modified and superseded by the new, which then itself becomes established over a period of time. The discomfort felt in, and temporary weakness entailed by, 'breaking the mould' are what

---

[98] 783a: the regimen for keeping hot sexual passion in check is in part lots of artistic *activity* of a disciplined kind ('Muses and the gods of competitions', cf. 790c–791a), in addition to the mental influences of 'fear, law, and right reason'. At 835e the Magnesians are said to have a life full of 'sacrifices, feasts, and dances', and at 858c ff. they are to be exposed to the legislator's 'writings and speeches' on how to live one's life. Note too how at 907c the atheists are to be brought by the arguments and addresses which form the 'preamble' to the law of impiety to 'hate themselves and cherish the opposite kind of character': the same two words are used as at 862d, 'hate and cherish' (*misein* and *stergein*).

[99] 797d–798b, cf. *Rep.* 404a, 406b.

we experience at having to abandon one habitual action or thought for another and better one.[100] The new action or thought, once achieved, becomes (as we have all experienced) gradually easier on the second and subsequent occasions; habituation brings ease and contentment, and the new pattern becomes in turn something it would be painful to abandon.[101]

The break-up of an existing pattern may be brought about by the person himself, who steels himself to put up with the pain in the interests of the change. But the break-up can also be induced by some-one else. How? Simply by causing the pain. For the causing of pain is necessarily a disruption of the regularity and equilibrium of the existing pattern: pain, like any other feeling, is embodied in and expressed by particular configurations and movements of the matter of the soul, which is affected by the conditions and movements of the body, and therefore by any pain imposed on the body direct; in other cases, say rebuke, the pain reaches the soul more immediately.

My suggestion, therefore, is that once Plato has denied punishment the status of recompense and retribution, he can treat it explicitly as not metaphorical but literal 'cure', or rather as part of cure's early stages. To acquire a new regimen the criminal necessarily experiences initial pain, which he may well not be willing to make the effort to bring on himself by attempting a reform of conduct. But we can impose that pain on him, by punishment, and so simultaneously and necessarily achieve the initial conditions essential for his change of regime, whether he likes it or not. So, whether he likes it or not, he has become at least a little less unjust than he was, for the unjust configurations and movements of his soul have been forcibly broken up, by an outside agent. Plato in the *Republic* recognized the imposition of 'another's justice' on an erring person, and in the *Laws* speaks of seeing a criminal *dikaioumenon*, 'being made just'; and when he says that the law will 'teach *and compel*' an offender to love justice and hate injustice, he means by the latter method exactly what he says.[102]

We have two elements; the break-up of the existing pattern of movement, and the pain of that break-up. The pain and break-up march together; neither is possible without entailing the other, just as one of two objects coupled rigidly cannot move without the other moving also.

---

[100] Cf. 646c ff.

[101] Cf. Belfiore (1986), esp. 429 ff., on the use of wine in re-education in *Laws* 1 and 2, the result-ing 'temporary weakness', and the eventual transition from *pathē* ('temporary emotional states') to *hexeis* ('permanent dispositions'). The criminal, I believe, passes through temporary *pathē*, temporary physical and emotional suffering, to a permanent (and hopefully better) *hexis*, condition. See too below on fear, especially p. 176 n. 110 on fear in *Laws* 1 and 2. As tools of moral re-education, wine and punishment operate in rather similar ways: they both re-prepare the soul for moral formation.   [102] *Rep.* 405ab, *Laws* 862d2 ff., cf. 934b.

The break-up is the physical, the pain the affective, element in an absolutely simultaneous twin process which is the initial stage in the change of regimen. The process may be brought about from within, by the person, or from without, by a punisher. In this sense, punishment *is* regimen, or more exactly, an integral and unavoidable part of the initial stage which any new regimen must have before it can begin to develop and consolidate over a period.

During that period the feelings of the person will be mixed: his pain will diminish, and pleasure at the new regimen will increase. In the establishing or impairing of the natural state, opposite experiences may take place simultaneously.[103] A person may be hot (*too* hot, I suppose), and cooled; or vice versa. The pain of the one experience is mixed with the pleasure of the other. It is not the case that in restoring a natural state only pleasure is felt. For 'everything happening contrary to nature is painful, everything happening in accordance with nature is pleasurable':[104] the new regime restores the natural state and so causes increasing pleasure, while the pain of the unnaturally disrupted state caused by punishment is diminished. But if the pre-existing regimen betokens an unnatural physical state, ought not the criminal to have been in some pain already, before being punished? Evidently not: we are told[105] that *gradual* disturbances of the natural state are imperceptible; and that makes good sense, for criminals rarely go to the bad suddenly; they glide into the condition gradually, and fail to notice because there is no pain to warn them.[106] The pain caused by punishment, however, is sudden and relatively violent: it serves to overwhelm the stable configurations of the unnatural but settled criminal state. One diseased state—a settled one—is overwhelmed by another and more fluid one, which offers potential for change of regimen. In this quite general sense, punishment, the infliction of pain, is homoeopathic.[107]

But it is also homoeopathic in a precise sense, in so far as the criminal is suffering from fear. Now fear arises from 'a poor condition of soul'.[108] The criminal's desire for the pleasure to be gained from wrong action induces fear of the pain he believes would come from other actions, in particular (in some cases) the pain of changing his way of life.[109] Now the

---

[103] *Phil.* 46cd, cf. 31d–32b.   [104] *Tim.* 81e.   [105] *Tim.* 64c ff.

[106] However, on Socratic principles they are also presumably suffering a sort of *covert* pain or loss, in the sense that were they living more virtuously they would be living more happily.

[107] *Tim.* 86b: pain is a disease of the soul; hence to apply pain to a bad/diseased soul is, presumably, to treat disease with disease.

[108] *Laws* 790c–791a, where the movement of Corybantic dancing, which has (I assume) a strong and regular beat, 'conquers' the fearful and frenzied internal movements of disturbed persons. This cure, however, seems to end here, in a feeling of peace and calm—unless that state is supposed to clear the ground for the inculcation of *better* psychic movements.

[109] As in the *Gorgias*, discussed on pp. 165–7; cf. 635bc, 636e, 653a–c, 727c, 875bc, Arist. *NE* 1104[b]10–12.

pain inflicted by punishment is deterrent: it induces, or is meant to induce, fear of further pain for further offences. The pain, in breaking up the existing state of the soul, imposes on the new state, with its potential for change, a new and *better* fear. The criminal now fears not the pain of doing good acts, but the pain of doing bad ones. This deterrent fear, which he should have had already by virtue of his education,[110] and which he has been unable or unwilling to overcome by himself, has been imposed upon him by the punisher. In the language of the *Laches*, he has learned to fear what should be feared: bad action; for the ultimate consequences for the agent and others of bad action are inferior to those of good action.[111]

To desist from bad action simply from a fear of its consequences is of course a humdrum level of virtue,[112] and Plato wishes his Magnesians to avoid bad action not merely because they recognize that it is reprobated and punished but because they believe it to be bad in some ultimate sense. To believe it bad, but to desire it and then to refrain from it simply because it is painful, shows a disaccord between reason and emotion.[113] But at least good habituation and moral conviction can be developed from the fear that deters in the short term. From a legislator's point of view, it is obviously preferable to bring the person to the point where he himself will attempt a change of regimen; for that does betoken a certain moral conviction, commitment, and resolution to put up with the pain involved. When punishers have to attempt the change on his behalf, by inflicting the pain he cannot steel himself to face, the omens are less good; indeed the person may simply suffer the pain, refuse in anger and resentment to respond to the 'teaching' part of the treatment, and resume his former regimen. In any case, the person can direct and control the effort to change more efficiently than a punisher can. Punishment is a relatively blunt instrument; for how can a punisher know that it will affect the relevant patterns and configurations in the

---

[110] 783a, 873a, 881a (passage 10). A good deal of the moral psychology of books 1 and 2, and many other passages in the *Laws*, indicate the importance of good fear in education, i.e. fear of the pain of doing bad things, and the corresponding *lack* of fear (courage) to overcome its pleasures, and to face the pain and effort of doing right. See especially 636de, 644c10 (fear = expectation of pain), 646e ff. (NB 647c7, 'make a man fearful with justice'), 649b ff. (NB 653c7, the 'wearing off' of correct feelings of pleasure and pain'), 699c (fear of law, amounting to 'modesty', cf. 647a1-2, 649c2, 671cd), 792c ff., 823c, 831a. Note too the sudden occurrence of fear, along with anger, as one of the 'painful' causes of offences at 863e5-864b4 (passage 1, steps 7(3) and 8; anger had been described in some detail a little earlier, but not fear): I take it this is the fear of doing right, and fear is of course painful. Fear and anger are bracketed at *Phil.* 40e, as true or false, i.e. 'true' in the sense of leading to advantageous results for the agent, 'false' in the sense of leading to disadvantageous ones: 'false' fear and anger is the state of being fearful or angry about the wrong things.

[111] 660d ff., 733d ff. His punishment is medicine/cure because it teaches, and so removes 'ignorance'; cf. *Crit.* 106b: 'knowledge is the best medicine'.

[112] *Phaedo* 68d ff., cf. *Rep.* 554de, 'commercial' virtue, on which see Hackforth (1955) 191-3 and Gallop (1975) 98 ff.   [113] Cf. 689a ff.

person? No doubt something can be achieved by linking in the person's mind a particular action or habit or way of life and the pain inflicted on it from outside, and encouraging him to draw his own conclusion, that in *this* or *this* respect his mode of life needs to be changed.

This reconstruction of the role of punishment in Plato has been worked out from first principles, by putting together in a Platonic spirit various strands in his thought whose connection he himself never made explicit, and perhaps never even made at all. In particular, I have tried to take the physiology of the *Timaeus* seriously, and to reconcile its conception of disease, pain, regimen, and cure with that of the *Laws*. The *Timaeus* is an advanced and technical work; certainly it requires sustained intellectual effort. The *Laws*, on the other hand, is a relatively popular work,[114] in which only selected subjects (e.g. theology in book 10, and certain parts of the penal code) are presented with much rigour or completeness. All too often, after sketching the outlines of something and tossing a few technical words about,[115] the Stranger refrains from taxing the brains of his interlocutors, clearly plain men who need *some* intellectual grasp of the reasons for the practical measures he recommends to them, but no philosophers. It would have been very bold to include even a condensed account of physiology, as part of an already lengthy discussion of penology. So in principle there is no reason why we should not assume the existence of a more esoteric idea of the way punishment actually works, in terms of the psychology and physiology of the *Timaeus*, than is actually articulated in the *Laws*.

However, if I have reconstructed Plato's ideas aright, the parallelism between medicine as cure and punishment as cure stands up almost but not quite completely. Medicine cures by regimen, drugs, cutting and burning; all these unavoidably entail pain, but pain is neither the purpose nor the means of the cure; and in Plato's view regimen takes pride of place. Punishment too, to judge from the 'teaching' element, consists in large part of regimen; and as in medical regimen such pain as there is seems to occur chiefly in the early stages.[116] It is also true both of medical and of penal regimen that pain is not the *purpose*; for penal regimen has mental health as its end, not the causing of pain as such either by way of compensation or by way of retribution. Where punishment, even *qua* regimen, does differ from medicine is in its *employment* of pain as a means of breaking up the existing bodily and psychic patterns, by way of a

---

[114] As Görgemanns (1960) has shown in detail.

[115] e.g. the low-level treatment of forms (or so I take them to be), of the unity of the virtues, and of other difficult topics, 960e ff. Even the elaborate theology of book 10 has argumentation that is loose and swift.

[116] Cf. 646d: the training imparted by drinking-parties has the advantage over physical exercises of being pain*less*; cf. 684c.

ground-clearing preparation for long-term moral regimen, and as a rudimentary method of inculcating immediately a low-level but desirable frame of mind (fear) as a preliminary to systematic re-training of character. This immediate application is limited to the inculcation of one moral virtue only, 'good fear'; to the others (temperance, wisdom, generosity, etc.) it is irrelevant.

At last one can see how it could make sense for Socrates to advise the punished person 'not to take into account the pain at all';[117] for what he will experience will be in large part regimen, in which pain occurs not as an end but as a tool in the early stages. However, he will have to take pain into account to the extent that part of the early stages of moral regimen is the inculcation of fear. But perhaps this is to read too much into what may be only a rhetorical *obiter dictum* in the *Gorgias*.

Plato's medical theory of punishment licenses him to do anything to the criminal, including the infliction of pain. But in fact he uses pain in only a limited and preparatory way, and he puts an emphasis on character-building regimen that is quite foreign to popular ideas. His conception of punishment differs almost *toto caelo* from that of the man in the ancient and modern street, for whom punishment must consist essentially and only in the deliberate infliction of pain, whether justified on retributive or deterrent grounds or in some other way. Indeed, Plato's conception of punishment goes a long way towards abolishing punishment as a conception.

MEDICAL PENOLOGY: PRACTICE

(a) Implications of consistency of purpose

Athenian jurors, faced with the welter of varied arguments paraded by litigants, were bound by no set penological policy, and had to rely on their own judgement and sense of justice, freely modified by considerations of private or public interest; and their animosities and prejudices were the frank target of the orators' pleas. Within the limits of laws which they themselves may have voted to establish, they could take any line they pleased from case to case and from day to day.

The Magnesian juror is in a quite different position. He has to administer a law and a penology which is not his own, but laid down for him, with the elaborate justifications which we have examined.[118] He has

---

[117] *Gorg.* 480c, cf. p. 166.

[118] Plato is anxious that the Magnesians should be conversant with law, not only through the 'preambles' to the various sorts of the legal code but from first hand experience: 767e, 855d, 957c. The principles of the law and its penology will not ordinarily be challengeable: 951a–952d, cf. 634de, 772cd, 796e ff. At 811c ff. the *Laws* is itself recommended as a sort of 'set book'.

essentially just two tasks: to *diagnose* the nature and extent of the criminal's psychic vice, and to *prescribe* the best means for curing it. His role is therefore simpler and tidier than that of an Athenian juror: he has a principled brief to achieve a specific purpose. On the other hand, that purpose is to be achieved by methods which go beyond the infliction of suffering; he must, it seems, prescribe also some form of teaching and regimen.

Consequently, a whole host of considerations which influenced Athenian juries must either become irrelevant or subtly change their meaning. The most important change is in the notions of justice and desert. A 'worthy' (*axia*) punishment in an Athenian court is one which a criminal deserves to suffer commensurably and reciprocally: it is a *just* infliction, in return for suffering inflicted. But Plato's penology is non-retributive; so a 'worthy' penalty is one which is 'deserved' as being appropriate to his particular psychic vice, in that it makes him a more just person: it is so to speak less 'just' than 'just-making'.[119] In either case the scale of the penalty may be arrived at by considering the objective seriousness of the crime, and to that extent the two calculations look the same—but they are not. In an ordinary court, the seriousness of the crime is a direct indication—perhaps modified, in cases of successful advocacy, by considerations of intent etc.—of the size of the 'worthy' penalty; in a Magnesian court, once recompense has been dealt with, the only relevance of the gravity of the offence is as one, and only one, indication of the type and intensity of the psychic vice; and it is the specific need to cure *this* disease in *this* individual that determines the penalty awarded. Magnesian justice focuses more on the criminal mind than on the criminal act. When an Athenian orator speaks of an accused's depravity, he refers, by a sort of shorthand, primarily to his criminal conduct, in mitigation or aggravation; in a Magnesian court the term will refer to his mental state, which stands in need of cure. The same sort of language may be used in either case, but the thrust of the assessment made will be different. Hence, if a Magnesian court thinks it proper to take into account a criminal's record of virtue, good service etc., it will do so not to determine what he is owed as a *quid pro quo* in mitigation of punishment, but as a help to diagnosing his psychic state.[120] The same will apply, as we shall see when we go through the code, to all those diverse pleas of status, age, ignorance, intent, blunder, deceit, etc., which were urged in Athenian courts as matters of justice: in Magnesia they will be simply tools of the diagnosis of psychic illness that precedes prescription of remedy.

---

[119] Cf. 934b (passage 12): *axias, dikaioumenon*, and p. 174.

[120] That Plato is prepared to treat the record as a guide to diagnosis is suggested not only by common-sense but by the cases of recidivism at 937c and 940c. Further, a number of passages show a belief that a propensity to crime may be genetic: 788c ff., 775b–e, 855a, 856cd.

Another and more obvious change in the use of a term will occur when a criminal is said by being punished to become 'better'.[121] An Athenian orator will mean that whatever the man's psychic state, he will be deterred by the memory and fear of suffering;[122] in Magnesia it should be his *character* that is reformed, in that he ought not even to wish to offend further. Again, all calculations are about the psychic state as the determinant of actions, not directly about the actions themselves.

A curable criminal deserves pity, not anger, for he is wretched.[123] To whip up anger against him in court to get a conviction is therefore, presumably, forbidden; and it would in any case militate against the calm deliberation Plato requires.[124] The turbulent atmosphere of Athenian courts is deprecated.[125] To win a case at all costs, by rhetoric and legal manœuvring, is punishable.[126]

The urging of wealth or social position to influence verdicts is, we may take it, strictly not permissible,[127] or at any rate they must not be urged as in Athenian courts; in Magnesia, one would have to show that they are relevant to diagnosing and remedying the psychic state of the person concerned. Further, to resort to lawsuits by way of political conflict or to gain social or financial advantage is surely, in any Platonic state, out of the question.[128] All this represents a considerable diminution in the range and variety of penological pleas heard in Athenian courts: the Magnesian juryman is to that extent set free to concentrate on Magnesian penology. His task will also be reduced and simplified because of the sharp reduction in the types of case and variety of subject-matter he will have to consider, thanks to Magnesia's very rudimentary economic system.[129]

Magnesian penology is state-directed: its principles and purposes constitute an orthodoxy. A single orthodox standard of belief and conduct applies also in every other department of life. Therefore in so far as any crime is a deviation from state-enforced norms, it may be treated as an offence against the public interest which is supposed to rest upon them. We have already seen[130] how the sense of injury to the public interest was strong in Athenian juries, and how the orators would attempt to represent private wrongs as involving it, in order to win verdicts and enhance penalties. Now Athenian society was a good deal more 'open' and varied than Magnesia was intended to be; so it is a fair guess—obviously it can be no more—that the weight of an officially sanctioned communal hostility to criminals, however 'private' their

---

[121] e.g. 944d (passage 15), cf. 784cd, 854d (passage 7); cf. 934a (passage 12).
[122] pp. 120-2.
[123] 731cd; against incurable criminals, however, anger may be given full rein. Cf. 927d1.
[124] 766de, 855c ff.   [125] 876b.
[126] 937e ff., cf. Lyc. *Leoc.* 11.   [127] Cf. 632c, 696ab, 706a.
[128] Cf. 679de.   [129] 842cd.   [130] pp. 102-4.

offence, would be brought to bear that much more readily in Magnesia than in Athens, or at any rate that this would be the intention of Plato, who is very ready to use communal pressure to arouse shame and enforce conformity in those who exhibit deviant behaviour.[131] Certainly the reflection that a criminal who offends against some state interest has been false to his training, or has been impervious to the social and educational pressures to which he has been exposed since childhood, is advanced as a reason for enhancing his penalty.[132] That is to say, whereas an appeal to the public interest in Athens takes a very crude form ('punish this man severely, O jurymen, in the interests of your own material well-being'), in Magnesia it would be couched in terms of the *kind of person* the material and other interests of the state require ('he has betrayed the common good by betraying his education—so punish him severely, since that will conduce efficiently to his cure'). The assertion of public interest in Magnesia is a distinct force, but it has changed its character. Once again, the emphasis is on the personality of the criminal.[133]

On the other hand, the assertion of communal interest in Magnesia would never go so far as to deny an injured party compensation, which could occur in Athens; for compensation is *de rigueur* in every case.[134]

Perhaps the most striking accommodation to be made to the Platonic way of thinking required of a Magnesian juryman would have to be made in his attitude to the death penalty.[135] In an Athenian court, it is thought to be the most severe penalty of all,[136] and is imposed retributively for serious crimes and for purposes of deterrence. But Plato rules out retribution, and sees the crucial issue as not the seriousness of the crime, but what that seriousness tells one about the criminal's state of mind. A very serious crime is evidence that the criminal is beyond cure, and that the normal policy of attempting to cure it is inappropriate. Only when this is so is the death penalty to be imposed, and in no other case whatever. The penalty will also serve to deter others, and cleanse the state of scoundrels.[137] Thus far, the policy is harsh but intelligible: one discards a harmful member of society, much as one might eliminate a

---

[131] e.g. 774c, 784e.

[132] 853b–854e (embracing passage 6), 942a (passage 14); cf. 884a ff.

[133] The public interest seems to be asserted in Magnesia in broadly the same kind of legal and procedural framework as existed in Athens; the Magnesian details are in many ways obscure, and we need not linger over them. See Morrow (1960) 264–70; the chief texts distinguishing public and private interests are 767bc and 767e–768a.

[134] 933e (passage 12).

[135] Guthrie V. (1978) 338: '. . . Plato by our standards makes pretty free with the death penalty.'

[136] Lyc. *Leoc.* 134, Lys. 12. 37; cf. Dem. 25. 59.

[137] 862e–863a (passage 1, step 6). cf. 855a (passage 7), 728c (passage 2), 942a (passage 14), 957e–958a (passage 16), and *Rep.* 410a, *Phaedo* 113e, *Gorg.* 525c.

sick animal from a herd;[138] and there is a 'spin-off' in the shape of deterrence to others.

However, Plato also seeks to justify the death penalty in terms of his curative penology, in spite of the facts that to all appearances death removes all possibility of cure, and that by definition the only persons to suffer this penalty are those who are incurable anyway. He resorts to a number of paradoxes, and it is worth trying to penetrate the thinking behind them.

1. *854de, in passage 7*. Reflecting that the incurable offender has not refrained from committing the greatest evils, the judge should punish him by the *dikē* of death, 'least of evils'.

2. *Ibid*. No *dikē* imposed by law aims at evil: it makes the person who suffers either better or less bad.

((1), in its last words, is a paradox in itself. (2) is not; but it becomes a double paradox when the *dikē* is death, because it is hard to see how death can make better or less bad, and because according to (1) death *is* an evil, albeit a small one.)

3. *862e, in passage 1, step 6*. It is 'better' for incurable offenders themselves to live no longer.[139]

4. *880e-881a, in passage 10*. The most extreme deterrent is the prospect of suffering in Hades; death is not an 'extreme' thing (apparently not extreme as a penalty, and therefore not extreme as the deterrent needed by the heinous offenders under discussion).

5. *957e-958a, in passage 16*. For incurables, death is a 'cure'.

Clearly, the purpose of these statements is to dissolve a dilemma generated by the new penology. On Socratic principles, one must *never* harm anyone; punishment, which causes pain, is justified by its curative effect; it is therefore no harm. But death, which *is* harm, precludes cure. How therefore can it be justified?

Paradox (4) is crucial. Plato apparently distinguishes between death as a quick transition from life to the bare *state* of being dead, or as that state itself, and the dead person's *post-mortem* punishments. Now if transition is an evil (the incurable offender suffers some pain in being executed, and perhaps also in the sense that he is deprived of the enjoyment, if any, he can derive from living), it is nevertheless a small, i.e. not an 'extreme', evil *when compared with* the punishments; hence the punishments are or should be a greater deterrent than the transition. Hence also the paradox of (1): death, considered in isolation from the *post-mortem* punishments, is 'least of evils'. Or perhaps the point is that death is a far lesser evil than remaining alive and becoming wicked and therefore

---

[138] Cf. 735a–736a (which concludes with passage 4), and 873b.
[139] Cf. 854c, Isoc. 5. 55.

more miserable. The paradox of (2) would then be similar: it would rest on the notion that death makes a man 'less bad' by *preventing* the moral deterioration that would take place if he were to go on living. Incurable he may be, but there can presumably be degrees of incurability: the fact that here and now he cannot respond to the legislator's curative effort does not preclude an even worse state or even greater inability to respond; for then he is, on a Socratic view, even more unhappy.[140] A similar thought is behind (3): to become no worse is 'better' than to become worse, and so be less happy in this life and more harshly punished in the next. (5) is perhaps a grim jest: the offender is cured of his bad moral state precisely because, being dead, he no longer has it.[141] (For the jest to work, we have of course to avert our eyes from the carry-over of the incurability into the next life: the offender starts his *post-mortem* punishments rather earlier than he would have done if he had survived to die a natural death.)

But why does Plato feel a need to resort to these paradoxes in the first place? He could perfectly well have justified the death penalty by reference to social considerations alone: the offender is incurable, we must be rid of him, and that's that. But in this case, would not exile suffice? The fact that he goes to some trouble to present death for incurables as a (necessary) evil, but a small one, or as even a benefit, suggests that even incurables are somehow under the benevolent impulse of Socratically inspired penology: even they must not be harmed, or only minimally, in response to social needs and policies. Or perhaps Plato simply wishes to persuade his Magnesian jurors to overcome a natural repugnance against inflicting the death penalty as often as he prescribes.

The man in the street naturally thinks of death as an extreme penalty because it is a deprivation of life. But that is not how Plato sees it. Its deterrent value apart, he regards it as simply that decisive moment when the virtuous go to their reward,[142] the incurables to their extreme penalties, and the curables cease to enjoy opportunities of moral improvement.[143] In itself, it is no great thing; what matters is the relationship between our conduct in this life and our experiences in the next.[144]

---

[140] See pp. 151 above, and cf. 661e ff., 716ab, 874d2.

[141] Compare the incurably sick carpenter in *Rep.* 406de, who dies and is quit of his troubles, and Soph. fr. 698 with references: Plato deploys a medical commonplace in the service of medical penology; cf. also Dodds on Eur. *Bac.* 1002–4.

[142] 959b; cf. 727d: we are not to suppose everything done in Hades is evil: the activities of the gods there may be the greatest of goods; cf. 828d.   [143] 959b.

[144] As I once heard a Christian priest say, 'People think death is the worst thing that can happen to you, but it isn't. The worst thing that can happen to you is to die in a state of sin.' The rhetoric of 908e (heretics deserve multiple deaths) presumably lies outside this network of thoughts: see p. 312 and cf. Dem. 19. 110, 302.

Conclusion

The technical legal and penological terminology Plato uses to describe the procedures and policies of the Magnesian courts is thoroughly Athenian, and when reading his penal code one finds it easy to forget that these old bottles have a great deal of new wine in them. The Magnesian juror will find himself listening to arguments and pleas couched in familiar language; but the arguments and the pleas themselves will be based on thoroughly Platonic principles and deployed for thoroughly Platonic ends.[145] Much vocabulary will be used with new meanings.[146] The reform of penology is radical, and the juryman will have to think in Platonic terms; but he may use conventional terminology. The political demiurge prefers to reform the use of the language, rather than replace the language itself by a fresh set of words. In intention at any rate, here is a major and far-reaching exercise in the political art.

(b) Diagnosis and prescription

Magnesian courts have a total discretion to decide whether an alleged offence took place or not, and within certain guidelines to settle on the penalties to be inflicted on persons found guilty.[147] How are they to set about their task? In what terms are they to *think*?

The individual offender

It is obvious from the assemblage of passages early in this chapter that jurors are expected to take a good deal of trouble to distinguish many different motives, intentions, characters, dispositions, and states of mind in general, in the light of the crime, its manner of commission, and a variety of attendant circumstances. Not every section of the code elaborates on these matters; but we may reasonably assume that the sections which do are paradigmatic for the sections which do not;[148] for there is nothing to distinguish the latter as essentially different in kind from the former: the cases they treat are in principle open to the same kind of elaboration. Plato gives several varied examples of the considerations jurors should bear in mind; and they should be studied and

---

[145] The language problem diminishes if he is from a place where Athenian terminology is not in use, or only partially (708ab), and ought in any case to disappear after the first generation or so, since Magnesia is fairly well insulated from the rest of the world.

[146] There are of course some overlaps of thought. For instance, *kolasis* both in Athens and Magnesia is to instill fear and to deter. Yet in Magnesia this is not the whole rationale of punishment, only a part.

[147] 875d ff., with specific reference to the law on wounding; but presumably it applies *mutatis mutandis* across the board: cf. 934bc.   [148] 876de, on 'patterns', *paradeigmata*.

applied by them in the light of the relevant preambles. He is attempting to train them to think in a responsible and principled manner.

Now all this elaboration has one important implication: Magnesian penal law is not to be a blunt instrument, but is calculated to cure criminals on the basis of accurate diagnoses of the diseased psychic state of *individuals*. For there can be no point in allowing for many different diagnoses unless there are to be many different criminal characters to whom they may be applied. Fragmentation and multiplication of diagnostic procedures and of the diagnoses themselves, to say nothing of the cures, imply a high degree of individual assessment.[149] Each diagnosis will therefore be fairly detailed: as I have put it elsewhere, Platonic criminal diagnosis is 'micropsychoscopically hexoboulo-metric'.[150]

The lack of medical terminology

In what terms are psychic diseases to be described? In principle, they are describable in physical terms, in that they are literally some kind of disorder of the physical constituents of the soul, as affected by the disorders of the body. Physiological disorders are expressed in pairs of extremes, which are physical and tangible: (A) hot/cold, wet/dry, heavy/light, hard/soft, etc.; and they have also a general capacity to be measured on conceptual scales: (B) proportion/disproportion, excess/deficiency, harmony/disharmony, balance/imbalance, more/less, weaker/stronger, rarity/frequency.[151]

Sometimes in the *Laws* there is language of the (A) kind: youths must not (by wine) pour 'fire' on the 'fire' already in their souls and bodies, and old men have a 'hard' character of soul, which can be made more malleable, like iron in a fire.[152] One could easily dismiss these cases as simply metaphorical, though in the light of the close connection between physical character and moral character in the *Timaeus* I should hesitate to do so. In specifically penal contexts too, (A) language occurs occasionally,[153] but not in the code itself, which makes virtually no attempt to relate criminal states to poor physiology.

---

[149] Note for instance the striking concern for precision in individual cases at 878e: 'should this criminal suffer a little more, or a little less, than death?' If indeed there was a practice or law in Athens that verdicts should be given for or against *individual* defendants, not groups of them, then Plato adopts for his own purposes a model which lies easily to hand (Xen. *Hell.* 1. 7. 23, Plato *Ap.* 32b).

[150] Saunders (1973a), 353. Plato needs a 'hexometer', a measure of states, or (as someone suggested to me) a 'depravitometer'. Compare the micropsychoscopy of *Phaed.* 270a ff., for the purpose of persuading different kinds of souls in the most efficient way; and note the comparison with medicine (270b).

[151] See Tracy (1969) 123–36 for the details, largely from the *Timaeus* and *Philebus*.

[152] 666a–c, cf. 775b–e.

[153] 853cd: criminals who are 'hornstruck', so tough *by nature* as not to be softened; cf. 880e.

The language of the code is that of (B). Plato proposes, it seems, that judges should diagnose the gravity or intensity or frequency of criminal psychic states on some sort of continuous quantitative scale. Such language does not exclude a physiological description of the states, but does not necessarily, on its own, presuppose it. At any rate, in spite of constant references to criminal states as 'diseases', Magnesian judges are not asked, when diagnosing those states on a sliding scale, to identify them individually in physiological terms; and it is clear why not. First, it would require very considerable knowledge of a complex compound, body and soul, of which much was still unknown, so that mistakes would be easy.[154] Second, even if mistakes of diagnosis were *not* made, one would need to have available a sophisticated and empirically effective range of physiological/penological treatments. That would be a tall order even today. The only practical course for Plato was to move on level (B), as did the orators; and the pain thereby inflicted by 'ordinary' punishment can still be understood, by those who know their *Timaeus*, as inducing the initial shake-up of the physical and psychic system as a preliminary to a change of regimen on both levels. And since the bad psychic configurations will presumably be bigger and more pronounced when a serious crime is committed, it makes sense to inflict a greater penalty, i.e. greater pain, which will cause a correspondingly greater change in those configurations.

The result is that Plato's penal code wears a very traditional look, in that most of the penalties it provides for consist of the infliction of pain, not the medical or quasi-medical regimen that would strictly be expected from his persistent statements that punishment is cure of disease. Behind it all looms the physiology of the *Timaeus*, a sort of hidden agenda whose implications are only partly followed up.[155] Central to it is the notion of regimen, which appears in the *Laws* not in an overtly physical form, but in the shape of the reforming programme of persuasion, re-education and training[156] that follows the preparatory

---

[154] See 636a, on the uncertainties of physical regimen.

[155] On the ideal and the practical in the *Laws*, see 739a ff. and 745e ff. Perhaps ideally Plato would have liked to impose 'cures' that worked in an entirely automatic way, independently of the will of the person; but he certainly did not wish to produce the sort of zombie depicted in Anthony Burgess's *A Clockwork Orange* (cf. my article, (1975)). In that novel Alec is 'cured', in that though he wishes to commit violence (his character remains unreformed) he simply cannot; whereas Plato's 'cures' must on the showing of his own physiology produce a person who has himself rationally embraced 'true justice', and whose actions proceed from internal 'movements', not those imposed from outside. It is the notion of acceptance that is somehow both constrained and willing that is absent from *A Clockwork Orange* but present in Plato. His penology is more radical than that of the Minister of the Interior in that novel, but more firmly founded on the realities of man as a rational animal with a will of his own. On constrained willingness, see 670cd, as well as the central text, 862d ('teach and constrain').

[156] See esp. 862d (passage 1, step 6) and 957d–958a (passage 16).

shock to the organism brought about by the pain of punishment and the inculcation of the right kind of fear. Here is medicine's greatest contribution to Plato's penology: the insistence that reform of an offender can properly be achieved only by regimen, by long-term renewal of the education he had when young, designed to affect his character and beliefs, so that his future conduct is securely determined by inner conviction rather than crudely painful and temporary physical pressures imposed from outside. The legal code and its punishments are a long-stop; they take over when education has failed.[157] The strictly penal measures do not in themselves form a substitute for more than a part of re-education, namely the instillation of good fear; the rest of the treatment is presumably supplied by the educational, social and cultural apparatus already in existence, and by the legal preambles.[158]

Diagnosis of psychic injustice

A man who deliberately abandons his weapons in battle and takes to his heels is acting from the species of fear we call cowardice. That much is, at least normally, obvious. The diagnosis is easy, and may well stop there.[159] But Plato realizes that if psychological diagnosis is to be useful, it must be considerably refined beyond the mere pinning of obvious labels on the moral dispositions that lead to offences. Given that there are no 'shrinks' in Magnesia, who might seek to plumb a criminal's state of mind by hypnosis or deep 'analysis' or whatever, how does he proceed? Naturally, he does not tell us tidily: the evidence has to be swept up from many texts. I present in systematic form what they suggest when inspected synoptically. His method seems to be as follows.

1. He entertains a large number of states of mind, or similar personal conditions, as contributory to or consequent upon the committing of offences.[160] The general term to describe them is 'injustice', *adikia*.[161] From the following list I exclude 'voluntariness' and 'involuntariness', which occur *passim.*

    ambition (*philotimia*): 870c
    anger (*thumos, orgē*): 863b,e, 934a
      (i) short-term ⎫ 866d ff.
      (ii) long-term ⎭

---

[157] 853a ff., cf. 718b, 783d.

[158] I take it that these would be bound to form part of the *logoi* which are included in the 'teaching' element of punishment at 862d (passage 1, step 6). The criminal would probably be directed to spend time in the company and conversation of good men: 728bc, 854bc (note the inducing in oneself of suitable belief); cf. Isoc. 2. 12–13.

[159] Once, that is, we have decided the abandonment really was voluntary: 943d ff. (passage 15).

[160] I list only those analyses of psychic states which occur in explicitly penological contexts. There are many others, especially in the early books.   [161] 863e (passage 7(3)), 869e.

avarice (*philochrēmatia, philochrēmosunē*): 938bc, cf. e.g. 870a
contentiousness (*philonikia*): 938b
cowardice (*deilia*): 856b, 870c, 873c, 934a; cf.943a, 944c
desire (*epithumia*), general or specific: 854ab, 863e, 864b, 869e-870a,
    934a
fear (*phobos*): 863e, 870c, 934a (cowardice);
    lack of fear (of gods): 880e
folly (*anoia*): 934a
    (i) of another (over-persuasion)
    (ii) own
ignorance (*agnoia*): 863cd, 864b (= (false) hopes and opinions), 881a
    (i) simple
    (ii) double (= conceit of wisdom, *doxosophia*) (*a*) with power (*b*)
    without power
illnesses (*nosoi*), literal: 864d
impulse (hormē), sudden: 866e
insanity (*mania*): 864d
jealousy, envy (*phthonoi*): 863e, 869e, 870c, 934a
longing (*himeros*): 870a
lust (*erōs*, 'love'): 870a, 941c
pain (*lupē*, i.e. the *fear* of it): 863e, cf. 864b, 934a
persuasion (*peithō*, implying a state of mind over-easy to persuade):
    934a
pleasure (*hēdonē*): 863b, e, 864b, 934a
premeditation, plotting, or the lack of it (*pronoia, epiboulē*, etc.):
    866d ff., 869e
repentance, or the lack of it (*metameleia*): 866e ff.
senility (*gēras*): 864d
sloth (*argia*): 873c
'uppitiness' (of a foreigner, *thrasuxenia*): 879e
yearnings (*pothoi*): 870a
youth (*paidia, neotēs*): 864d, 934a

Sometimes we find also the language of comparative strength and weakness: 'control' of the soul by desire, lack of ability to 'control' (*akrateia*) pleasure or pain, or 'defeat' by desire or pleasure.[162]

The length of this list is fairly impressive: Plato clearly wishes to make his Magnesian jurymen sensitive to the wide variety of possible criminal states of mind. Refinement of classification of moral 'disease' should then facilitate efficient 'cure'. It is in fact the very purpose of these identifications that differentiate them from the superficially similar

[162] 863e, 869e–870a, 934a.

identifications[163] made by the Attic orators of the moral states of defendants; for the orators were conducting partisan attacks, designed to win cases and maximize or minimize penalties, and it is often difficult to know whether they are referring to moral conditions or to actual offences.[164] By contrast, Plato is firm on the distinction;[165] and it is because the former lead to the latter that they need to be identified and cured.

Yet the list is something of an *omnium gatherum*, and is in certain respects unsystematic and unclear. (*a*) Four words—desire, lust, longing, yearning—seem virtually synonymous; the variation in terminology seems to have no diagnostic or functional significance. Over-fondness for money is termed, apparently indifferently, 'desire for money' and 'avarice'.[166] Voluntary and premeditated murders are said to arise from 'complete' injustice 'because of' defeat (*hēttas*) by pleasures, desires and feelings of jealousy;[167] yet a similar defeat or lack of control of emotions etc. (*akrateia*) is described as the cause of 'one's own folly':[168] what then is the relationship between 'complete' injustice and folly, and indeed between folly and ignorance? Or are they all the same thing? 'Impulse' and 'repentance' occur only in connection with anger: but why should they not apply to any offence? There is a haziness in the list which suggests that Plato is content to alert his jurors to the complexity of criminal psychology, rather than to give them a systematic analysis of it. Nor does he attempt to relate the disposition of offenders to their social circumstances, domestic background etc., as a modern social worker or lawyer would.

(*b*) The question about impulse and repentance raises a larger issue. Much of the material in the list is taken from general descriptions of 'unjust' psychic states in the penological preamble in book 9, and from the descriptions of the states of mind which lead to the three main categories of murder, and to theft. In most sections of the code indications of the state of mind relevant to the offence under consideration are absent or perfunctory. Plato is providing only models of procedure, and the discretion allowed to Magnesian jurors to decide on appropriate diagnoses for individual criminals will apparently be very great.

(*c*) However, it may be significant that the most elaborate analyses centre on the three 'parts' of the soul, as described in the *Republic*: (i) *Intellectual* causes of crime (see under 'ignorance'); there are important

---

[163] But Plato's list naturally includes some identifications absent from the orators, which arise from his special concerns, e.g. the 'conceit of wisdom'; no doubt he would be quicker to blame 'love of money' than would the average Athenian orator or juryman; and his analysis of anger is more elaborate than anything in the orators.   [164] See p. 116.

[165] 863b-d.   [166] 870a, 938ab.

[167] 869e.   [168] 934a4.

links with the treatment of heretics in book 10.[169] (ii) *Spirited* causes, specifically anger (see under 'anger'). (iii) *Emotional* and *appetitive* causes (jealousy, lust, pleasure etc.). But here again there is disregard for precise consistency: in one passage anger is bundled in with several emotions, and then a little later it forms a separate category along with fear alone, both being 'painful'.[170]

2. He grades the psychic states in an order of gravity. Some passages imply that a given state, otherwise undifferentiated, may exist at a higher or lower intensity; the higher is the more serious and attracts a higher penalty.[171] One state in particular, ignorance, is elaborated by two subdivisions, and climaxes with 'the conceit of wisdom with power', which is said to produce 'great and uncivilized offences', which are clearly more serious than those produced by the other and lesser forms of ignorance.[172] Some passages have rankings of two or more states: avarice is worse than contentiousness,[173] and cowardice is 'second' in point of vice to some other but unnamed condition.[174] The fullest ranking places, as causes of voluntary homicide, 'first' the love of money, 'second' ambition, and 'third' cowardly fears.[175] The love of money is said to be 'the greatest' ('cause'?), and to be a very great producer of the greatest trials, *dikai*, for voluntary murder. One assumes the other two causes are in some sense less serious, or at any rate less frequent; but the grading seems without practical effect, as in all cases there is no question of cure and the penalty is death.[176] Sometimes comparative wickedness is expressed in terms of hardness and softness of soul.[177]

In short, it seems that Magnesian jurors have to diagnose not merely which psychic state led to the offence in question, but also the level of intensity or force with which it was present, and its seriousness as compared with other psychic states.

3. He requires that the state of mind identified caused the offender to offend while in full possession of his faculties, with full and deliberate intent, without over-persuasion, and 'in character'. Hence lunatics, or senile persons, etc. are not punished at all, presumably because they are incapable of deliberation, and hence of a rational response to punishment;[178] and to the extent that the other conditions can be shown not to

---

[169] See pp. 309–12 below.

[170] 863e, 864b.

[171] 854c, the disease (a desire to commit sacrilege) *abates*, i.e. is felt less strongly; 867dc, *greater* anger in a killer, merits a *longer* exile; 934a, some desires etc. can be 'difficult to cure', implying others may be easier. Cf. 853b: general wickedness, *mochthēria*, has 'greater' (and presumably lesser) forms.

[172] 863cd, cf. 881a.

[173] 938c.   [174] 856bc.   [175] 870a ff.

[176] Plato *may* mean that avarice causes murders of parents, a super-heinous type of murder.

[177] Cf. p. 185. Other picturesque ways of expressing mental states: 854b (sting), 783ab (fire).

[178] 864de (murder etc., but presumably the rule applies universally); cf. p. 217 n. 3.

be fulfilled the standard penalty is abated;[179] in other words, to punish part-injustice with full severity is inefficient.[180]

4. He assumes that the gravity of the offence is itself a major indication of the extent of 'injustice' in the soul. His strict position, of course, is that the two things are not necessarily connected. A gift or a deprivation ought not to be called just or unjust 'unqualifiedly' (*haplōs*); what matters is whether the agent had a just disposition and character.[181] A robbery could be a just act, the giving of a gift an unjust one, depending on the disposition of the agent; and even if he does no harm, an unjust agent remains unjust.[182] These strong remarks occur in the penological preamble, and serve the purpose of driving home Plato's central point, that psychic states matter above all, and in principle may be assessed other than by reference to acts. In practice, however, when he comes to the details of the penal code, he takes the commonsensical position that psychic injustice can be read off from unjust acts, the gravity of the former being in direct ratio to the gravity of the latter.[183]

By 'gravity',[184] however, Plato clearly understands something far wider than the scale of the simple objective damage. Two offences may be identical in the damage they cause; but the manner, circumstances and purposes of their commission may differ widely. He therefore adopts 'adverbial' criteria for assessing the gravity of an offence; he pays regard not merely to *what* was done, but also to *how* it was done; for he believes that the manner of commission reveals the nature and scale of the injustice in the soul. He is sensitive to the following aggravations, *inter alia*:

(a) *The degree of violence or brutality used*: 843b, 856b, 864c, 942a. Some offences where the damage is the same may be committed violently or otherwise, 867d;[185] in other cases the damage presumably varies in proportion to the degree of the violence used: 878c, 933e.

(b) *Secrecy, fraud etc*: 843b, 864c, 908de.

---

[179] 934a, cf. 863bc, 865a ff., 943e. In murder in anger (866d ff.), sudden anger and repentance suggest the killer acted out of character, and is to that extent 'like' the involuntary killer. It is his normal self who is to be punished.   [180] See further p. 193 n. 192.

[181] 862b, cf. 934ab.   [182] 863e.

[183] 863cd and 870bc locate the causes of certain kinds of offences in states of mind, and suggest, though without actually saying, that *if* those offences occur, *then* the causes are as stated. It should be noted that nowhere in the *Laws* is one punished simply for *being* unjust: one has to commit an offence first (contrast the implications of Plut. *Di.* 9. 7). In the law of impiety Plato does not propose prosecutions of opinions as such; he confines himself to punishing their systematic expression and undesirable effects: see pp. 305–8.

[184] Plato seems to think in terms of 'bigness', 735e3, 853a5, 854e6, 863c7, cf. 870c4. 'Light' offences: 863c3.

[185] Note the particularly thorough investigation, over a long period, of the offender's actions, 867e.

(*c*) *Frequency and recidivism*: 937bc. Cf. 'recidivism' from generation to generation in the same family: 856cd.

(*d*) *Comparative status of offender and victim*: see chapter 15. To commit an offence against a superior in status is an indication of greater psychic vice than to commit it against an equal or inferior.

(*e*) *Exploitation of power and opportunity*: 761e ff., 777d, 863c, 933c, 934a; cf. the misuse of authority at 846b, 945bc, 946d, 955cd.[186]

Obviously more than one of these factors can be present in the same offence: 864c. Plato has therefore two windows into the soul of an offender: the objective gravity of the offence, and the mode of its commission.

The two modes of assessment are however not entirely easy to keep separate; and a nice example of the way they can modify each other is found in the law of murder in anger.[187] Two categories of killers are distinguished, initially on grounds of the comparative scale of their anger. The one who kills on a sudden impulse and straightway repents is 'like' an involuntary killer; the one who nurses his anger over a period, then kills without repentance, is 'like' a voluntary murderer; and the latter must be punished by a longer exile than the former. But Plato then admits that some cases do not run true to form. The 'more difficult' or 'tougher' criminal in the eyes of the law—presumably the embittered nurser of anger—might prove 'softer' or 'gentler'; and the 'gentler' (i.e. impulsive) one may prove 'tougher', having committed the murder 'in a more savage manner', whereas the embittered killer may have killed 'more gently'. The impulsive killer is in a sense gentler, since he repents; but *if he killed violently, he 'is' tougher*; conversely the embittered killer is tougher in the sense that he resolutely stokes up his anger; but *if he kills gently, he 'is' softer*. Each 'is' constitutes an inference from the manner of the killing to the character of the killer; and this assessment of character (and therefore of curability) cuts in a direction different from that of an assessment based on degrees of anger. And the Guardians of the Law, when deciding on pardon and return from exile, must go to considerable lengths to make a correct assessment of what was done. Anger and a propensity to violence do not exist in the same ratio in the character of all the members of this category of offenders; each character has to be assessed individually.

Prescription of penalty

If psychic 'injustice' is a 'disease' which is to be 'cured' by punishment, how should one set about matching punishments to the many and various psychic diseases which may be diagnosed? In his penological

---

[186] Cf. *Gorg.* 525d–526a.   [187] 866d ff.

manifesto (passage 1, step 6) Plato envisages 'words, deeds; pleasures, pains; honours, dishonours; fines or even gifts; or indeed *any* method' to make the (curable) criminal 'hate injustice and to love or not hate true justice'—in short, to cure him either wholly or partially. In the penal code, therefore, we shall expect to find individual unjust states of mind and individual penalties brought into some principled relationship. In particular, we shall expect at least the occasional prescription of measures which do not consist of the infliction of suffering, for example 'words, pleasures, honours, gifts'.

The code itself does indeed contain certain fairly generalized remarks on the necessity, and indeed difficulty, of settling on the right penalty in individual cases.[188] Juries are to 'attach to each offence (*hamartema*) the value/worth (*axia*) of (*a*) what has been done/suffered (*pathos*), and of (*b*) the action or doing (*praxis*)'.[189] (*a*) presumably points to the assessment of injury or damage, for purposes of recompense; (*b*) seems to indicate the offence itself with all its attendant circumstances (see above), as they enter into the calculation of the offender's injustice.[190] Jurors must aim, like a good archer, 'at the size of the punishment (*kolasis*) for the sake of each (offence?) and especially at the *deserved* (*axias*) punishment' (or, 'at the *value*', i.e. of the damage done).[191] Undeserved (*anaxias*) penalties must not be imposed on an undeserving (*anaxiōi*) person.[192]

It will become clear when we examine the complicated detail of the penal code that Plato does in fact apply a wide variety of gradations of penalty to a wide variety of analyses of psychic injustice. The most prominent distinction is between the death penalty for incurables and lesser penalties for curables. At this point, however, only certain broad observations are needed.

---

[188] e.g. 861c, 943e. The common formula is 'assess what he must suffer or pay' (e.g. 934b). As Gernet (1951) pp. cxlii–cxliv rightly stresses, Plato frees jurors in *timētoi agōnes* (see p. 101) from the crude necessity of choosing between the assessment of the prosecution and that of the defence: he allows them a free hand to fix (presumably after discussion among themselves: 766de) whatever penalty seems right; this reform obviously serves his penological purposes. He is perhaps following Hippodamus.

[189] 876d. I should now wish to confine to a footnote the expansion of *pathos* and *praxis* which (following the Budé version) I built into my Penguin translation. Bury's 'penalty merited by the wrong as suffered and committed' (Loeb) is neater.

[190] Cf. the use of *praxis* a little earlier, 864c, 867e, 874d. *Praxis* and *prattein* are often used of offences: *Gorg.* 525a1, *Rep.* 614d1.

[191] 934b: *tēs axias*, fem. sing. genitive, may be adjective or noun. I prefer the former: recompense having been dealt with at 933e6–10, the weight of the passage falls on cure, and 'and especially value' would be an awkward reversion to the subject of damage.

[192] Cf. 731cd (over-severity deprecated), 882bc and 949c–e (punishment ceases when it suffices), and above all 856cd (descendants not liable to punishment for ancestors' offences: contrast pp. 118–20); the single exception, ejectment from the estate when there is a family history of capital offences, is presumably precautionary rather than penal.

1. Injustice is persistently described as disease and punishment as cure; yet the penalties in the code are not literally medical.[193] They are couched in terms of comparative size or harshness, *vel sim.* Measures other than the infliction of pain are rare,[194] and the range of penalties Plato allows is largely traditional.[195] Certain remissions are permitted without regard to the state of mind of the offender.[196]

2. As a general rule, greater psychic injustice attracts more severe penalties. Hence the killer in anger who approximates to a voluntary killer is punished more severely than the one who approximates to an involuntary killer, a measure which is justified by appeal to the principle, 'that which is like a greater evil should be punished more greatly, that which is like a lesser evil should be punished less'. It is clear that the 'evils' here are states of mind: the higher penalty is imposed on the one killer because of the 'size' of his anger as compared with that of the other.[197]

3. Although close examination of the penal code to some extent dispels the impression, ostensibly at any rate Plato often grades penalties in the light of the gravity of the offence, not with reference to the state of mind of the offender. Up to a point, this is natural and justified on his own principles; for the objective act can indeed convey information about psychic state. The crucial word is *axios*, 'worthy'. It is of course utterly appropriate in calculations of damage and recompense; the offender must pay the injured party the 'value'. But Plato is capable of talking occasionally in terms of penalties that 'are worthy of' or 'fit' the crime, without reference to mental states, so as to appear to be operating on some retributive theory of punishment.[198] In these cases he may be incautious, or speaking popularly; for after all, if serious acts betoken serious mental states, to punish for acts retributively is in a crude way to punish states also. Equally, the language of desert is always open to construction in a reformative sense: it is 'right' or 'fitting' that such-and-such a penalty should be imposed, *as cure.*[199] But Plato also sometimes

---

[193] See above, pp. 185–7.

[194] 845b (admonition of a free foreigner, cf. 777e); 908e ff. (re-education of certain heretics—heresy being of course an offence with strong *intellectual* roots). So much for 'words'. Of 'pleasures', 'honours', and 'gifts' I find no instance; presumably they are incentives ('reform yourself, and you will be rewarded'); cf. Stalley (1983) 142–3, and perhaps 855a.

[195] 855c: death, imprisonment, whipping, fines, various humiliations (some exotic: see Gernet (1981) 240–51), and exile.

[196] e.g. 869a, contrast 876e–877a.

[197] 867b–e.

[198] e.g. 762e1, *axia dikē* (presumably 'penalty'); 778d3, 'acts of injustice worthy, *axia*, of death'; 855a7, b5–6; 882c1; 908e2, in a passage which pays much attention to states of mind.

[199] As at *Gorg.* 480cd. Note 941d3, 'the law *deems it fit* (*axioi*) to punish' on the basis of comparative curability, not with direct reference to the offences. Cf. 876e8, a criminal is not worthy (*axion*) to be pitied, i.e. pity would be useless treatment (cf. 731cd).

uses the language of 'need' or 'necessity' or 'propriety', in which suggestions of desert are only implicit.[200]

THE ROLE OF CRIME-SPECIFIC PUNISHMENTS

In the determination of punishments Plato pays little regard to crime-specificity. The principle is of course employed in some of the eschatological myths (see next chapter), to picturesque effect, and with stress on retribution. But I find no hint of it in the long theodical myth of the *Laws*, which is addressed to the young heretic in book 10.[201] He does however make striking use of it in the preambles to the law of homicide; intentional killers are fated to suffer, in their next reincarnation, precisely what they inflicted; in particular, killers of parents are fated to be killed by their own children.[202]

Similarly, few actual penalties in the *Laws* are crime-specific. A slave who intentionally kills a free man is to be scourged and executed within sight of the dead man's tomb.[203] There may be point in the requirement that heretics who become 'beast-like' are to be imprisoned in the 'wildest' terrain of Magnesia.[204] The clearest case is in the law relating to cowardice on military service. Plato remarks that it would be appropriate to transmogrify the coward into a woman; but since that is not possible, he must be made to suffer the disgrace of living for the rest of his life *without danger*, 'because of the love of life'; this penalty is 'as near as possible' to the other.[205] Of the major survival (if that is what it is) of crime-specificity in Athenian law, 'radishing' for adultery, there is no trace in the relevant part of Magnesia's penal code.[206]

Plato's lack of interest in crime-specific punishments is all of a piece with their rarity in the contemporary Athenian law. Since their main effect is to suggest retribution rather than reform, it would have been surprising if he had exploited them more than he did. Even in the case of the coward, he does not rely on the crime-specific punishment alone: he adds a conventional penalty in the shape of a fine. In the homicide law, the principle is confined to the preface of the section on the most serious homicides of all, and is no doubt to be justified in these extreme cases by its blood-curdlingly deterrent effect.

---

[200] e.g. 908b3–4, 869c4, 949d7.

[201] 903b–905d. It is however just possible that the penalty for bad souls at 904e, of being dispatched to join bad souls, is to be regarded as crime-specific.

[202] 870e, 872d–873a.

[203] 872b.

[204] 908a, 909a–c; cf. the soul which is 'wild' with desire, 870a. See also pp. 156–7 and 275 on rustication for assault C, on one's parents or grandparents.   [205] 944d–945a.

[206] 838a–842a, cf. pp. 82, 247.

6

THE PENOLOGY OF PLATO'S MYTHS

INTRODUCTION

The eschatological stories in Greek literature down to Plato have in common the central notion that offences for which the penalty has not been paid in this life will be punished after death by surrogate agencies. The purpose of the stories is twofold: to provide an incentive to good conduct, and to reassure injured parties that in the end they will obtain at least the satisfaction of their enemies' suffering. The punishments described are therefore purely retributive, and often described in lurid terms. Certain mystery-religions, however, developed the idea that *post-mortem* punishment could constitute a stage in a system of moral reform.[1]

Plato wrote several eschatological myths in this broad tradition: they were calculated to convince Socrates' interlocutors that injustice will be punished in the end. We need to review them briefly before considering the myth of the *Laws* itself and the mythical material incorporated into the legal 'preambles', whose penological doctrines are meant to exist in the minds of his citizens side by side with the 'official' penology which I have tried to reconstruct. I take the myths entirely at face value, seeking only to extract the penological ideas which they implicitly or explicitly present: I have no concern to rationalize or allegorize them.

The order in which I present the first four myths (those of the *Gorgias*, *Phaedo*, *Phaedrus*, and *Republic*) may or may not be the order of composition; for these matters are highly uncertain. But the *Laws* is by common consent the last of Plato's writings, and the *Timaeus*' strong affinity to it in point of eschatology is a pointer to a late date for that dialogue too. At any rate the eschatology of these two works is sharply different from that of the other four.

---

[1] This paragraph summarizes pp. 52–61. Cf. also Annas's quotation (1982, 123) from Sidgwick, and Dodds (1959) 373–4.

GORGIAS

The myth of the *Gorgias*[2] is simple: wicked souls, which carry the marks of their character on them, are punished in Tartarus, the prison of requital and penalty/justice (*dikē*). They are unhealthy, and their punishment is their cure, alike in this world and the next.[3] Incurables, who are beyond help, are visited with the most fearful penalties, apparently forever, and serve as an example to others.[4] The nature of the punishments for the curables is described only as 'fitting', and to undergo them is to become 'better'.[5] To live virtuously in this world is therefore advantageous 'for the next world too'.[6] What happens to us after *post-mortem* reform is however not stated: there is no mention of reincarnation.

Medical terminology is fairly pervasive,[7] but the manner in which cure is effected is indicated only by the words, 'those who are helped by being punished by gods and men are those who have committed curable offences; however, the help they get, both here and in Hades, comes through pains and sufferings'.[8] The word 'however' points up the paradox; for to be helped is not normally a painful experience. 'Through' translates *dia*, which is ambiguous as between the instrumental 'by means of', and the associative 'accompanied by', or 'in a context of'. The latter meaning could point to some process that did not consist of pain, but just happened to be painful. Deliberately or not, the same door is left open here as in the body of the dialogue.[9] A soul exhibits its nature (*phusis*) and experiences (*pathēmata*) as they have developed *as a result of* the person's unjust way of life (*epitēdeusis, adikia*); the judge sees his 'lack of health', which arises as a result of false nurture.[10] In other words, the unjust state, as in the body of the dialogue, is traced to bad regimen, brought about by bad education. The conclusion seems obvious that 'cure' would consist in a *change* of nurture and way of life—even, so to speak, after death, when improvement is professedly still possible. But the conclusion is not drawn, and the strong impression is given that the 'cure' is simply suffering and deterrence, without further influence on character and convictions.

---

[2] 523a ff.
[4] 525bc.
[6] 527ab.   [7] 524e ff.
[3] 525b.
[5] 525b, 526bc, 527bc.   [8] 525b.
[9] See pp. 165–7 above. At 525b1 *pathē* would then be (painful) 'experiences', not 'sufferings'.
[10] 524d ff., cf. *Phaedo* 107d.

PHAEDO

If we splice the relevant passages,[11] we find that a non-philosophic soul, on the death of the body, experiences the following.

1. Since its love of bodily pleasures has made it heavy with the corporeal, it remains for a period dragged back to the visible realm, somehow attracted to its corpse and flitting around the grave. It is compelled thus to flit as a *punishment*; and eventually it is again bound to some human or bestial body which is appropriate to its former misdeeds.

2. Its *daimon* drags it away from the body with considerable difficulty; but eventually it joins the other souls at a place of judgement, where they are divided into 3 categories: (*a*) those who have lived 'middlingly', who pay the penalty for their crimes (including any for which they have already been punished in this world, apparently), and are then 'absolved'; (*b*) the incurable, who have committed very heinous crimes such as murder, and are flung into Tartarus, never to emerge; (*c*) persons who have similarly committed great crimes, but with diminished guilt, because they acted in anger and repented; these remain suffering in Tartarus until they persuade their victims to let them off; for that is their penalty.

3. Those in category (*a*), and presumably eventually those in category (c) who have been let off, are reincarnated in new bodies. This is evidently the same reincarnation as takes place after the 'flitting' in stage (1): the judgement and punishment intervene between flitting and reincarnation.

Three rounds of penalties, therefore, are apparently envisaged:

1. Flitting.[12]
2. Penalties at Acheron or in Tartarus, leading to absolution and purification.[13]
3. Reincarnation in a body appropriate to the misdeeds which were thus punished, and of which the offenders have been 'cured', 'absolved', 'purified', or 'let off'.

The distinction between curable and incurable offenders is clear; and the way in which the latter are 'written off' anticipates the spirit of the *Laws*. But the medical terminology is perfunctory: the 'cure' seems to consist not of some medicine or treatment that might be painful, but only of pain; and *if* it amounts to moral reform, it ought to dispense from

---

[11] 81a ff., 107d–108c; 113a, and 113d–114c.
[12] 81d, *dikē*.
[13] 113d, 114b, *dikē* imposed by personal but unnamed judges, *dikastai*.

the further punishment of an undesirable reincarnation.[14] Even if 'cure' is supposed (not that the passage naturally suggests it) to take place subsequently, *during* that reincarnation, not before it, the unfairness is striking; for the slate has apparently been wiped clean by an 'absolution'. This idea of cure seems to have been somewhat implausibly grafted on to a procedure whose purpose is primarily retributive and vindictive (note how the satisfaction of the victim is crucial for offenders in category (*c*)).

Incoherent though the myth of the *Phaedo* may be in this respect, it does contain the important suggestion that a wicked soul, burdened by its devotion to the body, will by its own acquired corporeal heaviness *automatically sink* through space.[15] This notion of automaticity will be developed in the myth of the *Laws*.

PHAEDRUS

Some brief use of the notion of 'heaviness' is made in the description of how souls whose vision of the heavenly truths is inadequate become filled with forgetfulness and evil, and so sink to the earth, where they enter the body of a man—philosopher, king, politician, etc.—in descending order, according to the extent of the vision they have had.[16] They then enter on a period of ten lives, each followed by judgement and a period of a thousand years either of punishment or reward for conduct during it. After 10,000 years they recover their wings; those who were philosophers for three successive lives regain them after 3,000 years; and after the first incarnation souls may enter the bodies of beasts.[17] At the end of each 1,000 years' period the souls enter a new body, which is allocated to them after a process of lot-taking combined with their own wish and choice;[18] but no details are given of the relationship between choice and lot. Nor are we told what effect reward or punishment has on the character of the soul and the wisdom or otherwise of its selection of its next life. Medical vocabulary is absent; in particular, we hear nothing of eternal punishment for incurables.

The myth of the *Phaedrus* is therefore of limited penological interest. Its fundamental point is quite basic: conduct in this world is rewarded or punished in the next.[19] That punishment—and for that matter reward—can enlighten and improve a soul and enable it wisely to choose a next life which will be superior to its predecessor is perhaps implied; it is certainly not stated outright.

[14] Cf. Annas (1982) 127–8.
[15] 81c; cf. Annas (1982) 126.
[16] 248a ff.
[17] 248c–249b.
[18] 249b.
[19] 248e.

REPUBLIC

The penology of the myth of Er runs as follows.[20] After each death of the body, the soul is judged. It may be dispatched to some heavenly region for 1,000 years of bliss, as a reward for a just life, or to some subterranean spot for a similar period of punishment for an unjust one; each reward and punishment is on the scale of ten times the benefit or injury done in this life. Incurable offenders, after being consigned to Tartarus, never emerge; but both curable souls and just souls reunite after the 1,000 years, and draw lots to decide the order in which they shall choose their next reincarnation; a vast variety of human and animal lives, both good and bad, are on offer. The choice is absolutely for the soul itself to make: it is entirely unconstrained, open, and free; and the soul can blame no one but itself if it chooses unwisely. Two things influence the choice; (*a*) the soul's experiences during the preceding 1,000 years,[21] (*b*) its memories of how its habits in its previous existence caused it happiness or misery at that time.[22] By choosing a particular *type* of life—philosopher, tyrant, businessman, or whatever, with various qualities such as intelligence, weakness, etc. appropriate to that life—it necessarily chooses a particular *rank* or *nature* for itself, since particular types or modes of life necessarily confer on the soul particular characteristics. The 'better' life is one which will render it more just, and the 'worse' life one which will render it more unjust[23] (that is to say, on a Platonic view, happier or more miserable respectively). After their choices are ratified as unalterable, the souls drink from the river of forgetfulness, and are duly reincarnated.

The periods of 1,000 years, and the provision for lot and choice (now explained), clearly link this myth to that of the *Phaedrus*. Further, there is the same vagueness about the role of the punishments: not only are they inflicted, apparently, even if a penalty has already been paid in this world, but they seem to be primarily retributive. The curable/incurable distinction is made but not stressed.[24] Even a rewarded soul—admittedly one which was good out of mere habituation, not from philosophy—can display 'greed and folly'.[25] True, there is a suggestion (no more) that 'sufferings' (*ponoi*, 'labours') make the choices of the punished souls better than those of the rewarded souls;[26] however this is apparently not the result of moral conviction, but of prudent caution born of a memory

---

[20] 614a–616a, 617d–end.

[21] 619b–d.

[22] 620a ff., where (*b*) is said to be greater influence than (*a*). On the numbing penological and psychological consequences of feeling that one's present character is the result of choices a different 'I' made in a previous existence and after death, see Annas (1982) 132 ff.

[23] 618e–619a, cf. 618b.

[24] 615e.

[25] 619b.

[26] 619d1–6.

of pain which they do not wish to undergo again. In general, the lack of the resounding statements of the *Gorgias* that *post-mortem* punishment 'helps' and 'makes better' is remarkable. The emphasis of the *Republic's* myth is on the free choice a soul has to fare well or ill in its next reincarnation.

TIMAEUS

The treatment of *post-mortem* punishment is spare and simple,[27] having virtually none of the picturesque detail about judges and judgement and awful sufferings beneath the earth included in the earlier accounts. It is in effect an explanation of the creation of animals other than human beings. The soul of a person who has lived a morally good life is dispatched to the heavenly region where its own star is, i.e. to the highest of the four main cosmic masses, that of fire; but the soul of a man who has lived unjustly is reincarnated in the body of a woman; if it continues to be unjust in that and further lives, it is further demoted down the scale of animals of the air, land, and water. These three demotions, described as 'changes' (verb *metaballein*), arise from derangement in the rational, spirited, and appetitive part of the soul respectively; and they occur, for all one can tell, automatically, as a result of decrease of rationality in the soul.[28] On the other hand, we learn of certain personal agencies, who 'remould' the most stupid men into sea-animals.[29]

There may be something of the humorous in this; at any rate the punishments are in various ways 'crime-specific' (birds, for instance, coming from feather-witted men who thought that the best way to study the heavens is through the eye rather than the brain). But although such demotion is envisaged as punishment,[30] the purpose of the changes is not said to be in any way the 'betterment' of the souls;[31] in particular, medical concepts are entirely absent. It is notoriously hard to know how to interpret the mythical elements in the science of the *Timaeus*; but at least we do not seem to be confronted with a moral fable of the traditional kind, in which picturesque subterranean gods punish wrongdoers after infallible judgements. That kind of apparatus has been swept away. The *Timaeus* seems to present, with mythical colouring, a law of nature which operates automatically; in that case the soul's next

---

[27] 42b–d, expanded at 91d–92c; cf. 90e, where the initial transformation into women is described as a 'probable story'.

[28] 92c1–3. Note at 42cd (cf. 91e) the influence of the weight of corporeality, as in the *Phaedo*.

[29] 92b; the 'remoulders' I take to be the gods of 42de.　　　　　[30] 92b, *dikē*.

[31] However, promotion up the scale of beings is briefly envisaged at 92c.

reincarnation is not chosen by it, but merely falls to it by some impersonal procedure.

LAWS

The eschatological myth of the *Laws*[32] occurs in the course of the long theodicy which occupies almost the whole of book 10. It follows the philosophical proof of the existence of gods and of their concern for mankind, and is technically part of the preamble[33] to the law of impiety; it is described as 'words' or 'stories' designed to charm and persuade the imaginary interlocutor, an heretical young man, in addition to the formal proofs he has just heard.[34] As one expects in eschatology, there is a certain amount of vivid detail,[35] and a touch of protreptic rhetoric;[36] but the prevailing tone is plain and sober, though in places the text becomes decidedly murky. The following extended extract combines summary (square brackets), quotation, and at one point brief interpretative paraphrase (italics); it may be supplemented by my full analysis published elsewhere, on which I draw here.[37]

903b4–e1. [The universe is a teleological construction, in that all its parts, including all human beings, have been arranged by its Supervisor for the good of the whole; and men should realize that their position is best not only for that whole but for themselves as well.] And since a soul is allied with different bodies at different times, and perpetually undergoes all sorts of changes (*metaballei pantoias metabolas*), either self-imposed or produced by some other soul, the divine Draughts-Player has nothing else to do except promote a character which is becoming better to a better place, and relegate one that is deteriorating to a worse, as is appropriate in each case, so that they get the lot/portion that is suitable for them.

903e3–904a4. Thanks to the system and order present in the physical construction of the universe, the Supervisor and the gods find their task marvellously easy.[38]

904a5–905a1.

ATHENIAN: Our King saw (*a*) that all actions are a function of soul and involve a great deal of virtue and a great deal of vice, (*b*) that the combination of body and soul, while not an eternal creation like the gods sanctioned by law, is nevertheless indestructible[39] (because living beings could never have been

---

[32] 903b1–905c7.   [33] 907d4.   [34] 903b1–4.

[35] Rulers (903b7), a Draughts-Player (903d6), a Supervisor of the All (904a3), Our King (904a6), various anonymous gods (903e3 etc.), Hades (904d2 and 905b1), and a quotation from Homer (904e).

[36] 905a ff.   [37] Saunders (1973*b*).

[38] That is to say, the physical system described in the *Timaeus* ensures four relatively stable cosmic masses, change within and between them being subject to strict laws. For a defence of this interpretation of a very obscure passage, see Saunders op. cit.

[39] Presumably because it persists, in a sense, from generation to generation. The train of thought is none too clear.

created if one of these two constituent factors had been destroyed), (c) that one of them—the good element in soul—is naturally beneficial, while the bad element naturally does harm. Seeing all this he contrived a place for each constituent where it would most easily and effectively ensure the triumph of virtue and the defeat of vice throughout the universe. With this grand purpose in view he has worked out what sort of position, in what regions, should be assigned to a soul to match its changes of character; but he left it to the individual's acts of will to determine the direction of these changes. You see, the way we react to particular circumstances is almost invariably determined by our desires and our psychological state.

CLEINIAS: Likely enough.

ATHENIAN: So all things that contain soul change, the cause of their change lying within themselves, and as they change they move according to the ordinance and law of destiny. Small changes in unimportant aspects of character entail small horizontal changes of position in space, while a substantial decline into injustice sets the soul on the path to the depths of the so-called 'under'world, which men call 'Hades' and similar names, and which haunts and terrifies them both during their lives and when they have been sundered from their bodies. Take a soul that becomes particularly full of vice or virtue as a result of its own acts of will and the powerful influence of social intercourse. If companionship with divine virtue has made it exceptionally divine, it experiences an exceptional change of location, being conducted by a holy path to some superior place elsewhere. Alternatively, opposite characteristics will send it off to live in the opposite region. And in spite of your belief that the gods neglect you, my lad, or rather young man,

This is the sentence of the gods that dwell upon Olympus,[40]

to go to join worse souls as you grow worse and better souls as you grow better, and alike in life and all the deaths you suffer to do and be done by according to the standards that birds of a feather naturally apply among themselves. *905a1–c7.* [Flee where you will, this sentence is inescapable, either on earth or in Hades, or even if you go to some even more remote place: you and all other offenders inevitably pay an appropriate penalty. For the gods do not ignore the universe; and if you don't realize that, you can have no real idea about life's happiness and misery.]

This account seems to be a more elaborate version of that of the *Timaeus*. Again, the notion of change (*metaballein*) is prominent, and again the souls go up or down by a more or less automatic process, without the personal action in every instance on the part of Our King, the Draughts-Player and the other vague and mysterious characters who appear briefly.[41] In both dialogues the direction of the transfer is determined

[40] xix. 43.

[41] The language describing the journeys is quite neutral: 'travels', 'proceeds', 'falls', etc., not 'is sent' or 'is conducted' by some person. Even passive verbs such as 'brought' (e.g. *Laws* 905b2) need not imply a personal agency.

by the moral quality of the souls at the death of the body, and this quality has been chosen and acquired by the souls themselves. Their rational and moral qualities, and their location in space, are in a sense the same thing. Demotion consists in the *Timaeus* of transfer to lower animals at the next reincarnation, and presumably the same is true in the *Laws*. At any rate we are told that souls in the *Laws* are 'associated now with one body, now with another', that they have many deaths, and that they rise and fall spatially.[42] It appears that one is not necessarily either demoted or promoted: the 'small horizontal changes of position in space'[43] imply the possibility of rebirth as another human being, if one's moral record is not especially good or bad. If that is right, demotion would suggest rebirth in something lower than human. Nor does the *Laws* mention relegation to the body of a woman, conceivably because it would be an imprudently insulting thing to say openly in a state in which women play a fairly full public life, and their goodwill needs to be gained.[44]

The myth of the *Laws*, then, with its summary anticipation in the *Timaeus*, seems to be unique in the eschatology of Plato: it describes an automatic or semi-automatic system, perhaps initially established by gods, but not administered by them on a day-to-day basis, in which souls are promoted or demoted according to moral desert, in virtue of some physical and natural process that operates like any other process of the natural world. Hades seems to have no separate location; the next world seems to be simply *the* world, in which wicked souls sink and virtuous souls rise, much as in water a stone sinks and cork bobs up.

To take the measure of the difference between the earlier myths and that of the *Laws*, let us list what has been jettisoned: (1) elaborate and detailed descriptions of the topography of the next world; (2) the conducting of the souls by personal guides from one point to another within it; (3) the notion of a judgement in some sort of court, analogous to judgement in this world, by picturesque persons such as Minos and Rhadamanthus, after the soul has given an account of itself;[45] (4) details of exquisite punishments; (5) the curing of curable souls; (6) perpetual punishment for the incurable; (7) the idea of a personal choice, in the afterlife, of one's next reincarnation; (8) the relevance of the experience of *post-mortem* reward or punishment to the making of that choice.

Clearly it is not only vivid circumstantial detail that has disappeared: some important ideas have vanished with it. The earlier myths distinguished these stages:

---

[42] 903d, 904e, 904c ff.
[43] 904c.
[44] The disparaging remarks about women at 781a ff. are made in private between the interlocutors.
[45] But cf. 959a–c.

1. This life, lived wickedly or well.
2. Judgement of the soul after death, followed by reward or punishment.
3. The next reincarnation.

The myth of the *Laws* effectively suppresses stage 2, or rather collapses it into stage 3. The wicked soul effectively carries its own judgement with it, and sinks automatically into some inferior reincarnation, *which is its punishment*; judgement and punishment coincide. Neatness, economy, and infallibility are achieved at one blow.

We have to ask why these startling changes to the penology of the myths has taken place. I conceive that Plato's thought developed roughly as follows. His earlier myths stand firmly in the tradition that there exist surrogate punishers who punish wrongdoing in the end. Socrates' interlocutors, who are commonly sceptical of the need to cultivate the soul and to adhere to just conduct at any price, are confronted with edifying and powerful stories designed to appeal to their feelings and imagination, even if argument has failed to convince their intellect. So far so simple. But Plato, no doubt influenced by the mystery-religions, has grafted on to this tradition that quality which I call 'aspirational': wicked men are reincarnated, and reincarnation constitutes a second chance. Intervening between death and reincarnation comes punishment; and Plato supposed that just as punishment in this world is or should cure, so too should it be in the next. The question then arises (and the *Gorgias* does not answer it), what is a cured soul cured *for*? Hardly to 'live' a better 'life' after death; so surely to live a better life in *this* world, at its next reincarnation; for having learned the error of its ways as a result of *post-mortem* punishment, it chooses to live more virtuously next time it lives.

The earlier myths therefore simply project upon punishment in the next world the same hopeful view that is commonly held of punishment in this world, namely that it cures the criminal and makes him better. But there are implausibilities.

1. The very picturesqueness of the stories, and lack of hard evidence, could invite ridicule; intellectuals, at least, would be unlikely to believe in their literal truth;[46] and if we are not to regard them as literally true, why should we take any more notice of them than of any other passionate assurance that injustice does not pay, or even of dialectic to that effect?

2. Like punishment in this world, punishment *post-mortem* seems singularly inefficient as cure. If all curable souls were in fact cured in the next world, they would all choose blameless next lives and this world would be a better place than it is. But it is evident from the *Republic* that

---

[46] *Gorg.* 527a, cf. *Laws* 885c.

even the souls that have been horribly punished after death often choose their next life unwisely; admittedly, they choose with a certain care; but their choices are not invariably good. So to the extent that *post-mortem* punishments fail to cure, they must look purely retributive.

3. More conjecturally, if 'cure' in this world consists, as we have seen, not merely of the inculcation of fear through suffering, but of re-education, then cure in the next world ought presumably to consist of similar measures. But even if we can swallow the proposition that one may be punished *post-mortem* and so 'cured', it seems much more implausible to suggest that one can at that time be cured by being re-educated, i.e. by 'words, honours, and gifts',[47] and by some sort of regimen. This consideration may account for the very partial and unsatisfactory extent to which punished souls, conspicuously in the *Republic*, seem to be reformed. In the *Timaeus* and *Laws* the notion of *post-mortem* cure is then simply dropped.

At any rate, when he came to write the eschatology of the *Laws*, Plato had presumably worked out the physics of the *Timaeus*, and had come to see that a purely automatic and physical system could suit his purposes. Preserving a patina of myth, he wrote his eschatology chiefly in 'scientific' terms, which would not attract ridicule from clever atheists for being an 'old-wives' tale'; it provided for infallibility, a most desirable feature in penology;[48] and it neatly incorporated a theme already found in the myths, the upward and downward movement of the soul. But the crucial point is that he is able economically to embody in this physical system a point that is absolutely fundamental to his ethics, and already stressed in the early myths, namely that a wicked man brings his suffering upon himself. He possesses reason with which to control his emotions and appetites; if he does not, and so becomes unjust, he is already punished, for on Platonic principles he is unhappy; but more particularly, when he dies, his soul will simply be in such a state that it will inevitably sink into some inferior reincarnation, without any fallible intervention from personal judges in an afterlife whose very existence is uncertain. Old-hat mythical eschatology gives way to new-style physics, which lends a fresh sense to the fundamental truth that the good create their own heaven, the wicked their own hell. That is to say, thanks to physics, the tenet can be represented as applying as inevitably after death as it does in life. Plato himself draws attention to the parallel between the inevitable punishment of injustice in this world and its punishment in the next:

[47] 862d (passage 1, step 6).
[48] Note the mistakes that even Aeacus and Rhadamanthus can make, *Gorg.* 524a.

728bc (passage 2). [The greatest judgement, *dikē*, on wrongdoing, is] to grow to resemble men who are evil, and as the resemblance increases to shun good men and their wholesome conversation and to cut oneself off from them, while seeking to attach oneself to the other kind and keep their company. The inevitable result of consorting with such people is that what you do and have done to you is exactly what they naturally do and say to each other. Consequently, this condition is not really a 'judgement' at all, because justice and judgement are fine things: it is mere punishment, suffering that follows a wrongdoing.[49]

904e. And in spite of your belief that gods neglect you, my lad, or rather young man,

> This is the sentence of the gods that dwell upon Olympus,

to go to join worse souls as you grow worse and better souls as you grow better, and alike in life and all the deaths you suffer to do and be done by according to the standards that birds of a feather naturally apply among themselves.

Alike in life and in death, punishment of injustice is to join the company one deserves. If on death one deserves, owing to lack of justice, to become a beast, so be it; for beasts do not treat each other with justice.[50]

In the last sentence of the first quotation Plato notes briefly that such punishment, mere *timōria*, does not cure the criminal.[51] May one infer that the point applies also to the incorporation into the company of bad souls that takes place after death? If so, it would chime very well with the total absence of any mention of *post-mortem* cure in the myth of book 10.

If then Plato holds out no prospect that *post-mortem* punishment is cure, how does a demoted soul—say one now demoted to a dog—ever get itself promoted to the body of a man? Can you, as a dog, become more virtuous? Both the *Timaeus* and the *Laws* talk casually of promotion,[52] but perhaps that is only from the human state, not from the animal state. Nor is it clear to what higher state human beings may aspire. And if no living person can help much to reform you when you are dead,[53] can you help yourself? Or is one simply reincarnated punished but uncured? Two brief passages lying outside the myth of book 10 stress *post-mortem* punishment, but say nothing of cure (nor indeed of reincarnation).[54]

---

[49] Plato's insistence on the inevitability of the disagreeable social consequences of crime is reminiscent of Hesiod's.

[50] Cf. 937d, 'human life is graced by *dikē*', and Hes. *WD* 276–80.

[51] See the discussion above, pp. 150–1.

[52] 92c, 903d, 904c ff.

[53] 959c.

[54] 880c–881a (passage 10), 959a–c.

THE PREAMBLES

Certain preambles offer a somewhat different picture.

1. *Involuntary homicide, 865 de (cf. 866 b4–5)*

[The homicide] should not take lightly an old story that comes from our collection of ancient tales. It runs as follows:

Having lived in the full proud spirit of freedom, the man murdered by violence, freshly dead, turns his fury on the person responsible. The dead man is full of fear and horror at his own violent sufferings; he is horror-stricken at the sight of his own murderer going about localities once familiar to himself; to the full limit of his powers he visits his own anguish on the perpetrator of the crime, the man and his deeds; and his allies are the memories that haunt the murderer.

2. *Voluntary homicide, 870 de*

We must tell the story which is so strongly believed by so many people when they hear it from those who have made a serious study of such matters in these mystic ceremonies. It is this:

Punishment (*tisis*) is exacted for these crimes in Hades, and when a man returns to this world again he is ineluctably obliged to pay the penalty (*dikē*) prescribed by nature—to undergo the same treatment as he himself meted out to his victim, and to conclude his earthly existence by encountering a similar fate at the hands of someone else.

3. *Voluntary homicide of relatives, 872 d–873 a*

The 'myth', or 'explanation', or whatever the right word is, has come down to us in unambiguous terms from the lips of priests of long ago:

Justice (*Dikē*) stands on guard to exact punishment[55] for the spilling of the blood of relatives; she operates through the law we have just mentioned, and her decree is that a man who has done something of this kind is obliged to suffer precisely what he has inflicted. If ever a man has murdered his father, in the course of time he must suffer the same fate from violent treatment at the hands of his children. A matricide, before being reborn, must adopt the female sex, and after being born a woman and bearing children, be dispatched subsequently by them. No other purification is available when common blood has been polluted; the pollution resists cleansing until, murder for murder, the guilty soul has paid the penalty (*tinein*), and by this appeasement has soothed the anger of the deceased's entire line.

In (1) the dead man is not the criminal but his victim; but the passage is of interest because it presupposes some *post-mortem* period, perhaps limited to the time in which the victim is 'freshly' dead and is not yet

---

[55] Literally, '*Dikē* as punisher, avenger' (*timōros*), is a 'watcher', 'overseer' (*episkopos*); cf. 866a3.

undergoing whatever penalties or rewards lie in store for him, when he is able to punish his murderer, in a wholly retributive manner that can hardly be said to 'cure' him.

In (2) we again have unspecified penalties after death, but this time increased by a crime-specific punishment after reincarnation as a human being (not, be it noted, as an animal, even though he is a murderer). Here again it seems that although appropriate reincarnation is itself somehow a punishment, it may be preceded by *post-mortem* penalties in Hades.

In (3) the crime-specific nature of reincarnation and subsequent deaths is even more pointed than in (2);[56] but the *post-mortem* penalties are omitted. The reincarnation as a woman I take to be directed by the desire to provide a crime-specific penalty, not as an indication that there is a scale descending to animals; for if there were such a scale, one would expect murderers to be reincarnated far further down the scale of animals than into human females.

The myth of book 10's theodicy and the myths of the preambles seem then to operate on rather different levels. Both, it is true, have the notion of *some* kind of relationship between immoral conduct in this life and bad destiny in the next, and both promise reincarnation; and neither has anything to say about cure. The theodicy presents an 'automatic' system based on the *Timaeus'* physics; it seems to omit specific *post-mortem* punishments of the traditional kind in favour of inferior reincarnations which are themselves punishments, and it probably extends such reincarnations, as does the *Timaeus*, to animals. The preambles, however, speak in much more traditionally lurid terms; they suppose a murdered man is in some way still alive and can vent his fury on his killer; they utilize crime-specific punishments; but they make no reference to physics, and apparently envisage reincarnation into human form only. The crucial theme of the 'company of the wicked', and of suffering accordingly, appears in both, explicitly in the theodicy, where it seems to apply to animal-reincarnation (animals have no justice, so they are appropriate company for an unjust soul), and implicitly in the preambles, in which obviously the reincarnated soul does indeed suffer from the company of wicked men, by being killed at their hands.

These differences in content and tone are easily explicable. The theodicy is addressed to a young man of some intellectual pretensions. Before the myth, he has had to grasp some more or less sophisticated arguments about the nature of motion, the necessity of a prime mover, the priority of soul, and the existence of gods. The myth itself requires him to absorb an argument from teleology,[57] to understand some swift

---

[56] 872d makes clear that (3) is essentially a repetition of (2).
[57] 903b ff.

points about the psychology of action and—apparently—get some grasp of the essence of Platonic physics.[58] The eschatology expounded does contain some mythical apparatus, but of a thin and vague kind. Its main burden is the 'scientific' or 'automatic' account of the relationship between moral action in this life and one's *post-mortem* destiny. It is written in unspecific and allusive terms, and it attempts to make its appeal on the rational and the mythical level simultaneously. The preambles, on the other hand, are addressed to the Toms and Dicks and Harrys of Magnesia, especially those tempted to commit murder; now the appeal is unambiguously to primitive fears and inhibitions, by means of beliefs and stories professedly taken from traditional stock.

But there is perhaps a problem. As we have seen, considerations of religion did not bulk large in the pleadings before Attic courts;[59] but obviously Plato wishes his Magnesians' minds to be saturated in carefully specified religious orthodoxies, and their lives to be full of religious observances.[60] They have had it impressed on them that punishments inflicted under their penal code are intended to cure the criminal; yet if my interpretation of the myth, the preambles, and certain other passages is correct, they are to assume that *post-mortem* punishments traditionally inflicted by divine agencies do *not* cure. Further, even if in strict doctrine such punishments are not to be regarded as retributive, but simply the automatic results of crimes, thanks to the way the world is constructed, nevertheless they have a disagreeably retributive sound. Admittedly, the crime-specific reincarnations are of incurables; and we are told that in such cases anger can be let off its leash.[61] But the punishments of the curables (who are presumably among the the subjects of the myth of the theodicy), it seems, do not cure either.

Provided all this is explained carefully enough to the average Magnesian, I suppose he may escape penological schizophrenia. But it is more to the point that the threats of eschatology are essentially attempts to induce fear. Just as when someone commits a crime, *part* of his treatment consists of suffering, which induces 'good fear' as a basis for re-education, so too eschatological threats form only a small part of the preambles and constitute a last resort. We hear of them chiefly in connection with the young heretic, and those tempted to commit the most heinous crimes. Most of the preambles are positive in content and spirit; the savage ones are to be deployed only where education and persuasion have proved ineffective.[62] At this point Plato throws anything

60 e.g. 828a ff., 835de.
59 p. 121 above.
61 731d (passage 3).
62 e.g. 870a–d is a long and discursive preface of persuasion, sharply marked off from 870de (quoted above); cf. the remarks preceding 872d–873a, which make it clear that the tale of the crime-specific penalty is advanced only when education has failed. See also 783d on the priority of persuasion over law, and the celebrated passage 718–23, on preambles.

and everything at the potential criminal's head, however crude and primitive, regardless of inconsistency with his official penology. Indeed, it is not clear that there is inconsistency, for those who suffer these crime-specific penalties at their next reincarnation are incurable anyway.

This restricted role of *post-mortem* punishment in the social and educational system of Magnesia perhaps accounts for the complete absence of Erinues, Alastors *et al.* Such personified surrogates acting on behalf of individual injured parties are quite out of keeping with a state where they and their attackers are meant to be reconciled, where the legislator, not individuals, decides who is to be punished and how, and where an impersonal eschatology is at any rate the 'official' doctrine.

CONCLUSION

Some things remain the same throughout all the myths, some things change. The notion of moral responsibility is constant: if one suffers punishment in the next world, it is only because one has brought it on oneself. Moreover, like the automatic misery a wicked man brings upon himself in the shape of an unhappy life, *post-mortem* punishment is wholly inevitable. Reincarnation features in all the myths except that of the *Gorgias*, which could well be the earliest. But into this almost constant framework is fitted, more or less awkwardly, the suggestion that *post-mortem* punishments cure, as punishments in this world do or should do; and they cure in the sense that they facilitate a wise choice of reincarnation. Even in the *Republic*, however, there is far more emphasis on personal responsibility than on cure; in the *Timaeus* and *Laws* the notion of cure is dropped entirely; but reincarnation is retained, being given a 'scientific' explanation. Continuity of the consequences of moral action between one lifetime and the next is thus preserved; but moral improvement is confined to a man's incarnations in this world, and eliminated from his *post-mortem* existence, in which only inevitable *timōria*, 'the suffering that follows injustice',[63] takes place. Paradoxically, the very dialogue which stresses in an elaborate theoretical and practical penology that punishment is cure, holds out no hope that it can have that effect in the next world. Punishment as cure, and moral improvement in general, is the preserve of the legislator and under him of the judge, not of the theologian.[64]

[63] 728bc (passage 2).
[64] See *Polit.* 303e ff. (esp. 304d, 305bc) and 308c–309a, for the general doctrine of the supremacy of 'statesmanship'.

7

THE STRUCTURE OF MAGNESIA

INTRODUCTION

In chapters 8–14 I attempt to make a systematic comparison, crime by crime, between the penalties of Magnesian law and those of Attic law. The enterprise is difficult, because often there is some evidence from one side or the other but not from both, and one can easily stumble into comparing uncertainties with unknowns; and sometimes because Magnesian law is elaborate and extremely complex, and operates in terms and categories which are not on all fours with those of Attic law.[1] However, my attention centres on the punishments imposed,[2] and their justifications and purposes; I consider the details of the structure and procedures of the two legal systems only when they seem relevant to penology. This fairly narrow focus enables me to leave aside many problems which have no bearing on my enquiry, however important they may be to other students of Greek law.

My prime consideration is: how far does Plato attempt to embody his new penology in the penalties he lays down in the Magnesian code? In particular, how far are the alterations he makes to Attic law dictated by such an attempt? Obviously the alterations he makes to Attic penalties must have *some* penological purpose,[3] and *prima facie* it would be to put into practice the principles of his own penology; but those principles seem themselves to be subject to elaborate variation when applied in particular cases, for a variety of social, economic, and political reasons. The only way to assess these matters is to scrutinize the Magnesian penal code in detail.

---

[1] Little is known of other codes; I try to incorporate evidence from them as occasion offers, though of course the extent of Plato's own acquaintance with them is uncertain.

[2] The range of permissible punishments in Magnesia is to be found at 855b ff.: death, imprisonment, whipping, degrading postures, and fines. However, fines must not be imposed with such severity that a man is left with resources insufficient for the continued working of his estate. If he cannot afford to pay and his friends are not prepared to bail him out, he is subject to imprisonment and various humiliations. In this case the injured party has presumably to rest content with that form of 'satisfaction'.

[3] I make the reasonable assumption that he knew what the Attic penalties were, at least roughly. There is no reason to suppose that they changed substantially soon after his death in 347, and I have admitted evidence about them until the forensic sources cease, c. 322. Cf. Hansen (1976) 118.

THE SYSTEM OF COURTS

Morrow has an excellent account,[4] and the merest summary of the major features will suffice here. There are several types of court; the first three form a distinct sequence.[5]

1. *Arbitrators*, chosen privately by the litigants.

Dissatisfied ligitants may appeal to

2. *Dicasteries*, i.e. jury-courts, modelled on the Athenian.

Dissatisfied litigants may appeal again, to

3. The *Select Judges*, whose decision is final.

However, it seems that none of these may impose the death penalty, which is in most but not all cases the prerogative of

4. A combined court of the *Select Judges* and the *Guardians of the Laws*.[6]

But in addition, fines and other penalties, some severe, may be imposed, without right of appeal, in a wide range of matters by

5. *Boards of officials*, acting within their own special areas of responsibility.[7]

6. *The full popular assembly*, to deal with 'charges of crimes against the people'.[8]

7. Various specialized boards, which we shall notice as they occur in the code.

There are elaborate rules of procedure designed to ensure that all litigants are treated fairly, and that verdicts are reached after a calm consideration of all the issues.[9] We can only suppose that all these bodies are expected to apply the same penological principles and criteria, though perhaps each with a different emphasis according to its own special character and procedures; at any rate, Plato offers no guidance on the point.[10]

---

[4] Morrow (1960) 241 ff.

[5] See esp. 766d ff., 956b ff.

[6] 855c ff.

[7] Morrow (1960) 242 ff.

[8] 767e–768a. The relationship of this court to the others is obscure: see Morrow (1960) 265 ff.

[9] See esp. 766e, and Morrow's favourable assessment of Magnesia's procedure, (1960) 295–6, quoted in the Penguin *Laws*, 31–2.

[10] For instance, he may have expected arbitrators to lay more emphasis on reconciliation than on blame and penalties (see 766de, 956bc, Is. 2. 30–2, Arist. *Rhet* 1374^{b}19–22, and Morrow (1960) 256–7); and summary penalties inflicted by officials would ordinarily (but see 845b–d) consist simply of fines or physical chastisement.

THE SOCIAL STRUCTURE

Platonic law provides that, at least for some crimes, the penalty imposed should vary according to the social and political status of the criminal. There are four categories of inhabitants of Magnesia, which is a small agricultural state to be founded in a fairly remote position in Crete, with little foreign contact.

1. *Citizens,* politai.[11] 5,040 farmers and their families. They earn their bread from their farms alone, and are forbidden to engage in commerce. An intensive programme of state education, compulsory from the age of three, is directed to perfecting their moral fibre; and in adult life they are obliged to attend many cultural and religious occasions whose purpose is primarily educational.

2. *Resident aliens,* xenoi metoikoi. They are admitted to live in Magnesia not for an indefinite period, as were Athenian metics, but for twenty years only;[12] their purpose is to relieve the citizens of certain tasks Plato holds to be harmful to the soul, notably retail trade.[13] Some metics are to act as supervisors on the farms of the citizens; some will be craftsmen or doctors or nurses; others will be teachers, provided they are licensed: Plato lays down that these metics must be in agreement with the aims of Magnesian education before they are allowed to educate Magnesian youth, whereupon they may be employed as 'assistants'.[14] Such metics thus approach quite closely to citizens; but the traders among them are rather tolerated as a necessity to the state than welcomed as co-operators in its moral purpose. The metic class includes also freedmen.[15]

3. *Temporary visitors,* xenoi epidēmountes. Plato envisages four categories:[16] traders, visitors to the religious festivals, official ambassadors from other states, and private philosophers come to commune about the eternal verities with the high officials of the state. It is unlikely that these last two categories will ever be involved in legal proceedings; but traders and sightseers may, and it is presumably to these that Plato refers when he mentions temporary visitors in the penal code.

There is in fact a fundamental ambiguity in the position of the

---

[11] To be understood to refer to civic status, not to political role (cf. Arist. *Pol.* 1275ᵃ14 ff.). Plato clearly envisages that most political activity will be in the hands of men, though apparently women citizens may hold office from the age of 40 (785b), and in general they take a considerable part in public life. For other terms employed by Plato to denote categories of inhabitants, e.g. *astos* (citizen) and *oiketēs* (slave), see the full survey of his usage by Fouchard.

[12] 850a ff.

[13] 846d ff., 918a ff.

[14] 811e.

[15] 915a ff.

[16] 952d ff.

foreigner, *xenos*, in Magnesia. From one point of view, Plato frowns on him: he is banausic, he will import foreign customs into the state, he is a potential source of innovation and discord.[17] On the other hand, he is a free man, and all foreigners must be treated with respect and consideration, for Zeus the god of strangers watches over them; they have a special position in the state.[18]

4. *Slaves,* douloi. Apart from a small number of public slaves kept by the state, the slaves of Magnesia are owned by citizens and metics. Most of them will be employed on the farms; the slaves of citizens are forbidden to indulge in handicrafts and trade, so eager is Plato to cocoon his Magnesians in their non-commercial way of life.[19] Slaves are recognized as a species of property, and may accordingly be bought and sold in the market.[20] Plato is very much aware that slaves are difficult to deal with: he recommends[21] that the slaves of Magnesia should not all be of the same tongue—conspiracy is thus made more difficult—and that they should be treated firmly but humanely: a man will show himself a hypocrite in his regard for justice if he treats his slaves badly. But he should not become familiar with them; he should speak to them only by way of a simple command.

Now as we sometimes find in the *Laws* penalties of varying severity awarded to these four categories for identical crimes, it is reasonable to infer that the very status of the criminal is evidence, in Plato's eyes, for the amount of injustice in the soul. We might infer that the citizen, who has been subjected to a lifetime of education designed to eliminate injustice, is suffering from it the least, and that he has committed a crime not from any longstanding or deep-seated malady of the soul, but from a temporary and isolated derangement: he is already 'easy to persuade to virtue'.[22] The penalty, then, need not be a severe one. The metic, on the other hand, has not had such education, although he does belong to a group that includes teachers of the state's children; nevertheless the likelihood is that he is engaged in a business of some kind, and as Plato says, education for that kind of life is not real education;[23] such pursuits urge a man on the road to vice. The penalty will have to be higher than that given the citizen. The itinerant foreigner has not even the slight contact with Magnesian education enjoyed by the metic, and presumably the injustice in his soul is even greater; he has been educated by a 'bastard education'.[24] An even greater punishment is therefore indicated. The slave has had no education at all; he is 'no easy chattel', and he is not

---

[17] 952e. [18] 729e. [19] 846d, 920a.
[20] 916a ff., 936c–e. [21] 777b ff. [22] 718c.
[23] 643d–644a, 920ab. [24] 741a.

to be punished by judicial admonition, as one might punish a freeman, but by strict justice.[25] He has not the dignity and outlook of a free man; his soul must be positively overflowing with disease. Strong curative measures are therefore called for, and a heavy punishment will be imposed, heavier than that imposed on any of the other three. We should thus have an ascending scale of punishments, the citizen being comparatively lightly punished at one extreme, the slave being most severely punished at the other.

Matters will prove to be nothing like so simple; but these expectations may suffice for the moment, as we stand poised at last to plunge into the code. In chapter 15 I attempt a systematic analysis of the sociological differentiations in the punishments it prescribes.

Plato neither prescribes nor forbids differentiation of punishment by reference to the offender's sex.

Finally, it should be noted that when the code distinguishes, as special categories, offences against a parent, grandparent, or slave-master, it means of course the *offender's* parent etc., not that of any other person.

Note on the presentation of the penal code

Plato is not a tidy legal draftsman. He presents the offences one at a time and in a rational sequence; but within each category he varies considerably the order of topics and the extent and distribution of detail. He is also apt to break up his exposition by generous interlardings of 'preface' or 'preamble' material, which cannot be ignored, as it contributes to the interpretation of the positive laws themselves.

My method of handling these difficult texts has been to adopt Plato's categories and sub-categories and numerous refinements absolutely strictly, but to systematize their presentation in the interests of clarifying their structure and penological significance. Liberal sprinklings of (A) (B) (C) (i) (ii) (iii) etc. have enabled me to achieve some modest uniformity as between the major sections of the code (see Contents list); but in the finer detail it is inevitably much less than rigorous. At any rate, I hope that these measures will do something to render the often bewildering complexities intelligible.

[25] 777b ff.

8

HOMICIDE

INTRODUCTION

Plato obviously intends his Magnesians to live orderly, quiet and uneventful lives. What then are we to make of the fact that he devotes more space to homicide (*phonos*) than to any other part of his penal code?[1] It can hardly be because he expects murders to be frequent.[2] As we shall see, the reason is rather that attacks on persons necessarily involve important questions of policy within a carefully contrived social and political structure. The Magnesian law of homicide is accordingly not only very long but very elaborate. However, its exposition is, in the main, systematic and clear.

At 857a Plato has concluded the law relating to treason, temple-robbery, and subversion. The pages from then until 864c are occupied by the exposition of his new penology. The transition to homicide is now effected by way of part of a rider to the law of treason etc.: any offender shown to have been suffering from insanity at the time of the offence, or some state that is effectively insanity, must certainly pay simple damages for damage done, but 'should not be subject to the other just measures, *dikaiōmata*,' i.e. he should not be punished. This provision is entirely consistent with the principles of the penology: punishments are to be inflicted only on the 'unjust' psychic state of a person capable of the rational response necessary for its cure.[3]

The law that the insane person should not be liable to 'the other

---

[1] 10 Stephanus pages, about $\frac{1}{32}$ of the entire *Laws*.

[2] 872cd, cf. 853b ff.

[3] Cf. pp. 152–3, 190–1. But may not an insane person be just as much under the domination of fear, lust, etc. (= injustice) as a sane one? In which case, and *if* insanity implies incurability (as in the case of a senile person it usually does), why is such an offender not executed (for treason etc.) as incurable? Presumably because he was not 'responsible', and should be exempt from death on some grounds of reciprocal justice. But Plato has officially ruled that out as a consideration in sentencing policy: curability is all. Probably, to save his position, he would have argued that punishment can apply only to an intent arising from a degree of reformable moral reason. Lacking moral reason, the insane person is a sort of zombie or puppet, outside normal categories; his action is effectively involuntary (cf. Budé edn. ad loc.), and involuntariness, being uninformative about the state of the soul, cannot license punishment.

dikaiōmata' has one exception. If he proves to have killed someone in the commission of the offence, and is thus unclean of hands in respect of murder, he is (after some purifications) to go into exile for one year; if he returns before this period has elapsed, he is to go to prison for two years.[4] These provisions are revealing. In principle, a madman cannot be punished.[5] Exile and imprisonment are therefore, *at least in his case*, not punishments. They can only be measures of social and religious hygiene: they allow both the dead man[6] and his family a 'cooling off' period, in which the offender is out of sight and hopefully out of mind, and the pollution has a chance to wear off.[7] When exile and imprisonment are imposed on murderers who are *not* mad, are the implications the same?

At this point, 865a1, the law of homicide gets properly under way. The first three sections are arranged in an ascending scale of seriousness:

A: 865a1–866d4: Involuntary (*akousios*) homicide
B: 866d5–869e5: Homicide in anger (*thumōi*)
C: 869e5–873c1: Voluntary (*hekousios*) homicide

Then, after sections on suicide (873c2–d8), animals and inanimate objects as killers (873e1–874a3), and murder by person unknown (874a4–b5) we have

D: 874b6–d1: Justifiable homicide.

It is possible, though far from certain, that Plato intended *all* cases of homicide to be tried before the select and senior court described just before the penological excursus.[8] However, while this court is certainly said to try cases where death would be the penalty, which would obviously include some varieties of homicide,[9] its competence in other cases of homicide which do not entail that penalty is neither asserted nor excluded. Plato may therefore have envisaged that charges of homicide where the penalty would be less than death would be tried before the ordinary 'dicasteries'.[10] In either case, it is clear that the prosecutions

---

[4] 864e. I assume that it is by mere oversight that Plato does not specifically make similar provisions for madmen who commit *any* murder, not only in the course of treason etc.

[5] Hence the occurrence of *dikaiōmata*, a word used by Plato here only, may be significant. In Aristotle, *NE* 1135ª9 ff., a *dikaiōma* is a rectification of an act of injustice, *adikēma*. The injustice which Plato's penology aims to rectify is the criminal's state of mind. In the case of a madman, it cannot be achieved: hence he is dispensed from 'the other things, the makings-just, the *dikaiōmata*,' i.e. the measures of punishment, which are 'other' than the exile which he does have to undergo, but purely as a social and religious measure. On *dikaioun*, 'to make (a criminal) just', see p. 174 above, on 934b. 'The other x' in the sense of 'the other things, i.e. x' is a common Greek idiom.

[6] See 865de.

[7] The two-year period is prescribed, I take it, because in this case the offender is physically present in the state, and it would be felt that the pollution and resentment would thus take longer to fade away.

[8] 855c; so assumed by Goetz (1920) 11 ff., 15–16; cf. Piérart (1973*a*) 425.

[9] Cf. Morrow (1960) 267–8, and 871d.

[10] See p. 213.

would ordinarily be *dikai*, private suits, brought by a relative of the deceased.[11]

Plato's penological excursus in book IX laid stress on the psychological analysis of the criminal as a preliminary to his cure, and listed 3 major causes of offences:[12] (1) anger, (2) pleasures and desires, (3) ignorance (with subdivisions). It is obvious that the first of these looks ahead to Plato's second major category of murders, those committed in anger, which are neither voluntary nor involuntary but somewhere in between. The second cause, as he makes clear later,[13] describes the state of mind of criminals who lust after money or social position, and who commit voluntary homicide, the third of the major categories. But how the third cause, ignorance, can be related to the first of the categories, involuntary murder, is not at all obvious, chiefly because an involuntary murderer is not committing an offence at all, even a trivial one; for he is not acting from psychic *adikia*. It is best to treat ignorance as *moral* ignorance, the cause of any criminal action—including voluntary murder, conceivably—which the agent believes to be morally justified.[14]

A: INVOLUNTARY HOMICIDE (865a1–866d4)

(*a*) *Special cases*

865a1–b4 contains special cases prefacing the standard cases: (i) involuntary killing of a compatriot in contests, war, or military training required mere purification; (ii) doctors whose patients die as a result of treatment are not polluted at all. Both provisions are based firmly on Athenian law, though as far as one can tell no purification was required in either case;[15] scrupulous persons may have performed them nevertheless.

(*b*) *Standard cases and derelictions*

In 865b4–866d4 the standard cases and derelictions are stated at length, with sociological elaboration, and apparently applying to any context or circumstance except those in (*a*). There are two uniform preliminary requirements: (i) that the purifications, whether the victim is slave or

---

[11] Dem. 43. 57, 47. 72; Gagarin (1979*a*) 302–13.
[12] 863b–864c.
[13] 869e ff.
[14] It does not help to take the ignorance as merely technical, rather than moral. Cf. pp. 147–50.
[15] (i) *AP* 57. 3, Dem. 23. 53 ff., cf. 831a; (ii) Ant. *Tetr.* 3c. 5; Hewitt (1910), esp. 111 ff. These cases, and their inclusion under involuntary homicide, are dicussed also under D below, 'Justifiable Homicide'.

free, should be greater and more numerous than those employed in cases of killing in contests[16] (in deference to the anger of the victims, at least when they are free men); (ii) that the property of the exiles should not be confiscated.[17]

Standard cases

1. If a citizen or metic involuntarily kills a free man, he must go into exile for a year; an itinerant is to be exiled permanently. If the deceased is a foreigner, the killer must keep away from the victim's native land too.[18] After the year, the relatives of the deceased are to grant pardon to the killer and live on peaceable terms with him.[19]

The debt to Attic law, which prescribed exile (without confiscation of property), purification on return, and reconciliation, is direct and obvious, though there may be some curtailment of the length of exile, which in Athens was probably at the discretion of the victim's relatives.[20]

2. If a man[21] involuntarily kills his own slave, only purification is required; if another's, he must pay simple damages to the owner, and purify himself.[22]

The Attic penalties in such cases are uncertain;[23] indeed, it is not clear that Attic law made separate provision for the involuntary murder of a slave, as distinct from a voluntary.

Nothing is said about involuntary murder committed *by* slaves. Somewhat hazardous inferences may be made from the provision[24] that

---

[16] 865cd. On 865b4-c2 see p. 237 n. 101.   [17] Conformably with 855a.

[18] This last point presumably applies at 866bc as well as at 865e—though in the case of the itinerant killer it is hardly enforceable. I also assume ξένος (866b7) includes metics. On 866b7-c5 see my note 2 in (1963).

[19] 865d-866a5, b7-c5. The words ἐλεύθερον (865d3), ξένος (e9) and καί (e9) need careful attention. I assume ἐλεύθερος is any free man, ξένοι included, as opposed to the slave (c2 ff.), and not in the special sense of citizen alone (see Morrow (1960) 112 n. 51, 323 n. 88). For a study of this and similar ambiguities of technical terminology in Plato's homicide law, see Grace (1977). 865e9-866a1 adds a rider to the general rule applying to freemen: when ξένοι are killed, the killers must apparently keep away both from a killed metic's native land (metics are to stay for a maximum of 20 years in Magnesia, 850a ff.), and from a killed itinerant's, *as well as* (καί) from Magnesia itself. For in Magnesia the dead man himself is a danger, and in his native land his relatives. Gernet (1917) note 100, having omitted καί in his translation, supposes ξένος to be only the itinerant. But surely καί implies metics too; for when they are murdered there is *more* reason to insist on the murderer's avoiding Magnesia as well as elsewhere, since (as Gernet says) metics are more closely integrated into the city than itinerants. Further, if ξένος means an itinerant alone, the metic victim would either not be envisaged in the law, which would be strange, or would have to be included with the citizen in ἐλεύθερος, to the exclusion of the itinerant, which would be awkward and contrary to usage. Cf. Harrison i (1968) 188.

[20] IG I³ 104 (Draco's homicide law, still in use in the 4th century), 11 ff., Dem. 23. 44-5, 71-3 (cf. 21. 43), Harp. ὅτι οἱ ἁλόντες; MacDowell (1963) 117 ff., Lipsius (1905-15) 609 ff., BS II. 230-1. Inconclusive evidence for the length of exile: Lipsius (1905-15) 611 n. 42, Goetz (1920) 80-2. On the determination of court (Palladium), see Sealey (1983) 278-9. For Sparta, see Xen. Anab. 4. 8. 25.

[21] The τις at 865b5 presumably includes metics and other foreigners.   [22] 865cd.

[23] Suggestive but inconclusive considerations in Morrow (1937) esp. 213, 216-9; cf. Levinson (1953) 589-91.   [24] 869d.

a slave who kills a free man, even in self-defence, is executed, but not if he thus kills a slave: perhaps a slave who kills a free man, even involuntarily, may be subject to some penalty, but not if he thus kills a fellow slave.[25] Strictly, of course, on Plato's own principles, there being *ex hypothesi* no relevant *adikia* in the slave's soul, no *penalty* should be attracted, though purification could conceivably be relevant (but exile would not). Nothing is known of Attic practice.

Derelictions

Embedded within the standard cases there are punishments for failure to observe the rules relating to them:

1. Refusal to pay the value of the killed slave to the owner is punished by payment of twice the value.[26]

2. Refusal (i) to abstain from religious activities etc. (presumably in the period before exile), and (ii) to complete the period of exile: the next of kin must prosecute for murder, and all penalties, *timōrēmata*,[27] are doubled.

3. Failure of the next of kin to act in the circumstances of (2) renders him liable to prosecution by anyone, and five years of exile; for the dead man makes demands about his suffering.[28]

4. Voluntary return of *foreigners* exiled for involuntary murder: the penalty is death, and any property they possess is to be given to the murdered man's nearest relative.[29] Those who return involuntarily are simply sent away again as soon as possible.

(c) Discussion

Certain specific matters may be considered first.

1. In standard case (1), some reasonably sure comparison may be made with Athenian law. Exile from Athens probably lasted until a relative empowered to act granted pardon (*aidesis*), which could apparently be refused indefinitely. Plato's rule however, reads as if the exile has a *right* to return after the fixed period of one year, and the nearest relative will then be correct to live at peace with him; pardon is

---

[25] Cf. Goetz (1920) 87-8.

[26] 865c4-5. This provision is based on the Athenian *dikē blabēs*; cf. p. 319.

[27] 866a5-b2. Corresponding Athenian law: (i) Dem. 24. 105 (court decides what the offender should suffer or pay); but cf. 23. 80 and MacDowell (1963) 132-3, 139-40, Harrison ii (1921) 226-7; Gagarin (1979a) 313 ff. (ii) Dem. 23. 28, 31, 51, MacDowell (1963) 121-2, 140 (likelihood but not certainty of death; but on the restoration of IG I³ 104 (then I² 115) 30-1 see Stroud 54-6).

[28] 866b3-7. Dem. 22. 2 *may* imply that in Athens pressure to prosecute for (2i) could be brought to bear on the negligent relative by means of a suit for impiety (*graphē asebeias*): Hansen (1976) 111, Parker (1983) 123 n. 72, Treston (1923) 181 and 260, MacDowell (1963) 9-11, Piérart (1973a) 428, Gagarin (1979) 303 ff.   [29] 866c5-7.

not a *condition* of the return. '*Let him* grant pardon' may or may not imply that the pardon itself is compulsory.[30] At all events, it is clear that Plato is anxious to have the matter over and done with, and to see the offender reintegrated into society and back working his estate. This wish may have prompted him to impose somewhat tighter limits than Athens did on the discretion permitted to relatives to express their own resentment and, vicariously, that of the dead man (described in lurid terms in the lines immediately preceding). On the other hand he says nothing of a right of the prosecutor to grant pardon *after* the conviction but *before* the exile can take place.[31]

2. The range of penalties for dereliction (2(ii)), voluntary premature return from exile, is striking:

In Athens: Death.
In Magnesia: Citizen, doubling of period of exile.
          Foreigner, death.

Plato retains the probable Athenian penalty for the foreigner, but treats the citizen very leniently. The citizen, after all, merely wishes to re-enter society, a natural desire with which, as in (1), Plato sympathizes. But Magnesia is not the home of the foreigner, so his return can have no justification; presumably it betokens incurably insolent impiety towards Magnesia's religion. He would also be guilty, if a metic, of a breach of the requirement that he display 'moderate conduct'.[32]

3. So far as one can see, all free men—citizens, metics and itinerants—are accorded the same legal protection, in that the same impositions are prescribed whatever the social status of the freeman victim.[33] The only differentiation arises in the case of the itinerant *offender*, whose exile from Magnesia is to be permanent. No doubt he is less integrated into the state than the metic; yet it is hard to see why animosity against an itinerant too should not die down after a year.

4. The purifications are to be the same whether the victim is slave or free; in that respect the slave enjoys equal protection, as in some sense a member of the household. But the killer is not sent into exile: presumably dead slaves, not having lived 'in the full proud spirit of freedom',[34] are relatively powerless after death.[35] The killer has only to pay recompense; this requirement, though it obviously depends on a view of

---

[30] 866a3–4, ἐχέτω συγγνώμην; England (1921, 407) believes that it does so imply. Third-person imperatives may certainly convey legal obligation, e.g. 865c2. Compulsory pardon would be consistent with Plato's obvious desire to have punishment stop at the point where an offender is prepared to comply with requirements: cf. 847b1, 910c6, 949e1.

[31] Dem. 38. 22.   [32] 850b.

[33] Note 866c1: anyone may prosecute when a *xenos* is killed, presumably because there may not be relatives on hand to do so; his position in Athens seems to have been less well protected (Gagarin (1979) 307–13); further discussion in Panagiotou (1974) 428 ff.

[34] 865d ff.   [35] Cf. Gernet (1917a) n.95.

slaves as primarily property, does afford them some limited protection. In a curious way the owner of a killed slave is better off than the relative of a killed kinsman: he does receive some payment, whereas the relative, as in Athenian practice of the classical period,[36] evidently does not; he has to rest content with the satisfaction of observing the purifications and exile.

What of the penology? Either the unintentional killer is not suffering from a state of injustice in his soul, or, even if he is, the injustice is irrelevant to the offence. He cannot, therefore, be punished.[37] It follows that, at least in terms of Plato's official penology, the measures prescribed in his case are not punishments; for punishments are intended to cure criminals, and here there are no criminals to cure. Yet it is very obvious that the measures (polluted status, exile) are impositions: they inflict suffering, or at the very least inconvenience; and Plato is obviously aware that sometimes a killer will attempt to avoid them for that reason. If Demosthenes is any guide,[38] an Athenian juror too would have thought of them as *timōria*, punishment; and it goes without saying that the dead man himself is thinking in purely vindictive and retributive terms.[39] Moreover, like punishments, the impositions are *graded* in point of severity:

(*a*) The purifications in the standard cases are to be greater than those in the special cases.

(*b*) The impositions in dereliction (2), exile and abstention from religious activity, are 'doubled'; moreover they are actually termed *timōrēmata*.

(*c*) To anticipate, in his law of homicide in anger Plato prescribes exile of 2 or 3 years, depending on the anger's intensity, and it is clear that he envisages a continuous scale:

  (i) Involuntary killing (1 year's exile)
  (ii) Unpremeditated killing in anger (2 years' exile)
  (iii) Premeditated killing in anger (3 years' exile)

He refers to the imposition under (i) and (ii) as 'suffering', and to that under (ii) and (iii) as *timōria*.

A resident of Magnesia, therefore, who is made to suffer under the law of involuntary homicide could be forgiven for supposing that he is being made to suffer *punishment*. And so he is, in the intention of the dead man and possibly his relatives. But on strict Platonic principles he is not being punished by the state, whose interest is not to cure him—that is

---

[36] MacDowell (1963) 9.

[37] Cf. p. 219 above. Nor, strictly, can he be called an 'offender', natural though the usage is. Cf. involuntary woundings (879b), which are mere 'chance'.   [38] Dem. 23. 73.

[39] 865e4, 'being anguished himself he makes anguished the doer', with whom he is angry (*thumoutai* 865d7, cf. *thumon* 873a2).

unnecessary—but to prevent his being a source of friction, as a result of the popular belief, which Plato wishes at least to allow for and apparently even to encourage, that dead men are a danger to their killers and their community. Plato's desire to enmesh his Magnesians in religious belief and observance permits a vindictive penology to exist, confusingly, side by side with his reformative penology. He would have to say to the involuntary killer: 'It is not I, or my law, that is blaming and punishing you; it is your victim. There is nothing I can do about it; it as an objective fact of existence; even a lunatic who blunders into homicide is polluted; all I can do is ensure by my law that the situation be managed in an orderly and expeditious manner, and that your misfortune does not rebound on your community. Hence I insist that you satisfy the dead man; but that is so to speak a chthonic, not a legal, punishment. I accept that it is an evil—I would not myself want you to be absent for a year;[40] and as I say in my *Laws*,[41] any genuine penalties I prescribe are not intended to do you harm, but to cure you; and in your case I accept that that is not appropriate.'

We need not suppose that Plato himself believed in the anger of dead men, only that he expected the belief to exist antecedently among the Magnesians, and/or that a strong and effective framework of religious doctrine and inhibition was politically necessary for the cohesion and stability of the state. Now religious belief which includes the anger of dead men can operate desirably as a deterrent to murder; and when a murder is voluntary, any suffering inflicted by law can be represented both as the demand of the dead man for a measure of compensation *and* as punishment in its role of reform. When the murder is involuntary, religious belief and advanced penology conflict.

There is one residual matter. The intensity of a dead man's resentment is presumably the same whether he has died in a 'standard' or a 'special' situation;[42] why then does the latter require only lesser purifications, and no period of exile? I take it that the communal nature of the special situation diminishes the seriousness of the killing: it occurred as a sort of accidental by-product of a good cause, and society so to speak stifles or shouts down the indignant sufferers.[43] Rather similarly, as I have argued above, the dead slave is weaker than the dead free man, and can hardly demand the exile of his killer.

[40] Witness his wish to limit the period of exile and to get the person back into society (see above). The same wish may lie behind his implication (866a) that the purification should take place sooner rather than later, before not after exile: it is an earnest of later re-absorption into the community. I do not believe (*pace* Parker (1983) 374) that Plato misunderstood the link between the two.

[41] 854d: 'no penalty (*dikē*) imposed by law has an evil purpose, but generally ... makes the punished person either better or less bad'.

[42] See however Gernet (1917*a*) n. 86 on the significance of the word αὐτόχειρ, '(killing) with one's own hand', in the standard cases (865bc).   [43] Cf. 873e2, and Sealey 282–5.

B: HOMICIDE IN ANGER (866d5–869e5)

Attic law recognized voluntary, involuntary, and justified murder; homicide in anger was not a separate formal category. Possibly the presence of anger in a killer could either be a reason for prosecuting for involuntary murder only, or be used as excuse in reply to a charge of voluntary murder.[44] More probably,[45] the law distinguished between the presence or absence of *harmful intent* (*pronoia*), not between long-term intent (premeditation) and short-term intent (impulse). If that is right, Athenian law regarded all cases of homicide in anger as voluntary, and Plato's removal of such cases from that category is a major and striking modification. Other things being equal, *fewer* homicides will be classified 'voluntary' in Magnesia than in Athens.

Certainly Plato's intense interest in anger as a cause of crime stems from, and has considerable affinities with, his treatment of *thumos* as the middle 'part' of the soul in the *Republic*, and to reflect comtemporary discussion, as indeed Aristotle presumably does in parts of his *Nicomachean Ethics*. Philosophical psychology, it seems, is to be applied to legislation. With what result?

Plato's law of homicide in anger falls into five well-defined sections:[46]

(*a*) The psychological preamble, 866d5–867c2.
(*b*) The 'standard' cases and derelictions, 867c4–868a4, 868a6–b5;
(*c*) Slaves as killers and victims, 868a4–6, 868b5–c5;
(*d*) Murders within the family, 868c5–869c6;
(*e*) Murders in self-defence, 869c6–d7;
(*f*) A rider about pardon, 869d7–e4.

(*a*) The psychological preamble, 866d5–867c2

Homicide in anger may be committed in two ways. (1) The killer may act immediately, on sudden impulse, without previous intention; his anger bursts forth uncontrollably, and his act is followed by instant remorse. (2) The killer may be stung by insulting words or actions, and nurse his anger and pursue vengeance until some time later, he kills deliberately and without remorse.[47] (1) resembles, but is not, an involuntary killer; (2)

[44] On anger as an excuse, see p. 110 above. It is hard to know whether Arist. *NE* 1135^{b}26–7, 'acts of anger are not judged (*krinetai*) to be of intent (*pronoia*)' is a report of jurisprudential opinion, common opinion, or legal practice, and what relevance it has to homicide law in particular. Cf. 1111^{a}24 ff., 1149^{b}1 ff., *Rhet.* 1378^{a}30 ff.
[45] Loomis, building on MacDowell (1963) 59–60.
[46] I have however slightly rearranged the material at 868a–c, in the interests of clarity.
[47] On remorse, cf. *Phaedo* 114a, Is. 1. 19, Arist. *NE* 1110^{b}18 ff.

resembles, but is not, a voluntary killer. Each should be classified under what he resembles, the crucial consideration being the presence or absence of premeditation. That which resembles a greater evil should be punished on a greater scale, that which resembles a lesser evil on a lesser scale.

This is an elaborate and fine preamble, full of nice observation.[48] In effect, it argues that anger is quasi-rational: as the remark about insults implies, it is provoked; it is a revolt against some felt injustice.[49] But the sustained and calculated animosity of (2) is a graver evil than the sudden uncontrollable impulse experienced by (1).[50]

We hear nothing about 'cure'; we are merely told that the severity of punishment ought to vary in direct ratio to the evil which is the degree of premeditation. The suggestion sounds retributive, but is not: it is merely that the circumstances or manner of the killing is an indication of the degree of psychic vice to be dealt with by the infliction of suffering his anger by exile. In other words, if you wish to gauge a criminal's psychic injustice, look at what he actually did, and how. The difficulties and hazards of such a procedure do not escape Plato.[51]

(b) Standard cases and derelictions, 867c4–868a4 and 868a6–b5

1. The killer who acts without premeditation and therefore resembles the non-angry (i.e. involuntary) killer should in other respects 'suffer' what that killer 'suffers', but go into exile for *two* years, 'checking (*kolazein*) his passion';

2. The killer who acts with premeditation and therefore resembles the voluntary killer is subject to the same rule, except that his 'punishment' (*timōrētheis*) must be exile for *three* years.

The 'other respects' are the purifications, presumably; and more explicitly than before they are recognized as an infliction of suffering.[52] But we now find a significant change of emphasis. In involuntary murder, there was no state of soul needing cure, so the purifications and exile were interpreted as religious observances in deference to the dead man's desire for vengeance. Anger, however, does need cure; accordingly we now hear nothing whatever of the dead man, the purifications are only alluded to, and the stress is on exile as the killer's punishment.[53] How

---

[48] For discussion of its implications, see Woozley (1972) and Saunders (1973a). The full text is given as passage 9.

[49] Cf. *Rep.* 439e ff. for anger as an ally of reason. Nevertheless, no doubt Magnesian courts would take a harsh view of a killing done by someone angry at being called a rogue, if in fact he is one.

[50] Cf. Lys. 3. 39.   [51] See pp. 187–92.   [52] 867c7; cf. pp. 223–4.

[53] See Gernet (1917a) n. 114 on the significance of the technical term *pheugein*, 'be exiled', for homicide in anger, as opposed to the milder terms used in the case of involuntary homicide (Dem. 23. 44–5): 'depart', etc.

then is exile supposed to 'cure'? Plato focuses on its length: two years of it makes the first criminal 'buffet' 'chastise' or 'repress' or 'punish' his anger (*kolazein*), and three years of it presumably does the same for the greater scale of the anger of the other man. I take it that the rigours of life in exile is a species of regimen; the exile will attract danger if he indulges his anger, and in two or three years as the case may be he acquires the *habit* of controlling it. 'Longer exile for greater anger' sounds retributive; the dead man may interpret it thus, and so too may other thoughtless Magnesians; but in the brief words 'chastising his anger' we catch the purposes of a reformative penology: the criminal's moral character is to be 'cured' by the *kolasis* of exile.[54]

3. At the conclusion of the period of exile, twelve Guardians of the Laws are to assemble at the frontier and decide whether to grant permission to return, 'having examined in this time the actions of the exiled person still more exactly'.

Now that the exile is a genuine curative punishment, the pardon and permission to re-enter Magnesia is taken clean out of the hands of the victim's relatives and entrusted to high-ranking officials. 'This time' is the period of exile; and it would be nice to think that the examination is of the criminal's demeanour during it, to discover whether he now appears to be cured. But for various reasons[55] the 'actions' have to refer to the manner of the murder, which as we have seen Plato believes to convey information about the criminal's psychological state, i.e. how far he approximates to an involuntary or voluntary murderer. On Plato's own showing, categorizing murderers in anger is tricky; the process may therefore be supposed to take some time. Even so, one wonders how much more the Guardians could expect to learn. If the two-year man seems now to deserve three years, is he sent away again? If the three-year man now looks less wicked than he did, how is his unnecessary year of exile made up to him?

4. A returned exile who again murders in anger is exiled permanently;[56] and if he does return he is to be dealt with in the same way as the foreigner who returns (see involuntary homicide, dereliction (4)), i.e. if he returns voluntarily, he is killed.

Permanent exile presumably points to incurability; yet the criminal is not executed unless he returns voluntarily. I infer that Plato recognizes that incurability *tout court* is too crude a criterion for the death penalty: it must be incurability of a very serious state of *adikia*, not of a trivial one.

---

[54] Cf. *Soph.* 229a. Strictly, one could treat the first year (of the two or three) of exile as recompense only, the other(s), the 'extra', as cure; but probably that would be to over-refine the text.

[55] Given in my note 86 (1972), *contra* Goetz (64) and Reverdin (186–7).

[56] His property presumably passes to his heir; the case does not fall under the provisions of 855cd. Cf. my note 90 (1972).

In this case, the murderer in anger, though a recidivist, is not suffering from *adikia* of the most serious kind: that would be the state of the wholly voluntary murderer. The latter should die and cut his spiritual losses; that is not quite true of the former.[57]

5. If any killer ignores his pollution and enters public and holy places, both he and the relative of the victim who permits it become liable to prosecution (for impiety, *asebeia?*) by anyone, the relative being forced to exact 'double the money and other expenses'; and the prosecutor is entitled to keep for himself the money so exacted.

This regulation is similar to those for derelictions (2) and (3) in involuntary homicide. The 'other expenses' are probably those of the purification rituals, but what 'the money' means is not clear, unless it refers to the compensation for a slave (in which case does the prosecutor, as well as the owner, receive twice the value of the slave?) The chief difference is that the defaulting relative's punishment is not specified; in the case of involuntary homicide dereliction (3) he was exiled for five years. It is ironic that Plato is willing to allow money as an incentive to ensure enforcement of the law.

(c) Slaves as victims and killers, 868a4–6, b5–c5

1. If a man kills his own slave, let him purify himself; if he kills another's, let him pay double damages to the owner.

The first provision is the same as that for involuntary homicide of a slave; but the second doubles the exaction, the extra amount obviously functioning as a penalty.[58] However, the penalty is strikingly less than for killing a non-slave. Here again the objective seriousness of the offence is a measure of psychic *adikia*: the killer of a non-slave is more unjust than the killer of a slave; *adikia* is measured in a precise social context.

2. A slave who kills his master must be handed over to the relatives of the victim to be treated as they wish, provided they kill him; and for such killing they are to incur no pollution. (If the victim is *not* his master, the relatives are to carry out the execution in whatever manner they like; it is not clear whether this penalty is meant to differ substantially from the other.)

The resentment of the relatives is allowed full play, in one of the nastiest of Plato's laws: for in Athens such personal vindictiveness was prevented by having the slave killed by the public executioner.[59] Plato, true to his desire to allow scope to the dead man's resentment, makes his

---

[57] See the discussion of the death penalty, pp. 181–3 above.

[58] So too Levinson (1953) 589. This has the curious result that the owner, to whom it is all the same, at least in respect of mere property, whether his slave was killed unintentionally or in anger, receives in the latter case a bonus.   [59] Ant. 5. 48.

relatives his surrogates. A slave who kills his master in anger is in some sense violating *family* law, and in Magnesia's particular social structure is by definition incurable, it seems; and it would be dangerous to allow him to be handed over (perhaps as compensation) and allowed to live. To put it differently, social status overrides the fact that the slave's offence is by definition less than fully voluntary; and no distinction between a slight and a great degree of psychic injustice is allowed: the slave has no dignity to be offended by insults, and any righteous indignation he feels on that score must be misguided. The absence of pollution is clearly because *this* slave has thus no ground for resentment at being killed, unlike the slave killed involuntarily or the slave killed in anger, for both of whom purification was required.

(*d*) Murders within the family, 868c5–869c6

The unexpressed thought that the slave is in some way a member of the family now prompts a transition to the law governing murder in anger of one family-member by another. When

    parent kills offspring,
    spouse kills spouse,
    sibling kills sibling,

the penalty is purification and three years in exile; on return (which is apparently as of right), the offender is to be separated from his or her spouse[60] and permanently excluded from the family circle and its social and religious life. In each case, failure to observe the law, either by the offender or by the other members of the family, creates liability to a charge of impiety at the hands of anyone who wishes. But when offspring kills parent, the penalty is death, unless the killer is absolved by the deceased before he expires; in this case, the same purifications (and 'other actions', i.e. exile)[61] are demanded as for involuntary murder.

A certain pattern emerges:

(*b*) and (*c*(2)): free man kills free man (two or three year's exile); slave kills free man (death penalty).

(*d*) family-member kills family-member (three year's exile); offspring kills parent (death penalty).

The grand system of subordination that is Magnesia's social structure is obvious.

(*b*) allowed differentiation between periods of exile for impulsive (two years) and premeditated (three years) killings in anger, but (*d*) does not:

[60] This provision may be restricted to parents who kill their children: to forbid them to have further children would be only prudent, even if it is not penal. If it is penal, it is crime-specific.
[61] Cf. 869de.

evidently killings of either kind within the family have to be regarded as in principle at the serious end of the scale; yet impulsive murders within the family are in practice just as likely as premeditated ones. The differentiation of states of mind is again overridden by other considerations. It is overriden yet again in the provision for pardon (adopted from Attic law):[62] for the killer's state of mind is exactly the same whether his parent pardons him or not. Or perhaps the parent is supposed, even though near death, to gauge his offspring's state of mind and grant or withhold pardon accordingly.

Since the returned killers are now purified, there can be nothing on that score to prevent their re-absorption not only into Magnesia but into their families; perhaps that is why Plato justifies their continued exclusion from the family by reference to the law of property or theft: they have permanently robbed the family of a member.[63] At any rate, the permanent disabilities from which they are to suffer are striking.

869a7–c5 is the first of a series of impassioned preambles, which now become frequent in the remainder of the law of homicide, and in the law of woundings and assault (i.e. the rest of book 9). Plato 'throws the book' at the killer of a parent: he is guilty of assault, impiety, and temple-robbery, and deserves accordingly to die many deaths. *Nothing* justifies the killing of a parent, not even self-defence; even in those circumstances, the killer must, it seemed, be incurably unjust.[64] This apparently casual mention of self-defence prompts a transition to killings in self-defence as a separate category.

(e) Killings in self-defence, 869c6–d7

This section is in a sense a reversion to the standard relationships, for even when a brother kills a brother, the kind of occasion envisaged (e.g. a factional wrangle of some kind) is non-familial. Killing in self-defence as between all free persons, whether citizens or foreigners, has the same status as the killing of an enemy in war: no pollution is incurred; nor, presumably, is pollution incurred when a slave is killed by a free man in self-defence. A slave who kills a slave in self-defence (against an attack on his *life*?) is likewise free of pollution; but a slave who kills a free man in such circumstances is to be executed.

For a third time, a general rule is overridden:
(e) free men kill free men (no penalty or pollution); slave kills free man (death penalty).
The slave is 'subject to the same laws as the parricide': even in self-defence, killing a social (or familial) superior is a heinous act.

---

[62] See also (f) below.   [63] 868d4, e11.
[64] Cf. 717d, 879c. Their liability is in effect 'absolute'.

In general, Plato's law of homicide in self-defence is based closely on Attic law.[65] His inclusion of it under homicide in anger makes sense; for both are reactions to some provocation: insults etc. in the case of murder in anger, blows in the case of killing in self-defence.[66]

(f) A rider about pardon, 869d7–e4

The rules concerning absolution given by a father in (d) above are to apply to every absolution 'in such cases' or 'of such persons' (*tōn toioutōn*, genitive).

What is 'such'? Obviously not killings in self-defence, but apparently murders in anger in general. The pardon effectively renders such a killing involuntary and the killer liable to only one year's exile, whatever his state of mind. Great weight is given to the dead man's resentment:[67] in involuntary homicide it forced the killer, who *ex hypothesi* deserved no penalty, to go into exile nevertheless, for a year; in homicide in anger the dead man can relinquish his fury and release the killer, but only from up to two thirds of his exile (i.e. his exile will be of one year only, whereas without the pardon it would have been either of two or of three). Goetz notes that the pardon in Attic law was a *total* release;[68] Plato's law is more frugal of indulgence, possibly because the killer is after all at fault, and still needs to chastise his anger in order to reform. But an alternative, and sharper, interpretation of Plato's intentions may be more accurate. As the text says, the victim regards his killing as involuntary; and even if it was not, Plato is prepared to concede the point. Cure is therefore inappropriate, and the one year of exile constitutes recompense and satisfaction for the members of the family, to which *they* are entitled, whatever the victim may be willing to forgo on his own behalf.

It is not clear whether the provision for absolution applies more widely, to *voluntary* murder, or not; in Attic law it apparently did.[69] Nor do we learn whether it applies in Magnesian law to involuntary murder; if so, probably the killer would be dispensed from going into exile at all, as apparently in Attic law, since there would be not only no need to cure him, but none to provide satisfaction for the dead man or his family either.

---

[65] *IG* I³ 104 (I² 115) 33–6 possibly: see Stroud 56; Dem. 21. 71 ff. (cf. 23. 60 ff. on violent robbery), Ant. *Tetr.* 3d. 3; cf. Apol. *Bibl.* 2. 4, 9.

[66] 869d1; cf. p. 244 below.

[67] Cf. MacDowell (1963) 148; cf. also pp. 223–4.

[68] Goetz (1920) 8; cf. Gernet (1951) p. cxcvi.

[69] Dem. 37. 59; contrast Ant. 1. 29, Lys. 13. 42, and cf. p. 252.

C: VOLUNTARY HOMICIDE (869e5–873c1)

Plato's law of homicide in anger was a major innovation, which needed and received lengthy explanation. His law of voluntary homicide is however even longer. In it he certainly makes some significant departures from Athenian practice; yet most of the extraordinary length of this part of his code is caused by the elaborate moral, psychological, social, legal, and religious considerations which underpin it. The concrete regulations occupy correspondingly little space; it is their justifications that are penologically important.

(a) Introduction: Psychology and Penology

The opening lines distinguish sharply murder in anger from voluntary murder, and launch into a very full disquisition on one of the causes of crimes summarized at the end of the main penological excursus:[70] pleasures and desires. Voluntary murder is the result of 'complete injustice', the domination of pleasure, desire, jealousy, and ambition over the soul. Money, which is only the third of human 'goods' (perfection of soul being first, and of body second),[71] is typically the focus of the unjust person's aspirations. In other words, whereas murder in anger sprang from a quasi-rational emotion capable of a noble stand against injustice, voluntary murders are caused by a fundamentally vitiated ordering of moral priorities. In such cases the killers are incurable; every penalty for killing in this section is accordingly death (sometimes with grisly embellishments).

Reform of these killers is therefore necessarily ruled out. Nevertheless they are to be punished, by the extreme penalty.[72] For what purpose? As in the other categories of homicide, it is to satisfy the resentment of the dead man and his family.[73] A comparison with the scope allowed to that resentment in those other categories is instructive. In involuntary homicide, where for utterly different reasons there was equally no question of reform, the measures dictated by the deceased's resentment looked curious and even unjust, even though they were strictly limited. In homicide in anger, the exile demanded by the dead man could function as a species of regimen: the purposes of vengeance and reform could coincide. When, however, as in voluntary homicide, there is again no prospect of reform, and the crime is of the utmost gravity, the deceased's resentment may be given an unimpeded run. And so it

---

[70] 863b–864c.
[72] But see pp. 181–3.
[71] Cf. 631b ff., 679b, 743e, 831c.
[73] 871b, d, 872b, 873a.

proves. Not only is the killer executed, but he is denied burial in Magnesia, presumably by way of symbolical demonstration that the deceased has not forgiven him and he is therefore still (and presumably for ever) polluted.[74]

But that is not all. Immediately after the psychological preamble, which seems meant for readers and judges, we pass to a description of the beliefs which should deter potential killers: that there is 'payment' (*tisis*) for such things in Hades, and on coming back to this world a killer must suffer precisely what he did and end his own life by a similar fate (*moira*) at the hand of someone else; this is termed 'the penalty (*dikē*) according to nature'. This is strictly talionic; and a stronger and more pointed version of the same story is given in order to deter matricides and parricides: Justice exacts vengeance (*timōros Dikē*) for the blood of relatives; parricides after re-birth must be killed by their children, matricides must be re-born as women and be dispatched similarly.[75] Common blood knows no other purification than murder for murder, which soothes the anger (*thumos*) of the deceased's entire family.

Thus side by side with the anger of the dead man, which dictates certain provisions of the actual law, we have a talionic and deterrent doctrine of the most lurid kind; and it is presented not as something the legislator inflicts or can control, but as a fact of 'nature' (*phusis*), operated by a kind of goddess, *Dikē*. The implication is not only that voluntary killers are incurable in this world but in the next too: there is a total continuity of experience and desert as between the two worlds, in the matter of reform and cure as well as in the continued existence of the dead man and his resentment. Plato intends such beliefs to have a strong inhibitory effect on the minds of his Magnesians.[76]

(*b*) The standard cases and derelictions (871a2–e8)

When a man 'unjustly' (i.e. with his soul in an unjust state) and with forethought (*ek pronoias*) kills a fellow-citizen, a chain of requirements is created.

(1) The proclamation and prosecution (871a3–d4)

Relatives (within certain degrees)[77] of the dead man have the usual duty to proclaim a debarment of the killer from temples and other places of

[74] 871d: 'for the sake of lack of pardon, in addition to being impious', i.e. it *would* be impious to bury him in Magnesia. (So interpreted by Diès (Budé) and myself (Penguin), following England; alternatively 'because of the shamelessness in addition to the impiety [of his act]'; but probably ἕνεκα suggests a forward-looking *purpose*.)

[75] 872d5 ff. Clearly there would be no end to the sequence: cf. pp. 70–1.

[76] 870e4, 873a3.

[77] See Gernet (1951) p. cxcviii on Plato's apparent pruning of the list of relatives.

assembly, on grounds of pollution, and to prosecute him for murder.[78] However, the law is on permanent stand-by: it makes, and always will make, such a prohibition on behalf of the whole state, *whether or not* some individual does so.

The notion of a permanent prohibition by the law seems to be a Platonic innovation.[79] What is its purpose? Perhaps Athenians were growing remiss in these matters,[80] and that is the reason for Plato's obvious wish to secure observance of the procedures. At any rate his method of doing so makes use of the hallowed device of a surrogate punisher: a curse.[81] Its *modus operandi* is however not clear: if someone fails to bar by proclamation, or to prosecute, the pollution and the enmity of the gods should devolve upon him, 'for the curse of the law urges on the rumour/report (*phēmē*)'. Presumably the law says, 'undertake the proclamation, and if you don't you will incur the force of my curse, which is *publicity*, which will put you under pressure: for it will become well-known in society that *you* are now the polluted person'. The *miasma* which is the dead man's enmity,[82] and the publicity it somehow receives from the law, should be powerful stimuli to undertaking the prosecution by making the proclamation. Plato is determined that the procedures shall be observed, and that prosecutions shall not be neglected; and his provisions contain a greater degree of public and religious compulsion than prevailed, at least formally, in Athens.

Subsequent provisions point in the same direction.[83] Anyone who wishes to take vengeance (*timōrein*) for the deceased may prosecute the defaulting relative,[84] presumably for impiety; but he should also perform the proclamation and other observances, and *force* (*anankazein, cf. ex anankēs* 867c8) the killer to submit to the legal penalty. A similar apparent provision for prosecution under impiety law was made in involuntary homicide; but there that seemed to be the end of the

---

[78] MacDowell (1963) 17 ff.

[79] In Athens there were two relevant proclamations (MacDowell's B and C (1963) 24–5), by the relatives in the *agora* (B), and by the King Archon (*AP* 57. 2), after receiving the formal accusation (C). Of (C) there is no trace in Platonic law, though just conceivably the law's proclamation may be modelled on it, as an act expressing public will, especially if, as Gernet ((1917a) n. 139, cf. (1951) p. cxcvii and his Budé edn. of Antiphon, p. 141) suggests, the King's proclamation *replaced* that of the relatives at some point around the middle of the 4th century, perhaps for much the same reasons as I suggest for Plato's innovation. Cf. also MacDowell (1963) 26, on Paoli's view, and Piérart (1973b) and (1973a) 430–3.

[80] Dem. 24. 186 seems to complain of some general laxity; cf. MacDowell (1963) 9–11, on Dem. 22. 2 and the difficulty of dealing with the 'negative offence' of not prosecuting. At any rate, the *first* point Plato makes in the law of voluntary homicide is that proclamations are *de rigueur*; the actual penalties have to wait till a good deal later (871d). Hansen (1976) 111 n. 20, however, contests the view that the relatives had a *duty* to prosecute.   [81] 871b; cf. Vallois (1914) 261 n. 6.

[82] Cf. 866b.   [83] 871b5–c3.

[84] *Pace* England (1921), the persons thus described in 871b5 and 6 must surely be the same; cf. Piérart (1973a) 429.

matter.[85] In voluntary homicide, however, the person who 'wishes to avenge the deceased' then actually takes over the entire prosecution with its various observances. This may be a major departure from the Athenian principle, if indeed it existed, that only certain members of the family of the deceased, or persons in some analogous relationship, could prosecute.[86] To the constraints of law and religion Plato explicitly adds the action of 'whoever wishes'; and the purpose is clear: that the killer shall be punished.[87] In Magnesia, when voluntary homicide is committed, prosecutions *will* be brought and penalties *will* be imposed, or Plato will know the reason why.

(2) *The penalty (871d4–5)*

The significance of the penalty (death, but without burial in Magnesia) I have discussed above.[88] Death simply reproduces Athenian practice;[89] the extra provision seems to be Plato's.[90] In Athens, the property of the convicted killer was confiscated, whether he was executed or went into (permanent) exile (see (3) below);[91] in Magnesia, it presumably passed to his heir, conformably with Plato's desire to keep estates in the same family in perpetuity.[92]

(3) *Exile and illegal return (871d6–e2)*

In Athens, a person accused of voluntary homicide could go into life-long exile after making the first (of two) speeches in his defence at the trial.[93] Plato accords a similar permission, but the accused has apparently to leave before the trial gets under way.[94]

The voluntary killer who again sets foot in the country of the murdered man may be killed with impunity by a relative of the latter, or indeed any citizen, or handed over to the authorities for the same

[85] Cf. 866b, and p. 221 n. 28.

[86] MacDowell (1963) 16–19, 94–5, (1978) 111, but cf. now id., *CR*, 28 (1978), 175, and Hansen ((1976) 108–12, (1981) 13–17) have maintained that the right to prosecute for homicide was not thus restricted (contra, Gagarin (1979a) 304 ff., 322–3). If that was so, Plato is merely formalizing and stressing this point of procedure. Cf. p. 240 n. 116 below (the case of murdered slaves).

[87] 871c2–3.

[88] pp. 233.

[89] Unless the killer went voluntarily into exile: see below; Ant. 5. 10, Dem. 21. 43, 23. 80; but Gagarin (1981) 111–15 argues that exile was also an alternative *penalty*, not merely an option open to the accused. If that is right, Plato may wish to block off the alternative: see (iv) below. He makes no mention of the practice of permitting the accuser to watch the execution (Dem. 23. 69).

[90] Morrow (1960) 492 n. 277 gives references for the penalty of non-burial in Attica; cf. Parker (1983) 45 n. 47.

[91] Dem. 21. 43, Lys. 1. 50, *AP* 47. 2, MacDowell (1963) 115–17.

[92] Cf. p. 227 n. 56 above, on homicide in anger, and Saunders (1972) n. 90.

[93] Ant. 5. 13, Dem. 23. 69.

[94] 871d6 φυγών may imply, however, only *acquiescence* (see (4) below, on sureties), rather than permission: 'if he absconds'; at any rate the source of pollution would be far away from the sight of the dead man, and so no danger to Magnesia. The licence of exile is, perhaps significantly, not repeated in the provisions relating to voluntary murder within the family (873b); cf. Poll. 8. 117, who says that it was not allowed to killers of parents.

purpose. This is broadly similar to corresponding Athenian law; and we note again the insistence on the role of others besides the relatives.[95] Once more, the feelings of the deceased are kept at the front of our attention, by the description of Magnesia as the 'country of the murdered man'.

(4) Sureties (871e2–8)

The accused must supply three sureties to the accuser; if he cannot, he must be kept bound, pending the hearing. (If he flees into permanent exile, presumably either he does so at a very early moment or leaves the three sureties in the lurch.)

Again there is an evident anxiety that the procedures of accusation and trial should take place; the accused should be prevented, if possible, from fleeing abroad; at any rate the mention of sureties seems in the text to be prompted by the brief discussion of exile. In Athens, all *foreigners* could be required to produce sureties for their appearance in court, apparently in all types of cases,[96] obviously in view of the strong possibility that they might make off out of Athens before the trial; for to some at least, exile would matter little. In homicide cases, Plato applies this provision to all persons, citizen, foreigner, or slave, with the sole exception (discussed below) of murder by *bouleusis* of one citizen by another.[97] The overall effect of his introduction of sureties into homicide cases will presumably be to bring about an increase in the number of death sentences relative to the number of escapes into exile; he seems to feel that justice needs conspicuously to be seen to be done, and exile serves that purpose less well than death.

(c) Bouleusis (871e8–872a7)[98]

Attic law distinguishes between the plotter of an act resulting in death, and his agent; the planner (*ho bouleusas*) is not *autocheir*, that is, he does

---

[95] Refs. as on p. 221 n. 27 (ii), with discussion in last para. of Gernet (1917a) n. 153. It is however not clear that Plato enlarges the role of non-relatives in *this* matter: see Gagarin (1986) 113 n. 35 on Athenian practice.

[96] Isoc. 17. 12, 41, Dem. 32. 29, MacDowell (1978) 76, Whitehead (1977) 92–3, Harrison i (1968) 196 n. 1, Lipsius (1905–15) 811, Gauthier (1972) 138–41. In Magnesia, foreigners are apparently relieved of this duty.

[97] That is the upshot of the complex regulations at 871e2–872b4, in particular the repeated πλὴν τῆς ἐγγύης (a5, b2); see Saunders (1972) n. 89. They have the curious effect of providing that a citizen prosecuted by a foreigner for *bouleusis* must provide sureties, but not when prosecuted by a fellow citizen. But Plato is not above minor muddle: cf. Saunders (1972) n. 85, on involuntary homicide.

[98] In the tangled topic of *bouleusis* I rely on the careful work of MacDowell (1963) ch. VI, cf. 125–6, and Loomis (1972), who between them seem to me to have established that Attic law was as I have summarized it.

not kill 'with his own hand'. *Bouleusis* could be of two kinds: (1) of intentional killing, i.e. when the planner intends either the killing, *or other harm to the victim*, to be done by the agent, and it is so done, the harm leading to death;[99] (2) of unintentional killing, i.e. when the planner intends neither killing nor harm, but is responsible for acts, carried out by his agent, which result in a death.[100]

Plato shows no interest in (2); but he may have meant to include it in his law of involuntary homicide.[101] Nor does he say anything about cases of intention merely to do harm, which then results in death.[102] One can perhaps see why. If he had treated it as involuntary killing, which in a sense it is, he would have been imputing no 'injustice' at all to the killer—which is obviously unsatisfactory. If he were to treat it as voluntary killing, he would be ascribing exactly the same injustice to a desire to harm as to a desire to kill, which in a penology ostensibly concerned with motive is equally intolerable. At any rate, all he prescribes is that the plotter who intends his agent to kill and is thus responsible (*aitios*) in the psychic sense, is 'unclean of soul' (though not, of course 'of hands') and should be tried as a voluntary killer, except that (*a*) sureties are not required,[103] (*b*) he may, if executed, be buried in his native land. In effect, the plotter is thus exempted from the two additions to Attic law Plato made in the standard case of *autocheir* murder of citizen by citizen: sureties, and burial outside Magnesia.

Now although the penalty for *bouleusis* of voluntary homicide in Athens was death, and thus far Plato's law is identical, there too plotters of intentional murder seem, on at least one occasion,[104] to have been considered to have done something slightly less heinous than murderers 'with their own hand'. Perhaps plotters were thought, not being *auto-cheires*, or not being literally blood-stained, to attract less pollution; perhaps that is Plato's reason for permitting burial in Magnesia, within

[99] And. 1. 94, Ant. 1. 26, Dem. 54. 25; for this variety of *bouleusis* the penalty was death; but there is doubt (*AP* 57. 3 is ambiguous) whether it was the Areopagus or the Palladium court that tried the cases: see MacDowell (1963) 64 ff., Loomis (1972) 91 n. 45., Grace (1973) 23, Rhodes (1981) 643-4.
[100] Ant. 6. For this variety of *bouleusis* the penalty was exile.
[101] That is, if in αὐτὸς τῷ ἑαυτοῦ σώματι ἢ δι' ἑτέρων σωμάτων (865b7-c1) the word σῶμα is taken to refer to human bodies in each case and to point to a distinction between principals and agents. Alternatively we may have only a repetition/summary of the distinction in the preceding few lines between one's own body and things which could be termed 'other' bodies, i.e. tools etc., and the purpose could be to stress that he who kills unintentionally by some instrument is just as *responsible* as he who kills unintentionally 'by his own body'; cf. Plut. *Per.* 36, and Ant. *Tetr.* 2 (Plato would presumably support the prosecution). The physical means, the σῶμα, which they use is irrelevant: both are equally unintentional killers; but *both* are αὐτόχειρες (c1-2), and responsible (though not morally culpable), and cannot escape the consequences of exile etc. by blaming the victim or the instrument. Further discussion: Nörr (1986) 75-6, Maffi (1988) 113-14.
[102] See under 'woundings in anger', below.   [103] See p. 236 n. 97.
[104] *AP* 39. 5, perhaps implying persons merely implicated *politically* in the pogroms under the Thirty Tyrants, as distinct from those who actually killed; see Bonner (1924).

the sight of the victim. Or perhaps he is also concerned with the question of brutality:[105] since he himself did not commit violence, the plotter is less 'unjust'. Whatever his reasons, the minor concessions granted to the plotter are hard to square with a penology that concentrates on states of mind.

(d) Foreigners (872a7–b4)

The law is that the same arrangements are to apply when

   (i) foreigners prosecute foreigners,
   (ii) citizens prosecute foreigners and foreigners prosecute citizens,
   (iii) slaves prosecute slaves,

in regard both to *autocheiria* and to *bouleusis*, except as regards the sureties, which must be provided by all these defendants (i.e. the exemption granted to citizens accused by citizens of *bouleusis* is withdrawn). I assume 'foreigners' (*xenoi*) includes metics, and 'arrangements' ('things') include the death penalty and burial outside Magnesia.

Thus foreigners must always provide sureties, but citizens only when prosecuted by foreigners. It is not easy to see why: the citizen is hardly *more* likely to abscond if prosecuted by a foreigner. Perhaps the reason is simply reciprocal equity as between free men: if foreigners must provide sureties when prosecuted by foreigners, so too must citizens.

But Plato's major innovation is a penological one, and has been pointed out often enough.[106] In Athens, intentional murder of a foreigner was treated less seriously than that of a citizen: it was tried not by the Areopagus but at the Palladium, the court for unintentional killing, and presumably attracted the penalty not of death but only of exile.[107] Here again Plato seems anxious to accord all free men equal protection; and he does so by in effect extending to all foreigners the privilege, occasionally granted in Athens to a foreigner, of the same protection as a citizen, i.e. if he were killed, the murder would be punished in the same way as that of a citizen would be.[108]

---

[105] See on murder in anger, p. 192 above.

[106] Goetz (1920) 47–8, Gernet (1917a) n. 82, Morrow (1960) 147. Whitehead (1977) 133–4 remarks on the anomalous nature of the Athenian bracketing of foreigners with slaves in homicide law.

[107] *AP* 57. 3; *Lex. Seg.* 4 s.v. φονικόν. Harrison i (1968) 196–8 holds out the possibility that the Palladium could decide the killing warranted treatment as intentional, in spite of the general rule, and impose 'the harsher penalty': the general rule itself he cautiously regards as 'a probably but not absolutely certain deduction' from the venue of the trial. Clerc (1893) 100 suggests that while involuntary murder of a citizen was punished by only temporary exile, voluntary murder of a metic was punished by *permanent* exile. Cf. Grace (1973) 8–10, 16.

[108] MacDowell (1963) 126 gives some examples in inscriptions: IG II² 32, ll. 9 ff. (dating to 385) and 226, ll. 34–40 (c343); both specify that the death should have been 'violent'; cf. Dem. 23. 89.

It is also clear that foreign defendants in Magnesia in cases of voluntary homicide attract the same punishment as citizens; one assumes the same applied at Athens (unless of course the victim was himself a foreigner).[109]

(e) Slaves as killers (872b4–c2)

A slave who is convicted of killing a free man, either by his own hand or by *bouleusis*, is to be dragged to a point at which he may see the victim's tomb and be given as many strokes of the lash as the successful prosecutor directs; if after that he is still alive, he is to be killed.

As in Attic law,[110] the slave receives a trial and if found guilty is executed. We do not know whether it was Athenian law, or practice, to embellish the penalty for a slave.[111] The ostensible purpose of the embellishments which Plato prescribes are of course to give the fullest possible satisfaction to the dead man and his kin, by the sight of the slave's sufferings. For a free man to be killed is bad enough; but to be killed by a slave is an outrage, and atrociously violates both the victim's feelings and the settled order of society.[112]

Why is the slave to 'see' the tomb? So that he may have it 'rubbed into' him why he is to suffer. The excruciating sharpness of that knowledge, thus brought home to the condemned person, is itself part of the victim's satisfaction. The slave knows he is being watched by his victim, who knows the slave knows[113] he is to die to satisfy himself. His vengeance could thus not be sweeter. The 'appropriateness' of holding the execution near the tomb is not merely external and grimly picturesque, but psychological.

Plato envisages[114] that a slave (a relative of a victim, presumably) may prosecute a slave. In this case no social order is violated, except that if the prosecution is successful some free man loses a slave, since the penalty is death (but apparently unembellished). Nothing is said about satisfying the resentment of the slave who was murdered.

---

[109] Cf. Gauthier (1972) 141–4, Grace (1973) 21 ff.

[110] Ant. 5. 46–8, cf. Isoc. 12. 181, Morrow (1939) 71–2. Grace (1974), however, contests the right to a trial.

[111] At Ant. 1. 20 it is not clear whether the torture of a slave was by way of penalty, or to extract information.

[112] That is perhaps why the proceedings are carried out partly by the relatives (they dictate the number of lashes), and partly by the public executioner. On whipping as appropriate for slaves, see Glotz (1908). The slave is beyond cure; now his only role is to satisfy resentment—indeed the victim and his relatives can be compensated in no other way.

[113] Cf. pp. 18–19, and App. case A21.

[114] 872a8–b1.

(f) Slaves as victims (872c2–6)

In Athens, the murder of a slave was certainly actionable at law; the trials were held at the Palladium.[115] However, since the right—or duty—to prosecute belonged to the master,[116] who for various reasons may have been reluctant to pursue the matter,[117] the protection of slaves against murder was weaker than that enjoyed by free men; and the protection was of course at its weakest when the master was himself the killer.[118] Nevertheless, the law regarded the slave as more than a piece of property; he was to some degree a member of a religious community.[119]

What was the punishment for killing a slave? It was certainly not death: that is precluded by the fact that even the murder of a non-citizen free man attracted only the penalty of exile.[120] A passage of Lycurgus allows us to infer for his day the possibility of a fine; Demosthenes speaks of disfranchisement or exile.[121] There appears to be no other evidence, and one can only conclude tentatively that the court itself could fix a penalty to reflect the gravity of the circumstances of the killing.

Magnesian law provides that if a man kills a slave who is 'doing no wrong/injustice', fearing that the slave may inform against his own wicked and disgraceful conduct,[122] or from some similar motive, he must, in this case too,[123] when such a slave had died, likewise submit to trial, just as he would had he killed a citizen. Similarly, it is said later on that offical action has to be taken to prevent vengeance being taken on a slave-informer.[124]

Plato undoubtedly wished to encourage slaves to inform,[125] and is well aware of the fears of masters with something to hide.[126] It is a measure of his anxiety on this score that in this one instance only of the murder of a

---

[115] AP 57. 3, Ant. 5. 48, Dem. 59. 9–10 (if indeed the woman was a slave, as MacDowell (1963) 54 assumes).

[116] Ant. 5. 48: 'if he sees fit' (to prosecute). On Isoc. 18. 52 ff. and Dem. 47. 70 ff. see MacDowell (1963) 20–3 and Harrison i (1968) 169 esp. n. 3. Discussing Dem. 47. 72, MacDowell (1963) 20–2, 94–5 (cf. Harrison i (1968) 169 n. 4) believes others too may have been able to prosecute; but cf. Kells (1965) 207, Grace (1974 and 1975), Evjen (1971), and Kidd (1990) 216 ff.

[117] He may have disliked the slave or found him useless anyway and not worth the bother of avenging, or did not wish to offend the killer; cf. Evjen (1971) 263–4. In any case, the slave would not have been a blood-relation.

[118] But possibly not quite non-existent: see Morrow (1937) 214 ff., 220 ff., and n. 116 above; cf. Ant. 6. 4.

[119] Ant. 6. 4, who speaks of purifying oneself after killing a slave (perhaps lest one become liable to a graphē asebeias); cf. Isoc. 12. 181.   [120] Gernet (1917a) n. 159.

[121] Leoc. 65; Dem. 59. 10 (but see n. 115 above).

[122] Cf. 870cd.

[123] καί 872c5, i.e. 'as well as' in case of murder of a citizen.

[124] 932d.   [125] Cf. 914a, 917d.

[126] Cf. Lys. 7. 16, Ant. 5. 46–8, 52 (the last overtranslated by Morrow (1939) 53 n. 17).

slave does he prescribe a penalty, and the death penalty at that.[127] The murderer, being dominated by psychic injustice, is incurable; and Plato is determined that his punishment shall be as inevitable as society can make it.

It does not follow either (i) that Plato intended the death penalty to apply to all murders by free men of slaves, informers or not, or (ii) that all such murders of slaves *except* those of informers go unpunished. (i) has been rightly ruled out by Morrow:[128] Plato carefully excludes murder of a slave by a free man from the elaborate regulations at (*d*) above, providing only for the murder of a slave by a slave. (ii) may be dismissed by a series of inferences: as Morrow himself points out,[129] Plato (in (*e*) above) provides that 'a slave who has murdered his master is entitled to trial. . . . This would imply that it was unlawful to put such a slave to death without judicial sentence. And . . . *a fortiori* it would be illegal to put him to death for lesser offences.' And *a fortiori* again, we could argue, it would also be illegal to do so when he is 'doing no wrong/injustice', in our passage. This clause is merely a description of the general circumstances, within which the *particular* case of an informer is exceptional, as attracting the penalty of death for his killer. The implication is not that an innocent (or offending, for that matter) slave may be killed with impunity, but that such a killing normally attracts some penalty less than death, as apparently in Athens. Certainly purification would be required, as for involuntary murder and murder in anger,[130] and possibly on a greater scale, given that the murder is voluntary. Whether anything further would be inflicted on the killer is entirely uncertain.[131]

(*g*) Murder within the family (872c7–873c1)

We have already discussed the prefatory and deterrent material of this section.[132] Such murders are 'wholly unjust',[133] and no distinction is to be made between *autocheires* and plotters. The rules are as follows. Deliberate murder of one's own father, mother, brothers,[134] or children: proclamations of exclusion from public places and exaction of sureties

[127] This may well be a stiffening of Athenian law, which seems not to have distinguished murder of informer-slaves from that of others: Grace (1974), Morrow (1939) 56, Levinson (1953) 591.

[128] (1939) 52–3; but Levinson (1953) 590 argues the possibility, surely unrealistically: Plato would hardly rate a slave's life so highly, or think that his murder was as serious as that of a citizen.

[129] Morrow (1939) 51.   [130] 865cd, 868a.

[131] Cf. Morrow (1939) 54, who properly stresses that if the slave belonged to another, compensation would be required. If the master were the killer, who would prosecute—a member of the family, 'anyone who wishes', or officials (see 932e)?   [132] See pp. 208–11 above.

[133] 872cd. A touch of euphemism creeps in: the criminal has been overtaken by 'misfortune' (873a5, cf. Dem. 23. 42); but perhaps it is not a euphemism, in view of what will ineluctably happen to him in the next world.

[134] Though ἀδελφῶν (873a5) presumably includes sisters too.

should be as in other cases of intentional murder; but the execution to be
is elaborately embellished by expulsion of the body, naked, to a point
where three roads meet outside the city; all the officials concerned are to
throw a stone at the head of the corpse, so as to purify the entire state;
they must then eject it from Magnesia, without burial.

These embellishments are even more spectacular than those
prescribed for the slave who kills voluntarily. The free man who kills
within the family is at least executed first, apparently in the normal way,
and the embellishments affect only his corpse; but the slave is made to
suffer very great extra pain, for wholly vindictive reasons. The execution
of the slave involves joint participation of persons representing both the
public[135] and the private interests; that of the free man seems to be an
exclusively public event. As Plato himself explains, the stoning is a
purification on behalf of the entire state;[136] presumably the pollution is
transferred to the stone and swept away with detritus, much as the body
is itself then ejected from Magnesia. We have here a purification that is
fundamentally of the same kind as those specified in other forms of
homicide; but as the whole state is affected by voluntary murder of a
blood relative, the rite needs to be not only very public but peculiarly
solemn and thoroughgoing.

The emphasis on 'blood for blood' in the preamble seems to be meant
strictly, for murders as between spouses are not listed. As Gernet says,[137]
'c'est parmi les victimes du second rang qu'ils figurent', both in murder in
anger[138] and in the law of wounding:[139] a spouse is less venerable as a
spouse than as a parent. Again, Plato's law reflects and reinforces the
hierarchical structure of his state.

As for Attic law, there is no firm evidence that penalties for murderers
within the family were embellished in any way;[140] but if Pollux is to be
believed parricides were not entitled to the option of exile after the first
speech for the defence at the trial.[141]

---

[135] Cf. p. 230 n. 112. The slave guilty of killing a free man *in anger* (*c*2) is left to purely private
vengeance; but *voluntary* killing (*e*) is so serious that the state takes a hand in inflicting the penalty.

[136] Gernet (1981) 265-6. Note that the stoning is *not* the mode of execution, which is carried out
by officials, not by popular lynch law; so too the purification is an official act, on behalf of the state
(cf. Hirzel (1909) 234 ff., Gras (1984) 81, Cantarella (1984) 66-8). The proceedings are symbol and
spectacle, not participatory: the populace is kept at arm's length. The cross-roads is an 'appointed'
one: it is made known in advance where the event will be, at a place which is easy of access from
various directions. However, the religious significance of the location is probably more important:
for some discussion see Gernet (1917a) n. 166 on schol. to Aes. *Choe*. 98, Hirzel (1907) 234 n. 6 and
Halliwell (1986) esp. 188. I do not know why Plato directs that the stones be aimed at the head:
perhaps it is because the head is the location of the rational part of the soul, the part which in this
criminal has been radically corrupted. On the importance of the head, see Onians (1951) 95 ff.

[137] (1917a) n. 165.   [138] 868d–869c, cf. p. 229 above.

[139] 877bc.   [140] MacDowell (1963) 116, but cf. Soph. *OC* 407, Garner (1987)103.

[141] Pol. 8. 117.

TRANSITION: SUICIDES ETC. (873c2–874b5)

After this solemn close to the law of intentional homicide Plato passes to a consideration of suicides, no doubt prompted by the similarity between the disposal of the bodies of those who kill themselves, and that of the bodies of executed murderers. The disposal of animals or objects that kill is likewise similar, and so too would be that of an unknown killer's body could he but be found. In none of these cases is there a living human and convicted criminal available for cure, so they are of only secondary penological interest. But Plato persists in treating the 'offenders' as nearly as possible in the normal way. The suicide should 'suffer' something for the cowardice of imposing an 'unjust' judgement on himself; he must be buried alone, in anonymity and disgrace, in a remote part of the country.[142] Animals and objects must be prosecuted and tried, and if convicted ejected from Magnesia;[143] murderers unknown must have a proclamation made against them, and be publicly threatened with the penalties for intentional killing.[144] The justification for these elaborate procedures is presumably that all the 'offenders' have inflicted damage on the community; pollution is an issue in each case; and the rituals serve some didactic and social function. In particular Plato may suppose, or wish it to be supposed, that the suicide, on the assumption he has some existence after death, will be aware of his ignominy, and punished by his anguish.

D. JUSTIFIABLE HOMICIDE (874b6–d1)

(a) Conspectus

The term *phonos dikaios*[145] does not occur at all in Plato, perhaps because it misleadingly implies that when killers are exempted from penalty the law somehow regards the killings as legitimate.[146] But that cannot be true for the first of the several groups of penalty-free homicides recognized in Attic law:[147]

1. Killings of innocent persons in competitions, battles etc.; persons who die under a doctor's care.

---

[142] Cf. Arist. *NE* 1138ª4 ff.   [143] Cf. Aesch. 3. 244, Dem. 23. 76.
[144] Cf. *AP* 57. 4.   [145] e.g. Aesch. 2. 88, Dem. 23. 74; cf. 20. 158.
[146] e.g. Dem. 23. 53, 'the law grants permission' to kill apparently in regard to both 1 and 4; similarly *AP* 57. 3 treats these two categories of killings as 'according to law', which is equally misleading. Pausanias puts the matter better, 9. 36. 8: for some killings there is ἄδεια, 'immunity'. Cf. Gagarin (1978*a*) 119–20, (1978*b*) 301 n. 41.
[147] I follow in outline MacDowell (1963) ch. 7; cf. Gagarin (1978*a* and *b*), Lipsius (1905–15) 614 n. 50.

2. Killings of persons illegally returned from exile.
3. Killings in self-defence.
4. Killings of criminal aggressors (footpads, rapists, adulterers, etc.); these are special cases of (3), some of them involving the protection of third parties.
5. Killings of persons attempting to set up a tyranny or subvert the democracy.[148]

Clearly in (1) the law does not 'give permission' to kill; it certainly allows the risk of it, but then merely recognizes that error or mishap, however disastrous, should not attract punishment or pollution.[149]

If we now look back over the whole of Plato's homicide law, we can see how these categories have been distributed:

(1) is clearly a variety of unintentional homicide, and is placed right at the beginning of that section.

(2) is distributed in various forms throughout the law of homicide unintentional, in anger, and intentional, as occasion arises.[150]

(3) forms part of the law of homicide in anger, and is obviously appropriate there.[151]

(4) is clearly a variety of intentional homicide,[152] and effectively forms an appendix to that section.

(5), however, occurs nowhere; treason and subversion attract the death penalty,[153] but nothing is said about a licence to kill offenders.

(1) and (4), bundled together in Attic law, are thus kept widely separated, a device which silently meets the point that the victims in the two cases are very different: those in 1 are innocent, and killed unintentionally; those in 4 are criminals killed deliberately (or usually so, one assumes).

Our immediate concern, however, is with (4).

(b) Theft

(i) A man who catches a thief entering his home at night to steal his goods, and kills him, shall be 'pure' (katharos).

As Cohen has pointed out,[154] in Greek society theft is very often from private dwellings, at night. Demosthenes states that a *nocturnal* thief,

---

[148] MacDowell (1963) 77 ff. summarizes the evidence for this intermittent legislation.

[149] No pollution: Dem. 20. 158, Hewitt (1960) esp. 111 ff., Parker (1983) app. 5.

[150] And in more discriminating forms (see 866c, 868a, 871de) than the blanket provision reported by Dem. 23. 28, which allows the killing, apparently summarily, by any person, without necessarily arresting him (apagōgē) and taking him before officials, of *any* exiled murderer who returns.

[151] See pp. 230–1 above, and Gagarin (1978a) 118–19. As he points out, killings allegedly arising out of self-defence were likely to be more contentious than the relatively clear-cut special cases, in which the circumstances could be more surely reconstructed.   [152] 874b6–d1, cf. 876e.

[153] 856a–857a.   [154] Cohen (1983) 76–8, with references.

apparently in any place, may be killed with impunity by the offended party;[155] and that any thief who uses *force*, presumably on the person of the owner of the property, may similarly be killed, provided the killing took place at the time, without premeditation, and in defence of one's own goods; there is no restriction of place or time.[156]

In Plato, and no doubt in the Attic law, entering a house at night creates a presumption of intent to steal, and the need to defend one's property justifies the killing. He may have thought of the 'house' as simply part of the description of the typical case; or he may have intended it as a deliberate *restriction* on the apparent licence of Athenian law to kill a night-time thief anywhere. It is not clear whether simply entering a house constitutes 'force';[157] if so, then Plato's specification of *night-time* burglary may be similarly intended as a restriction on the scope of the law.[158]

(ii) A man who kills a 'clothes-stealer', *lōpodutēs*, in self-defence, shall be pure.

To suffer *lōpodusia* is to be 'mugged' and robbed of one's clothes[159] (and property carried about the person, notably money, one supposes). The offence seems to be a particular case of the robbery with violence for which the injured party could kill on the spot in defence of his own property.[160] *Apagōgē* was an alternative remedy, with a strong possibility of the death penalty.[161]

Now these two regulations of Plato form only an appendix to the law of homicide, and they may be written rather summarily; he presumably expects us to take a good deal for granted, notably the offender's use of force, and probably the immediacy of his being killed. Certainly the cases he mentions confine the right of killing to the offended party, as Demosthenes stresses.[162] Yet his restriction of the liability of thieves to be killed with impunity to muggers who steal clothes (and then only in self-defence),[163] and to burglars *at night*, looks like a deliberate narrowing of the scope of self-help.

---

[155] Dem. 24. 113; the owner might also wound the thief, or hale him before the Eleven.

[156] Dem. 23. 60–1, which supplies restoration of IG I³ 104, 37–8.

[157] The Attic term was *toichōruchos*, 'digger through a wall'.

[158] Cf. 864c.

[159] Cohen (1983) 79–83, Ar. *Birds* 496–8, *Eccl.* 668, Lys. 10. 10.

[160] Cf. (i) above, and Dem. 23. 53, in which ἐν ὁδῷ καθελών may refer only to brawls, but probably refers to mugging for the purpose of theft, including that of clothes etc.

[161] Aesch. 1. 91, *AP* 52. 1.

[162] Dem. 23. 60.

[163] Presumably some clothes-stealing was *stealthy* (cf. Aesch. 1. 91), i.e. when they were temporarily deposited somewhere, say at a baths or a gymnasium.

(c) Rape and seduction

(i) If a man rapes a free woman, or a boy, he may be slain with impunity by the victim of the outrage, and by the victim's father, brother or sons.

(ii) If a man discovers his wedded wife being raped, he may kill the rapist and be 'pure' in the eyes of the law.

Gernet raises the question why if both (i) and (ii) refer to rape,[164] as they seem to,[165] Plato did not simply add 'or by the [victim's] husband' to (i), thus dispensing with the separate provision (ii). He hazards that (ii), in spite of the description of the woman as *biazomenēi*, 'being forced', includes adultery as well as rape, and that only the husband (not the victim or other persons) has the right to kill the seducer or rapist. That seems paradoxical, in view of the more widely-distributed licence to kill a rapist in (i). Surely (ii) is only an additional, special case of (i):[166] *both* are instances of rape alone, as the language sufficiently indicates; and seduction of any person is left without formal penalty.[167] That would fit very well with Plato's expressed intention of leaving sexual misdemeanours to be dealt with by moral, social, and religious sanctions alone;[168] and his concentration on rape is all of a piece with his preoccupation with the manner of the commission of a crime, which we have noticed before.[169] Force or violence are peculiarly reprehensible, and bring that variety of sexual misconduct which is rape within the ambit of the criminal law. The licence to kill the rapist however, seems to be confined to the occasion of the offence; it is unclear what remedy would be available subsequently.

It is a nice question whether Plato has inverted Attic practice. According to Lysias, a rapist of a free man, boy, or woman[170] was liable to double damages.[171] Seducers, on the other hand, were treated more

---

[164] Gernet (1917a) n. 185.

[165] 874c3-6 *passim*: 'force'.

[166] Possibly marked out as such by ἐάν τε (καὶ ἐάν is the regular connection between *different* headings elsewhere in this section).

[167] Cf. Goetz (1920) 97. In practice, of course, a husband coming upon his wife in bed with another man might find it difficult to restrain himself, even if—or especially if—it were obvious that it was a case of seduction rather than rape; cf. Harrison i (1968) 34.

[168] 783b-785a, 841de, cf. 759c. Plato may realize that the relatively public role he wishes women to take (739c, 779e ff., 807b) will expose them to greater sexual risk than in Athens, but feels that the risk will be worth taking. Gernet (1951) p. clxviii describes the sanctions for seduction as 'assez aléatoires'; Becker (1932, 92 ff.) reviews the law of adultery in Greece and in Plato.

[169] e.g. in murder in anger; cf. 864c.

[170] Lys. 1. 32. ἐφ᾽ αἷσπερ applying to women looks restrictive, but taken with 31 and Dem. 23. 53 must in practice mean almost all free women. Cf. Plut. *Sol.* 23, who speaks simply of a 'free woman', without restriction.

[171] Presumably by way of a δίκη βιαίων and paid to the victim's *kurios*, or to the victim himself if an adult male: see Cole (1984) 99, 102-3; and 108-11 on practice at Gortyn. On 'double' see Harrison i (1968) 34 n. 2, Edwards and Usher (1985) 227, Carey (1989) 79.

severely, as permanently alienating the wife's affections and creating uncertainties about parentage.[172] They could be killed by the husband on the spot *if caught in the act*,[173] or at least when *not* so caught, they could be prosecuted by a *graphē moicheias* (suit for adultery), for which the penalty is uncertain;[174] they could alternatively pay the husband a sum of money, or (by custom if not in law) be subjected to various crime-specific penalties.[175]

If this statement of Athenian law is correct, Plato has made two important innovations: (i) because of the violence used in rape, he enhances the penalty from damages to death; (ii) he frees seduction of formal penalty. (i) constitutes a vast increase in severity; (ii) is a sharp decrease in the scope of punitive law. Both measures flow from the penological principles he enunciated earlier in the *Laws*. (ii) is particularly interesting: it shows a keen awareness of the limitations of law and the possibility and efficacy of formally punishing misconduct arising from strong natural urges—provided it is not accompanied by force.

However, the argument of the crucial witness, Lysias in speech 1, that rape was punished less severely than seduction, sounds paradoxical and has come under reasonable suspicion.[176] In order to cry up the seriousness of seduction as compared with rape, he omits almost entirely mention of the non-capital penalties for the former;[177] conversely, it is *prima facie* likely that rape could be punished by death (perhaps by way of a *graphē hybreōs*); but 'no extant Athenian law states this.'[178] On the other hand, if Lysias' paradox were not true, could he have expected to get away with it? Perhaps; but even if it is false, the second of Plato's innovations (the freeing of seduction from penalty) would still survive.

The persons listed in the Attic law providing for the summary killing of their *seducers* coincide very largely with those in Plato's law providing for the summary killing of *rapists*: a man's wife, mother, sister, and daughter.[179] But Plato adds 'boy', mentioned in the law about rape in Lysias,[180] thus giving to raped boys as well as to raped females the

[172] Lys. 1. 32 ff. See Cole (1984) 101-2 and 110 on the significance of the location of sexual offences.
[173] Lys. 1. 25, 30-3, 13. 66, Dem. 23. 53, *AP* 57. 3; cf. Xen. *Hiero* 3. 3, Paus. 9. 36. 8.
[174] *AP* 59. 3. 1. I do not know why Harrison (i (1968) 35) says the penalty 'would' be death; cf. Cole (1984) 103-4, Harris (1990) 374.
[175] Lys. 1. 49, Ar. *Cl* 1083, *Plut.* 168, App. case A6 (but see Cohen (1985)); for a fuller account of marital infidelity in Athenian law, see Harrison i (1968) 32 ff.; cf. Cole (1984) 108 n. 49 for practices in some other Greek states.   [176] Bateman 277-8, citing Paoli (1950) 164-5.
[177] Sections 25 and 29 do however mention the possibility of the payment.
[178] Edwards and Usher (1985) 227; on *hubris*, see Paoli (1950) 165, 168-9 (citing 874c as evidence for *Attic* law). Cf. now Harris (1990) 373.   [179] Dem. 23. 53.
[180] Lys. 1. 32, Carey (1989) ad loc.; seducers of *boys* seem not to have been liable to summary killing in Athens.

protection enhanced from monetary payment to risk of summary killing of the offender. He also adds that the victim himself/herself may summarily kill; we cannot say whether this was so in Athens. Finally, there is one provision he drops. Attic law embraced concubines kept for the procreation of free children;[181] but of course Plato would not tolerate, much less protect, such arrangements in Magnesia.

(d) Protection of family

Plato provides that one is completely 'pure' (katharos) if one kills in the course of protecting from death one's father, mother, children, siblings, or wife.

I find no parallel to such a law in Athens,[182] though no doubt the circumstances described would have been heard sympathetically by a jury, on the general ground, perhaps, that the victim was the aggressor. For it seems to be an extension of the preceding law of rape to aggression in general. However, Plato says nothing about aggression, and there are the tight restrictions that the killing must be to protect from death, not (presumably) from mere wounding, and that the person thus protected must not be engaged in an 'unholy' activity. Indeed, not to intervene could be construed as allowing the father or mother to be killed, which would be quite close to doing what must never be done in any circumstances, even in self-defence: killing parents.[183]

(e) Conclusion

Our chief result seems to be that the circumstances under which one may inflict the punishment of death on one's own authority are appreciably more circumscribed in Magnesia than in Athens. There is no licence to kill on political grounds, or so it seems (5). In (4) killing of thieves is restricted to footpads and nocturnal burglars, killing for sexual misconduct is limited to rapists (probably a more limited category than the seducers thus at risk in Athenian law), and the apparent enlargement of the law of self-defence to defence of third parties is restricted to cases where close relatives are in danger of death. The key to Plato's thought seems to be violence: those who resort to it in order to commit their crimes must be incurable, and in view of the pressing circumstances he allows injured parties or their defenders to punish them by summary death. But seducers are not violent, and may be handled in other ways.

---

[181] On the historical reasons for this provision see Harrison i (1968) 13–15, and Carey (1989) on Lys. 1. 31.

[182] Aesch. 1. 91, however, says that confessed murderers caught in the act may be put to death, but it is not clear whether this may be done by persons other than the potential victim.

[183] 869b7–c4.

As this review of the varieties of penalty-free killings has demon-strated, Plato has distributed his provisions throughout the law of homicide intelligently and tidily. In part, the distribution depends on the intentions of the killer: (1) and (4) are related to the main categories of involuntary and voluntary homicide respectively, and (3) to homicide in anger. But in justifiable homicide it is obviously the state of mind of the killed, not of the killer, that is all-important. The killed persons in (3) and (4) are all malevolent; and in (2), whereas Athenian law allowed the summary killing of *any* exiled murderer who returns, Plato permits it only for the voluntary murderer, the only one whose state of mind originally warranted death in any case.[184] Once again, Plato's main concern is psychological.

THE PENOLOGY OF THE HOMICIDE LAW

In spite of its gaps and obscurities, and the occasional piece of clumsy writing, Plato's law of homicide is an impressive structure.[185] It forms part of the last work of his life, but there is no evidence of intellectual decline. The major categories, if not the subordinate details, are marshalled in a logical sequence; and the logic is that of a penology which concentrates on states of mind. We advance from killers who have no 'injustice' in their souls to killers whose injustice is incurable; and along the way we find explanations, some very elaborate, of the thinking that dictates the procedures and penalties laid down.

The code's most prominent characteristic is scrupulous tightness of procedure. Plato is determined that the law shall be enforced. The law makes a permanent proclamation backed by a surrogate punisher, accused persons must give sureties, slave informers are heavily protected, and there are frequent carefully-drawn fall-back provisions, at least some of which may not have existed in Athenian law, requiring or allowing a wide range of persons to remedy dereliction of the duty to prosecute and failure to fulfil the verdicts of the courts. For law unenforced comes into disrepute; sureness of conviction and punish-ment subserves both justice and deterrence; and the complex socio-logical differentiations in penalties reinforce the social structure.

This list of innovations Plato makes or apparently makes to Attic penal practice is strikingly long. Some of them are on the face of it rationalizations or natural extensions of it. Yet in the end they all flow from one or more of the following concerns: (i) to match penalties to a

---

[184] 871de. The killings of returned exiles at 866c and 868a are not *summary*.
[185] See Piérart (1973a) 424 for a less favourable assessment.

psychological assessment of the criminal; (ii) to reintegrate him wherever possible into society; (iii) where that is not possible, to enable society to recover as rapidly as possible from his elimination; (iv) in general, to perpetuate and strengthen the social structure of the state, and especially its family life.

1. Above all, the invention of the formal new category of homicide in anger pays close attention to the psychology of the criminal and to gradation of punishments. To the extent that fewer death sentences may result than in Athens, there will be fewer permanent losses to families and society at large.

2. The sharp restrictions—and one notable extension (rapist)—to the range of persons who may be killed with impunity seem to stem partly from a belief that it is the use of violence that makes the difference between a curable and an incurable criminal, and perhaps partly from a desire to restrict the operation of self-help in favour of legal process.

3. Magnesian society is based on the family, and murders as between relatives are regulated in separate sections of the code, with enhanced penalties which seem to be Plato's innovations (for instance the denial of permission to the returned exile who has killed a *relative* in anger to re-enter the family circle). The extension of justifiable homicide to cases where a close relative is protected from death is similarly designed to protect the family.

4. The wide discretion allowed in certain types of homicide to relatives of the deceased to vary or increase the severity of punishment is presumably intended *inter alia* to permit an expression of group solidarity. Similarly, the solidarity not merely of individual families but of the community as a whole is encouraged by the spectacular enhancements of penalties, e.g. denial of burial in Magnesia for a voluntary killer, and the stoning of the head of the corpse of the parricide.

5. *Compulsory* purifications for killing in games etc. are presumably calculated to make absolutely sure of the restoration of normal relationships between the offender and the relatives of the victim.

6. Non-confiscation of property is extended from involuntary murderers to voluntary murderers, whose families are thus left in possession of the ancestral lot.

7. The requirement that a banished involuntary killer must avoid the country of his foreign victim ensures that he will avoid trouble with the victim's relatives, and will survive to return to Magnesia.

8. Similarly, exiled involuntary killers seem on certain conditions to have the *right* of return, without let or hindrance on the part of the victim's relatives.

9. According the foreigner the same protection from homicide as a citizen, by punishing a person who kills a foreigner on the same basis as

one who kills a citizen, strengthens the distinction between slave and free man that is fundamental to the code. The same is true of the embellished penalty (scourging and death within sight of the victim's grave) for the slave who kills a free man.

Now obviously in Plato's law of homicide reform has only a restricted role. Justified and involuntary killers have no psychic *adikia* to be reformed, voluntary killers are beyond cure, and only killers in anger can be affected. And so it proves: such killers, in their two or three years of exile, 'chastise' their anger.

The structure of the homicide law as a whole, the way the various categories of murder are related not only to the psychological excursuses in the law itself but to the psychology of the main penological policy-statement (passage 1), and in particular the introduction of murder in anger with its two subdivisions, all show that the leading, but not the exclusive, consideration is the morality of the motive of the agent. A number of secondary provisions display the same concern: for instance, did the involuntary foreign killer who has returned from exile *intend* to return, or not?

Short of a 'window into the souls of men', how does one perform psychological inspection of a criminal? Up to a point, one can recall his conversation and demeanour till the moment of the crime. And one can observe his conduct at that moment: he was visibly angry, visibly killed accidentally, his voluntary killing was obvious. Such visibility lets a lot of light into the soul that controlled the agent. But Plato goes further. He allows, as Athenian law allowed, the seriousness of the act itself to guide by inference a reconstruction of the state of the agent's soul. By this calculation, *ceteris paribus*, killing suggests greater psychic injustice than (say) wounding. In a hierarchical society, to kill your father, or your master if you are a slave, betokens more serious *adikia* than killing someone else; and to kill brutally argues for greater *adikia* than to do so non-brutally. But his discussion of murder in anger shows he is aware of the dangers of arguing directly from the act and the manner of its commission to the psychic state. He knows that these considerations will not necessarily tell him *all* he needs to discover about the criminal's mental condition, which is his central concern.

Nevertheless, the question has to be asked whether he does not allow consideration of the nature of the act to override psychology and modify the measures which psychology would suggest. For instance, (*a*) he who merely plots murder is punished slightly less severely than he who commits it; (*b*) the slave who kills a free man in self-defence is nevertheless to be killed; (*c*) pardon granted by a dying man diminishes the penalty. In (*a*), are not the plotter and the killer suffering from exactly the same *adikia*? At any rate they are both punished by death; but the plotter is allowed burial in Magnesia, apparently because he does not actually have blood on his hands. In (*b*) the *adikia* is the victim's, not the slave's—unless to kill a free man argues in principle for incurable psychic injustice, infinitely greater than that of the victim's. In (*c*) the killer's *adikia* is the same whether or not he is absolved. In (*a*) and (*b*) a psychic state may be supposed to be more or less serious, from the nature of the act; but in (*c*) the act is the same in either case, and the penalty is affected by contingent pardon by the victim. (When it comes to *voluntary* murder, however, state of mind is paramount: for pardon is no longer allowed, at least to judge from Plato's silence.) In short, Plato's law of homicide can all too readily give the impression of inflicting penalties in disregard of the crucial consideration that ostensibly controls them: psychic *adikia*.

That impression becomes overwhelming if we consider the frequency of the penalties, chiefly purification and exile, to say nothing of lurid embellishments of the death penalty, imposed in deference to the vindictive fury of the dead man and his relatives. Even killing in games etc. requires purification—if indeed that is a penalty; and the standard cases of involuntary killing demand exile in addition. Penalties are intended to cure *adikia*; but in these cases there is no *adikia* to cure; and such lack is indeed recognized for justifiable homicide and for doctors (no purifications are demanded). Further, the victim of a killing in games is innocent, whereas the victim of justifiable homicide is *ex hypothesi* guilty; but it seems paradoxical that the impositions to be undergone by the killer in the former case, and the dispensation from them in the latter, depend not on *his* state of mind but on his victim's. Is there, nevertheless, some explanation that would make sense in terms of Plato's penology?

The key to understanding what is going on lies in the deceased person. In Athenian thought and practice—doubtfully in the law itself[186]—the dead man's fury and that of his relatives, was objectivized as 'pollution',[187] a sort of 'spiritual *Doppelgänger* of the law', 'a vehicle through which social disruption is expressed'.[188] It provided reasons which reinforced motives for doing what would have been done under the law anyway, for other and secular reasons. The killer became liable to retaliation by his victim, and hence a source of possible danger. Distancing oneself from the act by purification, and literal distancing oneself for a period by exile from the anger of the dead man and his family, could restore the *status quo*: 'any action that restores the normal equilibrium of things becomes a purification'.[189] The need to purify from

---

[186] MacDowell (1963) 141 ff.

[187] Parker (1983) 107: '[The] co-extensiveness of pollution and the victim's anger.'

[188] Parker (1983) 116, 121.   [189] Parker (1983) 121.

pollution 'fits round' the demands of the law.[190] Murder-pollution is demon-driven, i.e. powered by the wrath of the dead; but in some cases the *miasma* (stain) seems to have had an independent dynamism.[191]

That the form of pollution Plato envisages in the *Laws* is demon-driven is very clear indeed.[192] His whole homicide law is saturated with the fury of the deceased, as we have often seen in analysing the detailed prescriptions. It is not only the killer who is polluted: relatives who fail to prosecute find the *miasma* transferred to themselves. In short, the dead and his relatives have a *claim* on the killer; they are angry at the injustice of an innocent man's death—and Plato (as we know) treats anger as a noble feeling. They are entitled to some satisfaction, which will restore normal relationships. However, the claim is not a quantity that cannot vary: it may have to be forgone altogether (as in justified killing, or for deaths at the hands of doctors), or modified (for killing in games etc. only purification is required, and no exile). In the other direction, it increases with the malign intent, status, and brutality of the killer: the dead man killed intentionally, by his son, and brutally, is more angry than one killed unintentionally, by a stranger, without brutality. The claim is a 'function' of the actions and state of mind of the dead person on the one hand, and the actions and state of mind of the killer on the other. But this function is modified by social contraints: doctors, for instance, would be in an impossible position if they had to be purified whenever a patient died,[193] and the communal utility of games requires that the claim of persons killed in them by mischance should not be great.[194] The anger of the dead man can be mild or furious; but the strength of the *claim* he is allowed to make is determined by Plato.

In Greece, there was a certain tension between pollution's ability to recognize and objectify moral guilt, and its tendency to spread on its own accord like a germ. It could indeed operate 'as a stern and discriminating upholder of the moral order',[195] but it did not do so invariably: there was a non-moral residue. Plato eliminates the residue completely.[196] In his hands pollution represents one form of one of the two primary elements in his penology: the just entitlement to recompense. That entitlement is ostensibly calculated by the dead man, by reference to a moral assessment of the offence;[197] the calculation, performed by the legislator, of the

---

[190] Parker (1983) 118. Pollution is 'the metaphorical justification for a set of conventional responses to the disruption of normal life through violent death' (120).
[191] Parker (1983) 109 ff.; cf. Dodds (1951) 36–7, esp. nn. 43 and 44.
[192] Cf. 926e ff.
[193] Hewitt (1910) 103.
[194] Cf. Parker (1983) 124.
[195] Ibid. 110.
[196] *Pace* Parker (1983) 113, following Reverdin (1945) 177 ff. Nor should a wedge be driven between 'social order' and 'moral intention': for a slave to kill a free man simply *is* morally worse than for a free man to kill a slave.
[197] Dead men killed *justly* have of course no entitlement at all.

penalty needed to reform the offender (needed in fact only for murderers in anger), is based on the same calculation. Hence the imposition for murder in anger, purification followed by two or three years' exile, is indivisibly recompense/appeasement for the dead, cure of the criminal, and a preparation for re-entry into society. Law, religion, and penology mesh.

The peculiarity of the claim of the dead, however, is that it cannot be met by ordinary simple or enhanced recompense, such as the restoration of something stolen, in kind or money. Such restoration, when made to a living person, returns matters to their former state, and generates satisfaction of the emotions of the injured party, who feels vindicated and enjoys the sight of the offender's suffering in being forced to give up what he took. But the dead man can get nothing except enjoyment: it is the only form of satisfaction available to him. Plato's constant insistence, therefore, on the necessity to satisfy the fury of the dead by exile and purification is an insistence on the need to *recompense* the injured party. Plato prepares the ground when listing the various ways in which compensation may be made:[198] sometimes it should be 'assuagement by requitals' (*apoinois exilasthen*). This does not sound like ordinary recompense to living persons, already adequately covered in the previous few lines: both words are *hapax legomena* in the *Laws*, as is the word used to convey the 'assuagement' of the anger of a murdered man's relations achieved by murder for murder: *aphilasamenē*.[199] Similarly, the rapist is to be killed *nēpoini*, 'without requital', i.e. without a claim that purification be carried out, just like the other aggressors who are killed justifiably, whose killers are *katharoi*, 'pure'; *nēpoini* is a *hapax legomenon* in Plato.[200] In short, he recognizes appeasement of feeling is a form of recompense. And like the other forms, it is intended to be a restoration of normalcy.[201] Demon-driven pollution, purification and exile thus slot into place as one part of Plato's penological purposes; and it is significant that the first two form a definite part of his law: they are not simply the strongly compelling beliefs and observances they seem usually to have been at Athens.

The result is a complete and comprehensive 'package' of homicide law, with a range of impositions of far greater variety and complexity

---

[198] 862c.

[199] 872d–873a. None of these words occur elsewhere in Plato, except *apoina* at *Rep.* 393e. In Homer *apoina* commonly means literal recompense in goods, but the metaphorical use for disaster or suffering of some kind in return for an offence is well attested later: Aes. *Pers.* 808; *Agam.* 1420 (exile for killing), Eur. *Bac.* 516. In order to incorporate satisfaction of feelings, Plato uses a word, rare in prose (see L+S), which is ambiguous as between the two ideas. ἐξιλάσκομαι and ἀφιλάσκομαι are *recherché* compounds. The vocabulary marks out the special nature of this form of recompense; it applies only in homicide.

[200] 874c. On the variation of νηποινί and καθαρός here, cf. Hewitt (1910) 106 and cf. And. 1.96–8.

[201] 862c, 866a, 873a.

than was achieved in Attic practice, at least to judge from our lacunose sources. Leaving aside the penalties for derelictions of various kinds, we have in Athens the following range of measures:[202]

Doctors:	No penalty. No purification.
Justified killing, including self-defence:	No penalty. No purification.
Accidental killing (games etc.):	No penalty. No purification.
Involuntary killing:	Exile at the discretion of deceased's relatives; property not confiscated. Purifications etc. required on return.
Voluntary killing:	Death or life-long exile, with confiscation of property.

In Magnesian law we have (confiscation applies in no case):

Doctors:	No penalty. No purification.
Justified killing, including self-defence:	No penalty. No purification.
Accidental killing (games etc.):	One year of exile. Purification.
Involuntary killing:	One year of exile. Purification.
Murder in anger (i):	Two years of exile. Purification.
Murder in anger (ii):	Three years of exile. Purification.
Plotters of murder:	Exile or death *with* burial in Magnesia.
Voluntary killing:	Exile, or death *without* burial in Magnesia.

These are standard cases; and to the denial of burial we may add various other enhancements of penalties for familial or sociological reasons:

Killing of parent in anger:	Death.
Slave who kills master in anger:	Killed as relatives of deceased decide.
Voluntary killing of parent:	Death and stoning of corpse.
Slave who kills free man voluntarily:	Scourging and death at tomb.

The extra elaboration of Magnesian law arises partly (1) from the introduction of murder in anger, and partly (2) from the embellishments, which in the nature of the case cannot be 'cure': they are varieties of recompense designed to satisfy various degrees of indignation in the

[202] In all cases where purifications are not *required*, I assume that both in Athens and in Magnesia scrupulosity could in practice prompt their performance.

dead person and his relatives; and compulsory (rather than optional) purifications serve the same purpose. It seems fair to say that Plato's firm distinction between punishment/cure and recompense has been carried through systematically into his law; the need to cure leads to the elaboration of (1), the need to supply recompense to that of (2), which serves to restore normalcy as well as to ensure publicity and deterrence. By such means did Plato seek to harness to his own penology a 'profound religious conservatism'.[203] He has drafted into his law, on a grand scale, a set of beliefs which were probably already waning in his day,[204] interpreted them in accordance with his penology as strictly a demand for recompense, and so used them as a means of reconciliation and restoration of normalcy.

Nevertheless, the line between recompense and punishment/cure is not invariably drawn with surgical precision. Involuntary murder entails purification and one year of exile; the offender has no *adikia* in his soul, so these impositions cannot be cure. The less heinous variety of murder in anger entails purification and exile of two years, during which the offender will chastise his anger. Where does the recompense end and the cure begin? The two seem to be rolled up together, possibly by the legislator's ingenuity in meeting two purposes by the same rules. But as I noted before,[205] the involuntary murderer may be forgiven for thinking that by one year's exile he is being punished unjustly, i.e. made to suffer in order to be cured of an *adikia* he does not have. On the other hand, Plato makes it very clear to him that his exile is in deference to the dead man's fury,[206] and imputes no blame to him at all. The real trouble is that the dead man's purpose is to *hurt*; so the offender may well feel resentment. To a lesser extent the killer in games may resent the necessity of purification, which was not imposed in Athens. Both offenders may reasonably ask, 'Why, Plato, do you tell us in your *Laws*[207] that one is not punished because of one's wrong-doing, for the sake of the past? Clearly I *am* being punished for the sake of the past, in being made to go into exile for a killing which I did not commit in a state of injustice—and therefore need no cure. It is very difficult to see, when you say "not for the sake of the past", what you intend to rule out.' To this natural protest Plato would reply: 'Read the passage more carefully. It is *punishment*, i.e. cure, that is forward-looking, and not for the sake of the past. The suffering you undergo, innocent of bad moral intent though you are, is not punishment, but the only form of recompense you can give your victim. Would you not expect to recompense your neighbour if you killed his slave[208] or pig, however accidentally? Or if you involuntarily wounded

---

[203] Parker (1983) 128.   [204] Cf. Parker (1983) 126–8.
[205] pp. 223–4.   [206] 865de.   [207] 934a.
[208] See 865c, and cf. the point made in Ant. *Tetr.* 2c. 7.

him?[209] That might indeed cause you hardship; but it is not punishment. My paragraph as a whole makes it clear that punishment is in *addition*[210] to recompense; and in your case no punishment is imposed. However vindictive and vengeful your dead victim feels, neither he nor I am *punishing* you. Any form of recompense is painful; *his* recompense is the pleasure he finds in your pain, and in the diminution of your *timē*; but although both recompense and punishment are painful, they are quite different things. You must not allow the vengeful (and therefore painful) purposes of your victim and the curative (and painful) purposes of my reformative punishment to become confused.'

[209] 879b.   [210] 934a1, προσεκτεισάτω.

9

WOUNDING

INTRODUCTION

The Athenian contrives a transition from homicide to woundings (*traumata*) by linking the former to the education and nurture of the 'living soul' (presumably because murder terminates that state), and woundings to the education and nurture of the body. The law on woundings is set out in an order which reverses that of the law of homicide, in that the most serious cases come first; it is preceded by one lengthy preamble and an even longer discussion on a principle of legislation; and the first substantive section (A) is supplemented by a passage on the adoption of an heir into families without male issue, from which the lot-holder is lost by execution or permanent banishment.[1]

A didactic preamble (874e8–875d6) may be summarized as follows: 'The necessity of making communal good paramount over the private, and the difficulty of finding an absolute ruler who is sufficiently wise and altruistic to follow that principle rather than line his own pockets, jointly require law and regulation, to prevent our lives becoming like those of wild beasts.'

This preamble has little specific relevance to wounding: it could be attached to any part of the code. The concluding reflection is that law and regulation cannot provide for every individual case, but must express general principles.

Next comes a discussion of the courts' discretion (875d6–876e5). It runs in summary: 'The degree of discretion allowed to courts ought to vary according to the quality of the jurymen and of their conduct in court. In Magnesia, both are likely to be good. So for woundings we shall sketch some *timōriai* as specimens, to keep jurymen within the bounds of *dikē*, but leave them wide discretion; for woundings are many and various in type and circumstance.'

This discussion is more directly relevant than the preamble, though in a general sense they obviously cohere, the former supplying a wide social framework for the latter. Three penological points arise: (i) the gaps in

[1] 877d5–878b3.

the lists of penalties may arise as much from Plato's willingness to permit discretion as from negligence on his own part; (ii) the penalties which wounders are to pay may take the form of 'suffering or fines';[2] (iii) the penalties should 'attach to each of the crimes, *hamartēmata*, the value of the suffering and doing'; that is, we have to ask both how much the victim has suffered, and the nature and circumstances (including the motives of the agent?) of the crime as an act.[3]

As for the Attic law of wounding, the evidence is less clear than one could expect and wish. It was certainly possible to prosecute before the Areopagus, by a *dikē* or a *graphē*,[4] for voluntary wounding.[5] (i) If it could be shown that the wound was inflicted in an attempt to kill, the penalty, at least in the *dikē*,[6] was permanent exile and confiscation of property. (ii) If there was no attempt to kill, we do not know what lesser penalty would have applied;[7] nor do we know whether recompense was paid to the injured party, and if so, how it was assessed. It is equally unclear how far woundings without intent to kill were graded: was it by reference to the nature and scale of the wound(s), or by reference to intent, or to both? At least the wounds seem to have embraced those received in brawls 'arising from drunkenness, rivalry, games, abuse, or about a mistress', i.e. situations which blow up quickly and are apt to be repented of later.[8] No doubt involuntary wounding could be prosecuted, but we have no evidence about the procedures and penalties.

A. WOUNDING WITH INTENT TO KILL (876e5–877d5)

Penalties vary according to social and familial status:

(*a*) Wounding of one citizen by another: after a trial for *murder*,[9] if the accused is found guilty, he should be banished to a neighbouring state for the rest of his life, but may continue to enjoy the revenues of his estate; damages are to be assessed by the court, and paid to the victim.

(*b*) Woundings of parent by child, of master by slave, and as between siblings: death.

---

[2] The standard formula, 875d7, 876c8.   [3] Cf. p. 193.

[4] MacDowell (1978) 124, citing Hansen (1976) 108–110; see now Hansen (1981) 17 and (1983).

[5] *AP* 57. 3, Dem. 54. 18, 23. 22, 24. The injury may have been limited to head, face, hands, and feet: Lys. 6. 15. The use of a weapon may have been necessary: MacDowell (1978) 124 on Lys. 4. 6.

[6] Hansen (1983) 317, on Lys. 3. 28, 43–4.

[7] Lys. 3. 28, 38–43 from which it is clear that a crucial point to be decided by the court was intention: he obviously implies that absence led to abated penalties; cf. MacDowell (1978) 123–4 on Dem. 54. 17–19. No doubt prosecutors, with more or less plausibility, commonly alleged its presence: Lys. locc. citt., Dem. 40. 32–3, 54. 10–12 (expert witnesses), Aesch. 2. 93, 3. 51, 212 (where 'payments' may mean recompense).   [8] Lys. 3. 43, cf. 4. 6–7.

[9] The court is the special court of 855c ff., which would have tried the case had the attempt to kill succeeded, 877b. Possibly Plato regards suits for woundings as *graphai*, but he does not say.

(c) Woundings as between spouses: permanent exile, the estate passing to an heir (or trustees *pro tem.*).[10]

Nothing is said of woundings with intent to kill inflicted on foreigners and slaves. (c) launches Plato into a long account of the procedure to be followed when a lot-holder is executed or permanently banished for *any* crime, and has no male issue. (b) and (c) are clearly aggravated cases; no parallels are known from Athens. (b) is very heinous, as involving blood relationships,[11] or insolence by a slave towards his superior; (c) is less heinous than (b), since relationship by blood is not present. (b), though it is the most serious case, is cleared off before (c), probably to allow the digression on the lack of male issue to take place last, without disruption of the exposition.

So far as we can tell, therefore, Plato substitutes a scale of punishments for the single punishment allowed by Attic law. (a) is less severe than Attic law, (b) more severe; (c) is equally severe in one sense (the offender loses his property anyway), but less severe in that the property is not taken by the state but kept within the family.[12] Social, familial, and economic concerns are very evident, and have led to a notably nuanced scale of penalties. It is possible, however, that his major innovation is to insist on tangible recompense for the victim, on top of the 'satisfaction' he would get anyway from seeing his wounder go into exile.

Nothing, however, is said about 'cure', no doubt because the offenders are psychologically exactly the same as voluntary murderers, and should be treated as such[13] and hence as incurable. But in cases not involving slaves and a blood relationship the death penalty is waived, and social considerations are then allowed to determine the two slightly different penalties imposed. The death penalty is waived because of the concrete *result* of the affair: the murderous intent was frustrated, the victim still lives. Plato glosses over this breach of his own principles by claiming the need to defer to the wishes of the *daimōn* (minor god) who has prevented a curse (the anger of the victim, had he died?) from descending on the head of the offender.[14] Possibly for the reason that he wished to do everything to ensure the permanent stability of one family in its own estate, possibly for reasons of reciprocal equity (robust common-sense suggests that you ought not to punish a man for something that has not happened[15]), or perhaps for both reasons, Plato

---

[10] Presumably only when the *husband* is exiled.   [11] Cf. p. 242 above.

[12] Cf. homicide, p. 227 above. On the difference between (a) and (c) in the matter of property, and the disputed reading at 877c6, see my (1972) note 90.

[13] 876e–877a.   [14] 877a.

[15] On 27 August 1861 one Martin Doyle was hanged for trying to kill a woman, with extreme violence. An editorial in *The Times* noted the rarity of the infliction of this penalty when the victim survived, and praised the 'moral courage' of the judge.

ignores the strict implications of the incurability of these offenders. The justification he advances is one of political piety; the other reasons, if he had them, he conceals. He exercises his own discretion, and does not allow Magnesian judges to exercise theirs.

B. WOUNDINGS IN ANGER (878b4–879b1)

As a formal category, this is of course Plato's innovation, though an incidental remark in Lysias suggests that the role of anger in woundings was recognized,[16] as indeed we should expect. It is not clear to which court Plato assigns the trials.

(a) Standard cases (878b8–d6)

Plato opens with a brief recapitulation of his discussion of anger,[17] but makes no mention of the two categories of acts caused by this motive; one assumes he takes it for granted and expects it to be used in the law of woundings as well as in the law of homicide. But at this point the text becomes puzzling. Is he still legislating for woundings with intent to kill? Or is the angry wounder's intent now only to wound? On the first alternative, the intent to kill will be somewhat less wicked, both because of the anger and because of the lack of success; and then woundings inflicted without an intent to kill at all, but just wound, will be left unprovided for. I assume therefore the second alternative, particularly since this section on woundings in anger says nothing at all about killing. However, if Plato *is* now dealing with wounds inflicted with intention to wound only, 'intent' in the two categories (A, B) will be different: to kill in the one case, to wound in the other. The same seems true of Attic law: the lesser, impromptu, cases of wounding described by Lysias and Demosthenes are lesser precisely because they are of intending to wound and wounding, not of intending to kill and failing to achieve more than bodily injury.[18] The discontinuity is probably more apparent than real. Woundings were probably thought of as being on a sliding scale; when they became very grievous, and endangered life, then an intention to kill could be presumed or argued;[19] and this presumed intention was then treated as an aggravation approximating the offence to murder, and meriting a more severe penalty (exile and confiscation of goods) than

---

[16] 3. 39.   [17] 878b, referring to 866d ff.

[18] Lys. 3. 43, Dem. 54. 19, cf. *Rep.* 465a. It is of course not always true that planned woundings are more serious than impromptu ones.

[19] See Dem. 54. 11 ff., esp. 13. After all, to kill a man one has to wound him in *some* way, however indirect, and if a wound is serious, it seems natural to assume an intention to kill. But of course such an intention may lead only to minor wounds.

less serious woundings. That is why, to judge from Lysias,[20] the notion of serious wounds inflicted with a view to wounding only was hardly envisaged. 'And again, I did not consider that *pronoia* existed, when a man wounded without intending to kill. For who is so stupid as to premeditate far in advance how some enemy of his shall suffer a wound?' In other words, *if* a man wounds and does not intend to kill, the wounds he inflicts *must* be of the lesser, heat-of-the-moment, kind. For no man premeditates how to wound *simpliciter*; if he does plan to wound, it must be with the intention of killing.[21] The result is to polarize the notion of wounding into two categories only: serious, with intention to kill, and lesser, with *intention* to wound indeed, but on the spur of the moment, not with premeditation. What this dichotomy leaves out is the possibility of *planning* to wound, seriously or not, but not to kill.[22]

Now if this reconstruction of Attic thinking and law is right, Plato has in his category of wounding in anger a perfect way of remedying the deficiency. For anger may result in sudden, more or less unpremeditated wounding; or it may be 'nursed', and result in wounding that is planned over a period of time. This may of course be serious—so serious as to make us treat the anger as shading into deliberate intent in its full sense. At any rate, Plato has the means to write a law of wounding which, so far as one can tell, would have nicer nuances than Attic law. The same was true in homicide: there too anger, subdivided as he describes, permitted differentiation between short-term intent (approximating to involuntary murder) and long-term premeditation (approximating to voluntary murder).

But Plato fluffs his chances. The law on wounding in anger not only fails to make the interval subdivision between short-term and long-term anger, but makes no mention whatever of state of mind in the calculation of penalties. True, psychological considerations are present by implication: there is no intent to kill, the state of mind is thus less grave, and the penalties are less severe than for wounding with that intent. But how far can reformative intent be read into the following scale of penalties?

For curable wounds: double damages.
For curable but acutely
    embarrassing wounds: triple damages.
For incurable wounds: quadruple damages.

---

[20] Lys. 3. 40 ff.

[21] Hence Lysias succeeds in eliminating *pronoia* to wound, in the sense of 'premeditation', from the actions of the defendant. A man who wounds (on the spur of the moment) without wishing to kill has no *pronoia* to wound (there is insufficient time); nor can he have had a long-term *pronoia* to wound, since that is not how men act (cf. 28); the only possibility left is the *pronoia* to *kill*, by wounding—the category he alleges the lawgivers recognize (42).

[22] Cf. Maschke (1926) 109.

Presumably the jurors are to categorize the wound; they will certainly need the discretion Plato promises them. One assumes also that the same mode of calculation of recompense will apply in the case of woundings with intent to kill.

The assessment of the penalties seems to be purely to ensure recompense, calculated wholly from the point of view of the wounded person; what is curable or incurable is the wound, not the wounder. It seems paradoxical that whereas for woundings with intent to kill Plato provided penalties (though non-curative) on top of recompense, he provides in the case of wounding in anger for recompense only;[23] for it is precisely here that one would expect an attempt to cure the offender by some measure adjusted to his state of mind and firmly separated from recompense. One is left to assume either that murder in anger is an indication of psychic injustice hardly worth bothering to cure, which seems unlikely, or that the seriousness of the injury itself is a sufficient gauge of the criminal's state of mind, and that the various multiples of recompense build in enough pain and suffering for the offender to cure him. If that is so, we have to conclude that although for Plato recompense and cure have sharply different purposes, in practice recompense can serve both. Will not the resentment of paying recompense vitiate its curative effect?

That Plato is preoccupied with injury and damage rather than with cure is indicated by the provision which follows immediately: a wounder who injures not just his victim but the state, because he has rendered the victim incapable of military service, must in addition to the other penalties recompense the state[24] by doing military service on the victim's behalf.[25] If he fails so to do, anyone who wishes may prosecute him for *astrateia*, evasion of military service; the punishment is not stated. A *graphē astrateias* is known in Athenian law, and Plato's version of it is set out later in the *Laws*.[26] His application of it to a wounder who fails to substitute for his victim is new, simply because the substitution itself seems to be his own innovation.

(b) Woundings within the family (878d6–879a2)

This intricate section has considerable penological implications.

1. 878d6–e4. If a relative (*homogonos*) injures a relative, the *gennētai*,[27] with the *sungeneis* (i.e. close relatives within certain degrees), are to meet,

---

[23] As in wounding with intent to kill, recompense itself may be a Platonic innovation.
[24] Cf. 875a ff. and 877d on the interests of the state.
[25] 878cd.
[26] 943a ff., see ch. 13.
[27] Of the victim *and* the aggressor, I take it, but the point is not clear. But what does *gennētai* mean? Either (i) parents or (ii) all adult members of the two immediate *oikoi* or (iii) relatives sharing

decide a verdict,[28] and entrust the assessment (i.e. of the injury) to the natural parents (of both victim and aggressor?). If the assessment is challenged, the relatives on the male side are to have the final say; if they themselves cannot agree, they must hand the matter over to the Guardians of the Laws.

2. 878e5–879a2. When children wound parents, the judges are (apparently) as in (1); but they must exclude those of their number who (i) are less than 60 years of age, (ii) have no natural children, (iii) are *sungeneis* of the culprit; and they must decide whether death, or something less severe, or something more severe,[29] is the right suffering to impose.

Who are the victims in these cases? (1) is introduced by the words 'If a relative wounds a relative in the same way as this'[30] (this way? this victim? this aggressor?). 'This' is singular, and points not to the variety of victims in general, but specifically to the victim who is incapacitated for military service, and whose injuries must therefore be severe. (2) mentions 'such' wounds, plural, and again it seems that the reference must be to incapacitated victims alone. For if it were to other wounded parents as well, in general, the penalty for wounding parents in anger would—or could—be as high as, if not higher than, the penalty for wounding them with intent to kill.[31] I take it therefore that 'such' means a plurality of injuries within a single restricted class, not a plurality of injuries spanning several classes; and that accordingly both (1) and (2) refer only to woundings which incapacitate for war.

The point is simple: in these remarkable elaborations on Attic law, Plato is still preoccupied by damage and recompense. Incapacitation for war is incapacitation for much else; not only are the victim and the state harmed, but his family too.[32] It is the family that can best decide the loss entailed *to it* by the incapacity: let it therefore form part of the court. Moreover, in aggravated cases, i.e. when parents are wounded by their children, the exclusion of the offender's *sungeneis*, who may be inclined to take his side, and the qualifications of age and natural children, which entail that the judges will feel strongly about aggressive juniors, ensure that offenders will not get off lightly.[33] True, this court has to make a

descent from the same male ancestor (founder of a *genos*) as the aggressor and/or the victim. (iii) seems too diffuse and unwieldy a group to form part of a quasi-court; (i) seems the same as 'the natural parents'; (ii) looks about right in point of numbers and acquaintance with aggressor and victim. 877c ff. (d7 and 878a2, *genos*), where the victim is not represented and penal matters are not in question, is hardly a guide; cf. Gernet (1917a) n. 205.

[28] The range of meanings of *sungeneia* is discussed by Bresson and Debord (1985), who do not, however, mention this passage.

[29] Such as denial of burial in Magnesia, one supposes.   [30] τὸν αὐτὸν τρόπον τούτῳ.

[31] 877b.   [32] Cf. 868d on losses to the family.

[33] If the 'natural parents' of (*a*) are or include those of the *victim*, there will be the same tendency to harshness on their part.

fairly delicate choice within a fairly narrow range of penalties, and in particular determine the psychological point of whether the offender is incurable or (barely) curable. To that extent, it has a penological role, distinct from the assessment of recompense. Yet the penalties sound vindictive, and designed to satisfy the victim further; for even if the offender is curable, we learn nothing about how he can be cured by some penalty which is 'slightly less than death'. The court is rigged, and administers something that could, given sufficient animosity in the judges, come uncomfortably close to lynch law. Presumably Plato is confident they will be above that; certainly he has granted the large discretion which he promised.

(c) Woundings by slaves (879a2–b1)

1. If a slave wounds a free man in anger, the owner must hand over the slave to the victim to do as he likes with him; if he does not hand him over, he must 'cure' the damage himself.

2. Anyone who wishes may prosecute the injured party for collusion (i.e. for conspiring with the slave to bring about a change of ownership); if he loses, he is to pay triple damages; if he wins, he is to prosecute the injured party on a charge of kidnapping.

There is little here of special penological interest. It is not clear that doing what he likes with the slave includes a licence to kill him;[34] at any rate, wounding of a free man by a slave is an 'aggravated' offence, analogous to the wounding of a parent by a child.[35] A procedure against kidnapping existed in Attic law; Plato does not say what penalty he had in mind.[36]

C. INVOLUNTARY WOUNDINGS (879b1–5)

This need not detain us: no legislator can rule chance, and only simple damages are payable. Rather curiously, the court which tries children who wound their parents has to be convened for the presumably limited job of assessing the injury.

---

[34] I suppose it does; but at least the victim is not *obliged* to kill him, in contrast with 868b (homicide in anger). If the wound were slight and the recompense small, the owner could reasonably opt to pay up and keep the slave.

[35] Cf. 877b.

[36] Cf. 955a and Morrow (1960) 286. On collusion, cf. 936cd.

266 PLATO'S PENOLOGY AND PENAL CODE

ASSESSMENT

The sources for our knowledge of the Athenian law of wounding are lacunose, and comparisons are tricky. The one penalty attested, permanent exile with confiscation of property for wounding with attempt to kill, is adopted by Plato in two milder forms ((A)a,c) that reflect his social and economic preoccupations; for the most heinous type of wounding ((A)b) it is replaced by the death penalty. The introduction of the category of wounding in anger, though in strict terms probably new, may well be only Plato's way of following Athenian law on unpremeditated woundings arising out of brawls etc., without intent to kill; however, he does not follow his own lead in the law of homicide, and differentiate motive on the basis of two different types of anger. It is under his category of anger that he introduces a scale of recompense which may well be more elaborate than the Athenian, if indeed there was one; it may however not be confined to that category, but apply also to woundings with intent to kill; at any rate recipients of such wounds are to have some recompense, and that may well be an innovation. Plato generates further complication by demanding special recompense for state and family when the victim is incapacitated for military service; the special family courts which convene in these cases may hark back to a much earlier state of Greek law, when the family had extensive powers;[37] Plato constitutes them in such a way that defendants found guilty are likely to be treated harshly; nevertheless these courts are not independent of the polis, but in the exercise of their discretion strictly under its control. Plato has in short produced a complex piece of legislation, in which concern for recompense, and for the economic effects of penalties, are prominent. Psychological considerations are implicit in the three main categories of wounding (*intent* to kill, *anger*, *involuntary* woundings), but nothing, so far as I can see, is said about the cure of any offender. Indeed in the 'standard' cases of woundings in anger there is on the face of it no measure, additional to recompense, which could be the vehicle of a cure. The best one can do for this element in Plato's penology is to suppose that the pain of supplying recompense, together with pressure and instruction from family and society, are to have a mixed deterrent and didactic effect on those convicted criminals who are not killed or exiled. And Plato's willingness for economic (and ostensibly religious[38]) reasons to refrain from executing a person who intended to

---

[37] Glotz (1904) 31 ff.

[38] After the pollution-laden air of the homicide law, the absence of pollution from the law of wounding is a relief. The wounded parties still live: they do not need pollution as the means of their satisfaction/recompense.

kill, is one more indication of how easily strict psychological considerations may be overridden.

The principle that incurability is a necessary but not a sufficient
condition for the death penalty is not confined to the law of wounding.
The following persons have the same unjust state of mind, i.e. an
intention to kill, but suffer different penalties: (*a*) the voluntary killer, (*b*)
(on the assumption that absolution is not confined to killers of parents,
in anger) the voluntary killer who is forgiven, (*c*) the plotter of a killing,
(*d*) the intending killer who wounds only. If they were curable, they
would have to attract, *ceteris paribus*, the *same* penalty; but they are
incurable, so psychology ceases to be, even in theory, the ruling
consideration, and the law may allow other concerns to influence penalties. The same thinking permits the various 'embellished' penalties for
especially heinous murders, by way of didactic publicity—though in a
sense one could argue that the voluntary killer of (say) a mother is 'more
incurable' than an 'ordinary' killer, and so deserves death-plus.

IO

ASSAULT

Like homicide and wounding, assault (*aikia*) is a crime of violence (*bia*); but since it involves mere rough treatment of the body by blows, without actual wounds, it is the least serious of the three.[1] Nevertheless, Plato lavishes a great deal of attention on it; his laws are a phenomenally complex and highly distinctive construction of considerable penological importance. Three Athenian suits are relevant to the understanding of it.

ATTIC LAW

(i) *Dikē aikias*.[2] The offence was deemed to be that of him who 'started it'; the penalty was a payment to the plaintiff, the court choosing between his assessment and the counter-assessment of the offender.[3]

(ii) *Graphē goneōn kakōseōs*. It was possible to bring suit for 'ill-treatment of parents' (and certain remoter forbears). The ill-treatment could take various forms, notably failing to support them in their old age, and/or hitting or beating them.[4] The penalty was complete *atimia*, 'disfranchisement', in the form of deprivation of the right to enter temples and market-place, to hold public office, and to speak in the assembly or a law-court (the latter entailing inability to prosecute).[5]

(iii) *Graphē hubreōs*. Seven complementary studies[6] facilitate discussion. The suit, which is of uncertain date, could be brought for an offence

---

[1] 879b; MacDowell (1978) 123–4; Dem. 54. 17–19 recounts the 'escalation' from blows to wounds to killing; ibid. 18 (cf. Lys. 4. 6 and 880a) seems to imply that *aikia* is mere 'fisticuffs', without the use of weapons.

[2] On the legal procedure see Harrison ii (1971) 21 and 22 and Rhodes (1981) 585 on *AP* 52. 2 and Dem. 37. 33.   [3] Isoc. 20. 1, 19, Dem. 47. 35, 45–8, Lys. fr. 64.

[4] Lys. 13. 91, Aesch. 1. 28, MacDowell (1978) 92, Harrison i (1968) 77–8, Rhodes (1981) 629 on *AP* 56. 6 for full sources.

[5] Dem. 24. 103, 105, Aesch. 1. 28; Harrison i (1968) 78; MacDowell (1978) 73–5, referring to Hansen (1976) 54–98.

[6] MacDowell (1976), (1978) 129–32, (1990) 17–23, 263–5, Gagarin (1979*b*), Murray (1990), Fisher (1976 and 1979, 1990); on *hubris* in Sparta, see Fisher (1989). I am much indebted to the last-

against 'a free or slave man, woman, or child';[7] to gain conviction it was necessary to show that the deed was of a particular 'nature' or 'type', i.e. hubristic.[8] A hubristic act is one committed in a markedly insulting manner, with gratuitous arrogance and selfishness, in such a way as to humiliate the victim and impair his honour and status (*timē*).[9] The young were naturally thought to be prone to committing this kind of offence.[10] Typically the act would be an assault (*aikia*), but the possible range of acts envisaged by the law as capable of being performed hubristically was apparently unlimited.[11] Nevertheless, few suits for *hubris* are known; some of them were merely threatened; and no actual conviction is recorded.[12] Probably the large number of intangibles militated against the bringing of such suits: how, after all, does one cogently assess the offender's motive, or damage to the victim's standing? Given the high level of feeling in such cases, the reconstruction of events in court would be even more hazardous than usual; and the manner in which an act is performed is much more difficult to establish than the act itself, especially if there is no visible injury.[13] Furthermore, the fine (which was fixed by the court) would go to the state,[14] not to the victims, who therefore not unnaturally preferred suits offering the chance of recompense.[15]

Yet to concentrate on the motive of the offender, and the manner in which his offence was committed, does not seem to me to take us to the heart of *hubris*. Athenian society contained categories of persons who were commonly in an exposed position, and who for various reasons and in various degrees formed part of the total community and deserved protection: women, children, foreigners, slaves, the elderly or infirm; and obviously adult male citizens too could often find themselves defenceless against attack. Hence the law of *hubris*[16] does not restrict the categories of persons to be protected: it is a 'blanket' provision, covering all free and

---

named, Dr N. R. E. Fisher, for a valuable exchange of views on the nature of *hubris*; but he must not be taken as necessarily endorsing the particular emphasis of my account.

[7] Law cited in Dem. 21. 47, cf. Aesch. 1. 15. On the significance of the rider 'or some unlawful/improper (*paranomon*) act against them', see MacDowell (1976) 25-6, Gagarin (1979*b*) 233-4, and cf. the discussion below.   [8] Dem. 21. 46.

[9] e.g. Dem. 21. 41 ff., 72, Isoc. 20. 5-6. On the nature of *hubris*, see Arist. *Rhet.* 1374ª13-15, 1378ᵇ23 ff.; 1402ª1-3 emphasizes the 'first blow'. Cf. Lipsius (1905-15) 425, Morrow (1939) 37 ff.

[10] Cf. 808d, 835de, Arist. *Rhet.* 1378ᵇ28, and in general MacDowell (1976) 15.

[11] Dem. 53. 16, 54. 3-9, cf. Fisher (1976) 181.

[12] MacDowell (1976) 29, presumably dismissing Dem. 21. 49, which claims that many men have been executed for *hubris* against slaves, as unreliable.

[13] Dem. 21. 72, cf. MacDowell (1978) 131.

[14] Dem. 21. 45, Isoc. 20. 16; evidently the death penalty also was possible: see Dem. 54. 23, Din. *Dem.* 23, Lys. fr. 64. On the evidence of Aesch. 1. 16, see MacDowell (1976) 31 n. 23.

[15] MacDowell (1976) 28-9. Prosecutors for *aikia* nevertheless liked to represent the alleged offence as *meriting* a charge of *hubris*, e.g. Isoc. 20, esp. 5 ff. (on which see Jebb ii. 215 n. 1), Dem. 54. 1 ff., 13.   [16] Dem. 21. 47.

slave men and women temporarily or permanently in a position of weakness. A very similarly worded[17] law for the protection of widows, orphans, and 'heiresses',[18] persons who are obviously vulnerable, cuts in the same direction: officials must seek to prevent anyone committing *hubris* against them, and 'if anyone commits *hubris* against them or does some unlawful/improper act against them', he may be fined. The central purpose of the law of *hubris* is to prevent, by a *graphē* open to all, and by penalties which could be as severe as death, ill-treatment of persons who have 'honour', status and valued function in society, but are in practical terms weak and incapable of defending that 'honour'. This is a point made by Gernet long ago, and it needs emphasizing.[19] The style or arrogance or motive of the offence is indeed an aggravation, a means of arousing a jury's anger; but the notion of the weakness of the victim needs to be built into any formulation of the offence.

PLATONIC LAW

It is quite clear that Plato's law of *aikia* is the counterpart of the Athenian *dikē aikias*;[20] but it has been considerably strengthened by certain elements of the two *graphai, goneōn kakōseōs* and *hybreōs*.

(i) *Goneōn kakōseōs*. Plato's law on this matter is written in wide and vague terms; it insists at length on the respect due to parents, the need to care for them and not ill-treat them; no penalty for neglect or ill-treatment is to be excluded.[21] No specific mention is made of *blows* as a form of ill-use: for Plato transfers this part of the Athenian law to his law of assault; and in so doing he extends enhanced protection to other senior persons also. He incorporates all this new content into a fully comprehensive law of *aikia* in various complicated ways which we shall examine in detail shortly.

(ii) *Hubreōs*. Plato has no statute on *hubris* as such, nor does the word or any derivation appear in the law of *aikia*; but he makes it clear that he

---

[17] Dem. 21. 47: ἐάν τις ὑβρίσῃ εἴς τινα (of the blanket list of protected persons) ἢ παράνομόν τι ποιήσῃ εἰς τούτων τινά; Dem. 43. 75: ἐάν τις ὑβρίζῃ ἢ ποιῇ τι παράνομον (against heiresses etc.).

[18] i.e. women left in possession of property after the death of their father: see MacDowell (1978) 95 ff., and cf. Is. 8. 40 ff.

[19] Gernet (1917*b*) 194–5; cf. Morrow (1939) 39 ff. Gagarin (1979*b*) 235 rightly stresses the significance of the procedure (*graphē*), and of the potentially high penalties. The vagueness of the law, and its obscure relation to other laws covering part of the same field (e.g. *kakōsis goneōn*), seem to me not a difficulty, but precisely the point: the law is a catch-all, an attempt to legislate comprehensively, in fierce terms, for a broad sweep of certain kinds of social relationships which resist precise enumeration.

[20] The word *aikia* occurs at 879b7, c2, 880b6, e8, 881d3; blows: 879c4, d5, d6, d7, 880a1 *et saepe*.

[21] 930e–932d.

regards that law, at least in so far as it covers assault on parents, as covering instances of *hubris*. For *after* the law of assault he turns to acts of violence (*biaia*), and after briefly mentioning robbery, remarks that the worst of the 'remaining' acts of violence are the insolences and *hubreis* (acts of *hubris*) of the young.[22] In descending order of heinousness these acts of violence are committed against

1. sacred objects owned communally,
2. sacred objects in private ownership,
3. parents, 'when someone commits *hubris* against them apart from those [presumably acts of *bia/ hubris*] already mentioned',
4. objects belonging to officials, by removing or using them,
5. *to politikon* of the individual citizen, *polités*.[23]

The acts of violence specified in (3), then, whatever they are,[24] seem to embrace *hubreis* in general against parents, as a category of *hubris* additional to those *hubreis* against them 'already mentioned'; and the latter must embrace at least *aikiai*, and presumably woundings and homicide too.

The Attic law of *hubris* was relatively narrow: it applied to assaults on *weaker people*. Plato adopts that law in its spirit, but widens its scope. He takes the broad communal concept of *hubris* which underlay the Athenian law—gratuitously arrogant and self-seeking conduct—and extends the range of things to be protected against it from weaker people to objects; and he distributes the concept widely in the various parts of his penal code. We have already seen that the protection given to parents, for instance, in the law of homicide and wounding, far exceeds that given in Attic law; and the concept of *hubris* is present in several other places too.[25] In Plato's hands the legal application of the general concept of *hubris* is pervasive: it covers virtually any act of violent aggression against people or property, especially, but not exclusively, those in need of special respect and protection, such as that given in the law of *aikia* to foreigners, parents, other seniors and (in some circumstances) slaves. The general concept is given legal teeth, *in specific contexts*.

---

[22] 884a ff.

[23] I am not clear precisely what (5) means: the totality of rights conferred by citizenship, I suppose (perhaps especially when attacked by *foreigners*?). An example might be the *hubris* committed against orphans (926d ff.), which could involve 'political' matters such as the inheritance of the family property.

[24] Perhaps the neglect of parents at 930e–932d: see especially the ill-treatment at 932c4.

[25] 761e (misuse of official powers), 849a (offences in markets), 874c (rape), 885b (impiety); cf. 637a (drinking parties), 713c, 906a, and of course n. 23 above on orphans. At 777de masters are urged not to commit *hubris* against slaves, and in general persons weaker than themselves.

THE *REPUBLIC* AND THE *LAWS*

Assault is one of those subjects for which Socrates says, with lofty disdain, and perhaps with tongue in cheek, that it will be unnecessary to legislate in the ideal state. 'We shall say that as between persons of the same age self-defence will in a sense be fine and just, and so compel them to look after their bodies'—presumably by the exercise thus afforded. Angry men can work off their anger thus, before things go too far; older persons will have charge of ruling and chastising the young, who will commit no violence or assault upon an elder, or dishonour him in any other way. Fear and respect will restrain them—respect which inhibits them from attacking elders because they regard them as their own parents, fear lest the victim be defended by persons who think of themselves as his relatives.[26] The provocatively casual attitude of these remarks is quite absent from the law of *aikia* in the *Laws*, whose tone is earnest and even obsessive. What survives is an emphasis on psychological inhibition and considerations of age and status.

THE PREFACES

A brief preface[27] to the law itself makes the following points. Age is to be more highly respected than youth; an assault by a younger man on an older is disgusting to gods and men; for the sake of the gods of birth, a young man, if struck by an old man, must always put up with his bad temper.[28] The general law, then, is that he should avoid crossing any person twenty years older than himself; he should think of such a person as a parent, since he is old enough to have given him birth.[29] Similar respect is due to foreigners, both metics and itinerants.[30]

A second preface occurs later,[31] just before the law dealing with those who do assault their parents. If any man refuses to observe the laws of civilized life, he must become liable to punitive laws which we would rather not have to use. If he assaults his father or mother or their forbears, it is because he fears punishment neither in this world nor the

---

[26] 425d, 461de, 464e–465b; cf. 463cd, 562e ff., Xen. *Con. Lac.* 4. 6.   [27] 879b7–d5.

[28] Cf. the prohibition of self-defence against a parent in the law of murder in anger, 869bc, cf. 717d. An elder has a mature judgement, which gives his anger a weighty claim: it will be a well-founded protest against some injustice.

[29] Cf. *Rep.* 461de: offspring are to be kept in ignorance of their real parents, and all who are born 7–10 months after a man's marriage are to call him 'father'. The situation in the *Laws* is no doubt influenced by this aspiration, but is very different: every Magnesian obviously knows perfectly well who his parents are. He is simply to revere all persons over 20 years older *as though* they were his parents. Cf. Ar. *Eccl.* 635 ff.   [30] Cf. 845c.

[31] 880d8–881b2.

next.[32] He needs an extreme deterrent, but death is not 'extreme', so his penalties in this world should as far as possible equal those beyond the grave.[33]

It is not clear whether Plato regards *aikia* as the subject of a *dikē* or of a *graphē*. His law has several sections, and runs as follows.[34]

A. STANDARD CASES (879e6–880a6)

(i) A man of any age who strikes another of the same age (or someone older but without children),[35] should be resisted by the use of bare hands, without a weapon. Apart from this injunction to resist, the law takes no further notice. (It is not clear what is to happen when an older victim is *not* childless.)

There is perhaps here a hint of Socrates' feeling in the *Republic* that *aikia* is beneath a legislator's notice. Certainly the difference from Attic law is striking: the victim receives no recompense. Yet the number of possible standard cases is reduced by:

(ii) Anyone over 40 who has the face to scrap with someone, either as aggressor or in self-defence, must suffer the 'shameful' penalty (*dikē*) of being spoken of as uncivilized boor and no better than a slave.

Plato's desire to punish by various forms of social pressure, which are presumably to 'cure', is obvious. It is remarkable that persons over 40 are not allowed even to resist: no doubt he thinks it inconsistent with their dignity. But the rule lends added point to the protection accorded to seniors: they merit respect and protection in their own right, but all the more so since they are forbidden to fight back. Plato seems to recognize that such restraint could not be expected of the natural vigour and self-assertion of a younger man.

B. SENIOR VICTIMS (880b1–d7)

Any citizen, metic, or itinerant who strikes someone 20 or more years older than himself, must suffer a prosecution for assault, and go to prison for

---

[32] He has a conceit of wisdom in this matter: cf. 701ab, 863cd.

[33] This passage is discussed in more detail above, pp. 156–7 and 182. Its bark is worse than its bite: we expect an 'enhanced' death penalty, but in fact the punishment for assault on parents etc. is rustication and ostracism.

[34] 879b7, 'type of assault', perhaps warns us that Plato's law of assault is not as unitary as the Athenian.

[35] Older by less than 20 years, presumably; for at that point different regulations apply (880b1 ff.).

(i) 1 year if he is a citizen,
(ii) 2 years if he is a non-resident alien,
(iii) 3 years if he is a metic.

The court may however prescribe a longer period, at least in cases (i) and (iii).[36]

Again, the victim receives no financial recompense; but unlike a victim of a contemporary he can have the 'satisfaction' of knowing his aggressor is suffering. Now although imprisonment as a punishment in itself is known in Athens,[37] it was apparently not imposed for assault. What kind of imprisonment does Plato have in mind, and what is its purpose? Magnesia is to have three prisons:[38] one near the market-place for large numbers of prisoners (evidently to ensure appearance at their trials: it is at least in part an administrative prison, a 'holding tank'),[39] one situated near where the Nocturnal Council assembles and called the 'reform-centre' (sōphronistērion: here heretics are re-educated by the Council members), and one in wild and deserted country, which is to have a name suggesting timōria, 'punishment'. It seems improbable that the Nocturnal Council would be prepared to spend two to three years re-educating mere assaulters (especially the foreigners among them).[40] So does Plato mean to send assaulters to the timōria-prison? If so, their incarceration, while of course capable of a deterrent effect on them (and on others), will hardly be reformative in any strong sense;[41] and in any case this prison sounds excessively grim for such offenders. The only offenders whom we know go to the sōphronistērion and the timōria-prison are heretics. So on the whole I agree with Knoch that the prison near the market is meant.[42] What Plato proposes to do, if anything, with his prisoners there is entirely obscure.

We may ask why the metic is punished more severely than the itinerant, for if the metic is to some degree assimilated into Magnesia and approximated to a citizen, the itinerant should be punished more severely than both. Probably the metic is regarded as harder to deter than the citizen, as not having enjoyed Magnesian education, and the itinerant is so to speak dismissed early, since the state will be quit of him

[36] αὐτῷ 880c2, d1. There seems no reason why the second αὐτῷ should not apply to itinerants ('him', i.e. a foreigner of either kind). But in so far as the incarceration is intended as reform, perhaps the discretionary longer period would not be appropriate for someone who will not be remaining in the state. Cf. p. 339 below.
[37] Barkan, Gernet (1917a) n. 27, MacDowell (1978) 256-7, Harrison ii (1971) 177.
[38] 908a.
[39] For the 'safety of bodies' (908a); heretics are imprisoned in the sōphronistērion for the 'safety of their souls' (909a).
[40] There is of course the possibility that assaulters do go to the sōphronistērion, but are not favoured by visits from the members of the Council.
[41] Just conceivably, the citizen would go to the sōphronistērion, and foreigners to the timōria-prison.   [42] Knoch (1960) 144.

soon in any case. If that is right, the purpose of *his* imprisonment, at least, will be to deter others who see him punished rather than the man himself.

C. PARENTS AND GRANDPARENTS AS VICTIMS
(881b3–882a1)

The penalty is permanent exile from the city, and residence somewhere else in Magnesia, with exclusion from all sacred places and social activities. Presumably this is to be regarded as a more severe penalty than the imprisonment of (B).

Again, there is no recompense for the victim. The penalty is harsher than the fine for *aikia* of Attic law; indeed it is not clear how life in the conditions specified would be possible, though if the offender were a lot-holder he would presumably be allowed to live off its revenues. This 'rustication' is Plato's version of the *atimia* imposed by Attic law for *kakōsis goneōn* in the form of assault,[43] and presumably entails much the same range of legal and political disabilities. Perhaps the point is that the offender is beast-like, and should therefore live in the country-side. One assumes that the penalty applies *mutatis mutandis* to foreigners also.

D. ASSAULT BY FOREIGNERS (879d5–e6)

(Assaults by foreigners on senior victims are covered by (B); thus (D) presumably covers only non-senior victims, like (A).) Foreigners, not mentioned for some reason in the law of wounding, are dealt with first and in some detail in the law of assault.[44] Both metics and itinerants, apparently of all ages, are to enjoy the same protection as seniors: they must never be struck, even in self-defence. But whereas a citizen senior has an absolute right not to be resisted, the foreigner's is limited; for if a citizen believes him to be in the wrong, he may hale him before the City-Wardens—but still without hitting him—so that the offender 'may be far from venturing to hit a Magnesian native (*epichōrios*) ever again'. The Wardens too must respect the god who protects foreigners; but if they conclude that the foreigner is in the wrong, they must put a stop to his 'foreign uppitiness' (*thrasuxenia*),[45] by giving him as many strokes of the

---

[43] The expression *aikia goneōn* (881d3) seems calculated to put one in mind of the Attic suit.
[44] I put them as (D) in my own sequence for the sake of the comparisons with parents (C) and slaves (E).
[45] A word evidently coined for the occasion: it occurs nowhere else in Greek literature.

lash as the blows he himself inflicted. If the foreigner is innocent, the other party must be rebuked; and then both are to be dismissed.

These detailed regulations perfectly reveal the ambiguous status of the foreigner: he has some role and 'honour' in Magnesia, and in virtue of his relatively exposed position is accorded enhanced protection against ill-treatment (*hubris*, though the word is not used in the text).[46] But if *he* proves unruly, his character as someone lacking in education comes into play: he is whipped (a punishment characteristic of slaves[47]), whereas it seems that for a citizen who was in the wrong only rebuke is in order. At any rate, the preventive purpose of both measures is clear. Whether a foreigner who hits a *foreigner* (one not 20 years older) would be treated less harshly is not clear: the word *epichōrios* suggests that a citizen has some greater protection against foreigners than foreigners have.

E. ASSAULT BY SLAVES (882a1–c4)

A slave who strikes any free man, citizen or foreigner, must be arrested by the passers-by and handed over to the victim, who may whip him as much as he likes, short of diminishing his value to his owner; he must then be handed over in chains to his master, and released only when he satisfies his victim that he deserves it.[48]

Nothing is said about assaults of slaves on slaves; but apparently free men enjoy the same 'protected' status *vis-à-vis* slaves as seniors *vis-à-vis* juniors. For to judge from the silence of the text about self-defence, slaves (who are naturally in an exposed position) are punished as described even if they are retaliating against the *hubris* which Plato firmly tells masters not to commit against them.[49] Plato recognizes the danger of assaults on slaves, but affords them no *formal* protection.[50] In this section of the law we are of course dealing only with blows, not injuries or murders; to cuff a slave would be routine, and Plato is not prepared to legislate for occasions when it is not deserved; social and religious pressures on the master must suffice.

---

[46] To give the foreigner enhanced formal protection against *aikia* seems to be an innovation; cf. the law of homicide, where he is put on the same footing as the citizen, unlike in Attic law.

[47] But at least the number of stripes is limited: contrast the whipping of a slave (E below).

[48] This amounts to a sort of *aidesis* for a slave (cf. 869a); I know no parallel. Cf. Morrow (1939) 70–1. Plato may expect the degradation followed by release to be reformative: notice 'deserve' (*axios*).

[49] 777d ff., 793e, cf. Morrow (1939) 48.

[50] See on the Attic *graphē hubreōs* above, pp. 268–70, and cf. Harrison i (1968) 168–9.

F. BACK-UP PROVISIONS

Embedded in A-E are elaborate back-up provisions, which I have kept back till this point so as not to complicate further an already complicated set of laws.

(i) 880b1–6, d2–7, 881b4–d3. A bystander has a duty in (A), (B), (C), and (D), if older than the combatants, to separate them; if the person attacked is his senior or contemporary,[51] he must go to his assistance as though it were his own brother or father etc. who is being wronged. If he fails to assist, the law will treat him as a coward, and he will be fined a sum (according to property class), by a special court of military officials.[52]

In the case of (C), various rewards for rendering assistance are offered to three of the four social groups, with penalties as under:

Metic:[53] permanent exile.
Itinerant: reprimand.
Slave: 100 strokes of lash.

The citizen (man, woman, and child) is offered no inducement, but must shout 'you wicked monster' at the attacker, and try to repel him; if he fails to try, he is liable to a curse from Zeus (on top of the fine and reputation for cowardice?).[54]

(ii) 881d3–7. Persons convicted of (C) who return from the country-side to the city are punished by death; if they fail to keep away from sacred places in the country-side, the Country-Wardens are to whip them or inflict some other penalty at their discretion.

(iii) 881d7–882a1. In (C), persons associating with those rusticated are polluted,[55] and if they go into temples and the city without being purified must be prosecuted by any official. If the official fails so to act, it will be one of the major charges against him in his *euthuna* (scrutiny) on demitting office.

These elaborate provisions are so far as we know foreign to the Attic law of assault; they arise because of considerations of status imported from the Attic laws *kakōsis goneōn* and *hubris*. The mandatory death penalty for exercising rights of which one had been deprived by *atimia*

---

[51] Hence a victim younger than the bystander would have to defend himself, without assistance.

[52] Morrow (1960) 181 n. 68 unduly restricts the authority of this court, to cases involving metics and other itinerants; and like my note in the Penguin version, 404 n. 2, he misleadingly suggests that the court deals with the assaults themselves (not just with delinquent bystanders). On the moral duty in the elderly to prevent a fracas, see Dem. 54. 22.

[53] In 881b6 either ἤ or ἤ ξένος must be deleted from Burnet's text.

[54] (E) too requires action from bystanders (882a1–4), but only the fine is mentioned (for free men).

[55] On *alitēriōdēs tuchē* (881e4), cf. pp. 287–9 under theft. The pollution arises only if the association was voluntary, 881e2; contrast its indifference to intent in involuntary homicide.

imposed for assaulting parents is probably more severe than the corresponding penalty (for breach of *atimia* imposed for ill-treatment of one's parents) in the law of Athens, which was a penalty fixed by the court.[56] The brief reappearance of pollution, reinforcing 'social ostracism',[57] for those who consort with offenders rusticated for assaulting a parent (and presumably for the offenders themselves) is startling; for it played no part in the law of wounding, a more serious offence.[58] So too is the special court of military officials for timorous bystanders, and the instances of whipping free men (convicted offenders against parents who enter sacred places). The slave who fails to assist an assaulted parent receives twice the maximum number of whip-lashes that may have been customary in the summary punishment of slaves in Athens.[59] Yet the death penalty is inflicted in no case for an initial offence, not even on a slave, only for the assaulter of his parents who returns from the rustication imposed on him for that offence.

ASSESSMENT

How does one assess such an amazing set of laws? There are traces of the insouciance of the *Republic*, an absence of penalty in the standard cases,[60] an abandonment of the compensations of Attic law, and a heavy reliance on social pressures and informal penalties.[61] By contrast, we have wholesale importation of status considerations, and some severe formal penalties, apparently under the influence of two Attic suits designed to protect parents and other parties in a weak position. Why the extraordinary elaboration? Even the homicide law looks simple by comparison. But the paradox of simplicity combined with complexity is only apparent. Assault may be the least serious of homicide, wounding, and assault; but if one thing leads to another—assault to wounding to homicide—then in a sense legislation about assault is primary and fundamental. Plato surrounds mere fisticuffs with such a mass of inhibitions that any bodily violence is likely to be nipped in the bud. Of these inhibitions penalties form only one kind; there are just a few hints of penalties that could be said to inform, persuade, and enlighten; but most are deterrent, and some savagely so; they are justified by crude considerations of how 'tough' characters need to be forcibly softened.

[56] Dem. 24. 103, 105, Hansen (1976) 66–7, 90–2, 96–7. It is noticeable that in the *Laws* returning to the city is much more harshly treated than going into sacred places (so much for the *real* importance of religion?); cf. 868de.

[57] Parker (1983) 194 and n. 17.   [58] Except, in a sense, at 877a.

[59] Morrow (1939) 68–9, accepting Glotz's suggestions, (1908) 572–8.

[60] Numerically, these may not be great, so wide is the range of the special cases.

[61] Cf. 880e, the wish that laws were unnecessary.

The 'teaching' element in the law comes not here,[62] but in the network of myth, exhortation and social pressures that envelops the man in the Magnesian street. The elaboration of the law of *aikia* reflects and reinforces the elaborately hierarchical nature of Magnesian society.[63]

[62] 88od ff. The subtleties of the analysis of anger, already diminished in the law of wounding, disappear without trace in the law of assault. Whether such considerations could affect the discretion to increase the length of imprisonment for assaults on seniors (88ocd) must remain uncertain.

[63] In this reinforcement, and in some other respects, Spartan practice probably exercised some influence: see Fisher (1989).

11

THEFT

'En cette matière, les *Lois* deviennent presque un modèle de confusion inintelligible.'[1] Plato's law of theft is indeed confusing. The six relevant texts have to be fetched from afar, from widely scattered locations in books 9 and 11-12 of the *Laws*; when compared, they seem mutually inconsistent. To understand their interrelationships, we have to consider Plato's literary strategy in the composition of the dialogue as a whole.

THE PLATONIC LAWS OF THEFT, NAKED

In order to clarify these exceptional problems I first set out the bare provisions of his laws of theft in full, but without reference to historical law, and sharply shorn of their contexts and the sometimes lengthy explanatory matter which penetrates and surrounds them.

Passage A: sacrilege (854d1-4, e1-2, 6-7, 855a1-2)

If a man is caught committing sacrilege,[2] and he is a slave or a foreigner, a brand of his misfortune shall be made on his face and hands, and he shall be whipped, the number of lashes to be decided by his judges. Then he shall be thrown out beyond the boundaries of the land, naked. . . . If a citizen is ever shown to be responsible for such a deed . . . his penalty is to be death . . . [and he will be] held in ignominy and banished from sight beyond the borders of the state.

Passage B: the comprehensive law (857a2-b3)

Again, a single law and legal penalty should apply to a thief, no matter whether his theft is great or small: he must first pay twice the value of the stolen article, if he loses a suit of this kind and has sufficient surplus property over and above this farm with which to make the repayment; if he has not, he must be kept in prison until he pays up or persuades the man who had had him convicted [to let him off]. If a man is convicted of stealing from public sources, he shall be freed from prison when he has either persuaded the state [tò let him off] or paid back twice the amount involved.

---

[1] Gernet (1917*a*) n. 49. This present chapter is an adapted version of Saunders (1990).
[2] That sacrilege, *hierosulia*, is a species of theft, *klopē*, is shown below, p. 286.

Passage C: 'diminished' theft (914b6–c3)

If ... someone picks up an object of no great value and takes it home, and he is a slave, he should be soundly beaten by any passer-by who is not less than thirty years of age; if he is a free man [*eleutheros*], in addition to being thought ungentlemanly [*aneleutheros*, literally 'unfree'] and no sharer in law, he must pay the person who left the article ten times its value.

Passage D: theft from private sources (933e6–934a)[3]

When one man harms another by theft or violence and the damage is extensive, the payment he makes to the injured party should be large, but smaller if the damage is comparatively trivial. The cardinal rule should be that in every case the sum is to vary in proportion to the damage done, so that the loss is cured. And each offender is to pay an additional penalty appropriate to his crime ...

Passage E: theft from public sources (941d4–942a4)

If anyone successfully prosecutes in court a foreigner or slave on a charge of theft of some piece of public property, a decision must be reached as to the fine or penalty he should pay ... If a citizen ... is convicted of plundering or attacking his fatherland, whether he is caught red-handed [*ep' autophōrōi*] or not ... he must be punished by death.

Passage F: theft from public sources by officials (946d2–e4)[4]

When they [the Scrutineers, *hoi euthunoi*] have sat in judgement, either privately and individually, or in association with colleagues, on those at the end of their term of office in the service of the state, they must make known, by posting written notice in the market place, what penalty or fine in their opinion each official ought to pay. Any official who refuses to admit that he has been judged impartially should haul the Scrutineers before the Select Judges, and if he is deemed innocent of the accusations he should accuse the Scrutineers themselves, if he so wishes. But if he is convicted, and the Scrutineers had decided on death as his penalty, he must die (a penalty which in the nature of the case cannot be increased); but if his penalty is one that it is possible to double, then double he must pay.

EXPULSION OF THE COMPREHENSIVE LAW

The puzzles are obvious. After the straightforward law of sacrilege (A), we have the very different set of provisions in (B), which are explicitly stated to apply whatever the amount of the theft, whether the source is

---

[3] The word *kleptōn*, 'stealing' (933e6), may have a wider reference than theft, and cover any kind of stealthy act, of which theft would be then a typical example; cf. Whitehead (1988). At any rate theft can hardly be *excluded*: note 'all' *(pantōn) klopaiōn*, 'acts of theft/stealth', 934c4.

[4] That this passage embraces theft is suggested below, pp. 295–6.

public or private (or indeed sacred), and apparently without sociological distinction between offenders, or any regard to motive or circumstances. A further set of provisions applies in (C) to the removal of property of little value which is not in the immediate custody of its owner. (D) presents another law, restricted to theft from *private* sources.[5] (E) presents yet another, restricted to theft from *public* sources. Finally, (F) presumably embraces *inter alia* theft by officials, presumably of public money or property; but at first sight it differs from (E) in not making the death penalty mandatory for the citizen.

This is a dissipated and unhelpful mode of lawgiving. Plato is capable of better. In the sections of the penal code we have examined so far the striving for order and clarity has been apparent.[6] Even in the less complicated sections of his legal code, in which the offences spill forth in only loosely systematic sequence and are often dismissed quite briefly, Plato usually rounds off his treatment of one before embarking on another. The fragmented nature of his law of theft is wholly exceptional. What accounts for it?

The key is the structure of the *Laws* and its penal code as a whole. By the end of book 8 some forty offences have been dealt with; many, as the Athenian Stranger notes in the opening paragraph of book 9, were concerned with agricultural affairs and were relatively trivial. In some cases the range of penalties was left open-ended; but the most swingeing penalties, notably death and exile, have not even been mentioned, let alone made mandatory. Now, however, more serious crimes are in prospect: 'sacrilege, and all the other similar crimes which are difficult or impossible to cure'.[7] The law of sacrilege follows accordingly ((A) and related material); a description of procedure in capital cases ensues. Subversion and treason are then described; both, like sacrilege, naturally attract the death penalty.

We now encounter passage (B). Its opening words are obviously intended to link it closely to the laws of subversion, treason and sacrilege. In those cases, a 'single law' prescribed a single legal procedure and mode of punishment.[8] Similarly, a 'single law and just penalty' is to apply 'again', this time to all thieves without distinction.[9] The connection is slightly strained, in that at least the law of sacrilege did permit a variation of punishment as between citizen and non-citizen; but the

---

[5] 933e6 *allon*, 'another *person*'.

[6] The genera, (*a*) homicide, (*b*) wounding, (*c*) assault, and the species of (*b*), come in descending order of seriousness; the species of (*a*) come in ascending order, followed by 4 brief appendices on special cases; (*c*) is a complex but principled sequence of regulations, dealing comprehensively with all the many varieties of assault.   [7] 854a.

[8] 856e5 ff.; but *dikōn* may mean not 'punishments' but 'trials'.

[9] 857a3-4. 'Just penalty' renders *dikēs timōria*, 'punishment of justice; on these two words, see pp. 150-1.

single law of theft permits no variation, at any rate in the sense that all thieves whatever pay double.

Now this latter proposal is a very odd one, as Kleinias immediately complains:

How on earth can we be serious, sir, in saying that it makes no odds whether his theft is large or small, or whether it comes from sacred or secular sources? And what about all the other different circumstances of a robbery? Should not a legislator vary the penalties he inflicts, so that he can cope with the variety of thefts?

The Athenian Stranger smilingly agrees: for this example has shown that the business of laying down laws has not yet been 'properly worked out'.[10] The three interlocutors have not yet achieved their aim of becoming legislators, and some further explanation is needed of how to legislate for sacrilege, all theft, and all acts of injustice.[11] In short, there is a strong presumption that in formulating (B) they have in some way got the law of theft *wrong*.

The function of (B) now emerges quite clearly. It is merely to serve as a foil to the long and crucial penological excursus which the Stranger now undertakes, with the purpose of showing the *right* way to prescribe penalties. As we have seen, the chief recommendation of this excursus was that punishments, in order to cure offenders, must be calculated to fit their states of mind. Hence the elaborate differentiations of punishments found throughout Plato's penal code. It follows that Plato would never tolerate a law of theft without a single such differentiation. The comprehensive law of theft in passage (B) is therefore bogus. It is a piece of coat-trailing,[12] destined to be corrected and superseded. When, after the laws of homicide, wounding and assault in book 9, and the lengthy theodicy that occupies the whole of book 10, we come at last to the genuine laws of theft in books 11 and 12, their defective predecessor has been entirely forgotten.

When the 'normal business' of legislation is resumed at the start of book 11, passage (C) occurs within two pages; it is prompted by a discussion of the unauthorised removal of buried treasure. Twenty pages later comes passage (D); it is part of a *generalized* description of the various ways in which one person may harm another, a description apparently stimulated by a set of laws relating to certain highly *specific* ways of inflicting injuries, i.e. by drugs etc. Passage (E) appears after a further eight pages; the mention of Hermes, a god who delights in theft, brings that topic into Plato's mind. Passage (F) then occurs after only a further six pages, in connection with the duties of Scrutineers. In all

[10] 857c.   [11] 859b.
[12] This is not a new suggestion: cf. e.g. Knoch (1960) 11, 'Kunstgriff'.

these cases Plato proceeds by a loose association of ideas: he allows one topic to trigger another. Seen in this light, his untidy mode of presenting his law of theft has a certain rationale, or at least an intelligible genesis.

It is, however, necessary to spend a little longer in the company of passage (B). For David Cohen, in two recent publications,[13] takes it very seriously indeed. He believes it to be the definitive statement of certain parts of Plato's law of theft, and to embody its central principle, 'one law, one penalty'; other passages are to be interpreted in harmony with it. This attempt to iron out the explicit and implicit discrepancies between (B) and every other passage seems to me unconvincing.[14]

1. Cohen does not explain certain suspicious, or at least striking, discrepancies between (B) and the law of Athens on the one hand, so far as we know it, and between (B) and the laws of Magnesia on the other.

(*a*) Indefinite imprisonment until payment of a fine—usually but not always when the state is itself the aggrieved party—is certainly known in Athens; but it is not known in the law of theft.[15] But this of course is an *argumentum ex silentio*; and even if the provision did not apply in that law, Plato may be making an innovation.

(*b*) Formal 'letting off' (*aidesis*, not that the word occurs in (B)) of an imprisoned person unable to pay a fine, seems similarly un-attested. It is, however, not wholly unlikely in practical terms,[16] and Plato may again wish to innovate, by building it into his law.

(*c*) The general arrangements for the execution of judgement in Magnesia, in disputes between private persons, make no provision whatever for imprisonment;[17] nor indeed, as we have seen, does any other passage relating specifically to theft.

(*d*) However, those regulations regarding inability to pay a fine which occur only just before passage (B) (but which may refer only to cases in which the state is the aggrieved party) do indeed specify 'long imprisonment open to public view, and various humili-ations'.[18] This suggests something like the stocks; but it is surely implausible to suppose that such exposed confinement, though long, would last indefinitely, at the pleasure of the victorious prosecutor—who is not even mentioned, let alone given licence to 'let off'.

---

[13] Cohen (1982 and 1983) is the first to have attempted a systematic study of Plato's law of theft in its relation to Athenian law, a most welcome venture.

[14] Not least because he ignores (D) and (F) entirely. 'It is not until 941 [E] that the promised consideration of theft (859b) finally comes', (1983) 121.

[15] Harrison ii (1971) 242-4; Rhodes (1972) 151; MacDowell (1978), 166-7, 257.

[16] In spite of the implications of prolonged or indefinite imprisonment in Dem. 24. 125, 135; cf. Barkan (1936) 339-40, Partsch (1909) 78 n. 2. *Aidesis* is of course known in homicide law.

[17] 958a-c.   [18] 855a-c.   [19] See 884 ff.

2. In (B) the private prosecutor and the state are obviously both injured parties. In a Platonic state, it is wholly unlikely that the penalty would not be more severe for injuring the state than for injuring a private person.[19]

3. Cohen takes the word which in (B) I translate 'from public sources', *dēmosiai*, as referring merely to 'theft of private property from public places'. But the passage clearly implies that the public is the *injured party*; the location is not at issue.[20] Moreover, if that is all *dēmosiai* means, there would be no separate provision here, in a law which is obviously intended to be comprehensive (as Kleinias notes), for theft from public sources, an omission which in a Platonic state is inherently unlikely. The vagueness of 'in a public way' is all Plato needs for the purpose of what is a non-law anyway.

4. Most crucially, Cohen supposes that Plato subscribes to 'one overriding principle: one law and one penalty for theft, regardless of amount or circumstances'.[21] But that would be quite alien to the elaborate attention Plato frequently pays to such considerations, as determinants of penalty, elsewhere in the code. Indeed, he would abominate the principle;[22] for as a tool of reform it is blunt. Plato is anxious to fit penalty/cure to the precise mental state, character and circumstance of each individual criminal. That penalties should be freely variable at the discretion of the judges is essential. (B) is therefore flatly inconsistent with Plato's radical and reformative penology, in particular with its fundamental distinction between recompense and cure.

Perhaps that is why Cohen does not notice the possible significance in (B) of the word 'first' (the thief must pay double). Conceivably, the double is merely recompense; 'second' would come punishment/cure. But as Plato has not yet drawn the distinction between recompense and cure, and (B) is to be abandoned anyway, he simply drops the point.[23] To be sure, a gap in the law does not rule it out as a law; but the oddity of a 'first' without a 'second' needs to be accounted for.

So I again conclude that as a serious statement of Platonic law, passage (B) is fundamentally vitiated both by its context and by its

---

[20] MacDowell (1984) 231: the contrast between 'persuades the man who has had him convicted' and 'has ... persuaded the state' clinches the matter. Cohen (1983, 120–1) sees no conflict between (B) (allegedly wholly about private property) and (E) (public property).

[21] Cohen (1983) 118.

[22] *Pace* also Schöpsdau (1984) 109. Note how 859bc recognizes 'every [variety of] theft', *pasēs klopēs*: it is a complex thing, and like assault (*to tēs aikias pan genos*, 879b, 'assault of every type'), requires a *range* of penalties.

[23] Note that even if (B) does confine itself to recompense, serious contradictions with (A) and (C)–(F) remain: notably, recompense in (D) seems only single recompense, not double, and in (A) and (E) an offender can hardly be executed *and* 'kept in prison till he pays' (B). (England (1921), on 857a5, says that '"first" distinguishes the case of the man who can pay from that of the man who cannot'. Perhaps; but 'first' suggests a sequence, not an alternative).

content. Contrary to his usual practice, and uniquely among the six passages,[24] Plato provides no explanation or justification—because none is
available. On the contrary, he indicates that (B) is quite unsatisfactory.[25]
It is therefore pointless to attempt to reconcile the other passages with
it.

We now turn to passages (A) and (C)–(F). Close examination of them
now duly clothed in their contexts demonstrates that the consideration
which controls their form and content, and their differences from
Athenian law, is Plato's new penology. We shall, however, be handicapped by the fact that no surviving forensic speech deals with theft; we
have only incidental references. The laws of theft seem not to have been
enacted as a single unified corpus, but at different dates and piecemeal,
without regard for overall consistency. At any rate, they exhibit
considerable variety and intricacy.

A. SACRILEGE (853a ff.)

Like the Athenian orators, Plato does not define sacrilege, but it seems
to me certain that he means at least broadly what they meant; if his
understanding of it had been substantially different, he would have
explained just how. In spite of Cohen's useful review of the evidence,[26] I
am not persuaded that Lipsius was far wrong in taking the word to mean
'theft of sacred objects from sacred places'.[27] By 'sacred objects' I mean
valuable sacred objects (statues, arms, money, implements, etc. of
precious metal or other material,[28] not the trivial things like wood and
water mentioned in the inscriptions Cohen marshalls).[29] As he says,[30]
'the "standard case" of *hierosulia* as theft of sacred property from temples
is clear, for this is the type of case described in what Athenian evidence
there is'. I have little doubt that theft of such objects from anywhere
would indeed constitute sacrilege;[31] but normally it is in temples that
they are found. Given the orators' lack of interest in the precise
definition of offences, this is about as far as we can go; and Plato makes
the same assumption as they do, namely that one just knows what
hierosulia is.[32]

[24] Except (F), where strong disapproval of misdemeanour by officials, and the appropriateness of
a possible death sentence, are simply taken for granted.
[25] Cf. the 'bare' law of marriage, which is, however, unsatisfactory not so much in itself as because
it lacks explanation: 720e–723d, with 772de, 774a, 785b.
[26] Cohen (1983) 93–100. Pol. 8. 40 indicates the charge was a *graphē*.
[27] Lipsius (1905–15) 442–3.
[28] e.g. the robes mentioned in Dem. 25 hypothesis 1–2.
[29] Cohen (1983) 99, cf. (1) on 102.
[30] Ibid. 115, and the sources on 96, esp. Dem. 57. 64.
[31] Cf. Cohen (1984) 97–100, esp. Xen. *Hell.* 1. 7. 22.

[*See opposite page for n. 32*]

The Athenian stranger introduces the law of sacrilege by explaining that slaves and foreigners are likely to be the most frequent offenders. The reasons are psychological, and are expressed partly in medical terms: not having had the education enjoyed by citizens, they will be open to the 'disease' of wishing to commit this and similar crimes, which are 'hard or impossible to cure'. The penalties now follow; they incorporate briefly their psychological/penological justifications:[33]

1. *A slave or a foreigner* should have a brand of his 'misfortune' (i.e. offence[34]) put on face and hands, be whipped as much as his judges decide, and be thrown naked out of Magnesia. For perhaps by paying that penalty he will become 'better', 'having been made restrained' (*sōphrōn*). No *dikē* imposed by law aims at evil, but usually makes the punished person 'either better or less wicked'.

2. *A citizen* who does 'such a thing'[35] must be regarded as incurable, suffer death ('least of evils'), and by being thrust out of sight beyond the borders of the state in ignominy serve as an example to others. The justification advanced for inferring incurability is that in spite of his education and nurture he has not refrained from the greatest evils. In short, the determinant of penalty is psychological assessment of curability.

The address to the person tempted to commit sacrilege runs in full:

My dear fellow, this thing that at present drives you to sacrilege is neither human nor divine. It is a sort of goad (*oistros*), innate as a result of acts of

---

[32] He speaks at 853d5–6 of a law *hierōn peri suleseōn*, which probably means 'pillaging temples', but could mean simply 'pillaging of sacred objects'; at 854a7–b1 *hierōn* probably has the latter sense. To judge from 955e–956b, the objects to be found in Magnesian temples will not be valuable; they will be cherished and protected precisely because they are holy. In historical states, of course, they needed protection not only for that reason but because of their sheer monetary value.

[33] 854d1–855a. 885b1 casually reveals that the law covers sacrilege 'by force and by stealth'.

[34] See p. 290 below.

[35] Glossed immediately (854e) as 'having committed one of the great and unspeakable acts of injustice in regard to gods or parents or state'. Cohen (1983, 128) rightly notes that thieves of public property also commit plunder (*sulan*) against their fatherland (942a). He could have added 931a, where we learn that parents are 'shrines', and 869b, where the killer in anger of a parent is liable to swingeing penalties of *hierosulia*, because he has 'plundered' (*sulēsas*) the soul from his begetter; likewise the voluntary killer of a parent at 873a 'deprives' the body of a parent of its soul. The gloss in question seems then to embrace not only *hierosulia* as such but theft from public sources and part of the law of homicide, not to speak of subversion and treason (856b–857a). But the wide casting of 'the net' (Cohen's term) has nothing to do with how 'narrowly' Plato 'defined' *hierosulia*. Plato is doing with *hierosulia* precisely what he did with *hubris* (see pp. 270–1 above): he takes a term that he hopes arouses horror, and injects, as he finds opportunity, its flavour into some of the offences described in various parts of his penal code. He has crude precedents in passages in the orators abusing opponents for *hierosulia*, when what they are accused of resembles it only very vaguely (see Parker (1983) 171 n. 152, and Cohen (1983) 95, both citing *inter alia* Lys. 30. 21.) That procedure tells us nothing about the specifically legal meaning of the term at 854. Cohen is nearer the mark with his suggestion that 'the broad language [is] part of Plato's attempt at exhortation and persuasion'.

injustice of long ago that remained unpurified (*akathartōn*) by men;[36] it travels around working destruction (*alitēriodēs*), and you should make every effort to take precautions against it. Now, take note what these precautions are. When any of these thoughts enters your head, seek the rites that free a man from pollution (*apodiopompēseis*), seek the shrines of the gods who avert evil (*theoi apotropaioi*), and supplicate them; seek the company of men who have a reputation in your community for being virtuous. Listen to them as they say that every man should honour what is fine and just—try to bring yourself to say it too. But run away from the company of the wicked, with never a backward glance. If by doing this you find that your disease abates somewhat, well and good; if not, then you should look upon death as the preferable alternative, and rid yourself of life.[37]

It is fundamental that at some time injustice has been committed, for which the injured party, whoever he is, has not received recompense in the form of purification. We are surely in the realm of homicide, or at least of some equally serious offence;[38] the injured party is probably a murdered person whose killer has not given satisfaction to him or his relatives in the form of purification, or perhaps exile or even death. His resentful desire for reciprocal justice in the only form available to him has as its tool the 'itch', *oistros*, to commit sacrilege; it is a tool that may be wielded either by himself or by a surrogate, perhaps the Erinues.[39] Neither dead men nor surrogates are *men*; but they are not gods either. They belong to some sinister intermediate world, where having lost track of the original offenders, they—or rather the itch—still wander round blindly trying to inflict reciprocal suffering on somebody, no matter who.[40] That suffering is not just the itch itself: it is the *punishment* for the offences the itch prompts the person to commit. This theme is an old one.[41]

The crudely vindictive reciprocal justice which the *oistros*-wielders seek to enforce is of course grossly unjust, in the sense that the person assailed by the urge to commit sacrilege has done nothing to offend.[42]

---

[36] *Oistros*: 'itch', 'strong yearning'; cf. 782e, *Tim.* 91b, *Phaed.* 240d, 251d.

[37] 854b1–c5. On the technical terms, see Parker (1983), esp. 109 (*alitērios*), 28–9, 220 (*apotropaios*), 373 (*apodiopompēsis*).

[38] e.g. assaults on parents (880e ff.; note (*alitēriōdēs*, 881e4); cf. *kathērasthai* and *apodiopompēsasthai* of the property of major criminals (877e).

[39] Cf. Euripides *IT* 1456, *oistrois Erinuōn*.

[40] Plato is obviously aware of the kind of 'subculture' of debased religion represented for example by the *katadesmoi*, 'binding spells', placed in tombs, whose operation depended on the assumption that a dead man's anger could be diverted to targets chosen by cursers: see *Republic* 364c, and p. 62 above. Much as he deprecates such practices (933a–e), he is prepared to exploit for his own ends the beliefs which inspire them. See further under 'Impiety' below.

[41] Herodotus 2. 139; Dem. 24. 121; Dover (1968a) 272, on *Clouds* 1458–61. Cf. p. 67 above.

[42] It is worth reminding ourselves that Plato distances himself from this injustice: it belongs neither to the world of men (where there is potentiality for good) nor to the world of gods (who do no evil); cf. 933a. The *oistros* is a wayward 'surd' in the scheme of things; but we have to take account

The temptation comes to him quite unbidden, like a disease; and a disease is precisely what the *oistros* is; for Plato seeks in this passage to marry religion and medical penology.[43] Religion and medicine had a noticeable overlap of vocabulary and concepts, notably 'purification'.[44] Plato exploits the overlap for his own purposes. If the *oistros* to commit sacrilege is a mental disease, it may be cured by mental *regimen*:[45] not only must the tempted person resort in pious faith to purificatory and prophylactic rites of religion, but he must associate with good men and say what they say, that everyone must honour what is fine and good. In other words, by echoing the moral doctrines of good men a tempted person can diminish his moral disease; for we all tend to believe what we ourselves say.[46] Social, religious, and mental regimen should be resorted to curatively and prospectively, in the hope that it may prevent the offence. In effect the cure for the *oistros* is simply a particular application of that regimen which is submission to the total educational and religious influences which bear on the Magnesian at every turn. Plato blends religion, psychology, and medicine: the *oistros* (goad) of religious thought = the *epithumia* (desire, lust) of psychology = the *nosos* (disease) of medicine; for, as we know from the *Timaeus*, mental diseases are, like physical diseases, physical configurations of a physical soul, and are curable, as they are, by the appropriate type of regimen.

A man who finds nevertheless that he still has the urge to commit sacrilege had better die; for it is better to die sinless than to suffer the pains of sin after death.[47] Does that mean he should commit suicide? If so, he will be justified by the second and/or third of the criteria given in the law about suicides: obedience to a legal decision of the state, and the compulsion of some excruciating and unavoidable disaster.[48] For sacrilege *is* a disaster (*sumphora*), which is branded on the face and hands of the slave or foreigner who commits it—a disaster in the sense that wickedness ineluctably entails suffering; hence one never really wants to be wicked, and if one does so want, it must be 'involuntarily', in the Socratic sense.[49]

After all this, it is easy to see why Plato regards a citizen who commits sacrilege as incurable. The penalty is the same as in Attic law: death

of it, just as we must the 'wandering cause' of the *Timaeus* (48a), to which England (on 854b) compares the 'wandering' *oistros*.

[43] The medical content occurs at 853d8, 854a3, c4, e4.
[44] Parker (1983) ch. 7, esp. 213–21.
[45] In medicine, Plato is a partisan of regimen, as against drugs: see p. 170 above.
[46] In committees, this is called 'falling for your own propaganda'. (England (1921), on 854c2, splendidly misses the point: 'a curious recipe for inducing belief').
[47] 959bc.   [48] 873cd.
[49] Cf. 881e4, the *alitēriodēs tuchē* catchable from an assaulter of a parent, and Parker (1983) 218–19, 268. *Oistros* leads to misery: *Rep.* 577b ff., esp. e; cf. 573b1 and *Laws* 734a ff. On suicide, see 873c ff.

without burial in the state;[50] but while Attic law also confiscated the offender's property, the peculiar conditions of land-tenure in Magnesia forbid it, as Plato goes on to explain immediately.[51]

When he describes the penalties for slaves and foreigners he explicitly (and incredibly) envisages that they may serve to 'cure'; such persons have not been exposed to the Magnesian education, and there remains hope that the pain and shock of punishment will induce self-control.[52] We cannot say exactly what the 'writing of the disaster on face and hands' means; presumably it is some sort of tattooing.[53] Expulsion naked beyond the confines of the country might be enough to kill. But even if the man survives, and is cured, Magnesia itself, apparently, will not benefit, since he will no longer be resident in it. At any rate, a metic in Athens would have suffered the same penalty as a citizen,[54] and so too presumably would an itinerant (and perhaps a slave—we simply do not know).[55] So formally the foreigner in Magnesia is punished for sacrilege less severely, though more elaborately, than the foreigner in Athens; and this innovation is a direct consequence of Plato's penology.

B. THE COMPREHENSIVE LAW (857a2–b3)

This is now irrelevant: see above.

C. 'DIMINISHED' THEFT (914b1 ff.)

When in passage (E) Plato deals with theft from public sources, he describes the thief of a small piece of public property as simply 'the thief', but the thief of a substantial piece as 'the remover of what he has not deposited'.[56] He thus brings theft of public property under the

---

[50] Diod. Sic. 16. 25; Xen. *Hell*. 1. 7. 22, *Mem*. 1. 2. 62, Lyc. *Leoc*. 65, Cohen (1983) 101, n. 22, cf. Parker (1983) 45, 170 ff. Hansen (1976) 45–6 argues that *hierosuloi* were liable to *apagōgē*: cf. pp. 293–4 below on 'aggravated' theft, Lipsius (1905–15) 443 n. 88 and Cohen (1983) 102–3.

[51] 855a ff: except in certain extreme cases (856c–e), Magnesia's *klēroi* are inalienable from the owner's family.

[52] At 854a3, 'hard to cure' may refer to the actions of foreigners and slaves, but 'impossible to cure' to those of citizens (cf. 854e4). In theft of public property too we see the same pattern: slaves and foreigners are punished less severely than citizens (passage E), though precisely how is not specified; but it is certainly, and interestingly, implied that the punishment even of non-citizens is cure: 941d4–942a1.

[53] See C. P. Jones 146–9, and esp. nn. 39, 47, 58.

[54] Lys. 5. 1 ff.

[55] There is no need to assume uniformity of practice. Unless an itinerant was a citizen of a state with which Athens had a judicial agreement, he could find himself in the same position as a slave: liable to summary punishment without trial. At any rate, the penalties of itinerants and slaves would hardly be *less* than that of the citizen and metic.

[56] 941c5–d1.

general prohibition of 'removing what one has not deposited',[57] which is in turn connected with the celebrated maxim, 'don't remove what is not to be moved'.[58] On the same grounds, just before passage (C), the simple removal, as distinct from outright theft, of lost or abandoned property is similarly forbidden.[59] Such property is under divine protection, and the case of any man removing valuable treasure-trove must be referred to Delphi (with a hint that some awful divine punishment awaits him). Plato then, in passage (C), applies 'the same rule' to every object, great or small, that has been 'left' or 'lost': if a slave removes it and takes it home,[60] and it is *small*, he must be whipped by any passer-by over 30 years of age; if a free man does so, he must be accounted 'ungentlemanly and no sharer in law', and he must pay the person who left the object ten times its value. (The restriction 'small' seems to apply to both thefts, though the Greek is not quite clear.) Plato then describes the procedure under which ownership may be settled in case of dispute.[61]

One is perhaps left to assume that removal of a *valuable* object would be dealt with by some further regulation; but none is given; or perhaps Plato believes he has already dealt with the point in the provisions about treasure; most probably, he would deal with it under regular theft (passage D). For the apparent restriction to 'small' makes good practical sense. On the whole, one does not 'lose' a large object of some value, like a wagon or a plough, except by outright theft—which is provided for under the relevant law of theft from private sources (D); and even if one 'loses' something automobile, such as a pig, one does not abandon ownership, but searches. But if one inadvertently loses something trivial, or deliberately leaves it somewhere for some reason, intending to collect it later, its status will not always be clear to the finder: is it just 'left', or actually abandoned? To appropriate it, on the blithe assumption[62] that the owner has effectively relinquished ownership, is neither theft nor not-theft:[63] it betokens some minor psychic injustice, that may be cured by a beating for a slave, and for a free man by social disgrace and repayment on a scale which in point of the multiple is large (ten times), but, since *ex hypothesi* the object is of small value, will not amount to much.[64]

Plato's discussion of 'lost property' is surprisingly lengthy, which may

---

[57] 844e.   [58] 684e, 842e.   [59] 913a–914a.

[60] As Cohen (1983) 126–7 notes, taking home may be 'an objective requirement for liability'. The remover can argue he is not stealing but 'removing for safe keeping', *vel sim.*; but the plea is less plausible if the article is (in use?) in his home.   [61] 914c3–e2.

[62] One can always find a reason: cf. 913b1–3.

[63] As Cohen (1983) 124 rightly notes, the words for 'theft' do not occur in this section. It is the concept of 'not removing what one has not deposited' that provides the link with theft.

[64] Cohen (1983) 125–6, however, regards the penalty as 'severe', and suggests a connection with the (debatable) tenfold fine for private theft (see p. 293 n. 68 below).

be some indication that he felt he was supplying a gap in Attic law, in which, as Cohen has pointed out,[65] the concepts of 'appropriating' and 'stealing' tend to merge, the word 'lose' being used ambiguously. Plato succeeds in effect in inventing a formal category of 'diminished' theft; and his ruling consideration is that to find and appropriate a small thing is less 'unjust' than to find and appropriate a large one such as treasure (where the assumption of abandoned ownership is implausible), and less unjust than 'regular' theft by force or fraud. Again, psychological considerations seem to have led to innovation and reform.

D. THEFT FROM PRIVATE SOURCES (933e6–934c6)

Whenever one man commits theft or violence against another, he must pay compensation up to the point at which the harm is cured. A further penalty should be suffered or paid; it is to be calculated in the light of a number of elaborately detailed psychological considerations, e.g. over-persuasion of youth, pleasure, pain, envy, anger. This penalty is not for the sake of the past crime, but to encourage 'abatement' of the offender's 'misfortune' (i.e. unjust state of mind).

It is quite clear that the passage legislates for theft from private sources, that the injured party is to receive simple (but full) recompense, and that any extra payment is curative.[66] No upper or lower limit is prescribed: apparently the scale of this 'extra' is to vary open-endedly in direct proportion to the seriousness of the psychic state. Here then is what we need: recompense and cure, firmly distinguished.

At the end of the passage Plato indicates that the legislator must sketch, for the guidance of judges, the types of penalties that ought to be imposed on the various categories of theft and violence. This apparent promise to relate specific penalties to specific crimes is never fulfilled, at least in the systematic form suggested. At any rate, Plato obviously envisaged a law of theft which is more finely graded than that of passage (B).

What was the law of Athens on private theft? Certainly a *dikē klopēs* existed;[67] the penalty varied according to whether the stolen article was recovered by the owner or not. If it was, the offender paid the injured

---

[65] Cohen (1983) 64–68, 126 on Dem. 24. 105, Lys. 29. 11, [Arist.] *Prob.* 952^{b}21, Hes. *WD* 348.

[66] It is not stated to whom the 'extra' is paid, whether to the injured party or to the state; but *mechriper*, 933e9, suggests *not* to the injured party, who receives payment 'right up to' (but not beyond?) full compensation. Nor is any indication given of the legal procedure: one assumes a simple *dikē klopēs*, private suit for theft.

[67] Dem. 24. 144; Cohen (1983) 62–8. On the possible existence of a *graphē klopēs* from *private* sources, see Dem. 22. 26–7, Cohen (1983) 44–9, MacDowell (1984) 229–30, Harrison i (1968) 207 n. 1.

party twice the value in addition; if not, he paid the article's value, *plus* that value multiplied either by two or by ten.[68] The court also had discretion to order five days and nights in the stocks in addition to the payment, by way of inflicting social disgrace.[69]

In certain circumstances[70] it was permissible to resort to self-help. (*a*) One could arrest (*apagōgē*) the thief and take him to the board of officials called 'The Eleven', who kept him in prison till the trial; the penalty on conviction was death. (*b*) Thieves who were caught red-handed (*ep' autophōrōi*) and confessed guilt, were summarily executed by the Eleven. (*c*) In the case of theft at night, or when force was used on the person of the owner, the latter could kill the thief with impunity.

This mixed picture is presumably the result of an historical development.[71] I assume, but cannot prove, that the extreme specificity of the provisions for those cases, which may be called collectively 'aggravated' theft (*a-c* above), indicates that this part of the law is a relic of unrestricted self-help: because these particular thefts were 'so serious' or 'so easy',[72] or because there were connected social problems, or for all these reasons, the law still permitted, or had at some point reintroduced, self-help—but self-help restricted to theft *at night, over certain sums, from certain places*. In the absence of a confession, there had to be a trial; and the infliction of the penalty had to be in the hands of officials, not of the arrester (except for theft at night, and when force was used). Thefts not meeting these criteria would presumably have had to be dealt with by a normal *dikē klopēs*, which I take to have been introduced either before or simultaneously with these restrictions.[73]

Now if that reconstruction is right, and if one may argue from Plato's silence on the topic of 'aggravated' theft,[74] he has achieved a radical

---

[68] The text of Dem. 24. 105 says 'ten'; but 'two' would make the position of the injured party the same in both cases, and Heraldus' emendation to that effect has been almost universally adopted. However, 'ten' should not be too firmly ruled out: see Cohen (1983) 62–4. On the location of the stocks, see Barkan (1936) 338–9.

[69] Dem. 24. 105, 114. The origin of the provision is discussed by Rhodes (1981) 161.

[70] Day-time theft of more than 50 dr., theft of equipment of a value higher than 10 dr. from harbours or gymnasia, theft of minor articles from certain public places: Dem. 23. 60, 24. 113–14, Isoc. 15. 90, Aesch. 1. 91, *AP* 52. 1, MacDowell (1978) 148–9, Hansen (1976) 36–53. Cf. also Dem. 22. 26, *ephēgēsis*, 'leading' the Eleven to the thief. The special provision relating to the use of force suggests that the kind of theft normally dealt with by a *dikē klopēs* was carried out by stealth alone; cf. Cohen (1983) 90. Red-handedness may have been the defining characteristic of theft in which self-help followed by the death penalty was possible: Cohen (1983) 52–61, but cf. MacDowell (1984) 230–1. Carawan (1984), however, argues that summary execution was distinctly unusual.

[71] Cf. Ruschenbusch (1984), Cohen (1983) 75, Gernet (1959) esp. 394–5, 399; cf. in general Latte (1968) 286–94.

[72] MacDowell (1978) 148.

[73] Dem. 24. 113–14, for what it is worth, attributes most of the regulations for aggravated theft to Solon.

[74] One slight indication that we can so argue is that Plato says 'red-handedness' is irrelevant to theft from public sources (passage E) and we may probably assume *a fortiori* that it is irrelevant to

simplification of Athenian law. He has pushed it even further in the direction in which it had already gone, of relying on public trials rather than on self-help. He has swept away most of the Athenian apparatus of self-help against private theft,[75] and with it the possibility of the death penalty for the theft of quite trivial things and in special circumstances. He (probably)[76] limits to simple damages the injured party's recompense, and certainly abandons the single inflexible penalty awarded in the *dikē klopēs*, a fine calculated in terms of a fixed multiple of the value of the theft. Crucially, he substitutes *open-ended* penalties, not necessarily related to the value of the theft, but adjusted to psychic states and calculated to promote the criminal's self-control.[77] The discretionary period of five days and nights in the stocks also disappears; but it could no doubt be used if the court decided it would constitute effective cure. In short, the crude twofold distinction of Attic law between 'simple' and 'aggravated' theft, and the crude alternatives—stocks apart—of a fine or death,[78] are largely replaced by a single category of theft from private sources, and by a single sliding scale of penalties based on motives and psychic states.

E. THEFT FROM PUBLIC SOURCES (941b2–942a)

F. THEFT FROM PUBLIC SOURCES BY OFFICIALS (946d2–e4)

A brief prelude to (E) decries crimes of violence and theft, and the belief that since the gods commit them they must be legitimate. Plato then argues, harshly, that thefts large and small of public property by citizens should attract 'the same *dikē*', penalty, since both the pilferer and the greater thief are suffering from 'the same lust', i.e. to steal public

private theft also. If so, then given its importance in Athenian aggravated theft, aggravated theft too may be taken to have been dropped as a separate category.

[75] Cf. Cohen (1983) 120–1. But there are two exceptions: the night-time thief and the *lōpodutēs*, snatcher-of-clothes, may be killed (874bc). Yet even here there is the same tendency to be parsimonious in the scope allowed to self-help: the thief has to be *breaking into the house*, and the *lōpodutēs* may be killed *only in self-defence*. Cf. Cohen (1983) 72–83 for a discussion of the relation of these provisions to Attic law, and pp. 244–5 above.

[76] The Athenian *dikē klopēs* seems to have been an 'estimated' suit (Dem. 24. 114; see p. 101 above): the estimate (presumably of the disputed object's value) adopted by the court was the basis of the assessment of the multiple. If Plato permitted 'estimates' in trials for private theft (914bc and 954b2 may suggest it), he limits its employment to the assessment of recompense, and entrusts the assessment of penalty to the discretion of the jurors: see 876a–e. In the law of theft as a whole, most of (A), all of (C), and part of (E), are on the face of it non-estimated.

[77] *Sōphronistuos heneka*, 'for the sake of 'self-control' 934a1; cf. *sōphrōn* in A(1), p. 287.

[78] In Athens, death of the offender presumably robbed the injured party of any 'extra' recompense: the death was his only 'satisfaction'. Plato *guarantees* him his (simple) recompense: note *para panta*, 933e8, 'above all'.

property.[79] Foreigners and slaves who steal from public sources are probably curable, and what they must suffer or pay in order to cure them has to be assessed; but citizens educated as they have been educated, should be executed as well-nigh incurable, if they thus plunder and do violence to their fatherland, whether they are caught red-handed or not. The basis of differentiation of punishment is therefore sociological, as in sacrilege. No mention of recompense is made, nor of the legal procedure to be used; possibly there would be a *graphē klopēs*.[80] Nor is the point of the proviso 'whether caught red-handed or not' made clear.[81]

What, in Athens, is the counterpart of this law? At first sight, it is the *graphē klopēs dēmosiōn chrēmatōn*, the public suit for theft of public money (or objects?); this charge could be brought at their 'scrutiny', *euthuna*, against officials about to demit office; the penalty was a fine of ten times the amount stolen.[82] Yet Plato, in passage (F), has his own special procedures for the conduct of audits: the Scrutineers are to judge the conduct (presumably including financial conduct)[83] of officials on the end of their term of office, and can apparently impose any penalty including death.[84] Obviously (E) is not in conflict with these provisions, and could indeed provide the justification for imposing the death penalty in (F) on officials judged at scrutiny to have stolen public property;[85] yet its scope seems far wider, covering *all* theft of *all* public property (*dēmosiōn*) in general, and embracing, among the potential thieves, the categories of foreigners and slaves, to whom scrutinies are irrelevant, since they could not hold public office.

(E) seems then simply to deal with theft of public property by a

---

[79] This summary assumes the interpretation advanced above, pp. 160-1. Cf. Arist. *Rhet.* 1374[b]30: the thief of three consecrated half-obols would stick at nothing. Luke 16: 10 has a similar thought.

[80] Perhaps under the provisions of 767bc.

[81] See Cohen (1983) 123-4. I suspect that if (E) is a Platonic innovation (see below), he wishes to make clear that just as (by implication, see pp. 293-4 above) in (D), the time and circumstances of the offender's *detection* do not affect assessment of his mental state.

[82] Cohen (1983) 49-51, *AP* 48. 4-5, 54. 2, Dem. 24. 112, 127, cf. Aesch. 3. 22-3, And. 1. 74 (who adds *atimia*, a disqualification from some citizen rights). MacDowell (1984) 229-30 believes the *graphē* could be brought other than at the audit. Another *graphē* (if indeed it existed) concerned theft of sacred property, *hierōn chrēmatōn*, for which also the penalty may have been ten times the sum at issue: Ant. *Tetr.* 1a. 6, Dem. 19. 293, 24. 111, Cohen (1983) 100-2. It was also possible to prosecute, at any time, by means of an 'impeachment' or 'denunciation', *eisangelia*, before the *boulē* or *ekklēsia* (e.g. Hansen (1975) case 143); in this case either the death penalty or a fine could be imposed. See in general Hansen (1975), and Rhodes (1979); the details are complex and controversial. On variations in penalties, see Cohen (1983) 51 n. 56; I have followed Hansen (1975) 33-6. On variations in procedure, see Hansen (1985) 352-3. (As Piérart (1973) 450 points out, Plato has suppressed *eisangelia*: no doubt he mistrusted such democratic procedures, and thought his select body of Scrutineers more suitable for the important and specialized job of examining officials: cf. Hyp. *Eux.* 1-3, Morrow (1960) 219-29, esp. 227-9.)   [83] Aesch. 3. 22-3.

[84] Evidently on their own authority, unlike in Athens, where cases were referred to courts; cf. n. 82 on *eisangelia*.

[85] Especially as the immediately preceding lines, 941a1-b1, concern misdemeanours by officials on embassies etc.

private person, whether citizen, foreigner or slave. Cohen reports that 'no text describes theft of public property by a private citizen [in Athens]'.[86] If the lacuna is not simply a lacuna in our sources but an indication of a gap in Athenian law,[87] then Plato, anxious as always to provide fully against offences against the communal interest, supplies the need. So (F) includes theft of public property by officials;[88] (E) deals with theft of public property by private persons; (D)[89] caters for theft of private property by private persons.

LEGISLATION AND PENOLOGY

What emerges from these lengthy complexities? In sum, that Plato has both abridged and expanded Athenian law, partly in order to rationalize and simplify, but chiefly under the guidance of a penology based on the psychology of the criminal. Once the law in (B) bas been ruled out as unsatisfactory, he can be seen to meet its deficiencies by providing a graduated set of penalties for a variety of thefts exhibiting psychic 'injustice', on an ascending scale.

C. *Mild* 'injustice' is catered for in a new formal category: quasi-theft, which is simply 'picking up' a small object the thief fondly hopes has been abandoned.

Penalties: (*a*) *Slave*: a whipping. (*b*) *Freeman*: reputation for un-gentlemanliness and tenfold repayment to depositor.

It is sufficient to rely on social pressure and a slap at the offender's pocket.

D. *Normal* 'injustice', shown in theft by private persons from private sources, is of variable intensity: the offender may be young and over-persuaded by the folly of someone else, or be a victim of his own foolish emotions and desires.

Penalties: Stated without sociological distinctions: suffering or fines graded open-endedly in direct ratio to the seriousness of the vice and its presumed curability. Psychic disorder thus becomes the single determinant of the severity or mildness of the penalty.[90]

Practically the entire self-help procedure against theft of Athenian law

---

[86] Cohen (1983) 49 n. 46.
[87] Obviously such offences had to be catered for somehow, perhaps by a *dikē* (or *graphē?*) *klopēs*, or by a *graphē klopēs dēmosiōn chrēmatōn*, independently of any *euthuna* (audit, scrutiny).
[88] Cohen's remark (1983, 122), about (E) public property, that 'no distinction is made . . . between theft by officials and theft by private citizens', though true, hardly matters, in view of (F).
[89] Not (*pace* Cohen (1983) 118 and 129) (B), which should not be 'read together' with (E), public property, as he suggests (121–2), in disregard of (D), private property.
[90] But *not* of the amount of the recompense, naturally.

is thrown overboard, and with it most of the differentiations of punishments depending on considerations of the hour and location of the theft, and the value of the stolen object.

E. *Serious* 'injustice' is displayed in theft from public sources. It is however not calculated by reference to the value of the theft. The main determinants of psychic state and hence of penalty are status-distinctions: slaves and foreigners who steal from public sources are 'probably' curable, but citizens are not.

Penalties: Slave and foreigner: suffering or fine calculated open-endedly. *Citizen:* death.

The law seems to cover all theft from public sources by all persons whatever. No separate provision is made for financial malfeasances of officials, but the law of (E) would justify or demand the death penalty at audit (see (F)). So whereas Attic law permitted death or fines for such official misconduct, probably according to procedure, Plato seems to permit, to judge from (E), only the former. *Eisangelia* is suppressed.

A. *Very serious* 'injustice' is exhibited in sacrilege; it is traced to an overpoweringly strong desire, which comes from some supernatural but not divine source. Elaborate advice based on religion, psychology, and medicine is given prophylactically.

Penalties: Slave and foreigner: branding and expulsion naked. *Citizen:* death, expulsion from state.

In (A), (C), and (E) the penalties are differentiated by socio-political groups; in (C) foreigners are bracketed with citizens as free, and are therefore not to suffer the degradation of a whipping, but with slaves in (A) and (E), in which the citizen is isolated as a particularly heinous offender against the gods and the state that nurtured him. There is a general tendency for incurability to be more readily assumed, and for penalties therefore to increase, in proportion to the grandeur of the interests offended: individuals (C and D), state (E and F), gods (A).[91]

Although the Attic penal code was certainly capable of distinguishing formally between voluntary and involuntary acts (e.g. in homicide), the law of theft, so far as we know, was framed without reference to intent; that is to say, it assumed that everyone knows roughly and intuitively what theft objectively is, and left the subjective elements, intentions and excuses, to be argued out in the speeches delivered at the trial.[92] In this

[91] Cf. 884a–885a. The open-endedness of some penalties, however, imports some uncertainty about what their application would have been in practice. Compare the tinge of uncertainty in (E) (*schedon*, 'pretty well' incurable, 942a3), with the confident inference in (A) (854e1).

[92] See Cohen (1983) 86–91. If, as he suggests (90), *AP* 52. 1 implies that thieves haled by *apagōgē* before the Eleven were killed if they merely admitted the objective act, even if they advanced apologies and excuses ('I genuinely but mistakenly thought the thing was mine', *vel sim.*), then in *apagōgē* 'objective liability' applied, and one would have to deny the deed itself to get a trial (so

respect it must have been typical of a great many offences; and indeed the lack of any reference to intent in any Athenian law of theft is natural enough: one can easily kill without wishing to, but if theft means something like 'stealthy removal of another's property', then it is difficult (but not impossible) to claim that one did *that* involuntarily (though one could plausibly claim to have acted on impulse, without premeditation). However that may be, Plato does for theft what in principle he does for his penal code as a whole: he provides an outline of the considerations jurymen should bear in mind in reaching verdicts and deciding sentences.[93] The discretion of Athenian jurymen to formulate their own criteria in such matters would have been far greater. Not that Plato is interested in excuses or aggravations as such, as a means of arriving at reciprocal justice; his sole concern, recompense apart, is to establish curability or incurability, and if the former applies, to estimate that punishment which will be the most effective cure. For efficient treatment of a disease demands its efficient diagnosis. Here as elsewhere his attention to mental states is in advance of Attic law: he builds them into his code.

Cohen rightly states Plato's position,[94] that 'the legislator's evaluation of an act must not be based upon external circumstances, but rather the moral state of the actor'. But he is quite wrong in supposing that this approach 'justifies the principle of uniform penalties', or 'one law, one penalty'. As my summary of Plato's law of theft shows, Plato applies, if anything, a more complicated, or rather a more flexible, range of penalties for theft than Attic law. His law is 'one' only in the sense that it provides for penalties in accordance with a single criterion: the relative intensity of the 'injustice' in the offender's soul.

Cohen also detects 'competing motivation',[95] in that Plato's 'philosophical theory' conflicts with his 'larger political concerns'. He claims 'clear inconsistency' between his penology and the provisions that 'two similarly situated offenders may meet with vastly different fates depending simply upon the fortuity of external circumstances; how much property they have, whether or not someone else is willing to lend

would it not always be denied?), or at least supply a *prima facie* title to the thing one is alleged to have stolen. (Objective liability would be appropriate to a procedure that obviously developed from self-help.) If that was indeed the practice, then Plato's apparent abolition of *apagōgē* for theft becomes the more significant: he is opposed to strict liability, precisely because it ignores calculation of states of mind.

[93] See especially 934bc (the closing remarks of (D)). Note too the brief assessment of an intention/state of mind at 874b8: the night-time entrant to a house is acting 'for purposes of (*epi*) theft'. The receiver of stolen goods must *know* them to have been stolen if he is to be punished as the thief is (955b; cf. Cohen (1983) 84–6).

[94] Cohen (1983) 119.

[95] Ibid. 119–20.

them the money,[96] whether or not they are let off by the injured party, etc.'. It is helpful here to remember Plato's firm distinction between backward-looking recompense and forward-looking curative penalty. If X is prepared to supply money to Y to enable Y to pay recompense, that is not a *penal* matter. Only if Y cannot pay a fine intended as a *penalty* would his bailing-out be inconsistent with Plato's penology, and then only if the bailing-out were a gift and not a loan.

Plato legislates for theft in a decidedly broken manner, for which the artistic structure of the *Laws* may in part be to blame. Naked, his scattered provisions are a puzzling and incongruous collection. Garbed in Plato's penology, and after the expulsion of the rogue law of (B), they are an impressive array, with a clear and consistent rationale. I find no sign that they were conceived and written by someone whose mental powers were failing. Plato the statesman and legislator is firmly in control, and knows exactly what he is doing. He takes Athenian law as basic; he excises, he supplements, he re-shapes; and he splices it to a reforming 'medical' penology. It is perhaps a tribute to the quality of the historical model that a philosopher of Plato's persuasion can see fit to retain many of its contours.

Appendix on the house-search (945a5–c2)

This passage describes the procedure for a 'house search'. If Y believes Z has an item of Y's property in Z's house, Y may demand that Z open his house for search. If Z refuses to open it (cf. Is. 6. 42), Y should 'go to law' and if Z is 'found guilty' he must pay as damages (*blabē*) double the value of the property as assessed by Y. This provision is naturally interpreted by Cohen ((1983) 129, cf. Glotz (1904) 206) to mean that Z is 'treated as a thief in accordance with the general penalty for theft of private property established in 857 [passage B]'. But it would be strange if that is all there is to it: is there no penalty for obstruction, the refusal to open up? In fact, the Greek seems to specify that it is this and this alone that is being punished: 'if [statement of offence, i.e. refusing to open up], then on a verdict of guilty, such and such a penalty'. At least part of the fine must be for obstruction (as at 844d, where he who causes damage to another, in defiance of an official's instructions, must pay the injured party double damages, 'not having obeyed the officials', i.e. precisely *for* not having obeyed). So it seems preferable to interpret the double damages in the house search in accordance with passage D: simple damages to the presumed owner to be paid by the presumed thief, plus as much again for obstruction and as 'cure'. At any rate, this passage is only hazardous support for the status of passage B as the genuine

---

[96] On bailing-out, see 855a ff. Unqualified 'letting-off' is however found only in (B).

Magnesian law of theft. Plato does not say whether, the house being searched with or without Z's consent, and the object being found, a further charge, of theft, would lie. If Z had not consented to the search, I would suppose not, since Y will already have retired with a profit; in that case would the search be made at all? On the house-search in Athenian law, see Harrison i (1968) 207.

12

IMPIETY

PLATO'S THEOLOGY

On a strict view, it is not possible to compare the Magnesian law of impiety with the Athenian. For to offend against the gods of Greek popular belief is to offend gods who were essentially human beings writ large. Although immortal and more powerful than we, they are subject to the same motivations and desires; they are sensitive to damage to their honour and interests, quick to make suffer those individuals and communities who offend them, and capable, like men, of being appeased by words and gifts. In particular, their devotion to justice in the world of men, and their exertions on its behalf, can not be relied upon. Platonic gods, by contrast, are wholly incorruptible. They supervise every detail of the world, and are unqualifiedly virtuous. As we saw,[1] in Plato's view the unjust man lives in a world so constructed that he makes his own hell; and one aspect of that hell is precisely the passion the gods have for virtue, and their zeal to punish vice—a punishment that cannot be evaded. At least in this life,[2] divine punishment, like punishment inflicted under the law, is benevolent: it is intended to make us morally better; to bribe the gods is therefore against our own interests. There is an alliance of kinship between gods and men, and the gods care for the world and its smallest parts. The wise man will attempt to imitate the gods, and make his own character like theirs.[3] The Platonic and Athenian laws of impiety are therefore based on radically different views of the nature of those beings against whom the impiety is committed, and therefore on radically different views of the nature of the offence itself.

It is worth contrasting briefly the position of Hesiod and Plato. According to Hesiod, Zeus' motivation in imposing justice on men is to

---

[1] Cf. pp. 150–2.

[2] See, however, ch. 6 on the apparent lack of 'cure' after death, at least in the *Laws*.

[3] This dogmatic summary needs considerable portions of the Platonic corpus to support it. Most of *Laws* 10 is essential, especially 885b and 899d–907c. Compare 715e ff., 803de, *Rep.* 613ab, *Th.* 176a ff. (modelling oneself on gods, and their virtue), *Rep.* 379a ff., *Phil.* 39e, *Tim.* 29e ff., *Phaed.* 247a (gods never a source of evil, only of good, and have no envy); Roloff (1970) 198–206, esp. 201 n. 12.

punish them, by making them work hard, and by ensuring that failure to work hard is in turn punished; Zeus is not a noticeably benevolent being. According to Plato, the gods rejoice at human virtue, because they are virtuous themselves; they are altogether warmer and closer[4] than Zeus, models of conduct rather than rods of chastisement. Both Plato and Hesiod give the gods a motive for the upholding of justice, but in radically different ways.

THE ATTIC LAW OF IMPIETY

The great bulk of the Athenian law of impiety, *asebeia*, concerned a wide variety of specific acts which were supposed to be disagreeable to the gods and which therefore ran the risk of attracting their retaliation on the offender and his society. The law was essentially prudential: it forbade the offending of gods much as it forbade the offending of human beings. When it forbade the advancing of certain opinions about the nature of the gods, it was simply to protect the fundamental popular conception of them as personal, offendable, and placable persons who, like men, could do great good or ill to those who pleased and displeased them—but not necessarily with a ruling passion for moral virtue. The focus of Plato's law of impiety is sharply and necessarily different. His prime concern is to ensure the 'happy' life of his citizens by ensuring that they lead a virtuous one; for on Socratic principles the virtuous life and the 'happy' life are the same. He therefore concentrates on a set of beliefs, and on certain practices, which tend to dissociate the gods from the protection of moral virtue, and to that extent to encourage vice and so inevitably promote 'unhappiness'. The intellectual content of the Magnesian law of impiety is therefore richer than that of the Athenian: it is a law which concerns bad opinions about certain elaborately argued theological matters, opinions which are the mainspring of bad actions;[5] it does not concern, or not primarily, bad actions themselves, which are catered for in other parts of the criminal code.[6] But both laws are fundamentally prudential, for both seek to maximize human good; and

---

[4] Note 716d: one should 'associate', *prosomilein*, with the gods, for nothing is more effective in securing the 'happy' life; cf. 888b, 907a2–3 (the gods are guardians of 'the greatest things for us'), 877e2 (wretchedness and impiety closely linked), 906a (gods are our 'allies' in the fight against evil). On gods as in some sense companions of men, see 653d, 665a, 666b, 796b–d.

[5] 907c2–3.

[6] Both Plato and the orators are of course capable of denouncing as 'impious', *asebē*, offences which fall under other headings and are not covered by the law of impiety as such (869b, 871d, 941a, Ant. 5. 88). That is natural enough in societies in which the gods were supposed to enter into all departments of life. Cf. too my remarks on the didactic manner in which Plato 'distributes' the notions of *hubris* and *hierosulia* in his code (pp. 270–1 and 287 n. 35).

Plato presents his law as more efficient in promoting it, since it is based on philosophically establishable truths about the gods.

This change of emphasis becomes evident from the merest glance at the Attic laws of impiety. The specific acts forbidden by them were many and various; and the procedures and penalties were accordingly numerous. The offences known to us may be summarized as follows.[7]

1. Infractions of religious ritual and procedure.
2. Insulting, damaging or otherwise unseemly behaviour in relation to the gods, their temples and property, or their images.
3. Revealing the 'mysteries' of certain cults.
4. Entering holy places when polluted or in a state of *atimia*.
5. Introducing into the state and worshipping new or foreign divinities.[8]
6. Atheism, and the propagation of doctrines concerning the heavenly bodies.

The coverage of these offences in the *Laws* is extremely selective. (1)–(5) are treated cursorily or not at all; but (6) is set out at enormous length.[9]

THE MAGNESIAN LAW OF IMPIETY

Of (1) and (2) Plato says nothing; but given that Magnesia has a considerable *Apparat* of priests etc., and a full programme of religious ceremonies, it is a safe bet that elaborate rules of procedure and behaviour, and appropriate penalties for infractions, would have existed. Perhaps mercifully, Plato has not bothered to describe them.[10] The nearest he comes to legislating on such matters is his firm provision that the dancing and singing at each religious festival should be unalterable: the Magnesians must decide which kinds of songs and dances are appropriate to which gods, and then never change them. Anyone who introduces different songs and dances at any festival must be expelled from it; and if he resists expulsion he is to be liable to a charge of impiety for the rest of his life, at the hands of anyone who wishes; no penalty is

---

[7] It is uncertain just how extensive and specific the laws of impiety were: see Rudhardt (1960), sensibly modified by MacDowell (1978) 199–200, and cf. Ostwald (1986) 535. Sources in Lipsius (1905–15) 358–68; brief review: MacDowell (1978) 192 ff. For comparisons of Attic and Magnesian law, see Morrow (1960) 470 ff., Reverdin (1945) 208 ff., Gernet (1951) pp. cxcii ff. Robbery from temples, *hierosulia*, is separate from the law of impiety, both in Athenian and in Magnesian law.

[8] Derenne (1930) 224 ff., Reverdin (1945) 211 ff., Rudhardt (1960) 92–3; cf. Morrow (1960) 493–4.

[9] Plato also devotes much attention to 'magic', as an offence originating in impious opinion (see below); but whether Attic law treated magic formally as impiety is not clear: see p. 322.

[10] 804a, 828b. At 941a offenders in diplomatic matters are said to be impious; but the *charge* against them would presumably be of *parapresbeia*, 'false embassy'.

stated.[11] This law is thoroughly Platonic: it springs from an extreme regard for the educational influence of doctrinal and artistic orthodoxy;[12] but since an unresisting offender is apparently not prosecuted, it looks as if the impiety consists simply in the resistance to expulsion. At any rate, it is significant that it is only in connection with a breach of artistic standards that Plato troubles to produce a law of impiety relating to conduct at religious festivals.

As to (3), it is wholly unlikely that mystery-religions will exist in Magnesia: with few exceptions, religious ceremonies are public.[13] (5) too is ruled out: the chances of any foreign gods being introduced are slender indeed, since the access of the Magnesians to the outside world is strictly controlled, and on their return they are carefully vetted for any undesirable ideas they may have picked up.[14]

The prominence of pollution in Plato's code, especially in the homicide law, entails that prosecutions for (4) are envisaged. But the involuntary murderer who incurs pollution by entering temples is to be prosecuted not for impiety but for murder,[15] and in certain connected cases the charge may indeed be of impiety but is left unspecified.[16] In murder in anger, however, the murderer who has killed a member of his own family and on return from exile associates with its surviving members is (with them, apparently) liable to a charge of *asebeia*.[17] With this one exception his homicide laws do not explicitly embrace laws against impiety.[18] Nor does his code contain laws of impiety relating to breaches of *atimia*.

So in regard to offences in the categories (1)–(5), the *Laws*, for diverse reasons, makes a meagre showing. The weight of Plato's attention to impiety falls on the Magnesian counterpart to (6), the Attic law against heresies.

THE ATHENIAN 'HERESY' LAW

At least some of the prosecutions of Socrates and other 'intellectuals' for impiety seem to have taken place under legislation originating in the

---

[11] 799ab, 800a ff., cf. 829c–e.

[12] Further elucidation in Morrow (1960) 354 ff., who suggests (475) Dem. 21. 51 as an analogy; the two cases do indeed have in common disrespect to an official, but the causes and circumstances are very different.

[13] 828a ff. describes Magnesian worship. The prohibition of private rites is at 909d ff.

[14] 742b, 950d ff., esp. 952b–d. Presumably resident aliens will have to be allowed their own cults, as in Athens (Whitehead (1977) 86–9), but in what would have been the appropriate passage (850d ff.) Plato says nothing at all on the matter.   [15] 866a.

[16] 868b, 871b.   [17] 868d–869a; the penalties are not stated; see homicide p. 229.

[18] 871d, however, if I interpret it aright, says that it would be impious to bury a voluntary killer in Magnesia; but nothing is said about a charge. At 869b the killer of a parent in anger is apparently subject to charges of murder, assault, impiety and sacrilege, all rolled up together.

'decree of Diopeithes', which probably dates from the early 430s and may have been recast later in the century in the shape of a regular *graphē asebeias*, suit for impiety.[19] According to Plutarch,[20] the decree provided, vaguely enough, that 'those who do not recognize the divine things, or who teach doctrines about the things in the sky' should be impeached (*eisangellesthai*). To judge from the accounts of the individual cases, the penalty was assessed by the court; instances of fines, exile and death are reported.[21]

The purpose of the decree and of any other legislation of a similar kind, was presumably not merely to discourage statements likely to irritate the gods and provoke their wrath against the community, but to protect the popular conception of them. For if they do not exist,[22] then they cannot receive our prayers and sacrifices, and we cannot be benefited by them; so too if the heavenly bodies are interpreted as material objects subject to merely natural forces rather than as personal beings. Thus far, Plato's law against impiety may have had solid Athenian antecedents;[23] for he too wishes to suppress expressions of atheism and of mere mechanical explanations of the working of the heavens.

A. THE MAGNESIAN 'HERESY' LAW

Just after the beginning of book 10 the Athenian says:[24]

No one who believes in gods as the law directs ever voluntarily commits an unholy act or lets any lawless word pass his lips. If he does, it is because of one of three possible misapprehensions: either, as I said, he believes (1) the gods do not exist, or (2) that they exist but take no thought for the human race, or (3) that they are influenced by sacrifices and supplications and can easily be won over.

The refutation of these three heresies then occupies most of the book, until we reach the formal statement of the law.[25]

The law, which is explicitly said to be 'of impiety', is long and discursively written. It is rich in penological interest, and presents ten

[19] On the date, see Frost (1964). Derenne's (1930) book is still the best starting-point for a study of these prosecutions (his discussion of Plato's law (248–52) is, however, brief); cf. Reverdin (1945) 208 ff., Rudhardt (1960) 90 ff., Ostwald (1986) 196–8, 274 ff., cf. 528–36. No such legislation is known in other states. Some considerable scepticism about the whole tradition is possible: see Dover (1976).   [20] *Per.* 32. 1; Diod. Sic. 12. 39.

[21] Derenne (1930) 244, Diog. Laert. 2. 12, 9. 51–2, and especially Plato *Ap.* 37bc. On the political aspects of these cases, see Ostwald (1986) 196–8.

[22] *Nomizein*, 'recognize', in Diopeithes' decree is a 'weasel' word covering both 'observe' (cult-practices) and 'acknowledge' (existence of something). See Fahr's (1969) extensive review of the evidence, esp. 158 ff., *contra* Derenne (1930) 217 ff.   [23] Cf. Cohen (1988).

[24] 885b. There is a rapid summary at 909b1 (where I retain μή).

[25] 907d ff.; the refutation constitutes its 'preface'; cf. 887a–c.

problems, most of them major, which I shall set out in full; not all of them are soluble.[26] Like the decree of Diopeithes, Plato's legislation is (I shall argue) realistic, in being directed not against the mere holding of heretical opinions *in petto*,[27] or even at their casual expression, but at their propagation. Clearly only one of the three heresies may be maintained by any one person at one time, for each logically excludes the other two; and at first sight, at least, it seems that for the purpose of calculating penalties it does not matter which heresy the heretic advances. What matters is the *damage* he does to others,[28] by converting them to his own opinions. In a certain way, the law of heresy is a species of the law of damage. But in what sense does converting someone to a heresy damage him? No doubt gods dislike heretics, the holders of false opinions about themselves: but Plato has a deeper point than that. To the extent that to believe any one of the three heresies is to believe in the possibility of committing injustice without detriment to the quality of one's life, the holding of a heresy constitutes 'damage'; for the heretic creates his own misery, by being unjust and so unfitting himself for his total social environment, which includes the gods, who turn away from him, just as his fellow-men do. The more firmly a man is converted to a heresy, the more damage he will proceed to attract to himself. Therefore the more *persuasive* the converter is in converting others to his heresy, the more damage he inflicts on them. What then becomes important in assessing a heretic's punishment is not the heresy itself, but his persuasiveness; and his persuasiveness is a function of his character, his intellect, his mastery of the arts of speech, and the seductive practices in which he expresses his beliefs and reinforces them in other people. If therefore his character and beliefs can be changed—if, that is, he can be 'cured'—he will cease to be a danger to society.

It is in accordance with such social and psychological considerations that Plato distinguishes two classes of heretic.[29] The first has a naturally just character, hates scoundrels, and lives an upright life; he holds his heresy because of foolishness; he will be utterly frank in his conversation about gods and sacrifices and oaths, and by poking fun at other people will probably make converts,[30] if he does not meet with punishment (*dikē*).[31] The second, by contrast, lacks control over his pleasures and

---

[26] There is a detailed and careful but strikingly complex analysis of the law in Wyller (1957). My interpretation of its structure differs somewhat from his, and indeed from certain features of the usual view, particularly in connection with problem 1.   [27] Cf. Wyller (1957) 298.

[28] 908c4–6, e3–5; cf. 890b1–2 and, the even stronger language at 909b5–6 (and in a different matter, 958c). See Rudhardt (1960) 103–4, Reverdin (1945) 220–1, on the way other crimes were *linked* with charges of impiety as such in Attic practice. As in Plato, impiety was thought to lead to other crimes, which then also became evidence for it.

[29] The first: 908b4–c1, c6–d1, e5–6; the second, at rather greater length: 908c1–4, d1–7, 909a8–b6.
[30] Cf. 891d2.   [31] Cf. 728bc.

pains; he has a powerful memory and is a shrewd learner; he has 'so-called natural gifts',[32] and is full of deceit and guile. From such people come seers who are keen on hocus-pocus, tyrants, demagogues, generals, plotters in private rites, and tricks of 'so-called sophists' ('wise men', literally). They are dissemblers; they are 'beast-like', they despise men, and bewitch many of the living; and by claiming to bewitch the dead and by promising to persuade the gods, alleging powers of sorcery through sacrifices, prayers, and charms, they try to wreck individuals, whole houses, and states for the sake of money.

This impassioned outburst, which recalls a celebrated passage in the *Republic*,[33] is an *omnium gatherum* of Plato's *bêtes noires*, and includes several categories of persons who will not exist in Magnesia. Presumably Plato is simply calling attention to what heresy can lead to,[34] in certain sorts of person with certain sorts of natural gifts; let the Magnesians beware. This consideration may explain two minor curiosities of Plato's exposition: the first account of the second class of heretics occurs in a description of atheists,[35] yet the heresy they chiefly employ, the third, is incompatible with atheism; and the third description[36] of them says paradoxically that in addition to holding one or other of the three heresies, including plain atheism, they promise 'to persuade the gods'. It seems that Plato's preoccupation with the third heresy, which is the worst and most impious of all,[37] that the gods are bribable, has run away with him. Or do the atheists *conceal* their view (see problem 3 below)?

Problem 1. Plato's *animus* against heretics also makes it difficult to see how far the apparent distinction between (i) holding and propagating heresies and (ii) acting on them, is functional in the law. The text has three sections.

A. 907d7–908d7. Procedure in case of impiety 'in word or deed'. Description of character of the two kinds of heretics, the 'just' and the

---

[32] 908d2, *euphuēs*, not *eutuchēs*, 'fortunate, blessed', *pace* Wyller (1957) 294 n. 1: cf. *Rep.* 365a, in a similar connection.   [33] 364b–e; cf. Reverdin (1945) 226.

[34] Note 908d3 ἐξ ὧν, d5 ἐξ αὐτῶν ἔστιν ὅτε, 909a8 ff. 'they *become* beastlike *by* certain practices' which are firmly distinct (πρός, 909b1) from the heresies themselves. Note too the political flavour of the list. For the political motivation of prosecution for impiety in Athens, see Morrow (1960) 473–4. Briefly, the difference between Athens and Magnesia in this respect is that in Athens the impiety law could be *exploited* for political and factional purposes, whereas in Magnesia, where factions will hardly exist, impiety is itself an offence with political implications: it breaks up the 'body politic' by encouraging fatal and socially destructive moral beliefs, and in particular by fostering precisely the kind of person who will resort to factional politics—demagogues etc. For the kind of political assumptions to which impiety leads, see 889e–890a. As Dodds notes (1951, 222), more than 'minor charlatans' are in question (and more even than the 'unlicensed' private practitioners of ritual purification, who are his own suggestion).

[35] 908b4 ff., esp. 908d1–2: they hold 'the same beliefs' (i.e. atheism) as the first type.
[36] 909a8 ff.   [37] 907b.

'dissembling', culminating in the list of occupations and activities to which the latter give rise (magicianship etc.).

B. *908d7–909d2*. The penalties (imprisonment) for heresy, again with an extended description of the dissemblers: in addition to their heresies, they become 'beastlike' by (*inter alia*) professing to influence gods, and try to destroy whole cities for money.

C. *909d3–910d4*. Penalties (in *no* case imprisonment) for founding private shrines, introduced as measures to check impiety 'in word and deed'. Similarly, in book 11, magicians etc. are punished, but *not* by imprisonment, nor, so far as the text goes, for impiety as such.[38]

Now clearly the penalties in (C), which are for specific actions, cannot be inflicted simultaneously on someone already being punished under the provisions of (B). In spite of the polar cliché 'words and deeds', it therefore looks as if (A) and (B) refer to the heretics' character, belief, and speech only. (A), however, develops the theme of what heretics can turn into. (B), as a close inspection of the text shows, confines itself, the penalties apart, almost wholly to a description of the heretics' assertions, attitudes, policies and general tendencies;[39] but here again there is a (brief) description of their actions: 'they destroy whole cities for the sake of money'. I suggest that, *juridically and penologically*, (A) and (B) deal only with heretical belief and speech, and the character and outlook of the heretics. The concrete offences stimulated by those beliefs and words are indeed mentioned in (A) and (B), but dealt with in (C), under legislation which is separate and distinct.

Problem 2 concerns the precise number of categories of heretics functional in the law. Plato initially distinguishes six: two categories of heretics, the amiable and vicious, each of whom may hold any one of the three heresies.[40] These six need '*dikē* which is neither equal nor similar'. This sixfold analysis is, however, overtaken a little later[41] in the prescription of penalties, which relies exclusively on the two-fold distinction. It is possible that, if the third heresy (that gods are bribable) is the worst of all,[42] simple atheism would attract the full five years in prison, the second heresy (say) six years, and the third (say) seven years. But that still yields only four categories, as the vicious, clever heretics are in all cases, whatever their heresy, imprisoned for life. Though carefully drawn, the sixfold classification seems to be without penological effect.[43]

[38] 932e ff., discussed in more detail below.
[39] 909b2: they 'despise', 'charm' (their hearers), 'claim', 'promise . . . on the grounds that . .'.
[40] 908a7–b4.　　　　　　　　　[41] 908d7 ff.　　　　　　　　　[42] 907b, cf. 948c.
[43] See further Morrow (1960) 490–1. Wyller's (1957) diagram (307) is wildly misleading: 'Magiker' would never be admitted to the reform prison (*sōphronistērion*), which is to house the amiable, *just* heretics.

Problem 3 is the precise meaning of 'dissembling', *eirōnikon*, in the description of the second class of heretic.[44] It surely amounts to more than mock-modesty. The point lies in the contrast with the 'frankness' (*parrhēsia*) of the first. A convert of the first knows what he is being converted to, but a convert to the second does not; for the converter dresses up the heresy in some form of plausible reasoning which makes it look like intellectual sense and religious orthodoxy; the convert is 'played for a sucker', contemptuously.[45] For instance, a priest can persuade one that to try to 'square' a god by a gift or sacrifice is fair and reasonable *and pious*—whereas of course the concealed assumptions of the argument are, on Plato's view, flatly impious. So 'ironic' means here, I suggest, 'arguing one's case tricksily, unfrankly, dissemblingly': the speaker knows perfectly well that bribing the gods is an act of impiety.[46]

Problem 4. Some of the dissembling heretics engage in *psuchagōgia*, 'soul-leading' or 'bewitchment' of the dead, and perform sacrifices etc. for pay; in other words, in addition to propagating heresy, they put it into practice in order to find money with which to gratify the appetites they cannot control.[47] What exactly are these rites, incantations, etc.? The mention of 'soul-leading the dead' suggests strongly that what Plato has in mind includes at least the 'bindings' by which one may seek to harm another by harnessing a dead person's resentments.[48] His disapproval of this belief and practice generates a dilemma for him, as we shall see.[49]

(a) Magnesian re-education

Both heretics, the foolish and the clever, are to be imprisoned.[50] The foolish is evidently curable, given time and trouble: he is to be sent for a period of at least five years[51] to the 'reform centre' or 'sound-mind centre' (*sōphronistērion*) which is situated near the meeting-place of the Nocturnal Council. During this period he must meet no one except that Council's members. At the end of the imprisonment, if he seems 'to be sound of mind' (*sōphronein*), he should live with others who are 'sound of mind'; if not, and he is convicted again on such a charge, he must be punished by death.

---

[44] 908e2.

[45] Cf. *kataphronountes* (909b2) with Arist. *Rhet.* 1379^{b}31: *kataphronētikon eirōneia*, 'irony is something that shows contempt'.

[46] Cf. *Soph.* 268a, where the more intelligent ironists are uneasily aware of the dialectical frailty of what they put forward so confidently, and Vlastos (1987), esp. 80.

[47] 909b6, which I take to be implicitly connected with 908c2–3.

[48] See p. 62.   [49] See under 'poisoning', pp. 320–3 below.

[50] On the legal procedure, see Morrow (1960) 488.   [51] 908e ff.

Problem 5 is Plato's confusing way of wording the provisions for release. 'If' and 'if not' read as if they refer to the same point in time, i.e. when the possibility of release arises. But that can hardly be; for obviously 'such a charge' can occur only in society, *after* release. Hence 'if' implies: 'but if he does *not* seem to be of sound mind, he is not released'; in effect his sentence, subject to the minimum period stipulated initially, was an 'indefinite' one, terminable not by a decision of a court but at the discretion of officials. 'If not' will mean, 'if the appearance of soundness of mind proves (after release) to have been deceptive'. The heretic, though released, is on probation.

Problem 6 is what actually happens to the curable heretic while in the 'sound-mind centre'. Plato speaks of 'his bonds' (*desmoi*);[52] this term may indicate that in addition to being incarcerated the heretic is also chained; but it may only be another way of saying merely that he is kept in prison (*desmōtērion*). The stipulation that no citizen (apart from members of the Nocturnal Council) is to associate with him presumably protects the general public from exposure to his heresies, but allows slaves (and doubtfully foreigners) to act as warders and give him food.[53] Presumably also he may not meet even his fellow-heretics—for such contacts would generate fellow-feeling and tend to confirm them in their heresies. At any rate, Plato says that only members[54] of the Nocturnal Council may come together with them, 'associating (*homilountes*) with them for the purpose of admonition (*nouthetēsis*)[55] and the safety of the soul (*sōtēria tēs psuchēs*)'. Now Plato is very keen on the formative power of association: by mixing with good men one tends to become good oneself; by *homilia* with X one becomes *like* (*homoiousthai*) X.[56] So under the psychological pressure, isolation from society, and by associating with such sterling characters as members of the Nocturnal Council, and with them alone, the heretic is likely to be improved morally. That is to say, his punishment is *dikē*, not *timōria*,[57] for instead of suffering the *timōria* of wrongdoing, which is to associate with bad men and become like them and so 'unhappy,' he is *forced* to associate with good men. The 'compelling' and the 'teaching' element in punishment thus far go hand in hand.[58]

But clearly an intellectual and persuasive element comes into play in addition; for as Wyller well points out,[59] *nouthetēsis* means literally the 'placing' or 'implanting' of mind or sense or reason, *nous*. Are the heretics treated to five years of Platonic theology? If so, how? The

[52] 909a5–6, cf. 908a1, e3.
[53] 909a3–4; cf. c2, of the heinous heretics.
[54] But 909a4 *koinōnountes*, 'sharers in', perhaps would not preclude trusted agents who were not actually members of the Council: cf. 951e ff.
[55] Cf. 908e3.
[56] e.g. 728bc, 854bc, 904d, cf. *Th.* 176a ff.
[57] 908d1.
[58] 862d.
[59] Wyller (1957) 311, referring also to 888a1–2.

members of the Council are certainly supposed to master theology,[60] and no doubt their dialectic would be more than a match for 'foolish' heretics. Would they base their instruction on readings from *Laws* 10? Certainly Plato seems to commend the *Laws* as suitable for educating the young, or at any rate its content, and at any rate down as far as a certain point in book 7.[61] It is useless to speculate further; but five years of re-education will have to consist of *something* systematically intel-lectual;[62] retraining of the emotions is hardly called for, since these offenders already hate the bad and love the just.[63]

The expression 'for the safety of the soul' is striking, for we seem now to be concerned not with the effect of his heresy on the heretic's fellow-men, but simply with the state of his own soul. A 'safe' soul, that is in the context one with correct theological opinions, is of course a 'happy' one, on Socratic principles. But the social dimension rapidly reasserts itself: an unsafe soul is unsafe for society, and recidivism attracts the death penalty. It is not only, nor even primarily, for his own sake that the heretic's soul is to be made 'safe'.

This is a remarkable piece of legislation, sharply different from anything in Athens. Plato is prepared to require high-ranking officials to spend five years—at least five years, in fact—on reintegrating somewhat foolish persons into society.[64] Unlike the Athenian law of impiety, Magnesian law formally distinguishes characters and states of mind, with the result that at least some, perhaps even most, offenders are not subjected to the sharply more severe penalty inflicted on the other heretics (for which see below); recidivism, however, is treated harshly. No doubt a successfully cured heretic would do the cause of religion in Magnesia great good; and in any case we have noticed in other parts of the code Plato's tendency to create whole categories of offenders who can after a time be reabsorbed into society; and for this he has social, political, and economic motives.[65] But although he sets out his categories of heretics in psychological terms, we notice that his assessment of curability here as elsewhere is crucially affected by his assessment of the harm done: relatively trivial harm is done by the curable heretic, but very

[60] 966c ff.

[61] See 811c–e. Not for nothing, after all, do some religious orders require edifying literature to be read to them during their communal meals.

[62] Some astronomy perhaps, as conducive to piety? See not only book 10 in general, but 821a ff. and 967a ff. (in contrast to the decree of Diopeithes).

[63] Cf. 907c6–7 and 908b5–c1 with 862d7–8.

[64] Nothing, however, is said about the *frequency* of the sessions spent with the members of the Nocturnal Council. And are they to be held throughout the period of incarceration, or for only part of it? At 919e–920a binding or imprisonment is used again, as a penalty for a citizen who follows an unworthy occupation (retail trade); but nothing is said about instruction or reform. Conceivably enforced abstention from such activity is intended to be habit-forming.

[65] See notably on homicide in anger, 'diminished' theft, etc.

grave harm is done by the incurable: act for act, those of the latter are more damaging than those of the former. He seems to assume that really serious damage can only be caused by really serious, i.e. incurable, psychic vice.

(b) The heinous heretics

Heretics of the second class, the 'beast-like' ones, are to be sentenced to imprisonment for life in a prison whose name is to be suggestive of *timōria*, in a spot where the terrain is at its wildest.[66] No free man is to approach them, and they are to receive their ration of food from slaves; at death their bodies are to be cast out (out of Magnesia, presumably) unburied. This final point recalls the penalties imposed on voluntary killers and temple-robbers;[67] and these heretics are ejected from society, not only after death, but before it, since from the date of their conviction their children must be treated as orphans.

Problem 7. One wonders why these more heinous heretics, who are dominated by 'pleasures and pains', are not simply executed, for they seem to be incurable; at any rate no attempt is made to cure them.[68] The very name of their prison shows that they are not to undergo the curative *dikē* undergone by the other heretics.[69] Perhaps Plato is content to use them as 'examples' or lessons, *paradeigmata*, to others, in spite of their being out of sight.[70] On the other hand the very fact that they are not executed suggests that they are in principle curable; but does Plato fear that, if an attempt at cure were made, the dialectic of the Nocturnal Council would not be proof against the intellectual sharpness of the prisoners? Or that some of these heretics do after all believe in gods, and are therefore not beyond hope? Or that they have not actually *done* anything except speak? Does Plato believe that mental states are accurately assessable only by reference to *acts*?[71]

---

[66] 908a, 909bc; cf. 766a. A 'wild' terrain is crime-specifically suitable for 'beast-like' persons; and their being 'bound' at 909c1 *may* indicate that they are to be 'chained up' or 'tied up' like animals (but the just heretics are also 'bound', 908a1, e3, 909a5–6).

[67] 871d, 873b, 854e–855a.

[68] 908c3; they deserve to die many deaths (908e), which on the principles of 862e–863a and 957e–958a betokens incurability. (But I have heard it suggested that, if death is 'the smallest of evils' (854e, cf. 862e), to be kept alive in physical and spiritual misery may be intended to be an extremely severe *retributive* punishment.)

[69] 728bc, 908a6–7, d1.   [70] Cf. 854e–855a.

[71] In that case, 'errors worthy of not one but two deaths' at 908e1 will have to mean *intellectual* errors and their 'ironical' propagation, not actual offences, e.g. the founding of private shrines.

(c) Private shrines

Immediately after stating provisions for the 'orphans' of heretics in the second (clever) class, Plato, with apparent reference to both[72] classes, states a 'common' law for them which will have the effect, he says, of reducing offences against the gods by word and deed, and in particular of making them less witless (*anoētous*), 'owing to its not being permitted to engage in religious practices (*theopolein*) against the law'.[73] The law seems, then, to rely on the power of habit: by observing it, heretics grow less heretical.[74] It provides simply that no one is to possess shrines in private houses; all worship must be public.[75] The reason is that religion is a difficult thing to get right, and it is undesirable that shrines should be founded all over the place, in an impulsive manner, by persons who wish to thank or supplicate the gods for some benefit, or in some fear arising from a vision in sleep.[76] These practices are undesirable, one supposes, because they encourage a 'commercial',[77] *do ut des* relationship with the gods; for dealings with them become *ex opere operato*, divorced from considerations of 'virtue' and real desert.

Plato now says:[78] 'Because of/for the sake of (*heneka*) *all* (reasons? people?) one must act in accordance with the law now stated; and in addition to *these* (reasons? people?) because of/for the sake of those who are impious, in order that [. . .] they may not bring reproaches/charges (*enklēmata*)[79] from the gods both on themselves and on those who let them (*sc.* 'act', 'go unpunished?'), who are better than they, so that the whole city catches the infection[80] of their impious actions.' The missing material indicated in the square bracket consists of four participial clauses which describe *how* the 'impious' draw divine reproach on themselves etc.:

(i) by 'secreting these things too,' in their actions;

(ii) by founding shrines and altars in private dwellings;

---

[72] 909d3, 7: 'all' heretics, i.e. all those who hold the third heresy, that gods are bribable (Morrow (1960) 492 n. 278).

[73] 909d3-7.

[74] Even those in prison? For there they will have no chance to engage in illegal religious activities.

[75] 909d7-e2. As Morrow (1960, 463) says, the prohibition of private shrines does not exclude the worship of ancestral gods (forbears?) within the household: 717b, cf. Reverdin (1945) 230-1.

[76] 909e3-910a6.

[77] *Eu.* 14e; cf. 885d: 'we do wrong first and try to put it right later' (i.e. try to persuade the gods to turn a blind eye).

[78] 910a6-b6.

[79] This word is rather mild; so too the 'blame' which the god will not level at the legislator (910b). Contrast the *timōria* the gods are supposed to want at Lys. 6. 13 (cf. Dem. 59. 109). In Plato, do the gods react to impiety more in sorrow than in anger?

[80] On *apolauō* here in a medical sense, see Saunders (1972) note 100; cf. *nosos* 888b8. *Pathos* 900b3 and 908c5 (cf. *paschōn* 885b6) probably has a medical flavour, but it is impossible to be sure.

(iii) by intending secretly to make the gods propitious by sacrifices and prayers;

(iv) by [thus?] increasing their injustice to infinity.

I am inclined to treat 'all' and 'these' as *reasons*, rather than people, since otherwise we would seem to have a contrast between the people who impulsively found shrines, and the impious; but those impulsive people too are, presumably, impious themselves, if only slightly; moreover the impious too found shrines. So I take the whole passage[81] to describe the impious as a class, including the impulsive persons.

(i)–(iii) obviously describe actions: the impious are not now simply propagating their heresies, but putting them into practice. In (i), 'these things too' probably refers, as England says, to *asebēmata*, 'acts' of impiety;[82] 'too' means 'in addition to their opinions.' We saw that the heretics of the second class were 'ironic' or 'dissembling', concealing their real opinions under a cloak of piety; and this concealment of opinion is now paralleled by the concealment of practices in private homes. In (iv), what was the injustice before it was infinite? Surely it was simply to *speak* heresy; but to *apply* it by founding private shrine is 'injustice' on an 'infinite' scale. Whether the 'injustice' refers to the psychic state of the agents, or simply to the quality of their actions, is however not clear.

If this reasoning is right, the two penalties of imprisonment described above apply only to heretics who disseminate heresy, however serious that heresy is, and however corrupt the character of the disseminators. Simply stating impious opinions does not argue for incurability: only impious actions do that, and even then not all of them, as shown by the two regulations that follow.[83]

1. Possession of and worshipping at private shrines, if the possessor does no great act of impiety, must be reported[84] to the Guardians of the Laws, who should give orders for the private shrines to be removed to public places/temples; cases of disobedience are to be punished till the shrines are so removed. (The punishments are not further specified; fines seem likely.)

2. If someone is found to have committed an act of impiety which is typical not of children but of adults, either by founding a shrine on private property/or by sacrificing to 'whatever gods'[85] in public places/

---

[81] 909e3–910b6.   [82] England (1921) on 910b1, pointing to *asebēma* in c7.

[83] 910b8 till the end of book 10.

[84] εἰσαγγελλέτω 910c4: *pace* Morrow (1960) 488 n. 269, I doubt if this intended to suggest the Attic procedure of *eisangelia*. Initially, all the Guardians do is to try to shift the shrines; only in case of disobedience do formal legal procedures come into play. Cf. Piérart (1973 a) 451–2, Reverdin (1945) 228 n. 2, Gernet (1951) p. cxxxvi n. 1.

[85] 910c8–d1, θεοῖς οἱστιαινοῦν, which comes in suddenly and suprisingly. What does the expression mean? To sacrifice to the approved Magnesian gods would hardly be an offence, unless it

shrines, he must be punished by death, as sacrificing in a state of pollution,[86] and the Guardians are to judge whether the offence was 'childish' or not, before taking the matter to court 'in the light of their decision.'[87]

Problem 8 is to know whether these two categories of offenders precisely reproduce the two categories of heretics. I think not. Certainly I take it that the impulsive founders of shrines[88] and the 'childish' worshippers at them[89] are the same people; but neither of them are the same people as the 'frank' heretics, who seem to have dropped out of sight; for they could hardly 'scoff at'[90] others' religion and found shrines themselves. Rather they are ordinary gullible men or women in the street, without intellectual pretensions, as distinct from the committers of 'great'[91] unholy acts, whom I suppose to be both the clever, dissembling heretics[92] and those who persistently and wholeheartedly accept their teaching and patronize their practices. The sharpness of the distinction between the childish offenders and the others is noticeable; and it seems to be psychological, in that the lesser offenders seem to be witless rather than ill-intentioned. At all events, they are punished only if they *resist* the removal of their private shrines. The heinous heretics, by contrast, who take the initiative in these offences, are executed. The distinctions between the two sets of offenders here, and between the two sets of heretics, therefore seem not to be on all fours.

The law forbidding private shrines rests upon the belief that such unregulated worship not only constitutes a focus of religious loyalty rivalling and therefore weakening the official state cults,[93] but encourages the 'commercial' view of relations with the gods. The law is largely a Platonic innovation.[94]

---

were done with the wrong intentions or manner or state of mind, i.e. 'heretically'. Plato probably means that; but he may also be indicating that the interdiction of private shrines is also an interdiction of foreign cults.

[86] *Pace* Dodds (1951, 235 n. 87) more than mere 'ritual' is at stake here: such offences would hardly attract the death penalty. The pollution lies in approaching the gods in a deeply offensive manner, i.e. by ritual constructed on the assumption of their venality.

[87] This seems to be the force of οὕτως, 910d3; 'accordingly', says England (1921) ad loc. The procedural point, however, is not clear: perhaps it is that only if the Guardians decide the offence is *not* childish does it go before the Court for Capital Offences (855c ff.). For acts done 'childishly' (and under pressure), cf. 934a2.

[88] 909e5 ff.

[89] 910c2 ff.

[90] 908c8.

[91] 910c2; what these acts are is not clear—perhaps 'plotting in sacred rites' (see 908d6), with political implications?

[92] Observe the similarity between 909b3-4 and 910b3.

[93] A focus that is, moreover, out of sight, 910b2; cf. Plato's desire to 'flush out' women from their homes, 780a ff., and note the special mention of women at 909e.

[94] 'Largely', because of p. 303 (5). If Plato's indignant description of the frequency with which private shrines were founded is even half true, it is a good indication that in Athens, at any rate, the practice was unregulated by law.

SUBSIDIARY LEGISLATION

In the impiety law as a whole we find two further laws:

1. Anyone who comes across impiety in word or deed is to report it to officials, and the first officials to hear of it are to bring the matter to the relevant court. Any official who has heard of it and fails to act thus, is to be liable to a charge of impiety at the hands of anyone who wishes to *timōrein* on behalf of the laws. No penalty is stated.[95]

Plato relies on private informers, but requires that prosecutions be brought by officials, possibly as a means of filtering out prosecutions of a trivial or spiteful kind. Nothing is said to indicate that failure to inform is actionable; but failure to act on the part of an official is open to remedy by anyone. The regulation shows the same anxiety as Plato has in the homicide law and elsewhere, to ensure that crime should not go unpunished because of a lack of zeal to prosecute it.[96]

2. Heretics of the second kind, when they die, are to be expelled unburied. If any free man helps to bury such a heretic, he is to be liable to charges of impiety at the hand of whoever wishes. No penalty is stated.[97]

'Free man' presumably includes a foreigner. The insulation of these heretics from anyone but slaves is obviously intended to prevent their beliefs spreading, and could no doubt be justified also on grounds of pollution, though nothing is said about that. When it comes to burial, however, no other reason can apply—though again Plato is silent on the point. Pollution is very much under the control of the state: it conveniently stops with the slaves who (we suppose) are to eject the body, and does not affect the free men who come into contact with *them*.

Both regulations spring from Plato's characteristic concerns, and neither has an Athenian counterpart. One wonders what the Magnesian penalties would be—hardly imprisonment?

CONCLUSION

Plato's law of impiety is a highly distinctive product of his theology. He acts within the tradition of Athenian anti-intellectual impiety legislation,

---

[95] 907de.

[96] Cf. Reverdin (1945) 217, who speaks of the absence in Athens of 'répression systématique du délit.' In Magnesia, one should always remember the young men who act as the eyes/spies of the Nocturnal Council, 964e–965a.

[97] 909c; cf. 871d: it would be impious to bury a voluntary murderer in Magnesia.

but with radically different assumptions and purposes, and with wholly different categories of offenders in mind. Indeed, any Athenian who in Athens ventured to use the Athenian law to prosecute someone who believed in non-squareable gods would himself run the risk of prosecution in Magnesia.

Imprisonment for impiety is probably a Platonic innovation;[98] and which of the two very different varieties of it is to be imposed in a particular case depends on an assessment of the offender's state of mind. In rough terms, such an assessment took place in Athens too: obviously an incidental expression of some outrageous theological view would hardly attract prosecution; to judge from the prosecutions that did take place, and from the mention of 'teaching' in the decree of Diopeithes, the law was directed against well-known intellectuals whose opinions were thought likely to spread if not checked. Plato invents a formal category of lesser impiety, not indeed directed against the holding of heretical views, or the casual or occasional expression of them,[99] but against persons who more or less systematically 'scoff at' the orthodox, but without pernicious character or intent, and without (it seems) great intellectual subtlety. The crucial difference between the two categories is that this latter is persuadable, whereas the other, being under the unjust domination of pleasure and pain, is not. Psychological assessment of character, motive, intent, and intellectual capacity is therefore central to the operation of the Magnesian impiety laws.[100] Re-education will take at least five years, but it applies only to heretics whose characters are fundamentally just to start with. So although on the face of it heresy, which is the holding of certain incorrect opinions, is a natural area for curative re-education, the scope of that re-education is much more limited than a quick reading of the final pages of book 10 would suggest. It does not touch the more dangerous type of heretic.

The existence of the less serious category of heretics meshes with Plato's general desire not to leave any estate without a head, if he can help it, but to reintegrate offenders into society. The more serious offenders, however, are cut off completely: their children are treated as orphans, and presumably the choice of heir to their estates gets under way immediately.[101]

So much for impious opinions. When it comes to impious actions, Plato again distinguishes between the naïve offender and the clever, but as I indicated, the naïve heretics and the naïvely impulsive founders of

[98] But see *Ap.* 37bc; that, however, would certainly not have been *reformative* imprisonment.

[99] Note that even some thoughtless impious *actions* are not actually punished, provided the agents desist (910c).

[100] See also 885b5 on 'voluntary' impiety, and MacDowell (1978) 198–9 on knowledge and intent in the Athenian impiety law.   [101] 909cd.

shrines can hardly be the same persons. But the clever heretic can indeed be the clever practitioner of rites etc. When he is, he is incurable. So long as he is not, but merely mouths opinions which however religiously horrible do not result in religiously horrible actions, he is—to judge from the fact that he is not executed—*not* incurable. The line between curability and incurability lies here, in action. So long as wicked opinions remain opinions, and do not become unalterable, i.e. incurable, by being finally solidified by the habituation of action, the person is in principle curable. Wet concrete, so to speak, has not yet set hard. It is good Platonic (and Aristotelian) doctrine that it is by *doing* actions of a certain kind that one's character is formed; so it is by *doing* impious actions that one becomes totally impious, not just by holding and expressing impious opinions. In practice, of course, the Magnesians may not be able to cure the 'clever' heretic, even if he were curable, because they may not be clever enough themselves. The most they can do, then, is to hold him in prison. Just conceivably, by being prevented from committing impious acts, his psychic disease can be arrested just short of incurability. As elsewhere, one's psychic condition is assessed crucially by what one does. But his opinions make him far too dangerous to be let loose on society. It would have been easy for Plato to prescribe the death penalty; that he did not do so is a curious instance of a rigorous and consistent application of a moral and psychological doctrine.

B. POISONING (932e1–933e5)

In this intriguing and ingenious set of laws we meet again our old friends the magicians of the law of impiety. There, they were imprisoned for life if they 'dissemblingly' spread heretical opinions, and executed if in some systematic manner they took part in private rites which presuppose venality in the gods. In the law to which we now turn such people are bracketed with malicious doctors under the general heading of 'poisoners': just as doctors may, if they so wish, poison the bodies of men directly, charlatans 'poison' them on another level, intellectual or spiritual, by a set of practices[102] which I shall compendiously call 'magic'.

(a) Doctors

This law covers non-fatal poisoning of human beings and any kind of poisoning, fatal or not, of animals. It is evidently a particular application

---

[102] *Manganeiai*, 'tricks', 'hocus pocus'; *epōidai*, 'charms'; *katadeseis*, 'bindings'; *goēteuein*, 'sorcery'; *epagōgai* 'leadings, bewitchments' (933a, c, d). The reminiscences of the law of impiety are obvious (908d, 909b).

of the law of damage, *blabē*.[103] The essentials are: (i) if a doctor deliberately and with intent, by food or drink or unguents, poisons a person, with a view to non-fatal harm to that person or a person 'belonging to' him[104] (or of his flocks or bees with a view to fatal or non-fatal harm), he is to be executed; (ii) if a layman does so, the court is to assess what he must suffer or pay.

The Attic law of *blabē* provided simple restitution of involuntary damage, double restitution for voluntary.[105] Plato probably assumes that a doctor who causes damage involuntarily will not be liable to prosecution, and that a layman would pay simple recompense.[106] However, instead of the doubling in Attic law he leaves the penalty for voluntary poisoning by a layman open-ended; the doctor is killed. One may probably reconstruct his reasoning as follows. A doctor has a skill; his potential for harm is very great; he has betrayed the trust put in him; he must therefore be incurably wicked. The layman may be an ignoramus, or have some degree of technical knowledge; the open-ended penalty allows this point to be taken into account; perhaps even in his case death may be indicated. Plato says nothing about recompense to the injured party; but it looks as if in place of the fixed twofold penalty of Attic law (where no special provision for malicious doctors is known) he wishes to apply a wider range of punishments based on considerations of the extent of technical expertise possessed by the offender; for his misuse of it is a measure of his psychic vice. Once again, psychology is at the centre of Plato's attention.

(b) Magicians

The chief interest of the law of poisoning lies however in the clever way in which Plato extricates himself from a penological difficulty, by likening the 'magicians' to doctors. The main points of the discussion of the 'magicians' may be presented quite blandly, but interpretation of their precise import is difficult:

932e4–933a5 distinguishes two types of poisoning: (i) the evil effect of body on body according to nature [i.e. a purely physical type, used by malicious doctors]; (ii) the sort that proceeds by trickery, charms and bindings, which persuades both aggressor and victim of the efficacy of such practices in the infliction of harm.

[103] 933d1 ff. Plato has no specific law of damage: the concept appears in various contexts, wherever there is need of it.   [104] ἀνθρώπων ἐκείνου, 933d3.
[105] Dem. 21. 43 (cf. 23. 50), Lipsius (1905–15) 653 ff. It was a law of very wide application to persons or objects, and could presumably be used in cases of poisoning.
[106] Cf. 865b ff.: as in Attic law, medics who kill involuntarily are 'pure' (they would be in an impossible position otherwise); but laymen are not 'pure': see p. 219 (a).

933a5–b5. Here full translation is needed: 'On these and similar matters it is neither easy to discover how things really stand,[107] nor, if one were to find out, simple to persuade others. It is not worth trying to persuade about such matters persons scowling at each other by the souls of men,[108] that if some people sometimes see somewhere images fashioned from wax at doorways or crossroads or on tombs of their ancestors—to bid them ignore all such things, since/when/if/although they/we have no clear opinion about them'.[109]

933b5–c7. Our law about poisoning needs to take two forms, depending on the type of poisoning attempted. First there should be an injunction against attempting such a thing [apparently of the second type], and against scaring men like children and forcing the legislator to cure men of such fears[110]—since the attempter of poisoning does not know what he is doing, in the case of bodies if he is ignorant of medical art, about trickeries (*manganeumata*) if he is not a seer or watcher of portents.

[*933d1–7.* The punishment of doctors and laymen, already described.]

933d7–e5. If someone [by using] trickeries or charms or bindings or any[111] such poisonings seems 'like a harmer', he must die if he is a seer or watcher of portents; but if he is without the art of the seer, and is convicted, the same assessment for him too, of what he must suffer or pay, must be made by the court.

Problem 9. 'Persons scowling at each other by the souls of men' is obscure on any count. My Penguin version essentially followed England: 'people whose heads are full of mutual suspicion'; and that may indeed be right, though it leaves the 'men' somewhat otiose.[112] As for the lack of a 'clear opinion' (*problem 10*), there seems to be no sense to be made of it except as a *ground* for ignoring the waxen images; but to bid superstitious persons to ignore them on the ground that they themselves have no clear opinion is to give them the very reason they have for not ignoring them; for not to ignore them is only prudence, because they may after all turn out to be effective. On the other hand, if the *legislator* says that 'we' (the Stranger and his companions) have no clear opinion, he simply leaves the field wide open for the magicians, who most certainly do have a clear opinion. So what is the drift of these mysterious remarks?

---

[107] ὅπως ποτε πέφυκεν, 933a6.

[108] ταῖς ψυχαῖς τῶν ἀνθρώπων δυσωπουμένους πρὸς ἀλλήλους a7–8. Conceivably, τῶν ἀνθρώπων is partitive genitive: 'scowlers among men'.

[109] μὴ σαφὲς ἔχουσι (participle) δόγμα περὶ αὐτῶν, b4–5.

[110] Note the medical language, which is presumably meant seriously: fear is a species of injustice, if related to what should not be feared (cf. pp. 175–7 above).

[111] 933e1 αἰστισινοῦν Barrett: see Saunders (1972) n. 115.

[112] Morrow (1960) 433 takes the same view. 'Men' are strangely frequent in this whole passage: 932e5, 933a8, c2, c4, d3.

We need to interpret *de novo*. Morrow cannot be right in thinking that Plato is entering 'a curious suspension of judgement' about the falsity of the belief that the gods are venal, in his remark that it is difficult to know 'how things really stand about such matters'.[113] On that issue Plato is immovable: he cannot be expressing a suspension of judgement about the venality of gods. What then causes him difficulty? I suggest it is that dark world of the dead, intermediate between the gods and men, and alluded to in the address on the law of sacrilege.[114] He has encouraged, indeed demanded, notably in the regulations about pollution in the law of homicide, belief in the ability of the dead malevolently to affect the living. Moreover, a dead man's living relatives stand shoulder to shoulder with him in demanding punishment for the killer. In this light, the beliefs of magicians sound rather plausible. By their rites etc. they 'soul-lead' (i.e. bewitch) many of the living, and 'by claiming to "soul-lead" the dead[115] and by promising to persuade gods . . . wreck . . . whole cities . . .' Users of 'bindings' reckoned to harness the resentments of the dead to injure the living. Plato's problem is to show how, given the continuity between this world and that of the dead on which he has himself insisted in the homicide law, influence of the dead on the living is possible, while influence of the living on the dead, at least of the kind envisaged by magicians,[116] must be ruled out. No doubt it could be shown; but it would not be easy to persuade others, even if one found out—and I take it Plato reports a puzzlement he really does feel. At all events, he knows that presenting such a probably wire-drawn case to observers of waxen images is 'not worth it'; they will take the prudential option every time. The best he can do is to urge them, as he urged the young heretic, to bear in mind that they do not have a sure opinion, and to await a more mature one. The remark about 'sure opinion' is therefore a piece of protreptic, enjoining suspension of judgement.[117]

The dead may then be a clue to 'the souls of men' that are connected with those who scowl at each other. Could the words mean, in full, 'scowl at each other *because of* the souls of men', i.e. each thinking that the other has incited some soul (of a dead man) to attack him? Or perhaps 'scowling *with*, *by means of*, the souls', i.e. using them in a hostile manner? This is not very easy to extract from the Greek; neither is anything else; but at least it fits what seems to be the train of thought.[118]

In effect, then, Plato is worried by the problem of distinguishing magic

---

[113] Morrow (1960) 432 n. 120.

[114] 854b ff.

[115] 909b3.

[116] I take it that the Magnesian worship of ancestors by their living descendants has the effect of *influencing* their conduct towards the descendants: see 927a, 932a.

[117] Note the similarity of language at 888c and 933b: *saphes dogma*, 'sure opinion'.

[118] Note well the *tombs* at 933b3: the role of the dead is very much in the issue.

from medicine.[119] For magic was not simply a matter of charms and incantations, but embraced the use of philtres. In the early days of medicine, before the systematic use of clinical trials, it was difficult to distinguish a genuine drug from a potion whose efficacy, if any, depended for its effects on the charms etc. which accompanied its administration.[120] Plato's remarks[121] on the way magic convinces both the victim and the aggressor of the reality of its effects suggest that his uncertainty centres on whether magic really works, like medicine, and has the results it claims. On the other hand, he says that while the ignorance of a non-doctor is connected with bodies, the ignorance of a non-seer is connected with *manganeumata*, 'hocus-pocus', which suggests technical ignorance of procedures and rituals rather than of their effects on body or mind. At any rate, he seems to think that in so far as the magician has or claims to have technical skills, he may as well be compared with any other technical expert, say a farmer or cook or carpenter or doctor.

Whatever Plato's doubts, he gives the magicians the benefit of them. To judge from the distinction between skilled and unskilled persons, the skilled magician does 'know what he is doing'.[122] The concession is however more deadly than real. For it immediately puts him on the same footing as the doctor: it makes him liable to the death penalty if he uses trickeries, spells, and conjurations, although, in the strict wording of the law, he is only 'like' a harmer.[123] This expression perhaps sufficiently reveals Plato's scepticism about the real efficacy of magic. But he is faced with a practice which, whether a genuine skill or not, he obviously considers undesirable; for it encourages private punishing divorced from the legal apparatus, fosters a belief that certain supernatural beings[124] can be persuaded to assist in retaliation which may or may not be justified, and constitutes a focus of religious loyalty rivalling the official one. As for the non-expert magician, Plato stresses the open-endedness of his penalty,[125] presumably to indicate that there can be degrees of skill that is misused, and therefore of psychic vice.

There are a few scattered indications that sorcery could be repressed under Attic law too, perhaps as a species of impiety.[126] What seems to be

[119] The list of 'foods, drinks, and unguents' at 932e3 is apparently relevant to both.
[120] See Edelstein (1937), and Lloyd (1979) 15 ff., esp. 29 n. 98 on the passages in *Laws* 10.
[121] 933a.
[122] 933c ff., esp. c5. Contrast the alleged *ignorance* of 'quacks' in Hipp. *Morb. Sacr. init.*
[123] 933e1-2. Note too the frequency of the word to 'try': it is as if Plato is hinting at the futility of the charlatans' efforts: 933c1, c4, cf. 909b6; but at 933b6 it applies to doctors too.
[124] Not only dead men, but gods: Guthrie (1950) 272; cf. *Rep.* 364c.
[125] 933e3-5.
[126] e.g. Dem. 25. 79 with Harp. (echoing Philochorus) *Theoris*, Dodds (1951) 204-5, esp. n. 98, Reverdin (1945) 215-16. But it is not clear to me, given the assumptions of Greek religion, just how magic ranks as impiety.

peculiar to Platonic law is the grouping of doctors and magicians in one 'package', subjection of them to essentially the same law, and the firm distinction between the wickedness of expert and non-expert poisoners. The strong caveats about the efficacy of magic probably express the state of knowledge at the time; it is a pity Plato is not more explicit.[127] At all events, as best he can, he once again puts the measurement of psychic states at the centre of his formal law.

[127] Reverdin (1945) justly describes his exposition as 'sibylline' (237).

13

MILITARY OFFENCES

INTRODUCTION

Up to a point, Plato bases himself firmly on Attic law; but beyond that point his special social and psychological concerns become evident, and his reforming hand is busy, not always to clear effect.

Certain suits for naval misdemeanours were known in Athens, but naturally they have no counterparts in Magnesia. Apart from them, three offences were distinguished:[1]

1. failure to serve (*astrateias*)
2. desertion (*lipotaxiou*)
3. abandonment of shield (*apobeblēkenai tēn aspida*)

All were *graphai*, tried before special military courts; the penalty was *atimia*, entailing loss of certain citizen rights, but with no fine or confiscation of property.[2]

Plato recognizes the same three suits,[3] treats them all apparently as *graphai*,[4] and provides for similar courts, apparently for all three.[5] However, the penalties he prescribes are not those of Attic law; he discusses failure to serve and desertion together, and provides the same penalty for both; the suit for abandonment of arms he reserves for separate and more elaborate treatment, and supplies a different penalty. The reason why he draws a line between the first two offences and the third is fairly obvious. All three are of course caused by cowardice;[6] but in the case of the first two, the facts can rarely be in dispute. Either the man reported for duty, went and stayed on military service, or he did not.

---

[1] And. 1. 74; Lys. 14. 5, 9; 15; Dem. 15. 32, 21. 103, 110, 24. 103, 105, 59. 27; Aesch. 1. 29, 2. 148, 3. 175. Lipsius (1905–15) (455 n. 10) seems right to follow Thalheim in deleting the mention of confiscation of property in Lys. 14. 9. Discussions: Harrison ii (1968) 32 (171 on the *atimia*: ban on entering agora, addressing council and assembly, entering holy places etc.); Lipsius (1905–15) 452–4; MacDowell (1978) 160. On *atimia* in Sparta, see MacDowell (1986) 44–6.

[2] There is some talk in the orators about a suit for *deilia*, cowardice: see Lipsius (1905–15) 453 n. 6. If it was a separate suit, Plato has simply absorbed it into the others.

[3] The third he seems to regard (944c ff., e5 ff.) as one of abandoning arms, *hopla*, in general, not only the shield; no doubt in practice the same was true in Athens (see Lys. 10. 1). Plato mentions a shield, however, at 944b7, c2, d8. [4] See 943a5, d2, for the first two suits, at least.

[5] See 943ab, d, for the first two suits, at least. [6] 943a5, 944c6 (retaining κάκης).

True, one can envisage circumstances in which absence could be excused or justified; but the absence itself can hardly be in doubt. The third suit, however, requires investigation[7] into the circumstances arising in the press of battle; and as Plato explains at length, there is a danger of reconstructing them wrongly, and of imposing penalties unjustly.

A. FAILURE TO SERVE

B. DESERTION (942a5–943d4)

A lengthy preface to the military offences as a group insists on total obedience to officers, and on willingness to put up with the rigours of active service.[8] If when called up a man fails to serve,[9] or if on active service he deserts,[10] the penalty is threefold:

(*a*) permanent debarment from competing for any military distinction;[11]

(*b*) permanent debarment from prosecuting anyone for failure to serve, or acting as an accuser in these matters;[12]

(*c*) an additional imposition of 'suffering' or 'paying', to be assessed by the court.

(*a*) and (*b*) are obviously intended to replace the limited *atimia* imposed under Attic law.[13] They are much milder: they are confined to certain disabilities in military matters only, and do not exclude the offender from large areas of communal life. Except in times of war, they would be virtually without effect;[14] and they do not prevent or exempt the offender from serving subsequently. (*c*) is new, and may be intended to make up for the limited severity of (*a*) and (*b*). One assumes Plato hopes, by a combination of (say) a fine calculated according to the presumed degree of cowardice, and by continued licence to engage in normal life, to effect a 'cure'; but he does not say so.

---

[7] Cf. 943c.

[8] 942a5–943a3. On the relevance of this passage to civilian life, see Silverthorne.

[9] 943a3–b7.

[10] 943c8–d4.

[11] 943b4 ὅλης ἀριστείας, cf. 943c1, ἀριστείων. But conceivably the point of ὅλης is to extend the prohibition to cultural and athletic distinctions, and to those to be won for success in military *training* (828e ff.)

[12] 'Prosecuting' and 'accusing' seem different. Perhaps 'accusing' is to speak in court in an official capacity in a case brought by someone else: see MacDowell (1978) 61–2.

[13] The total *atimia* forbidden at 855c, which included confiscation of property, hardly comes into question.

[14] But see n. 11 above.

C. ABANDONMENT OF WEAPONS (943d4-945b2)

The penalties are: (a) not to be employed ever again as a soldier nor in any other rank/position whatever; (b) a fine of 1,000, 500, 300 or 100 *drachmai*, according to property-class.[15] They differ from the others not only in content but in presentation.

(i) It is embedded in colourful material. The offender is described in abusive terms.[16] Grand moral personifications are briefly introduced to justify the rationale of (a).[17] There is an extended example of a loss of arms taken from myth,[18] and a briefer mythological reference to make clear that (a) is a 'crime-specific' penalty: it marks the offender out as a womanish coward.[19]

(ii) It is founded on a distinction, set out at length, between the voluntary *abandonment* and the involuntary *loss* of weapons. The purpose of the distinction, which Plato admits is not easy to draw with precision,[20] is to prevent punishment being imposed on someone who is not in fact a coward, but who has merely lost his armour against his will in face of some superior force—either the enemy or something else. Such a penalty would be a 'false' *timōria*, that is, one which is unrelated to the mental state of the person, and therefore not a *timōria* at all; for in this case there is no vice to which it may relate; both the offender and the charge against him would then be 'unworthy'.[21]

At first these precautions seem designed only to prevent mistakes in apportioning retributive justice. But Plato makes clear that his purpose is as always, reform.[22] His reasoning is presumably that the coward is psychically a woman; his soul may therefore efficiently be affected by the *pain* of the disgrace of having this disposition made public, by permanently not being required to run risks like a man, in accordance with his womanly nature; this is his *prosphoros zēmia*, 'appropriate punishment', the nearest approximation we can manage to actually changing him into a woman, which would be his 'fitting penalty',

---

[15] (b) applies also to any officer who disregards (a).

[16] Notably 944e2-5.

[17] 943e, *Aidōs* and *Dikē*, Respect/Modesty and Justice.

[18] 944a2-8.

[19] 944d3 ff. To the extent that the punishment for the other two offenders cuts them off from military life, it too could be interpreted in a weak crime-specific sense. On the 'effeminizing' of offenders, cf. App., case A13. The mirroring punishment Plato imposes, by comparison with the dressing in female clothes imposed on military offenders by Charondas (Diod. Sic. 12. 16. 1), is fairly attenuated: it is simply the negative one of not serving in the army henceforth. On the other hand, it is permanent, whereas the exhibition in female clothes lasted for only three days. On the use of disgrace and derision in Sparta to punish *tresantes*, 'tremblers', see David (1989) 14-15. Cf. in general Dover (1978) 144.

[20] 943e7-944a2.

[21] 943d4-e7.

[22] 944d2-3: 'it's the coward you need to punish (*kolazein*), so that he may be better, not the unlucky man.'

prepousa timōria.[23] But (we ask) will this pain, which is apparently deterrent, *cure* him? If so, one would expect him to be enlisted again; if not, how can Plato justify the penalty by reference to the need to *kolazein* a coward, to make him better? Can a man's 'nature' be improved, or is it fixed? Perhaps the improvement could never be great enough to justify re-employment as a soldier, but it might manifest itself in some general stiffening of the offender's moral fibre. This is speculation; but at all events Plato has made an attempt to harness the concept of a crime-specific punishment to his reformative penology. It is not entirely convincing, perhaps because of the intrusion of the idea of 'nature'.

(iii) The severity of the punishment of shameful exclusion from military activity is clearly intended to be greater than that of the mere prohibition of bringing suit for military offences and of competing for military honours. So desertion and failing to serve apparently betoken less cowardice than abandoning arms. One could indeed argue that it is especially in battle, when one's blood ought to be up, that courage should be shown, whereas the cowardice that prevents one from even going on military service and enduring its discomforts is relatively venal. Or should we argue that if one cannot even do that, one must be very cowardly indeed? However that may be, Plato clearly believes the abandoning of arms to be the more serious offence (it does after all directly endanger companions); and that may account for the fixed fine, in place of the variable penalty for the other two offenders.

(iv) There is however this similarity between the two sets of penalties: in both cases the fine or other measure is said to be 'in addition to' the penalties of disgrace.[24] That recalls the distinction between recompense, and the cure in 'addition'.[25] But it is hard to see how the penalties of disgrace could constitute recompense, unless the coward's fellow-citizens, aggrieved as they are at his cowardice, are to enjoy the sight of their infliction. Or are the fines etc. recompense, and the disgrace the cure? In that case, who is the injured party? Presumably the state.[26] At any rate, Plato prescribes a twofold penalty as a package, each part inflicting pain, but in a different manner—one directed at self-esteem and relying on social pressures, the other directed at the offender's pocket.[27]

---

[23] Note too the irony of 944e3–5, φιλοψυχία: he loves his life, so he shall have it. Is there also some significance in the offence of deliberately 'letting' go armour (944c, ἀφείς, ἀφῇ, and the penalty of not being 'let' undertake manly risks (945a6, ἀφείσθαι)? Probably not: cf. 943a5.

[24] 943b6, 945a6, 7.   [25] 862d4, 934a1.   [26] Cf. 878c.

[27] He thus uses two (or three, if 'pains' are counted) of the eight modes of punishment enumerated at 862d.

CONCLUSION

Plato recognizes the same three offences as Attic law. But in place of the single penalty of *atimia*, which applied to all three offences, and which he probably thought had an undesirable effect in cutting the offender off from society to an undue degree, Plato supplies a new and flexible set of penalties, consisting partly of social disgrace and partly of fines or other measures, all to be calculated in the light of what can be learned of the offender's state of mind. The first two offences reveal less cowardice than the third; but before extreme cowardice may be inferred in that third case, we must make sure we take every precaution. Perhaps Plato had observed instances of apparently hasty or partisan judgements about these matters in Athenian courts.[28] He attempts to utilize a crime-specific punishment to effect improvement in the offender, but seems to have little faith in its efficacy; at any rate he allows no possibility of recognizing such a cure by permitting or requiring the cured person to fight again. However, the main thrust of this law is fundamentally directed by his penology.

[28] Note 944d1–2, on possible carelessness in a judge. It would be easy to infer cowardice from loss of armour (cf. 944b3, εὐδιάβολον). The special courts of soldiers ought in theory to be experienced in these matters. For an extreme disregard of circumstances (in Sparta), see Her. 7. 232.

14

OFFENCES IN COURT

There is a short but revealing sequence of offences and penalties at the end of book 11, which deals with offences by witnesses and unscrupulous advocacy.

A. OFFENCES BY WITNESSES

(*a*) *Failure to act* (*936e6–937a3*) [1]

The function of a witness in a modern English court is to assist in the establishment of the truth, by stating his own version of events and by answering questions put by both prosecution and defence. His role in an Athenian court was conceived differently, and was quite restricted: it was to *support* the litigant who arranged for him to appear, by testifying to the truth of a written deposition composed either by himself or by the litigant.

A right of *subpoena*, exercised by litigant or court, to force an unwilling witness to appear at the trial, has often been supposed,[2] but is hard to demonstrate; more probably, a litigant who could not persuade a witness to appear had no recourse.[3] He could however persuade a witness to enter into an agreement (we cannot say how formal this would have been) to appear in court on the appointed day. Two legal processes then became possbie: (i) A *dikē lipomarturiou*, 'desertion of witnessing', brought by the litigant against a witness who failed to appear. The suit was effectively for damages (*blabē*) for breach of contract:[4] it did not in

---

[1] In these exceptionally uncertain matters I owe much to Todd's (1990) paper, which marks a considerable advance on earlier discussions (e.g. Rentzsch (1901) 17 ff., Leisi (1908) 49 ff., Harrison ii (1971) 136–45, MacDowell (1978) 243–4). I describe practice after *c*.380, when there was a change from oral to written evidence.

[2] e.g. Bonner and and Smith ii (1938) 136 ff., esp. 141–2, MacDowell (1978) 243; *contra*, Harrison ii (1971) 138.

[3] A potential witness could be subject to all sorts of pressure, and there were certain dangers in acting: see Todd (1990), and Lyc. *Leoc.* 20.

[4] Pol. 8. 36, Dem. 49. 19. In the Demosthenes passage the speaker seems to mean he proposes to drop the *dikē lipomarturiou* and enter a *dikē blabēs*; or perhaps he means he will enter both; or perhaps the latter is only a loose description of the former, since success in either would yield him damages.

itself force the witness to appear and act. Presumably the penalty was a fine payable to the litigant. (ii) A witness present in court who failed either to confirm the litigant's deposition or to deny on oath (*exōmosia*) knowledge of the facts was fined 1,000 dr., after formal summons (*klēteuein*).[5]

Plato provides that failure by a witness to present himself at the trial when summoned by a litigant makes him liable to a *dikē blabēs*; the *dikē lipomarturiou* is not so much as mentioned. Nor is it clear whether the witness must have *agreed* to appear; indeed, the passage reads very much as if Plato is providing for an unqualified right of *sub poena*; if so, it may well be a considerable innovation.[6] However that may be, the litigant on appearance must, as in Attic law, either confirm the depositions or affirm his ignorance on oath; but no provision is made for *klēteuein* and a fine if he refuses to do so. Is Plato deliberately and pointedly omitting it, or is he merely taking it for granted, in a piece of swift composition on a not very interesting matter? Surely the latter: a refusal to act in court could hardly go unpunished by it.

A plain *dikē blabēs* seems then to replace the *dikē lipomarturiou* of Attic law, at any rate for sheer non-attendance. But what is the significance of this? Possibly Plato intends to achieve some simplification, by collapsing two rather similar derelictions into one, under the general heading of 'damage'.[7] At all events, a penalty for damage will presumably include both recompense to the litigant and an 'extra' (paid to the state?) by way of encouragement to moral reform.[8] Whatever other provisions Plato may be taking for granted, the one he does see fit to make follows Athenian law in treating the matter as a private issue between litigant and witness, presumably with the unspoken consideration that the public and social interest is to be served by the 'extra'.

(b) False testimony (937b7-c5)

Both Attic and Magnesian law permit suits for false witness, *pseudo-marturiōn*;[9] it suffices here to focus on the penalties inflicted on someone found guilty of such a charge.

Although in a sense it is true to say[10] that in Athens there was no penal action against false evidence as such, i.e. against a false assertion of

---

[5] Lyc. *Leoc.* 20, Aesch. 1. 46, Dem. 59. 28, Harrison ii (1971) 139-40. It is doubtful if the witness was permitted to give an *alternative* account of his own.

[6] Plato says 'deliberately refuses' (to witness), i.e. when not forcibly prevented (see 954e); forcible prevention would be a defence against a *dikē blabēs* for non-appearance.

[7] Cf. p. 319 n. 105 above.   [8] See 933 ff.

[9] Discussions are numerous: Rentzsch (1901) 27 ff., Wyse (1904) 425-6, Leisi (1908) 120 ff., Bonner (1905) 88 ff., Calhoun (1906), Bonner and Smith ii (1938) 261 ff., Harrison ii (1971), 192 ff., MacDowell (1978) 244-5.   [10] Harrison ii (1971) 144.

the truth of a deposition, a litigant injured by such an assertion was able to claim damages by way of a *dikē pseudomarturiōn*,[11] the amount being decided by the court after consideration of the 'estimate' and 'counter-estimate' of the litigants. However, Plato does not provide for damages; again, he may take a practice for granted.

More interestingly, in Attic law if a man was convicted twice on a charge of false testimony, he was permitted, but not compelled, to decline to give evidence on a third occasion.[12] If he chose not to refrain and was convicted a third time he was punished by *atimia*;[13] this had *inter alia* the effect of barring him from acting as a witness again.[14] Plato's rules are similar. After two convictions, the culprit is not *obliged* to give evidence; after a third, he is not *allowed*. Thus far, Plato merely imposes for the third conviction not the general *atimia* of Attic law, but a restricted *atimia* of debarment from acting as a witness. He adds, however, that if a thrice-convicted person is *then* convicted of giving evidence (even true evidence, it seems), he must be executed. In Athens, the penalty in such cases, if indeed in defiance of *atimia* they ever occurred, would probably have been at the discretion of the court, after hearing 'estimate' and 'counter-estimate', the death penalty being permissible and not mandatory. In one respect, therefore, Plato's law regarding a third conviction is less severe than Attic law, but in another it may be harsher.[15]

But how far is exemption (on second conviction, both in Attic and in Platonic law) from the obligation to give evidence a *penalty*? Its purpose seems less penal than to warn and protect the court: it is a statement of 'the man's standing as a possible witness'.[16] Hyperides' suggestion that the state was reluctant to compel a liar to disfranchise himself, and that if he did so it would be by his own readiness to be a witness when he did not have to be, may be only an edifying rationalization.[17] At all events the exemption is penal in the sense that it conveys public disgrace; so too, of course, does *atimia* on third conviction. And whether the *atimia* is wide (as in Athens) or narrow (as in Magnesia), it is a disability, a diminution of the privileges of being a citizen, and of one's opportunities to assist one's friends in court as occasion arises.

Owing to uncertainty as to how much Plato takes for granted, it is not entirely easy to compare the severity of his law on false evidence with that of his law on failure to act as a witness. Certainly, to judge from the

[11] Dem. 45. 46; or perhaps the exaction was a fine, payable to the state: MacDowell (1962) 66 and Calhoun (1916) 388–9. See now Hansen (1977) 113–14, 119.   [12] Hyp. *Phil.* 12.
[13] And. 1. 74; cf. Ant. *Tetr.* 1d. 7, Dem. 29. 16; Harrison ii (1971) 172.
[14] Dem. 59. 26 ff., Harrison ii (1971) 137.
[15] I infer the Athenian penalties from those for cognate offences: see Harrison ii (1971) 231.
[16] Morrow (1960) 286–7 n. 120.
[17] *Phil.* 12. MacDowell (1978) 245 terms the provision 'humane'.

greater elaboration of the former,[18] he takes it to be the more serious offence: he imposes a mild *atimia* on third conviction, and the death penalty for ignoring it; but he is presumably aware of the pressures to which witnesses may be subjected, and imposes, like Attic law, no penalty (except probably damages) until the offence is repeated for a second time. All this contrasts with the mere imposition of damages for failing to testify. Lying betokens a more serious psychic disorder than simply neglecting one's duty, which is at least overt; to state untruth is deceit (*apatē*);[19] it misleads the jury, not merely fails to inform it.

B. UNSCRUPULOUS ADVOCACY (937d6-938c5)

Plato concludes his trinity of offences in court by considering unscrupulous advocacy (*kakodikia*) at some length. This offence seems to have two elements:

(a) the use of rhetorical techniques to win a case, with any argument that works, without regard to justice;

(b) the taking of fees for so doing.

It is obvious that he is attempting to suppress practices considered normal in Athenian courts; naturally, therefore, no counterpart to this law of Plato exists in Attic law.[20]

Plato defines the offence as follows: 'trying to turn in an opposite direction the force, *dunamis*, of just things, *dikaiön*, in the souls of the jurymen and to multiply suits or collaborate in a suit contrary to what is opportune, *kairon*, of such things'. 'Of such things' I take to mean 'of just things'.[21] The point of the definition is that sufficiently unscrupulous ingenuity of argument can make a jury doubt its own sense and understanding of justice, and prompt an unsuccessful litigant to force the same set of facts under the heading of another suit, and so 'multiply suits' when it is already clear where justice lies. The offence seems to be at bottom an intellectual one: it corrupts the minds of juries,[22] and provides

---

[18] 937b3, b7-c5, as compared with 937a1-3.

[19] Cf. 864c.

[20] Dem. 46. 26 reports a law against taking fees for *speaking* in a court. But that did not touch the taking of fees from litigants for composing speeches to be delivered there in person by litigants, which was standard practice, and is Plato's chief target (Morrow (1960) 294-5). As Morrow says, there were laws to check 'sycophancy' in Athens, but this does not seem to be what Plato is thinking of in this passage, though doubtless his law could be used against it. The money he mentions is a *fee*, not money extorted by blackmail or other aggressive exploitation of the legal system (though 'multiply suits' *may* be a hint of it). On 937e6 see Saunders (1972) n. 117.

[21] So England (1921) ad loc., following Ritter (1896).

[22] See Morrow (1960) 290 on the honest judgement mentioned in the jurors' oath of both Athens and Magnesia (856a and references in n. 130).

more or less plausible justifications for the misuse of the legal machinery in a way that frustrates justice.

The suit is a *graphē*, and is tried before the Select Judges, the court empowered to inflict the death penalty.[23] The offence may be committed from one or other of two motives: (i) *contentiousness*, in which case the penalty is a period, to be decided by the court, of debarment from bringing or helping to bring a suit against anyone; a second conviction entails a mandatory death penalty; (ii) *avarice*, in which case a foreigner must leave Magnesia on pain of death if he returns, and a citizen must be executed, 'because the love of money is in every way honoured by him'.[24]

As Morrow notes,[25] contentiousness is connected with the spirited element in the soul, and 'is not intrinsically bad', whereas avarice, at least in a citizen, is incurable; but the contentious offender who is not 'cured' by a period of non-litigation is as incurable as the avaricious one. The contentious first offender suffers pain in the form of disgrace; but the debarment is in a sense a regimen: for *not* litigating for a period ought to cool his ardour and accustom him to a less aggressive mode of conduct. As for the avaricious citizen offender, incurability is presumably inferred from his resistance to Magnesian education.

CONCLUSION

I suggest then that we have a gradation of offences, largely based on Attic law but with some adjustments and innovations made in the light of Platonic social, psychological and penological preoccupations:

Offence	*Penalty*
Failure to bear witness: *hindering* litigant and court, by failing to confirm the deposition of (alleged) facts.	Damages, probably including a penal element, to litigant.
False witness: *misleading* litigant and court, by confirming false (alleged) facts.	Damages? At any rate *atimia* for recidivists, then death for further recidivism.
Unscrupulous advocacy: *corrupting* the court's sense of justice by bad arguments.	*Citizen*: *either* debarment then death for recidivism (contentiousness), *or* immediate death (avarice).
	Foreigner: for contentiousness apparently as for citizen, but for avarice banishment on pain of death.

[23] 855c ff.
[24] Note that it is the *love* of money, *philochrēmosunē*, that is 'honoured', not just money. The offender seems not just greedy, but to have a principled *view* of life—that love of money is a motive to be esteemed in society; and his own actions follow suit.   [25] Morrow (1960) 294.

15

CLASS-DISTINCTIONS IN PLATO'S PENAL CODE

Membership of the four social and political groups in Magnesia, citizen, resident alien, itinerant alien, and slave,[1] plays some part in the determining of penalties. Most instances of such differentiations occur in the sections of the code which we have examined in detail; but there are a few others in other sections too. It is time to attempt a synoptic view of all these cases, and to compare Plato's principles and practices with the Athenian.

In the Table of Comparative Penalties I use these abbreviations:

C Citizen
F Foreigner, undifferentiated
Fr Foreigner, resident (metic)
Fi Foreigner, itinerant
S Slave

Sequences of these letters indicate punishments inflicted in order of increasing severity; categories in brackets receive the *same* punishment. The views I have taken of the relative severity of certain punishments are not in all cases self-evidently true: some justifications are advanced in the discussion. In particular, I may not be justified in treating the whipping inflicted on a slave as in all cases a more severe penalty than the penalties inflicted on the other social classes; but it assists schematization to do so, pending discussion. The table is also necessarily summary; full details of each offence and penalty are in chapters 8–14.

Two questions arise immediately:

1. Why are there only 21 cases? There are very many[2] other offences catered for in the code, both important and trivial; but in laying down the penalties for them Plato makes no distinction at all between the

---

[1] For a description of them, and some preliminary considerations, see pp. 214–16.
[2] In the Penguin (539–44) I listed a total of 115 offences, some of them having several subdivisions. Obviously much depends on one's mode of enumeration; and in any case the very nature of certain offences entails that members of some classes cannot commit them.

social classes. What do the cases in which he draws distinctions have in common, as opposed to all the others? What is special about them?

To this question I see only one plausible answer. There is *nothing* special about them. The distinctions he draws are simply possible patterns, to be applied appropriately, under the guidance of the 'younger legislators' and/or at the discretion of the courts, in the whole of the rest of the code. For the most part, Plato does not bother to spell out the detail. He leaves the standard formulation, 'if someone commits such and such an offence, let him be punished in such and such a way', to be elaborated later, in the light of these models, by the Magnesians themselves.[3]

2. This formulation may be elaborated into not one pattern only, but into no less than eleven: $CFiFrS$, $(CFr)FiS$, $(CF)S$, (CF), CS, FS, $C(FS)$, CF, $S(FC)$, $(SF)C$, FC. What considerations control the distributions, and require that *this* pattern is to be applied to *these* offenders for *this* offence? There is no way of answering this question except by inductive spotting of trends.

The table has been constructed on the assumption that it makes sense to grade the various punishments for each crime in terms of comparative severity. The clearest example of such gradation is the sequence of one, two and three years of imprisonment in case 2; for here the threefold gradation is of penalties that are commensurable. But problems arise when one (or more) of the penalties in a sequence is different in kind from the others. To take case 2 again, imprisonment for free men replaced by a whipping for slaves. Is a whipping to be regarded as a heavier or a lighter penalty than imprisonment, or as of the same degree of severity? Set out as in the table, the sequence at any rate suggests, by extrapolation, that it is heavier. But in a way it is lighter, because it is of only brief duration; whereas the shortest period of imprisonment is a whole year. The probable truth is that to reform or at any rate punish a slave by imprisonment is simply unthinkable; it would be an inconvenient and expensive way of dealing with a comparatively worthless and irrational person. Plato therefore simply falls in with the common belief that whipping is an appropriate punishment for a slave. In this case appropriateness tends to replace severity as the ruling factor in the gradation. In case 4, however, severity and appropriateness coincide: the scourging which is imposed on top of death is not only the type of penalty commonly thought appropriate to a slave but also of a severity designed to achieve publicity and assuage the feelings of the dead. Case 15, though in a way trivial, is nevertheless revealing. It is the only

___

[3] See in general 772a ff., 875d–876e, 934bc, 956e ff.

TABLE OF COMPARATIVE PENALTIES

Col. 1 *CFS*	Col. 2 (*CF*)*S*	Col. 3 *C*(*FS*)	Col. 4 *S*(*FC*)	Col. 5 (*SF*)*C*
CFiFrS				
1. Failure to help assaulted parent (881b ff.) *C* Curse in the name of Zeus *Fi* Reprimand *Fr* Permanent Exile *S* Whipping	4. Homicide: deliberate (871a ff.) (*CF*) Death *S* Severe scourging; if still alive, death	13. Assault 3[f] (897c, 882ab) *C* No penalty (*FS*) Whipping	17. 'Diminished' theft (914bc) *S* Whipping (*FC*) Reputation for illiberality, and repayment 10 × value	18. Sacrilege (854d ff.) (*SF*) Whipped, branded, and expelled naked *C* Death
2. Assault 1[a] (880bc, 882ab) Imprisonment: *C* One year *Fi* Two years *Fr* Three years *S* Whipping (*CFr*) *FiS*	5. Homicide: in anger (867c ff.) (*CF*) Exile *S* Death	14. Market offences (764bc) *C* Fine (*FS*) Whipping in chains		19. Theft of public property (941d) (*SF*) Fine or other penalty *C* Death *FC*
3. Homicide: Involuntary (865a ff.) Exile *C* One year *Fr* One year *Fi* Permanent *S* Death[b]	6. Homicide: in self-defence (869a ff.) (*CF*) No penalty *S* Death unless pardoned by victim	15. Offences near schools (794b) *C* Chastisement,[g] with right to appeal (*FS*) Chastisement,[g] with no right to appeal *CF*		20. Following inappropriate occupation (847ab) *F* Imprisonment, fines, expulsion *C* Reproof and degradation
	7. Wounding: deliberate (876e ff.) (*CF*) Exile *S* Death	16. Premature return from exile after involuntary homicide (866a ff.) *C* Doubling of exile and other impositions *F* Death		21. Unscrupulous pleading for gain (938a) *F* Exile *C* Death
	8. Wounding: in anger (878c, 879b) (*CF*) Damages *S* To be punished as victim pleases[c]			
	9. Failure to inform about buried treasure (914a) (*CF*) Reputation for vice *S* Death			

(*CF*)

10. Assault 2[d] (881d)
   (*CF*) Rustication
     CS

11. Picking dessert fruit
   without owner's
   permission (844e ff.)
   C Fine?[e]
   S Whipping
     FS

12. Picking coarse fruit in
   ignorance of law (845b)
   F Admonition
   S Whipping

[a] Attacks on free persons more than 20 years older than the attacker (assembled from Assault BE).

[b] Even for homicide in self-defence (case 6) the slave is put to death, so the same is presumably true of involuntary homicide. See under 'homicide', pp. 220–1.

[c] 868b7–c1: some decidedly brutal treatment seems to be implied.

[d] Attacks on parents (Assault C).

[e] The text appears to refer to 843b, on the removal of boundary stones, where what the person found guilty must 'suffer or pay' is to be assessed by the court. Presumably for mere fruit-picking a fine would suffice.

[f] Attacks on citizens not 20 years older than the attacker, committed by a foreigner or citizen, and *any* attack on a free man by a slave (assembled from Assault ADE).

[g] *Kolazein*, 'buffet', 'punish', perhaps falling short of a whipping.

instance[4] in the code of physical chastisement (*kolazein*: whipping?) of a citizen in full standing, and he is allowed to appeal against it. But such treatment is appropriate to slaves and foreigners, who are therefore, by a curious kind of extra severity, not so allowed.

But there is a subjective element too, which imports further complications. Case 14 may be considered in the light of a passage[5] in which Plato claims that blame and reproach are a heavier penalty 'for a man of sense' than large fines. Blame and reproach are social pressures, appealing to one's sense of shame.[6] Whipping, one supposes, is effective not just because of the pain but because it is shameful. The foreigner, as a free man and thus a man of sense, may be supposed to feel his whipping as 'heavier' than the citizen's fine. But the slave is hardly 'a man of sense'. How is *he* to regard his whipping? Is he supposed to feel shame as well as pain, or pain alone? In a curious way, to whip a slave may be *less* severe than to whip a free man.[7] On the other hand the reproof and disgrace in case 20 are presumably, on Plato's own criterion, to be regarded as more severe than the fines etc.

No fewer than 13 out of the 21 cases exhibit patterns of punishment that call for a bracket because two classes out of the three are grouped together and punished exactly alike. The simple threefold distinction—citizen, foreigner, slave—which we should expect occurs never; but surprisingly in view of that, we are presented with three crimes (those in column 1) where the most elaborate distinction of all is drawn, between the *four* social groups. However, two of the three cases reveal the same broad pattern: two classes—here citizens and other free men (foreigners)—are grouped as against the other one (slaves). In assault 1 (case 2) the citizen and foreigner suffer various terms of imprisonment, whereas the slave is flogged; and in the case of involuntary homicide (case 3) the free men are again exiled for various periods while the slave is (probably) put to death. Thus far, the first column could be assimilated to the second. But case 1 is hard to interpret: how are these four penalties to be graded in point of severity? The curse in the name of Zeus could be the severest, if he could be relied upon to act; the itinerant's reprimand also, if he is 'a man of sense', could be interpreted as very severe; on the other hand permanent exile, even if the offender will eventually leave anyway, looks more severe than mere disgrace. In the text, Plato presents the citizen's penalty separately, and the others in the sequence *FrFiS*; but he may not have meant that as an order of

[4] See pp. 339-40 below. I take the offenders in case 15 to be adults, not children, who would surely not be permitted to contest summary chastisement.
[5] 926d.   [6] Cf. p. 108 above.
[7] Another parodoxical result can be reached if one takes Plato at his word, that death is the 'smallest evil' (see pp. 181-3). In that case death, in e.g. case 3, is *milder* than exile etc.

severity. On the whole, it looks as if appropriateness is the ruling criterion—but then why is a reprimand *peculiarly* appropriate for an itinerant?

Column 1 is revealing in other ways too. It is not at all clear what features the three cases have, individually or in common, to justify a more elaborate and various set of penalties than any other case in the entire code. Again, the desire to provide *paradeigmata* seems to be the only plausible reason. But what accounts for the variation in sequence as between foreigners? In assault 1 (case 2), perhaps the metic is punished more severely than the itinerant foreigner because, however remotely, he has had the chance to absorb some of the special ethos of Magnesia and has now betrayed it: why in that case is the citizen not punished more severely than both, as having had the Magnesian education directly? It is on any account remarkable that Plato is prepared to devote trouble and expense to the imprisonment (and reform?) of an itinerant alien, who will presumably leave the state shortly after his release. In involuntary homicide (case 3), there is a sense in which the penalty imposed on the itinerant foreigner is hardly a penalty at all: for what trouble is it, if one is not a metic with some modest stake in the place, to stay away from Magnesia, even permanently? And is this penalty intended to 'cure'? Its main purpose seems to be not to put into practice an explicitly reformative penology, but to achieve other ends, notably elimination of a troublesome presence.

In seven cases (3–9) *a priori* expectations are confirmed: the slave is punished most severely of all, often being treated as incurable and killed. What then accounts for the reversal of the pattern in cases 18 and 19, in which it is the citizen who is killed? In sacrilege (18), he has acted in a way which is a betrayal of his education, as Plato says;[8] he is incurable and deserves to die. But any crime is, in a sense, a betrayal of one's education; what makes crimes 18 and 19 special? Let us broaden induction to cases 20 and 21, in which the citizen is punished more severely than the *foreigner*. All four offences are committed with a view to financial gain (so too case 17), which is peculiarly something which the citizen, more than anyone else, must not covet unduly. What is serious in a slave (or foreigner) is infinitely more so in a citizen. When Plato inveighs against the love of riches, and exhorts the Magnesians to live moderately,[9] it is not mere moral uplift: his protreptic has legal teeth.

Whipping is appropriate for slaves, and it is sometimes inflicted on foreigners too (cases 13 and 14). The citizen, however, while he may be punished *more* severely than a slave, is in the table only once punished *as*

[8] 854e.   [9] e.g. 631c, 697bc, 743d, 870a ff.

severely, by undergoing a whipping, or at any rate some form of physical chastisement.[10] This possible case apart, in the *Laws* as a whole he is whipped only in five special cases assembled by Morrow,[11] where he is punished in this manner only if he is already under some *atimia*, or under the age of 30. As Morrow says, whipping seems not to be inflicted on a citizen 'of mature age and in good repute'. In other words, the principle that citizens are not whipped holds good: the only citizens who suffer this penalty are so to speak slightly less than citizens anyway. Again, status matters: an incurable citizen can certainly be 'written off' by the death penalty, but if he is curable he is not to be affected by direct assault on his body. Only slaves, and sometimes foreigners, are coarse enough for that.

The patterns are much complicated by the presence of the foreigner, who in column 2 finds himself grouped, if grouped at all, with the citizen, but in column 3 with the slave. Can we divine any reasons? Six of the relevant crimes in column 2 are concerned with life and limb; but it is far from clear why a foreigner who commits any of these offences deserves to be ranked with the citizen in receiving a lighter penalty than the slave. Perhaps Plato believes that slaves are more prone to physical violence than free men, whether citizen or foreigner, and/or that physical violence is peculiarly something slaves must avoid, as disrupting the clear boundaries of the social system.

Assault 3 (case 13), on the other hand, concerns the foreigner who attacks a citizen in a way too violent to be tolerated on the ground that the foreigner is a guest-friend; the other two relevant offences in column 3 (cases 14 and 15) are likewise cases of being unruly in public places, and this is especially inappropriate to the status of a foreigner: if we respect him as a guest-friend, he should reciprocate the friendship and show deference to his social superiors. If he does not, then his injustice is considerable, and he sinks to the moral level of a slave. But this is not really very cogent, for the same line of reasoning could equally well be applied to the cases in column 2. Possibly the explanation is that to group the stranger with the slave in column 2 would entail inflicting the death penalty too frequently, and respect for Zeus the god of strangers restrains Plato.[12] However, he does not hesitate to impose it on a foreigner in the case of deliberate homicide, when it is imposed on the citizen also (case 4).

In columns 4 and 5 there is the same oscillation as in 2 and 3: the foreigner is ranked once with the citizen (case 17), and twice with the slave (18 and 19); and in cases 20 and 21 he is sharply distinguished from

---

[10] Case 15; but he has a right to appeal (see pp. 335–6 above).
[11] Morrow (1939) 66 n.32: 762c, 784d, 845c, 881d, 932b.
[12] See 879e2.

the citizen. Again, a possible reason is that Plato hesitates to execute the stranger in column 5 (execution is involved in three of the four cases). When execution is not involved, as in column 4, then the foreigner can be grouped with the citizen, as a free and rational man open to social pressures. But in that case one would expect citizen and foreigner to be bracketed in case 20 too.

Some clue to the thinking behind the penalties in case 18, and perhaps (*mutatis mutandis*) 19 too, may be found in a passage of Lysias[13] in which it is argued that a religious offence is more serious if committed by a citizen than if committed by a foreigner; for in the latter circumstance it is 'alien', in the former 'domestic'. That is to say, a citizen should have greater loyalty to the religion of his state than a foreigner, and owes a greater duty; so his offence in this regard is that much more dangerous and heinous. He has done something which he least of all people should have done.

In Plato's penal code penalties are supposed to be matched, in scale and type, to the scale and type of the psychic 'injustice' which they are intended to cure. Now psychic injustice can be gauged by reference to the objective seriousness of the offence. It can also be gauged by reference to the objective status of the offender: a foreigner, and even more a slave, is without benefit of the systematic training given to the citizen and calculated to produce a 'just' state of mind. Even the citizen, however, is not completely just; and foreigners and slaves come even further down the scale.[14] *Prima facie*, therefore, when a citizen and a slave commit the same offence, one can arrive at a good estimate of the psychic injustice present in each by as it were lumping together (*a*) the injustice implied by the offence itself, objectively considered (this injustice would be the same in both cases), and (*b*) the injustice implied by the psychic character of the offender—this second injustice being invariably greater in the slave than in the citizen. On the further principle that greater injustice calls for more stringent cure, the slave will invariably attract a more severe punishment. And that is what seems to happen generally in columns 1–3.

Yet this analysis will not do. There is no reason, other things being equal, why an identical offence should require for its commission a greater degree of injustice in one agent than in another;[15] and an identical degree of injustice in two agents ought to call for identical

---

[13] Lys. 6. 17.

[14] Some, however, are less far down than others: 776d ff., cf. Isoc. 15. 286. A common scale of injustice for citizens, foreigners and slaves is implied by e.g. 941c–942a (passage 14).

[15] Foreigners and slaves do not commit a given crime as a result of greater psychic injustice than that of the citizen who commits it, who has simply sunk down the scale to their level; but they may be expected to commit it *more frequently* (853de), each of them having as a rule a lower level of justice in the soul than a citizen.

severity of punishment for purposes of cure. There must be further factors, which account for the general practice of punishing slaves more severely, for the inversions of that tendency, and likewise for the variable treatment of the foreigner. In some cases, obviously, it will suffice to assume that the citizen's injustice, though equal to that of a slave, is nevertheless only a temporary derangement, and his education will make him more easily curable, so that a lighter penalty is appropriate. Yet the principles on which Plato is working are, I think, much more elaborate.

Let us consider certain complexities which the table conceals. In all four cases of homicide in columns 1 and 2 (cases 3–6), the penalty stated is for the killing of a free man, both when the killer is himself a free man and when he is a slave: both killers are after all committing the 'same' crime, objectively considered. Yet it is quite clear from the relevant texts, that when a *slave* kills a free man, Plato does not think of it as the 'same' crime at all: for the slave kills not an equal in status, but a superior. Thus the penalty for a slave who kills a *slave* is less than if he had killed a free man: at any rate, in deliberate homicide (case 4) the severe scourging is apparently omitted, and for homicide in self-defence (case 6) there is (apparently) no penalty at all, not even the need to obtain cleansing from pollution.[16] In other words, the slave is not now punished more severely than free men, but on exactly the same basis: that is, when in these two cases (homicide deliberate and homicide in self-defence) no considerations of status are involved, the slave is *not* singled out for heavier punishment. May one generalize, and say that an offence against a fellow-member of one's own social class is of this or that seriousness, but always of a greater seriousness when committed against a member of a higher class?

There is quite a lot to suggest that this general principle does in fact hold good, in respect not only of the four social classes, but of relationships of family and age, and indeed of the whole grand system of subordination on which Magnesia depends. In the homicide law we noticed many times that killings of relatives, especially parents, are of special gravity; and a glance at the specifications of Assault 1, 2, and 3 at the bottom of the table will serve to remind us that Plato prescribes penalties for assault only when the assaulted person has some status which is higher than that of the attacker. If we may again adopt the principle that Plato is providing paradigms, we may conclude that status-distinctions of the appropriate kinds would come into play across the board. In that case, Plato's penal code is absolutely drenched in considerations of status.

---

[16] In cases 3 and 5 no rule is given regarding the killing of a slave *by a slave*.

Admittedly, it is not always easy to see how the system would work. Take involuntary homicide (case 3): *if* death is the penalty for a slave who kills a free man, as I have inferred, and some lesser penalty would be exacted for his killing of a fellow-slave, what would that penalty be? One can hardly send a slave, like a free man, into exile. But in woundings in anger (case 8), where again no separate penalty for a slave's wounding of a slave is shown, the slave offender (or more probably his master)[17] could presumably be made to pay damages on the same basis as the free man who wounds a free man in anger. A further obscurity is that in deliberate wounding (case 7) the death penalty applies to the slave only if his free man victim was his master. What would happen in the presumably less heinous case of killing a free man who was not his master is not stated.[18] But on any showing, status is vitally important to the assessment of penalties. If, say, a slave commits an offence against a fellow-slave today, and the same offence against a citizen tomorrow, this second offence will be a more serious one, and committed in virtue of greater psychic injustice, than the first. It is worth asking just why. After all, to be more indignant at the second offence may be the normal gut-reaction, but is it not at bottom merely a social prejudice, similar to the unreasoning anger at such cases found in historical courts?[19]

Plato no doubt reflects and utilizes that prejudice; but his real reasons for differentiating punishments by status run rather deeper, and are ultimately metaphysical. Magnesia is part of a more or less rationally ordered cosmos, in which living beings of greater rationality control, or should control, those of lesser: gods, senior persons, citizens, foreigners, slaves, animals (themselves graded in point of rational faculties).[20] Human reason is exercised prudentially: its object is knowledge of human good. Certain members of the state—elders, high officials, the Nocturnal Council—understand that good more fully than others, and so have a greater capacity for conferring benefit on the community. An attack on (say) a citizen by a citizen is an attack on the presence in the state of a certain degree of human rationality. That is serious. But the offence is committed by a person of similar rationality, who—thanks to that very rationality, duly refined by education—may perhaps be cured of his psychic injustice, i.e. irrational domination by emotion, appetite, etc. in his soul. But an attack on a citizen by a slave is an attack from below of unreason on reason; it is an attack which threatens the very hierarchy of reason so painstakingly constructed by the legislator, and on the social cohesion in which it is embodied and on which it relies. A slave and a

---

[17] Cf. 936cd; slaves would own little or no money or other (movable) property.
[18] 868bc perhaps suggests the death penalty would stand, but with diminished ill-treatment beforehand.
[19] See pp. 107–8.   [20] *Tim.* 91d ff.

free man who rob a free man may be equal in the injustice that is their greed, *tout court*; but the greed/injustice of the slave is such as to threaten the social, intellectual and moral structure of the state. It is for this reason in particular, not simply because he must *a priori* be supposed to be less just, that the slave commits a greater offence; it is this greater offence that is evidence of greater injustice; and it is the greater injustice that calls for a more severe penalty/cure. On the other hand a slave who robs a slave with the same degree of greed as a citizen who robs a citizen does not threaten the social order so much; for the slave victim contributes less to society, so any damage done to him matters less than the same damage done to a citizen. What a slave can do, *in his position*, to threaten the social order, is to attack someone in a superior position; this is the one thing which, as a slave, he must peculiarly not do.

It is by some such rationale that we should seek to explain the various oscillations and inversions in the punishments meted out to citizens and foreigners. As we saw, what is particularly disapproved of in the citizen is undue desire for wealth. In his position, that is one of the most effective things he can do to undermine the rationally ordered structure of society; for in the end it will convert the state from a judicious compromise between monarchy and democracy[21] into a timocracy. Another thing he must peculiarly not do, in his position, is to offend by sacrilege (case 18) the gods, who in some sense direct and protect the state of which he is a member. The one thing that a foreigner must not do, in his position, is indulge in unruly behaviour in a wide sense,[22] for this is to undermine the carefully cultivated Magnesian standards of conduct. And modifying these considerations are considerations of 'appropriateness', and of respect to the god of strangers. The result is a penal code of puzzling complexity, in which the reasons for the various patterns of punishment are not always clear, though some can be divined by induction and speculation. Faced with such a plurality of criteria, Magnesian juries could well feel in need of enlightenment. Yet clearly their discretion in modifying and supplementing the patterns Plato provides will be great indeed.

That discretion, however wide, is subject to the guidance of certain gradations, intricate and confusing though they are. By contrast, the Athenian juror had no formal guidance at all: there seems to have been no general policy or regulation that slaves and foreigners should be punished more or less severely than citizens.[23] Such variations as

---

[21] 756e, cf. 697b ff., 741e–744a.

[22] Column 3; cf. the only metic-tax, 'moderate behaviour', 850b.

[23] Dem. 22. 55 and 24. 167 state that free men are liable in point of their property, but slaves in their person. But the practice of punishing slaves appropriately (i.e. by whipping) does not in itself demonstrate an intention to punish them more severely (cf. p. 108 above): whipping, though it

occurred would have been entirely the result of the discretion of juries guided only by their own social beliefs and the arguments of the orators. Plato's innovation is to embrace slaves and foreigners as offenders within a comprehensive set of penological criteria and rules. To speak strictly, citizens alone constitute the *polis*; but it is obviously prudent to try to ensure that the moral virtue of non-citizens be as high as possible; for that is in the interests of the citizens themselves.

That the penology of Magnesia is intended to effect moral improvement in non-citizens is suggested by several more or less incidental remarks.[24] The clearest statement of the principle occurs in Plato's extended discussion of the 'possession and chastisement (*kolasis*) of slaves'.[25] I summarize: 'For practical purposes men have to be divided into free and slave; and slaves should be made to bear the yoke easily. They should be treated with respect not only for their sake but even more for our own.[26] One should not be arrogant, impious, or unjust towards them; such restraint will sow the seeds of virtue.[27] Slaves should be punished justly (*kolazein en dikēi*), not warned like free men; otherwise it will be difficult for us to maintain our authority and for them to submit to it.' Plato is apparently anxious that slaves should have moral understanding as far as slaves can,[28] and thus attain that share of human felicity which is open to them; but his concern is hard-eyed. That slaves should be virtuous is in the interests primarily (as he says) of free men; for free men cannot attain their own share of felicity if troubled by unruly slaves. Now the chief responsibility for the training of slaves in virtue must obviously rest with their masters, on an informal level; but the penal code, it seems, has some residual or back-up function, just as it has for free men themselves, when their own initial education has proved ineffective. In that sense, and to this degree, Plato's concern in his penal code is to cure slaves too. And if that is true, *a fortiori* his concern must extend also to those free men who are not citizens but foreigners.

shames, is simply the *counterpart* of fines. But see Morrow (1939) 67–8 (cf. J. W. Jones (1956) 281) for a collection of chiefly non-Athenian laws of various dates, some of which clearly do punish the slave more severely than the free man. On the possible restriction in Athens to *non-citizen* defendants of the penalty of being sold into slavery, see Harrison ii (1971) 168–9.

[24] The foreigner is 'warned and taught' at 845b (though for an offence committed in ignorance of the law); 879e, he is to be checked from 'foreign uppitiness' by a whipping; 941d, foreigners and slaves are 'probably curable'.

[25] 777b; the discussion about slavery in general runs from 776b to 778a.

[26] ἐκείνων ἕνεκα, πλέον δὲ αὐτῶν προτιμῶντας 777d2–3. If the second genitive implies 'for our *benefit*', then presumably the first implies that of slaves, even though, as I argue, Plato's concern for slaves' virtue/happiness is *also* instrumental (cf. Xen. *Hell.* 5. 3. 7). At any rate I see no reason to rule out benevolent intent, so far as it goes.

[27] In *slaves*, I take it (so too Morrow (1939) 43), though the Greek is not utterly clear.

[28] Morrow (1939) 43–4, with useful references (though 794b does not support the thesis: see Saunders (1972) n. 51 and Vlastos (1941) 94–5).

The systematic incorporation of the slave into the Magnesian tariff of penalties for the purpose of curing him is thus not quite the enlightened and benevolent reform which it may seem. There is some evidence that the punishments Plato inflicts on slaves are in general severe. In Athens, for certain offences for which slaves were summarily whipped, the number of stripes was less than in certain other states, and subject to a strict maximum which had to be reduced, if necessary, in order to achieve some reasonable correlation with the gravity of the offence. Plato, however, specifies either no limit, or one higher than in Athens.[29] Case 13 is revealing. For assault on a citizen, a foreigner and a slave are both whipped; but the former receives stripes only to the precise number of blows he inflicted, while the latter receives as many as the victim pleases (provided the master's interests are not affected), and is put in fetters until the victim agrees to his release. Evidently Plato takes a pessimistic view of the curability of slaves: they are persons of crass reactions, and offenders are hard to influence by any treatment short of considerable bodily pain.

Morrow claims that Platonic law is regressive in recognizing, in contrast with Attic law, the principle of private vengeance in the punishment of slaves:[30] 'in most cases' it is the injured party or his representative who is to inflict the penalty in person, not an official. But 'most' seems an exaggeration, at any rate if we look beyond homicide. The principle is indeed applied in four cases of life and limb;[31] but in cases in which the slave's offence is not of that kind the text is either unspecific or specifies officials;[32] it is also unspecific in one case of murder.[33] If there is some further pattern to be discerned, it is that in homicide law Plato has regard for the vengeful feelings of the dead man and his representative, both when the killer is free and (especially) when a slave; in lesser but still serious cases, wounding and assault, he allows the expression of such feelings by the living too, but only when the offender is a slave. Of course, both in Athens and Magnesia most punishments of slaves would be inflicted not under the provisions of a law but in private domestic contexts. Even in Athens, an injured party

[29] See Morrow (1939) 67 ff., building on Glotz (1908), though the bogus law of theft (857a) should not be called in evidence (68): cf. J. W. Jones (1956) 281.

[30] Morrow (1939) 70, perhaps generalizing from the prohibition of private vengeance at Ant. 5. 48, which is however restricted to homicide.

[31] 868bc (murder of master or other free man, in anger), 872bc (voluntary murder of free man; but only a partial application of the principle), 879a (wounding of the free man, in anger), and 882ab (assault on free man).

[32] 845a (stealing fruit), 854d (sacrilege), 881c (failing to help assaulted parent), and 914a (failure to inform about the removal of treasure).

[33] 869d, killing of free man in self-defence. The slave is certainly to die; but if we may argue *ex silentio* that he is not to be executed 'privately', perhaps it is the fact of self-defence that has earned him the exemption. (Some comfort.)

may have been allowed to punish in person even in legal contexts: we simply do not know enough to rule out the possibility. One would expect the punishment of slaves to be an area in which private vengeance would disappear late or not at all.

As we have seen, for certain offences Athenian law differentiated penalties by social class, sometimes making the status of the victim the crucial consideration, sometimes that of the offender. If I am right in thinking that Plato wished to apply such distinctions throughout his code, then he probably goes far beyond Athenian law in a concern for status. This concern is readily explicable by reference to his own special political assumptions. Yet it is possible that part of his historical inspiration may be Cretan. One section of the law code of Gortyn,[34] on rape and seduction, provides for penalties which differ systematically according to the social position[35] of offender and victim. It is clear that an offence committed by the same offender *against* a free person is a more serious wrong than one against (say) a slave, and an offence committed *by* a slave is more serious than one committed by a free person, where the victim is the same. The offences are apparently seen merely as private torts, and the penalties are without exception financial;[36] the purpose of the law is to ensure recompense only; at any rate, the fines seem not to be paid to the public purse, and the regulations are innocent of overt penological reflection. Presumably the framers simply took a deterrent effect for granted. It is possible that socially differentiated penalties applied also in other portions of the code in which they would have been appropriate, but which are not now extant; as in Plato, differentiation in some areas probably implies differentiation in all. If that is so, it is not only geographically that Magnesia is close to Gortyn.

Note. Class-distinctions of a quite different kind are found at several points in the penal code,[37] when citizens are fined according to their property-class. Members of the wealthiest of the four property-classes are fined a high sum, which diminishes by steps to a low sum in the case of the poorest class (e.g. 100 dr., 70 dr., 60 dr., 30 dr., or 1,000 dr., 500 dr., 300 dr., 100 dr.).[38] I know of no precedents in Athens; but as we saw,[39] there was uncertainty about how far a man's punishment should be

---

[34] Col. 2, ll. 2 ff. The code was probably inscribed in the 5th cent., but seems to incorporate many relatively primitive principles and usages: Willetts (1967) 8–9.

[35] Free citizens, *apetairoi* (free persons without political rights), 'serfs' (on whom see Cole (1984) 108 n. 53), and slaves; nothing is said of freedmen and foreigners.

[36] The variations are extreme: see Willetts (1967) 10.

[37] The details are assembled by Knoch (1960) 158–9.

[38] The various gradations are presumably paradigmatic; it is hard to say more.

[39] p. 108.

influenced by his wealth. Plato's innovation is a clear attempt to solve the problem. Economically, it ensures that no citizen of modest means is reduced to penury by a fine that is beyond his ability to pay. Penologically, since a small fine is felt as grievously by a poor man as a large one by a rich, it achieves the important purpose of inflicting suffering equally, or roughly so, on equal offenders, i.e., offenders with equal injustice in their souls; the penalties are kept within a certain range, becoming neither excessive nor insufficient in individual cases.[40] After all, punishment-by-deprivation is a kind of regimen, and regimen must be neither too strict nor too lax.[41] Plato ensures that equal offenders receive a roughly equal stimulus, in part painful, to a more abstemious and self-controlled life.

[40] Cf. *Ap.* 38b.
[41] See 835e ff. for the connection of restraint in wealth with restraint in desire, and cf. 841a.

16

SUMMARY AND ASSESSMENT

In the *Laws*, Plato is a political 'demiurge' (craftsman). Just as a carpenter works with the grain wherever possible, but imposes his own shape on the wood, so Plato adopts contemporary institutions without change if possible, but freely and skilfully adapts them to his own purposes. In legislation, to use his own metaphor,[1] his aim is to *build*, after a judicious choice from among the materials available. Plato looks for institutions which are acceptable to, and preferably approved by, ordinary men, but which offer opportunities for manipulation and reworking into something which embodies, to the maximum extent practicalities allow, Platonic purposes. Sometimes popular acceptability and Platonic principles conflict; the result is then some compromise.[2] In more favourable circumstances, Plato sees that some popularly acceptable institution, whether desirable to him, or undesirable but inevitable, offers possibilities of improvement. The craftsman-legislator with a reforming bent is then really in business; for he can do precisely that—re-form his material into something better, by utilizing its existing popular acceptability.

Punishment comes into the category of institutions which are undesirable but inevitable. In Plato's view, an ideal state would be one in which all the inhabitants either had full moral knowledge, so that on Socratic principles they would never commit injustice, or were so thoroughly conditioned by training and education, on the level of 'right opinion', that the same result would be achieved. Punishment is undesirable, then, in that a legislator would much prefer to be operating in a state in which it was unnecessary. It is simply a back-up or long-stop in a state whose population is indeed conditioned, but not fully effectively; it is a mark of a society that is imperfect. Such a society is Magnesia. On the other hand, punishment is not merely acceptable to but demanded by ordinary men, who can hardly envisage or tolerate a society in which offenders are not to suffer for the suffering they inflict. Thus far, the

---

[1] 858a ff.
[2] e.g. Plato would like a state with no private property; clearly that is not 'on'; he therefore allows it, under sharp restrictions (739a–745b).

carpenter can work with the grain. More importantly, the institution is capable of improvement: it offers, as Mr Brown (a craftsman of another kind) would have said, 'capabilities'.

Plato's manipulation of the historical institution of punishment is decidedly thoroughgoing:

1. Since Magnesia has but rudimentary commercial and economic arrangements and limited foreign relations, he is able to sweep away whole areas of historical penal law. It is true that some areas which are retained are elaborated beyond historical usage, and he adds certain new areas of his own. Nevertheless, though its groaning readers may not realize it, Plato's penal code, however lengthy and replete with preambles and exhortation, covers a smaller range of human activity than the Athenian. But within that range his attention to penology is great: though it does not receive the weight of attention theology receives, it is certainly the subject of an excursus that is among the lengthiest in the whole work.

2. He provides a penology that does not change. To the Magnesian juror, the justification and purposes of punishment are not to be argued about: they are official orthodoxy, in which he has been instructed. Not for him are the fluctuations of the principled arguments that could be heard by his Athenian counterpart. Such consensus on principles as existed in Athenian courts is far exceeded in strength by the state-directed consensus of Magnesia. The Magnesian jurymen have much discretion in range and severity of the penalties they award; but they are, or are intended to be, unanimous in their understanding of the purpose of awarding them. If they feel doubt or hesitation, it would be only about means, not ends.

3. Plato provides for a legal apparatus which is equally firm. The trials are to be strictly controlled, and rationally conducted in a calm atmosphere conducive to the finding of that punishment which is exactly right.[3] He regards it as a major danger if an offender goes unpunished; for he becomes habituated to injustice and greater danger than before. Plato does not shrug his shoulders and think of the damage as only that of the injured party. Accordingly, without ceasing to rely on fundamentally the same system of law-enforcement and prosecution as was employed in Athens, he follows a decidedly interventionist policy: he often goes out of his way, by back-up provisions such as incentives to informers and penalties for those who fail to prosecute when they should, to ensure that no one shall offend without being duly punished. These provisions, so far as we can tell, are at least sometimes more stringent than the pressures applied in Athens.[4]

---

[3] 768b, 855d–856a, 937d ff., 957a–958a.   [4] Cf. Morrow (1960) 274–6.

4. He redefines the *aims* of punishment. To speak broadly, plaintiffs and jurors in Athenian courts assumed that it served these purposes:[5]

(*a*) Appropriate compensation for the injured party.

(*b*) 'Satisfaction' for the injured party, the pleasure of triumphing over an opponent.

(*c*) The betterment of the offender, by deterrence.

(*d*) The betterment of society by (*c*), and if necessary through the elimination of the offender by exile or death.

Plato proceeds as follows:

(*a*) *Compensation.* He wholly accepts this as a proper aim. No doubt he would disapprove of any overestimating of damage on the part of the plaintiff; but he is insistent that injured parties must in every case be fully recompensed. However, he does not treat this as a penal matter: the strictly penal element in punishment is the 'extra'. The purpose of recompense is not just to make amends to the victim, but (how absurd this would sound to Athenian litigants![6]) to encourage amity between him and the offender. This policy amounts to a very considerable narrowing of the very concept of punishment. From the undifferentiated package of punishment thought in Athens to subserve recompense and deterrence simultaneously, Plato simply excises the element of recompense. He can do this the more easily because of the existing distinction between recompense and extra, which went right back to Homer.

(*b*) *Satisfaction.* Plato can hardly prevent an injured party from gloating privately not merely over his recompense but at the sight of the punishment strictly conceived; but he can and does refrain from encouraging him, for obviously such animus militates against the restoration of friendship. Here again there is a sharp narrowing: neither the award of recompense nor the imposition of a punishment in the strict sense must be influenced by consideration of the *Schadenfreude* the injured party may (but should not) feel.

(*c*) *Betterment of the offender.* The ground is thus cleared for Plato to devote the whole of his attention to the forward-looking purpose of punishment, the reform of the criminal's soul. Obviously he is able to build on the existing belief that punishment betters the offender, by deterrence, and also on the apparent and somewhat ambiguous

---

[5] Cf. pp. 120–2 for a fuller statement.

[6] A large population such as Athens' was no doubt able to absorb a good deal of litigious animosity; perhaps amity as an aim would have been more readily understandable in smaller, more intimate, and less commercially active states—precisely the kind Magnesia is intended to be.

suggestions in the orators that offenders are punished for their bad characters, not merely for their actions. But he takes this tendency a great deal further: he treats the offence not as that 'for' which a punishment is imposed (here recompense suffices), but only as that 'in view of' which, i.e. as evidence; it is a source of information about the psychic state that is to be cured, to prevent repetition of the criminal action. He focuses, far more narrowly and exclusively than in Athenian practice, on cure; and he allows, at least in principle, that cure may be effected by means other than the imposition of suffering. This last suggestion is new, and wholly contrary to popular orthodoxy.

(d) *Betterment of society.* This aim too is accepted by Plato, but with the restriction that the death penalty may be imposed only on incurables.

5. The total effect is to make punishment continuous with education. If the purpose of the educational programme of the state is to integrate into society, the purpose of punishment is to *re*integrate. In Athens, the forward-looking purposes of punishment were tied intimately to backward-looking purposes: plaintiffs urged deterrence as one more reason for inflicting the penalties they demanded. But in Magnesia the state, having discharged its historical duty of controlling the dispute, ushers the plaintiff, clutching recompense, off the scene; it then turns its attention to reforming the criminal, in part by 'teaching', in an atmosphere now disinfected of hostility—the kind of atmosphere in which education is conducted normally. The ultimate inspiration, for Plato, of this educational thrust is the Socratic paradox, 'no one does wrong willingly'; but an anticipation of the notion that the purpose of punishment is to educate is to be found in Protagoras. Indeed the idea goes even further back, in embryo: the Homeric heroes were apt to say 'I will make you suffer, so that you may know . . .'.

6. Efficient punishment, whether by 'teaching' or 'compelling' or both, requires exact knowledge of that which is to be compelled or taught. Hence Plato's interest in psychology: he enlarges the passing references to states of mind in the orators into a potentially comprehensive psychic map. The terms in which he himself is apt to talk are however medical: specific psychic diseases are to be diagnosed, treated and cured. Here again he builds on existing usage. The orators referred to offences as 'incurable'; Plato extends the terminology to the criminal, or rather to his soul.

7. The refinement of assessment, or diagnosis, prompts Plato to bring into play a whole host of considerations relating to the offender's record, motives and demeanour, and of the manner and circumstances of the commission of the offence. Such considerations are known in Athenian

courts; but Plato is inquisitorial, and ranges far more widely. The crucial point is that they function not as indicators of mitigation or increase of penalty, on grounds of desert, but as indicators of psychic conditions; and it is psychic condition that is the decisive indicator of punishment. Hence the seriousness of the offence itself ceases to be a direct determinant of the scale of punishment, but takes its place as simply one—though an important one—of a range of indicators of psychic state, which intervenes between it and the penalty. The result in Magnesia is that serious offences do indeed often attract heavy penalties; but since these penalties are cures, the way is in principle open for them to be modified by reference to the psychic state to be cured, without necessary reference to the act itself. Conspicuous among indicators of psychic 'injustice' are the degree of damage caused to the public or other important interests, the use of deception and/or violence, moral ignorance, and the social class of the offender in relation to that of his victim. Plato exploits assumptions which were already powerful in Attic law or forensic practice.[7]

8. The punishments imposed in Magnesia are broadly similar in range to those imposed in Athens. Fines, exile, death, and various forms of *atimia* are the most common. Plato makes some limited use of imprisonment (most conspicuously for heretics); and like Athenian law he resorts only rarely to criime-specific penalties (though he utilizes the idea in some preambles). Both Magnesian and Athenian law are sparing in the scope they allow to self-help, and in the imposition of corporal penalties on free men. Plato suppresses, for social and economic reasons, total confiscation of property. That apart, the political craftsman finds that existing penalties, appropriately deployed, suit his purposes.[8]

9. The general similarity of Magnesian punishments to historical punishments is only one of the reasons why to a casual observer Plato's penal code looked fairly conventional in its operation. That is indeed

---

[7] In the case of moral ignorance, I am thinking of the Athenian impiety law, as used against intellectuals.

[8] Whether Plato uses this or that penalty more or less frequently than did the Athenian code is a natural question, but a hard one to make precise. Since Magnesia never existed, penalties actually imposed cannot be compared even if we knew every example of every imposition of every type of penalty in Athens, which obviously we do not. One could try to examine each crime in both states, and find out how often each code specifies each punishment. Yet the gaps in our knowledge of Athenian law are huge, and the penal code of the *Laws* is itself not complete. Further, some crimes in Magnesia have no parallel in Athens, or vice-versa; and even when the same crime exists in both, with the same content and label, the way it is conceived, defined, and classified can vary considerably, in the light of the differing social and political assumptions of each state. So one would not be comparing like with like. But that of course is the point. It is because of such differences of conception that the penalties vary. Perhaps a systematic survey would be revealing on the question of frequency; but I have not attempted it. The death penalty occurs with sickening frequency in the pages of the *Laws*; would not a continuous reading of Athenian laws and practice be equally sickening?

part of the cleverness of its construction. The new colonists, the Magnesians who will first operate it, will see *punishments*, suffering inflicted as a result of suffering inflicted; they will at every point be surrounded by penological institutions, concepts, and terminology that strike them as familiar, but which if properly understood have justifications, relationships, and purposes that differ, often sharply, from those of contemporary practice. For instance, a Magnesian juror has in some contexts to take into account the new, special meanings of the ordinary words *dikē* and *timōria*; he may continue to use both words loosely, as indeed Plato does; but he ought to remember the technical penological difference. Again, asked to consider what an offender 'deserves' to suffer or pay, he will feel faced with a familiar question; and so in a sense he is. For Plato does at least require him to assess recompense accurately. Yet, if properly instructed, the juror will understand his further task to be not the assessment of what the offender 'deserves' to pay or suffer retributively, to satisfy a vengeful plaintiff, but what he 'deserves' to pay or suffer as a measure of reform. 'Deserve' takes on a new meaning: what suffering does the offender's state of mind call for in order to be cured?[9] Cocooned in familar words and practices, the juror is nevertheless encouraged to *think* in a new way.

It is clear from this summary that Plato's penology is a coherent and impressive whole. He has lavished a lot of attention on elucidating it and making it acceptable to his Magnesians; and our detailed examination of major parts of the criminal code has made clear that he has written it with his penological principles very much in mind. Nevertheless, in the course of that examination certain doubts and difficulties arose. The question underlying them all is this: can a radically reformative penology of the kind espoused by Plato legitimately be given practical expression in terms of traditional penal practices consisting essentially of the infliction of suffering?

    1. The policy that criminals should be dealt with in part by being taught seems to promise more than it delivers. Although Plato goes out of his way, in his official policy, to allow a wide range of measures of persuasion, as distinct from the infliction of suffering, none of them are common in the penal code and some are not used at all. We may plausibly suppose that 'teaching' will be carried out by some formal means of re-exposing the convicted criminal to the educational influences of the state, and/or social pressures of some kind. If so, those means are not specified in detail for each offence. They seem to be taken for granted, and to apply indifferently to all offenders, except incurables.

---

[9] See 934b, 'the deserved penalty', in connection not just with recompense but with reform; cf. p. 193 n. 191 for a justification of this interpretation.

2. Most of the penalties in the code consist of the infliction of pain in some form or other. Even if, against the odds, Plato were to succeed in persuading a criminal condemned to pay double damages to his victim that the first unit is only recompense and not a punishment at all, the fact remains that the second unit, the 'extra', is certainly so, and the suffering it inflicts will or may provoke resentment. Further, the first unit, being exactly the same as the second in size and kind, may well come to be seen in the same light; the two units seem insufficiently distinct.[10] Now resentment is not a secure basis for reform, except perhaps when assuaged by 'teaching', or held in check by fear of the pain of renewed punishment. On the face of it, despite the 'teaching', Plato often seems to mean by 'cure' little more than conventional deterrence. It may be, however, that there is some other explanation of the operation of pain and fear, cast in terms of physiology (see 7 below).

3. Plato's penology is non-vindictive: aggressor and victim are to be restored to friendship. Yet the ostensible justification for the belief in pollution which the Magnesians are to have is that the dead man is pressing for his satisfaction. Admittedly, a dead man and a living one can hardly be friends; but it is curious that such weight is given to the former's venomous feelings. If we must reconcile this feature of the code with the official penology, we shall have to reinterpret his satisfaction as a form of recompense; and to call it recompense legitimizes it in terms of the penal theory. Nevertheless, the tension is uncomfortable.

4. Plato's attempts to bring particular punishments into systematically fine-tuned relationship to the particular 'unjust' states of mind which he so carefully distinguishes are intermittent; often the level of punishment seems to depend directly and only on the seriousness of the offence. Yet even if one grants (which Plato officially does not) that that seriousness is invariably a reliable indicator of psychic state, nevertheless the vague connections between the psychic state and the penalty are apparently to be taken as models for universal application. One hardly knows whether to be irritated by the sketchiness of the scheme, or gratified by the wide discretion Plato permits the Magnesian jurymen.

5. By contrast, the complexities of the tariff of penalties prescribed on the basis of age, family relationship, and social class are almost unbelievable.

6. The death penalty is imposed for the worst offences; yet it is stated not to be an extreme penalty. The paradox can be resolved, but only if we contemplate it through spectacles heavily tinted by Socratic/Platonic assumptions about morality, 'happiness', and *post-mortem* existence. Plato goes to some trouble, but not great trouble, to supply those spectacles in

---

[10] A good example is 843cd; here the extra is itself double.

Magnesia. For neither he nor the average Greek found anything unusual or untoward in a fairly high rate of executions.

7. If the medical language which pervades the penology is more than metaphor, it is necessary to interpret it in the light of Plato's physiology. Plato himself makes no such connection, at least explicitly. Yet if we follow up some indications in a Platonic spirit, it is possible to do the work for him. Whether he ever did it himself will never be known. If he did, it is a pity he did not tell us about it; but then he was not writing for us. So far as his readership was intellectuals of the Academy, they might have known anyway; so far as he wrote for the Magnesian farmers, they may well not have understood, or been bothered in the slightest.

8. As in the matter of the 'satisfaction' of the dead man, different penological rules seem to apply in the next world. In the eschatological myth of the *Laws* there is no mention of the 'cure' of wicked souls: punishment is simply retributive, and possibly takes a form (reincarnation as animals) which actually precludes cure.

In discussing all these problems I have done my best for Plato, in the sense that when lacunae and obscurities and inconsistencies occur I have tried to make the connections which he either made and omitted, or would have made had he been tackled; for in deference to the prejudices and capacities of the Magnesians he may not have revealed his full hand. Having examined his penology and his penal code in this spirit, my conclusion is that they are, at least in potential, consistent internally and mutually.

Consistency, however, does not, protect from criticism. The major drawback of any penology such as Plato's is that to permit 'any' method of punishment which will prevent the criminal from offending again is an unconscionable infringement of his status as a responsible person, and is likely in practice to lead to treating him as a sort of animal suitable only for conditioning. Such an extreme reformative position has to be tempered by some notion of desert, which permits suffering to be imposed only in some reasonable relationship to the gravity of the offence. In its strictest form, Plato's theory allows for no such thing; but in practice, at least in the earliest stages of its operation in the new state, some such result is more than likely. For Plato has chosen to present his theory in ordinary language, in terms of concepts which both look and are similar to conventional ones—but into which new meanings are to be injected. To the extent that the Magnesians fail to understand, and temper the rigour of Plato's resolutely forward-looking policies by reference to some notion of desert, a result very broadly acceptable to his critics will occur. It is one more indication that the institutions of the *Laws*, radically Platonic though they are, have flexibility and compromise built into them.

APPENDIX

CRIME-SPECIFIC PUNISHMENTS: ASSEMBLAGE OF EVIDENCE

The fullest review known to me is by Hirzel (1908); it includes much material which is post-fourth century, Roman, medieval, and modern. The early and classical Greek evidence which it contains is abundant, but by no means complete. No doubt the same is true of this assemblage too, which is compiled chiefly from my own reading of the literary sources, with some supplementation from Hirzel.[1] A fully systematic trawl of all sources, not only literary but epigraphical, papyrological, sculptural, and graphic, is very much needed; and it could be subjected to all kinds of analyses: historical, sociological, anthropological, artistic, religious, and thematic. This large task lies beyond the scope of this book; indeed, it would require a book in itself.

Crime-specific punishments are easy to miss if one is not alert to them (commentators on texts miss them constantly); but alertness, once achieved, imports the danger of seeing in one's imagination significant connections between offence and penalty which may not, to the ancients, have been significant at all. I therefore exclude all cases about which I do not feel reasonable confidence. I have divided the cases into two categories:

A. *Historical*: here the evidence seems to report an event or practice which either is historical, or, if not itself historical, at least reflects something which is.

B. *Imaginative*: here the evidence describes not fact but fiction, or more or less fanciful ideas expressed in the form of wishes, threats, predictions, jokes, and jingles.

The distinction between (A) and (B), though apparently straightforward, is in fact somewhat crude: in Greek antiquity the boundary between myth and history is particularly hazy, and obviously many Greeks would wish to resist my treating the activities of gods as 'imaginative' rather than true. But the twofold division will suffice as a first approximation.

Crime-specific punishments in Plato are considered in their proper location in the penal code, and on p. 195. Chapter 3 attempts an analytical survey of the role of such punishments in Greek thought and culture, with some references to this assemblage of evidence.

---

[1] In view of Sourvinou-Inwood's exhaustive discussion of Tityus, Sisyphus, and Tantalus, I omit references to them.

A. Historical

In this category some rough clusterings are discernible. First, there is a certain obsession about eyes:

1. Dem. 24. 139 ff., 'an eye for an eye' in the penal code of seventh-century Locri. Cf. Diod. Sic. 12. 17. 4–5, where the same story is located in Catana. Diog. Laert. 1. 57 reports the provision about the one-eyed man as a law of Solon.
2. Ael. *VH* 13. 24: Zaleucus of Locri provided that adulterers should be blinded; cf. blinding inflicted by raped bride, Paus. 2. 20. 1.
3. Soph. *OT* 1268 ff.: self-blinding is symbolic self-castration(?), as penalty for incest. See Devereux (1973) for the historicity of the practice, with further references, and discussion on p. 83.
4. Her. 8. 116: eyes torn out for seeing what should not have been seen.
5. Her. 9. 93: destruction of eyes, for sleeping on duty.

(2) and (3) concern sexual trespass; so too do:
6. Ar. *Cl.* 981, 1083, *Plut.* 168: 'radishing' and depilation of adulterers, in order to effeminize them: Dover (1968) 227, (1978) 105–6. *Possibly* part of the Athenian penal code; see discussion, p. 82.
7. (*a*) Her. 1. 2–4: seizure for seizure, 'equal for equal'; (*b*) id. 8. 105–6: castration of offender's son *by offender himself* (as part-punishment for the offence, castration), followed by castration of offender *by them*; and Panionius is perhaps a 'significant' name.
8. In Xen. *Cyr.* 5. 2. 28 castration is the penalty not for castration but for some other sexual offence.

Four cases of removal of bodily parts:
9. Her. 9. 112: object of sexual anger has her breasts cut off (among other mutilations).
10. Aesch. 3. 244: hand by which a man committed suicide cut off and buried separately.
11. Diod. Sic. 1. 78. 3 (apparently an old Egyptian law): cutting off of tongues of those who give information to enemy, and of hands of those who falsify coinage, weights, records, etc.
12. Plut. *Dem.* 28: tongue of offending orator pulled out.

'Trans-sexual' punishments:
13. Her. 7. 11, Diod. Sic. 12. 16. 1, Ael. *VH* 12. 12, cf. Hesych. στέφανον ἐκφέρειν, Hirzel (1908) 435 n. 173, Latte (1931, in Berneker) 312 n. 29: 'effeminization' of a military coward or sexual offender, by being treated as a woman. Cf. A6 and Ar. *Cl.* 680.

Two cases concerning animals:
14. Aesch. 1. 182: unchaste girl to be killed by a horse, symbol of strong sexual appetite (Arist. *HA* 572ᵃ8 ff., Ael. *NH* 4. 11, Virgil *Georgic* 3. 266). Cf. Nic. Dam., *FGrH* IIA fr. 103 l(3).

15. Scholiast to xviii. 29 claims it as a Cyprian law that a pig which eats another's crops should have its teeth knocked out. Cf. Ael. *NH* 5. 45, and case B3.

Two dissimilar cases concerning statues:

16. Lyc. *Leoc.* 117–19: Hipparchus punished vicariously for treason by the melting down of his bronze statue into a pillar on which the names of traitors were inscribed.

17. Arist. *Poetics* 1452ᵃ7–9: statue of Mitys fell on his killer and killed him; cf. [id.] *MH* 846ᵃ22–4, Plut. *LVD* 553d.

Two dissimilar cases concerning buildings:

18. Xen. *Anab.* 4. 4. 14: soldiers who had wantonly burned houses punished by being allocated poor accommodation.

19. Plut. *Alex.* 38: burning of Persian buildings urged in return for Xerxes' burning of Athens a long time before.

Pointed hopes:

20. False accuser should be punished by the penalty the falsely accused person *would have* suffered: Isoc. 17. 21; cf. Dem. 31. 6. At Her. 6. 68–9, there is a wish that slandermongers should themselves suffer what they allege; cf. 3. 65 *fin.*

Significant location:

21. Her. 1. 45: Adrastus, having accidentally killed Atys, punished himself by suicide at Atys' tomb (presumably the victim gets 'satisfaction' from seeing his killer's death, cf. XXIV. 14–16, Arist. fr. 166, *Pol.* 1274ᵃ31); and pointed publicity is achieved. Cf. Her. 1. 11, 7. 88; and compare Aes. *Choe.* 571 ff. with Soph. *El.* 1493–6. Significant location of wound: Her. 3. 64.

(Such observances survived till late. The *Bath Chronicle* for 5 July 1804 reported that a recent case of theft from a barge on the Somerset Coal Canal was punished in part by a whipping at the inclined plane at Combe Hay and at the bridge at Radstock.)

Significant time:

22. Diod. Sic. 20. 70. 3.

Significant weapon:

23. Plut. *LVD* 553d. Cf. case B11, and the 'men of bronze (armour)' in Her. 2. 151–2.

Miscellaneous:

24. Her. 1. 189: Cyrus enfeebles the river Gyndes, as penalty for its offence against the Sun, by dividing it into 360 channels, the approximate number of days into which the sun divides the year. *Note*: Cyrus may be attempting to effeminize (cf. 13) the river Gyndes by a disgustingly coarse joke: he threatened that even a woman would then be able to go across without getting her knees wet (is Apol. *Bibl.* 3. 14. 6 relevant?).

25. Her. 7. 133: messengers demanding earth and water thrown into pit and well.

26. Her. 1. 212–14: Queen Tomyris denounces Cyrus as a glutton for blood and threatens to give him more blood than he can drink; then when her forces

defeated his, she cut off the head from his body and put it in a skin full of human blood, saying 'now I'll give you your fill of blood'.

27. Her. 6. 86: Glaucus contemplates cheating those who had deposited money with him by failing to return it to their sons, and is punished by having no descendants himself.

28. Lys. 12. 36, 82–3 (cf. Dem. 19. 310), killing of offenders' children in return for killing of other children.

B. Imaginative

These are hard to group; the pack can be shuffled in any order:

1. viii 266–369: Ares and Aphrodite punished for adulterous copulation by being forced to continue adulterous copulation.
2. Hes. *Th.* 147 ff.: Uranus suppressed some progeny of his by Gaea; Cronus, a son of theirs, punished him by removal of his private parts, during his copulation with Gaea. Perhaps multiple appropriatenesses: deprivation of sexual pleasure and further progeny, during procreative activity itself.
3. xviii. 27–9, 98–100 (cf. μακών here with xix. 454, the cry of the boar): Irus threatens to treat Odysseus like a pig and smash his teeth out, but is then felled by Odysseus and clenches (?) his teeth, presumably in agony (or does he smash them in by falling heavily on his face?). Cf. case A15.
4. Dem. 25. 40, 'they say that dogs that taste mutton should be chopped to bits'.
5. Hes. *Astr.* 4: Orion threatened to kill all animals, and is killed by a scorpion.
6. Punishments inflicted by Zeus for Prometheus' offences:
    (*a*) Hes. *Th.* 535 ff.: Zeus punished Prometheus for depriving him of meat by depriving mankind (Prometheus' protégés) of fire, so that the meat could not be cooked (see West's edition on l. 562);
    (*b*) Aes. *PV* 20, 269–72: for preserving mankind, Prometheus is punished by being deprived of their presence; 7, 23, *anthos* repeated: Prometheus steals fire from Zeus, who thereupon 'toasts' him.
7. Retaliation by deities in their own special areas: *Hom. H.* 2. 305 ff., Eur. *Hel.* 1327 ff., Stes. 12, Her. 1. 105, 8. 129, Apol. *Bibl.* 1. 9. 17, Paus. 1. 14. 6, 9. 2. 3; Diog. Laert. 5. 91 (Pythian snake). Cf. Lys. 6. 1–2, a composition which 'adopts and exploits the most primitive religious fears, prejudices and beliefs' (Dover (1968*b*) 80): offender against Demeter, goddess of the fruits of the earth, punished by being placed before a feast which proved to stink, so that he could not eat.
8. Call. *Dem.* 31 ff., esp. 63 ff.: Erysichthon cut down trees of Demeter to build a banqueting-hall, and is punished by insatiable appetite.
9. Certain metamorphoses are crime-specific penalties. On Iunx as wryneck and Ixion as *iunx*, see Vernant 143–6. Cf. Eur. *Hecuba* 1265: Hecuba becomes a savage dog as penalty for savagery.
10. Ovid *Met.* 11. 100; Hyg. *Fab.* 191: Midas punished for avarice by his 'golden' touch and for stupidity by the ears of an ass.
11. On the identity and significance of the murder-weapon(s) in the *Oresteia*,

see Fraenkel (1950) 806–9, Davies (1987), and Sommerstein (1989*a*); the iconographic evidence is in Prag (1985) esp. 82, 88 ff.

12. xx. 66 ff. with scholiast: Pandareus stole a golden dog from Zeus; his daughters were punished by being handed over to the Erinues, i.e. dogs (Aes. *Choe.* 924, 1054, cf. *Eum.* 111, 132, 247, Soph. *El.* 1388, Eur. *El.* 1252, *Or.* 260).

13. XXIV. 211–14: Hecuba wishes to eat the liver of Achilles, as requital for the death of her son Hector, whose body gluts dogs.

14. i. 376–80: the suitors, thinking to offend without suffering reprisals, will die without their killers suffering reprisal.

15. Eur. *Bac.* 458, 469, 485–6, 510, 549: Pentheus punished Dionysus' night-time offences by imprisoning him in the dark.

16. Jingles are frequent, e.g. Aes. *Agam.* 1430, 1560–4, *Choe.* 309–14, Soph. *OT* 100.

17. xiv. 68–9, a grim pun: 'would that the whole breed of Helen had perished utterly, πρόχνυ, since she loosed the knees, γούνατα, of many men' (πρόχνυ is probably from πρό + γόνυ).

18. xx. 296 ff., xxii. 285 ff.: Ctesippus, one of the suitors and unwelcome guests, threw an *ox*-foot at Odysseus, and is struck by a *herds*man, who ironically describes the blow as a 'gift to a guest'.

19. xx. 390 ff., xxi. 428: a nice indication of the strength of the feeling that a punishment should picturesquely 'mirror' the offences: the massacre of the suitors, who are eating Odysseus out of house and home, is described as their 'supper'. Cf. 'to don a coat of stone' = be stoned to death, III. 57, possibly with sarcastic reference to Paris' handsome appearance.

20. V. 292: Pandarus, *boasting* that he had 'done for' Diomedes, is pierced by Diomedes' spear, which cuts off his *tongue*; or perhaps the point is that he has breached his *oath* (see Willcock (1976) ad loc.). Cf. A12.

21. Miscellaneous vague formulations of the means or manner or type of requital, using especially the notion of 'same', e.g. Aes. *Agam.* 1430, *Choe.* 274, 556–8.

22. Eur. *Bac.* 241 with 1139–41: Pentheus threatens to behead Dionysus; his own head is later carried by his mother. See Dodds (1960*b*) 192 on Dionysus' ironic concern with Pentheus' clothing (925–44, contrast 493–7) shortly before Pentheus' death.

23. Non-burial for disrespect to Ajax's corpse: Soph. *Aj.* 1175 ff.

24. Phineus blinded for misusing gift of foresight: Ap. Rh. 2. 177 ff.

25. Hes. *Astr.* 4: blinding for sexual offence (cf. A2 and 3).

26. Aesop *Fab.* 1: eagle eats fox's cubs, fox eats eagle's chicks; cf. Arch. 174 ff.

BIBLIOGRAPHY

Abbreviations follow the usage of *L'Année philologique*

ACTON, H. B. (ed.) (1969), *The Philosophy of Punishment: a Collection of Papers* (London).

ADELAYE, G. (1983), 'The Purpose of *dokimasia*', *GRBS*, 24, 285–306.

ADKINS, A. W. H. (1960*a*), *Merit and Responsibility: a Study in Greek Values* (Oxford).

—— (1960*b*), '"Honour" and "Punishment" in the Homeric Poems', *BICS*, 7, 23–32.

—— (1970), *From the Many to the One* (London).

—— (1971), 'Homeric Values and Homeric Society', *JHS*, 91, 1–14.

—— (1972*a*), *Moral Values and Political Behaviour in Ancient Greece: From Homer to the End of the Fifth Century* (London).

—— (1972*b*), 'Homeric Gods and the Values of Homeric Society', *JHS*, 92, 1–19.

—— (1975), Review of Zuntz (1971), *CR*, 25, 239–41.

—— (1982), 'Values, Goals, and Emotions in the *Iliad*', *CPh*, 77, 292–326.

—— (1987), 'Gagarin and the "Morality" of Homer', *CPh*, 82, 311–22.

ANDERSEN, O. (1976), 'Some Thoughts on the Shield of Achilles', *SO*, 51, 5–18.

ANDREWES, A. (1962), 'The Mytilene Debate, Thucydides 3. 36–49', *Phoenix*, 16, 64–85.

ANNAS, J. (1982), 'Plato's Myths of Judgement', *Phronesis*, 27, 119–43.

ANTON, J. P. (1980), 'Dialectic and Health in Plato's *Gorgias*: Presuppositions and Implications', *AncPhil*, I, 49–60.

BARKAN, I. (1936), 'Imprisonment as a Penalty in Ancient Athens', *CPh*, 31, 338–41.

BATEMAN, J. J. (1958), 'Lysias and the Law', *TAPhA*, 89, 276–85.

BECKER, W. G. (1932), *Platons Gesetze und das griechische Familienrecht* (Munich).

BELFIORE, E. (1986), 'Wine and Catharsis of the Emotions in Plato's *Laws*', *CQ*, 36, 421–37.

BENN, S. I. (1958), 'An Approach to the Problem of Punishment', *Philosophy*, 33, 325–41; see also Benn and Peters (1959).

—— and PETERS, R. S. (1959), *Social Principles and the Democratic State* (London). Incorporates Benn (1958).

BERNEKER, E. (ed.) (1968), *Zur griechischen Rechtsgeschichte* (Darmstadt).

BLUCK, R. S. (1958*a*), 'The *Phaedrus* and Reincarnation', *AJPh*, 79, 156–64.

—— (1958*b*), 'Plato, Pindar and Metempsychosis', *AJPh*, 79, 405–13.

BONGERT, Y. (1982), 'Travail et justice chez Hésiode', *RD*, 60, 187–206.

BONNER, R. J. (1905), *Evidence in Athenian Courts* (Chicago,).

—— (1924), 'Notes on Aristotle, *Constitution of Athens* xxxix 5', *CPh*, 19, 175–6.

— and SMITH, G. (1930 and 1938), *The Administration of Justice from Homer to Aristotle* (2 vols., Chicago).

BRANDON, S. G. F. (1967), *The Judgement of the Dead* (London).

BRESSON, A., and DEBORD, P. (1985), 'Syngeneia', *REA*, 87, 191–211.

BROWN, A. L. (1982), 'Some Problems in the *Eumenides* of Aeschylus', *JHS*, 102, 26–32.

— (1983), 'The Erinyes in the *Oresteia*', *JHS*, 103, 13–34.

BURKERT, O. (1972), *Lore and Science in Ancient Pythagoreanism* (Cambridge Mass.).

BURKERT, W. (1985), *Greek Religion, Archaic and Classical* (Blackwell, Oxford).

BUXTON, R. G. A. (1980), 'Blindness and Limits; Sophocles and the Logic of Myth', *JHS*, 100, 22–37.

CALHOUN, G. M. (1916), "Ἐπίσκηψις and the δίκη ψευδομαρτυρίων', *CPh*, XI, 365–94.

— (1927), *The Growth of Criminal Law in Ancient Greece* (Berkeley).

CALOGERO, G. (1957), 'Gorgias and the Socratic Principle *Nemo sua sponte peccat*', *JHS*, 77 i, 12–17.

CANTARELLA, E. (1979), *Norma e sanzione in Omero* (Milan,).

— (1984), 'Per una preistoria del castigo', in *Du Châtiment dans la cité: supplices corporels et peine de mort dans le monde antique* (Collection de l'École Française de Rome, 79, Paris), 37–73.

CARAWAN, E. M. (1984), '*Akriton apokteinai*: Execution Without Trial in Fourth-Century Athens', *GRBS*, 25, 111–21.

CAREY, C. (1989), *Lysias, Selected Speeches*, ed. with introd., text and comm. (Cambridge).

CARTLEDGE, P. A., MILLETT, P. C., and TODD, S. C. (edd.) (1990), *Nomos: Essays in Athenian Law, Politics and Society* (Cambridge).

CLERC, M. (1893), *Les Métèques athéniens* (Paris).

COHEN, D. (1983), *Theft in Athenian Law* (Münchener Beiträge zur Papyrus-forschung und Antiken Rechtsgeschichte, 74). (Incorporates, in a slightly changed form, 'Theft in Plato's *Laws* and Athenian Legal Practice', *RIDA*, 29 (1982), 121–43.)

— (1984), 'The Athenian Law of Adultery', *RIDA*, 31, 147–65.

— (1985), 'A Note on Aristophanes and the Punishment of Adultery in Athenian Law', *ZRG*, röm. Abt. 102, 385–7.

— (1988), 'The Prosecution of Impiety in Athenian Law', *ZRG*, röm. Abt. 105, 695–701.

COLE, S. G. (1980), 'New Evidence for the Mysteries of Dionysos', *GRBS*, 21, 223–38.

— (1984), 'Greek Sanctions against Sexual Assault', *CPh*, 79, 97–113.

CONACHER, D. J. (1956), 'Religious and Ethical Attitudes in Euripides' *Suppliants*', *TAPhA*, 87, 8–26.

CONSIDINE, P. (1986), 'The Etymology of *mēnis*', in J. H. Betts *et al.* (edd.), *Studies in Honour of T. B. L. Webster* (Bristol), 53–68.

CORNFORD, F. M. (1937), *Plato's Cosmology* (London).

DAUBE, B. (1939), *Zu den Machtsproblemen in Aischylos' Agamemnon* (Zurich and Leipzig).

DAVID, E. (1989), 'Laughter in Spartan Society', in A. Powell (ed.), *Classical Sparta: Techniques behind her Success* London), 1–25.

DAVIES, M. (1987), 'Aeschylus' Clytemnestra: Sword or Axe?', *CQ*, 37, 65–75.

DAVIES, M. (1989), 'Sisyphus and the Invention of Religion ('Critias' *TrGF* 1 (43) F19 = B 25 DK)', *BICS*, 36, 16–32.

DERENNE, E. (1930), *Les Procès d'impiété intentés aux philosophes à Athènes au Vme et au IVme siècles avant J.-C.* (Liège and Paris).

DE ROMILLY, J. (1979), *La Douceur dans la pensée grecque* (Paris).

DEVEREUX, G. (1973), 'The Self-blinding of Oedipus in Sophocles: *Oidipous Tyrannos*', *JHS*, 93, 36–49.

DICKIE, M. W. (1978), '*Dikē* as a Moral Term in Homer and Hesiod', *CPh*, 73, 91–101.

DODDS, E. R. (1951), *The Greeks and the Irrational* (Berkeley, Los Angeles, and London).

—— (1959), *Plato, Gorgias*, rev. text with introd. and comm. (Oxford).

—— (1960a), 'Morals and Politics in the *Oresteia*', *PCPhS*, 186, 19–31. Repr. in id., *The Ancient Concept of Progress* (Oxford 1973), 45–63.

—— (1960b), *Euripides, Bacchae*, ed. with introd. and comm. (2nd edn., Oxford).

DORJAHN, A. P. (1930), 'Extenuating Circumstances in Athenian Courts', *CPh*, 25, 162–72.

DOVER, K. J. (1957), 'The Political Aspects of Aeschylus' *Eumenides*', *JHS* 77 (ii), 230–7. Repr. in id., *Greek and the Greeks* (Oxford 1987), 161–75.

—— (1968a), *Aristophanes, Clouds*, ed. with introd. and comm. (Oxford).

—— (1968b), *Lysias and the Corpus Lysiacum* (Berkeley and Los Angeles).

—— (1973), 'Some Neglected Aspects of Agamemnon's Dilemma', *JHS*, 93, 58–69. Repr. in id., *Greek and the Greeks* (Oxford 1987), 135–50.

—— (1974), *Greek Popular Morality in the Time of Plato and Aristotle* (Oxford).

—— (1976), 'The Freedom of the Intellectual in Greek Society' *Talanta*, 7, 24–54. Repr. with additional notes in id., *The Greeks and their Legacy* (Oxford 1978), 135–58.

—— (1978), *Greek Homosexuality* (London).

—— (1981), 'The language of Classical Attic Documentary Inscriptions', *TPhS*, 1–14. Repr. in id., *Greek and the Greeks* (Oxford 1987), 31–41.

DREWS, R. (1962), 'Diodorus and his Sources', *AJPh*, 83, 383–92.

DYER, R. R. (1969), 'The Evidence for Apolline Purification Rituals at Delphi and Athens', *JHS*, 89, 38–56.

EASTERLING, P. E. (1973), 'Presentation of Character in Aeschylus', *G & R*, 20, 3–19.

EDELSTEIN, L. (1937), 'Greek Medicine in its Relation to Religion and Magic', *Bull. Inst. Hist. Med.*, 5, 201–46. Repr. in O. Tomkin and C. L. Tomkin (edd.), *Ancient Medicine: Selected Papers of Ludwig Edelstein* (Baltimore 1967), 205–46.

EDWARDS, M., and USHER, S. (1985), *Greek Orators*, i. *Antiphon and Lysias*, trans. with comm. and notes (Warminster). [Selected speeches.]

ENGLAND, E. B. (1921), *The Laws of Plato*, text ed. with introd., notes, etc. (2 vols., Manchester).

EVANS, E. P. (1906), *The Criminal Prosecution and Capital Punishment of Animals* (London, repr. 1987).

EVJEN, H. D. (1971), '(Dem.) 47. 68–73 and the δίκη φόνου', *RIDA*, 18, 255–65.

FAHR, W. (1969), Θεοὺς νομίζειν: *Zum Problem der Anfänge des Atheismus bei den Griechen* (Hildesheim and New York).

FARAONE, C. A. (1985), 'Aeschylus' ὕμνος δέσμιος (*Eum.* 306) and Attic Judicial Curse Tablets', *JHS*, 105, 150–4.

FINLEY, J. H. (1942), *Thucydides* (Cambridge, Mass.).

FINLEY, M. I. (1978), *The World of Odysseus* (2nd rev. edn. London; Pelican edn. Harmondsworth 1979).

FISHER, N. R. E. (1976 and 1979), 'Hybris and Dishonour', I: *G & R*, 23, 177–93; II: *G & R*, 26, 32–47.

—— (1989), 'Drink, *Hybris* and the Promotion of Harmony in Sparta', in A. Powell (ed.), *Classical Sparta: Techniques behind her Success* (London), 26–50.

—— (1990), 'The Law of *Hubris* in Athens', in Cartledge *et al.* (1990), 123–38.

FLEW, A. (1954), 'The Justification of Punishment', in Acton (1969), 83–102 (originally in *Philosophy*, 29 (1954)), with a postscript dated 1967, 102–4.

—— (1973), *Crime and Disease* (London).

FLOYD, E. D. (1990), 'The Sources of Greek "Ιστωρ, "Judge, Witness"', *Glotta*, 68, 157–66.

FOUCAULT, M. (1973), *Discipline and Punish* (London).

FOUCHARD, A. (1984), '*Astos, politès* et *épichôrios* chez Platon', *Ktèma*, 9, 185–204.

FRAENKEL, E. (1950), *Aeschylus, Agamemnon*, ed. with comm. (3 vols., Oxford).

FROST, P. J. (1964), 'Pericles, Thucydides, Son of Melesias, and Athenian Politics before the War', *Historia*, 13, 385–99.

FURLEY, D. J. (1981), 'Antiphon's Case against Justice', in G. B. Kerferd (ed.), *The Sophists and their Legacy* (*Hermes* Einzelschriften, 44, Wiesbaden), 81–91. Repr. in Furley's *Cosmic Problems* (Cambridge 1989), 66–76.

FURLEY, W. D. (1989), 'Andokides IV ('Against Alcibiades'): Fact or Fiction?', *Hermes*, 117, 138–56.

GAGARIN, M. (1973), '*Dikē* in the *Works and Days*', *CPh*, 68, 81–94.

—— (1974a), 'Hesiod's Dispute with Perses', *TAPhA*, 104, 103–11.

—— (1974b), '*Dikē* in Archaic Greek Thought', *CPh*, 69, 186–97.

—— (1976), *Aeschylean Drama* (Berkeley, Los Angeles, and London).

—— (1978a), 'Self-defence in Athenian Homicide Law', *GRBS*, 19, 111–20.

—— (1978b), 'The Prohibition of Just and Unjust Homicide in Antiphon's *Tetralogies*', *GRBS*, 19, 291–306.

—— (1979a), 'The Prosecution of Homicide in Athens', *GRBS*, 20, 301–24.

—— (1979b), 'The Athenian Law against Hybris', in G. W. Bowersock *et al.* (edd.), *Arktouros: Hellenic Studies presented to Bernard M. W. Knox on the occasion of his 65th birthday* (Berlin and New York), 229–36.

—— (1981), *Drakon and Early Athenian Homicide Law* (New Haven and London).

—— (1986), *Early Greek Law* (Berkeley, Los Angeles, London).

—— (1987), 'Morality in Homer', *CPh*, 82, 285–306.

—— (1990), 'The nature of proofs in Antiphon', *CPh*, 85, 22–32.

GALLOP, D. (1975), *Plato, Phaedo* (Oxford).

GARNER, R. (1987), *Law and Society in Classical Athens* (Beckenham).

GAUTHIER, P. (1972), *Symbola: Les Étrangers et la justice dans les cités grecques* (Nancy).

GERNET, L. (1917a), *Platon, Lois Livre IX: traduction et commentaire* (Thesis, Paris).

—— (1917b), *Recherches sur le développement de la pensée juridique et morale en Grèce* (Paris).

—— (1951), *Les Lois et le droit positif* (2nd part of the introduction to the Budé *Lois*, pp. xciv–ccvi).

—— (1955), *Droit et société dans la Grèce ancienne* (Paris).

—— (1959), 'Note sur la notion de délit privé en droit grec', in *Mélanges H. Lévy-Bruhl* (*Droits de l'antiquité et sociologie juridique*) (Publications de l'Institut de droit Romain de l'Université de Paris, 17), 393–405.

—— (1981), *The Anthropology of Ancient Greece* (Baltimore and London; trans. by J. Hamilton and B. Nagy of *Anthropologie de la Grèce antique* (Paris, 1968)).

—— (1984), *Le Droit pénal de la Grèce ancienne*, in *Du Châtiment dans la cité: supplices corporels et peine de mort dans le monde antique* (Collection de l'École Française de Rome, 79, Paris), 9–35.

GIOFFREDI, C. (1974), 'Responsabilità e sanzione nell'esperienza penalistica della Grecia arcaica', *SDHI*, 40, 1–51.

GLOTZ, G. (1904), *La Solidarité de la famille dans le droit criminel en Grèce* (Paris).

—— (1908), 'Les Esclaves et la peine du fouet', *CRAI*, 571–86.

GOETZ, W. (1920), *Legum Platonis de Jure Capitali Praecepta cum Jure Attico Comparantur* (diss. Darmstadt).

GOMME, A. W. (1956–81), *A Historical Commentary on Thucydides* (5 vols., Oxford: vols. iv and v by A. Andrewes and K. J. Dover in addition).

GÖRGEMANNS, H. (1960), *Beiträge zur Interpretation von Platons Nomoi* (Zetemata 25, Munich).

GOSLING, J. (1973), *Plato* (London).

GRACE, E. (1973), 'Status Distinctions in the Draconian law', *Eirene*, 11, 5–30.

—— (1974), 'The Legal Position of Slaves in Homicide Cases', *VDI*, 128, 34–56. (Russian, and English summary.)

—— (1975), 'Note on Dem. XLVII 72: τούτων τὰς ἐπισκήψεις εἶναι', *Eirene*, 13, 5–18.

—— (1977), 'Status Distinctions in Plato's Homicide Law', *VDI*, 139, 71–81. (Russian, and English summary.)

GRAS, M. (1984), 'Cité grecque et lapidation', in *Du Châtiment dans la cité: supplices corporels et peine de mort dans le monde antique* (Collection de l'École Française de Rome, 79, Paris), 75–89.

GUTHRIE, W. K. C. (1950), *The Greeks and their Gods* (Boston).

—— (1962–81), *A History of Greek Philosophy* (5 vols., Cambridge).

HACKFORTH, R. (1955), *Plato's Phaedo*, trans. with introd. and comm. (Cambridge).

HALLIWELL, S. (1986), 'Where Three Roads meet: a Neglected Detail in the *Oedipus Tyrannus*', *JHS*, 106, 186–90.

HAMMOND, N. G. L. (1965), 'Personal Freedom and its Limitations in the *Oresteia*', *JHS*, 85, 42–55.

HANSEN, M. H. (1975), *Eisangelia* (Odense).

—— (1976), *Apagoge, Endeixis and Ephegesis against Kakourgoi, Atimoi and Pheugontes* (Odense).

—— (1977), '*Atimia* in Consequence of Private Debts?', in J. Modrzejewski and D. Liebs (edd.), *Symposion 1977* (Vorträge zur griechischen und hellen- istischen Rechtsgeschichte (Chantilly, 1.-4. June 1977); publ. Cologne/ Vienna 1982), 113–20.

—— (1978*a*) '*Demos, Ecclesia and Dicasterion* in Classical Athens', *GRBS*, 19, 127–46. Repr. with additions in id., *The Athenian Ecclesia* (Copenhagen 1983), 139–60.

—— (1978*b*) '*Nomos* and *Psephisma* in Fourth-century Athens', *GRBS*, 19, 315– 30. Repr. with additions in id., *The Athenian Ecclesia* (Copenhagen 1983), 161–77.

—— (1979), 'Did the Athenian *Ecclesia* Legislate after 403/2 BC?', *GRBS*, 20, 27–53. Repr. with additions in id., *The Athenian Ecclesia* (Copenhagen 1983), 179–206.

—— (1981), 'The Prosecution of Homicide in Athens: a Reply', *GRBS*, 22, 17–30.

—— (1981–2) 'The Athenian *Heliaia* from Solon to Aristotle', *C & M*, 33, 9–47.

—— (1983), 'Graphē or Dikē Traumatos?', *GRBS*, 24, 307–20.

—— (1985), 'Athenian *Nomothesia*', *GRBS*, 26, 345–71.

—— (1990), 'The Political Power of the People's Court in Fourth-Century Athens', in O. Murray and S. Price (edd.), *The Greek City from Homer to Alex- ander* (Oxford), 215–43.

HARRIS, E. M. (1990), 'Did the Athenians regard Seduction as a Worse Crime than Rape?', *CQ*, 40, 370–7.

HARRISON, A. R. W. (1968 and 1971), *The Law of Athens* (2 vols., Oxford).

HART, H. L. A. (1968), *Punishment and Responsibility* (Oxford).

HEWITT, J. W. (1910), 'The Necessity of Ritual Purification after Justifiable Homicide', *TAPhA*, 41, 99–113.

HIRZEL, R. (1907), *Themis, Dike und Verwandtes* (Leipzig).

—— (1908), 'Die Talion', *Philologus*, Suppl. XI. 4, 405–82.

—— (1909), 'Die Strafe der Steinigung', *Abh. d. K. S. Gesellsch. d. Wissensch., phil- hist. Kl.*, XXVII. 7, 223–66. Repr. Darmstadt 1967.

HOFFMANN, M. (1914), *Die ethische Terminologie bei Homer, Hesiod und der alten Elegikern und Jambographen* (Tübingen).

HONDERICH, T. (1969), *Punishment: the Supposed Justifications* (London).

HUMPHREYS, S. (1983), 'The Evolution of Legal Process in Ancient Attica', in E. Gabba (ed.), *Tria Corda: Scritti in onore di Arnaldo Momigliano* (Biblioteca di Athenaeum, 1, Como), 229–56.

IVES, G. (1914), *A History of Penal Methods* (London; Repr. Montclair, NJ, 1970).

JANKO, R. (1984), 'Forgetfulness in the Golden Tablets of Memory', *CQ*, 34, 89–100.

JEBB, R. C. (1893), *The Attic Orators from Antiphon to Isaeus* (2nd edn., 2 vols., London).

JEFFERY, L. H. (1955), 'Further Comments on Archaic Greek Inscriptions', *ABSA*, 50, 67–84.

JENSEN, M. S. (1966), 'Tradition and Originality in Hesiod's *Works and Days*', *C & M*, 27, 1–27.

JOLOWICZ, H. F. (1926), 'The Assessment of Penalties in Primitive Law', in P. H. Winfield and A. D. McNair (edd.), *Cambridge Legal Essays* (Cambridge), 203–22.

JONES, C. P. (1987), 'Stigma: Tattooing and Branding in Graeco-Roman Antiquity', *JRS*, 77, 139–55.

JONES, J. W. (1956), *The Law and Legal Theory of the Greeks* (Oxford).

JORDAN, D. R. (1985), 'A Survey of Greek *defixiones* not Included in the Special Corpora', *GRBS*, 26, 151–97.

KASACHKOFF, T. (1973), 'The Criteria of Punishment: Some Neglected Considerations', *CJPh*, 2, 363–77.

KELLS, J. H. (1965), Review of MacDowell (1963), *CR*, 15, 205–7.

—— (1973), *Sophocles, Electra*, ed. with introd., text, and comm. (Cambridge).

KENNY, A. J. P. (1969), 'Mental Health in Plato's *Republic*', *PBA*, 55, 229–53.

KEULS, E. (1974), *The Water-carriers in Hades: a Study of Catharsis through Toil in Classical Antiquity* (Amsterdam).

KIDD, I. G. (1990), 'The Case of Homicide in Plato's *Euthyphro*', in E. Craik (ed.), *Owls to Athens: Essays on Classical Subjects for Sir Kenneth Dover* (Oxford), 213–21.

KIRK, G. S. (1962), *The Songs of Homer* (Cambridge).

——, RAVEN, J. E., and SCHOFIELD, M. (1983), *The Presocratic Philosophers* (2nd edn., Cambridge).

KNOCH, W. (1960), *Die Strafbestimmungen in Platos Nomoi* (Wiesbaden).

LATTE, K. (1931), 'Beiträge zum griechischen Strafrecht', *Hermes*, 66, 30–48, 129–58. Repr. in (i) id., *Kleine Schriften* (Munich 1968); (ii) Berneker (1968).

—— (1946), 'Der Rechtsgedanke im archaischen Griechentum', *A &A*, 2, 63–76. Repr. in (i) id., *Kleine Schriften* (Munich 1968); (ii) Berneker (1968).

LEISI, E. (1908), *Der Zeuge im attischen Recht* (Frauenfeld).

LEVINSON, R. B. (1953), *In Defense of Plato* (Cambridge, Mass.).

LIPSIUS, J. H. (1905–15), *Das attische Recht und Rechtsverfahren* (3 vols., Leipzig).

LLOYD, G. E. R. (1979), *Magic, Reason and Experience* (Cambridge).

LLOYD-JONES, H. (1956), 'Zeus in Aeschylus', *JHS*, 76, 55–67.

—— (1962), 'The Guilt of Agamemnon', *CQ*, 12, 187–99.

—— (1983), *The Justice of Zeus* (2nd edn., Berkeley, Los Angeles, and London).

—— (1985), 'Pindar and the After Life', in *Pindare* (Entretiens sur l'antiquité classique, 31, Geneva), 245–83.

—— (1987), 'A Note on Homeric Morality', *CPh*, 82, 307–10.

—— (1990), 'Erinyes, Semnai Theai, Eumenides', in E. Craik (ed.), *Owls to Athens: Essays on Classical Subjects for Sir Kenneth Dover* (Oxford), 203–11. (French version: 'Les Erinyes dans la tragédie grecque', *REG*, 102 (1989), 1–9.)

LONG, A. A. (1970), 'Morals and Values in Homer', *JHS*, 90, 121–39.

LOOMIS, W. T. (1972), 'The Nature of Premeditation in Athenian Homicide Law', *JHS*, 92, 86–95.

MACCLOSKEY, H. J. (1962), 'The Complexity of the Concepts of Punishment', *Philosophy*, 37, 307–25.

MACDOWELL, D. M. (1962), '*Andocides, On the Mysteries*', text, ed. with introd., comm., and appendices (Oxford).

—— (1963), *Athenian Homicide Law in the Age of the Orators* (Manchester).

—— (1968), 'Unintentional Homicide in the *Hippolytos*', *RhM*, 111, 156–8.

—— (1975), 'Law-making at Athens in the Fourth Century BC', *JHS*, 95, 62–74.
—— (1976), '*Hybris* in Athens', *G & R*, 23, 14–31.
—— (1978), *The Law in Classical Athens* (London).
—— (1984), Review of Cohen (1983), *CR*, 34, 229–31.
—— (1985), 'The Length of Speeches on the Assessment of the Penalty in Athenian Courts', *CQ*, 35, 525–6.
—— (1986) *Spartan Law* (Edinburgh).
—— (1990), *Demosthenes, Against Meidias (oration 21)*, ed. with introd., trans., and comm. (Oxford).

MacKenzie, M. M. (1981), *Plato on Punishment* (Berkeley, Los Angeles, and London).

Macleod, C. M. (1978), 'Reason and Necessity: Thucydides iii. 9–14, 37–48', *JHS*, 98, 64–78.

McPherson, T. (1967–8), 'Punishment: Definition and Justification', *Analysis*, 28, 21–7.

Macurdy, G. H. (1940), 'The Quality of Mercy: the Gentler Virtues in Greek Literature' (Yale).

Maffi, A. (1988), Bibliographical review in *RD*, 66, 96–116.

Maschke, R. (1926), *Die Willenslehre im griechischen Recht* (Berlin).

Merkelbach, R. (1951), 'Eine Orphische Unterweltsbreschreibung auf Papyrus', *RhM*, 8, 1–11.

—— (1967), 'Die Heroen als Geber des Guten und Bösen', *ZPE*, 1, 97–9.

Miller, H. W. (1962), 'The Aetiology of Diseases in Plato's *Timaeus*', *TAPhA*, 93, 175–87.

Morris, I. (1986), 'The Use and Abuse of Homer', *ClAnt*, 5, 81–138.

Morrow, G. R. (1937), 'The Murder of Slaves in Attic Law', *CPh*, 32, 210–27.

—— (1939), *Plato's Law of Slavery in its Relation to Greek Law* (Urbana, Illinois).

—— (1960), *Plato's Cretan City* (Princeton).

Moulinier, L. (1952), *Le Pur et l'impur dans la pensée des Grecs* (Paris).

Moulton, C. (1972), 'Antiphon the Sophist, *On Truth*' *TAPhA*, 103, 329–67.

Murray, O. (1983), 'The Greek Symposion in History', in E. Gabba (ed.), *Tria Corda: Scritti in onore di Arnaldo Momigliano* (Biblioteca di Athenaeum, 1, Como), 257–72.

Murray, O. (1990), 'The Solonian Law of *Hubris*', in Cartledge *et al.* (1990), 139–45.

Nörr, D. (1986), *Causa Mortis* (Münchener Beiträge zur Papyrusforschung und antiken Rechtsgeschichte, 80, Munich).

O'Brien, M (1967). *The Socratic Paradoxes and the Greek Mind* (Chapel Hill).

Onians, R. B. (1951), *The Origins of European Thought* (Cambridge).

Osborne, R. (1985), 'Law in Action in Classical Athens', *JHS*, 105, 40–58.

Ostwald, M. (1969), *Nomos and the Beginnings of the Athenian Democracy* (Oxford).

—— (1986), *From Popular Sovereignty to the Sovereignty of Law*, (Berkeley, Los Angeles, and London).

Palmer, L. R. (1950), 'The Indo-European Origins of Greek Justice', *TPhS*, 149–68.

Panagiotou, S. (1974), 'Plato's *Euthyphro* and the Attic Code on Homicide', *Hermes* 102, 419–37.

PAOLI, U. E. (1948), 'Le Développement de la "polis" athénienne et ses conséquences dans le droit attique', *RIDA*, I, 153–61.

—— (1950), 'Il reato di adulterio (*moicheia*) in diritto Attico', *SDHI*, 16, 123–82.

—— (1959), 'Zum attischen Strafrecht und Strafprozessrecht', in id., *Altri studi di diritto greco e romano* (Milan 1976), 309–22. (Repr. from *ZRG*, röm. Abt. 76, 97–112.)

PARKER, R. (1983), *Miasma*: Pollution and Purification in Early Greek Religion (Oxford).

PARTSCH, J. (1909), *Griechisches Burgschaftsrecht*, i (Leipzig and Berlin).

PETRIE, A. (1922), *Lycurgus: the Speech against Leocrates*, introd. with text and comm. (Cambridge).

PIÉRART, M. (1973a), *Platon et la cité grecque* (Brussels).

—— (1973b), 'Note sur "prorrhesis" en droit attique', *AC*, 42, 427–35.

PODLECKI, A. J. (1989), *Aeschylus, Eumenides* (Warminster).

PORCHEDDU, R. (1980), 'La concezione platonica della sanzione penale in rapporto alla evoluzione storica della "polis" e allo stato "giusto"', *Sandalion*, 3, 19–52.

POST, L. A. (1939), 'Notes on Plato's *Laws*', *AJPh*, 60, 93–104.

PRAG, A. J. N. W. (1985), *The Oresteia: Iconographic and Narrative Tradition* (Warminster and Chicago).

QUINTON, A. M. (1954), 'On Punishment', in Acton (1969), 55–64 (originally in *Analysis*, 14, 133–42).

RAWLS, J. (1955), 'Two Concepts of Rules', in Acton (1969), 105–14 (originally in *PhR*, 64, 3–32).

RENTZSCH, J. (1901), *De δίκη ψευδομαρτυρίων in iure Attico, comparatis Platonis imprimis legum libris cum oratoribus Atticis* (diss. Leipzig).

REVERDIN, O. (1945), *La Religion de la cité platonicienne* (Paris).

RHODES, P. J. (1972), *The Athenian Boule* (Oxford; repr. with add. and corr. 1985).

—— (1979) 'Εἰσαγγελία in Athens', *JHS*, 99, 103–14.

—— (1981), *A Commentary on the Aristotelian* Athenaion Politeia (Oxford).

RICHARDSON, N. J. (1974), *The Homeric Hymn to Demeter*, introd. with text and comm. (Oxford).

RITTER, C. (1896), *Platos Gesetze, Kommentar zum griechischen Text* (Leipzig).

ROBERTS, J. (1987), 'Plato on the Causes of Wrongdoing in the *Laws*', *AncPhil*, 7, 23–37.

ROBERTS, S. (1979), *Order and Dispute* (Harmondsworth).

ROBINSON, J. V. (1990), 'The Tripartite Soul in the *Timaeus*', *Phronesis*, 35, 103–10.

RODGERS, V. A. (1971), 'Some Thoughts on *dikē*, *CQ*, 21, 289–301.

ROLOFF, D. (1970), *Gottähnlichkeit, Vergottlichung und Erholung zu seligem Leben* (Berlin).

ROSE, H. J. (1936), 'The Ancient Grief', in *Greek Poetry and Life: Essays presented to Gilbert Murray on his 70th birthday, Jan. 2 1936* (Oxford), 79–96.

ROSEN, F. (1989), 'Tyranny, Eros and the Theme of Punishment in Plato's *Gorgias* and *Republic*', in K. Moors (ed.), *Politikos*, i (Pittsburgh), 45–59.

RUDHARDT, J. (1960), 'La Définition du délit d'impiété d'après la législation attique', *MH*, 17, 87–105.

RUSCHENBUSCH, E. (1960), 'Φόνος: Zum Recht Drakons und seiner Bedeutung fur das Wenden des athenischen Staates', *Historia*, 9, 129-54.

— (1965), " Ὕβρεως γραφή: Ein Fremdkörper in athenischen Recht des 4. Jahrhunderts v. Chr.", *ZRG*, röm. Abt. 82, 302-9.

— (1968), *Untersuchungen zur Geschichte des athenischen Strafrechts* (Gräzistische Abhandlungen, 4, Graz).

— (1984), Review of Cohen (1983), *HZ*, 23, 397-9.

— (1988) 'Das Vergehen und dessen Ahndung im griechischen Recht', *Gymnasium*, 95, 369-74.

RUTENBER, C. G. (1946), *The Doctrine of the Imitation of God in Plato* (New York).

SAMEK, R. A. (1966), 'Punishment: A Postscript to Two Prolegomena', *Philosophy*, 41, 216-32.

SAUNDERS, T. J. (1963), 'Two Points in Plato's Penal Code,', *CQ*, 13, 194-9 (note 1, on 728bc = note 23 in id. (1972); note 2, on 866bc = note 85 in id. (1972)).

— (1968), 'The Socratic Paradoxes in Plato's *Laws*: a Commentary on 859c-864b', *Hermes*, 96, 421-34.

— (1970), *Plato, The Laws* (Penguin trans., Harmondsworth).

— (1972), *Notes on the Laws of Plato* (*BICS*, Supplement 28).

— (1973*a*), 'Plato on Killing in Anger: a Reply to Professor Woozley', *PhilosQ*, 23, 350-6.

— (1973*b*), 'Penology and Eschatology in Plato's *Timaeus* and *Laws*', *CQ*, 23, 232-44.

— (1975-6), 'Plato's Clockwork Orange', *DUJ* 37, 113-17.

— (1977-8), 'Antiphon the Sophist on Natural Laws (B44DK)', *PAS*, 78, 215-36.

— (1979), *Bibliography on Plato's Laws: 2nd edition, 1920-1976, with additional citations through March 1979* (New York).

— (1981*a*), 'Talionic and Mirroring Punishments in Greek Culture', *Polis*, 4/i, 1-16.

— (1981*b*), 'Protagoras and Plato on Punishment', in G. B. Kerferd (ed.), *The Sophists and their Legacy* (*Hermes* Einzelschriften, 44, Wiesbaden), 129-41.

— (1984), 'Plato, *Laws* 728bc: A Reply', *LCM*, 9, 23-4.

— (1986), 'Gorgias' Psychology in the History of the Free-will Problem', in *Gorgia e la sophistica* (Atti del convegno internationale, Lentini-Catania, 12-15 dic. 1983, Catania 1986 = *Siculorum Gymnasium*, 38 (1985)), 209-28.

— (1990), 'Plato and the Athenian Law of Theft', in Cartledge *et al.* (1990), 63-82.

SCHÖPSDAU, K. (1984), 'Zum Strafrechtsexkurs in Platons *Nomoi*', *RhM*, 127, 97-132.

SCHOFIELD, M. (1986), '*Euboulia* in the *Iliad*', *CQ*, 36, 6-31.

SEAFORD, R. (1986), 'Immortality, Salvation, and the Elements', *HSP*, 90, 1-26.

SEALEY, R. (1983), 'The Athenian Courts for Homicide', *CPh*, 78, 275-96.

SEGAL, C. P. (1962), 'Gorgias and the Psychology of the Logos', *HSPh*, 66, 99-155.

SILVERTHORNE, M. J. (1973), 'Militarism in the *Laws*? (*Laws* 942a5-943a3)', *SO* 49, 29-38.

SIMONETOS, G. S. (1943), 'Die Willensmängel in den Rechtsgeschäften nach altgriechischen Recht', Ἀρχεῖον ἰδιωτικοῦ δικαίου, 14, 290–313. Repr. in Berneker (1968).

SKEMP, J. B. (1947), 'Plants in Plato's *Timaeus*', *CQ*, 41, 53–60.

SOLMSEN, F. (1944), 'The Tablets of Zeus', *CQ*, 38, 27–30.

—— (1955), 'Antecedents of Aristotle's Psychology and Scale of Beings', *AJPh*, 76, 148–64.

—— (1968*a*), 'Two Pindaric Passages on the Hereafter', *Hermes*, 96, 503–6.

—— (1968*b*), "Ἀμοιβή in the Recently Discovered 'Orphic' *Katabasis*", *Hermes*, 96, 631–2.

SOMMERSTEIN, A. H. (1989*a*), 'Again Klytemnestra's Weapon', *CQ*, 39, 296–301.

—— (1989*b*), *Aeschylus, Eumenides* (Cambridge).

SOURVINOU-INWOOD, C. (1986), 'Crime and Punishment: Tityos, Tantalos and Sisyphos in *Odyssey 11*', *BICS*, 33, 37–58.

STALLEY, R. F. (1983), *An Introduction to Plato's Laws* (Oxford).

STANFORD, W. B. (1947 and 1948), *The Odyssey of Homer*, ed. with introd., notes, and comm. (2 vols., London).

STROUD, R. S. (1968), *Drakon's Law on Homicide* (Univ. Calif. Publ. Class. Studies, 3, Berkeley and Los Angeles).

SUTTON, D. (1981), 'Critias and Atheism', *CQ*, 31, 33–8.

TAPLIN, O. (1977), *The Stagecraft of Aeschylus* (Oxford).

TAYLOR, A. E. (1928), *A Commentary on Plato's Timaeus* (Oxford).

THOMAS, C. G. (1977), 'Literacy and the Codification of Law', *SDHI*, 43, 455–8.

TODD, S. C. (1990), 'The Purpose of Evidence in Athenian Courts', in Cartledge *et al.* (1990), 19–39.

TRACY, T. J. (1969), *Physiological Theory and the Doctrine of the Mean in Plato and Aristotle* (Chicago).

TRESTON, H. J. (1923), *Poine: A Study in Ancient Greek Blood-vengeance* (London).

TSANTSANOGLOU, K. and PARASSOGLOU, G. M. (1987), 'Two Gold Lamellae from Thessaly', Ἑλληνικά, 38, 3–17.

TSOUYOPOULOS, N. (1966), *Strafe im frühgriechischen Denken* (Symposium, 19, Munich).

TZITZIS, S. (1983), 'Le Délinquant-malade chez Platon et chez les partisans de la défense sociale', *Revue pénitentiaire et de droit pénal*, 4, 383–91.

VALLOIS, R. (1914), "Ἀραί", *BCH*, 38, 250–71.

VERNANT, J. P. (1980), *Myth and Society in Ancient Greece*, trans. J. Lloyd (Brighton).

VLASTOS, G. (1941), Review of Morrow (1939), *PhR*, 50, 93–5.

—— (1946), 'Solonian Justice', *CPh*, 41, 65–83.

—— (1987), 'Socratic Irony', *CQ*, 37, 79–96.

VON FRITZ, K. (1943), '*Noos* and *noein* in the Homeric Poems', *CPh*, 38.

—— (1945, 1946), 'Νοῦς, νοεῖν and their derivatives in Pre-Socratic Philosophy (excluding Anaxagoras)', *CPh*, 40, 223–42; 41, 12–34. Reprinted in A. P. D. Mourelatos (ed.), *The Presocratics: A Collection of Critical Essays* (New York, 1974), 23–85.

—— (1957), "Ἐστρὶς ἑκατέρωθι in Pindar's second Olympian and Pythagoras' Theory of Metempsychosis', *Phronesis*, 2, 85–9.

WALCOT, P. (1963), 'Hesiod and the Law', *SO*, 38, 5–21.

—— (1978), 'Herodotus on Rape', *Arethusa*, 11, 137–47.

WELLES, C. B. (1967), 'Hesiod's Attitude towards Labor', *GRBS*, 8, 5–23.

WEST, M. L. (1966), *Hesiod, Theogony*, ed. with prolegomena and comm. (Oxford).

—— (1974), *Studies in Greek Elegy and Iambus* (Berlin and New York).

—— (1978), *Hesiod, Works and Days*, ed. with prolegomena and comm. (Oxford).

—— (1982), 'The Orphics of Olbia', *ZPE*, 45, 17–28.

—— (1983), *The Orphic Poems* (Oxford).

WHITEHEAD, D. (1977), *The Ideology of the Athenian Metic* (*PCPhS* suppl. 4).

—— (1988), "Κλοπὴ πολέμου: Theft in Ancient Greek Warfare", *C & M*, 39, 43–54.

WILLCOCK, M. M. (1976), *A Companion to the Iliad* (Chicago and London).

WILLETTS, R. F. (1967), *The Law Code of Gortyn*, ed. with introd., trans., and comm. (*Kadmos* Suppl. 1, Berlin).

WOLFF, H. J. (1946), 'The Origin of Judicial Litigation among the Greeks', *Traditio*, 4, 31–87.

WOOZLEY, A. D. (1972), 'Plato on Killing in Anger', *PhilosQ*, 22, 303–17.

WRIGHT, M. R. (1981), *Empedocles: the Extant Fragments*, ed. with introd., comm., and concordance (New Haven and London).

WÜNSCH, T. (1897), *Defixionum Tabellae* (Corpus Inscriptionum Atticarum, III/3 App.).

WYLLER, E. A. (1957), 'Platons Gesetz gegen die Gottesleugner', *Hermes*, 85, 292–314.

WYSE, W. (1904), *The Speeches of Isaeus*, text with critical and explanatory notes (Cambridge).

ZANKER, G. (1986), 'The *Works and Days*: Hesiod's Beggar's Opera?', *BICS*, 33, 26–36.

ZUNTZ, G. (1971), *Persephone* (Oxford).

—— (1976), 'Die Goldlamelle von Hipponion', *WS*, 89, 129–51.

INDEX LOCORVM

Hesiod

Homeric Hymns

Hyginus
Fabulae

Hyperides

Against Demosthenes

In Defence of Euxenippus

Against Philippides

GENERAL INDEX

Abians 37 n.
Achaeans 12, 19
Acheron 198
Achilles 13, 14, 17–18, 19, 25–6, 30 n.,
    35 n., 37, 52 n., 361
    scene on his shield 90 n.
action out of character 15, 110, 191 n.
admonition, reproof 133, 135, 165, 337,
    345 n.
Adrastus 109, 359
adultery 82, 84, 101–2
    see also seduction
advocacy, unscrupulous 332–3, 336
Aeacus 206 n.
Aegisthus 22–3, 70, 73 n., 74
Aeneas 13, 14
Agamemnon 13, 16, 19, 25, 26 n., 37, 50 n.,
    54, 63 n., 66–73
Agenor 14
aggravations see excuses and aggravations
aggression 3–4
    by gods 11 n.
    in Homer 12–21
    in drama 132
Ajax 361
Alcinous 22
Alexander 131
ambition 187, 190, 232
analogous punishments 77–8
anger, spirit 17, 39, 43, 124, 151–2, 180,
    187, 190, 224, 251, 279 n., 343
    as cause of offences 145–7, 155–6
    in courts 98–100, 110
    in Diodotus' speech 128
    of gods 37
    in Homer 18–19, 24, 98
    homicide in 225–31
    wounding in 261–3, 266
    of Zeus 39, 44, 47
    see also dead person's animosity
Antilochus 12, 15, 20, 25
Antimachus 13
Antinous 15

Antiphon (philosopher) 125–7, 131, 132
anxieties see surrogates
Aphrodite 19, 78–9, 84, 360
Apollo 12–13, 17, 19, 67, 69–73
apportionment (moira) 63, 66 see also
    Moira
appropriateness 17, 18, 30, 39 n., 77–87
    passim, 326–7, 335–8, 344
arbitrators 213
Archias 115
Areopagus 73, 91–3
Ares 14, 19, 37, 72, 78–9, 360
Argives 12
Argos 132
Aristocrates 100
Aristogeiton 117
arrest 96 n., 244–5, 290 n., 293–4, 297 n.
Artemis 69
assault 110 n., 268–79, 336–7, 346
    in Republic and Laws 272–3
assembly (ekklēsia) 92, 213, 295 n.
assimilation, argument from 22–5
archons 91, 93
atē or Atē see delusion, ruin
atheism 303, 305, 307
Athena 14, 16 n., 38 n., 71–3, 132
atimia see disfranchisement
Atreidae 12
Atreus 68, 69
Atys 359
authority, argument from 27–31
autocheir see killing with own hand
automaticity, of punishment 199, 201,
    203–7, 209–11
avarice 159–60, 188, 190, 333, 339, 344

Babylon 78
basic, the 25–7, 30, 106 n.
    see also extra, recompense
blame 12–13, 16, 128–9, 130–1, 213 n.
boulē 93–4, 295 n.
bouleusis see plotting
boundary-stones 337 n.